PETERSON'S

JOB OPPORTUNITIES IN BUSINESS

1996

Peterson's
Princeton, New Jersey

Visit Peterson's Education Center on the Internet (World Wide Web) at
http://www.petersons.com

To order additional copies of these books, call Peterson's Customer Service
at 800-338-3282.

Editorial inquiries concerning this book should be addressed to the editor at
Peterson's Guides, P.O. Box 2123, Princeton, New Jersey 08543-2123.

ISSN 1070-6615
ISBN 1-56079-510-7

Printed in the United States of America

10 9 8 7 6 5 4 3 2 1

CONTENTS

HOW TO USE THIS BOOK

Peterson's Job Opportunities in Business 1996 provides job hunters with vital information on approximately 2,000 of America's major employers. With this information, readers can identify and research companies that are seeking their skills and, by surveying the opportunities presented, build a picture of the various career alternatives possible at major businesses.

About Employer Profiles

This guide is not a definitive listing of America's largest organizations. If you do not find a particular company within the pages of this guide, it doesn't necessarily mean that the company has no employment opportunities. Similarly, a listing in the guide does not mean that the organization has immediate openings in the field of expertise mentioned. It simply means that the organization, by virtue of its business, typically seeks employees with the background cited.

Companies and other organizations profiled in this guide were selected based on the number of people they employ and were then contacted for specific information on the type of employees sought and appropriate contacts for employment inquiries. Employers were also asked to provide a contact for recent college graduates, if college recruiting is handled separately from overall employment recruiting within the organization. In addition to the above, profiles contain a business description; annual sales and number of employees (last reported publicly available figures as of December 1994); and in most instances a founding date. Founding dates generally refer to the year in which the organization was first established. However, they may in some cases indicate when the organization underwent the most recent major change resulting in its current corporate structure. Profiles also contain the number of professional and managerial hires, if the company surveyed was able to provide this information.

About Employer Descriptions

Some organizations have chosen to augment their profile with narrative information about their activities and job opportunities. In these cases, a short description follows the organizational profile. Longer descriptions, in which organizations provide detailed information about their businesses, future employment opportunities, quality of work life, and application information, appear in a separate section following the Employer Profiles.

In addition to the information about specific organizations, this book also includes the following valuable features:

Preparing for Workplace 2000: Business

What companies are looking for in employees today—what makes an employee valuable—has changed. As a job seeker, are you prepared to take the initiative in your career? Do you thrive on constant change and ambiguity? Can you adjust your sights toward a mobile career path in a global marketplace? Are you willing to keep expanding your knowledge and skills—both technical and interpersonal—to keep yourself employable? Read how changes in Corporate America are affecting today's employment picture and how you as a job seeker can address the needs of today's hiring managers.

Making Yourself a Stand-Out Candidate

Simply keeping your résumé neat and updated isn't enough in today's competitive job market. Read this section for tips of how to tackle the job of landing a job.

Finding Jobs in Small, Rapid-Growth Companies

It's probably not news to you that smaller companies create a large portion of today's jobs. Learn how to track trends that will help you find these rising stars and how to position yourself for potential employment in a smaller, fast-moving organization.

BUSINESS

by Susan Camardo

Globalization. Downsizing. Outsourcing. Instantaneous communication. Virtual offices. Flatter organizational structures. Welcome to the brave new world of business.

Business in America is currently going through a turbulent period of change so profound that some experts compare its impact to that of the Industrial Revolution. Gone is the model of the large, paternalistic corporation providing lifetime employment and benefits to employees. In its place, a very different prototype is evolving—the lean and aggressive firm operating in the global marketplace, staffed by mobile and empowered employees who are flexible and creative in producing more with fewer resources.

This competitive and entrepreneurial environment offers opportunities as well as challenges for the 16 million businesses in the United States today—and for those who work in them. To position yourself to be a winner in the job market of the next century, it's important to understand the major trends influencing American business today that are defining the workplace of tomorrow.

The Changing Face of American Business

Over the past few decades, the United States has been shifting from an industrial society that produces goods to an information society that produces services. As more manufacturing is done overseas, where costs are lower, America is producing fewer tangible goods in factories. But it is delivering more services, many of which involve the generation, transfer, and analysis of information. The U.S. Bureau of Labor Statistics (BLS) estimates that of the 26.4 million new jobs that will be created by the year 2005, 24.5 million will be in service-producing industries, such as communications, finance, and insurance.

The information society we're now living in has been driven in part by a steady stream of technological advances that have created a vast new array of high-tech business tools. Quantum leaps in the development of computers in the past few years—making them smaller, more affordable, and more user-friendly—have made the use of the computer essential in just about every aspect of business. At the same time, rapid advances in the field of telecommunications have made instantaneous communication possible. Whether you're using a computer network like the Internet or a cellular phone and a fax machine, you can reach people anywhere on the globe in a matter of minutes. That means that business is being conducted at a faster rate—and in more far-flung locations—than ever before.

Another factor influencing business today is the emergence of the global economy. With every passing year, the economies of the nations of the world are becoming more interrelated. Countries in the same region are joining into larger trading blocs, such as the European Community and the North American Free Trade Association. More and more American companies have manufacturing facilities and regional offices in other countries, just as corporations headquartered in other nations have operations here. American businesses are realizing that they have competitors—as well as opportunities—around the globe.

A trend that has had a major impact on American business over the past decade is the "downsizing" or "rightsizing" of corporations. For a number of reasons—reorganizations after mergers and acquisitions, cuts in the federal budget, the need to be more competitive in the global marketplace—companies have laid off hundreds of thousands of employeees since the mid-1980s. But just because certain industries and companies are downsizing doesn't mean that there aren't jobs out there—they are just in different places than they were before. For example, more employment is being created by small and medium-sized firms. And many large firms are "outsourcing" certain types of work, such as marketing and employee training, hiring smaller companies or individuals that specialize in that area to handle these jobs for them.

Downsizing also has implications for how the employees of tomorrow will do their jobs. Companies are learning to "do more with less," which means that employees have to be more productive with fewer resources. And leaner companies are tending to have flatter structures, dismantling the old hierarchical "chain of command" to emphasize project teams that have greater responsibility and authority for making decisions and getting the work done.

The Workplace of the Future

As we move into the next century, all of the trends described above will radically affect where, when, and how we work. Many people still have a traditional image of what it's like to work in corporate America—you go to a nice office from nine to five, spend forty years in the same company, and retire with a gold watch and a comfortable pension. But the workplace of the future is shaping up to be a very different

environment. Here's what experts think it will look like.

- Americans will change jobs—and even careers—a number of times over the course of their working lives. Most companies no longer promise their employees lifetime employment. Instead, they give employees an opportunity to learn and practice marketable skills that can be taken elsewhere. And employees do move on—experts estimate that most Americans will change jobs anywhere from six to ten times, and professions three times, over the course of their work lives.

- People will often work from their homes or other locations. Because the development of technology is moving at warp speed, the devices that allow people to communicate instantaneously from any location are becoming ever more portable and affordable. So employees won't need to work together in one central location. Instead, they'll have "virtual offices," communicating from wherever they are by cellular phone, laptop computer, and modem.

- Working hours will become more flexible. Trends like the increasing numbers of working mothers and the need to do business with people in different times zones across the country and around the world are causing businesses to rethink the nine-to-five workday. In the future, more people will be working flexible hours that suit their lifestyles as well as their job responsibilities. Many will also

be sharing jobs, with two or more people working part-time to fill one position.

- Businesses will have flatter, more horizontal structures. Traditionally, American corporations have been structured as hierarchies, with decisions made at the top and passed on by management at each level below. But now this authoritarian, chain-of-command style of management is being replaced by an emphasis on cross-functional project teams that have more responsibility—and authority—to make decisions. And there will be more "virtual teaming," with people in different locations working together on a project, linked by sophisticated telecommunications devices.

- The workplace will be much more diverse. Women and minorities are continuing to join the workplace in increasing numbers. Workforce 2000, a study produced by the Hudson Institute in 1987, predicted that women and minorities would make up about 85 percent of the people entering the workforce between 1988 and 2000. At this point, however, experts aren't making optimistic predictions about large numbers of women and minorities moving up to the ranks of top management. A federal government study by the Glass Ceiling Commission released in 1995 noted that while white men constitute about 43 percent of the U.S. workforce, they hold about 95 out of 100 senior management positions (vice president and above).

■ More jobs will be created by smaller firms than by large corporations. Although big companies will always need employees, the real spurt in job growth into the next century is expected to come from small and medium-sized firms. A survey conducted by Olsten Corporation, a temporary placement firm, revealed that small businesses showed a 45 percent increase in hiring in 1993—twice the rate of major corporations. And economic researcher David Birch, president of Cognetics, Inc., and author of Job Creation in America, predicts that 77 percent of the jobs created over the next few years will be generated by just 5 percent of companies now in existence—and 98 percent of those companies currently have under 100 employees. Experts think that the most rapid job growth will come from companies that have a unique market niche and offer a highly innovative product or specialized service.

The Employee of the 21st Century

Since the workplace of tomorrow will be a fluid, continually evolving environment, you need to be prepared to meet the challenges and seize the opportunities it offers. Whatever profession or industry you work in, you will need to bring to your job a variety of skills and attitudes—technical skills in your chosen field, interpersonal skills that help you to communicate and work well with others, and a flexible, positive attitude.

Experts believe that since the employees of the future can expect to change jobs and even professions a number of times in their working lives, it's important to develop "portable skills" that they can take from one employer to another. Economist Herbert Striner, who served as a consultant to two U.S. Secretaries of Labor and spent several years as pro-

---

THE WORKPLACE: WHERE IT'S BEEN, WHERE IT'S GOING

The Past: Employees could expect to be employed by one company for their entire working life.
The Future: Employees can expect to change jobs at least half a dozen times and switch careers several times.

The Past: Most employees worked in an office environment.
The Future: Many employees will work from their homes or temporary locations or travel the globe, linked by computer and fax.

The Past: People worked a structured nine-to-five workday.
The Future: There will be much more flextime and job sharing.

The Past: Most corporations had a hierarchical structure, with a clear and rigid chain of command.
The Future: Corporations are being structured horizontally, with more cross-functional teams given more responsibility to make decisions.

The Past: The workforce was dominated by white males.
The Future: Women and minorities will make up a much larger percentage of America's employees.

The Past: Job growth stemmed from the expansion of large corporations.
The Future: More jobs will be created in small and medium-sized firms.

---

gram director of the W. E. Upjohn Institute for Employment Research, encourages employees to always keep an eye on the future. "There's a difference between getting a job and preparing for continuing employability, which hinges on flexibility and willingness to change as you move from one type of activity to another," says Striner. "So rather than train for one specific job, learn as much as you can about the entire field so you'll be ready to go into different jobs as the need arises."

There are some skills common to all professions and industries that every employee will need to know. Computer literacy is an absolute must. Since more and more business is being transacted through computers, employees have to be able to store, access, and analyze information and communicate with colleagues through computer networks. And you will have a big advantage if you speak other languages and understand other cultures. Companies competing in a global economy and dealing with an increasingly multicultural workforce both here and abroad will value employees who can function across cultural and linguistic lines. Communication skills, which have always been important in the workplace, will become even more so in the future. Whatever job or field you're working in, you need to be able to write and speak clearly and persuasively to work effectively with others. It's also important to be self-motivated— with the mobile offices and flexible hours of the future, there won't be someone constantly direct-

ing your work, and you'll be expected to take the initiative.

The business world is now putting great emphasis on teamwork and values team players who have the ability to cooperate and work productively with others to get the job done, putting the goals of the group above their own personal needs and opinions. "It's important to learn how to create a shared vision instead of a solo vision," observes consultant Ann McGee-Cooper, whose Dallas-based firm specializes in such areas as interdependent teaming and future skills. "And every

member of a team has to be both a leader and a follower. Each person has a clear sense of what he or she brings to the team— creativity, leadership, autonomy—but also has an accountability back to everyone else on the team."

And finally, the employee of the future must have a lot of flexibility. Situations will change rapidly, you'll move from job to job, and new skills will be required of you. You have to be open and adaptable and willing to change if you want to stay competitive. Experts suggest that the successful employees of the future will be those

HAVE SKILLS, WILL TRAVEL

No matter what job you hold and what industry you work in, you'll need to be proficient in a number of important skills if you want to prosper in the ever more mobile and ever more global business world of the next century.

Communication skills: Speaking and writing clearly and persuasively.

Computer literacy: Being adept at accessing, analyzing, and storing data and communicating with other employees via computer.

Flexibility: Having a "go with the flow" mentality that allows you to do different tasks— and even switch jobs—in response to changing business conditions.

Team player: Demonstrating the ability to cooperate and work with others productively to achieve a common goal, putting the needs of the group above your own.

Self-motivation: Getting things done on your own, without having someone else give you guidance and direction on what to do and how to do it.

Cross-Cultural Skills: Being able to communicate in other languages and understand different cultures.

SUCCESS AND SATISFACTION? IT'S UP TO YOU . . .

Consultant Ann McGee-Cooper, whose Dallas-based firm's areas of expertise include work skills for the future, has been examining the qualities, skills, and attitudes employees need to be successful—and satisfied—in their jobs. Here, she offers some advice on how to make the most of what she sees as "a very exciting time of change when you can write your own script—and your own ticket."

- Learn to welcome change as an opportunity instead of seeing it as a traumatizing, stressful event. We used to think security was getting hired by a well-established company. But the only security there ever really was for anyone is to trust yourself and bring value to others. Your security is the confidence you have in yourself, your ability to work with others, and your ability to see problems as opportunities. If you can be creative in turning problems into opportunities, then you've always got a job or a new business. The faster things change, the more people have needs they didn't have last year, and the more business opportunities you have.

- Create a dream for yourself and make it real. If you live that dream, you'll be motivated, because you'll be preparing for it. And that will help you to make life—even the dreary parts—fun.

- Forget about what makes money. If you're bright and motivated, you're going to make money. If you're doing something you hate, you'll have a lousy attitude and won't be able to manage yourself, much less work with other people. It's a great waste of talent to go in that direction.

- Learn how to learn. Without question, everyone now must be a lifelong learner. But each of us has a different learning window. Notice how you learn most easily—is it by having someone tell you, or show you, or do a task with you?

- Look for mentors. Throughout your life, look for people who are doing what you'd like to do and make yourself valuable to them. Figure out what you can do for them, so they'll spend time with you. This is one of most important ways to learn—you don't absorb just facts and strategies, but you breathe in how your mentors think, what their attitude about life is, how they organize themselves.

- Think of yourself as a business of one, no matter who you work for. This doesn't mean look out for #1—it means that if you don't bring value to your work, you're history. Make it your job to bring profit to everyone around you. If you can help them to be successful, you'll always have a role—in the future, the people you've worked with will see that if they want a successful project, they need you.

- Take responsibility for your own attitude and mental well-being. Be enthusiastic and happy about yourself and what's happening to you, and learn how to work and interact effectively with others. Don't wait to have a balanced life—do it now. We can't maintain quality in products and services long-term unless we create an equal dedication to the quality of our lives. That means making your job and your life fun and bringing a spiritual dimension to whatever you do.

dedicated to lifelong learning to keep abreast of new developments in their field and changes in the business environment and to keeping their skills up-to-date and acquiring new ones. As Christopher Byrne, a principal in Byrne-McCoy Worldwide, a marketing and publishing venture, notes, "In this increasingly mobile and global environment where things are constantly changing, the most valuable skill you can develop is learning how to learn."

Where the Jobs Will Be

In general, the availability of jobs depends on both economic factors and population trends. The factors that are affecting the evolution of American business are not yielding the same results in every industry. Some types of businesses are growing by leaps and bounds, while others are shrinking. And different areas of the country are growing at different rates, which means that the presence of businesses—and the demand for employees—will vary from region to region. So in addition to looking at the "big picture" for employment opportunities, it's important to examine specific industries and locations to see where the jobs will be.

Industry Trends

As we move into the next century, the bulk of new jobs will be created in industries that provide services. These include transportation, communications, public utilities, retail and wholesale trade, finance, insurance, real estate, government, and businesses that supply personal, automotive, legal, educational, health, business, and social services. The BLS projects that by the year 2005, 109.2 million people will work in service-producing industries.

The largest and fastest-growing area in this sector is businesses that deliver various services, where employment is expected to rise 40 percent by 2005, accounting for almost two thirds of all new jobs. Positions will be found in small firms and in large corporations and across most industries. Companies providing services to other businesses, such as temporary help agencies and consulting firms, are expected to generate many more jobs, especially in the computer and data processing area.

According to data from the BLS, employment in finance, insurance, and real estate is expected to increase by 21 percent by the year 2005. Despite the recent turbulence on Wall Street, the strong demand for financial services is expected to continue. Holding and investment offices, as well as

HOW TO TRACK A COMPANY

Once you have checked the overall performance of a company's industry, you can use the library or your computer to gather more information about the company itself. Perform database searches to look for mention in the press of new products or new contracts, along with comments from industry analysts. You invariably will impress the people who are conducting an interview by informing yourself about their company before you get there. An hour's worth of research time will make you look sharp and prepared and put you in a position to interview them while they are interviewing you.

If a company is publicly traded on a stock exchange, you can also take advantage of a good indicator of a company's future performance. Look at the P/E (price to earnings) ratio of companies you are interested in over the last year or so. Compare this ratio to other companies in the same industry. You can find up-to-date figures for most publicly traded companies in the Wall Street Journal or Barron's. If the P/E of a company in a healthy industry is significantly higher than other similar companies, the stock market's judgment is that the near- to mid-term prospects for profitability of that company are good.

Companies that are achieving profitability through sales growth and high profit margins typically will be hiring. The stock market is full of smart people doing their best to judge the prospects of companies year in and year out. They are not always right, of course, but they have more sources of information at their disposal than the average job seeker. Take advantage of them.

HOW TO TRACK AN INDUSTRY

Once you have used this book to identify employers you may be interested in, take the time to investigate their industry group. The current financial performance and future prospects of an industry, as a whole, in which you take a job will directly affect your job security, along with your chance for raises and promotions. It is easy to become better informed. Consult with general business magazines such as Business Week, Forbes, or Fortune. They do most of the work for you.

For instance, each year these magazines publish industry-by-industry analyses of the top corporations in the United States. Use the industry-by-industry figures provided to judge the overall prospects of a company you are interested in, regardless of whether it is actually listed. Look for industries that are rated above average in sales growth, profits as a percentage of sales, and growth in the number of employees. Keep in mind that one or two years of bad results for an industry do not necessarily mean the industry is in permanent decline; some industries are more sensitive to short-term economic conditions than others.

The point is that tracking an industry takes many different forms. You should study the raw data—the numbers—but look at the intangibles and, especially, at the future.

---

mortgage bankers and brokers, are targeted as the fastest-growing areas. The largest numerical increase in jobs is expected to be among agents, brokers, and services in the insurance industry. But changes in the banking industry look like they will limit job growth in commercial banks and savings and loan institutions.

Employment in the transportation sector is expected to increase by 24 percent, with good growth in the passenger transportation arrangement industry, which includes travel agencies. Despite the general decline of jobs in manufacturing, there will be a continuing need for professionals (like operations research analysts) and industrial managers. And there are a few types of manufacturing com-

panies that are expected to show some employment growth, such as those producing plastic products, printing, and chemicals.

Demographics will be driving the growth industries of the future, says Paul Queally, a general partner in Sprout Group, the venture capital affiliate of Donaldson, Lufkin & Jenrette. "The baby boom generation is like a bubble going through a snake," he notes, referring to the 76 million Americans born between 1946 and 1964. He sees a surge in the need for health-care services as the population ages; this bodes well for those pharmaceutical, medical supply, and service companies that provide health-care-related products and services. And as baby boomers contemplate retirement, he expects

them to create more demand for financial services (especially for retirement savings and estate planning) and vacation planning.

In looking to the future, other experts suggest you keep your eye on increasingly "hot" fields like computers, marketing, medical technology, robotics, telecommunications, biotechnology and genetics, and communications and entertainment.

Occupational Trends

The continuing expansion of the services-producing sector means that many new job opportunities will be created for employees with managerial, professional, and technical skills. The fastest-growing occupations will be those that require the most formal education and training.

According to the BLS, the job group expected to grow most rapidly through the year 2005 is professional specialty occupations, with a projected increase of 37 percent. Reflecting the continuing importance of technology in the information society, many of these jobs will be in computer-related fields. Corporate America will need professionals to work in the information systems area. High on the BLS's list of the fastest-growing jobs through the year 2005 are systems analysts and computer scientists (up over 75 percent) and computer programmers (up over 50 percent).

More executives, administrators, and managers—the people who direct the strategies and activities of an organization—will be needed to oversee increasingly complex business operations. The BLS lists these jobs among the fastest-growing occupational groups, projecting that employment will increase by 26 percent through the year 2005. But demand will vary by industry. For example, there will be more job openings available to health services managers than for wholesale and retail buyers.

In the field of finance, the BLS lists accountants and auditors among the fastest-growing occupations requiring a college degree or more education. By the year 2000, employment of economists is expected to be up 27 percent, as companies increasingly depend on sophisticated quantitative methods of analyzing business trends, forecasting sales, and planning purchasing and production. Changes in the regulation of the financial services industry is leading to an explosion in the number and types of services being offered by banks, insurance companies, and other financial firms. This opens up opportunities for financial analysts, financial planners, insurance agents and underwriters, and securities and financial services representatives.

Prospects for marketing, advertising, and public relations specialists and managers look good into the next century. According to the BLS, employment in marketing and sales occupations is projected to grow by 21 percent, to 15.7 million jobs by 2005. Up-and-coming areas include consumer services, marketing to children, and international financial marketing. Since many companies have reduced their in-house marketing staffs over the past decade, a lot of job growth is likely to come from outside agencies.

In the human resources area, the BLS projects that the number of personnel, training and labor relations specialists, and managers will grow faster than the average for all occupations through the year 2005. Much of this job growth will come from companies that specialize in providing human resources services, such as executive recruiters, training and development firms, and personnel placement agencies, since businesses are contracting out more and more of their human resources functions to these firms. Two human resources areas expected to be very hot into the next century are workforce diversity and employee benefits. As the American workforce becomes increasingly multicultural, many human resources departments and consultants are focusing on how to develop employees into a cohesive and productive group who respect and value the contributions of employees of all backgrounds. Companies are also recognizing the changing needs of American employees by creating more flexible benefits packages that can include, for example, parental leave, child and elder care, and wellness programs.

Although manufacturing in general is not the place to look for job growth in the next century, there are a few niches of opportunity. According to data from the BLS, employment in executive, administrative, and managerial occupations in manufacturing should increase about 8 percent through the year 2005, while professional specialty occupations are

---

HOT JOBS FOR THE NEXT CENTURY

While good employees will be needed in all professions in Workplace 2000, these are some occupations that look especially promising.

Information Systems Specialist (Computer Scientist/Systems Analyst/
    Computer Programmer)
Accountant/Auditor
Economist
Insurance Agent/Underwriter
Financial Services Representative
Marketing, Advertising, and Public Relations Specialist/Manager
Product Development/Brand Manager
Employee/Management Training Professional
Employee Benefits Specialist
Workforce Diversity Specialist
Industrial Manager
Operations Research Analyst
Lawyer
Environmental Policy and Management Specialist

expected to grow about 16 percent. Industrial managers will be needed to supervise plants, production, materials, operations, purchasing, and traffic. The job of operations research analyst is identified by the BLS as one of the fastest-growing professional specialty occupations, with employment projected to rise by over 70 percent through 2005. These professionals, who use logical analysis and mathematical applications to find solutions to managerial and administrative problems, are also employed in other industries, such as banking, insurance, and airlines, as well as in consulting firms.

Geographic Trends

No matter where you live, there will be jobs available in the next century. But not all areas of the U.S. are growing at the same pace. Since population growth affects the demand for various goods and services—and the demand for employees in different occupations and industries—it's important to look at what's happening in the part of the country you want to be in. The Bureau of the Census projects that the fastest-growing regions of the U.S. over the next decade will be the West, with a population increase of 24 percent, and the South, up 16 percent. Experts also note that the Midwest is experiencing an economic resurgence, fueled by aggressive entry into world markets, increasing entrepreneurship, and innovative policies on the part of state and local governments.

To give you an idea of how job growth will be distributed across

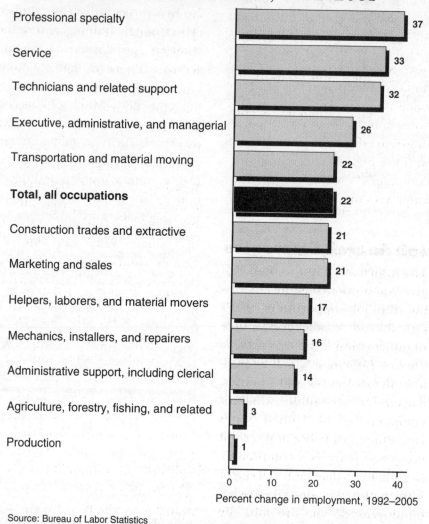

PROJECTED EMPLOYMENT GROWTH BY OCCUPATIONAL GROUP, 1992–2005

Professional specialty — 37
Service — 33
Technicians and related support — 32
Executive, administrative, and managerial — 26
Transportation and material moving — 22
Total, all occupations — 22
Construction trades and extractive — 21
Marketing and sales — 21
Helpers, laborers, and material movers — 17
Mechanics, installers, and repairers — 16
Administrative support, including clerical — 14
Agriculture, forestry, fishing, and related — 3
Production — 1

Percent change in employment, 1992–2005

Source: Bureau of Labor Statistics

the U.S. in the next few years, here are some statistics forecast by Regional Financial Associates in West Chester, Pennsylvania, based on regional employment growth in 1993. The strongest growth will be in the Mountain states (+3.1%), followed by the South Central area (+1.7%), the Southeast (+1.2%), and the Midwest (+1.1%). The two areas losing jobs will be the Northeast (–0.9%) and the Pacific region (–1.8%).

Regional trends are one part of the picture. But job growth also varies on a state-by-state basis. Companies tend to set up operations in states where it costs them less to do business. They also look at quality-of-life issues. Urban areas with high levels of pollution, crime, and poverty are not as attractive as places without these negatives that also have affordable housing and good educational resources. As a result, many companies are attracted to the "edge cities" springing up across America. This designation is given to areas where 24,000 or more jobs are concentrated outside of traditional downtowns; among the most prosperous are the Bishop Ranch area near San Francisco, Great Neck on Long Island, and the I-270 corridor north of Washington, D.C. Small companies in particular are drawn to edge cities—the 10 areas with the highest concentration of companies with fewer than 50 employees are all edge cities.

Job Search Strategies

The information in this book will give you a good start in identifying the job opportunity that's right for you. Another good source of information is the *Occupational Outlook Handbook,* which is available in bookstores and libraries. This reference guide, which is compiled by the United States Department of Labor and revised every two years, is a comprehensive and up-to-date source of career information. It describes what employees do on the job, the training and education needed, earnings, working conditions, and future job prospects in a wide range of occupations.

One of the benefits of living in an electronic age is being able to tap into a wealth of resources through a computer and modem. Now, you can go job hunting in cyberspace by connecting with the Internet as well as various on-line services. There are already many employment bulletin boards and job banks available to savvy searchers, and more will be sure to follow as usage grows. America Online, for example, offers access to a Career Center that includes a wide variety of services, including career counseling; examples of résumés and cover letters; a Career Guidance Service with a database of over 13,500 career options; an Occupational Profiles Database with information on over 245 jobs; a Help Wanted-USA Database listing thousands of current job openings; a Worldwide Resume/Talent Bank in which you can list yourself; an Employer Contacts Database; an Employment Agency Database; and a Career Resource Library. A vast array of similar services is available on the World Wide Web.

While print and electronic resources are enormously helpful, there is no substitute for face-to-face contact when you're conducting a job search. Most successful professionals will tell you that a great deal of business is done—and jobs found—through networking. Don't be shy about "working" your personal and professional connections to get the information you need about a job or field that interests you. Join industry groups to make contacts in your chosen field, talk to friends, family members, and business associates to see if they can refer you to an appropriate person, or identify someone in a company or job that appeals to you and ask them for an information interview.

As you explore the many possibilities open to you, remember that finding the right job involves not only following your head—being smart about getting into a field with growth potential—but also your heart—doing work that interests, excites, and satisfies you. As the German poet and dramatist Johann Wolfgang von Goethe once wrote, "Whatever you can do, or dream you can, begin it. Boldness has genius, power and magic in it."

Susan Camardo is a business writer and corporate communications consultant based in New York City.

MAKING YOURSELF A
STAND-OUT
CANDIDATE

Getting up to speed on current business trends and deciding what kind of job opportunities you want to tap are important steps in the job hunting process. Your next task is to communicate that knowledge and your particular assets to potential employers. In other words, you need to build an airtight case for hiring you by letting a company know precisely how you can contribute to its success. This is the time to express your passion and to strut out some new search strategies. And here are some guidelines that could help.

■ *Adopt an actor's mentality.* As the old joke goes, how do you get to Carnegie Hall . . . ? Practice. The same theory applies to honing your job seeking "craft." Be ready for the audition. Don't take rejection personally. Rehearse your lines. Pay attention to the casting director. And use feedback to improve your performance skills.

■ *Tailor your tools to your targets.* Sending out hundreds of resumes may feel like an industrious activity, but generic mailings typically get minimal to no results. Of 1,500 successful job seekers surveyed by the *National Business Employment Weekly*, most

got in through contacts, only 2 percent through unsolicited mailings.

■ *Create your own job security.* Finding a job doesn't mean you will never have to network, trend-track, or update your résumé again. Research indicates that most people will work for 10 or more employers over a lifetime. Job security, then, comes not from your current employer but from taking charge of your career and keeping yourself employable.

■ *Make change a way of life.* The old order changeth . . . what about you? In a survey of senior managers conducted by EquiPro International, their most frequently cited complaints were about employees accepting the status quo, not taking risks, reacting instead of initiating—in other words, resisting change. As companies live or die based on their ability to manage change, it's fairly obvious that they want to hire people who view change as a challenge and an opportunity.

■ *Learn.* The American Society for Training and Development (ASTD) projects that by the year 2000 more than 65% of all jobs will require some education beyond high school; 23 million people will be employed

in professional and technical jobs—the largest single occupational category—that require ongoing training. The key is to determine the kind of education and training that is valued by your market niche (or one you'd like to enter) at different stages of your career.

■ *Upgrade your computer-ease.* The need to be technologically literate is no longer limited to programmers, number crunchers, and data processors. Technology will continue to transform virtually every working environment, affecting how work gets done and, thus, the types of jobs available.

■ *Join the team.* Scrap the phrase "it's not in my job description" from your vocabulary. Potential employers want to hear that you're willing to roll up your sleeves and do whatever it takes to get the job done. Any evidence you can offer of your ability to both lead teams and be a good team player will win you points.

■ *Get personal.* Whenever possible, present yourself to potential employers either in person or through a person. Résumés and cover letters have their place, and certain variations on the theme may be useful (such as the "Me, Inc." proposal idea mentioned previously). But paper is often best used—especially by job seekers who have several years' experience or want to switch fields—to support your image rather than establish it.

■ *Get noticed.* Seize every chance to become known or better known (note: this is another activity that shouldn't stop once you land a job). Take an active role in an industry association or a civic group. Publish an article in a trade journal and send "FYI" copies to key contacts and potential employers. Send an item of interest to employers with whom you had a good interview but who weren't hiring at the time. Teach. Give speeches. And always send thank-you letters.

■ *Take the scenic route.* One nontraditional way to approach the job market is to become part of the growing contingent work force—"temporary professionals" or "interim executives" who are matched with needy employers by employment firms that specialize in this area. Assignments are usually specific and short-term (3 to 18 months), which lets you check out different employers and career options and sometimes leads to full-time employment. It tends to work out best if your skills are easily transferable and/or highly specialized and you can handle the uncertainty of when and where you'll be assigned next.

FINDING JOBS

IN SMALL, RAPID-GROWTH COMPANIES

Warning: If you've got your heart set on working for a large company, stop reading now. Otherwise, you may find yourself considering another viable option.

It's probably not news to you that smaller companies create a large portion of today's jobs. These job gains occurred at twice the rate of major corporations, a trend expected to continue throughout 1995 and beyond. The forecast from David Birch, president of the Massachusetts-based firm Cognetics Inc. and author of *Job Creation in America,* is that two thirds of the jobs created over the next few years will be created by just 5 percent of the companies now in existence and that 98 percent of those companies currently have under 100 employees.

Small business in general has had its share of economic struggles in recent years and has concerns at present about increasing government regulations, corporate tax legislation, and the impact of the impending health care plan. Cautionary attitudes, however, were laying the groundwork for 1995—which those same analysts predicted to be a breakout year for small business.

The economy continues to perk up. Banks are healthier, enabling more financing and credit for small business investment and expansion. And while small com-

panies are just as keen as large corporations on operating lean and mean, they also stand to benefit from some of the same overarching business trends, including globalization and the advent of the Information Superhighway. "As the adage goes, a high tide raises small ships," says Olsten president Stuart Olsten.

Net job gains in the small business sector happen predominantly in rapid-growth companies scattered across the country—many of which have the potential to be tomorrow's corporate leaders. Accompanying this section is a list of small, fast-growing companies, which are meant to be illustrative of the type of prospects to include in your job search.

When approaching this particular job market, you'll want to determine what is unique or special about any given company—in other words, what makes it stand out from the crowd? And you'll want to be aware of some of the major trends driving growth in the small business sector: outsourcing activitities of larger companies; the ever-increasing reliance on technology; the expanding service sector of the economy; the waves of growth stemming from trade liberalization south of the border; and the job gains being yielded by women-owned businesses.

Define the "Unique Proposition"

Small companies cover a broad range of industries and geographic locations. Here again, as in big business, most job creation will occur in the services sector. High-tech companies in particular have long graced the rosters of *Inc.* magazine's annual Inc. 100 list of fastest-growing small public companies. Indeed, the sluggish Silicon Valley has made a comeback, with small biotechnology and software companies redressing the defense industry fallout. Small companies are also finding success in servicing health-related industries, as evidenced by increasing numbers showing up in the Inc. 100 and other barometers of high-growth businesses.

In any industry, the area in which small companies tend to shine is in supplying goods and services to their larger counterparts. The best of them capitalize on an uncommon business strategy or a unique market niche, offering a highly innovative product or specialized service. One example is Integrated Communications Corp., a Parsippany, New Jersey-based advertising agency that averaged 50 percent annual growth in its first eight years of operation. The company's niche is in providing coordinated marketing, educational, and creative advertising services to the pharmaceuticals industry. Its proximity to several major drug companies headquartered in New Jersey has boosted its success. Integrated Communications also exemplifies the fact that service businesses often offer excellent job opportunities: the company looks to hire not only support staff but also account supervisors and executives, market research specialists, accountants, and a variety of other positions with growth potential.

Keeping up with trends—in business, among consumers, in society at large—pays off in a job search focused on rapid-growth companies every bit as much as with corporate giants. It's a useful means of determining whether a company's "unique proposition" makes good business sense and has staying power. If your instincts tell you "that's a smart idea," you just might want to get in touch! Consider these success stories:

- Cobra Golf (Carlsbad, CA), the King Cobra line of oversized golf clubs, including the first-ever oversized iron used for advancing the ball onto the putting green, garnered a 14 percent share of the irons market and saw overall sales soar by a projected 50 percent in 1994.
- Education Alternatives (Minneapolis, MN) tapped into the malaise among public school systems across the country by offering school-oriented business management and consulting services—and raised its sales 875 percent in five years.
- PictureTel (Danvers, MA), in the business of developing, manufacturing, and marketing

visual communications systems for videoconferencing, grew from 97 to 741 employees in approximately five years.
- Wonderware Software Development Corp. (Irvine, CA) developed a software product called InTouch, which lets operators control factory machinery by touching icons on a computer screen. The software was even used to maneuver the giant mechanical borers that dug the "chunnel" under the English Channel. Wonderware's sales skyrocketed from $322,000 in 1989 to roughly $20 million in 1993, and nearly all of its employees are white-collar technical and computer professionals.

These are just a few examples of small companies that turned big dreams into major payoffs. Of course, it isn't always—or only—the brand-spanking-new product or service that dictates success. The "unique proposition" for some small companies is simply that they do what they do very well, perhaps in a better or different way than it's been done by competitors for awhile. Papa John's International Inc. (Louisville, KY) and Outback Steakhouse (Tampa, FL), for example, each took traditional fare—pizza and steaks—to new heights with smart management practices and meals that appeal to value-conscious consumers.

The battle between fad and fashion rages wildly in the small business sector, however. The overall failure rate is high; today's hot commodity becomes tomorrow's fond memory. In particular, small

companies with a fresh idea are delectable prey for large company copycats. Typically, big business has more resources at its disposal to churn out, and often improve, products introduced by smaller competitors. Yet small companies have speed and flexibility on their side. And those that effectively manage change and can recreate their businesses even in the midst of success are the ones that stick around.

So how can you assess the elusive factor of "staying power"? One key task, when interviewing with small rapid-growth companies, is to ask about their plans for the future. While a company's not apt to pull out the blueprints or divulge trade secrets, try to get a sense of how it's planning to build on its current success and whether it's already thinking of ways to diversify its product lines or tap into new markets. And if you can throw out some ideas of your own for them to consider (meaning you did a little homework and "imagineering" before you got to the interview), you're likely to shine.

Habla Español?

Rapid-growth companies have a penchant for being in the right places at the right time. And the right places in the next few years could well be Mexico and Latin America.

Several regions or individual countries around the globe—including Eastern Europe, India, and the Pacific Rim countries—are currently ripe for U.S. business expansion, but none more so than those south of the border. Over the last few years, small businesses provided a wellspring of support for the passage of the North American Free Trade Agreement (NAFTA), opening up trade opportunities in Mexico, and for GATT (General Agreement on Tariffs and Trade), the global trade compact under which trade liberalization in Latin America is covered. Large U.S. corporations already have sparked a surge of business activity in both regions. However, the wealth of import and export opportunities in these regions is equally significant for small businesses that are geared up and ready to take the plunge.

Mexico is currently the world's second-largest importer of U.S. manufactured goods and the third-largest importer of U.S. agricultural products. As local companies in Mexico and its neighboring countries in Latin America emerge into a free-market, global economy, U.S. businesses can help pave the way. High on the list of priorities in these regions is state-of-the-art technology. But that list goes on, and it encompasses a wide variety of needs: office equipment, food-processing equipment, gas and oil-field equipment, electricity and gas distribution equipment, construction machinery, lumber, computers, telecommunications gear, iron and steel tubing, cars and car parts, and medical supplies. These needs translate to small business opportunities in the manufacture, distribution, and/or direct sales of products to a burgeoning marketplace. Additional opportunities are surfacing in the pursuit of joint ventures with local companies and certain government entities.

Symbol Technologies of Bohemia, New York, for example, makes bar-code scanners and hand-held computers. The company's sales to Latin American markets have spiraled upward at not less than 40 percent annually since entering those markets six years ago.

Telular Inc., based in Buffalo Grove, Illinois, has reported spectacular growth in sales of its cellular telephone interfaces in Mexico as well as in Latin American markets such as Guatemala, Costa Rica, Venezuela, Chile, and Argentina. Cellular facilities are on the rise in these regions, and Telular's interface allows businesses and residences to connect to these facilities through standard telephone and fax equipment. Telular's foray into Latin America alone has resulted in sales amounting to more than one fourth of the company's world-wide sales.

The upshot is that small companies will be major players in these emerging economies. To get in on the action, bone up on your knowledge of Mexican and Latin American markets. Learn about the ways and means of doing business there. Learn about the culture. Learn Spanish. If you're a bi-lingual marketing pro, market yourself to ad agencies or companies in any industry as being able to prepare brochures and sales materials in Spanish. If account management is your trade, dazzle potential employers with your cross-cultural negotiating skills and knowledge of the intricate document and contract preparation required in these regions. There's room for everyone from human resources specialists to computer whizzes in small companies that aim to be in Mexico and Latin America at the right time.

Cherchez Les Femmes

Among the rapid-growth companies not to be overlooked—perhaps especially if you're a woman—are women-owned businesses.

There are six and one-half million women-owned businesses in the U.S. today, virtually all of them with fewer than 250 employees. In each of the last five years, more than half of the three million businesses formed in the U.S. were started by a woman. Moreover, the gender profile of the personnel in a woman-owned company is typically two thirds female. By simple arithmetic, one can see that women are being recruited by growth companies more frequently than men.

While women entrepreneurs are starting new businesses at a faster clip than their male counterparts, the facts of business life are that they typically cannot attract capital as easily. According to A. David Silver, president of Santa Fe, New Mexico-based ADS Financial Services, Inc., and author of *The Venture Capital Sourcebook*, fewer than a dozen women-founded businesses have received $1 million or more of institutional venture capital. Consequently, rather than asset-based or capital equipment manufacturing companies, women tend to start trust-based businesses—those in which the customer pays in advance. They also substitute labor for capital, and the labor most in demand is skilled in affinity-marketing, communicating with suppliers to extend credit, desktop publishing, information gathering, and servicing customers. Have a skill in these areas? It's for hire by a woman-owned small business.

Silver notes that "The assets of women-owned companies are information, networks, insight, and trained people who will follow them to hell and back." And, he adds, "The sensitivity to community service and the needs of young, female employees is a distinctly gender thing."

Women entrepreneurs have proven themselves heroines in the current U.S. economic recovery. With the best and most expansive of them growing from an average initial capital of $38,000 to an average valuation of $90 million in 15 years, they also are providing training grounds for their employees to leave and launch their own businesses, which creates an ever-widening circle of women hiring mostly women. A shared work ethic is key, but male job seekers can rest assured that EEO regulations still apply: Connections to the old-boy network may not carry much weight, but inimitable, in-demand business skills count.

Acclimating to the Small Business Environment

Just as certain types of people tend to start and grow successful small businesses, employees of a certain temperament tend to thrive in a small business setting. If you'd like to put rapid-growth companies into your mix of employment prospects, keep in mind these hints and caveats:

- Small companies could give lessons to the giants on doing more with less. Dealing with resource constraints and, presuming you're financially conscientious, treating every dollar of the company's money as if it were your own are typical of small company life.
- Be prepared to wear many hats. Resource constraints often extend to personnel, with employees playing various roles, filling in for each other, and doing without an extensive support staff. The good news is that you get to try your hand at different functions, find out what you like best and are best at, and can develop multiple skills to bring to your next employer.
- Starting salaries may be lower than big company offerings. Frequently, though, other forms of compensation come into play, not only equity opportunities (such as stock options) but the "psychic rewards" of having a more immediate, direct, and visible impact on the business.
- On the other hand, some rapid-growth companies offer big bucks to bring new employees

aboard—especially those in urgent need of specialized or technical skills. (But remember the trade-off: small businesses tend to fall into the high risk category, considering their overall failure rate.)

- It's no different than in big business: you gotta sell yourself, your skills, and the way in which you, unlike anybody else, can add value to the company. Small companies simply can't afford to hire nonproductive, noncontributing employees; the impact on the business is too immediate. They also have access now to experienced folks "downsized" by big companies so you've got to communicate your edge on the competition.
- Some job seekers are attached to the prestige of working for a "brand-name" large corporation. However, proponents of working for lesser-known, rapid-growth companies cite the personal satisfaction of getting in on, or slightly above, the ground floor and helping the company make a name for itself.
- Enthusiasm goes far in a small company. So do hard work, long hours, bright ideas, self-motivated work habits, calculated risk-taking, an ability to pitch in wherever needed and to shift gears quickly, and a healthy respect for authority (the CEO) tempered with the ability to question authority (the CEO)—diplomatically, of course.

The working environment in rapid-growth companies is usually exciting, chaotic, and ever-changing. Just keep in mind that not every rapid-growth company keeps growing rapidly. Again, examine the company's "unique proposition." Ask about future growth projections and product/service lines. Ask about employee turnover rates. Talk to a few different employees to get their take on the business and day-to-day office life. Discreetly explore sources and adequacy of financing. And definitely get a sense of a company's management style and philosophy. If you pick a winner in the rapid-growth ranks, and the climate suits you, the opportunity is there for you to grow with the business and make your mark.

Thanks are extended to A. David Silver for his assistance in preparation of this article.

EMPLOYER PROFILES

*A listing of major U.S. companies, organized in alphabetical order,
and selected government organizations*

AAF MCQUAY, INC.
13600 INDUSTRIAL PARK BOULEVARD
MINNEAPOLIS, MINNESOTA 55441

OVERVIEW: Manufactures air conditioning equipment and filtration products. Established: 1982.

KEY STATISTICS Annual Sales: $750.0 million. Number of Employees: 6,600.

HIRING HISTORY Number of professional employees hired in 1994: 45.

EXPERTISE/EDUCATION SOUGHT: Mechanical engineering, accounting

CONTACT: For individuals with previous experience: Ms Dina L Duchene, Human Resources Representative; Phone (612) 553-5330.

A B CHANCE COMPANY
210 NORTH ALLEN STREET
CENTRALLA, MISSOURI 65240-1302

OVERVIEW: Manufactures electrical switchgear apparatus. Established: 1987.

KEY STATISTICS Annual Sales: $162.0 million. Number of Employees: 1,400.

HIRING HISTORY Number of professional employees hired in 1994: 30.

EXPERTISE/EDUCATION SOUGHT: Mechanical engineering, electrical engineering

CONTACT: Ms Areta Mayes, Manager Employment and Benefits; Phone (314) 682-5521.

AB DICK, INC.
5700 WEST TOUHY AVENUE
NILES, ILLINOIS 60714-4628

OVERVIEW: Manufactures and distributes office equipment.

KEY STATISTICS Annual Sales: $513.0 million. Number of Employees: 5,500.

HIRING HISTORY Number of professional employees hired in 1994: 30.

EXPERTISE/EDUCATION SOUGHT: Sales, marketing, mechanical engineering, accounting

CONTACT: For individuals with previous experience: Ms Susan Guziak, Manager of Employment and Employee Relations; Phone (312) 763-4455.

ABB POWER T&D COMPANY, INC.
501 MERRITT 7, PO BOX 5308
NORWALK, CONNECTICUT 06856-5302

OVERVIEW: Manufactures power distribution equipment.

EXPERTISE/EDUCATION SOUGHT: Administration, accounting, law, finance, human resources, benefits administration

CONTACT: Ms Sally Lint, Manager of Employee Relations; Phone (203) 329-0771.

ABB VETCO GRAY, INC.
10777 NORTHWEST FREEWAY
HOUSTON, TEXAS 77092-7325

OVERVIEW: Manufactures oil and gas drilling equipment. Established: 1906. Parent Company: Asea Brown Boveri, Inc.

KEY STATISTICS Annual Sales: $324.0 million. Number of Employees: 3,200.

EXPERTISE/EDUCATION SOUGHT: Accounting, finance, manufacturing engineering, mechanical engineering

CONTACT: Ms Sharon Clarkson, Director of Human Resources; Phone (713) 878-5244.

ABBOTT LABORATORIES
1 ABBOTT PARK ROAD
ABBOTT PARK, ILLINOIS 60064-3500

OVERVIEW: Develops, manufactures, and markets pharmaceutical and nutritional products. Established: 1888.

KEY STATISTICS Annual Sales: $8.0 billion. Number of Employees: 50,000.

HIRING HISTORY Number of professional employees hired in 1993: 497.

EXPERTISE/EDUCATION SOUGHT: Biological sciences, chemistry, pharmacology, chemical engineering, mechanical engineering, electrical engineering, finance, accounting, human resources, computer science

CONTACT: Ms Jean Jackson-Swopes, PhD, Manager of College Relations; Phone (708) 937-9016.

ABCO MARKETS, INC.
3001 WEST INDIAN SCHOOL ROAD
PHOENIX, ARIZONA 85017-4168

OVERVIEW: Operates chain of food stores stores. Established: 1984.

KEY STATISTICS Annual Sales: $630.0 million. Number of Employees: 5,700.

EXPERTISE/EDUCATION SOUGHT: Accounting

CONTACT: For individuals with previous experience: Mr Darryl Simmons, Human Resources Specialist.

ABEX, INC.
LIBERTY LANE
HAMPTON, NEW HAMPSHIRE 03842

OVERVIEW: Manufactures fabricated metal products. Established: 1968.

KEY STATISTICS Annual Sales: $728.0 million. Number of Employees: 4,000.

EXPERTISE/EDUCATION SOUGHT: Accounting, finance, data processing

CONTACT: Ms Sherry Loudon, Director of Personnel; Phone (603) 929-2440.

ABF FREIGHT SYSTEM, INC.
3801 OLD GREENWOOD AVENUE
FORT SMITH, ARKANSAS 72903-3721

OVERVIEW: Provides trucking and shipping services. Established: 1935. Parent Company: Arkansas Best Corporation.

KEY STATISTICS Number of Employees: 10,582.

HIRING HISTORY Number of professional employees hired in 1994: 200. 1993: 200.

EXPERTISE/EDUCATION SOUGHT: Sales, marketing, transportation, business, accounting

CONTACT: Mr Dan Griesse, Director of Personnel, 301 South 11th Street, Fort Smith, AR, 72902-0048; Phone (501) 785-8710.

ACE HARDWARE CORPORATION
2222 KENSINGTON COURT
OAKBROOK, ILLINOIS 60521

OVERVIEW: Manufactures and sells hardware and tools. Established: 1974.

KEY STATISTICS Annual Sales: $2.0 billion. Number of Employees: 3,766.

EXPERTISE/EDUCATION SOUGHT: Sales, merchandising, marketing, accounting, finance, management information systems, information systems

CONTACTS: For college students and recent graduates: Ms. Meg Marshinski, Human Resource Representative; Phone (708) 990-6600. For individuals with previous experience: Mr Don Wallner, Human Resources Representative; Phone (708) 990-6600.

ADC TELECOMMUNICATIONS, INC.
4900 WEST 78TH STREET
MINNEAPOLIS, MINNESOTA 55435-5410

OVERVIEW: Designs and markets cable management, transmission, and networking products. Established: 1952.

KEY STATISTICS Annual Sales: $316.0 million. Number of Employees: 2,400.

EXPERTISE/EDUCATION SOUGHT: Sales, marketing, accounting, management

CONTACT: Human Resources Department; Phone (612) 938-8080.

ADELPHIA COMMUNICATIONS CORPORATION
5 WEST 3RD STREET
COUDERSPORT, PENNSYLVANIA 16915-1141

Overview: Provides cable television services. Established: 1952.

Key Statistics Annual Sales: $305.0 million. Number of Employees: 1,518.

Hiring History Number of professional employees hired in 1993: 12.

Expertise/Education Sought: Communications, television broadcasting, human resources, marketing, finance, sales, electrical engineering, mechanical engineering, design engineering

Contact: Mr Kenneth Cole, Recruitment Compliance Coordinator; Phone (814) 274-9830; Fax (814)274-9623.

ADIA PERSONNEL SERVICES, INC.
100 REDWOOD SHORES PARKWAY
REDWOOD CITY, CALIFORNIA 94065

Overview: Provides temporary personnel services.

Key Statistics Annual Sales: $918.0 million. Number of Employees: 252,050.

Expertise/Education Sought: Management information systems, computer programming, management

Contact: Ms Petrice Espinosa, Employee Relations Manager; Phone (415) 610-1197.

ADOBE SYSTEMS
411 1ST AVENUE SOUTH
SEATTLE, WASHINGTON 98104

Overview: Develops desk top publishing software.

Expertise/Education Sought: Accounting, data processing, software engineering/development, financial analysis, computer programming

Contact: Ms Jill Gilbert, Staffing Assistant; Phone (206) 622-5500.

ADVANCE AUTO PARTS
1342 8TH STREET SOUTHWEST
ROANOKE, VIRGINIA 24015

Overview: Distributes retail automotive parts and accessories. Established: 1932.

Key Statistics Number of Employees: 6,500.

Expertise/Education Sought: retail, store management

Contact: For college students and recent graduates: Mr Daryl G Porter, Human Resources Director; Phone (703) 345-4911; Fax (703) 344-1118.

CORPORATE STATEMENT

Advance Auto provides rewarding opportunities in the retail sector. With store operations in nine states, and as a leading retailer of automotive parts and accesssories, the company seeks qualified professionals for corporate office, distribution, and store management positions.

Send inquiries to: Advance Auto Parts, P.O. Box 2710, Roanoke, VA 24001, attention: Human Resources.

ADVANCE DIAL COMPANY
3439 NORTH HARLEM AVENUE
ELMHURST, ILLINOIS 60126-1131

Overview: Manufactures custom injection molded plastics. Parent Company: Anderson Industries, Inc.

Key Statistics Annual Sales: $26.0 million. Number of Employees: 300.

Expertise/Education Sought: Injection molding, mechanical engineering, accounting, data processing, finance

Contact: For individuals with previous experience: Mr George Stratton, Director of Engineering; Phone (312) 993-1700.

ADVANCE PUBLICATIONS, INC.
950 FINGERBOARD ROAD
STATEN ISLAND, NEW YORK 10305-1453

Overview: Publishes books, magazines, and newspapers and operates cable television systems. Established: 1949.

Key Statistics Annual Sales: $3.0 billion. Number of Employees: 19,000.

Expertise/Education Sought: Journalism, sales

Contact: For individuals with previous experience: Mr Jack Furnari, Marketing Manager; Phone (718) 981-1234.

ADVANCED LOGIC RESEARCH, INC.
9401 JERONIMO ROAD
IRVINE, CALIFORNIA 92718-1908

Overview: Manufactures and markets personal computers. Established: 1984.

Key Statistics Annual Sales: $169.0 million. Number of Employees: 560.

Expertise/Education Sought: Computer programming, computer engineering, sales

Contact: Ms Irene Rios, Human Resources Director; Phone (714) 581-6770.

ADVANCED MICRO DEVICES, INC.
1 AMD PLACE
SUNNYDALE, CALIFORNIA 94008-3453

Overview: Manufactures microprocessors and computer memory products. Established: 1969.

Key Statistics Annual Sales: $2.0 billion. Number of Employees: 12,060.

Expertise/Education Sought: Electrical engineering, computer engineering, materials science

Contacts: For college students and recent graduates: Mr Jim Johnston, Manager of Human Relations. For individuals with previous experience: Mr Gary Albright, Manager of Employment; Phone (408) 732-2400.

ADVANCED SCIENCES, INC.
6739 ACADEMY ROAD NORTHEAST
ALBUQUERQUE, NEW MEXICO 87109-3345

Overview: Researches and develops environmental and nuclear studies. Established: 1977.

Key Statistics Annual Sales: $51.0 million. Number of Employees: 675.

Hiring History Number of professional employees hired in 1994: 84.

Expertise/Education Sought: Environmental engineering, nuclear engineering, civil engineering, mechanical engineering, design engineering, chemical engineering, electrical engineering, health and safety, physics

Contact: Mr Kurt Tippin, Corporate Recruiter; Phone (505) 828-0959; Fax (505)823-6829.

ADVENTIST HEALTH SYSTEMS/WEST
2100 DOUGLAS BOULEVARD
ROSEVILLE, CALIFORNIA 95661-3804

Overview: Owns and operates hospitals and medical centers. Established: 1973.

Key Statistics Annual Sales: $858.4 million. Number of Employees: 13,200.

Expertise/Education Sought: Data processing, nursing, computer programming

CONTACTS: For college students and recent graduates: Mr Roger Ashley, Director of Human Resources; Phone (916) 781-4740. For individuals with previous experience: Ms Cathy Clark, Human Resources Specialist; Phone (916) 781-4740.

ADVO, INC.
1 UNIVAC LANE
WINDSOR, CONNECTICUT 06095-2629

OVERVIEW: Provides direct mail advertising services. Established: 1971.

KEY STATISTICS Annual Sales: $788.0 million. Number of Employees: 10,800.

EXPERTISE/EDUCATION SOUGHT: Marketing, sales, finance, accounting, auditing, business management, computer science, human resources

CONTACT: Mr Byron Peterson, Director of Human Resources; Phone (203) 285-6128; Fax (203) 285-6236.

ADVOCATE HEALTHCARE
2025 WINDSOR DRIVE
OAK BROOK, ILLINOIS 60521

OVERVIEW: Provides managed health care services. Established: 1897. Parent Company: Evangelical Health Systems Corporation.

KEY STATISTICS Annual Sales: $673.0 million. Number of Employees: 10,500.

EXPERTISE/EDUCATION SOUGHT: Accounting, marketing, finance, sales, nuclear technology, pharmacy, management information systems

CONTACT: For individuals with previous experience: Ms Laura Prescott-Smith; Phone (708) 990-5002, ext. 5380.

AEGON USA
4333 EDGEWOOD ROAD NORTHEAST
BALTIMORE, MARYLAND 21201-5544

OVERVIEW: Provides insurance and financial services. Parent Company: Aegon US Holding Corporation.

KEY STATISTICS Assets: $5.5 billion. Number of Employees: 5,474.

EXPERTISE/EDUCATION SOUGHT: Accounting, underwriting, finance, computer programming, finance, actuarial

CONTACT: Ms Wendy Murray, Human Resources Representative; Phone (319) 398-8511.

AETNA CAPITAL MANAGEMENT, INC.
151 FARMINGTON AVENUE
HARTFORD, CONNECTICUT 06156

OVERVIEW: Provides insurance.

KEY STATISTICS Annual Sales: $2.0 billion.

CONTACT: For individuals with previous experience: Ms Maryann Champlin, Director of Human Resources; Phone (203) 273-0123.

AETNA LIFE INSURANCE COMPANY
151 FARMINGTON AVENUE
HARTFORD, CONNECTICUT 06156

OVERVIEW: Provides group insurance, pensions, commercial insurance and individual life, auto and homeowners' coverage. Established: 1853. Parent Company: Aetna Life and Casualty Company.

KEY STATISTICS Number of Employees: 42,000.

EXPERTISE/EDUCATION SOUGHT: Business, actuarial, computer science, management information systems

CONTACTS: For college students and recent graduates: Mr Leo Collins, College Internship Recruiter; Phone (203) 273-1350. For individuals with previous experience: Ms CaroLee Zdanis, Director of Staffing; Phone (203) 273-1594.

AFFILIATED COMPUTER SERVICES, INC.
2828 NORTH HASKELL AVENUE
DALLAS, TEXAS 75204-2990

OVERVIEW: Provides information processing, software development, and various computer services. Established: 1988.

KEY STATISTICS Annual Sales: $227.0 million. Number of Employees: 2,600.

EXPERTISE/EDUCATION SOUGHT: Accounting, finance, marketing, data processing

CONTACT: Mr Kevin Frederick, Personnel Administrator; Phone (214) 841-6111.

AFLAC, INC.
1932 WYNNTON ROAD
COLUMBUS, GEORGIA 31999-0001

OVERVIEW: Provides health insurance. Established: 1973.

KEY STATISTICS Assets: $4.0 billion. Number of Employees: 3,618.

HIRING HISTORY Number of professional employees hired in 1994: 100.

EXPERTISE/EDUCATION SOUGHT: Health insurance, auditing, accounting, finance, computer programming

CONTACT: Ms Bev Alexander, Vice President of Human Resources; Phone (706) 323-3431.

AG PROCESSING, INC.
12700 WEST DODGE ROAD
OMAHA, NEBRASKA 68103-2047

OVERVIEW: Produces soybean based products. Established: 1942.

KEY STATISTICS Annual Sales: $1.0 billion. Number of Employees: 1,985.

HIRING HISTORY Number of professional employees hired in 1994: 200. 1993: 140.

EXPERTISE/EDUCATION SOUGHT: Merchandising, agricultural engineering, marketing, operations, agricultural science, project management, chemical engineering

CONTACT: Ms Linda Brown, Manager of Human Resources; Phone (402) 496-7809, ext. 223.

AGFA
100 CHALLENGER ROAD
RIDGEFIELD PARK, NEW JERSEY 07660

OVERVIEW: Designs, manufactures, and markets photographic equipment and film. Established: 1920. Parent Company: Bayer, Inc.

KEY STATISTICS Number of Employees: 5,000.

EXPERTISE/EDUCATION SOUGHT: Graphics engineering, sales, accounting

CONTACTS: For college students and recent graduates: Mr Guy Pedelini, Director of Human Resources; Phone (201) 440-2500. For individuals with previous experience: Mr Tim Romps, Vice President of Human Resources; Phone (201) 440-2500.

AGWAY, INC.
333 BUTTERNUT DRIVE
DEWITT, NEW YORK 13214-1879

OVERVIEW: Manufactures and distributes agricultural supplies and products. Established: 1964.

KEY STATISTICS Annual Sales: $3.0 billion. Number of Employees: 7,900.

EXPERTISE/EDUCATION SOUGHT: Chemical engineering, agricultural science, energy/energy management, physics, animal sciences, biology, agricultural engineering, accounting, finance, data processing

CONTACT: Mr Robert Engfer, Vice President of Human Resources; Phone (315) 449-7061.

AIR-A-PLANE CORPORATION
3040 EAST VIRGINIA BEACH BOULEVARD
NORFOLK, VIRGINIA 23504-4107

OVERVIEW: Manufactures air conditioning and heating equipment. Established: 1946.

KEY STATISTICS Annual Sales: $29.0 million. Number of Employees: 352.

EXPERTISE/EDUCATION SOUGHT: Production, electrical engineering, mechanical engineering, HVAC engineering

CONTACT: Ms Kimberly King, Human Resources Manager; Phone (804) 622-5761.

AIR LIQUIDE AMERICA CORPORATION
2121 NORTH CALIFORNIA BOULEVARD, SUITE 700
WALNUT CREEK, CALIFORNIA 94596

OVERVIEW: Manufactures and distributes industrial gases, welding apparatus, and metal working machinery.

EXPERTISE/EDUCATION SOUGHT: Chemical engineering

CONTACT: Ms Debra Alfred, Manager of Employment and College Relations, 3602 West 11th Street, Houston, TX, 77008; Phone (713) 868-0660.

AIR PRODUCTS AND CHEMICALS
7201 HAMILTON BOULEVARD
ALLENTOWN, PENNSYLVANIA 18195-1526

OVERVIEW: Manufactures industrial gases, chemicals, and environmental/energy systems. Established: 1940.

KEY STATISTICS Annual Sales: $4.0 billion. Number of Employees: 13,000.

EXPERTISE/EDUCATION SOUGHT: Finance, marketing

CONTACTS: For college students and recent graduates: University Relations; Phone (610) 481-7050. For individuals with previous experience: Mr Robert Schmelzer, Human Resources Recruiter; Phone (610) 481-4911, ext. 7152.

AIRBORNE EXPRESS
3101 WESTERN AVENUE
SEATTLE, WASHINGTON 98121

OVERVIEW: Provides package delivery, courier, and freight forwarding services. Established: 1947. Parent Company: Airborne Freight Corporation.

KEY STATISTICS Annual Sales: $1.0 billion. Number of Employees: 17,000.

HIRING HISTORY Number of professional employees hired in 1993: 50.

EXPERTISE/EDUCATION SOUGHT: Sales, accounting, data processing, program analysis, systems analysis, avionics, operations engineering, customer service and support

CONTACT: Mr Andrew Herman, Employment Representative.

AIRBORNE EXPRESS
145 HUNTER DRIVE
WILMINGTON, OHIO 45177-9390

OVERVIEW: Provides package delivery and courier services. Established: 1980. Parent Company: Airborne Freight Corporation.

KEY STATISTICS Annual Sales: $535.2 million. Number of Employees: 5,600.

EXPERTISE/EDUCATION SOUGHT: Computer science, electrical engineering, mechanical engineering, systems analysis, program analysis

CONTACTS: For college students and recent graduates: Ms Edna Puca, Employment Coordinator; Phone (513) 382-5591. For individuals with previous experience: Mr Hank Stroup, Recruitment Supervisor; Phone (513) 382-5591.

AK STEEL CORPORATION
703 CURTIS STREET
MIDDLETOWN, OHIO 45044-5812

OVERVIEW: Manufactures stainless steel and related products.

KEY STATISTICS Annual Sales: $1.0 billion. Number of Employees: 6,400.

EXPERTISE/EDUCATION SOUGHT: Metallurgical engineering, electrical engineering, mechanical engineering, electrical engineering

CONTACT: Mr Michael Lehman, Senior Human Resources Representative; Phone (513) 425-6405.

AKZO NOBEL, INC.
300 SOUTH RIVERSIDE PLAZA
CHICAGO, ILLINOIS 60606-6613

OVERVIEW: Manufactures chemicals. Established: 1928.

KEY STATISTICS Annual Sales: $2.0 billion. Number of Employees: 10,650.

HIRING HISTORY Number of professional employees hired in 1993: 25.

EXPERTISE/EDUCATION SOUGHT: Accounting, finance, computer science, law, data processing, chemical engineering

CONTACT: For individuals with previous experience: Ms Melissa Van, Manager of Recruiting; Phone (312) 906-7500, ext. 7769; Fax (312) 906-7014.

ALADAN CORPORATION
2926 COLUMBIA HIGHWAY
DOTHAN, ALABAMA 36303

OVERVIEW: Manufactures latex gloves and condoms. Established: 1986.

KEY STATISTICS Annual Sales: $61.0 million. Number of Employees: 438.

HIRING HISTORY Number of professional employees hired in 1993: 200.

EXPERTISE/EDUCATION SOUGHT: Engineering, accounting

CONTACT: Ms Belinda Bracewell, Director of Personnel; Phone (205) 793-4509; Fax (205) 792-2753.

ALBANY INTERNATIONAL CORPORATION
1373 BROADWAY
ALBANY, NEW YORK 12204-2697

OVERVIEW: Manufactures felt. Established: 1895.

KEY STATISTICS Number of Employees: 5,286.

EXPERTISE/EDUCATION SOUGHT: Marketing, finance, sales, business management, process engineering, chemical engineering, mechanical engineering, electrical engineering

CONTACT: Mr Barry Jessee, Director Human Resources; Phone (518) 445-2200.

ALBERTSON'S, INC.
250 PARK CENTER BOULEVARD
BOISE, IDAHO 83706-3999

OVERVIEW: Operates chain of food and drug stores. Established: 1939.

KEY STATISTICS Annual Sales: $10.0 billion. Number of Employees: 77,100.

HIRING HISTORY Number of professional employees hired in 1993: 35.

EXPERTISE/EDUCATION SOUGHT: Accounting, electrical engineering, architecture, civil engineering, law, computer programming, marketing, sales, mechanical engineering, computer operations

CONTACT: Ms Natalie Bridges, Employment Administrator; Phone (208) 385-6397.

ALCAN ALUMINUM CORPORATION
100 ERIEVIEW PLAZA
CLEVELAND, OHIO 44114-1824

OVERVIEW: Produces aluminum. Established: 1960.

KEY STATISTICS Annual Sales: $3.0 billion.

EXPERTISE/EDUCATION SOUGHT: Auditing, finance, law, accounting

CONTACT: Mr Tom Skeen, Vice President of Human Resources; Phone (216) 523-6800.

ALCATEL CABLE SYSTEMS, INC.
2512 PENNY ROAD
CLAIRMONT, NORTH CAROLINA 28610

OVERVIEW: Manufactures wire and cable.

EXPERTISE/EDUCATION SOUGHT: Electrical engineering, mechanical engineering, materials engineering

CONTACT: Mr Wayne Cole, Vice President of Human Resources; Phone (704) 459-9787, ext. 8314.

ALCO STANDARD CORPORATION
825 DUPORTAIL ROAD
WAYNE, PENNSYLVANIA 19087-5589

OVERVIEW: Distributes paper products and office equipment. Established: 1928.

KEY STATISTICS Annual Sales: $6.0 billion. Number of Employees: 28,500.

HIRING HISTORY Number of professional employees hired in 1994: 20.

EXPERTISE/EDUCATION SOUGHT: Accounting, finance, tax

CONTACT: Ms Elizabeth Barrett, Director of MIS and Personnel; Phone (610) 296-8000.

ALCO THERMOPLASTICS, INC.
1400 INDUSTRIAL DRIVE
MISHAWAKA, INDIANA 46544-5720

OVERVIEW: Manufactures injection molded plastics. Established: 1985.

KEY STATISTICS Annual Sales: $31.0 million. Number of Employees: 318.

EXPERTISE/EDUCATION SOUGHT: Plastics engineering, injection molding, chemical engineering, mechanical engineering, accounting, finance, data processing

CONTACT: Ms Tracy Kerrigan, Personnel Supervisor; Phone (219) 256-0277, ext. 247; Fax (219)255-2579.

ALCOA FUJIKURA, LTD.
105 WESTPARK DRIVE, SUITE 200
BRENTWOOD, TENNESSEE 37027

OVERVIEW: Manufactures motor vehicle parts and accessories. Established: 1984. Parent Company: Aluminum Company of America.

KEY STATISTICS Annual Sales: $590.0 million. Number of Employees: 9,500.

HIRING HISTORY Number of professional employees hired in 1993: 40.

EXPERTISE/EDUCATION SOUGHT: Accounting, finance, marketing, sales

CONTACT: For individuals with previous experience: Mr Gus Agustinelli, Vice President of Human Resources; Phone (615) 370-2100.

ALCON LABORATORIES
6201 SOUTH FREEWAY
FORT WORTH, TEXAS 76134-2099

OVERVIEW: Manufactures eye care products and ophthalmic instruments. Established: 1981.

EXPERTISE/EDUCATION SOUGHT: Computer programming, data processing, information systems, product management, production control, production management, quality control, pharmaceutical

CONTACT: Placement Division; Phone (817) 293-0450.

JOHN ALDEN LIFE INSURANCE COMPANY
7300 CORPORATE CENTER DRIVE
MIAMI, FLORIDA 33126-1232

OVERVIEW: Provides life insurance and financial investment services. Established: 1961.

KEY STATISTICS Annual Sales: $1.0 billion. Number of Employees: 3,126.

EXPERTISE/EDUCATION SOUGHT: Finance, computer programming, network analysis, accounting

CONTACTS: For college students and recent graduates: Mr Jay Rombach, Recruiter; Phone (305) 715-2802. For individuals with previous experience: Ms April Harris, Senior Personnel Associate; Phone (305) 715-2000.

ALEX LEE, INC.
120 4TH STREET SOUTHWEST
HICKORY, NORTH CAROLINA 28602-2947

OVERVIEW: Wholesales to food stores.

KEY STATISTICS Annual Sales: $1.0 billion. Number of Employees: 4,500.

EXPERTISE/EDUCATION SOUGHT: Accounting, marketing, distribution, management, information systems, human resources

CONTACT: For individuals with previous experience: Mr Glenn DeBiasi, Vice President of Human Resources; Phone (704) 323-4403.

ALEXANDER AND ALEXANDER OF NEW YORK, INC.
1211 AVENUE OF THE AMERICAS
NEW YORK, NEW YORK 10036-8701

OVERVIEW: Provides insurance and management consulting services. Established: 1899.

KEY STATISTICS Annual Sales: $2.0 billion. Number of Employees: 14,200.

EXPERTISE/EDUCATION SOUGHT: Systems integration, accounting, marketing, finance, actuarial, underwriting

CONTACT: Ms Shani Loren, Human Resources Specialist; Phone (212) 840-8500.

ALL TRI-R, INC.
108 SOUTH POPLAR STREET
PANA, ILLINOIS 62557-1404

OVERVIEW: Provides general contracting services. Established: 1979.

KEY STATISTICS Annual Sales: $29.0 million. Number of Employees: 500.

EXPERTISE/EDUCATION SOUGHT: Accounting, finance, data processing

CONTACT: Ms Marilyn Peifer, Office Manager; Phone (217) 562-5113; Fax (217)562-5093.

ALLDATA CORPORATION
9412 BIG HORN BOULEVARD
ELK GROVE, CALIFORNIA 95758-1100

OVERVIEW: Provides information retrieval and repair services. Established: 1986.

KEY STATISTICS Annual Sales: $31.0 million. Number of Employees: 292.

HIRING HISTORY Number of professional employees hired in 1993: 140.

EXPERTISE/EDUCATION SOUGHT: Accounting, finance, electrical engineering, mechanical engineering, software engineering/development, sales

CONTACT: Ms Debbie Lewis, Recruiting Coordinator; Phone (916) 684-5200.

ALLEGHENY POWER SYSTEMS, INC.
12 EAST 49TH STREET
NEW YORK, NEW YORK 10017

OVERVIEW: Electric utility.

EXPERTISE/EDUCATION SOUGHT: Computer science, electrical engineering, mechanical engineering, applied engineering

CONTACT: Ms Jane Downey, Director of Employment, 800 Cabin Hill Drive, Greensburg, PA, 15601; Phone (412) 837-3000.

ALLEN-BRADLEY COMPANY, INC.
1201 SOUTH 2ND STREET
MILWAUKEE, WISCONSIN 53204-2410

OVERVIEW: Manufactures industrial automation control equipment and systems. Established: 1903. Parent Company: Rockwell International Corporation.

Allen-Bradley Company, Inc. (continued)

KEY STATISTICS Annual Sales: $2.0 billion. Number of Employees: 11,200.

EXPERTISE/EDUCATION SOUGHT: Mechanical engineering, sales, electrical engineering, applied engineering, industrial engineering, human resources, marketing, data processing, communications, computer programming

CONTACTS: For college students and recent graduates: Ms Susan Hagen, Human Resources Representative; Phone (414) 382-2000, ext. 4550. For individuals with previous experience: Ms Joy Aleksick, Professional Employment Representative; Phone (414) 382-2000, ext. 2603.

ALLERGAN, INC.
2525 DUPONT DRIVE
IRVINE, CALIFORNIA 92715-1599

OVERVIEW: Manufactures ophthalmic, optical, and pharmaceutical products. Established: 1948.

KEY STATISTICS Annual Sales: $859.0 million. Number of Employees: 4,749.

EXPERTISE/EDUCATION SOUGHT: Sales, pharmaceutical, research and development, science

CONTACT: Mr Rob Quinn, Manager of Human Resources.

ALLIANT TECHSYSTEMS, INC.
600 SECOND STREET NORTHEAST
HOPKINS, MINNESOTA 55343-8367

OVERVIEW: Manufactures military hardware and navigation equipment.

KEY STATISTICS Annual Sales: $775.0 million. Number of Employees: 4,900.

HIRING HISTORY Number of professional employees hired in 1994: 10.

EXPERTISE/EDUCATION SOUGHT: Mechanical engineering, electrical engineering, computer science, accounting, finance, management information systems

CONTACTS: For college students and recent graduates: Ms Cheri Harlan, Staffing Administrator; Phone (612) 931-5753. For individuals with previous experience: Ms Jeanne Jakel, Manager of Staffing; Phone (612) 931-5752.

ALLIANZ INVESTMENT CORPORATION
55 GREENS FARMS ROAD
WESTPORT, CONNECTICUT 06880-6149

OVERVIEW: Provides property and casualty insurance. Established: 1976.

KEY STATISTICS Annual Sales: $3.0 billion. Number of Employees: 10,000.

EXPERTISE/EDUCATION SOUGHT: Actuarial, law, underwriting, product design and development, health insurance, sales, marketing, data processing, claims adjustment/examination, program analysis

CONTACT: Mr Ed Fitzpatrick, Assistant Vice President of Human Resources; Phone (612) 347-6500.

ALLIED SECURITY, INC.
2840 LIBRARY ROAD
PITTSBURGH, PENNSYLVANIA 15234-2621

OVERVIEW: Provides security guard and detective services. Established: 1957.

KEY STATISTICS Number of Employees: 7,200.

EXPERTISE/EDUCATION SOUGHT: Sales, marketing, management

CONTACT: For individuals with previous experience: Mr Philip B Schugar, Manager of Human Resources; Phone (412) 884-2636.

ALLIED-SIGNAL, INC.
101 COLUMBIA ROAD
MORRISTOWN, NEW JERSEY 07962-4638

OVERVIEW: Manufactures aerospace and automotive components, and engineered materials. Established: 1899.

KEY STATISTICS Annual Sales: $12.0 billion. Number of Employees: 86,400.

EXPERTISE/EDUCATION SOUGHT: Electrical engineering, mechanical engineering, industrial engineering, civil engineering, metallurgical engineering

CONTACT: Ms Louise Monahan, Director of Staffing and Recruitment; Phone (201) 455-2000, ext. 2267.

ALLIED-SIGNAL TECHNICAL SERVICES CORPORATION
1 BENDIX ROAD
COLUMBIA, MARYLAND 21045-1832

OVERVIEW: Provides technical services to the aerospace industry. Established: 1950. Parent Company: Allied-Signal, Inc.

KEY STATISTICS Annual Sales: $546.0 million. Number of Employees: 7,000.

HIRING HISTORY Number of professional employees hired in 1993: 100.

EXPERTISE/EDUCATION SOUGHT: Electrical engineering, computer engineering, mechanical engineering, aerospace engineering, computer science, mathematics

CONTACT: Ms Pamela Bridges, Supervisor of Staffing; Phone (410) 964-7000.

ALLIED VAN LINES
215 WEST DIEHL ROAD
NAPERVILLE, ILLINOIS 60563-8457

OVERVIEW: Provides trucking and moving services. Established: 1928.

KEY STATISTICS Annual Sales: $900.0 million. Number of Employees: 4,000.

EXPERTISE/EDUCATION SOUGHT: Operations, customer service and support, transportation

CONTACT: Mr William C Buckland, Vice President of Human Resources; Phone (708) 717-3151.

ALLINA HEALTH SYSTEM
5601 SMETANA DRIVE
MINNETONKA, MINNESOTA 55343-5000

OVERVIEW: Manages hospitals and home care agencies.

KEY STATISTICS Annual Sales: $948.0 million. Number of Employees: 16,000.

EXPERTISE/EDUCATION SOUGHT: Collection, accounting, marketing, computer programming, operations, finance

CONTACT: For individuals with previous experience: Ms Anne Remy, Vice President of Human Resources; Phone (612) 992-2900.

ALLMERICA FINANCIAL CORPORATION
440 LINCOLN STREET
WORCESTER, MASSACHUSETTS 01653-0002

OVERVIEW: Provides life insurance. Established: 1844.

KEY STATISTICS Assets: $3.0 billion. Number of Employees: 10,000.

EXPERTISE/EDUCATION SOUGHT: Accounting, information systems, law, advertising, graphic arts, mathematics

CONTACT: Ms Kathy Vroman, Manager of Human Resources; Phone (508) 853-7200.

ALLSTATE INSURANCE COMPANY
2755 SANDERS ROAD, SUITE A1
NORTHBROOK, ILLINOIS 60062

OVERVIEW: Provides property, casualty, life, business, and mortgage insurance and motor club services. Established: 1931. Parent Company: Allstate Corporation.

KEY STATISTICS Number of Employees: 49,000.

EXPERTISE/EDUCATION SOUGHT: Actuarial, accounting, finance, mathematics, investment, administration

CONTACT: Mr Edwin Felice, Manager of Human Resources; Phone (708) 402-7182.

ALLTEL CORPORATION
ONE ALLIED DRIVE
LITTLE ROCK, ARKANSAS 72203

OVERVIEW: Supplies telecommunications equipment and services. Established: 1960.

KEY STATISTICS Annual Sales: $3.0 billion. Number of Employees: 16,300.

EXPERTISE/EDUCATION SOUGHT: Telecommunications, communications, accounting, finance, customer service and support, marketing

CONTACT: For individuals with previous experience: Ms Cindy Thomas, Staff Manager Employment Services, PO Box 2177, Little Rock, AR, 72203-2177; Phone (501) 221-5100.

ALLTEL INFORMATION SERVICES, INC.
4001 NORTH RODNEY PARHAM ROAD
LITTLE ROCK, ARKANSAS 72212-2442

OVERVIEW: Provides data processing services for financial, telecommunications, and health care industries. Established: 1970. Parent Company: Alltel Corporation.

KEY STATISTICS Annual Sales: $861.0 million. Number of Employees: 7,800.

HIRING HISTORY Number of professional employees hired in 1993: 200.

EXPERTISE/EDUCATION SOUGHT: Computer programming, program analysis, database management, network analysis, telecommunications

CONTACT: For individuals with previous experience: Cindy Thomas, Staff Manager Employment Services, PO Box 2177; Phone (510) 220-5100.

ALLTEL MOBILE COMMUNICATIONS
ONE ALLIED DRIVE
LITTLE ROCK, ARKANSAS 72203

OVERVIEW: Provides cellular telephone services. Established: 1985. Parent Company: Alltel Corporation.

KEY STATISTICS Annual Sales: $321.0 million. Number of Employees: 1,600.

HIRING HISTORY Number of professional employees hired in 1993: 50.

EXPERTISE/EDUCATION SOUGHT: Communications, accounting, finance, data processing, customer service and support, marketing, telecommunications

CONTACT: For individuals with previous experience: Ms Cindy Thomas, Staff Manager Employment Services, PO Box 2177, Little Rock, AR, 72203-2177; Phone (501) 220-5100.

ALTEC INDUSTRIES, INC.
210 INVERNESS CENTER DRIVE
BIRMINGHAM, ALABAMA 35242-4808

OVERVIEW: Manufactures utility trucks. Established: 1929.

KEY STATISTICS Annual Sales: $222.0 million. Number of Employees: 1,500.

HIRING HISTORY Number of professional employees hired in 1994: 43. 1993: 12.

EXPERTISE/EDUCATION SOUGHT: Research, accounting, sales, information systems, computer programming, program analysis

CONTACT: Mr Bill Riley, Director of Human Resources Administration; Phone (205) 991-7733.

ALTERNATE CIRCUIT TECHNOLOGY, INC.
46 ROGERS ROAD
WARD HILL, MASSACHUSETTS 01835-6969

OVERVIEW: Manufactures printed circuit boards. Established: 1982.

KEY STATISTICS Annual Sales: $23.8 million. Number of Employees: 220.

HIRING HISTORY Number of professional employees hired in 1994: 121.

EXPERTISE/EDUCATION SOUGHT: Manufacturing engineering, electrical engineering, electronics/electronics engineering

CONTACT: Ms Lucy Wiciel, Manager of Personnel; Phone (508) 372-0200; Fax (508)521-0773.

ALUMAX, INC.
5655 PEACHTREE PARKWAY
NORCROSS, GEORGIA 30092

OVERVIEW: Produces aluminum. Established: 1973.

EXPERTISE/EDUCATION SOUGHT: Accounting, auditing, law, risk management, systems integration, marketing, finance, management information systems, computer programming, public relations

CONTACT: Ms Krista Wilbanks, Employment Manager; Phone (404) 246-6775.

ALUMINUM COMPANY OF AMERICA
425 6TH AVENUE
PITTSBURGH, PENNSYLVANIA 15219-1819

OVERVIEW: Produces aluminum and aluminum products. Established: 1888.

KEY STATISTICS Annual Sales: $9.0 billion. Number of Employees: 62,000.

EXPERTISE/EDUCATION SOUGHT: Accounting, finance, computer science, law, environmental

CONTACT: For individuals with previous experience: Mr T L Carter, Vice President of Education and Training, 1501 Alcoa, Pittsburgh, PA, 15219; Phone (412) 553-4545.

ALUSUISSE FLEXIBLE PACKAGING
5303 SAINT CHARLES ROAD
BELLWOOD, ILLINOIS 60104-1048

OVERVIEW: Manufactures flexible packaging for food. Established: 1985. Parent Company: Alusuisse-Lonza America, Inc.

KEY STATISTICS Number of Employees: 480.

EXPERTISE/EDUCATION SOUGHT: Accounting, graphic arts, printing

CONTACT: For individuals with previous experience: Ms Joann Brooke, Human Resources Administrator, 6700 Midland Industrial Drive, Shelbyville, KY, 40065; Phone (502) 633-6800.

AM INTERNATIONAL, INC.
1800 WEST CENTRAL ROAD
MOUNT PROSPECT, ILLINOIS 60056-1218

OVERVIEW: Manufactures industrial equipment for the printing industry. Established: 1924.

KEY STATISTICS Annual Sales: $535.0 million.

EXPERTISE/EDUCATION SOUGHT: Sales, accounting, finance, marketing, management information systems

CONTACT: For individuals with previous experience: Ms Mary Anne Gruber, Director of Corporate Human Resources; Phone (708) 292-0600.

AMCEL CORPORATION
1 GALEN STREET
WATERTOWN, MASSACHUSETTS 02172-4501

OVERVIEW: Manufactures plastic garbage can liners. Established: 1977.

KEY STATISTICS Annual Sales: $75.0 million. Number of Employees: 300.

EXPERTISE/EDUCATION SOUGHT: Data processing, computer programming, finance, accounting

Amcel Corporation (continued)

CONTACT: Mr Paul Vogel, Human Resources Controller; Phone (617) 924-0800; Fax (617)924-2931.

AMDAHL CORPORATION
1250 EAST ARQUES AVENUE
SUNNYVALE, CALIFORNIA 94086-4730

OVERVIEW: Manufactures mainframe computers, communications equipment, and software. Established: 1970.

KEY STATISTICS Annual Sales: $2.0 billion. Number of Employees: 5,552.

EXPERTISE/EDUCATION SOUGHT: Accounting, finance, marketing

CONTACT: For individuals with previous experience: Ms Regine Von Aspe, Staffing Specialist; Phone (408) 746-6000.

AMERADA HESS CORPORATION
1185 AVENUE OF THE AMERICAS
NEW YORK, NEW YORK 10036-2601

OVERVIEW: Produces oil, gas, and petroleum based products. Established: 1920.

KEY STATISTICS Annual Sales: $6.0 billion. Number of Employees: 10,173.

EXPERTISE/EDUCATION SOUGHT: Marketing, finance, sales, accounting, management information systems, chemical engineering, mechanical engineering

CONTACT: Mr Larry Fox, Manager of Employee Relations; Phone (212) 997-8500; Fax (212)536-8318.

AMERCO
1325 AIRMOTIVE
RENO, NEVADA 89502-3201

OVERVIEW: Provides truck and trailer rental services. Established: 1971.

KEY STATISTICS Annual Sales: $1.0 billion. Number of Employees: 10,900.

EXPERTISE/EDUCATION SOUGHT: Marketing, finance, sales, data processing

CONTACT: Ms Joann Hoffman, Manager of Employment; Phone (602) 263-6011.

AMERICA NATIONAL INSURANCE
1 MOODY PLAZA
GALVESTON, TEXAS 77550

OVERVIEW: Provides insurance services. Established: 1905.

KEY STATISTICS Assets: $9.0 billion. Number of Employees: 1,500.

HIRING HISTORY Number of professional employees hired in 1994: 20.

EXPERTISE/EDUCATION SOUGHT: Actuarial, marketing, accounting, computer programming, management

CONTACT: Mr William H McCollum, Personnel Director; Phone (409) 763-4661.

AMERICAN AIRLINES, INC.
4333 AMON CARTER BOULEVARD
FORT WORTH, TEXAS 76155-2664

OVERVIEW: Passenger airline. Parent Company: AMR Corporation.

KEY STATISTICS Annual Sales: $15.0 billion. Number of Employees: 95,800.

EXPERTISE/EDUCATION SOUGHT: Accounting, management information systems, finance, marketing, sales, computer science, computer programming, computer analysis

CONTACTS: For college students and recent graduates: Ms Dorothy Mattingly, Administrator/College Relations, PO Box 619616, MD 5105, DFW Airport, TX, 75261-9616; Phone (817) 963-1146; Fax (817) 967-4380. For individuals with previous experience: Ms Mary Jordan, Vice President of Personnel Resources, PO Box 619616, MD 5123, Fort Worth, TX, 76155; Phone (817) 963-1234.

AMERICAN AUTOMOBILE ASSOCIATION
1000 AAA DRIVE
HEATHROW, FLORIDA 32746-5063

OVERVIEW: Provides insurance, travel, and related automotive services to members. Established: 1910.

KEY STATISTICS Annual Sales: $399.5 million. Number of Employees: 3,200.

EXPERTISE/EDUCATION SOUGHT: Accounting, publishing, health insurance, public relations, human resources, market research, publishing, management, finance, management information systems

CONTACT: Mrs Jamie Croteau, Staffing Employee Relations Analyst; Phone (407) 444-7000.

AMERICAN BRANDS, INC.
1700 EAST PUTMAN AVENUE
OLD GREENWICH, CONNECTICUT 06870-1321

OVERVIEW: Manufactures and markets consumer products. Established: 1904.

KEY STATISTICS Annual Sales: $15.0 billion. Number of Employees: 47,000.

EXPERTISE/EDUCATION SOUGHT: Finance, accounting

CONTACTS: For college students and recent graduates: Ms Alean N Timm, Assistant Manager Corporate Office Personnel; Phone (203) 698-5000. For individuals with previous experience: Mr Robert M Garber, Manager Corporate Office Personnel; Phone (203) 698-5000.

AMERICAN BROADCASTING COMPANIES
77 WEST 66TH STREET
NEW YORK, NEW YORK 10023-6201

OVERVIEW: Operates radio and television stations and networks. Established: 1986. Parent Company: ABC Holding Company, Inc.

KEY STATISTICS Annual Sales: $919.0 million. Number of Employees: 8,000.

EXPERTISE/EDUCATION SOUGHT: Finance, accounting, law, marketing, computer programming, electrical engineering

CONTACT: For individuals with previous experience: Mr Brendan Burke, Director of Employee Relations; Phone (212) 456-7777.

AMERICAN BUILDING MAINTENANCE INDUSTRIES
50 FREMONT STREET
SAN FRANCISCO, CALIFORNIA 94105-2230

OVERVIEW: Provides janitorial, security, and building maintenance services. Established: 1909.

KEY STATISTICS Annual Sales: $760.0 million. Number of Employees: 40,000.

EXPERTISE/EDUCATION SOUGHT: Mechanical engineering, electrical engineering, human resources, management, real estate, accounting, finance

CONTACT: Ms Nancy Tatum, Director of Human Resources; Phone (415) 597-4500.

AMERICAN COMMERCIAL LINES
1701 EAST MARKET STREET
JEFFERSONVILLE, INDIANA 47130-4747

OVERVIEW: Manufactures and repairs ships. Established: 1972. Parent Company: American Commercial Lines, Inc.

KEY STATISTICS Annual Sales: $127.2 million. Number of Employees: 1,200.

HIRING HISTORY Number of professional employees hired in 1994: 4. 1993: 10.

EXPERTISE/EDUCATION SOUGHT: Naval architecture, mechanical engineering, design engineering, manufacturing engineering, metallurgical engineering, drafting

CONTACT: Mr Robert Heree, Vice President of Engineering; Phone (812) 288-0162; Fax (812)288-0452.

AMERICAN CYANAMID COMPANY
1 CYANAMID PLAZA
WAYNE, NEW JERSEY 07470-8428

OVERVIEW: Produces agricultural, animal health and nutrition, and medical products. Established: 1907.

KEY STATISTICS Annual Sales: $4.3 billion. Number of Employees: 26,550.

EXPERTISE/EDUCATION SOUGHT: Sales, marketing, finance, chemistry, biochemistry, manufacturing engineering

CONTACT: For individuals with previous experience: Mr Robert Koegel, Director of Personnel Resources; Phone (201) 831-2000, ext. 3085.

AMERICAN DRUG STORES, INC.
1818 SWIFT DRIVE
HINSDALE, ILLINOIS 60521-1576

OVERVIEW: Operates chain of drug stores. Established: 1930. Parent Company: American Stores Company.

KEY STATISTICS Annual Sales: $4.0 billion. Number of Employees: 25,000.

EXPERTISE/EDUCATION SOUGHT: Management, pharmacy

CONTACT: For individuals with previous experience: Ms Elizabeth Cardello, Director of Recruitment; Phone (708) 572-5000, ext. 5294.

AMERICAN ELECTRIC POWER COMPANY
1 RIVERSIDE PLAZA
COLUMBUS, OHIO 43215-2373

OVERVIEW: Electric utility. Established: 1906.

KEY STATISTICS Annual Sales: $15.0 billion. Number of Employees: 20,007.

EXPERTISE/EDUCATION SOUGHT: Computer programming, computer engineering, engineering, finance, law, accounting

CONTACT: Ms Mary G Cofer, Manager of Personnel Services and Equal Employment Opportunity; Phone (614) 223-1000.

AMERICAN EXPRESS COMPANY
AMERICAN EXPRESS TOWER
NEW YORK, NEW YORK 10285

OVERVIEW: Provides credit cards, travelers checks, and other financial services. Established: 1850.

KEY STATISTICS Annual Sales: $14.0 billion. Number of Employees: 72,412.

HIRING HISTORY Number of professional employees hired in 1994: 7,919.

EXPERTISE/EDUCATION SOUGHT: Marketing, finance, accounting, auditing, data processing, human resources, operations, sales

CONTACT: For individuals with previous experience: Mr Neil Begley, Senior Director of Human Resources; Phone (212) 640-5050.

AMERICAN FAMILY ASSURANCE COLLECTIVE
1932 WYNNTON ROAD
COLUMBUS, GEORGIA 31999-0001

OVERVIEW: Provides health insurance. Established: 1973. Parent Company: Aflac, Inc.

KEY STATISTICS Annual Sales: $3.9 billion. Number of Employees: 3,500.

HIRING HISTORY Number of professional employees hired in 1993: 225.

EXPERTISE/EDUCATION SOUGHT: Customer service and support, telecommunications, computer engineering, actuarial, computer programming, finance, law, marketing, underwriting, accounting

CONTACT: Ms Beverly Alexander, Assistant Vice President of Human Resources; Phone (706) 323-3431.

AMERICAN FINE WIRE CORPORATION
907 RAVENWOOD DRIVE
SELMA, ALABAMA 36701-6724

OVERVIEW: Manufactures bonding wire. Established: 1977. Parent Company: Circle S Industries, Inc.

KEY STATISTICS Annual Sales: $48.0 million. Number of Employees: 300.

EXPERTISE/EDUCATION SOUGHT: Mechanical engineering, accounting, data processing, finance

CONTACT: Mr Charles Morello, Manager of Personnel; Phone (205) 875-4040.

AMERICAN FROZEN FOODS
355 BENTON STREET
STRATFORD, CONNECTICUT 06067

OVERVIEW: Provides shop at home food service. Established: 1921.

KEY STATISTICS Number of Employees: 1,200.

HIRING HISTORY Number of professional employees hired in 1994: 200. 1993: 200.

EXPERTISE/EDUCATION SOUGHT: Sales

CONTACTS: For college students and recent graduates: Mr Rich Silva, Recruitment Coordinator; Phone (800) 233-5554. For individuals with previous experience: Ms Debra Russo, Director of Recruitment; Phone (800) 233-5554.

CORPORATE STATEMENT

*A*merican Frozen Foods is one of the largest shop-at-home food services in the country. The company processes, packages, sells, and delivers food products directly to the consumer.

American General Finance

A Subsidiary of American General Corporation

AMERICAN GENERAL FINANCE
601 NORTHWEST 2ND STREET
EVANSVILLE, INDIANA 47701-0059

OVERVIEW: Provides consumer financing and insurance services. Established: 1920. Parent Company: American General Corporation.

KEY STATISTICS Annual Sales: $1.0 billion. Number of Employees: 8,500.

EXPERTISE/EDUCATION SOUGHT: Computer science, industrial engineering, software engineering/development, accounting, finance, business, statistics/QBA

CONTACT: Mr Darryl Farrow, Employment Consultant, PO Box 59, Evansville, IL, 47701-0059; Phone (812) 468-5677.

American General Finance (continued)

CORPORATE PROFILE

American General Finance, founded in 1920, has grown to become a consumer finance leader, with over 1,300 branch offices in 41 states, Puerto Rico, and the Virgin Islands.

American General Finance offers traditional consumer loans, retail sales financing, and real estate secured loans as well as life, health, and property insurance nationwide.

American General Finance is a subsidiary of American General Corporation and is one of three major business segments of this $54-billion financial services company.

American General Finance is searching for qualified candidates to become Systems Control Consultants. Systems Control Consultants are professional-level internal consultants who work with designated managers to develop, maintain, and improve American General's operating systems, i.e., budget, approval control, audit, and policies and procedures systems. Successful candidates will have a bachelor's degree (master's preferred), a GPA of 3.0 or better, and three to five years of experience in industrial engineering, systems design, accounting, methods and procedures, or other similar areas.

American General Finance also offers the Delta Program, which is an intensive training program designed to develop individuals for management positions in American General's branch network. Delta Associates are responsible for the profitable management of a branch. Qualified individuals must have a bachelor's degree with a minimum of two years of experience in marketing, retail, supervision, management, or sales training. Relocation is required.

American General Finance also may have opportunities for qualified candidates in the following disciplines: accounting, actuarial science, auditing, budget and financial analysis, legal, human resources, marketing, programming or information systems, credit card, mortgage lending, and others.

Individuals interested in these positions or other opportunities should submit their résumé to American General Finance's employment department.

American General Finance is an equal opportunity employer.

American General Finance may also have branch opportunities. Challenging and rewarding opportunities exist in the nationwide branch network. For information regarding branch, sales, service, or management positions, contact the nearest American General Finance office.

AMERICAN GOLF CORPORATION
1633 26TH STREET
SANTA MONICA, CALIFORNIA 90404-4023

OVERVIEW: Operates public golf courses. Established: 1968.

KEY STATISTICS Annual Sales: $239.0 million. Number of Employees: 6,000.

EXPERTISE/EDUCATION SOUGHT: Accounting, human resources, marketing, law, sales, management

CONTACT: For individuals with previous experience: Mr Mike Norman, Recruiter; Phone (310) 315-4200.

AMERICAN GREETINGS CORPORATION
10500 AMERICAN ROAD
CLEVELAND, OHIO 44144-2301

OVERVIEW: Manufactures greeting cards, gift items, and party goods. Established: 1906.

KEY STATISTICS Annual Sales: $2.0 billion. Number of Employees: 21,400.

HIRING HISTORY Number of professional employees hired in 1994: 150.

EXPERTISE/EDUCATION SOUGHT: Sales, marketing, accounting, public relations, industrial engineering, information systems

CONTACT: For individuals with previous experience: Mr Ron D Novak, Manager of Human Resources; Phone (216) 252-7300.

AMERICAN-HAWAII CRUISES
2 NORTH RIVERSIDE PLAZA
CHICAGO, ILLINOIS 60606

OVERVIEW: Operates cruise line. Established: 1979.

EXPERTISE/EDUCATION SOUGHT: Accounting, management information systems, travel/tourism

CONTACT: For individuals with previous experience: Ms Karen Kaufman, Manager/Employment and Benefits.

AMERICAN HOME PRODUCTS
5 GIRALDA FARMS
MADISON, NEW JERSEY 07940

OVERVIEW: Manufactures and distributes pharmaceuticals, consumer products, medical supplies, and food products. Established: 1909.

KEY STATISTICS Annual Sales: $8.0 billion. Number of Employees: 50,653.

EXPERTISE/EDUCATION SOUGHT: Biochemistry, marketing, public relations, nursing, sales

CONTACT: Mr Shawn Powell, Director of Human Resources; Phone (201) 660-5000.

AMERICAN INTERNATIONAL GROUP
72 WALL STREET
NEW YORK, NEW YORK 10270

OVERVIEW: Provides life, property, and casualty insurance.

EXPERTISE/EDUCATION SOUGHT: Underwriting, accounting, actuarial, marketing, finance

CONTACT: For college students and recent graduates: Ms Susan Poryles, Manager of College Relations; Phone (212) 770-7000.

AMERICAN LIFE INSURANCE COMPANY
600 KING STREET
WILMINGTON, DELAWARE 19801

OVERVIEW: Provides life insurance, health insurance, and annuities. Established: 1968. Parent Company: American International Group.

KEY STATISTICS Assets: $3.0 billion. Number of Employees: 4,000.

HIRING HISTORY Number of professional employees hired in 1994: 69. 1993: 39.

EXPERTISE/EDUCATION SOUGHT: Underwriting, accounting, administration, actuarial, finance, marketing

CONTACTS: For college students and recent graduates: Mr Richard Moore, Human Resources Representative; Phone (302) 594-2098. For individuals with previous experience: Ms Cathy Jones, Manager of Human Resources; Phone (302) 594-2000.

AMERICAN MANAGEMENT SYSTEMS, INC.
4050 LEGATO ROAD
FAIRFAX, VIRGINIA 22033-4003

OVERVIEW: Information technology consulting firm. Established: 1970.

KEY STATISTICS Annual Sales: $460.0 million. Number of Employees: 5,000.

HIRING HISTORY Number of professional employees hired in 1994: 500. 1993: 800.

EXPERTISE/EDUCATION SOUGHT: Computer science, computer programming, computer engineering, management information systems, software engineering/development

CONTACT: Mr Allan Jones, Manager of Corporate Recruitment; Phone (703) 267-5084; Fax (703) 267-8555.

CORPORATE STATEMENT

Our Business *AMS helps large organizations achieve their strategic and operational goals through the application of information technology. Our services range from strategic business analysis to full implementation of solutions.*

Our Requirements *AMS seeks candidates with innovative problem-solving skills, strong academic performance, entrepreneurial spirit, and a long-term interest in the application of information technologies.*

AMERICAN MOTORISTS INSURANCE COMPANY
KEMPER CENTER, 1 KEMPER DRIVE
LONG GROVE, ILLINOIS 60049

Overview: Provides commercial and personal auto insurance. Parent Company: Lumbermens Mutual Casualty Company.

Key Statistics Number of Employees: 8,000.

Expertise/Education Sought: Actuarial, human resources, accounting, finance, law, management information systems

Contact: Human Resources Department; Phone (708) 320-2000.

AMERICAN NATIONAL CAN COMPANY
8770 WEST BRYN MAWR AVENUE
CHICAGO, ILLINOIS 60631-3542

Overview: Manufactures flexible packaging, glass, and cans. Established: 1901.

Key Statistics Annual Sales: $4.0 billion. Number of Employees: 14,300.

Hiring History Number of professional employees hired in 1994: 60. 1993: 60.

Expertise/Education Sought: Sales, marketing, finance, chemical engineering, management information systems, mechanical engineering, electrical engineering, metallurgical engineering, accounting

Contact: Mr W Jerome Hatch, Director of Staffing; Phone (312) 399-3000.

AMERICAN POWER CONVERSION CORPORATION
132 FAIRGROUNDS ROAD
WEST KINGSTON, RHODE ISLAND 02892-1511

Overview: Manufactures electronic components for personal computers, engineering work stations, and communications equipment.

Key Statistics Annual Sales: $93.6 million. Number of Employees: 914.

Expertise/Education Sought: Manufacturing, operations, sales, marketing, administration, management information systems, research and development, production, technical

Contact: For individuals with previous experience: Ms Lisa DeFiuscio, Human Resources Manager; Phone (401) 789-5735, ext. 2444.

AMERICAN PRESIDENT COMPANIES, LTD
1111 BROADWAY
OAKLAND, CALIFORNIA 94607

Overview: Provides containerized shipping services.

Expertise/Education Sought: Accounting, business administration

Contact: For individuals with previous experience: Department of Personnel; Phone (510) 272-8000.

AMERICAN PUBLISHING COMPANY, INC.
111 SOUTH EMMA STREET
WEST FRANKFORT, ILLINOIS 62896-2729

Overview: Owns and operates 300 daily and weekly newspapers.

Key Statistics Annual Sales: $185.0 million. Number of Employees: 5,000.

Expertise/Education Sought: Publishing

Contact: For individuals with previous experience: Human Services Department; Phone (618) 932-2146.

AMERICAN RACING EQUIPMENT
19200 SOUTH REYES AVENUE
COMPTON, CALIFORNIA 90221-5813

Overview: Manufactures aluminum wheels for automobiles. Established: 1988. Parent Company: Noranda Aluminum, Inc.

Key Statistics Annual Sales: $233.0 million. Number of Employees: 2,500.

Hiring History Number of professional employees hired in 1994: 25.

Expertise/Education Sought: Sales, accounting, management information systems, marketing

Contact: Ms Adriana Davis, Manager of Personnel; Phone (310) 635-7806.

THE AMERICAN RED CROSS
8111 GATEHOUSE ROAD
FALLS CHURCH, VIRGINIA 22042

Overview: Provides humanitarian, social, and medical services. Established: 1881.

Key Statistics Number of Employees: 25,394.

Expertise/Education Sought: Finance, military/defense, public relations, chemistry, biology

Contact: For individuals with previous experience: Mr James E Thomas, III, Vice President of Human Resources.

 American Red Cross

AMERICAN RED CROSS - BIOMEDICAL DIVISION
1616 NORTH FORT MYER DRIVE
ARLINGTON, VIRGINIA 22209

Overview: Collects and distributes blood, human tissue, and plasma derivatives. Established: 1881.

Key Statistics Number of Employees: 14,500.

Hiring History Number of professional employees hired in 1994: 246.

Expertise/Education Sought: Biological sciences, information systems, marketing, training and development, transfusion medicine

Contact: For college students and recent graduates: Mr Ed Grant, Director of Recruiting and Staffing; Phone (703) 312-5866; Fax (703) 312-5585.

CORPORATE STATEMENT

*I*n 1941, the American Red Cross began recruiting blood donors for the military, laying the groundwork for what later would become the American Red Cross Blood Services program. The first Red Cross blood center was established in New York in 1948. Today, 15,000 professional staff and volunteers operate in thirty-nine Red Cross Blood Services regions across the U.S.

AMERICAN SAFETY RAZOR COMPANY, PERSONNA INTERNATIONAL, LTD. DIVISION
HIGHWAY 612
VERONA, VIRGINIA 24482

Overview: Manufactures razor blades and shaving cream.

Key Statistics Annual Sales: $150.0 million. Number of Employees: 1,300.

Hiring History Number of professional employees hired in 1993: 12.

Expertise/Education Sought: Engineering, plastics engineering, design engineering, manufacturing engineering, accounting, sales

Contact: Ms June Wilson, Personnel Administrator; Phone (703) 248-8000; Fax (703) 248-0522.

AMERICAN SAVINGS BANK

400 EAST MAIN STREET
STOCKTON, CALIFORNIA 95290-0299

OVERVIEW: Savings and loan institution. Established: 1922.

KEY STATISTICS Annual Sales: $1.0 billion. Number of Employees: 3,694.

EXPERTISE/EDUCATION SOUGHT: Credit/credit analysis

CONTACT: Ms Denyce Lancaster, Employee Relations Representative; Phone (209) 546-3956; Fax (209)546-3454.

AMERICAN SOURCE

300 CHESTERFIELD PARKWAY
MALVERN, PENNSYLVANIA 19355-9726

OVERVIEW: Distributes pharmaceuticals and health care products. Established: 1933.

KEY STATISTICS Number of Employees: 2,403.

EXPERTISE/EDUCATION SOUGHT: Management, accounting, finance

CONTACT: Mr Robert Gregory, Vice President of Human Resources; Phone (610) 296-4480.

AMERICAN STANDARD, INC.

PO BOX 6820
PISCATAWAY, NEW JERSEY 08855-6820

OVERVIEW: Manufactures plumbing fixtures. Established: 1929.

KEY STATISTICS Annual Sales: $4.0 billion.

EXPERTISE/EDUCATION SOUGHT: Technical engineering, product design and development, quality control, mechanical engineering

CONTACTS: For college students and recent graduates: Mr Steve Wilson, Human Resource Generalist; Phone (908) 980-6000. For individuals with previous experience: Director of Recruiting; Phone (212) 703-5100.

AMERICAN STERILIZER COMPANY

2424 WEST 23RD STREET
ERIE, PENNSYLVANIA 16506

OVERVIEW: Manufactures sterilizers for hospitals and laboratories. Established: 1894. Parent Company: Amsco International, Inc.

KEY STATISTICS Annual Sales: $498.0 million. Number of Employees: 3,300.

EXPERTISE/EDUCATION SOUGHT: Management information systems, finance, purchasing, sales, marketing

CONTACT: Mr Carl Zorn, Director of Human Resources Operations; Phone (814) 452-3100.

AMERICAN STUDIOS, INC.

11001 PARK CHARLOTTE BOULEVARD
CHARLOTTE, NORTH CAROLINA 28273-8860

OVERVIEW: Provides portrait photography services.

KEY STATISTICS Annual Sales: $94.0 million. Number of Employees: 2,300.

EXPERTISE/EDUCATION SOUGHT: Management, sales

CONTACT: For individuals with previous experience: Mr Charlie McGintey, Director of Recruiting; Phone (704) 588-4351.

AMERICA'S FAVORITE CHICKEN COMPANY

6 CONCOURSE PARKWAY
ATLANTA, GEORGIA 30328-5352

OVERVIEW: Operates chain of fast food chicken restaurants.

KEY STATISTICS Annual Sales: $434.0 million. Number of Employees: 13,000.

EXPERTISE/EDUCATION SOUGHT: Retail management, management, administration

CONTACT: For individuals with previous experience: Ms Shanna Lucien, Manager People Services.

AMERITECH

225 WEST RANDOLPH STREET
CHICAGO, ILLINOIS 60606-1824

OVERVIEW: Provides telephone and telecommunications services. Established: 1984. Parent Company: Ameritech Corporation.

KEY STATISTICS Number of Employees: 17,785.

EXPERTISE/EDUCATION SOUGHT: Telecommunications, finance, marketing, management information systems, computer programming

CONTACT: For individuals with previous experience: Ms Benita Kyle, Manager of Human Resources; Phone (312) 220-8450.

AMERITECH

444 MICHIGAN AVENUE
DETROIT, MICHIGAN 48226-2557

OVERVIEW: Provides telecommunications services. Established: 1984. Parent Company: Ameritech Corporation.

KEY STATISTICS Number of Employees: 14,561.

EXPERTISE/EDUCATION SOUGHT: Engineering science, telecommunications, accounting, marketing, finance, business administration

CONTACT: For individuals with previous experience: Ms Diane Kludt, Employment Manager; Phone (313) 223-9900.

AMERITECH ADVERTISING SERVICES

100 EAST BIG BEAVER ROAD, SUITE 200
TROY, MICHIGAN 48083

OVERVIEW: Publishes telephone directories. Established: 1984. Parent Company: Ameritech Corporation.

KEY STATISTICS Annual Sales: $1.0 billion. Number of Employees: 2,955.

EXPERTISE/EDUCATION SOUGHT: Customer service and support

CONTACT: For individuals with previous experience: Human Resources; Phone (810) 524-7300.

AMERITECH CORPORATION

240 NORTH MERIDIAN STREET
INDIANAPOLIS, INDIANA 46204-1983

OVERVIEW: Provides telecommunications services. Established: 1984.

KEY STATISTICS Number of Employees: 5,077.

EXPERTISE/EDUCATION SOUGHT: Engineering, business management, finance, accounting, marketing, business administration

CONTACTS: For college students and recent graduates: Ms Stephanie Scheitler, Manager of College Recruiting; Phone (312) 750-5977. For individuals with previous experience: Ms Joanne Persinger, Management Recruiter; Phone (317) 265-4884.

AMERITECH CORPORATION

30 SOUTH WACKER DRIVE
CHICAGO, ILLINOIS 60606-7402

OVERVIEW: Provides communications services. Established: 1984.

KEY STATISTICS Annual Sales: $12.0 billion. Number of Employees: 67,192.

EXPERTISE/EDUCATION SOUGHT: Accounting, finance, data processing, sales, business administration, marketing, engineering, computer analysis

CONTACT: Ms Stephanie Scheitler, Manager of Recruiting; Phone (312) 750-5977.

AMERITECH MOBILE COMMUNICATIONS

2000 WEST AMERITECH CENTER DRIVE
HOFFMAN ESTATES, ILLINOIS 60195-5000

OVERVIEW: Provides cellular communications services. Established: 1983. Parent Company: Ameritech Corporation.

KEY STATISTICS Annual Sales: $84.0 million. Number of Employees: 1,200.

HIRING HISTORY Number of professional employees hired in 1993: 200.

EXPERTISE/EDUCATION SOUGHT: Accounting, finance, data processing, electronics/electronics engineering, electrical engineering, customer service and support

CONTACT: Ms Christie Moran, Assistant Director of Staffing; Phone (708) 706-7600.

AMERITECH NETWORK SERVICE, INC.
45 ERIEVIEW PLAZA
CLEVELAND, OHIO 44114-1814

OVERVIEW: Provides telecommunications services. Established: 1984. Parent Company: Ameritech Corporation.

KEY STATISTICS Number of Employees: 10,023.

HIRING HISTORY Number of professional employees hired in 1994: 10. 1993: 10.

EXPERTISE/EDUCATION SOUGHT: Technical, engineering, operations, management

CONTACT: Mr Fred Mertes, Director of Human Resources; Phone (216) 822-6038.

AMERITECH SERVICES, INC.
2000 WEST AMERICA CENTER DRIVE
HOFFMAN ESTATES, ILLINOIS 60196-5000

OVERVIEW: Provides telecommunications services. Established: 1984. Parent Company: Ameritech Corporation.

KEY STATISTICS Annual Sales: $1.0 billion. Number of Employees: 6,993.

EXPERTISE/EDUCATION SOUGHT: Customer service and support, data processing, computer programming

CONTACT: For individuals with previous experience: Ms Bernethea Carter, Manager of Recruiting; Phone (708) 248-2000, ext. 5182.

AMES DEPARTMENT STORES, INC.
2418 MAIN STREET
ROCKY HILL, CONNECTICUT 06067-2550

OVERVIEW: Operates chain of department stores.

EXPERTISE/EDUCATION SOUGHT: Retail, management

CONTACTS: For college students and recent graduates: Ms Lori Rodden, Manager of Field Recruiting and Placement; Phone (203) 257-5766. For individuals with previous experience: Ms Cathy Berey, Vice President of Organizational Development; Phone (203) 257-2584.

AMITAL SPINNING CORPORATION
197 BOSCH BOULEVARD
NEW BERN, NORTH CAROLINA 28562-6924

OVERVIEW: Manufactures acrylic yarn.

KEY STATISTICS Annual Sales: $37.3 million. Number of Employees: 340.

EXPERTISE/EDUCATION SOUGHT: Accounting, management

CONTACT: Mr David Jones, Director of Personnel; Phone (919) 636-3435.

AMOCO CHEMICAL COMPANY
200 EAST RANDOLPH DRIVE
CHICAGO, ILLINOIS 60601-6436

OVERVIEW: Manufactures petrochemicals, industrial chemicals, and consumer products. Established: 1945. Parent Company: Amoco Company.

KEY STATISTICS Number of Employees: 15,400.

EXPERTISE/EDUCATION SOUGHT: Sales, purchasing, chemical engineering, mechanical engineering, geoscience, accounting, business

CONTACT: For individuals with previous experience: Mr Don Wilson, Director of Staffing and Employment Services; Phone (312) 856-3200, ext. 6621.

AMP, INC.
441 FRIENDSHIP ROAD
HARRISBURG, PENNSYLVANIA 17111-1203

OVERVIEW: Manufactures electrical, electronic, and optic connection devices. Established: 1941.

KEY STATISTICS Annual Sales: $3.0 billion. Number of Employees: 26,400.

HIRING HISTORY Number of professional employees hired in 1993: 200.

EXPERTISE/EDUCATION SOUGHT: Computer science, electrical engineering, mechanical engineering, design engineering, sales

CONTACTS: For college students and recent graduates: Ms Linda Spotts, Manager of College Relations, PO Box 3608, Harrisburg, PA, 17111; Phone (717) 780-6680. For individuals with previous experience: Mr Brian Cain, Manager of Employment and Employee Relations; Phone (717) 564-0100.

AMPEX
401 BROADWAY, MS-3A-01
REDWOOD CITY, CALIFORNIA 94063

OVERVIEW: Manufactures photographic equipment and supplies. Parent Company: Newhill Partners, LP.

KEY STATISTICS Annual Sales: $870.0 million. Number of Employees: 6,500.

EXPERTISE/EDUCATION SOUGHT: Electrical engineering, software engineering/development, computer programming, mechanical engineering

CONTACT: For individuals with previous experience: Ms Sharon Genberg, Director Human Resources; Phone (415) 367-3310.

AMPHENOL CORPORATION
358 HALL AVENUE
WALLINGFORD, CONNECTICUT 06492-3555

OVERVIEW: Manufactures electrical connectors and cables.

KEY STATISTICS Annual Sales: $604.0 million. Number of Employees: 5,300.

EXPERTISE/EDUCATION SOUGHT: Marketing, accounting, sales, electronics/ electronics engineering

CONTACT: For individuals with previous experience: Mr Bart Gerardi, Manager of Human Resources; Phone (203) 265-8900.

AMR CORPORATION
204 WEST 1ST STREET
FORT WORTH, TEXAS 76155-2605

OVERVIEW: Provides passenger and freight airline services. Established: 1934.

KEY STATISTICS Annual Sales: $16.0 billion. Number of Employees: 118,800.

EXPERTISE/EDUCATION SOUGHT: Aviation, accounting, customer service and support, electronics/electronics engineering, sales, marketing

CONTACT: For individuals with previous experience: Ms Mary Ann Lynch, Director of Recruiting, PO Box 619616, Dallas-Fort Worth Airport, Fort Worth, TX, 75261; Phone (817) 963-1234.

AMSTED INDUSTRIES, INC.
205 NORTH MICHIGAN AVENUE
CHICAGO, ILLINOIS 60601-5999

OVERVIEW: Provides railroad and industrial construction services. Established: 1902.

KEY STATISTICS Annual Sales: $827.0 million. Number of Employees: 7,900.

HIRING HISTORY Number of professional employees hired in 1994: 3.

EXPERTISE/EDUCATION SOUGHT: Law, mechanical engineering, treasury management, marketing, accounting, chemical engineering, human resources, marketing

CONTACT: For individuals with previous experience: Ms Deborah J Hampton, Manager of Personnel; Phone (312) 645-1700.

AMTECH CORPORATION
17304 PRESTON ROAD, BUILDING E-100
DALLAS, TEXAS 75252-5613

OVERVIEW: Manufactures electronic identification equipment. Established: 1983.

KEY STATISTICS Annual Sales: $40.0 million. Number of Employees: 272.

HIRING HISTORY Number of professional employees hired in 1994: 40. 1993: 85.

EXPERTISE/EDUCATION SOUGHT: Computer science, software engineering/ development

CONTACT: Ms Ronnie Barber, Staffing Coordinator; Phone (214) 733-6600; Fax (214)733-6699.

AMWAY CORPORATION
7575 EAST FULTON ROAD
ADA, MICHIGAN 49355-0001

OVERVIEW: Markets consumer and household products through independent distributors. Established: 1959.

KEY STATISTICS Annual Sales: $5.0 billion. Number of Employees: 10,000.

EXPERTISE/EDUCATION SOUGHT: Marketing, accounting, chemical engineering

CONTACTS: For college students and recent graduates: Ms Linda McCarter, Senior Advisor of College Relations; Phone (616) 676-6000. For individuals with previous experience: Mr Ron Schut, Manager of Professional Recruiting; Phone (616) 676-6000.

ANADIGICS, INC.
35 TECHNOLOGY DRIVE
WARREN, NEW JERSEY 07059-5197

OVERVIEW: Manufactures integrated circuits. Established: 1985.

KEY STATISTICS Annual Sales: $20.2 million. Number of Employees: 200.

HIRING HISTORY Number of professional employees hired in 1994: 50.

EXPERTISE/EDUCATION SOUGHT: Manufacturing engineering, mechanical engineering, electrical engineering

CONTACT: Human Resources Department; Phone (908) 668-5000.

ANALOG DEVICES, INC.
1 TECHNOLOGY WAY
NORWOOD, MASSACHUSETTS 02062-2634

OVERVIEW: Manufactures integrated circuits, semiconductors, and related devices. Established: 1965.

KEY STATISTICS Annual Sales: $567.0 million. Number of Employees: 5,300.

HIRING HISTORY Number of professional employees hired in 1993: 15.

EXPERTISE/EDUCATION SOUGHT: Management information systems, finance, mechanical engineering, electrical engineering, accounting, marketing, sales

CONTACT: Ms Marsha Terrelonge, Senior Human Resources Representative, PO Box 9106, Norwood, MA, 02062; Phone (617) 329-4700.

ANALYSAS CORPORATION
9620 WAYNE AVENUE, SUITE 500
SILVER SPRING, MARYLAND 20910

OVERVIEW: Provides data processing and environmental support services. Established: 1979.

KEY STATISTICS Annual Sales: $22.8 million. Number of Employees: 410.

EXPERTISE/EDUCATION SOUGHT: Computer programming, environmental engineering

CONTACT: Manager of Personnel.

ANALYSIS AND TECHNOLOGY, INC.
ROUTE 2
NORTH STONINGTON, CONNECTICUT 06359-9801

OVERVIEW: Develops software and computer systems. Established: 1969.

KEY STATISTICS Annual Sales: $109.0 million. Number of Employees: 1,558.

EXPERTISE/EDUCATION SOUGHT: Accounting, software engineering/ development, systems analysis

CONTACT: Ms Cheryl Kay, Human Resources Administrator; Phone (203) 599-3910, ext. 2343; Fax (203)599-2561.

ANALYSTS INTERNATIONAL CORPORATION
7615 METRO BOULEVARD
MINNEAPOLIS, MINNESOTA 55439-3050

OVERVIEW: Provides computer consulting, systems analysis, and programming services. Established: 1966.

KEY STATISTICS Annual Sales: $160.0 million. Number of Employees: 2,270.

HIRING HISTORY Number of professional employees hired in 1994: 169.

EXPERTISE/EDUCATION SOUGHT: Accounting, finance, sales

CONTACTS: For college students and recent graduates: Mr Tim Smith, Technical Staffing Manager; Phone (612) 835-2330. For individuals with previous experience: Ms Linda Larson, Supervisor/ Recruitment; Phone (612) 835-5900.

THE ANALYTIC SCIENCES CORPORATION
55 WALKERS BROOK DRIVE
READING, MASSACHUSETTS 01867-3238

OVERVIEW: Provides integrated systems and information services. Established: 1991. Parent Company: Primark Applied InformationTechnologies.

KEY STATISTICS Annual Sales: $279.0 million. Number of Employees: 2,000.

EXPERTISE/EDUCATION SOUGHT: Electrical engineering, computer science, technology research

CONTACT: Mr Peter McKallagat, Manager of Corporate Employment; Phone (617) 942-2000; Fax (617)942-7100.

ANAMET, INC.
698 SOUTH MAIN STREET
WATERBURY, CONNECTICUT 06706-1430

OVERVIEW: Manufactures wiring devices, industrial machinery, and motor vehicle parts and accessories. Established: 1984.

KEY STATISTICS Annual Sales: $150.0 million. Number of Employees: 1,200.

HIRING HISTORY Number of professional employees hired in 1993: 10.

EXPERTISE/EDUCATION SOUGHT: Finance

CONTACT: Mr Brian D McCormick, Vice President of Human Resources; Phone (203) 574-8500; Fax (203)574-8622.

ANCHOR GLASS CONTAINER CORPORATION
4343 ANCHOR PLAZA PARKWAY
TAMPA, FLORIDA 33634-7537

OVERVIEW: Manufactures and distributes glassware and glass containers. Established: 1983.

KEY STATISTICS Annual Sales: $1.0 billion. Number of Employees: 6,900.

EXPERTISE/EDUCATION SOUGHT: Accounting, marketing, finance, ceramic engineering, electrical engineering, mechanical engineering, process engineering, quality engineering

CONTACTS: For college students and recent graduates: Mr Mark Karrenbauer, Vice President of Human Resources; Phone (813)

884-0000. For individuals with previous experience: Ms Linda Lee, Human Resources Specialist; Phone (813) 884-0000.

ANCHOR HOCKING GLASS COMPANY
PO BOX 600
LANCASTER, OHIO 43130-0600

OVERVIEW: Manufactures consumer glassware, plastics, and household hardware. Established: 1905. Parent Company: Newell Operating Company.

KEY STATISTICS Annual Sales: $2.0 billion. Number of Employees: 15,000.

EXPERTISE/EDUCATION SOUGHT: Accounting, marketing, finance, human resources, production

CONTACT: Mr Karl Salmon, Vice President of Human Resources; Phone (614) 687-2500.

ANDERSEN CORPORATION
100 4TH AVENUE NORTH
BAYPORT, MINNESOTA 55003-1096

OVERVIEW: Manufactures windows, doors, and related accessories. Established: 1903.

KEY STATISTICS Number of Employees: 3,700.

EXPERTISE/EDUCATION SOUGHT: Marketing, chemical engineering, computer programming, finance, design engineering, sales, management information systems, accounting, computer science, mechanical engineering

CONTACTS: For college students and recent graduates: Mr Warren Schade, Employment Manager; Phone (612) 439-5150. For individuals with previous experience: Mr Paul Wiemerslage, Manager of Human Resources; Phone (612) 439-5150.

ANDOVER CONTROLS CORPORATION
300 BRICKSTONE SQUARE
ANDOVER, MASSACHUSETTS 01810-1430

OVERVIEW: Manufactures environmental controls. Established: 1989. Parent Company: BICC USA, Inc.

KEY STATISTICS Annual Sales: $64.4 million. Number of Employees: 310.

EXPERTISE/EDUCATION SOUGHT: Computer science, software engineering/development

CONTACTS: For college students and recent graduates: Mr Neil Parmenter, Director of Educational Services; Phone (508) 470-0555; Fax (508) 470-0946. For individuals with previous experience: Ms Patricia Abate, Director of Human Resources; Phone (508) 470-0555; Fax (508) 470-0946.

ANDREW CORPORATION
10500 153RD STREET
ORLAND PARK, ILLINOIS 60462-3099

OVERVIEW: Manufactures telecommunications equipment.

KEY STATISTICS Annual Sales: $558.0 million. Number of Employees: 3,281.

HIRING HISTORY Number of professional employees hired in 1994: 150.

EXPERTISE/EDUCATION SOUGHT: Electrical engineering, mechanical engineering, accounting, sales, computer programming, law, human resources, structural engineering

CONTACT: For individuals with previous experience: Mr Scott Golas, Human Resources Manager; Phone (708) 349-3300.

ANHEUSER-BUSCH, INC.
ONE BUSCH PLACE
SAINT LOUIS, MISSOURI 63118-1852

OVERVIEW: Manufactures beer and food products. Parent Company: Anheuser-Busch Companies, Inc.

KEY STATISTICS Number of Employees: 15,225.

EXPERTISE/EDUCATION SOUGHT: Accounting, finance, marketing, sales, management information systems

CONTACT: For individuals with previous experience: Human Resources Department.

ANIXTER BROTHERS, INC.
4711 GOLF ROAD
SKOKIE, ILLINOIS 60076-1224

OVERVIEW: Distributes wire and cable. Established: 1957. Parent Company: Itel Corporation.

KEY STATISTICS Annual Sales: $1.0 billion. Number of Employees: 4,000.

HIRING HISTORY Number of professional employees hired in 1993: 100.

EXPERTISE/EDUCATION SOUGHT: Accounting, finance, operations, sales, information systems, telecommunications, electrical engineering, network analysis, software engineering/development

CONTACT: For individuals with previous experience: Ms Pat Richmond, Director of Employee Benefits; Phone (708) 677-2600.

ANN TAYLOR, INC.
142 WEST 57TH STREET
NEW YORK, NEW YORK 10019-3396

OVERVIEW: Operates chain of women's apparel stores. Established: 1954.

KEY STATISTICS Annual Sales: $502.0 million. Number of Employees: 3,741.

EXPERTISE/EDUCATION SOUGHT: Retail management, sales

CONTACT: For individuals with previous experience: Ms Sara Robbins, Human Resources Director; Phone (212) 541-3300.

ANR PIPELINE COMPANY
500 RENAISSANCE CENTER
DETROIT, MICHIGAN 48243-1902

OVERVIEW: Natural gas transport company.

EXPERTISE/EDUCATION SOUGHT: Finance, accounting, mechanical engineering, chemical engineering, environmental engineering, civil engineering, laboratory technology, computer science

CONTACTS: For college students and recent graduates: Ms Nicole Rudel, Employment and Placement Specialist; Fax (313) 496-5742. For individuals with previous experience: Ms Cindy Trotta, Manager of Human Resources; Fax (313) 496-5723.

ANSON PARTNERS, LP.
3814 NORTH SANTA FE AVENUE
OKLAHOMA CITY, OKLAHOMA 73118-8524

OVERVIEW: Explores for petroleum and gas and produces related products. Established: 1984.

KEY STATISTICS Annual Sales: $100.0 million. Number of Employees: 410.

HIRING HISTORY Number of professional employees hired in 1993: 4.

EXPERTISE/EDUCATION SOUGHT: Accounting, data processing

CONTACT: Ms Katherine Willingham, Personnel Director; Phone (405) 528-0525; Fax (405) 523-3175.

ANSTEC, INC.
10530 ROSEHAVEN STREET
FAIRFAX, VIRGINIA 22030-2840

OVERVIEW: Provides computer systems and integration design services. Established: 1983.

KEY STATISTICS Annual Sales: $43.0 million. Number of Employees: 575.

HIRING HISTORY Number of professional employees hired in 1993: 150.

EXPERTISE/EDUCATION SOUGHT: Computer programming, production control, customer service and support

CONTACT: For individuals with previous experience: Mr Curt White, Staffing Manager; Phone (703) 591-4000.

A. P. GREEN INDUSTRIES, INC.
GREEN BOULEVARD
MEXICO, MISSOURI 65265

Overview: Mines, processes, manufactures, and distributes specialty minerals, including industrial lime products and refractories. Established: 1910.

Key Statistics Annual Sales: $170.0 million. Number of Employees: 1,975.

Hiring History Number of professional employees hired in 1994: 6.

Expertise/Education Sought: Ceramic engineering, computer science, finance, accounting, business management, information systems, management information systems

Contact: Mr David Adams, Manager Human Resources Development; Phone (314) 473-3454; Fax (314) 473-3500.

A-PLUS COMMUNICATIONS, INC.
2416 HILLSBORO ROAD
NASHVILLE, TENNESSEE 37212-5318

Overview: Provides paging and messenger services. Established: 1983.

Key Statistics Annual Sales: $35.0 million. Number of Employees: 700.

Expertise/Education Sought: Accounting, data processing, finance, telecommunications

Contact: Mr Earl Posey, Director of Human Resources; Phone (615) 385-4500; Fax (615) 385-4265.

APOLLO SKI PARTNERS
2 MANHATTANVILLE ROAD
PURCHASE, NEW YORK 10577-2118

Overview: Diversified company with operations in beef products and ski resorts.

Key Statistics Annual Sales: $1.0 billion. Number of Employees: 3,900.

Expertise/Education Sought: Finance, business, real estate

Contact: Human Resources Department; Phone (914) 694-8000.

APPLE COMPUTER, INC.
1 INFINITE LOOP
CUPERTINO, CALIFORNIA 95014-6202

Overview: Develops, manufactures, and markets personal computer products. Established: 1977.

Key Statistics Annual Sales: $8.0 billion. Number of Employees: 11,963.

Expertise/Education Sought: Business administration, software engineering/development, finance, computer programming, marketing, computer science, computer engineering

Contacts: For college students and recent graduates: College Relations Manager, 1 Infinite Loop, M/S 75-2CE, Cupertino, CA, 95014-2084; Phone (408) 996-1010. For individuals with previous experience: Human Resources; Phone (408) 996-1010.

APPLE TREE MARKETS
7676 HILLMONT, SUITE 300
HOUSTON, TEXAS 77040

Overview: Operates chain of food stores.

Expertise/Education Sought: Accounting, finance, sales, marketing

Contact: For individuals with previous experience: Ms Denise Bennett, Human Resource Specialist; Phone (713) 460-5000.

APPLIED POWER, INC.
13000 WEST SILVER SPRING DRIVE
BUTLER, WISCONSIN 53007-1018

Overview: Manufactures and distributes hydraulic power equipment. Established: 1910.

Key Statistics Annual Sales: $434.0 million. Number of Employees: 3,220.

Expertise/Education Sought: Accounting, marketing, sales, finance, distribution, transportation

Contact: Ms Gaye L Puccio, Manager of Human Resources Programs; Phone (414) 781-6600.

APPLIED SYSTEMS, INC.
20821 CICERO AVENUE
MATTESON, ILLINOIS 60443-1600

Overview: Provides computer systems and integration design services. Established: 1976.

Key Statistics Annual Sales: $44.0 million. Number of Employees: 525.

Expertise/Education Sought: Software engineering/development, computer programming, program analysis

Contact: Ms Janet Van Haren, Director of Human Resources; Phone (708) 748-2300; Fax (708) 481-3217.

ARAMARK CORPORATION
ARA TOWER, 1101 MARKET STREET
PHILADELPHIA, PENNSYLVANIA 19107

Overview: Provides concession and food services. Established: 1940.

Key Statistics Annual Sales: $6.0 billion. Number of Employees: 131,000.

Hiring History Number of professional employees hired in 1993: 79.

Expertise/Education Sought: Accounting, computer science, dietetics, finance, food services, hospitality/hotel and restaurant management, information systems, administration

Contact: For individuals with previous experience: Ms Barbara Jarvis, Manager of Human Resources; Phone (215) 238-3000.

ARAMARK UNIFORM SERVICES, INC.
115 NORTH 1ST STREET
BURBANK, CALIFORNIA 91502-1856

Overview: Provides industrial laundry services. Established: 1977. Parent Company: ARAMARK Corporation.

Key Statistics Annual Sales: $485.0 million. Number of Employees: 10,500.

Expertise/Education Sought: Accounting, finance, management information systems, sales, operations

Contact: For individuals with previous experience: Mr Keith Oreson, Vice President of Human Resources; Phone (818) 973-3700.

ARBOR DRUGS, INC.
3331 WEST BIG BEAVER
TROY, MICHIGAN 48007

Overview: Operates chain of retail drug stores. Established: 1968.

Key Statistics Annual Sales: $700.0 million. Number of Employees: 5,000.

Hiring History Number of professional employees hired in 1994: 140.

Expertise/Education Sought: Retail management, management information systems

Contact: Mr Wayne Melton, Management Recruiter; Phone (810) 637-1805.

ARCADIAN PARTNERS, LP.
6750 POPLAR AVENUE, SUITE 600
MEMPHIS, TENNESSEE 38138-7419

Overview: Manufactures fertilizers and industrial chemicals.

Key Statistics Annual Sales: $803.0 million. Number of Employees: 1,119.

Expertise/Education Sought: Chemical engineering, chemistry, agricultural engineering, industrial engineering, environmental engineering, agriculture

Contact: Mr Charles Williams, Vice President of Finance; Phone (901) 758-5200.

ARCH COMMUNICATIONS GROUP, INC.
1800 WEST PARK DRIVE
WESTBOROUGH, MASSACHUSETTS 01581-3912

Overview: Provides telephone paging services. Established: 1986.

Key Statistics Annual Sales: $45.3 million. Number of Employees: 376.

Expertise/Education Sought: Accounting, administration, sales

Contact: For individuals with previous experience: Ms Molly Dubis, Director of Human Resources; Phone (508) 898-0962.

ARCHER DANIELS MIDLAND COMPANY
4666 EAST FARIES PARKWAY
DECATUR, ILLINOIS 62526-5666

Overview: Processes, markets, and transports agricultural goods. Established: 1902.

Key Statistics Annual Sales: $10.0 billion. Number of Employees: 13,524.

Hiring History Number of professional employees hired in 1994: 125. 1993: 125.

Expertise/Education Sought: Engineering, business administration, agricultural science, economics

Contact: Mr Doug Farney, College Recruiting Coordinator; Phone (217) 424-5230; Fax (217) 424-2688.

ARCO ALASKA, INC.
700 G STREET
ANCHORAGE, ALASKA 99501-3439

Overview: Oil and gas exploration and production company. Established: 1866. Parent Company: Atlantic Richfield Company.

Key Statistics Annual Sales: $2.0 billion. Number of Employees: 2,450.

Hiring History Number of professional employees hired in 1993: 10.

Expertise/Education Sought: Chemical engineering, mechanical engineering, finance, accounting, information systems

Contact: Ms Marva Watson, Human Resources Consultant; Phone (907) 265-6494.

ARCO CHEMICAL COMPANY
3801 WESTCHESTER PIKE
NEWTOWN SQUARE, PENNSYLVANIA 19073-2387

Overview: Manufactures industrial chemicals and petrochemicals. Established: 1965. Parent Company: Atlantic Richfield Company.

Key Statistics Annual Sales: $3.0 billion. Number of Employees: 4,309.

Expertise/Education Sought: Chemistry, chemical engineering, management information systems, finance

Contact: For individuals with previous experience: Mr Frank Welsh, Vice President Human Resources; Phone (610) 359-2000.

ARIZONA PUBLIC SERVICE COMPANY
400 NORTH 5TH STREET
PHOENIX, ARIZONA 85004-3902

Overview: Electric and gas utility. Established: 1886. Parent Company: Pinnacle West Capital Corporation.

Key Statistics Annual Sales: $2.0 billion. Number of Employees: 7,062.

Hiring History Number of professional employees hired in 1994: 100.

Expertise/Education Sought: Electrical engineering, finance, electronics/electronics engineering, energy/energy management, mechanical engineering, environmental science, government affairs/relations, economics, accounting

Contact: Mr Jesse Delgado, Human Resource Department; Phone (602) 250-1000; Fax (602) 250-3803.

ARKANSAS BEST CORPORATION
3801 OLD GREENWOOD ROAD, PO BOX 10048
FORT SMITH, ARKANSAS 72917-0048

Overview: Provides worldwide freight transportation and distribution, truck tire remanufacturing, and information services company. Established: 1935.

Key Statistics Annual Sales: $1.0 billion. Number of Employees: 13,000.

Hiring History Number of professional employees hired in 1994: 11. 1993: 15.

Expertise/Education Sought: Information systems, systems analysis, computer science, industrial engineering

Contact: Mr Christopher J Cook, Lead Systems Analyst/ Programmer; Phone (501) 784-8524.

ARKANSAS BLUE CROSS AND BLUE SHIELD
601 GAINES STREET
LITTLE ROCK, ARKANSAS 72201-2181

Overview: Provides health insurance. Established: 1949.

Key Statistics Annual Sales: $478.0 million. Number of Employees: 1,600.

Expertise/Education Sought: Nursing, licensed practical nursing, computer programming, accounting

Contact: Ms Theresa Smith, Recruiting Coordinator; Phone (501) 378-2000.

ARKANSAS POWER AND LIGHT COMPANY
425 WEST CAPITOL AVENUE
LITTLE ROCK, ARKANSAS 72201

Overview: Electric utility. Established: 1946. Parent Company: Entergy Corporation.

Key Statistics Annual Sales: $2.0 billion. Number of Employees: 2,916.

Expertise/Education Sought: Mechanical engineering, electrical engineering, industrial engineering, chemical engineering, marketing, sales, finance, accounting

Contact: Mr Clifford T Allen, Human Resource Operations, PO Box 551, Little Rock, AR, 72203; Phone (501) 377-3620.

ARMCO, INC.
1 OXFORD CENTER 301 GRANT STREET
PITTSBURGH, PENNSYLVANIA 15219

Overview: Manufactures industrial equipment, steel and carbon products, and construction products; provides insurance. Established: 1899.

Key Statistics Annual Sales: $2.0 billion. Number of Employees: 10,500.

Expertise/Education Sought: Chemical engineering, manufacturing engineering, mechanical engineering, quality control, chemistry, biochemistry

Contact: For college students and recent graduates: Mr Greg Karavanich, Corporate Director Industrial Relations; Phone (412) 255-9800.

ARMSTRONG WORLD INDUSTRIES, INC.
WEST LIBERTY AND CHARLOTTE STREETS
LANCASTER, PENNSYLVANIA 17604

OVERVIEW: Manufactures interior furnishings including flooring, ceilings, furniture and industrial products for the construction , automotive, and textile industries. Established: 1860.

KEY STATISTICS Annual Sales: $3.0 billion. Number of Employees: 20,000.

HIRING HISTORY Number of professional employees hired in 1994: 30. 1993: 41.

EXPERTISE/EDUCATION SOUGHT: Electrical engineering, sales, mechanical engineering, marketing, computer science, accounting

CONTACTS: For college students and recent graduates: Mr Patrick L Bradford, Manager of College Recruiting, PO Box 3001, Lancaster, Pa, 17604; Phone (717) 396-2360. For individuals with previous experience: Mr Bing G Spitler, Manager of Professional Employment, PO Box 3001, Lancaster, PA, 17604; Phone (717) 396-2541.

CORPORATE STATEMENT

Armstrong is among the top 200 industrial corporations in the U.S. with annual sales exceeding $2.5 billion. With 80 plants worldwide and 21,000 employees, Armstrong manufactures a comprehensive range of products including floor coverings, building products, furniture, and a variety of industrial specialty products.

ARMY AND AIR FORCE EXCHANGE SERVICE
PO BOX 660202, ATTN: HR-C
DALLAS, TEXAS 75266-0202

OVERVIEW: Operates world wide retail stores and Burger King restaurants on Army and Air Force installations. Established: 1895.

KEY STATISTICS Number of Employees: 65,000.

EXPERTISE/EDUCATION SOUGHT: Business management, marketing, restaurant management, retail

CONTACT: Human Resources Department.

CORPORATE PROFILE

The Army and Air Force Exchange Service (AAFES) is one of the nation's largest retailers. Operations are located on military bases throughout the world, but being in the military is not required for employment.

AAFES usually has openings for Retail Manager Trainees (college degrees required) and for Assistant Burger King Manager Trainees. Significant related work experience is highly desirable. Rigorous on-the-job training programs exist.

Benefits include medical, hospital, dental, retirement, life insurance, and 401(k) savings plans, relocation allowances, credit union services, and exchange-store shopping privileges.

Since AAFES operates facilities at locations all over the world, new associates must be willing to relocate frequently.

AAFES is an equal opportunity employer.

ARROW-COMMUNICATIONS LABORATORIES, INC.
185 AINSLEY DRIVE
SYRACUSE, NEW YORK 13210-4202

OVERVIEW: Manufactures communications equipment. Established: 1983. Parent Company: Northern CATV Sales, Inc.

KEY STATISTICS Annual Sales: $26.0 million. Number of Employees: 300.

HIRING HISTORY Number of professional employees hired in 1994: 5. 1993: 4.

EXPERTISE/EDUCATION SOUGHT: Accounting, data processing, finance, electrical engineering, electronics/electronics engineering

CONTACT: Mr Darryl Dickinson, Vice President of Operations/Human Resources Director; Phone (315) 422-1230; Fax (315)422-2963.

ARROW ELECTRONICS, INC.
25 HUB DRIVE
MELVILLE, NEW YORK 11747-3509

OVERVIEW: Distributes computer and electronics products. Established: 1935.

KEY STATISTICS Annual Sales: $3.0 billion. Number of Employees: 4,100.

HIRING HISTORY Number of professional employees hired in 1994: 500. 1993: 100.

EXPERTISE/EDUCATION SOUGHT: Management information systems, finance, human resources, accounting, marketing, electrical engineering, sales

CONTACT: For individuals with previous experience: Recruiting Office.

ARTHUR ANDERSEN AND COMPANY
69 WEST WASHINGTON STREET
CHICAGO, ILLINOIS 60602

OVERVIEW: Provides accounting and consulting services. Established: 1913.

EXPERTISE/EDUCATION SOUGHT: Accounting, finance, marketing, education, budgeting

CONTACT: For individuals with previous experience: Mr William Johnson, Director of Human Resources; Phone (312) 580-0069.

ARVIN INDUSTRIES, INC.
ONE NOBLITT PLAZA
COLUMBUS, INDIANA 47201-6079

OVERVIEW: Manufactures automotive products. Established: 1919.

KEY STATISTICS Annual Sales: $2.0 billion. Number of Employees: 15,900.

EXPERTISE/EDUCATION SOUGHT: Accounting, marketing, finance, management information systems, automotive engineering, mechanical engineering, electrical engineering

CONTACT: For individuals with previous experience: Mr Raymond Mack, Vice President of Human Resources; Phone (812) 379-3000.

ASA INTERNATIONAL, LTD.
10 SPEEN STREET
FRAMINGHAM, MASSACHUSETTS 01701-4661

OVERVIEW: Develops software and provides hardware support, software support and network systems services. Established: 1969.

KEY STATISTICS Annual Sales: $31.4 million. Number of Employees: 200.

EXPERTISE/EDUCATION SOUGHT: Computer programming, program analysis, software engineering/development, analysis

CONTACT: Mr Katpady Shenoy, Vice President of Operations; Phone (508) 626-2727; Fax (508)626-0645.

ASARCO, INC.
180 MAIDEN LANE
NEW YORK, NEW YORK 10038-4925

OVERVIEW: Operates mine facilities. Established: 1899.

KEY STATISTICS Annual Sales: $2.0 billion. Number of Employees: 8,900.

EXPERTISE/EDUCATION SOUGHT: Chemical engineering, mining

CONTACT: For individuals with previous experience: Mr Robert Grevani, Director of Human Resources; Phone (212) 510-2177.

ASC, INC.
1 SUNROOF CENTER
SOUTHGATE, MICHIGAN 48195-3044

OVERVIEW: Manufactures motor vehicle parts and accessories. Established: 1965.

KEY STATISTICS Annual Sales: $350.0 million. Number of Employees: 2,000.

HIRING HISTORY Number of professional employees hired in 1994: 75.

EXPERTISE/EDUCATION SOUGHT: Marketing, data processing, accounting, finance, management, sales

CONTACT: Staffing Department; Phone (313) 285-4911; Fax (313) 246-2609.

ASHLAND CHEMICAL, INC.
5200 PAUL G. BLAZER MEMORIAL PARKWAY
DUBLIN, OHIO 43017

OVERVIEW: Manufactures and distributes chemicals, polymers, and plastics.

EXPERTISE/EDUCATION SOUGHT: Sales, marketing, chemical engineering, chemistry

CONTACT: For individuals with previous experience: Ms Marian Jones, Human Resources Manager for Engineering Recruiting.

ASHLAND, INC.
1000 ASHLAND DRIVE
RUSSELL, KENTUCKY 41169

OVERVIEW: Refines crude oil and produces gas, petroleum, chemical, and coal products. Established: 1918.

KEY STATISTICS Annual Sales: $10.0 billion. Number of Employees: 33,682.

EXPERTISE/EDUCATION SOUGHT: Engineering, computer science, sales, auditing, accounting, chemical engineering

CONTACT: Mr Brad Binder, Employer Representative and Corporate Recruiter, PO Box 391, Ashland, KY, 41114; Phone (606) 329-3023.

ASMO MANUFACTURING, INC.
500 FRITZ KEIPER BOULEVARD
BATTLE CREEK, MICHIGAN 49015-1006

OVERVIEW: Manufactures washer tanks and headlights. Established: 1986.

KEY STATISTICS Annual Sales: $60.0 million. Number of Employees: 600.

HIRING HISTORY Number of professional employees hired in 1994: 10.

EXPERTISE/EDUCATION SOUGHT: Accounting, finance, data processing, maintenance

CONTACT: Ms Ingrid Effenberger, Human Resources Manager; Phone (616) 962-8257; Fax (616) 962-8283.

ASPECT TELECOMMUNICATIONS CORPORATION
1730 FOX DRIVE
SAN JOSE, CALIFORNIA 95131-2311

OVERVIEW: Manufactures automated telephone call distribution equipment. Established: 1985.

KEY STATISTICS Annual Sales: $71.0 million. Number of Employees: 380.

HIRING HISTORY Number of professional employees hired in 1994: 180.

EXPERTISE/EDUCATION SOUGHT: Telecommunications, accounting, finance, marketing, electrical engineering

CONTACT: Ms Penny Mangam, Staffing Manager; Phone (408) 441-2200; Fax (408) 441-2260.

ASPLUNDH TREE EXPERT COMPANY
708 BLAIR MILL ROAD
WILLOW GROVE, PENNSYLVANIA 19090-1701

OVERVIEW: Provides tree trimming and removal services. Established: 1928.

KEY STATISTICS Annual Sales: $710.0 million. Number of Employees: 19,000.

EXPERTISE/EDUCATION SOUGHT: Computer programming, accounting, finance

CONTACT: Ms Lilian Staiger, Director of Personnel; Phone (215) 784-4214.

ASSOCIATED NATURAL GAS CORPORATION
370 17TH STREET, SUITE 900
DENVER, COLORADO 80202-5609

OVERVIEW: Natural gas utility. Established: 1983.

KEY STATISTICS Annual Sales: $1.0 billion. Number of Employees: 750.

EXPERTISE/EDUCATION SOUGHT: Petroleum/petrochemical engineering, construction engineering, mechanical engineering, accounting, finance

CONTACT: Ms Lynn Abrahamson, Manager of Personnel; Phone (303) 595-3331.

ASSOCIATES CORPORATION OF NORTH AMERICA
250 EAST CARPENTER FREEWAY
IRVING, TEXAS 75062

OVERVIEW: Provides consumer and business loans and financing. Established: 1971. Parent Company: Associates First Capital Corporation.

KEY STATISTICS Annual Sales: $4.0 billion. Number of Employees: 12,409.

EXPERTISE/EDUCATION SOUGHT: Marketing, accounting, law, underwriting, real estate, actuarial, mortgage, customer service and support, finance, credit/credit analysis

CONTACT: Ms P Ruth Wadsworth, Human Resources Director.

ASTRO-VALCOUR, INC.
18 PECK AVENUE
GLENS FALLS, NEW YORK 12801

OVERVIEW: Manufactures plastic and plastic foam products. Established: 1985.

KEY STATISTICS Annual Sales: $135.0 million. Number of Employees: 760.

EXPERTISE/EDUCATION SOUGHT: Accounting

CONTACT: Ms Barbara Nelson, Human Resource Manager; Phone (518) 793-2524; Fax (518) 745-5321.

ASTRONAUTICS CORPORATION OF AMERICA
4115 NORTH TEUTONIA AVENUE
MILWAUKEE, WISCONSIN 53209-6731

OVERVIEW: Designs and manufactures aircraft instruments, navigation systems, robotics equipment and computer systems. Established: 1959.

KEY STATISTICS Annual Sales: $382.0 million. Number of Employees: 4,200.

EXPERTISE/EDUCATION SOUGHT: Electrical engineering, mechanical engineering, computer science, business, software engineering/development

CONTACT: For individuals with previous experience: Ms Donna McSorley, Senior Personnel Administrator; Phone (414) 447-8200, ext. 132.

AT&T GLOBAL INFORMATION SOLUTIONS
1700 SOUTH PATTERSON BOULEVARD
DAYTON, OHIO 45479

OVERVIEW: Develops telecommunications services. Parent Company: American Telephone & Telegraph.

EXPERTISE/EDUCATION SOUGHT: Systems engineering, computer science, electrical engineering, marketing, finance

CONTACTS: For college students and recent graduates: Mr Harvey Beldner, Manager of Recruiting and College Relations; Phone (513) 445-5000. For individuals with previous experience: Mr Don Townsend, Director of Strategic Staffing; Phone (513) 445-1551.

THE ATCHISON TOPEKA AND SANTA FE RAILWAY COMPANY
1700 EAST GOLF ROAD
SCHAUMBURG, ILLINOIS 60172

Overview: Provides freight transportation services. Established: 1869. Parent Company: Santa Fe Pacific Corporation.

Key Statistics Annual Sales: $2.0 billion. Number of Employees: 14,794.

Expertise/Education Sought: Law, electrical engineering, accounting, finance, computer programming, mechanical engineering, logistics

Contact: For individuals with previous experience: Ms Carol Berbaum, Vice President of Human Resources; Phone (708) 995-6000.

ATEC ASSOCIATES, INC.
8665 BASH STREET
INDIANAPOLIS, INDIANA 46250-6970

Overview: Provides environmental consulting services. Established: 1958.

Key Statistics Annual Sales: $90.2 million. Number of Employees: 1,600.

Hiring History Number of professional employees hired in 1993: 250.

Expertise/Education Sought: Management information systems, accounting, environmental engineering, geotechnical engineering, materials engineering, environmental science, geoscience

Contact: Mr Pat Monheim, Manager of Recruiting; Phone (317) 842-4463.

ATLANTA GAS AND LIGHT COMPANY
235 PEACHTREE STREET NORTHEAST
ATLANTA, GEORGIA 30303-1407

Overview: Distributes natural gas. Established: 1856.

Key Statistics Annual Sales: $995.0 million. Number of Employees: 3,748.

Hiring History Number of professional employees hired in 1993: 12.

Expertise/Education Sought: Data processing, computer programming, sales, marketing, finance, drafting

Contact: For individuals with previous experience: Mr Porter Gnann, Personnel Manager, PO Box 4569, Atlanta, GA, 30302-4561; Phone (404) 584-4164.

AT&T
100 SOUTHGATE PARKWAY
MORRISTOWN, NEW JERSEY 07960

Overview: Provides telecommunications services. Established: 1869.

Key Statistics Annual Sales: $67.0 billion. Number of Employees: 308,700.

Expertise/Education Sought: Sales, marketing, accounting, finance, information systems

Contact: For college students and recent graduates: College Recruiting Manager.

For more information, see full corporate profile, pg. 206.

ATWOOD AUTOMOTIVE
1400 EDDY AVENUE
ROCKFORD, ILLINOIS 61103-3171

Overview: Manufactures motor vehicle parts and accessories. Established: 1909. Parent Company: Anderson Industries, Inc.

Key Statistics Annual Sales: $267.0 million. Number of Employees: 2,800.

Hiring History Number of professional employees hired in 1994: 65. 1993: 50.

Expertise/Education Sought: Accounting, finance, marketing, management

Contact: Mr Robert Yocum, Director of Human Resources; Phone (815) 877-5771, ext. 429.

AU BON PAIN COMPANY, INC.
19 FID KENNEDY AVENUE
BOSTON, MASSACHUSETTS 02210-2497

Overview: Operates chain of bakery cafes.

Key Statistics Annual Sales: $96.9 million. Number of Employees: 3,269.

Expertise/Education Sought: Management, hospitality/hotel and restaurant management

Contact: For individuals with previous experience: Mr Art Healey, Human Resources Representative.

THE AUSTIN COMPANY
3650 MAYFIELD ROAD
CLEVELAND, OHIO 44121-1734

Overview: Provides architectural and engineering services. Established: 1878.

Key Statistics Annual Sales: $350.0 million. Number of Employees: 1,095.

Expertise/Education Sought: Architecture, drafting, accounting, marketing

Contact: For individuals with previous experience: Mr Dennis Raymond, Director of Personnel; Phone (216) 382-6600.

AUSTIN INDUSTRIES CORPORATION
3535 TRAVIS, SUITE 300
DALLAS, TEXAS 75204

Overview: Provides commercial and industrial construction services.

Expertise/Education Sought: Mechanical engineering, civil engineering, accounting, chemical engineering, industrial engineering

Contact: For individuals with previous experience: Human Resources Department, PO Box 1590, Dallas, TX, 75221; Phone (214) 443-5500.

AUTODESK, INC.
2320 MARINSHIP WAY, 111 MC INNIS PARKWAY
SAN RAFAEL, CALIFORNIA 94903-1473

Overview: Develops computer software. Established: 1982.

Key Statistics Annual Sales: $353.0 million. Number of Employees: 1,565.

Expertise/Education Sought: Software engineering/development, computer analysis, computer programming, graphics engineering

Contact: Mr Joseph Barrett, Systems/Recruiter; Phone (415) 332-2344; Fax (415)507-5100.

AUTOMATIC DATA PROCESSING
1 ADP BOULEVARD
ROSELAND, NEW JERSEY 07068-1728

Overview: Provides computerized business services. Established: 1949.

Key Statistics Annual Sales: $2.0 billion. Number of Employees: 20,500.

Expertise/Education Sought: Accounting, sales, marketing, finance, computer science

Contact: Mr David Gluck, Senior Technical Recruiter; Phone (201) 994-5000.

AUTOMATION RESEARCH SYSTEMS

4480 KING STREET
ALEXANDRIA, VIRGINIA 22302

OVERVIEW: Develops medical and banking software. Established: 1984.

KEY STATISTICS Number of Employees: 14.

CONTACT: For individuals with previous experience: Ms Lisa Morrow, Human Resources Specialist; Phone (703) 824-6400.

AUTOMOTIVE CONTROLS CORPORATION

ROUTE 1 AND EICHLIN ROAD
BRANFORD, CONNECTICUT 06405

OVERVIEW: Manufactures automotive parts. Established: 1915. Parent Company: Eichlin, Inc.

KEY STATISTICS Annual Sales: $2.0 billion. Number of Employees: 25,000.

HIRING HISTORY Number of professional employees hired in 1994: 10.

EXPERTISE/EDUCATION SOUGHT: Finance, program analysis, network analysis, sales, marketing, computer programming, accounting

CONTACTS: For college students and recent graduates: Mr Paul Bahner, Employment Manager; Phone (203) 481-5771, ext. 1315. For individuals with previous experience: Mr John F Donovan, Employee Relations Manager; Phone (203) 481-5771, ext. 1223.

AUTOMOTIVE INDUSTRIES, INC.

EAST QUEEN STREET
STRASBURG, VIRGINIA 22657

OVERVIEW: Manufacturers and distributes automotive trim and accessories.

KEY STATISTICS Annual Sales: $272.0 million. Number of Employees: 3,500.

EXPERTISE/EDUCATION SOUGHT: Accounting, finance, sales, marketing

CONTACT: Mr Daniel Clinton, Corporate Personnel Manager; Phone (703) 465-3741.

AUTOZONE, INC.

3030 POPLAR AVENUE
MEMPHIS, TENNESSEE 38111-3552

OVERVIEW: Operates chain of retail automotive parts and supplies stores. Established: 1979.

KEY STATISTICS Annual Sales: $1.0 billion. Number of Employees: 15,700.

EXPERTISE/EDUCATION SOUGHT: Accounting, computer programming, finance, marketing, law, data processing

CONTACT: For individuals with previous experience: Mr William Poytner, Corporate Recruiter; Phone (901) 325-4600.

AVCO CORPORATION

40 WESTMINSTER STREET
PROVIDENCE, RHODE ISLAND 02903-2525

OVERVIEW: Manufactures aircraft parts and equipment. Parent Company: Textron, Inc.

KEY STATISTICS Annual Sales: $3.0 billion. Number of Employees: 28,500.

EXPERTISE/EDUCATION SOUGHT: Accounting, finance, marketing, aerospace engineering, technical engineering, industrial engineering, computer programming

CONTACTS: For college students and recent graduates: Ms Jennifer Hill, Human Resources Department; Phone (401) 421-2800. For individuals with previous experience: Mr Andrew Regan, Manager of Employer and Employee Relations; Phone (401) 421-2800.

AVCO FINANCIAL SERVICES, INC.

3349 MICHELSON DRIVE
IRVINE, CALIFORNIA 92715-1606

OVERVIEW: Provides consumer loans and financing. Established: 1927. Parent Company: Textron, Inc.

KEY STATISTICS Annual Sales: $1.0 billion. Number of Employees: 6,900.

EXPERTISE/EDUCATION SOUGHT: Accounting, graphic arts, finance, mathematics, marketing, human resources, computer programming, business, tax

CONTACT: For individuals with previous experience: Ms Marcy Becker, Recruiter; Phone (714) 553-7814.

AVIS RENT-A-CAR SYSTEM

900 OLD COUNTRY ROAD
GARDEN CITY, NEW YORK 11530

OVERVIEW: Provides automobile rental services. Established: 1946.

KEY STATISTICS Annual Sales: $1.0 billion. Number of Employees: 10,500.

EXPERTISE/EDUCATION SOUGHT: Sales, marketing, accounting, auditing, business management, computer science, computer programming

CONTACT: For individuals with previous experience: Ms Allison Atwood, Employment Specialist; Phone (516) 222-3000, ext. 3267.

AVNET, INC.

80 CUTTERMILL ROAD
GREAT NECK, NEW YORK 11021-3107

OVERVIEW: Distributes computer products and provides computer maintenance services. Established: 1955.

KEY STATISTICS Annual Sales: $2.0 billion. Number of Employees: 8,100.

EXPERTISE/EDUCATION SOUGHT: Accounting, law, marketing, sales, software engineering/development

CONTACT: For individuals with previous experience: Mr Robert Zierk, Vice President of Human Resources, 10950 West Washington Boulevard, Culver City, CA, 90232; Phone (310) 558-2000, ext. 2674.

AVON PRODUCTS, INC.

9 WEST 57TH STREET
NEW YORK, NEW YORK 10019-2600

OVERVIEW: Markets cosmetics and apparel. Established: 1886.

KEY STATISTICS Annual Sales: $4.0 billion. Number of Employees: 29,700.

EXPERTISE/EDUCATION SOUGHT: Accounting, finance, marketing, law, business management

CONTACT: Ms Romaine Needam, Manager of Human Resources; Phone (212) 546-6015.

AVX CORPORATION

750 LEXINGTON AVENUE
NEW YORK, NEW YORK 10022-4299

OVERVIEW: Manufactures electronic capacitors. Established: 1972.

KEY STATISTICS Annual Sales: $733.0 million. Number of Employees: 9,379.

EXPERTISE/EDUCATION SOUGHT: Accounting, finance, marketing, data processing

CONTACTS: For college students and recent graduates: Mr Scott Radwide, Employment Manager, PO Box 867, Myrtle Beach, SC, 29508; Phone (803) 946-0395; Fax (803) 444-0424. For individuals with previous experience: Mr Richard Aiosa, Corporate Vice President of Human Resources, PO Box 867, Myrtle Beach, SC, 29578; Phone (803) 448-9411.

BAILEY CONTROLS

29801 EUCLID AVENUE
WICKLIFFE, OHIO 44092

OVERVIEW: Manufactures and distributes automotive parts and components. Established: 1982.

KEY STATISTICS Annual Sales: $196.0 million. Number of Employees: 2,275.

EXPERTISE/EDUCATION SOUGHT: Marketing, finance, accounting, data processing, sales

Bailey Controls (continued)

CONTACTS: For college students and recent graduates: Mr Art Quinn, Director of Human Resources. For individuals with previous experience: Mr David Norgard, Group Vice President of Human Resources; Phone (216) 585-8500.

BAKER HUGHES, INC.
3900 ESSEX LANE, SUITE 1200
HOUSTON, TEXAS 77027-5112

OVERVIEW: Provides oil field services and manufactures oil well equipment. Established: 1913.

KEY STATISTICS Annual Sales: $3.0 billion. Number of Employees: 18,400.

EXPERTISE/EDUCATION SOUGHT: Accounting, finance, environmental engineering, computer programming, law

CONTACT: For individuals with previous experience: Ms Sharon Nini, Corporate Recruiter; Phone (713) 439-8600.

BAKERS AND LEEDS
501 NORTH BROADWAY
SAINT LOUIS, MISSOURI 63102-2196

OVERVIEW: Operates women's fashion shoe stores. Established: 1922. Parent Company: Edison Brothers Stores, Inc.

KEY STATISTICS Annual Sales: $1.0 billion. Number of Employees: 20,000.

EXPERTISE/EDUCATION SOUGHT: Business, education, liberal arts

CONTACT: For individuals with previous experience: Mr John Mathews, Vice President; Phone (800) 458-3305.

CORPORATE STATEMENT

Edison Brothers Stores, Inc. seeks committed, talented, and self-motivated persons ready to advance quickly. An executive development program sets a fast track of opportunity to rapidly move from sales to store management. The company's strength is built on promotion from within. Proven ability is the only criterion for advancement. Inquiries from two-year college graduates are encouraged.

BALL CORPORATION
345 SOUTH HIGH STREET
MUNCIE, INDIANA 47305-2326

OVERVIEW: Manufactures packaging, consumer products, and aerospace systems. Established: 1880.

KEY STATISTICS Number of Employees: 13,807.

HIRING HISTORY Number of professional employees hired in 1993: 6.

EXPERTISE/EDUCATION SOUGHT: Accounting, finance, data processing

CONTACT: Ms Rhonda Thomas, Manager of Human Resources; Phone (317) 747-6202.

BALL, INC.
1509 SOUTH MACEDONIA AVENUE
MUNCIE, INDIANA 47302-3664

OVERVIEW: Manufactures commercial glass. Parent Company: Ball Corporation.

KEY STATISTICS Annual Sales: $650.0 million. Number of Employees: 6,000.

EXPERTISE/EDUCATION SOUGHT: Chemistry, aerospace engineering, computer science, metallurgical engineering, machinery, plastics engineering

CONTACT: For individuals with previous experience: Mr Steve Bolander, Director Human Resources, 345 High Street, Muncie, IN, 47302-3664; Phone (317) 741-7000.

BALLY MANUFACTURING CORPORATION
8700 WEST BRYN MAWR AVENUE
CHICAGO, ILLINOIS 60631-3507

OVERVIEW: Manufactures coin operated game equipment, gaming equipment, and operates health and fitness equipment. Established: 1931.

KEY STATISTICS Number of Employees: 31,700.

EXPERTISE/EDUCATION SOUGHT: Accounting

CONTACT: For individuals with previous experience: Ms Lois Balodis, Director of Personnel; Phone (312) 399-1300, ext. 7641.

BALTIMORE GAS AND ELECTRIC COMPANY
GAS AND ELECTRIC BUILDING, 39 WEST LEXINGTON AVENUE
BALTIMORE, MARYLAND 21201

OVERVIEW: Electric and gas utility. Established: 1816.

KEY STATISTICS Number of Employees: 7,000.

EXPERTISE/EDUCATION SOUGHT: Electrical engineering, mechanical engineering, nuclear engineering, accounting

CONTACT: Mr John Pazourec, Employment Representative; Phone (410) 234-5000, ext. 5791.

BANANA REPUBLIC, INC.
1 HARRISON STREET
SAN FRANCISCO, CALIFORNIA 94105-1600

OVERVIEW: Operates chain of retail clothing stores. Established: 1983.

KEY STATISTICS Annual Sales: $223.0 million. Number of Employees: 3,000.

EXPERTISE/EDUCATION SOUGHT: Drafting, data processing, computer programming, finance, law, accounting, customer service and support, design

CONTACT: For individuals with previous experience: Human Resources Department; Phone (415) 777-0250.

BANC ONE OHIO CORPORATION
100 EAST BROAD STREET
COLUMBUS, OHIO 43215

OVERVIEW: Provides commercial banking, mortgages, and related financial services.

EXPERTISE/EDUCATION SOUGHT: Accounting, finance, actuarial, business administration, economics, management

CONTACTS: For college students and recent graduates: Ms Susan Brevoort, Manager of College Relations; Phone (614) 248-8818. For individuals with previous experience: Ms Glynis Jackson, Human Resources Recruiter; Phone (614) 248-4109, ext. 4109.

BANK OF AMERICA
231 SOUTH LA SALLE STREET
CHICAGO, ILLINOIS 60697-1407

OVERVIEW: Commercial bank. Established: 1969.

KEY STATISTICS Number of Employees: 4,206.

EXPERTISE/EDUCATION SOUGHT: Accounting, finance, business administration

CONTACTS: For college students and recent graduates: Ms Laurel Sanford, Manager of College Relations; Phone (312) 828-7441. For individuals with previous experience: Ms Jasmine Blaise, Recruiting Coordinator; Phone (312) 828-2345.

BANK OF AMERICA CORPORATION

PO BOX 37000, DEPARTMENT 9959
SAN FRANCISCO, CALIFORNIA 94137

OVERVIEW: Full service commercial bank. Established: 1972.

KEY STATISTICS Number of Employees: 23.

EXPERTISE/EDUCATION SOUGHT: Accounting, finance, management information systems, law, real estate

CONTACTS: For college students and recent graduates: Ms Jan Maderious, Manager. Corporate College Relations; Phone (415) 241-3072. For individuals with previous experience: Ms Marcia Gordon, Vice President of Human Resources; Phone (415) 241-3072.

BANK OF BOSTON CORPORATION

100 FEDERAL STREET
BOSTON, MASSACHUSETTS 02110

OVERVIEW: Bank holding company.

EXPERTISE/EDUCATION SOUGHT: Accounting, finance, marketing, underwriting, real estate

CONTACTS: For college students and recent graduates: Mr Patrick McBride, Manager of Human Resources; Phone (617) 434-2200. For individuals with previous experience: Ms Helen Drinan, Executive Director of Human Resources; Phone (617) 434-2200.

BANK OF HAWAII

111 SOUTH KING STREET
HONOLULU, HAWAII 96813-3597

OVERVIEW: State commercial bank. Established: 1971. Parent Company: Bancorp Hawaii, Inc.

KEY STATISTICS Number of Employees: 4,162.

EXPERTISE/EDUCATION SOUGHT: Accounting, credit/credit analysis, computer programming, finance

CONTACT: Mr Craig Hashimoto, Manager of Staffing; Phone (808) 537-8828.

THE BANK OF NEW YORK

48 WALL STREET
NEW YORK, NEW YORK 10005-2996

OVERVIEW: Commercial bank. Established: 1784. Parent Company: Bank of New York Company, Inc.

KEY STATISTICS Number of Employees: 15,621.

EXPERTISE/EDUCATION SOUGHT: Computer programming, accounting, program analysis, marketing, systems analysis, sales, credit/credit analysis, law, banking, investment

CONTACT: Ms Mary Ladrigan, MBA Recruiter - Human Resources, 1 Wall Street, New York, NY, 10286; Phone (212) 635-7751.

BANK ONE, INC.

100 EAST BROAD STREET
COLUMBUS, OHIO 43271

OVERVIEW: Commercial banking, leasing, and financial services. Established: 1868.

KEY STATISTICS Annual Sales: $7.0 billion. Number of Employees: 45,300.

EXPERTISE/EDUCATION SOUGHT: Administration, computer programming, finance, accounting, account management

CONTACT: Mr Ernie Sullivan, Manager of Employment; Phone (614) 248-1531.

BANK ONE OF WISCONSIN CORPORATION

111 EAST WISCONSIN AVENUE
MILWAUKEE, WISCONSIN 53202

OVERVIEW: National commercial bank.

EXPERTISE/EDUCATION SOUGHT: Finance, accounting, marketing, business administration, sales, communications

CONTACT: For individuals with previous experience: Ms Andrea Vugrinec, Employee Relations and Staffing Specialist; Phone (414) 765-3000.

BANK UNITED TEXAS

3200 SOUTHWEST FREEWAY
HOUSTON, TEXAS 77027

OVERVIEW: Savings and loan association.

KEY STATISTICS Annual Sales: $607.0 million. Number of Employees: 3,059.

EXPERTISE/EDUCATION SOUGHT: Investment, credit management, credit/credit analysis, banking

CONTACT: For individuals with previous experience: Ms Ann Miesen, Human Resources Representative, PO Box 1370, TX, 77251-1370; Phone (713) 965-6557.

BANKAMERICA NATIONAL TRUST SAVINGS ASSOCIATION

555 CALIFORNIA STREET
SAN FRANCISCO, CALIFORNIA 94104-1502

OVERVIEW: Savings and loan institution. Established: 1904. Parent Company: Bankamerica Corporation.

KEY STATISTICS Number of Employees: 70,000.

EXPERTISE/EDUCATION SOUGHT: Accounting, finance, marketing, auditing, banking

CONTACTS: For college students and recent graduates: Ms. Carrie Herman, College Relations Recruitment; Phone (415) 241-3773. For individuals with previous experience: Ms Kathleen Burke, Executive Vice President of Human Resources; Phone (415) 622-3456.

BANKERS LIFE AND CASUALTY COMPANY

222 MERCHANDISE MART PLAZA
CHICAGO, ILLINOIS 60654-1016

OVERVIEW: Provides life and casualty insurance. Established: 1984. Parent Company: Southwestern Life Insurance Company.

KEY STATISTICS Number of Employees: 1,500.

EXPERTISE/EDUCATION SOUGHT: Accounting, finance, health insurance, marketing, computer programming

CONTACT: Ms Maureen Haas, Manager of Staffing; Phone (312) 396-7170.

BANKERS TRUST COMPANY

280 PARK AVENUE
NEW YORK, NEW YORK 10017

OVERVIEW: Commercial bank.

EXPERTISE/EDUCATION SOUGHT: Accounting, finance, data processing, engineering, marketing, management information systems, mathematics, actuarial, economics

CONTACTS: For college students and recent graduates: Ms Deborah Barry, Assistant Vice President of College and University Relations, 130 Liberty Street 12th Floor, New York, NY, 10006; Phone (212) 250-1956. For individuals with previous experience: Ms Liz Lieberman, Vice President of Human Resources; Phone (212) 454-1762.

C.R. BARD, INC.

730 CENTRAL AVENUE
MURRAY HILL, NEW JERSEY 07974-1199

OVERVIEW: Develops, manufactures, and markets health care products and instruments. Established: 1907.

KEY STATISTICS Annual Sales: $971.0 million. Number of Employees: 8,450.

EXPERTISE/EDUCATION SOUGHT: Sales, chemical engineering, biomedical engineering, quality control, government regulation

CONTACTS: For college students and recent graduates: Mr Mark Sickles, Vice President of Human Resources; Phone (908) 277-8000, ext.

8384. For individuals with previous experience: Mr Eugene Schultz, Vice President of Personnel; Phone (908) 277-8000, ext. 8370.

BARNES AND NOBLE, INC.
122 5TH AVENUE
NEW YORK, NEW YORK 10011-5605

OVERVIEW: Owns and operates chain of book stores.

KEY STATISTICS Annual Sales: $1.0 billion. Number of Employees: 13,000.

EXPERTISE/EDUCATION SOUGHT: Accounting, finance, retail management

CONTACTS: For college students and recent graduates: Ms Wendy Ellis, Manager of Training, 105 5th Avenue, New York, NY, 10011; Phone (516) 633-3300. For individuals with previous experience: Ms Karen Livie, Employment Specialist, 14 Old Country Road, Westbury, NY, 11590; Phone (516) 338-8000.

BARNETT BANKS, INC.
50 NORTH LAURA STREET
JACKSONVILLE, FLORIDA 32202-3664

OVERVIEW: Commercial bank. Established: 1877.

KEY STATISTICS Assets: $3.0 billion. Number of Employees: 18,649.

EXPERTISE/EDUCATION SOUGHT: Sales, accounting, mechanical engineering, finance, mortgage, real estate, credit/credit analysis, investment

CONTACTS: For college students and recent graduates: Mr Jon Kendrick, College Relations Manager, 9000 Soutohside Boulevard, Jacksonville, FL, 32256. For individuals with previous experience: Human Resources Department; Phone (904) 791-7720.

BARNETT TECHNOLOGIES, INC.
9000 SOUTHSIDE BOULEVARD
JACKSONVILLE, FLORIDA 32256-0769

OVERVIEW: Provides data processing services. Established: 1981. Parent Company: Barnett Banks, Inc.

KEY STATISTICS Annual Sales: $223.0 million. Number of Employees: 3,200.

HIRING HISTORY Number of professional employees hired in 1993: 140.

EXPERTISE/EDUCATION SOUGHT: Accounting, marketing, sales

CONTACT: Mr Paul Lowrance, Recruiter, PO Box 40789, Jacksonville, FL, 32256-0789; Phone (904) 464-4988.

BASF CORPORATION
8 CAMPUS DRIVE
MOUNT OLIVE, NEW JERSEY 07828

OVERVIEW: Manufactures industrial and agricultural chemicals, plastics, fibers and pharmaceutical preparations.

EXPERTISE/EDUCATION SOUGHT: Accounting, marketing, logistics, chemical engineering, computer science

CONTACT: For individuals with previous experience: Ms Pat Murray, Manager of Human Resources; Phone (201) 426-2600, ext. 3130.

BASIN ELECTRIC POWER CORPORATION
1717 EAST INTERSTATE AVENUE
BISMARCK, NORTH DAKOTA 58501-0542

OVERVIEW: Generates and transmits electricity, produces natural gas, and mines coal. Established: 1961.

KEY STATISTICS Number of Employees: 1,850.

HIRING HISTORY Number of professional employees hired in 1994: 10.

EXPERTISE/EDUCATION SOUGHT: Computer analysis, electrical engineering, mechanical engineering, data processing, finance, human resources, management

CONTACT: Mrs Sharon Klein, Employment and Equal Employment Opportunity Coordinator; Phone (701) 223-0441, ext. 2430.

BASSETT FURNITURE INDUSTRIES, INC.
629 MAIN STREET
BASSETT, VIRGINIA 24055

OVERVIEW: Manufactures household furniture and mattresses.

KEY STATISTICS Number of Employees: 7,800.

EXPERTISE/EDUCATION SOUGHT: Sales, production management, marketing, accounting

CONTACT: For individuals with previous experience: Employment Office; Phone (703) 629-6000.

BASSETT-WALKER, INC.
WALKER ROAD
MARTINSVILLE, VIRGINIA 24112

OVERVIEW: Manufactures textiles. Established: 1941.

KEY STATISTICS Annual Sales: $380.0 million. Number of Employees: 7,000.

EXPERTISE/EDUCATION SOUGHT: Accounting, finance, mechanical engineering, electrical engineering, textiles

CONTACT: Human Resources Department; Phone (703) 634-3000.

BATH IRON WORKS CORPORATION
700 WASHINGTON STREET
BATH, MAINE 04530-2574

OVERVIEW: Provides ship building services. Established: 1884. Parent Company: Bath Holding Corporation.

KEY STATISTICS Annual Sales: $800.0 million. Number of Employees: 9,000.

HIRING HISTORY Number of professional employees hired in 1994: 25.

EXPERTISE/EDUCATION SOUGHT: Mechanical engineering, electrical engineering, marine engineering, naval architecture, information systems

CONTACT: Mr Marty Johnson, Supervisor of Employment; Phone (207) 443-3311, ext. 3463.

BATTELLE MEMORIAL INSTITUTE
505 KING AVENUE
COLUMBUS, OHIO 43201-2681

OVERVIEW: Provides research, development, and application of technology services for government and industrial contracts. Established: 1929.

KEY STATISTICS Number of Employees: 2,829.

HIRING HISTORY Number of professional employees hired in 1994: 54. 1993: 96.

EXPERTISE/EDUCATION SOUGHT: Mechanical engineering, chemical engineering, computer engineering, nuclear engineering, materials engineering, systems analysis, computer programming, aerospace engineering, combustion engineering

CONTACT: Mr Richard Shaw, Manager of Employment; Phone (614) 424-6324.

BAXTER INTERNATIONAL, INC.
1 BAXTER PARKWAY
DEERFIELD, ILLINOIS 60015-4625

OVERVIEW: Distributes health care and pharmaceutical products. Established: 1931.

KEY STATISTICS Number of Employees: 35,500.

EXPERTISE/EDUCATION SOUGHT: Finance, information systems, computer science, marketing, sales, credit management, life sciences

CONTACT: Ms Sylvia Grote, Manager of Staffing; Phone (708) 578-2215.

BAYBANKS, INC.
175 FEDERAL STREET
BOSTON, MASSACHUSETTS 02110-2277

OVERVIEW: Commercial bank. Established: 1928.

KEY STATISTICS Annual Sales: $10.0 billion. Number of Employees: 6,000.

HIRING HISTORY Number of professional employees hired in 1994: 2,000.

EXPERTISE/EDUCATION SOUGHT: Auditing, customer service and support, sales, investment, finance, accounting, credit/credit analysis

CONTACT: Mr Maurice Wright, Manager of Employment; Phone (617) 482-1040, ext. 6160.

BAYER CORPORATION

1 MELLON BANK CENTER, 500 GRANT STREET
PITTSBURGH, PENNSYLVANIA 15219

OVERVIEW: Develops, manufactures, and distributes pharmaceuticals, chemicals, and imaging products.

KEY STATISTICS Annual Sales: $6.0 billion. Number of Employees: 23,500.

EXPERTISE/EDUCATION SOUGHT: Marketing, sales, finance, accounting, pharmacy, biology, chemistry, physics, chemical engineering, mechanical engineering

CONTACT: Mr Mark Sappir, Director of Staffing; Phone (412) 394-5500.

BDM TECHNOLOGIES, INC.

7915 JONES BRANCH DRIVE
MCLEAN, VIRGINIA 22102

OVERVIEW: Provides information technology services. Established: 1960. Parent Company: BDM International, Inc.

KEY STATISTICS Annual Sales: $774.0 million. Number of Employees: 7,000.

EXPERTISE/EDUCATION SOUGHT: Computer science, computer programming, management information systems, electrical engineering, mathematics, business (MBA), organizational behavior

CONTACTS: For college students and recent graduates: Mr Seth Feit, College Recruiting Coordinator; Phone (703) 848-6276. For individuals with previous experience: Ms Sue Krieger, Corporate Employment and Equal Employment Opportunity Manager; Phone (703) 848-5023.

BEALLS, INC.

1806 38TH AVENUE EAST
BRADENTON, FLORIDA 34208-4708

OVERVIEW: Operates chain of family clothing stores.

KEY STATISTICS Annual Sales: $252.0 million. Number of Employees: 3,288.

EXPERTISE/EDUCATION SOUGHT: Management

CONTACT: For individuals with previous experience: Mr Mike Ross, Human Resources Director; Phone (813) 747-2355.

BEAR STEARNS SECURITIES CORPORATION

1 METROTECH CENTER NORTH
BROOKLYN, NEW YORK 11201-3872

OVERVIEW: Provides securities and investment brokerage services. Established: 1923. Parent Company: Bear Stearns & Company, Inc.

KEY STATISTICS Annual Sales: $552.0 million. Number of Employees: 2,000.

EXPERTISE/EDUCATION SOUGHT: Finance, accounting, actuarial

CONTACT: For individuals with previous experience: Ms Anne Corwin, Associate Director of Personnel, 115 South Jefferson Road, Whippany, NJ, 07981.

BEATRICE CHEESE, INC.

770 NORTH SPRINGDALE ROAD
WAUKESHA, WISCONSIN 53186-1849

OVERVIEW: Manufactures and processes cheese.

KEY STATISTICS Annual Sales: $1.0 billion. Number of Employees: 2,300.

EXPERTISE/EDUCATION SOUGHT: Marketing, sales, production management

CONTACT: Human Resources Department; Phone (414) 782-2750.

BECHTEL GROUP, INC.

50 BEALE STREET
SAN FRANCISCO, CALIFORNIA 94105-1813

OVERVIEW: Provides engineering and construction services.

EXPERTISE/EDUCATION SOUGHT: Computer science, engineering, environmental engineering, automation, mechanical engineering, nuclear engineering, construction engineering, accounting, business, industrial engineering

CONTACT: Mr Robert W Kilbourne, College Relations Manager, PO Box 193965, San Francisco, CA, 94119-3965; Phone (415) 768-5216.

THE BECKER GROUP

1920 CONCEPT DRIVE
WARREN, MICHIGAN 48091-1385

OVERVIEW: Manufactures injection molded plastics. Established: 1973.

KEY STATISTICS Annual Sales: $290.0 million. Number of Employees: 2,700.

EXPERTISE/EDUCATION SOUGHT: Management, administration, marketing, accounting

CONTACT: Mr Bill Walker, Director of Human Resources, 6600 East 15 Mile, Sterling Heights, MI, 48312-1079; Phone (810) 795-7865.

BECTON DICKINSON AND COMPANY

ONE BECTON DRIVE
FRANKLIN LAKES, NEW JERSEY 07417

OVERVIEW: Manufactures medical supplies and diagnostic systems. Established: 1897.

KEY STATISTICS Annual Sales: $3.0 billion. Number of Employees: 19,500.

EXPERTISE/EDUCATION SOUGHT: Accounting, marketing, sales, mechanical engineering, medical technology, manufacturing engineering, chemical engineering, chemistry, biomedical technology

CONTACT: Human Resources Department; Phone (201) 847-6800.

BELCAN CORPORATION

10200 ANDERSON WAY
CINCINNATI, OHIO 45242-4700

OVERVIEW: Provides engineering consulting services. Established: 1958.

KEY STATISTICS Annual Sales: $190.0 million. Number of Employees: 4,500.

EXPERTISE/EDUCATION SOUGHT: Accounting, finance, marketing

CONTACT: Mr Eric Bostian, Manager of Human Resources; Phone (513) 891-0972.

BELK ENTERPRISES, INC.

2801 WEST TYVOLA ROAD
CHARLOTTE, NORTH CAROLINA 28217-4525

OVERVIEW: Operates chain of department stores.

KEY STATISTICS Annual Sales: $261.0 million. Number of Employees: 4,000.

EXPERTISE/EDUCATION SOUGHT: Management, accounting, information systems, retail management

CONTACTS: For college students and recent graduates: Ms Carolyn McGinnis, Vice President Personnel-Belk Store Services; Phone (704) 357-1000. For individuals with previous experience: Mr Tom Westall, Executive Recruiting and Planning Human Resources Manager; Phone (704) 357-1000.

BELL AND HOWELL COMPANY

5215 OLD ORCHARD ROAD
SKOKIE, ILLINOIS 60077-1035

OVERVIEW: Manufactures mail handling equipment and provides microfilm and CD-ROM publishing systems and services. Established: 1907.

KEY STATISTICS Number of Employees: 5,700.

Bell and Howell Company (continued)

EXPERTISE/EDUCATION SOUGHT: Finance, systems integration, law, computer science

CONTACTS: For college students and recent graduates: Ms Mary Fairbanks, Human Resources Administrator; Phone (708) 470-7100. For individuals with previous experience: Ms Julie Foran, Manager of Corporate Human Resources; Phone (708) 470-7100.

BELL ATLANTIC BUSINESS SYSTEMS SERVICES
50 EAST SWEDESFORD ROAD
FRAZIER, PENNSYLVANIA 19355-1488

OVERVIEW: Provides computer and telecommunications services. Established: 1970.

KEY STATISTICS Annual Sales: $403.0 million. Number of Employees: 3,500.

HIRING HISTORY Number of professional employees hired in 1993: 400.

EXPERTISE/EDUCATION SOUGHT: Computer engineering, marketing, sales, network analysis, customer service and support, computer programming, accounting, finance

CONTACT: For individuals with previous experience: Human Resources Department; Phone (610) 296-6000.

BELL ATLANTIC CORPORATION
540 BROAD STREET
NEWARK, NEW JERSEY 07102

OVERVIEW: Provides telecommunications services. Established: 1879.

KEY STATISTICS Annual Sales: $13.0 billion. Number of Employees: 73,700.

EXPERTISE/EDUCATION SOUGHT: Information systems, strategic planning, communications, electrical engineering

CONTACT: Ms Dolores Watson, Manager of College Relations and Recruiting, 540 Broad Street, Room 903, Newark, NJ, 07102; Phone (201) 649-2301.

BELLCORE
290 WEST MOUNT PLEASANT AVENUE
LIVINGSTON, NEW JERSEY 07039-2747

OVERVIEW: Provides telecommunications research, development, and services. Established: 1984.

KEY STATISTICS Annual Sales: $1.0 billion. Number of Employees: 6,700.

EXPERTISE/EDUCATION SOUGHT: Computer science, computer engineering, sales, marketing, accounting, finance

CONTACT: Ms Gwen P Taylor, Vice President of Human Resources; Phone (201) 740-3410.

BELLSOUTH ADVERTISING AND PUBLISHING CORPORATION
2295 PARKLAKE DRIVE
ATLANTA, GEORGIA 30329-2218

OVERVIEW: Publishes telephone books and yellow page directories. Established: 1984. Parent Company: Bellsouth Enterprises, Inc.

KEY STATISTICS Annual Sales: $1.0 billion. Number of Employees: 3,000.

HIRING HISTORY Number of professional employees hired in 1993: 50.

EXPERTISE/EDUCATION SOUGHT: Sales, graphic arts

CONTACT: For individuals with previous experience: Ms Beverly Trimble, Manager of Employment, 2295 Park Lake Room 490, Atlanta, GA, 30345; Phone (404) 491-1908.

BELLSOUTH CELLULAR CORPORATION
1100 PEACHTREE STREET NORTHEAST
ATLANTA, GEORGIA 30309

OVERVIEW: Provides cellular telephone services. Established: 1986. Parent Company: Bellsouth Enterprises, Inc.

KEY STATISTICS Annual Sales: $209.0 million. Number of Employees: 3,000.

EXPERTISE/EDUCATION SOUGHT: Accounting, finance, purchasing, electronics/electronics engineering, field engineering, telecommunications

CONTACT: For individuals with previous experience: Mr Ted Manly, Human Resources Manager; Phone (404) 249-0432.

BELLSOUTH CORPORATION
1780 CENTURY CIRCLE
ATLANTA, GEORGIA 30345-3600

OVERVIEW: Provides telecommunications products and services. Established: 1984.

KEY STATISTICS Annual Sales: $16.0 billion. Number of Employees: 95,100.

EXPERTISE/EDUCATION SOUGHT: Marketing, electrical engineering, mechanical engineering, electronics/electronics engineering, information systems, computer science

CONTACTS: For college students and recent graduates: Job Hotline; Phone (404) 391-2300. For individuals with previous experience: Mr H C Henry, Senior Vice President of Human Resources; Phone (404) 249-2480; Fax (404)321-8123.

BELLSOUTH TELECOMMUNICATIONS
1760 CENTURY CIRCLE, SUITE 6
ATLANTA, GEORGIA 30345

OVERVIEW: Provides telecommunications services. Established: 1984. Parent Company: Bellsouth Corporation.

KEY STATISTICS Number of Employees: 81,400.

EXPERTISE/EDUCATION SOUGHT: Accounting, marketing, finance, purchasing, telecommunications

CONTACTS: For college students and recent graduates: Mr Martin Jenkins, Director of Employment; Phone (404) 329-9467. For individuals with previous experience: Ms Rebecca Dunn, Vice President of Human Resources; Phone (404) 529-2526.

BELOIT CORPORATION
1 SAINT LAWRENCE AVENUE
BELOIT, WISCONSIN 53511

OVERVIEW: Manufactures paper processing and recycling equipment. Established: 1884. Parent Company: Harnischfeger Industries, Inc.

KEY STATISTICS Annual Sales: $2.0 billion. Number of Employees: 12,200.

HIRING HISTORY Number of professional employees hired in 1994: 25.

EXPERTISE/EDUCATION SOUGHT: Mechanical engineering, electrical engineering, pulp and paper science

CONTACT: Mr Tim Monahan, Director of Human Resources; Phone (608) 365-3311.

BEMIS COMPANY, INC.
222 SOUTH 9TH STREET, SUITE 2300
MINNEAPOLIS, MINNESOTA 55402-4099

OVERVIEW: Manufactures packaging materials and products. Established: 1858.

KEY STATISTICS Number of Employees: 7,565.

HIRING HISTORY Number of professional employees hired in 1993: 5.

EXPERTISE/EDUCATION SOUGHT: Finance, auditing

CONTACT: Ms Marilyn Pearson, Human Resources Representative; Phone (612) 376-3018.

BEMIS MANUFACTURING COMPANY
300 MILL STREET
SHEBOYGAN FALLS, WISCONSIN 53085-1807

OVERVIEW: Manufactures flexible packaging, film, wallpaper, and roll goods. Established: 1901.

KEY STATISTICS Annual Sales: $175.0 million. Number of Employees: 1,300.

EXPERTISE/EDUCATION SOUGHT: Sales, mechanical engineering

CONTACT: Mr Ed Collins, Vice President of Human Resources; Phone (414) 467-4621.

BENEFICIAL CORPORATION
400 BELLEVUE PARKWAY
WILMINGTON, DELAWARE 19801-3974

OVERVIEW: Provides banking, mortgage, financial, and credit card services. Established: 1914.

KEY STATISTICS Number of Employees: 8,200.

HIRING HISTORY Number of professional employees hired in 1993: 6.

EXPERTISE/EDUCATION SOUGHT: Banking, auditing, accounting, marketing, finance, computer programming, sales

CONTACT: Mr Calvin H Christopher, Vice President of Human Resources, PO Box 15551, Wilmington, DE, 19899-1555.

BENJAMIN MOORE AND COMPANY
51 CHESTNUT RIDGE ROAD
MONTVALE, NEW JERSEY 07645

OVERVIEW: Manufacturers paints, stains, and finishes. Established: 1883.

KEY STATISTICS Annual Sales: $500.0 million. Number of Employees: 1,600.

EXPERTISE/EDUCATION SOUGHT: Chemistry, chemical engineering, sales, marketing, finance, data processing

CONTACT: For individuals with previous experience: Corporate Human Resources; Phone (201) 573-9600.

BERGEN BRUNSWIG CORPORATION
4000 METROPOLITAN DRIVE
ORANGE, CALIFORNIA 92668

OVERVIEW: Distributes pharmaceuticals, cosmetics, and medical equipment and supplies. Established: 1969.

KEY STATISTICS Annual Sales: $6.0 billion. Number of Employees: 2,965.

HIRING HISTORY Number of professional employees hired in 1993: 115.

EXPERTISE/EDUCATION SOUGHT: Accounting, sales, computer programming, finance

CONTACT: Ms Teresa Bach, Manager of Human Resources; Phone (714) 385-4000.

LM BERRY AND COMPANY
3170 KETTERING BOULEVARD
DAYTON, OHIO 45439-1975

OVERVIEW: Yellow pages advertising sales. Parent Company: Bell South.

KEY STATISTICS Annual Sales: $100.0 million. Number of Employees: 2,400.

EXPERTISE/EDUCATION SOUGHT: Sales, marketing, graphic arts, administration

CONTACT: For individuals with previous experience: Ms Carol Bucklew, Employment Services Coordinator; Phone (513) 296-2070.

THE BETH ISRAEL HOSPITAL ASSOCIATION
330 BROOKLINE AVENUE
BOSTON, MASSACHUSETTS 02215-5491

OVERVIEW: Nonprofit private hospital specializing in acute and trauma care. Established: 1915.

KEY STATISTICS Annual Sales: $283.0 million. Number of Employees: 5,000.

EXPERTISE/EDUCATION SOUGHT: Registered nursing, physical therapy, occupational therapy, respiratory therapy, networking

CONTACTS: For college students and recent graduates: Ms Mary Ellen Kiley, Nurse Recruiter; Phone (617) 735-2000. For individuals with previous experience: Ms Dianne Murphy, Employment Manager; Phone (617) 735-2000.

BETHLEHEM STEEL CORPORATION
1170 8TH AVENUE
BETHLEHEM, PENNSYLVANIA 18016

OVERVIEW: Produces steel and manufactures steel products. Established: 1904.

KEY STATISTICS Annual Sales: $5.0 billion. Number of Employees: 4,500.

HIRING HISTORY Number of professional employees hired in 1994: 24.

EXPERTISE/EDUCATION SOUGHT: Engineering, sales, marketing, finance, accounting, research

CONTACT: Mr Merlin Davidson, Manager of Planning and Development, 701 East 3rd Street, Bethlehem, PA, 18016; Phone (610) 694-5068.

BEVERLY ENTERPRISES
511 RODGERS AVENUE, SUITE 40A
FORT SMITH, ARKANSAS 72919

OVERVIEW: Operates pharmacy chain and nursing facilities, including retirement living centers and home health centers.

EXPERTISE/EDUCATION SOUGHT: Accounting, marketing, computer science, law, quality control, administration, management information systems, nursing

CONTACTS: For college students and recent graduates: Mr Bill Barrett, Manager of Recruiting, PO Box 3324, Fort Smith, AK, 72913; Phone (501) 452-6712; Fax (501) 484-8343. For individuals with previous experience: Ms Pat Powell, Personnel Manager, 1200 South Waldron Road, Suite 155, Fort Smith, AK, 72903; Phone (501) 452-6712, ext. 430.

BICC CABLES CORPORATION
1 CROSFIELD AVENUE
WEST NYACK, NEW YORK 10994-2221

OVERVIEW: Manufactures electrical cables. Established: 1984. Parent Company: BICC USA, Inc.

KEY STATISTICS Annual Sales: $474.0 million. Number of Employees: 2,500.

EXPERTISE/EDUCATION SOUGHT: Accounting, finance, sales, manufacturing engineering, electrical engineering

CONTACT: Mr Rick Matkins, Manager of Employment and Administration; Phone (914) 353-4000.

BIG B, INC.
2600 MORGAN ROAD
BESSEMER, ALABAMA 35023-5608

OVERVIEW: Operates chain of drugstores. Established: 1968.

KEY STATISTICS Annual Sales: $596.0 million. Number of Employees: 5,000.

EXPERTISE/EDUCATION SOUGHT: Sales, accounting, finance, marketing, data processing

CONTACT: For individuals with previous experience: Mr Charles Underwood, Corporate Recruiter, PO Box 10168, Birmingham, AL, 35202-0168; Phone (205) 424-3421, ext. 240.

BIG BEAR STORES COMPANY
770 GOODALE BOULEVARD
COLUMBUS, OHIO 43212

OVERVIEW: Operates chain of food stores and discount department stores.

EXPERTISE/EDUCATION SOUGHT: Accounting, computer programming, sales, marketing

CONTACT: Mr Robert Slee, Manager of Employee Relations; Phone (614) 464-6500.

BIG V SUPERMARKETS, INC.
176 NORTH MAIN STREET
FLORIDA, NEW YORK 10921-1021

OVERVIEW: Operates chain of food stores. Established: 1942.

KEY STATISTICS Number of Employees: 4,600.

Big V Supermarkets, Inc. (continued)

EXPERTISE/EDUCATION SOUGHT: Finance, marketing, sales, business administration, accounting, management

CONTACT: Ms Roseanne Morgan, Manager of Personnel; Phone (914) 651-4411, ext. 2432.

BIOSYM TECHNOLOGIES, INC.
9685 SCRANTON ROAD
SAN DIEGO, CALIFORNIA 92121

OVERVIEW: Provides computer programming services. Established: 1984.

EXPERTISE/EDUCATION SOUGHT: Computer programming, program analysis

CONTACT: For individuals with previous experience: Ms Kimberly Ellstrom, Human Resources Director; Phone (619) 458-9990.

BLACK AND DECKER U.S., INC.
701 EAST JOPPA ROAD
TOWSON, MARYLAND 21286

OVERVIEW: Manufactures and markets power tools and home appliances. Established: 1910.

EXPERTISE/EDUCATION SOUGHT: Management information systems, distribution, transportation, planning, finance

CONTACT: For individuals with previous experience: Human Resources Department; Phone (410) 716-3900.

BLOCK DRUG COMPANY, INC.
257 CORNELISON AVENUE
JERSEY CITY, NEW JERSEY 07302

OVERVIEW: Manufactures and distributes consumer dental care products, over-the-counter products, household products, and pharmaceuticals. Established: 1907.

KEY STATISTICS Annual Sales: $800.0 million. Number of Employees: 3,700.

EXPERTISE/EDUCATION SOUGHT: Marketing, sales, finance, pharmacy, accounting, chemical engineering, environmental engineering, law

CONTACT: For individuals with previous experience: Ms Mary Shevlin, Senior Personnel Administrator; Phone (201) 434-3000, ext. 1225.

H & R BLOCK TAX SERVICES, INC.
4410 MAIN STREET
KANSAS CITY, MISSOURI 64111-1812

OVERVIEW: Provides income tax services including on line financial and tax preparation software. Established: 1946.

KEY STATISTICS Annual Sales: $1.0 billion. Number of Employees: 80,000.

HIRING HISTORY Number of professional employees hired in 1994: 26. 1993: 21.

EXPERTISE/EDUCATION SOUGHT: Accounting, purchasing, law, operations, human resources, software engineering/development, computer programming, information systems, customer service and support, tax accounting

CONTACT: Ms Donna Morgan, Associate Relations Supervisor; Phone (816) 753-6900.

BLOCKBUSTER ENTERTAINMENT CORPORATION
200 SOUTH ANDREWS AVENUE
FORT LAUDERDALE, FLORIDA 33301

OVERVIEW: Diversified company with operations in video rental, music, film production, television, and recreation. Established: 1982.

KEY STATISTICS Annual Sales: $1.0 billion. Number of Employees: 23,000.

EXPERTISE/EDUCATION SOUGHT: Retail, marketing, management information systems, management, accounting, merchandising, planning, computer programming, finance

CONTACT: Mr Michael Werner, Corporate Recruiter; Phone (305) 832-3000.

BLOOMINGDALES, INC.
1000 3RD AVENUE
NEW YORK, NEW YORK 10028

OVERVIEW: Operates chain of department stores. Established: 1872.

EXPERTISE/EDUCATION SOUGHT: Retail, sales, marketing, graphic arts, finance

CONTACT: Ms Margaret Hofbeck, Senior Vice President of Personnel and Labor Relations; Phone (212) 705-2383, ext. 2387.

BLUE CROSS AND BLUE SHIELD
344 SOUTH WARREN STREET
SYRACUSE, NEW YORK 13202-2008

OVERVIEW: Provides health insurance. Established: 1946.

KEY STATISTICS Annual Sales: $500.1 million. Number of Employees: 920.

EXPERTISE/EDUCATION SOUGHT: Management information systems, accounting, marketing, registered nursing

CONTACT: For individuals with previous experience: Ms Nancy Meacham, Employment Coordinator; Phone (315) 448-3798.

BLUE CROSS AND BLUE SHIELD OF ALABAMA
450 RIVERCHASE PARKWAY EAST
BIRMINGHAM, ALABAMA 35298-2858

OVERVIEW: Provides health insurance. Established: 1934.

KEY STATISTICS Annual Sales: $5.0 billion. Number of Employees: 2,379.

EXPERTISE/EDUCATION SOUGHT: Accounting, actuarial, finance, marketing, computer programming, sales, registered nursing

CONTACT: For individuals with previous experience: Ms Elizabeth Hanlin, Human Resources Manager; Phone (205) 988-2100.

BLUE CROSS AND BLUE SHIELD OF ARIZONA
2444 WEST LAS PALMARITAS DRIVE
PHOENIX, ARIZONA 85021-4883

OVERVIEW: Provides health insurance.

KEY STATISTICS Number of Employees: 920.

EXPERTISE/EDUCATION SOUGHT: Registered nursing, computer programming, claims processing/management, and administration, auditing

CONTACTS: For college students and recent graduates: Job Hotline; Phone (602) 864-4339. For individuals with previous experience: Ms Sue Broadman, Staffing Specialist, PO Box 13466, Phoenix, AZ, 85002-3460.

BLUE CROSS AND BLUE SHIELD OF CONNECTICUT
370 BASSETT ROAD
NORTH HAVEN, CONNECTICUT 06473

OVERVIEW: Provides health insurance. Established: 1937.

KEY STATISTICS Annual Sales: $188.0 million. Number of Employees: 290.

EXPERTISE/EDUCATION SOUGHT: Sales, health insurance, actuarial, mathematics, human resources, computer programming, network analysis, law

CONTACT: Ms Sheila Vallombroso, Staffing Consultant; Phone (203) 239-4911.

BLUE CROSS AND BLUE SHIELD OF DELAWARE
1 BRANDYWINE GATEWAY
WILMINGTON, DELAWARE 19889-2762

OVERVIEW: Provides health, life, and liability insurance.

KEY STATISTICS Number of Employees: 728.

EXPERTISE/EDUCATION SOUGHT: Computer programming, accounting, underwriting

CONTACT: Ms Vicki Skomsky, Director of Human Resources; Phone (302) 421-3000.

BLUE CROSS AND BLUE SHIELD OF FLORIDA
532 RIVERSIDE AVENUE
JACKSONVILLE, FLORIDA 32202-4918

OVERVIEW: Provides health insurance. Established: 1944.

KEY STATISTICS Annual Sales: $2.0 billion. Number of Employees: 5,727.

EXPERTISE/EDUCATION SOUGHT: Accounting, finance, actuarial, underwriting, real estate, law, nursing

CONTACTS: For college students and recent graduates: Human Resources, PO Box 44088, Jacksonville, FL, 32231-4088. For individuals with previous experience: Mr Robert Croteau, Director of Human Resources; Phone (904) 791-6111.

BLUE CROSS AND BLUE SHIELD OF GEORGIA
3350 PEACHTREE ROAD NORTHEAST
ATLANTA, GEORGIA 30326-1040

OVERVIEW: Provides health insurance. Established: 1937.

KEY STATISTICS Annual Sales: $939.7 million. Number of Employees: 3,551.

EXPERTISE/EDUCATION SOUGHT: Claims adjustment/examination

CONTACT: Mr Jim Burns, Manager of Human Resources, PO Box 4445, Atlanta, GA, 30302; Phone (404) 842-8000, ext. 8208.

BLUE CROSS AND BLUE SHIELD OF KANSAS
1133 SOUTHWEST TOPEKA BOULEVARD
TOPEKA, KANSAS 66629-0001

OVERVIEW: Provides health insurance. Established: 1983.

KEY STATISTICS Annual Sales: $658.9 million. Number of Employees: 2,000.

EXPERTISE/EDUCATION SOUGHT: Accounting, finance, data processing, nursing

CONTACT: For individuals with previous experience: Mr Mike Valdivia, Manager of Personnel, PO Box 1712, Topeka, KS, 66601-1712; Phone (913) 291-7000, ext. 8638.

BLUE CROSS AND BLUE SHIELD OF MARYLAND
10455 MILL RUN CIRCLE
OWINGS MILLS, MARYLAND 21117-5559

OVERVIEW: Provides comprehensive managed healthcare insurance services. Established: 1950.

KEY STATISTICS Annual Sales: $2.0 billion. Number of Employees: 3,900.

EXPERTISE/EDUCATION SOUGHT: Computer programming, accounting, customer service and support, marketing, finance, clinical services

CONTACT: Ms Kay Keim, Human Resources Assistant; Phone (410) 998-7634.

BLUE CROSS AND BLUE SHIELD OF MASSACHUSETTS
100 SUMMER STREET
BOSTON, MASSACHUSETTS 02110-2190

OVERVIEW: Provides health insurance. Established: 1937.

KEY STATISTICS Annual Sales: $4.0 billion. Number of Employees: 5,323.

EXPERTISE/EDUCATION SOUGHT: Actuarial, real estate, underwriting, law, accounting, finance

CONTACT: For individuals with previous experience: Mr Bob Martin, Director of Human Resources Delivery.

BLUE CROSS AND BLUE SHIELD OF MICHIGAN
600 EAST LAFAYETTE
DETROIT, MICHIGAN 48226

OVERVIEW: Provides health insurance. Established: 1939.

KEY STATISTICS Number of Employees: 6,200.

EXPERTISE/EDUCATION SOUGHT: Business management, finance, computer programming, accounting, marketing, sales

CONTACT: Ms Mary Smith, Human Resources Representative; Phone (313) 255-9000.

BLUE CROSS AND BLUE SHIELD OF MINNESOTA
3535 BLUE CROSS ROAD
SAINT PAUL, MINNESOTA 55122-1154

OVERVIEW: Provides health insurance. Established: 1972.

KEY STATISTICS Annual Sales: $560.0 million. Number of Employees: 3,200.

EXPERTISE/EDUCATION SOUGHT: Computer programming, sales, case management, marketing, claims adjustment/examination

CONTACTS: For college students and recent graduates: Mr Ron Maye, Recruiter, PO Box 64560, Saint Paul, MN, 55164; Phone (612) 456-8000. For individuals with previous experience: Mr Brian Mullen, Recruiter, PO Box 64560, St Paul, MN, 55164; Phone (612) 456-8000.

BLUE CROSS AND BLUE SHIELD OF MISSOURI
1831 CHESTNUT STREET
SAINT LOUIS, MISSOURI 63103-2275

OVERVIEW: Provides health insurance. Established: 1936.

KEY STATISTICS Annual Sales: $926.0 million. Number of Employees: 1,761.

EXPERTISE/EDUCATION SOUGHT: Underwriting, actuarial, customer service and support, data processing, physicians, nursing, human resources, finance, claims processing/management, and administration

CONTACT: For individuals with previous experience: Ms Cindy Powers, Manager of Human Resources; Phone (314) 923-4444.

BLUE CROSS AND BLUE SHIELD MUTUAL OF OHIO
2060 EAST 9TH STREET
CLEVELAND, OHIO 44115-1304

OVERVIEW: Provides health insurance. Established: 1945.

KEY STATISTICS Annual Sales: $2.0 billion. Number of Employees: 2,900.

EXPERTISE/EDUCATION SOUGHT: Systems analysis, computer programming, accounting, sales, registered nursing, claims processing/management, and administration, customer service and support

CONTACT: For individuals with previous experience: Ms Cindy Cardwell, Manager of Employee Relations; Phone (216) 687-7000, ext. 7933.

BLUE CROSS AND BLUE SHIELD OF NATIONAL CAPITOL AREA
550 12TH STREET SOUTHWEST
WASHINGTON, D.C. 20065-0001

OVERVIEW: Provides health insurance. Established: 1939.

KEY STATISTICS Annual Sales: $292.3 million. Number of Employees: 2,500.

EXPERTISE/EDUCATION SOUGHT: Computer programming, finance, accounting, marketing, customer service and support, management

CONTACT: Ms Dana Tayag, Manager of Recruitment; Phone (202) 479-8000.

BLUE CROSS AND BLUE SHIELD OF NEW JERSEY
3 PENN PLAZA EAST, PPO 6A
NEWARK, NEW JERSEY 07105-2200

OVERVIEW: Provides health insurance. Established: 1932.

KEY STATISTICS Number of Employees: 3,200.

HIRING HISTORY Number of professional employees hired in 1994: 150. 1993: 150.

EXPERTISE/EDUCATION SOUGHT: Law, actuarial, operations, finance, communications, accounting, marketing, sales, auditing

CONTACT: Ms Sandra Rula, Recruiter; Phone (201) 466-4000.

BLUE CROSS AND BLUE SHIELD OF NORTH CAROLINA
5901 DURHAM CHAPEL HILL BOULEVARD
DURHAM, NORTH CAROLINA 27702

OVERVIEW: Provides health insurance. Established: 1968.

KEY STATISTICS Annual Sales: $1.0 billion. Number of Employees: 2,090.

HIRING HISTORY Number of professional employees hired in 1993: 300.

EXPERTISE/EDUCATION SOUGHT: Actuarial, computer programming, allied health, accounting, sales, underwriting, registered nursing, human resources, managed health care

CONTACT: Mr Mike Plueddemann, Manager of Employee Relations; Phone (919) 489-7431, ext. 2349.

BLUE CROSS AND BLUE SHIELD OF OREGON
201 HIGH STREET SOUTHEAST
SALEM, OREGON 97301-3612

OVERVIEW: Provides health insurance. Established: 1976. Parent Company: Blue Cross and Blue Shield of Oregon.

KEY STATISTICS Annual Sales: $82.0 million. Number of Employees: 410.

EXPERTISE/EDUCATION SOUGHT: Health insurance, claims adjustment/ examination, computer science, computer programming, accounting

CONTACTS: For college students and recent graduates: Job Hotline; Phone (800) 231-1617. For individuals with previous experience: Ms Barbara Gregerson, Office Supervisor; Phone (503) 364-4868.

BLUE CROSS AND BLUE SHIELD OF OREGON
100 SOUTHWEST MARKET STREET
PORTLAND, OREGON 97201-5747

OVERVIEW: Provides health insurance. Established: 1941.

KEY STATISTICS Annual Sales: $1.0 billion. Number of Employees: 2,110.

HIRING HISTORY Number of professional employees hired in 1993: 150.

EXPERTISE/EDUCATION SOUGHT: Accounting, marketing, information systems, underwriting, claims adjustment/examination, finance, data processing, nursing, computer programming

CONTACTS: For college students and recent graduates: Job Hotline; Phone (800) 231-1617. For individuals with previous experience: Ms Connie Schweppe, Supervisor of Employee Relations and Employment, PO Box 1271, 97207; Phone (503) 225-5221.

BLUE CROSS AND BLUE SHIELD OF RHODE ISLAND
444 WESTMINSTER STREET
PROVIDENCE, RHODE ISLAND 02903-3279

OVERVIEW: Provides health insurance.

KEY STATISTICS Annual Sales: $716.0 million. Number of Employees: 1,652.

EXPERTISE/EDUCATION SOUGHT: Data processing, computer programming, finance

CONTACT: For individuals with previous experience: Ms Jackie Girard, Recruiter; Phone (401) 459-1000.

BLUE CROSS AND BLUE SHIELD OF SOUTH CAROLINA
I-20 EAST AT ALPINE ROAD
COLUMBIA, SOUTH CAROLINA 29219

OVERVIEW: Provides health insurance. Established: 1946.

KEY STATISTICS Annual Sales: $1.0 billion. Number of Employees: 3,400.

EXPERTISE/EDUCATION SOUGHT: Computer programming, registered nursing, data processing, accounting, underwriting, computer programming

CONTACT: Ms May Rhea, Supervisor of Recruiting.

BLUE CROSS AND BLUE SHIELD OF TENNESSEE
801 PINE STREET
CHATTANOOGA, TENNESSEE 37402-2520

OVERVIEW: Provides health insurance. Established: 1945.

KEY STATISTICS Annual Sales: $1.3 billion. Number of Employees: 2,200.

EXPERTISE/EDUCATION SOUGHT: Information systems, managed health care

CONTACT: Ms Karen Sherrill, Corporate Recruiter; Phone (615) 785-8066.

BLUE CROSS AND BLUE SHIELD OF TEXAS, INC.
901 SOUTH CENTRAL EXPRESSWAY
RICHARDSON, TEXAS 75080-7302

OVERVIEW: Provides health insurance. Established: 1939.

KEY STATISTICS Annual Sales: $1.0 billion. Number of Employees: 4,300.

HIRING HISTORY Number of professional employees hired in 1993: 200.

EXPERTISE/EDUCATION SOUGHT: Computer programming, marketing, nursing, accounting, actuarial, mathematics, data processing, underwriting

CONTACT: For individuals with previous experience: Mr Ed Toogood, Director of Employment; Phone (214) 766-6440.

BLUE CROSS AND BLUE SHIELD OF UTAH
2455 PARLEY'S WAY
SALT LAKE CITY, UTAH 84109-1217

OVERVIEW: Provides health insurance.

KEY STATISTICS Annual Sales: $336.0 million. Number of Employees: 746.

EXPERTISE/EDUCATION SOUGHT: Accounting, data processing, computer programming

CONTACT: For individuals with previous experience: Ms Denise Rickins, Employment Coordinator; Phone (801) 487-6441.

BLUE CROSS AND BLUE SHIELD OF VERMONT
1 EAST ROAD
MONTPELIER, VERMONT 05602

OVERVIEW: Provides health care services. Established: 1980.

KEY STATISTICS Annual Sales: $204.0 million. Number of Employees: 295.

EXPERTISE/EDUCATION SOUGHT: Accounting, finance, data processing, information systems

CONTACT: For individuals with previous experience: Ms Louisa Neveau, Human Resources Secretary; Phone (802) 223-6131.

BLUE CROSS AND BLUE SHIELD OF VIRGINIA
2015 STAPLES MILL ROAD
RICHMOND, VIRGINIA 23230-3108

OVERVIEW: Provides health insurance.

KEY STATISTICS Annual Sales: $2.0 billion. Number of Employees: 4,012.

HIRING HISTORY Number of professional employees hired in 1993: 300.

EXPERTISE/EDUCATION SOUGHT: Actuarial, underwriting, law, claims adjustment/examination, information services, claims processing/ management, and administration, nursing, customer service and support

CONTACT: Ms Lyn Runnett, Manager of Staffing; Phone (804) 354-8000.

BLUE CROSS OF CALIFORNIA
21555 OXNARD STREET
WOODLAND HILLS, CALIFORNIA 91367

OVERVIEW: Provides health insurance. Established: 1982.

KEY STATISTICS Annual Sales: $10.0 billion. Number of Employees: 3,600.

EXPERTISE/EDUCATION SOUGHT: Accounting, finance, actuarial, marketing

CONTACT: For individuals with previous experience: Mr Steven Wesson, Human Resources Field Representative; Phone (818) 703-2205; Fax (818) 703-3389.

BLUE CROSS OF IDAHO HEALTH SERVICE

1501 FEDERAL WAY
BOISE, IDAHO 83705-2550

OVERVIEW: Provides health insurance. Established: 1945.

KEY STATISTICS Annual Sales: $235.0 million. Number of Employees: 375.

EXPERTISE/EDUCATION SOUGHT: Accounting, finance, business administration, nursing, licensed practical nursing, data processing

CONTACT: For individuals with previous experience: Ms Cece Schnuerle, Human Resources Administrator; Phone (208) 345-4550, ext. 232.

BLUE CROSS INSURANCE COMPANY

120 MONUMENT CIRCLE
INDIANAPOLIS, INDIANA 46204-4906

OVERVIEW: Provides health insurance. Established: 1944.

KEY STATISTICS Annual Sales: $3.0 billion. Number of Employees: 6,779.

EXPERTISE/EDUCATION SOUGHT: Auditing, real estate, actuarial, accounting, human resources

CONTACT: For individuals with previous experience: Ms Kathy Minx, Manager of Corporate Human Resources; Phone (317) 488-6000.

BLUE CROSS OF WESTERN PENNSYLVANIA

120 5TH AVENUE
PITTSBURGH, PENNSYLVANIA 15222-3099

OVERVIEW: Provides health insurance. Established: 1937.

KEY STATISTICS Annual Sales: $2.0 billion. Number of Employees: 3,000.

EXPERTISE/EDUCATION SOUGHT: Utilization review, quality control, customer service and support, marketing, medical records, case management, sales, claims adjustment/examination

CONTACT: Mr Wayne Nelson, Corporate Vice President of Human Resources; Phone (412) 255-7000, ext. 8202.

BMG MUSIC

1540 BROADWAY
NEW YORK, NEW YORK 10036

OVERVIEW: Publishes music.

EXPERTISE/EDUCATION SOUGHT: Sales, publishing, law, graphic arts, engineering, communications, computer science, business, accounting

CONTACT: For individuals with previous experience: Personnel Department; Phone (212) 930-4000.

BOATMEN'S BANCSHARES, INC.

1 BOATMENS PLAZA
SAINT LOUIS, MISSOURI 63101-2602

OVERVIEW: Commercial bank holding company. Established: 1969.

KEY STATISTICS Assets: $2.0 billion. Number of Employees: 14,370.

EXPERTISE/EDUCATION SOUGHT: Accounting, finance, auditing, real estate

CONTACT: Ms Terri Goslin-Jones, Vice President of Human Resources; Phone (314) 466-6000.

BOB EVANS FARMS, INC.

3776 SOUTH HIGH STREET
COLUMBUS, OHIO 43207-4012

OVERVIEW: Produces sausage products and operates chain of restaurants. Established: 1957.

KEY STATISTICS Annual Sales: $900.0 million. Number of Employees: 23,800.

HIRING HISTORY Number of professional employees hired in 1994: 625.

EXPERTISE/EDUCATION SOUGHT: Accounting, sales, finance, marketing, quality control, nutrition, food science

CONTACT: Mr Robert G White, Director of Human Resources; Phone (614) 497-4387.

BOC GASES

575 MOUNTAIN AVENUE
MURRAY HILL, NEW JERSEY 07974-2097

OVERVIEW: Manufacturers compressed gases, anesthetics, turbines, pumps, and flow measuring devices. Established: 1938. Parent Company: BOC Group, Inc.

KEY STATISTICS Annual Sales: $2.0 billion. Number of Employees: 10,500.

EXPERTISE/EDUCATION SOUGHT: Accounting, finance, chemical engineering, mechanical engineering, industrial engineering, chemistry, computer programming, marketing

CONTACT: Ms Sue Schanz, Manager of Human Resources; Phone (908) 665-2400; Fax (908) 464-9015.

BOEHRINGER INGELHEIM PHARMACEUTICALS

900 RIDGEBURY ROAD
RIDGEFIELD, CONNECTICUT 06877

OVERVIEW: Manufactures pharmaceuticals.

KEY STATISTICS Annual Sales: $300.0 million. Number of Employees: 1,800.

EXPERTISE/EDUCATION SOUGHT: Sales, marketing, research and development, data processing, finance

CONTACTS: For college students and recent graduates: Mr Jim Conklin, Associate Director of Human Resources; Phone (203) 798-5364. For individuals with previous experience: Mr John Petraglia, Senior Human Resources Specialist; Phone (203) 798-9988.

BOLDT GROUP, INC.

2525 NORTH ROEMER ROAD
APPLETON, WISCONSIN 54911-8623

OVERVIEW: Provides construction services for pulp and paper, engineering, and construction industries. Established: 1984.

KEY STATISTICS Annual Sales: $320.0 million. Number of Employees: 2,200.

HIRING HISTORY Number of professional employees hired in 1993: 20.

EXPERTISE/EDUCATION SOUGHT: Management information systems, accounting, finance, marketing, management

CONTACT: Mr Gary Tornes, Vice President of Human Resources; Phone (414) 739-7800.

THE BON MARCHE

1601 3RD AVENUE
SEATTLE, WASHINGTON 98101

OVERVIEW: Operates chain of department stores.

EXPERTISE/EDUCATION SOUGHT: Accounting, finance, marketing, sales

CONTACTS: For college students and recent graduates: Mr Dean Allen, College Recruiter; Phone (206) 506-6000. For individuals with previous experience: Ms MaryAnn Short, Director Personnel Services; Phone (206) 506-6000.

BON SECOURS HEALTH SYSTEMS

1505 MARRIOTTSVILLE ROAD
MARRIOTTSVILLE, MARYLAND 21104-1301

OVERVIEW: Provides health insurance; operates medical and surgical hospital.

KEY STATISTICS Annual Sales: $562.0 million. Number of Employees: 10,000.

EXPERTISE/EDUCATION SOUGHT: Administration

CONTACT: For individuals with previous experience: Ms Virginia Rounsaville, Personnel Manager.

BON TON STORES, INC.

2801 EAST MARKET STREET
YORK, PENNSYLVANIA 17402

OVERVIEW: Operates chain of department stores. Established: 1897.

Bon Ton Stores, Inc. (continued)

KEY STATISTICS Annual Sales: $253.0 million. Number of Employees: 4,213.

HIRING HISTORY Number of professional employees hired in 1993: 15.

EXPERTISE/EDUCATION SOUGHT: Management, merchandising, business administration, marketing, finance

CONTACT: For individuals with previous experience: Mr Joseph Culver, Vice President of Employment, PO Box 2821, York, PA, 17402; Phone (717) 757-7660.

BONNEVILLE POWER ADMINISTRATION
905 NORTHEAST 11TH AVENUE
PORTLAND, OREGON 97232-4100

OVERVIEW: Electric utility. Established: 1937.

KEY STATISTICS Annual Sales: $1.6 billion. Number of Employees: 3,655.

EXPERTISE/EDUCATION SOUGHT: Economics, finance, accounting, sales, auditing, biology

CONTACTS: For college students and recent graduates: Ms Judith Canja, Personnel Management Specialist, PO Box 3621, Portland, OR, 97208-3621; Phone (503) 230-3484. For individuals with previous experience: Ms Julie Adams, Manager of Recruiting, Staffing, and Health, PO Box 3621, Portland, OR, 97208-3621; Phone (503) 230-3055.

BORDEN, INC.
180 EAST BROAD STREET
COLUMBUS, OHIO 43215

OVERVIEW: Manufactures and markets a variety of food, non-food consumer, and industrial products. Established: 1857.

KEY STATISTICS Annual Sales: $6.0 billion. Number of Employees: 32,400.

EXPERTISE/EDUCATION SOUGHT: Marketing, finance, sales, accounting, chemical engineering

CONTACT: Ms Esther Adkins, Director of Corporate Recruiting; Phone (614) 255-4000.

BORDERS, INC.
311 MAYNARD STREET
ANN ARBOR, MICHIGAN 48104-9717

OVERVIEW: Operates chain of book and record stores.

KEY STATISTICS Annual Sales: $116.0 million. Number of Employees: 3,012.

EXPERTISE/EDUCATION SOUGHT: Retail management, purchasing, finance, distribution, management information systems, accounting, marketing, retail, real estate, human resources

CONTACT: For individuals with previous experience: Ms Cathy Zukowski, Employment Specialist; Phone (313) 913-1328.

BORG-WARNER AUTOMOTIVE CORPORATION
200 SOUTH MICHIGAN AVENUE
CHICAGO, ILLINOIS 60604

OVERVIEW: Provides armored transport and security systems services.

KEY STATISTICS Annual Sales: $400.0 million. Number of Employees: 6,700.

EXPERTISE/EDUCATION SOUGHT: Accounting, electrical engineering, electronics/electronics engineering, finance, computer programming, computer science, research and development

CONTACT: Ms Angela D'Aversa, Director of Management and Organizational Development; Phone (312) 322-8648.

BORG-WARNER AUTOMOTIVE, INC.
200 SOUTH MICHIGAN AVENUE
CHICAGO, ILLINOIS 60604-2402

OVERVIEW: Manufactures automotive components. Established: 1928. Parent Company: Borg-Warner Security Corporation.

KEY STATISTICS Annual Sales: $985.0 million. Number of Employees: 6,610.

EXPERTISE/EDUCATION SOUGHT: Electrical engineering, mechanical engineering, accounting, finance

CONTACT: For individuals with previous experience: Personnel Department; Phone (312) 726-4400.

BORLAND INTERNATIONAL, INC.
100 BORLAND WAY
SCOTTS VALLEY, CALIFORNIA 95066-3249

OVERVIEW: Develops and markets database, spreadsheet, and programming language software. Established: 1983.

KEY STATISTICS Annual Sales: $470.0 million. Number of Employees: 1,800.

EXPERTISE/EDUCATION SOUGHT: Public relations, customer service and support, management, sales, program analysis, management information systems, computer programming, computer science

CONTACT: Ms Jill Stinger, Human Resource Administrator, PO Box 6601, Scotts Valley, CA, 95060; Phone (408) 431-1000; Fax (408)431-4141.

BOSE CORPORATION
THE MOUNTAIN
FRAMINGHAM, MASSACHUSETTS 01701-9168

OVERVIEW: Manufactures and markets audio speakers. Established: 1964.

KEY STATISTICS Annual Sales: $531.0 million. Number of Employees: 3,100.

EXPERTISE/EDUCATION SOUGHT: Sales, law, accounting, marketing, finance

CONTACT: Central Recruiting Department; Phone (508) 879-7330.

THE BOSTON COMPANY, INC.
1 BOSTON PLACE
BOSTON, MASSACHUSETTS 02108-4402

OVERVIEW: Provides financial services and investment management. Established: 1867. Parent Company: Shearson Lehman Brothers, Inc.

KEY STATISTICS Annual Sales: $933.0 million. Number of Employees: 3,467.

EXPERTISE/EDUCATION SOUGHT: Accounting, management, business administration, finance

CONTACT: For individuals with previous experience: Ms Kristin Zaepfel, Manager of Human Resources; Phone (617) 382-9178.

BOSTON EDISON COMPANY
800 BOYLSTON STREET
BOSTON, MASSACHUSETTS 02199-8003

OVERVIEW: Electric utility. Established: 1886.

KEY STATISTICS Number of Employees: 4,500.

EXPERTISE/EDUCATION SOUGHT: Sales, mechanical engineering, marketing, industrial engineering, accounting, civil engineering, finance, structural engineering, electrical engineering, computer programming

CONTACT: Mr Jerome McKinnon, Senior Staffing Specialist; Phone (617) 424-2000.

BOWATER, INC.
55 EAST CAMPERDOWN WAY, BOX 1028
GREENVILLE, SOUTH CAROLINA 29601-3511

OVERVIEW: Manufactures newsprint, coated paper, and computer forms. Established: 1964.

KEY STATISTICS Number of Employees: 5,986.

EXPERTISE/EDUCATION SOUGHT: Finance, auditing, law, business management, human resources, sales, accounting, marketing, mechanical engineering, printing

CONTACT: Ms Linda Garrison, Personnel Manager; Phone (803) 271-7733.

BOZELL JACOBS KENYON ECKHARDT, INC.
40 WEST 23RD STREET, 2ND FLOOR
NEW YORK, NEW YORK 10010-5200

OVERVIEW: Advertising agencies.

KEY STATISTICS Annual Sales: $232.1 million. Number of Employees: 2,340.

EXPERTISE/EDUCATION SOUGHT: Advertising, marketing, account management

CONTACT: For individuals with previous experience: Ms Sherry Schneiderman, Human Resource Assistant; Phone (212) 727-5000.

BP AMERICA
200 PUBLIC SQUARE II-B
CLEVELAND, OHIO 44114

OVERVIEW: Integrated petroleum company. Established: 1870.

KEY STATISTICS Number of Employees: 12,000.

EXPERTISE/EDUCATION SOUGHT: Mechanical engineering, chemical engineering, retail, business management

CONTACT: Ms Dee Walters, Recruiting Manager; Phone (216) 586-8097.

CORPORATE PROFILE

Well-known refiners, small independents, and even convenience store chains all want a piece of one of America's most fiercely competitive industries—retail petroleum marketing. It is little wonder. A major site in a prime location may represent a seven-figure investment. The rewards are equally high: every hour BP America sells more than 1 million gallons of gasoline, oil, and other refined petroleum products worldwide.

People looking to build their marketing skills, and apply unique talents with an industry leader, belong with BP America's retail marketing group. The first step toward a potentially rewarding career with a global marketing leader is to be selected for one of BP America's entry-level positions. Most new hires have business or management degrees, but astute graduates from all technical, business, or liberal arts disciplines are considered. All candidates must have superior interpersonal and communication skills. Assertiveness, confidence, and the ability to motivate others are all key qualities for success.

BRADLEE'S, INC.
1385 HANCOCK STREET
QUINCY, MASSACHUSETTS 02169

OVERVIEW: Operates chain of discount department stores. Established: 1961.

EXPERTISE/EDUCATION SOUGHT: Finance, accounting, computer programming, marketing

CONTACT: Ms Donna Sweeney, Manager of Employment; Phone (617) 380-5387.

BRIDGESTONE/FIRESTONE, INC.
50 CENTURY BOULEVARD
NASHVILLE, TENNESSEE 37124

OVERVIEW: Manufactures tires. Established: 1900.

KEY STATISTICS Number of Employees: 40,000.

EXPERTISE/EDUCATION SOUGHT: Marketing, sales, mechanical engineering, chemical engineering

CONTACT: Mr Frank Doman, Director of Human Resources; Phone (615) 391-0088.

BRIGGS AND STRATTON CORPORATION
12301 WEST WIRTH STREET
MILWAUKEE, WISCONSIN 53222-2110

OVERVIEW: Manufactures small engines. Established: 1909.

KEY STATISTICS Annual Sales: $1.0 billion. Number of Employees: 7,950.

EXPERTISE/EDUCATION SOUGHT: Marketing, finance, accounting, electrical engineering, mechanical engineering, chemical engineering, design engineering, data processing

CONTACTS: For college students and recent graduates: Ms Carol Finses, Salaried Personnel Representative, PO Box 702, Milwaukee, WI, 53201-0702; Phone (414) 259-5326. For individuals with previous experience: Ms Judith Whipple, Salaried Personnel Manager, PO Box 702, Milwaukee, WI, 53201-0702; Phone (414) 259-5333.

BRINK'S, INC.
1 THORNDAL CIRCLE
DARIEN, CONNECTICUT 06820-5460

OVERVIEW: Provides security armored car services, coin processing, currency processing, and ATM services. Established: 1956. Parent Company: The Pittston Company.

KEY STATISTICS Number of Employees: 11,000.

EXPERTISE/EDUCATION SOUGHT: Accounting, finance, information systems, operations

CONTACT: For individuals with previous experience: Ms Ellie Peterson, Director of Human Resources Administration; Phone (203) 662-7800, ext. 7931.

THE BROADWAY STORES, INC.
3880 NORTH MISSION ROAD
LOS ANGELES, CALIFORNIA 90031-3179

OVERVIEW: Operates chain of regional department stores. Established: 1896. Parent Company: Zell/Chilmark Fund, LP.

KEY STATISTICS Number of Employees: 23,000.

HIRING HISTORY Number of professional employees hired in 1993: 300.

EXPERTISE/EDUCATION SOUGHT: Merchandising, purchasing, marketing, business management

CONTACT: For individuals with previous experience: Mr Neal Lenarsky, Director of Staffing and Recruiting; Phone (213) 227-2143.

BROWN AND WILLIAMSON TOBACCO
1500 BROWN AND WILLIAMSON TOWER
LOUISVILLE, KENTUCKY 40202

OVERVIEW: Manufactures and markets cigarettes and other tobacco products. Established: 1927. Parent Company: BAT USA Tobacco Services, Inc.

KEY STATISTICS Number of Employees: 5,200.

HIRING HISTORY Number of professional employees hired in 1994: 35.

EXPERTISE/EDUCATION SOUGHT: Accounting, marketing, business management, data processing, human resources, auditing

CONTACT: Ms Carolyn Cravl, Recruiter; Phone (502) 568-7000.

BROWN GROUP, INC.
8300 MARYLAND AVENUE
SAINT LOUIS, MISSOURI 63105-3645

OVERVIEW: Provides footwear and fabric retailing services. Established: 1878.

KEY STATISTICS Number of Employees: 800.

EXPERTISE/EDUCATION SOUGHT: Sales, marketing, finance, accounting, data processing

CONTACT: Ms Christina Miller, Personnel Specialist; Phone (314) 854-4000.

BROWN-FORMAN CORPORATION
850 DIXIE HIGHWAY
LOUISVILLE, KENTUCKY 40210-1038

OVERVIEW: Produces alcoholic beverages, glassware, and luggage. Established: 1870.

KEY STATISTICS Annual Sales: $2.0 billion. Number of Employees: 6,700.

EXPERTISE/EDUCATION SOUGHT: Marketing, business administration, human resources, computer programming, finance, chemical engineering

CONTACT: Mr Mike Mimnaugh, Vice President of Staffing and Executive Search; Phone (502) 585-1100.

BROWNING-FERRIS INDUSTRIES
757 NORTH ELDRIDGE PARKWAY
HOUSTON, TEXAS 77079-4435

OVERVIEW: Provides waste collection and disposal services. Established: 1913.

KEY STATISTICS Number of Employees: 31,600.

HIRING HISTORY Number of professional employees hired in 1994: 20.

EXPERTISE/EDUCATION SOUGHT: Accounting, law, sales, marketing

CONTACT: Ms Kim Bors, Director of Compensation and Human Resources Services; Phone (713) 870-8100, ext. 7633.

BRUNO'S, INC.
800 LAKESHORE PARKWAY
BIRMINGHAM, ALABAMA 35201-2486

OVERVIEW: Operates food store chain with diversified business interests.

EXPERTISE/EDUCATION SOUGHT: Accounting, marketing, finance, management information systems, business administration, law, retail management, data processing, sales

CONTACT: For individuals with previous experience: Mr Richard Marty, Vice President of Human Resources, PO Box 2486, Birmingham, AL, 35201; Phone (205) 940-9400, ext. 2346.

BRUNSWICK CORPORATION
1 NORTH FIELD COURT
LAKE FOREST, ILLINOIS 60045

OVERVIEW: Manufactures recreation and leisure products. Established: 1845.

KEY STATISTICS Number of Employees: 17,000.

HIRING HISTORY Number of professional employees hired in 1994: 25. 1993: 20.

EXPERTISE/EDUCATION SOUGHT: Business management, auditing, accounting

CONTACT: Ms Mary Bottroff, Director of Human Resources; Phone (708) 470-4700.

BRYAN FOODS, INC.
100 CHURCH HILL ROAD
WEST POINT, MISSISSIPPI 39773

OVERVIEW: Manufacture food. Established: 1937.

KEY STATISTICS Annual Sales: $711.0 million. Number of Employees: 3,685.

EXPERTISE/EDUCATION SOUGHT: Marketing, sales, finance, accounting, operations

CONTACT: For individuals with previous experience: Mr John Dixon, Division Human Resources Manager.

BTR, INC.
333 LUDLOW STREET
STAMFORD, CONNECTICUT 06902

OVERVIEW: Manufactures rubber products. Established: 1976.

EXPERTISE/EDUCATION SOUGHT: Accounting, finance, data processing, law

CONTACT: For individuals with previous experience: Mr Robert Mac Queen, Vice President of Human Resources, 9 Riverside Road, Weston, MA, 02193; Phone (617) 899-3300, ext. 19.

THE BUDD COMPANY
3155 WEST BIG BEAVER ROAD
TROY, MICHIGAN 48084-3002

OVERVIEW: Manufactures automotive parts and accessories. Established: 1912. Parent Company: Thyssen, A.G.

KEY STATISTICS Annual Sales: $2.0 billion. Number of Employees: 9,600.

EXPERTISE/EDUCATION SOUGHT: Mechanical engineering, manufacturing engineering

CONTACT: Ms Linda Bayly, Corporate Personnel Manager; Phone (810) 643-3613.

BUDGET RENT-A-CAR CORPORATION
4225 NAPERVILLE ROAD
LISLE, ILLINOIS 60532

OVERVIEW: Provides automobile and truck rental services. Established: 1958.

KEY STATISTICS Number of Employees: 10,500.

HIRING HISTORY Number of professional employees hired in 1994: 40.

EXPERTISE/EDUCATION SOUGHT: Sales, marketing, finance, accounting, auditing, human resources, information systems, law, public relations

CONTACT: For individuals with previous experience: Ms Joan Tuzzolino, Corporate Recruiter; Phone (708) 955-1900.

BUFFETS, INC.
10260 VIKING DRIVE, SUITE 100
EDEN PRAIRIE, MINNESOTA 55344-7230

OVERVIEW: Operates chain of family style restaurants.

KEY STATISTICS Annual Sales: $335.0 million. Number of Employees: 13,000.

EXPERTISE/EDUCATION SOUGHT: Administration, accounting, payroll, construction

CONTACT: For individuals with previous experience: Ms Elise Reiser, Director Human Resources.

BUILDER'S SQUARE, INC.
9725 DATA POINT DRIVE
SAN ANTONIO, TEXAS 78229-2029

OVERVIEW: Operates chain of home improvement stores. Established: 1983. Parent Company: Kmart Corporation.

KEY STATISTICS Annual Sales: $3.0 billion. Number of Employees: 18,500.

EXPERTISE/EDUCATION SOUGHT: Accounting, sales, marketing, computer programming

CONTACT: Ms Liz Keller, Corporate Human Resources Manager; Phone (210) 616-8000.

H. N. BULL INFORMATION SYSTEMS
TECHNOLOGY PARK
BILLERICA, MASSACHUSETTS 01821

OVERVIEW: Manufactures large computer systems and communications equipment. Established: 1955. Parent Company: Bull Data Systems, Inc.

KEY STATISTICS Annual Sales: $1.0 billion. Number of Employees: 9,100.

EXPERTISE/EDUCATION SOUGHT: Accounting, computer programming, finance, sales, marketing, data processing, systems integration, project management, technical

CONTACT: For individuals with previous experience: Mr Norm Gauthier, Director of Human Resources; Phone (508) 294-4969.

BUNGE CORPORATION
11720 BORMAN DRIVE
SAINT LOUIS, MISSOURI 63146-4129

OVERVIEW: Produces grain, feed products, oils, and processed foods. Established: 1923.

KEY STATISTICS Number of Employees: 3,000.

HIRING HISTORY Number of professional employees hired in 1994: 30. 1993: 30.

EXPERTISE/EDUCATION SOUGHT: Data processing, agricultural engineering, accounting, finance, auditing, human resources

CONTACT: Ms Tammy Jordan, Employment and Training Coordinator; Phone (314) 872-3030.

BUNZL USA, INC.
701 EMERSON ROAD, SUITE 410
SAINT LOUIS, MISSOURI 63141-6754

OVERVIEW: Distributes paper and styrofoam products. Established: 1959.

KEY STATISTICS Annual Sales: $1.0 billion. Number of Employees: 2,500.

EXPERTISE/EDUCATION SOUGHT: Auditing, accounting, finance, human resources, purchasing, sales, management information systems

CONTACT: For individuals with previous experience: Corporate Director of Human Resources; Phone (314) 997-5959, ext. 278.

BURDINE'S
22 EAST FLAGLER STREET
MIAMI, FLORIDA 33131-1004

OVERVIEW: Operates chain of department stores. Established: 1898.

KEY STATISTICS Annual Sales: $1.0 billion. Number of Employees: 12.

HIRING HISTORY Number of professional employees hired in 1994: 200.

EXPERTISE/EDUCATION SOUGHT: Retail, purchasing, planning, distribution

CONTACTS: For college students and recent graduates: Ms Laura Coller, Manager of College Recruitment; Phone (305) 835-5151. For individuals with previous experience: Ms Bonnie Weintraub, Manager Executive Placement; Phone (305) 835-5151.

BURGER KING CORPORATION
17777 OLD CUTLER ROAD
MIAMI, FLORIDA 33157-6325

OVERVIEW: Operates chain of fast food restaurants. Established: 1954.

KEY STATISTICS Annual Sales: $889.0 million. Number of Employees: 41,000.

EXPERTISE/EDUCATION SOUGHT: Human resources, law, management information systems, quality control, accounting, retail, finance

CONTACT: Mr Steven Cerrone, Director of Resourcing and Development, PO Box 20783, Miami, FL, 33102-0783; Phone (305) 378-7011.

BURLINGTON AIR EXPRESS, INC.
18200 VON KARMAN AVENUE
IRVINE, CALIFORNIA 92715-1029

OVERVIEW: Provides air freight services. Established: 1972. Parent Company: The Pittston Company.

KEY STATISTICS Annual Sales: $998.0 million. Number of Employees: 5,500.

EXPERTISE/EDUCATION SOUGHT: Marketing, sales, accounting, finance, data processing, computer programming

CONTACT: Mr Lee Sininger, Manager of Employee Relations and Benefits; Phone (714) 752-4000, ext. 2267.

BURLINGTON COAT FACTORY
1830 ROUTE 130
BURLINGTON, NEW JERSEY 08016-3020

OVERVIEW: Apparel manufacturer and retailer. Established: 1972.

KEY STATISTICS Annual Sales: $1.0 billion. Number of Employees: 12,800.

EXPERTISE/EDUCATION SOUGHT: Accounting, marketing, sales, computer programming

CONTACT: For individuals with previous experience: Ms Sarah Orlick, Director of Recruiting and Training/Human Resources; Phone (609) 387-7800.

BURLINGTON INDUSTRIES, INC.
3330 WEST FRIENDLY AVENUE
GREENSBORO, NORTH CAROLINA 27420

OVERVIEW: Manufactures textiles. Established: 1923.

KEY STATISTICS Annual Sales: $2.0 billion. Number of Employees: 26,000.

EXPERTISE/EDUCATION SOUGHT: Manufacturing management, marketing, engineering, finance, computer science

CONTACT: Mr Tony Michaels, Manager of Organization Planning and Development; Phone (919) 379-2000.

BURLINGTON NORTHERN, INC.
3800 CONTINENTAL PLAZA
FORT WORTH, TEXAS 76102

OVERVIEW: Operates railroad and provides freight transportation services. Established: 1850.

KEY STATISTICS Annual Sales: $5.0 billion. Number of Employees: 30,502.

EXPERTISE/EDUCATION SOUGHT: Computer science, data processing, computer programming, accounting, finance

CONTACT: For individuals with previous experience: Mr James Mills, Assistant Vice President of Human Resources Planning; Phone (817) 333-7085.

LEO BURNETT COMPANY
35 WEST WACKER DRIVE
CHICAGO, ILLINOIS 60601-1614

OVERVIEW: Advertising and direct marketing company. Established: 1935.

KEY STATISTICS Number of Employees: 2,500.

EXPERTISE/EDUCATION SOUGHT: Advertising, graphic arts, finance, accounting, marketing, sales

CONTACT: For individuals with previous experience: Mr Tom Nossem, Vice President/Director of Human Resources-USA, 35 East Wacker Drive, Suite 2200, Chicago, IL, 60601; Phone (312) 220-5959.

BURROUGHS WELLCOME COMPANY
3030 CORNWALLIS ROAD
RESEARCH TRIANGLE PARK
NORTH CAROLINA 27709

OVERVIEW: Develops and manufactures pharmaceuticals. Established: 1924.

KEY STATISTICS Annual Sales: $1.0 billion. Number of Employees: 4,814.

EXPERTISE/EDUCATION SOUGHT: Pharmacy, chemistry, computer programming, research, data processing, biology, biochemistry

CONTACT: For individuals with previous experience: Ms Ann Jones, Manager of Human Resources; Phone (919) 315-8347.

CABLE NEWS NETWORK, INC.
1 CNN CENTER
ATLANTA, GEORGIA 30335

OVERVIEW: Broadcasts cable news programs.

EXPERTISE/EDUCATION SOUGHT: Telecommunications, camera operations, graphic arts, editing, production

CONTACT: Mr Allan DeNiro, Vice President of Human Resources; Phone (404) 827-1500.

CABLE TELEVISION OF MONTGOMERY
20 WEST GUDE DRIVE
ROCKVILLE, MARYLAND 20850-1151

OVERVIEW: Provides cable television services. Established: 1986.

KEY STATISTICS Annual Sales: $58.0 million. Number of Employees: 435.

HIRING HISTORY Number of professional employees hired in 1993: 15.

EXPERTISE/EDUCATION SOUGHT: Communications, customer service and support, accounting, finance, data processing, customer service and support, electrical engineering

CONTACT: For individuals with previous experience: Ms Grace Killelea, Director of Human Resources; Phone (301) 294-7600.

CABLEVISION SYSTEMS, INC.
320 CROSSWAY PARK DRIVE
WOODBURY, NEW YORK 11797

OVERVIEW: Owns and operates cable television systems. Established: 1985.

EXPERTISE/EDUCATION SOUGHT: Accounting, customer service and support, finance, account management, telecommunications, television broadcasting

CONTACT: Ms Diana Sabato, Director of Corporate Human Resources, One Media Crossways, Woodbury, NY, 11797; Phone (516) 496-1192.

CABOT CORPORATION
75 STATE STREET
BOSTON, MASSACHUSETTS 02109

OVERVIEW: Refines metals and manufactures carbon black, silica, electronic materials, and plastics. Established: 1882.

EXPERTISE/EDUCATION SOUGHT: Chemistry, chemical engineering

CONTACT: For individuals with previous experience: Ms Karen Morrissey, Vice President of Human Resources; Phone (617) 345-6221.

CACI, INC.
1100 NORTH GLEBE ROAD
ARLINGTON, VIRGINIA 22201-4798

OVERVIEW: Develops computer systems and software; provides engineering and communication services.

KEY STATISTICS Annual Sales: $145.0 million. Number of Employees: 2,900.

EXPERTISE/EDUCATION SOUGHT: Computer science, information systems

CONTACT: Mr Robert Luniford, Technical Recruiter; Phone (703) 841-7800.

CALDOR, INC.
20 GLOVER AVENUE
NORWALK, CONNECTICUT 06801

OVERVIEW: Operates discount department store chain. Established: 1951.

KEY STATISTICS Annual Sales: $3.0 billion. Number of Employees: 21,000.

EXPERTISE/EDUCATION SOUGHT: Merchandising, management information systems, finance, distribution

CONTACT: Ms Denise B Henry, Senior Human Resources Specialist.

CALIFORNIA FEDERAL BANK
5700 WILSHIRE BOULEVARD
LOS ANGELES, CALIFORNIA 90036

OVERVIEW: Savings and loan institution. Established: 1925.

KEY STATISTICS Number of Employees: 2,300.

EXPERTISE/EDUCATION SOUGHT: Banking, finance, economics

CONTACT: For individuals with previous experience: Employment Department; Phone (213) 932-4129.

CALIFORNIA PHYSICIANS SERVICE
2 NORTH POINT STREET
SAN FRANCISCO, CALIFORNIA 94133-1598

OVERVIEW: Provides medical insurance. Established: 1939.

KEY STATISTICS Annual Sales: $2.0 billion. Number of Employees: 3,731.

EXPERTISE/EDUCATION SOUGHT: Systems analysis, accounting, finance, marketing, sales, health care, administration

CONTACT: For individuals with previous experience: Ms Deborah LeFevre, Manager of Human Resources; Phone (415) 445-5000.

CALTEX PETROLEUM CORPORATION
125 EAST JOHN CARPENTER FREEWAY
IRVING, TEXAS 75062

OVERVIEW: Refines and markets petroleum products. Established: 1936.

KEY STATISTICS Number of Employees: 8,000.

EXPERTISE/EDUCATION SOUGHT: Chemical engineering, mechanical engineering, accounting, finance

CONTACT: For individuals with previous experience: Ms Gretchen Remick, Professional Recruiter; Phone (214) 830-1000.

CAMPBELL SOUP COMPANY
CAMPBELL PLACE
CAMDEN, NEW JERSEY 08103-4303

OVERVIEW: Manufactures soups and processed foods. Established: 1869.

KEY STATISTICS Annual Sales: $7.0 billion.

HIRING HISTORY Number of professional employees hired in 1994: 50. 1993: 50.

EXPERTISE/EDUCATION SOUGHT: Accounting, finance, engineering, product design and development, law

CONTACTS: For college students and recent graduates: Mr Scott Simon, Corporate Recruiter; Phone (609) 342-4800. For individuals with previous experience: Ms Julie Hoy, Manager of Staffing; Phone (609) 342-4800.

CAMPBELL TAGGART, INC.
8400 MARYLAND AVENUE
SAINT LOUIS, MISSOURI 63105-3647

OVERVIEW: Distributes baked goods. Established: 1927. Parent Company: Anheuser-Busch Companies, Inc.

KEY STATISTICS Number of Employees: 18,270.

EXPERTISE/EDUCATION SOUGHT: Accounting, finance, marketing, data processing

CONTACT: Ms Maria Traina, Manager of Employment/Administrative Services.

CANADIAN PACIFIC RAIL SYSTEM
105 SOUTH 5TH STREET
MINNEAPOLIS, MINNESOTA 55402

OVERVIEW: Provides railway freight transportation services. Established: 1949. Parent Company: Soo Line Corporation.

KEY STATISTICS Annual Sales: $622.0 million. Number of Employees: 4,528.

EXPERTISE/EDUCATION SOUGHT: Engineering, systems analysis, accounting

CONTACT: For individuals with previous experience: Mr Paul Pfeiffer, Director of Staffing; Phone (612) 347-8394.

CANON USA, INC.
1 CANON PLAZA
NEW HYDE PARK, NEW YORK 11042-1119

OVERVIEW: Manufactures office equipment and cameras. Established: 1966.

KEY STATISTICS Annual Sales: $5.0 billion. Number of Employees: 5,500.

EXPERTISE/EDUCATION SOUGHT: Marketing, sales, finance, accounting, auditing, merchandising, business management

CONTACT: Mr Cevero Mancebo, Recruiter; Phone (516) 488-6700, ext. 5050.

CAPITAL BLUE CROSS, INC.
2500 ELMERTON AVENUE
HARRISBURG, PENNSYLVANIA 17110-9763

OVERVIEW: Provides health insurance. Established: 1938.

KEY STATISTICS Annual Sales: $1.0 billion. Number of Employees: 1,878.

Hiring History Number of professional employees hired in 1994: 30.
Expertise/Education Sought: Claims adjustment/examination, accounting, market research, program analysis, systems analysis
Contact: Mr David Staskin, Manager of Employee Relations.

CARDINAL HEALTH, INC.
655 METRO PLACE SOUTH, SUITE 925
DUBLIN, OHIO 43017-3313

Overview: Distributes wholesale pharmaceuticals. Established: 1979.
Key Statistics Annual Sales: $2.0 billion. Number of Employees: 1,600.
Expertise/Education Sought: Accounting, finance, data processing, law, pharmacology
Contact: Mr Ted Diabisi, Director of Human Resources, 655 Metro Place South, 9th Floor, Dublin, OH, 43017-3377; Phone (614) 761-8700.

CAREMARK, INC.
2215 SANDERS ROAD
NORTHBROOK, ILLINOIS 60062-6100

Overview: Provides home health care services. Established: 1987. Parent Company: Caremark International, Inc.
Key Statistics Annual Sales: $2.0 billion. Number of Employees: 6,900.
Expertise/Education Sought: Accounting, finance, pharmacy, physical therapy, occupational therapy
Contact: For individuals with previous experience: Human Resources; Phone (708) 559-4700.

CARGILL, INC.
PO BOX 5697, MS 63
MINNEAPOLIS, MINNESOTA 55440-5697

Overview: Merchandises, transports, and processes commodities. Established: 1865.
Key Statistics Number of Employees: 70,000.
Expertise/Education Sought: Accounting, information technology, commodity merchandising, business, agriculture, human resources, chemical, mechanical, electrical, and milling science engineers to fill production management positions
Contacts: For college students and recent graduates: Cargill Jobline; Phone (800) 741-7431; Fax (612) 742-7022. For individuals with previous experience: Human Resources.

CORPORATE PROFILE

Cargill is a privately held U.S. corporation that was founded as a grain warehousing and merchandising company. Today, Cargill is one of the most diversified companies in the world.

In addition to merchandising and transporting bulk commodities, Cargill processes and mills grains, fruits, and juices; manufactures fertilizer; operates beef-, pork-, and poultry-processing plants; mines salt; produces and fabricates steel; conducts research; sells and provides animal nutrition services, feed, seed, and fertilizer to farmers; and offers a wide range of financial services. Cargill operates from approximately 800 locations in 60 countries and employs over 70,000 people.

Career development and management training are an integral part of Cargill employee development and the Cargill experience. Employees are given the tools to have a rewarding career— challenging responsibilities, ample opportunities, and educational enrichment. Cargill's philosophy is to promote its employees from within. Effort and expertise are rewarded with a competitive compensation and benefits package.

The company's success record combined with the talent and vision of its management team provide a promising future for engineers. Cargill seeks chemical, biochemical, and mechanical engineers who desire a hands-on process production environment. Employment positions blend engineering

expertise with production management and supervision skills. Cargill engineers become managers of production departments or engineering projects with opportunities to become operations managers of production facilities. Most positions require relocation during an individual's career.

Orientation for new employees is held at Cargill's world headquarters in suburban Minneapolis, Minnesota.

CARLISLE PLASTICS FILMS DIVISION
1401 WEST 94TH STREET
MINNEAPOLIS, MINNESOTA 55431

Overview: Manufactures garbage bags and construction film.
Expertise/Education Sought: Accounting, finance, sales, marketing, computer science, management information systems, manufacturing engineering
Contact: For individuals with previous experience: Ms Mary Beth Volvis, Director of Human Resources; Phone (612) 884-7281; Fax (612)885-9355.

CARLSON COMPANIES, INC.
CARLSON PARKWAY-701 TOWER
MINNEAPOLIS, MINNESOTA 55459

Overview: Operates hotels and resorts. Established: 1938.
Key Statistics Number of Employees: 112,000.
Expertise/Education Sought: Computer programming, program analysis, finance, hospitality/hotel and restaurant management, marketing
Contacts: For college students and recent graduates: Mr Mike Frommett, Senior Human Resources Generalist; Phone (612) 540-5000. For individuals with previous experience: Mr Ron Brooks, Manager of Corporate Human Resources; Phone (612) 591-7239.

CARNIVAL CRUISE LINES, INC.
3655 NORTH WEST 87TH AVENUE
MIAMI, FLORIDA 33178-2418

Overview: Operates cruise ships and hotels. Established: 1974.
Key Statistics Annual Sales: $2.0 billion. Number of Employees: 15,650.
Expertise/Education Sought: Food services, hospitality/hotel and restaurant management, sales, data processing, law, accounting, finance
Contact: Mr Herb Schleier, Recruiting Specialist; Phone (305) 599-2600, ext. 3059.

CAROLINA FREIGHT CARRIERS CORPORATION
HIGHWAY 150 EAST
CHERRYVILLE, NORTH CAROLINA 28021

Overview: Provides trucking and transport services. Established: 1932. Parent Company: Carolina Freight Corporation.
Key Statistics Annual Sales: $658.3 million. Number of Employees: 8,116.
Expertise/Education Sought: Accounting, finance, marketing, auditing, computer programming
Contact: Mr Ken Marks, Manager of Personnel; Phone (704) 435-6811, ext. 2327.

CAROLINA POWER AND LIGHT COMPANY
411 FAYETTEVILLE STREET MALL
RALEIGH, NORTH CAROLINA 27601

Overview: Electric utility. Established: 1908.
Key Statistics Number of Employees: 8,100.
Expertise/Education Sought: Marketing
Contact: Mr Ray Giemza, Director of Corporate Recruiting; Phone (919) 546-6705.

E. R. CARPENTER COMPANY, INC.
5016 MONUMENT AVENUE
RICHMOND, VIRGINIA 23230-3620

Overview: Manufactures cushions and mattresses. Established: 1949.

Key Statistics Number of Employees: 6,000.

Hiring History Number of professional employees hired in 1993: 50.

Expertise/Education Sought: Sales, chemical engineering, electrical engineering, mechanical engineering, accounting

Contact: For individuals with previous experience: Mr Bobbie Richardson, Corporate Recruitor; Phone (804) 359-0800.

CARRIER CORPORATION
1 CARRIER PLACE
FARMINGTON, CONNECTICUT 06054-4015

Overview: Manufactures heating and air conditioning equipment. Established: 1979. Parent Company: United Technologies Corporation.

Hiring History Number of professional employees hired in 1994: 15. 1993: 15.

Expertise/Education Sought: Management, business administration

Contact: For individuals with previous experience: Ms Pamela Hamilton, Manager of Professional Recruiting; Phone (203) 674-3000.

CARSON PIRIE SCOTT AND COMPANY
331 WEST WISCONSIN AVENUE
MILWAUKEE, WISCONSIN 53203-2201

Overview: Operates chain of department stores. Established: 1854.

Key Statistics Annual Sales: $1.0 billion. Number of Employees: 18,000.

Expertise/Education Sought: Business, accounting, finance, management, information services

Contact: For individuals with previous experience: Ms Heather Page, Executive Recruiter; Phone (414) 347-5288.

CARTER-WALLACE, INC.
1345 AVENUE OF THE AMERICAS
NEW YORK, NEW YORK 10105

Overview: Manufactures pharmaceuticals, diagnostics, toiletries, and pet products. Established: 1880.

Expertise/Education Sought: Chemical engineering, mechanical engineering, accounting, finance, marketing, sales, management information systems, pharmacy

Contact: For individuals with previous experience: Ms Tina Scudere, Representative for Recruitment; Phone (212) 339-5000.

CASCADE DIE CASTING GROUP, INC.
3040 CHARLEVOIX DRIVE SOUTHEAST
GRAND RAPIDS, MICHIGAN 49546-7085

Overview: Provides die casting services. Established: 1985. Parent Company: TCH Industries, Inc.

Key Statistics Annual Sales: $42.0 million. Number of Employees: 500.

Hiring History Number of professional employees hired in 1993: 25.

Expertise/Education Sought: Accounting, finance, payroll, data processing, electrical technology, electrical engineering, project engineering, process engineering, benefits administration

Contact: For individuals with previous experience: Ms Miki Horton, Director of Human Resources; Phone (616) 956-0966.

CASE CORPORATION
700 STATE STREET
RACINE, WISCONSIN 53404

Overview: Manufactures agricultural machinery and equipment. Established: 1964.

Expertise/Education Sought: Information systems, finance, electrical engineering, mechanical engineering

Contacts: For college students and recent graduates: Mr Dennis Winkleman, Director of Organizational Development and Planning. For individuals with previous experience: Ms Judy Murray, Director of Corporate Human Resources; Phone (414) 636-6011, ext. 6249.

CASINO MAGIC CORPORATION
711 CASINO MAGIC DRIVE
BAY SAINT LOUIS, MISSISSIPPI 39520-1808

Overview: Operates casino hotels and eating and drinking establishments. Established: 1990.

Key Statistics Annual Sales: $202.4 million. Number of Employees: 3,000.

Expertise/Education Sought: Accounting, marketing, administration

Contact: Human Resources Department; Phone (601) 467-9257.

CASTROL, INC.
1500 VALLEY ROAD
WAYNE, NEW JERSEY 07470-2040

Overview: Manufactures and markets lubricants and petroleum products. Parent Company: Burmah Castrol USA, Inc.

Key Statistics Annual Sales: $550.0 million. Number of Employees: 1,800.

Expertise/Education Sought: Chemical engineering, product management

Contact: Ms Janet Tuffy, Director of Staffing and Development; Phone (201) 633-2200.

CATERAIR INTERNATIONAL CORPORATION
6550 ROCK SPRING DRIVE
BETHESDA, MARYLAND 20817-1132

Overview: Provides airport ground services. Parent Company: Caterair Holdings Corporation.

Key Statistics Annual Sales: $1.0 billion. Number of Employees: 22,000.

Expertise/Education Sought: Management, food services, hospitality/ hotel and restaurant management, business, accounting

Contact: Mr Bruce Murray, Vice President Human Resources; Phone (301) 309-7800.

CATERPILLAR, INC.
100 NORTHEAST ADAMS STREET
PEORIA, ILLINOIS 61629-1324

Overview: Manufactures farm and construction equipment. Established: 1925.

Key Statistics Number of Employees: 51,250.

Expertise/Education Sought: Accounting, computer science

Contact: Mr Chuck Williams, Supervisor of Professional and Technical Employment; Phone (309) 675-4279.

CAWSL CORPORATION
7 EAST WYNNEWOOD ROAD
WYNNEWOOD, PENNSYLVANIA 19096-1923

Overview: Manufactures steel tubing. Established: 1981.

Key Statistics Annual Sales: $2.0 billion. Number of Employees: 5,835.

Expertise/Education Sought: Mechanical engineering, industrial engineering, accounting, marketing

Contact: For individuals with previous experience: Mr Thomas Pezick, Director, PO Box 540, Wynnewood, PA, 19096; Phone (610) 649-3210.

CBI INDUSTRIES, INC.
800 JORIE BOULEVARD
OAK BROOK, ILLINOIS 60521-2216

OVERVIEW: Manufactures and installs storage tanks and industrial gases. Established: 1889.

KEY STATISTICS Annual Sales: $2.0 billion. Number of Employees: 13,920.

EXPERTISE/EDUCATION SOUGHT: Accounting, electrical engineering, metallurgical engineering

CONTACT: For individuals with previous experience: Mr Jim Morgan, Manager Employment and Equal Employment Opportunity.

CBS, INC.
51 WEST 57TH STREET
NEW YORK, NEW YORK 10019

OVERVIEW: Provides network broadcasting services.

EXPERTISE/EDUCATION SOUGHT: Accounting, finance

CONTACT: For individuals with previous experience: Recruitment and Placement Department, 524 West 57th Street, New York, NY, 10019; Phone (212) 975-4321.

CCH, INC.
4025 WEST PETERSON STREET
RIVERWOODS, ILLINOIS 60015-3888

OVERVIEW: Publishes books and reports for legal and tax professionals. Established: 1927.

KEY STATISTICS Number of Employees: 5,728.

EXPERTISE/EDUCATION SOUGHT: Accounting, marketing, purchasing, customer service and support, data processing, law, finance

CONTACTS: For college students and recent graduates: Mr Patrick Carney, Recruiting Specialist; Phone (708) 940-4600. For individuals with previous experience: Ms Coco Hirstel, Human Resource Manager; Phone (708) 267-7000.

CEDARS SINAI MEDICAL CENTER
8700 BEVERLY BOULEVARD
LOS ANGELES, CALIFORNIA 90048

OVERVIEW: Hospital and medical center.

EXPERTISE/EDUCATION SOUGHT: Research and development, finance, information services

CONTACTS: For college students and recent graduates: Job Hotline; Phone (310) 967-8230. For individuals with previous experience: Ms Jeanne Flores, Director of Employee Recruitment; Phone (310) 967-8230.

CENEX/LAND O'LAKES
5500 CENEX DRIVE
INVER GROVE HEIGHTS, MINNESOTA 55077-1733

OVERVIEW: Manufactures fertilizers, farm supplies, and feed products. Established: 1927.

KEY STATISTICS Number of Employees: 3,000.

EXPERTISE/EDUCATION SOUGHT: Marketing, sales

CONTACT: Mr Richard Baldwin, Director of Human Resources, PO Box 64089, St. Paul, MN, 55164-0089; Phone (612) 451-5151, ext. 4514.

CENTEL CORPORATION
8725 WEST HIGGINS ROAD
CHICAGO, ILLINOIS 60606

OVERVIEW: Provides local telephone and cellular communications services.

KEY STATISTICS Annual Sales: $1.0 billion. Number of Employees: 9,000.

HIRING HISTORY Number of professional employees hired in 1994: 50.

EXPERTISE/EDUCATION SOUGHT: Telecommunications, computer programming, engineering

CONTACT: For individuals with previous experience: Human Resources Department; Phone (312) 399-2500.

CENTERIOR ENERGY CORPORATION
6200 OAK TREE BOULEVARD
CLEVELAND, OHIO 44131-2510

OVERVIEW: Electric utility. Established: 1985.

KEY STATISTICS Annual Sales: $2.0 billion. Number of Employees: 6,748.

EXPERTISE/EDUCATION SOUGHT: Electrical engineering, mechanical engineering, nuclear engineering

CONTACT: Mr Jerry Smith, Manager of Employee Relations and Human Resources Services; Phone (216) 447-3189, ext. 3189.

CENTEX CORPORATION
PO BOX 19000
DALLAS, TEXAS 75219

OVERVIEW: Provides construction and real estate development services. Established: 1950.

EXPERTISE/EDUCATION SOUGHT: Management, training and development, information systems, architecture

CONTACT: For individuals with previous experience: Mr Richard Sconyers, Executive Vice President.

CENTRAL AND SOUTHWEST CORPORATION
1616 WOODALL RODGERS FREEWAY
DALLAS, TEXAS 75202-1234

OVERVIEW: Operates and manages utilities. Established: 1925.

KEY STATISTICS Number of Employees: 8,900.

HIRING HISTORY Number of professional employees hired in 1993: 60.

EXPERTISE/EDUCATION SOUGHT: Marketing, computer programming, finance, mechanical engineering, electrical engineering, accounting

CONTACT: Ms Diana Wright, Lead Human Resources Consultant; Phone (214) 777-1000.

CENTRAL ILLINOIS LIGHT COMPANY
300 LIBERTY STREET
PEORIA, ILLINOIS 61602-1238

OVERVIEW: Electric utility. Established: 1985.

KEY STATISTICS Annual Sales: $585.0 million. Number of Employees: 2,844.

EXPERTISE/EDUCATION SOUGHT: Program analysis, customer service and support, computer programming, electrical engineering

CONTACT: Ms Sue Hagel, Senior Employment Administrator; Phone (309) 677-5128.

CENTRAL PARKING CORPORATION
2401 21ST AVENUE SOUTH, SUITE 200
NASHVILLE, TENNESSEE 37212-5397

OVERVIEW: Operates parking lots and garages. Established: 1968.

KEY STATISTICS Annual Sales: $372.2 million. Number of Employees: 4,500.

HIRING HISTORY Number of professional employees hired in 1994: 60.

EXPERTISE/EDUCATION SOUGHT: Management

CONTACT: Mr Bob Mitchell, Vice President Human Resources; Phone (615) 297-4255.

CENTRAL SOYA COMPANY, INC.
1300 FORT WAYNE NATIONAL BANK BUILDING
FORT WAYNE, INDIANA 46802

OVERVIEW: Manufactures soybean products. Established: 1934.

EXPERTISE/EDUCATION SOUGHT: Mechanical engineering, chemical engineering, accounting

Central Soya Company, Inc. (continued)

CONTACT: For individuals with previous experience: Mr Tom Theard, Director of Human Resources, 1946 West Ciik Road, Fort Wayne, IN, 46818; Phone (219) 425-5100.

CERIDIAN CORPORATION
8100 34TH AVENUE SOUTH
BLOOMINGTON, MINNESOTA 55425-1672

OVERVIEW: Provides transaction processing, computer systems integration and payroll services. Established: 1957.

KEY STATISTICS Number of Employees: 7,600.

EXPERTISE/EDUCATION SOUGHT: Statistics, mathematics, computer programming, quality control, electrical engineering

CONTACT: For individuals with previous experience: Mr Glenn Jeffrey, Vice President of Organizational Resources; Phone (612) 853-8100.

CERTAINTEED CORPORATION
750 EAST SWEDESFORD ROAD
VALLEY FORGE, PENNSYLVANIA 19482

OVERVIEW: Manufactures building and construction materials. Established: 1976.

KEY STATISTICS Number of Employees: 8,000.

HIRING HISTORY Number of professional employees hired in 1993: 80.

EXPERTISE/EDUCATION SOUGHT: Marketing, accounting, finance

CONTACT: Mr Ken Chiarello, Manager of Personnel; Phone (610) 341-7000, ext. 7067.

CERTIFIED GROCERS OF CALIFORNIA, LTD.
2601 SOUTH EASTERN AVENUE
LOS ANGELES, CALIFORNIA 90040-1401

OVERVIEW: Distributes groceries and frozen food products. Established: 1925.

KEY STATISTICS Annual Sales: $2.0 billion. Number of Employees: 2,500.

EXPERTISE/EDUCATION SOUGHT: Systems analysis, computer programming

CONTACT: For individuals with previous experience: Mr Leonard Soebbing, Interviewer.

CESSNA AIRCRAFT COMPANY
2 CESSNA BOULEVARD, PO BOX 7704
WICHITA, KANSAS 67277-7704

OVERVIEW: Manufactures aircraft. Established: 1926. Parent Company: Textron.

KEY STATISTICS Annual Sales: $800.0 million. Number of Employees: 6,146.

HIRING HISTORY Number of professional employees hired in 1993: 165.

EXPERTISE/EDUCATION SOUGHT: Accounting, business administration, business management, mechanical engineering, manufacturing engineering

CONTACTS: For college students and recent graduates: Ms Wanda Meyers, Professional Recruiter; Phone (316) 941-6417. For individuals with previous experience: Mr Bill Quattlebaum, Director, Employment; Phone (316) 941-6157; Fax (316) 941-7865.

CHAMBERLAIN MANUFACTURING CORPORATION
845 NORTH LARCH AVENUE
ELM HURST, ILLINOIS 60126

OVERVIEW: Manufactures home improvement products.

EXPERTISE/EDUCATION SOUGHT: Marketing, mechanical engineering, finance, electrical engineering, accounting, sales, law, advertising

CONTACT: For individuals with previous experience: Ms Joanne Finger, Human Resources Administrator; Phone (708) 279-3600.

CHAMBERS DEVELOPMENT COMPANY, INC.
10700 FRANKSTOWN ROAD
PITTSBURGH, PENNSYLVANIA 15235

OVERVIEW: Provides waste disposal services. Established: 1971.

KEY STATISTICS Annual Sales: $289.0 million. Number of Employees: 1,500.

HIRING HISTORY Number of professional employees hired in 1993: 12.

EXPERTISE/EDUCATION SOUGHT: Sales, operations, accounting

CONTACT: For individuals with previous experience: Dr Alan Pass, Vice President of Human Resources; Phone (412) 242-6237.

CHAMPION HEALTHCARE CORPORATION
14340 TORREY CHASE BOULEVARD, SUITE 320
HOUSTON, TEXAS 77014-5947

OVERVIEW: Owns and manages hospitals. Established: 1983.

KEY STATISTICS Annual Sales: $44.0 million. Number of Employees: 612.

EXPERTISE/EDUCATION SOUGHT: Marketing, finance, accounting

CONTACT: For individuals with previous experience: Mr Randy Stone, Vice President of Administration.

CHAMPION INTERNATIONAL CORPORATION
1 CHAMPION PLAZA
STAMFORD, CONNECTICUT 06921

OVERVIEW: Produces wood and paper products. Established: 1937.

EXPERTISE/EDUCATION SOUGHT: Management information systems, accounting, management

CONTACT: Ms Leslie Forst, Manager of College Relations and Planning; Phone (203) 358-7004.

CHARMING SHOPPES, INC.
450 WINKS LANE
BENSALEM, PENNSYLVANIA 19020

OVERVIEW: Operates chain of apparel stores. Established: 1969.

EXPERTISE/EDUCATION SOUGHT: Merchandising, sales, accounting, marketing, finance, management information systems

CONTACT: Ms Patricia Kidder, Corporate Director of Human Resources; Phone (215) 245-9100.

CHART HOUSE ENTERPRISES
115 SOUTH ACACIA AVENUE
SOLANA BEACH, CALIFORNIA 92075-1803

OVERVIEW: Operates eating and drinking establishments. Established: 1961.

KEY STATISTICS Annual Sales: $140.0 million. Number of Employees: 5,200.

EXPERTISE/EDUCATION SOUGHT: Hospitality/hotel and restaurant management, management

CONTACTS: For college students and recent graduates: Mr Steward Newbold, Director of Training East Coast, 741 Boston Post Road, PO Box 11, Guilford, CT, 06437; Phone (203) 458-7545. For individuals with previous experience: Mr Duke Howard, Director of Training West Coast; Phone (619) 755-8281.

CHARTER MEDICAL CORPORATION
577 MULBERRY STREET
MACON, GEORGIA 31298-2728

OVERVIEW: Operates psychiatric and acute care hospital. Established: 1969.

KEY STATISTICS Annual Sales: $898.0 million. Number of Employees: 8,300.

EXPERTISE/EDUCATION SOUGHT: Accounting, finance, marketing, computer programming, data processing

CONTACT: For individuals with previous experience: Mr Al Joyner, Employment Manager; Phone (912) 742-1161.

CHASE MANHATTAN BANK, INC.
1 CHASE MANHATTAN PLAZA
NEW YORK, NEW YORK 10081

OVERVIEW: Commercial and retail bank. Established: 1955. Parent Company: Chase Manhattan Corporation.

KEY STATISTICS Number of Employees: 34,540.

EXPERTISE/EDUCATION SOUGHT: Accounting, finance, marketing

CONTACT: For individuals with previous experience: Human Resources Department; Phone (212) 552-2222.

CHECKERS DRIVE-IN RESTAURANTS
600 CLEVELAND STREET
CLEARWATER, FLORIDA 34617-4161

OVERVIEW: Operates chain of fast food restaurants. Established: 1985.

KEY STATISTICS Annual Sales: $189.5 million.

EXPERTISE/EDUCATION SOUGHT: Finance, marketing, accounting, management

CONTACT: For individuals with previous experience: Ms Sara Mills, Manager Human Resources; Phone (813) 441-3500.

CHESAPEAKE CORPORATION
1021 EAST CARY STREET
RICHMOND, VIRGINIA 23219-4000

OVERVIEW: Manufactures pulp and paper products. Established: 1918.

KEY STATISTICS Number of Employees: 4,833.

EXPERTISE/EDUCATION SOUGHT: Accounting, communications, electrical engineering, mechanical engineering, pulp and paper science, finance, accounting

CONTACTS: For college students and recent graduates: Ms Mary Bourne, Human Resources Administrator, PO Box 311, West Point, VA, 23181; Phone (804) 843-5169. For individuals with previous experience: Ms Joanne Boroughs, Manager of Employee Services.

CHEVRON CORPORATION
ROOM 1246 575 MARKET STREET
SAN FRANCISCO, CALIFORNIA 94105

OVERVIEW: Produces and refines oil and gas. Established: 1879.

KEY STATISTICS Annual Sales: $35.0 billion.

HIRING HISTORY Number of professional employees hired in 1994: 75. 1993: 75.

EXPERTISE/EDUCATION SOUGHT: Accounting, marketing, finance, industrial relations

CONTACT: For individuals with previous experience: Mark Witzke, Team Leader-Employment Services; Phone (415) 894-4322.

CHI-CHI'S, INC.
10200 LINN STATION ROAD
LOUISVILLE, KENTUCKY 40223-3815

OVERVIEW: Operates chain of restaurants. Established: 1965. Parent Company: Foodmaker, Inc.

KEY STATISTICS Annual Sales: $404.0 million. Number of Employees: 20,000.

EXPERTISE/EDUCATION SOUGHT: Marketing, finance, accounting, business development, auditing, business management, sales

CONTACTS: For college students and recent graduates: Ms Dee Shaughnessy, Manager of Recruiting; Phone (502) 426-3900, ext. 319. For individuals with previous experience: Ms Karen Hamilton, Manger of Personnel; Phone (502) 426-3900, ext. 400.

CHICAGO AND NORTHWESTERN TRANSPORTATION COMPANY
1 NORTHWESTERN CENTER
CHICAGO, ILLINOIS 60606-1512

OVERVIEW: Provides freight rail transportation services. Established: 1848.

KEY STATISTICS Annual Sales: $839.0 million. Number of Employees: 6,158.

EXPERTISE/EDUCATION SOUGHT: Transportation, data processing, business management, business, operations, marketing

CONTACT: Mr Robert M Kraft, Director of Human Resources; Phone (312) 559-6747.

CHICAGO TITLE AND TRUST COMPANY
171 NORTH CLARK STREET, 5TH FLOOR HUMAN RESOURCES
CHICAGO, ILLINOIS 60601-3203

OVERVIEW: Provides title insurance. Established: 1847. Parent Company: Allegheny Corporation.

KEY STATISTICS Number of Employees: 8,600.

EXPERTISE/EDUCATION SOUGHT: Accounting, finance, law, database management, computer operations, program analysis, computer programming

CONTACTS: For college students and recent graduates: Ms Kristine Annen, Human Resources Representative, 171 North Clark Street, 5th Floor Human Resources, Chicago, IL, 60801. For individuals with previous experience: Ms LaNette Zimmermann, Senior Vice President of Human Resources; Phone (312) 223-2000.

CHICAGO TRANSIT AUTHORITY
MERCHANDISE MART
CHICAGO, ILLINOIS 60654

OVERVIEW: Provides local and suburban transit services. Established: 1945.

KEY STATISTICS Number of Employees: 12,500.

HIRING HISTORY Number of professional employees hired in 1994: 30. 1993: 50.

CONTACT: For individuals with previous experience: Mr Thomas Czech, Vice President, Human Resources, PO Box 3555, Chicago, IL, 60654-0555; Phone (312) 664-7200, ext. 3440.

CHIQUITA BRANDS INTERNATIONAL
250 EAST 5TH STREET
CINCINNATI, OHIO 45202

OVERVIEW: Produces fresh fruits, vegetables, and prepared foods. Established: 1899.

EXPERTISE/EDUCATION SOUGHT: Marketing, business management, sales, accounting, food science, food engineering, food services, production control

CONTACT: For individuals with previous experience: Ms Ande Taylor, Human Resources Representative.

CHRYSLER CORPORATION
12000 CHRYSLER DRIVE, CIMS 416-21-01
HIGHLAND PARK, MICHIGAN 48288-0001

OVERVIEW: Manufactures cars, trucks, and automotive components. Established: 1925.

KEY STATISTICS Annual Sales: $50.0 billion. Number of Employees: 92,015.

HIRING HISTORY Number of professional employees hired in 1994: 176. 1993: 92.

EXPERTISE/EDUCATION SOUGHT: Finance, sales, human resources, administration, materials management

CONTACT: For college students and recent graduates: College Relations; Phone (313) 956-1268.

Chrysler Corporation (continued)

CORPORATE PROFILE

Chrysler designs, engineers, manufactures, and distributes cars, light trucks, automotive components and systems, aftermarket parts, and electronic products. Operations are primarily in the United States, Canada, and Mexico; headquarters and major engineering, manufacturing, and administrative activities are concentrated in the Greater Detroit area.

At Chrysler, imagination leads to innovation. An entrepreneurial spirit pervades the organization. Yet, at the same time, it enjoys a wealth of skills and experience gained from over 70 years of auto making. This combination makes Chrysler an ideal place to grow professionally. Chrysler seeks candidates who can satisfy immediate operational needs and who also have the potential to become managers of the company. Academic records must show mastery of relevant skills. In addition, the company looks for evidence of leadership skills and capacity for long-range growth. New graduates typically enter Chrysler either by direct assignment with immediate assumption of specific duties and responsibilities or by rotational training programs, which feature rotating work assignments over a fixed period of six months to two years.

CHRYSLER CREDIT CORPORATION
27777 FRANKLIN ROAD
SOUTHFIELD, MICHIGAN 48034-8286

OVERVIEW: Provides automobile financing services. Established: 1967.

KEY STATISTICS Annual Sales: $2.0 billion. Number of Employees: 3,100.

EXPERTISE/EDUCATION SOUGHT: Finance, accounting, credit/credit analysis, general insurance, marketing, management information systems, auditing, tax accounting

CONTACT: For individuals with previous experience: Ms Dawn Eaglin, Employee Relations Manager; Phone (810) 948-3008.

CHUBB AND SON, INC.
15 MOUNTAINVIEW ROAD
WARREN, NEW JERSEY 07039

OVERVIEW: Provides property, casualty, life, and health insurance. Established: 1882.

KEY STATISTICS Annual Sales: $5.0 billion.

HIRING HISTORY Number of professional employees hired in 1994: 48. 1993: 303.

EXPERTISE/EDUCATION SOUGHT: Underwriting, claims adjustment/examination, controlling, operations, accounting, computer programming

CONTACT: For individuals with previous experience: Ms Mary Scelba, Recruiting Coordinator; Phone (908) 903-2927.

CHURCH AND DWIGHT COMPANY, INC.
469 NORTH HARRISON STREET
PRINCETON, NEW JERSEY 08540

OVERVIEW: Manufactures baking soda and cleaning agents. Established: 1846.

HIRING HISTORY Number of professional employees hired in 1994: 25.

EXPERTISE/EDUCATION SOUGHT: Accounting, marketing, sales

CONTACT: For individuals with previous experience: Mr Jim Blauvelt, Manager of Human Resources Staffing and Development; Phone (609) 683-7044.

CIBA-GEIGY CORPORATION
444 SAW MILL RIVER ROAD
ARDSLEY, NEW YORK 10502

OVERVIEW: Develops and manufactures pharmaceuticals. Established: 1903.

EXPERTISE/EDUCATION SOUGHT: Computer science, finance, law, human resources, communications

CONTACT: For individuals with previous experience: Ms Janine Petroro, Human Resources Department; Phone (914) 479-5000.

CIGNA CORPORATION
1601 CHESTNUT STREET
PHILADELPHIA, PENNSYLVANIA 19192

OVERVIEW: Provides life and health insurance. Established: 1865. Parent Company: Connecticut General Corporation.

KEY STATISTICS Number of Employees: 24,260.

HIRING HISTORY Number of professional employees hired in 1993: 200.

EXPERTISE/EDUCATION SOUGHT: Finance, underwriting, management, actuarial

CONTACT: Ms Pam Lawless, Assistant Vice President of Management Planning, 1 Liberty Place, 1650 Market Street, Philadelphia, PA, 19192; Phone (215) 761-1000.

CIGNA HEALTH PLANS OF CALIFORNIA
505 NORTH BRAND BOULEVARD
GLENDALE, CALIFORNIA 91203

OVERVIEW: Provides health insurance.

EXPERTISE/EDUCATION SOUGHT: Registered nursing, licensed practical nursing, human resources, accounting, information systems, data processing, accounting, patient services

CONTACT: For individuals with previous experience: Mr Steve Barder, Assistant Vice President Human Resources; Phone (818) 500-6502.

CINCINNATI BELL TELEPHONE COMPANY
201 EAST 4TH STREET
CINCINNATI, OHIO 45202-4192

OVERVIEW: Provides telecommunications services.

KEY STATISTICS Number of Employees: 3,000.

EXPERTISE/EDUCATION SOUGHT: Electrical engineering, software engineering/development, finance, accounting, marketing

CONTACT: For individuals with previous experience: Mr Brian Keating, Director Employee Relations and Staffing; Phone (513) 397-1480.

CINCINNATI MILACRON, INC.
4701 MARBURG AVENUE
CINCINNATI, OHIO 45209

OVERVIEW: Produces manufacturing systems, machinery, and related industrial products for the metalworking and plastics processing industries. Established: 1884.

KEY STATISTICS Annual Sales: $2.0 billion. Number of Employees: 10,000.

EXPERTISE/EDUCATION SOUGHT: Mechanical engineering, business administration, electrical engineering, manufacturing engineering, industrial engineering, chemical engineering

CONTACTS: For college students and recent graduates: Mr Joseph Roberts, Human Resources Administrator-Plastics Machinery Group; Phone (513) 841-8100. For individuals with previous experience: Mr Steve Kuebbing, Human Resources Administration-Machine Tool Group; Phone (513) 841-8100.

CINEMARK USA, INC.
7502 GREENVILLE AVENUE
DALLAS, TEXAS 75231-3891

OVERVIEW: Operates movie theaters; provides video rental services.

KEY STATISTICS Annual Sales: $194.7 million. Number of Employees: 4,800.

EXPERTISE/EDUCATION SOUGHT: Accounting, real estate, marketing

CONTACT: For individuals with previous experience: Ms Julie Higgins, Executive Assistant; Phone (214) 696-1644.

CINTAS CORPORATION
6800 CINTAS BOULEVARD, PO BOX 2625737
CINCINNATI, OHIO 45262-5737

OVERVIEW: Manufactures, rents, and sells industrial uniforms. Established: 1968.

KEY STATISTICS Annual Sales: $523.0 million. Number of Employees: 8,581.

EXPERTISE/EDUCATION SOUGHT: Management

CONTACT: For individuals with previous experience: Ms Sally Hart, Management Recruitment.

CIRCUIT CITY STORES, INC.
9950 MAYLAND DRIVE
RICHMOND, VIRGINIA 23233

OVERVIEW: Retailer of brand name consumer electronics, major appliances, personal computers and music software. Established: 1949.

KEY STATISTICS Annual Sales: $6.0 billion. Number of Employees: 31,183.

EXPERTISE/EDUCATION SOUGHT: Business, computer science, management information systems, accounting, finance, marketing, economics, liberal arts

CONTACT: For college students and recent graduates: College Recruiter; Phone (804) 527-4000.

CORPORATE PROFILE

COMPANY OVERVIEW. *A major NYSE company with over 40 years of experience in retailing and 352 stores, Circuit City Stores, Inc. consists of the following operations:*

Superstores. *Free-standing consumer electronics and major appliance stores featuring a wide selection of name-brand items, including computers and music software. Superstores range in size from 15,000 to 45,000 square feet and are tailored to the size of each market.*

Circuit City Express. *Mall-based, leading-edge electronics stores targeting the gift-oriented, convenience-driven shopper. Typical size is 3,000 square feet.*

Roadshops. *Installation centers for mobile electronics products, including car stereos, security systems, and cellular phones.*

Service Centers. *Product repair facilities providing factory-authorized service for virtually all products sold.*

Distribution Centers. *Product distribution facilities meeting the high-volume inventory requirements of the store network. Circuit City also has several new regional businesses.*

COMPANY PERFORMANCE. *Controlled growth and nationwide expansion have allowed Circuit City over the last ten years to have sales increase at an annual rate of 28 percent and earnings grow at a 31 percent compounded annual rate. Fiscal year 1994 sales were more than 35 percent higher than the sales of the next-largest competitor. By the end of the decade, Circuit City Stores, Inc. is expected to be a $15-billion company.*

CAREER OPPORTUNITIES. *Circuit City recruits college and graduate-level students for formalized training programs in the Superstore Division, which leads to placement in sales, operations, or store management. The Circuit City Express stores offer a six-month program of formal training that covers selling, product knowledge, store operations, and management/supervisory skills leading to placement as store manager. At Circuit City's corporate office in Richmond, the company recruits for positions in merchandising, accounting, human resources, MIS, advertising, marketing, real estate, and construction. The accounting division, which includes accounting, treasury, and the wholly owned credit card bank, First North American National Bank (FNANB), offers a specialized Finance Trainee Program that involves three to four assignments over a 24+-month period in various positions within the division. Promotions at Circuit City depend on the trainee's performance and the availability of positions. The ability to relocate is also an important factor in field store assignments.*

COMPANY LOCATIONS. *The corporate office, with over 3,400 associates, is located in Richmond, Virginia. Division offices are located in Richmond, Atlanta, and Los Angeles.*

CIRCUS CIRCUS ENTERPRISES
2880 LAS VEGAS BOULEVARD SOUTH
LAS VEGAS, NEVADA 89109-1138

OVERVIEW: Owns and operates hotels and casinos. Established: 1968.

KEY STATISTICS Annual Sales: $955.0 million. Number of Employees: 13,600.

EXPERTISE/EDUCATION SOUGHT: Accounting, finance, business, management, marketing

CONTACT: Department of Human Resources; Phone (702) 734-0410.

CITGO PETROLEUM CORPORATION
6100 SOUTH YALE AVENUE
TULSA, OKLAHOMA 74102-3758

OVERVIEW: Distributes oil and gasoline products. Established: 1943.

EXPERTISE/EDUCATION SOUGHT: Petroleum/petrochemical engineering, design engineering, civil engineering

CONTACT: Ms Beth Ezarik, Personnel Manager; Phone (918) 495-4000.

CITIBANK SOUTH DAKOTA
701 EAST 60TH STREET NORTH
SIOUX FALLS, SOUTH DAKOTA 57104-0432

OVERVIEW: Provides credit cards.

KEY STATISTICS Assets: $3.0 billion. Number of Employees: 4,200.

EXPERTISE/EDUCATION SOUGHT: Data processing

CONTACT: For individuals with previous experience: Ms Sandy Vietor, Recruiter, PO Box 6000, Sioux Falls, SD, 57117-6000; Phone (605) 331-2626.

CITICORP FINANCIAL CORPORATION
1 PENNS WAY
NEW CASTLE, DELAWARE 19720-2437

OVERVIEW: Commercial and investment banking, credit cards, and financial services company. Established: 1968. Parent Company: Citicorp.

KEY STATISTICS Annual Sales: $584.0 million. Number of Employees: 7,500.

EXPERTISE/EDUCATION SOUGHT: Computer science, accounting, finance, business, computer programming

CONTACT: Director of College Recruiting.

CLAIRES BOUTIQUES, INC.
1501 NORTH MICHAEL DRIVE
WOOD DALE, ILLINOIS 60191-1095

OVERVIEW: Operates chain of apparel, accessories, gift, and stationery stores.

KEY STATISTICS Annual Sales: $280.0 million. Number of Employees: 5,200.

HIRING HISTORY Number of professional employees hired in 1994: 250.

EXPERTISE/EDUCATION SOUGHT: Retail management, management information systems, computer programming, design

CONTACT: For individuals with previous experience: Ms Tina Perkins, Director of Human Resources; Phone (708) 860-5400.

CLAIROL, INC.
345 PARK AVENUE
NEW YORK, NEW YORK 10154

OVERVIEW: Manufactures hair care products, cosmetics, and personal electric appliances. Established: 1941.

HIRING HISTORY Number of professional employees hired in 1994: 20.

EXPERTISE/EDUCATION SOUGHT: Chemical engineering, mechanical engineering, electrical engineering, marketing, finance

CONTACT: For individuals with previous experience: Mr David Roche, Director of Human Resources, 1 Blachley Road, Stamford, CT, 06922.

CLARION MANUFACTURING CORPORATION

237 BEAVER ROAD
WALTON, KENTUCKY 41094

OVERVIEW: Manufactures car stereos and cellular phones. Established: 1986.

KEY STATISTICS Annual Sales: $82.0 million. Number of Employees: 309.

HIRING HISTORY Number of professional employees hired in 1994: 20.

EXPERTISE/EDUCATION SOUGHT: Accounting, finance, data processing, electrical engineering, electronics/electronics engineering, purchasing

CONTACT: Ms Mary Schumer, Manager of Personnel and Administration; Phone (606) 485-6600.

CLARK REFINING AND MARKETING, INC.

8182 MARYLAND AVENUE
SAINT LOUIS, MISSOURI 63105-3786

OVERVIEW: Petroleum refining, marketing, and distribution company. Established: 1932.

KEY STATISTICS Annual Sales: $2.0 billion. Number of Employees: 6,746.

EXPERTISE/EDUCATION SOUGHT: Management information systems, retail, management, accounting, marketing, petroleum/petrochemical engineering

CONTACT: For individuals with previous experience: Ms Juli Sherman, Manager Human Resources; Phone (314) 854-1530.

CLARK CONSTRUCTION GROUP, INC.

75 OLD GEORGETOWN ROAD
BETHESDA, MARYLAND 20814

OVERVIEW: Provides construction and contracting services. Established: 1906.

EXPERTISE/EDUCATION SOUGHT: Accounting, law, finance

CONTACT: For individuals with previous experience: Director of Personnel; Phone (301) 657-7100.

CMC KALMAZOO, INC.

2016 NORTH PITCHER STREET
KALAMAZOO, MICHIGAN 49007-1894

OVERVIEW: Manufactures automotive stampings. Established: 1923.

EXPERTISE/EDUCATION SOUGHT: Quality control, accounting, management information systems, program analysis

CONTACT: Ms Marcia Koestner, Assistant Vice President of Human Resources; Phone (616) 343-6121, ext. 201.

CMS ENERGY CORPORATION

330 TOWN CENTER DRIVE
DEARBORN, MICHIGAN 48126-2711

OVERVIEW: Supplies nonregulated energy. Established: 1886.

KEY STATISTICS Assets: $3.0 billion. Number of Employees: 9,811.

EXPERTISE/EDUCATION SOUGHT: Accounting, law, finance, human resources, computer programming, program analysis, mechanical engineering, electrical engineering

CONTACT: Ms Sue Wright, Senior Human Resources Administrator; Phone (313) 436-9200.

For All the Commitments You Make®

CNA INSURANCE COMPANIES

CNA PLAZA - 41 SOUTH
CHICAGO, ILLINOIS 60685

OVERVIEW: Provides life, property, and casualty insurance. Established: 1897.

KEY STATISTICS Annual Sales: $40.0 billion. Number of Employees: 14,000.

EXPERTISE/EDUCATION SOUGHT: Systems analysis, finance, computer science, accounting, business, mathematics, statistics, auditing

CONTACTS: For college students and recent graduates: Mr John McGinley, Director of Employment; Phone (312) 822-5000. For individuals with previous experience: Ms Pamela DeLagarza, Recruiter; Phone (312) 822-5000.

CORPORATE PROFILE

CNA...FOCUSED ON THE FUTURE. *The CNA Insurance Companies are a dynamic, diverse, and energized organization committed to success.*

CNA is one of the nation's leading insurance organizations. The nature of its product portfolio allows CNA to serve the insurance needs of virtually every buyer: individuals, families, and businesses of any size.

Typical Entry-Level Opportunities in CNA's Chicago Home Office include the following:

Actuary. *Degrees: Math, Actuarial Science, or Statistics majors with successful completion of at least one actuarial exam or 30 credits.*

Rotational Accountant. *Degrees: Accounting majors.*

Systems Professional Associate. *Degrees: Computer Science or Business majors with strong concentrations in Computer Science or Information Systems.*

Summer Internships are also available.

Rewards. *Initiative and independent thinking are rewarded with performance-based compensation and comprehensive benefits including Life/Health/Dental insurance and an exceptional employee savings plan. CNA's work environment is designed to challenge employees' abilities and recognize their accomplishments. Applicants should send résumés to CNA's Home Office: The CNA Insurance Companies, Attn: Manager of College Relations, P.O. Box V V, Dept. PG, Chicago, IL 60685.*

The CNA Insurance Companies are an affirmative action employer M/F/D/V.

COASTAL POWER PRODUCTION COMPANY

9 GREENWAY PLAZA
HOUSTON, TEXAS 77046

OVERVIEW: Provides energy cogeneration services. Established: 1955.

KEY STATISTICS Annual Sales: $10.0 billion. Number of Employees: 14,400.

EXPERTISE/EDUCATION SOUGHT: Chemical engineering, data processing, computer programming

CONTACT: For individuals with previous experience: Mr Lloyd Healy, Director Employment.

THE COCA-COLA COMPANY

1 COCA COLA PLAZA NORTHWEST
ATLANTA, GEORGIA 30313-2499

OVERVIEW: Produces soft drinks and citrus products. Established: 1886.

KEY STATISTICS Annual Sales: $14.0 billion. Number of Employees: 34,000.

HIRING HISTORY Number of professional employees hired in 1993: 300.

EXPERTISE/EDUCATION SOUGHT: Marketing, business management, sales, finance, accounting, operations

CONTACTS: For college students and recent graduates: Ms Monica Simpson, Senior Staffing Specialist, PO Box 1734, Atlanta, GA, 30301; Phone (404) 676-2121. For individuals with previous experience: Mr Steve Bucherati, Manager of Staffing Operations; Phone (404) 676-5133.

COLGATE-PALMOLIVE COMPANY

300 PARK AVENUE
NEW YORK, NEW YORK 10022

OVERVIEW: Manufactures personal care and household products. Established: 1806.

EXPERTISE/EDUCATION SOUGHT: Sales, treasury management, marketing, finance, accounting, public relations

CONTACT: For individuals with previous experience: Mr Brian Smith, Corporate Staffing Manager.

COLLINS AND AIKMAN PRODUCT COMPANY
701 MCCULLOUGH DRIVE, PO BOX 32665
CHARLOTTE, NORTH CAROLINA 28232

OVERVIEW: Manufactures textiles. Established: 1843.

KEY STATISTICS Annual Sales: $2.0 billion.

HIRING HISTORY Number of professional employees hired in 1994: 100.

EXPERTISE/EDUCATION SOUGHT: Manufacturing engineering, mechanical engineering, engineering, industrial engineering, chemistry, accounting, finance, textiles

CONTACT: For individuals with previous experience: Mr Roger Eads, Director of Training and Development; Phone (704) 548-2340.

COLOR TILE, INC.
515 HOUSTON STREET
FORTH WORTH, TEXAS 76102

OVERVIEW: Operates chain of retail tile and floor covering stores. Established: 1978.

EXPERTISE/EDUCATION SOUGHT: Accounting, computer programming

CONTACT: For individuals with previous experience: Ms Marjorie Cassity, Supervisor of Employment; Phone (817) 870-9400.

COLUMBIA GAS SYSTEM, INC.
20 MONTCHANIN ROAD
WILMINGTON, DELAWARE 19807-3094

OVERVIEW: Gas utility. Established: 1926.

KEY STATISTICS Number of Employees: 10,000.

HIRING HISTORY Number of professional employees hired in 1993: 75.

EXPERTISE/EDUCATION SOUGHT: Accounting, finance

CONTACT: Mrs Lois Hubbs, Personnel Administrator; Phone (302) 429-5273.

COLUMBIA/HCA
1 PARK PLAZA
NASHVILLE, TENNESSEE 37203

OVERVIEW: Manages and owns hospitals. Established: 1985.

EXPERTISE/EDUCATION SOUGHT: Information systems, purchasing, hospital administration, finance, accounting

CONTACTS: For college students and recent graduates: Human Resources Department, Attn: Staffing Assistant, PO Box 550, Nashville, TN, 37203; Phone (615) 383-4444. For individuals with previous experience: Mr John Steele, Assistant Vice President of Human Resources; Phone (800) 251-2561.

COLUMBIA/HCA
201 WEST MAIN STREET
LOUISVILLE, KENTUCKY 40202

OVERVIEW: Provides healthcare services.

KEY STATISTICS Annual Sales: $202.0 million. Number of Employees: 4,300.

EXPERTISE/EDUCATION SOUGHT: Hospital administration, human resources, management, business, finance

CONTACTS: For college students and recent graduates: Mr Terry Brock, Director of Staffing; Phone (502) 572-2000. For individuals with previous experience: Mr Michawl Moore, Manager of Human Resources; Phone (502) 572-2204.

COLUMBIA/HCA
13455 NOEL ROAD, SUITE 2000
DALLAS, TEXAS 75240

OVERVIEW: Owns and operates specialty outpatient care facilities.

EXPERTISE/EDUCATION SOUGHT: Licensed practical nursing, nursing

CONTACT: For individuals with previous experience: Benefits Department; Phone (214) 701-2200.

COMBINED INSURANCE COMPANY OF AMERICA
123 NORTH WACKER DRIVE
CHICAGO, ILLINOIS 60640-1700

OVERVIEW: Provides life, home, and automobile insurance. Established: 1980. Parent Company: AION Company.

KEY STATISTICS Number of Employees: 10,000.

HIRING HISTORY Number of professional employees hired in 1994: 40.

EXPERTISE/EDUCATION SOUGHT: Customer service and support, claims adjustment/examination, computer programming, accounting, sales, program analysis, administration, technical writing

CONTACT: For individuals with previous experience: Mr Robert Dinocola, Staffing Manager.

COMCAST CORPORATION
1234 MARKET STREET
PHILADELPHIA, PENNSYLVANIA 19107-2146

OVERVIEW: Provides cable television services. Established: 1961.

KEY STATISTICS Annual Sales: $1.0 billion. Number of Employees: 5,391.

EXPERTISE/EDUCATION SOUGHT: Electrical engineering, design engineering, mechanical engineering, telecommunications, accounting, finance, construction engineering, sales, marketing

CONTACTS: For college students and recent graduates: Executive Secretary of Human Resources, 1234 Market Street 16th Floor, Philadelphia, PA, 19107; Phone (215) 665-1700. For individuals with previous experience: Mr Al Peddrick, Director of Human Resources.

COMDISCO, INC.
6111 NORTH RIVER ROAD
ROSEMONT, ILLINOIS 60018-5159

OVERVIEW: Provides computer leasing and disaster recovery services. Established: 1969.

KEY STATISTICS Annual Sales: $2.0 billion. Number of Employees: 2,000.

EXPERTISE/EDUCATION SOUGHT: Computer science, software engineering/development, telecommunications

CONTACT: Ms Pamela Heinz, Senior Manager of Human Resources; Phone (708) 698-3000.

COMERICA BANK
500 WOODWARD AVENUE
DETROIT, MICHIGAN 48226-3407

OVERVIEW: Provides financial services. Established: 1849. Parent Company: Comerica, Inc.

KEY STATISTICS Assets: $2.0 billion. Number of Employees: 12,670.

HIRING HISTORY Number of professional employees hired in 1993: 144.

EXPERTISE/EDUCATION SOUGHT: Accounting, finance, business, computer science, banking, data processing, credit/credit analysis

CONTACTS: For college students and recent graduates: Ms Jill Niebieszczanski, Human Resources Representative, PO Box 75000, Department JS, Detroit, MI, 48275-3121; Phone (313) 222-5607. For individuals with previous experience: Mr Richard Collister, Vice President of Human Resources, 100 Renaissance Center, Suite 3900, Detroit, MI, 48243; Phone (313) 222-6030.

COMMERCE BANCSHARES
720 MAIN STREET
KANSAS CITY, MISSOURI 64105

OVERVIEW: Commercial bank. Established: 1880.

KEY STATISTICS Assets: $6.0 billion. Number of Employees: 1,800.

EXPERTISE/EDUCATION SOUGHT: Computer programming, network analysis, finance, accounting

CONTACT: For individuals with previous experience: Ms Debra Sprayberry, Manager of Human Resources; Phone (816) 234-2000, ext. 2047.

COMMERCIAL UNION CORPORATION
1 BEACON STREET
BOSTON, MASSACHUSETTS 02108-3106

OVERVIEW: Provides Insurance.

KEY STATISTICS Annual Sales: $2.0 billion. Number of Employees: 6,600.

HIRING HISTORY Number of professional employees hired in 1993: 70.

EXPERTISE/EDUCATION SOUGHT: Accounting, actuarial, business administration, information services, general insurance

CONTACT: For individuals with previous experience: Human Resources Department; Phone (617) 725-6000.

COMMONWEALTH EDISON COMPANY
1 FIRST NATIONAL PLAZA, PO BOX 767
CHICAGO, ILLINOIS 60690

OVERVIEW: Electric utility. Established: 1887.

KEY STATISTICS Annual Sales: $5.0 billion. Number of Employees: 19,000.

EXPERTISE/EDUCATION SOUGHT: Electrical engineering, mechanical engineering, accounting, finance, data processing, nuclear engineering, chemical engineering

CONTACT: For individuals with previous experience: Ms Mary Kay McMahon, Supervisor of Professional Placement, PO Box 767, Chicago, IL, 60690; Phone (312) 394-4321.

COMMONWEALTH LIFE INSURANCE COMPANY
680 SOUTH 4TH AVENUE
LOUISVILLE, KENTUCKY 40202

OVERVIEW: Provides life insurance. Established: 1969. Parent Company: Capital Holding Corporation.

KEY STATISTICS Annual Sales: $1.0 billion. Number of Employees: 2,147.

EXPERTISE/EDUCATION SOUGHT: Business, case management, sales, statistics, actuarial, health insurance

CONTACT: For individuals with previous experience: Ms Marilyn Reis, Vice President of Human Resources; Phone (502) 587-7371.

COMMUNICATIONS DATA SERVICES
1901 BELL AVENUE
DES MOINES, IOWA 50315-1099

OVERVIEW: Provides information retrieval, data processing and magazine/newspaper subscription fulfillment services.

KEY STATISTICS Annual Sales: $86.0 million. Number of Employees: 2,750.

EXPERTISE/EDUCATION SOUGHT: Computer programming, auditing

CONTACT: For individuals with previous experience: Ms Jan Thomas, Recruitment Specialist; Phone (515) 280-4130.

COMMUNITY MUTUAL INSURANCE COMPANY
221 EAST 4TH STREET, SUITE 2600
CINCINNATI, OHIO 45202-4151

OVERVIEW: Provides health insurance.

KEY STATISTICS Annual Sales: $2.0 billion. Number of Employees: 3,100.

EXPERTISE/EDUCATION SOUGHT: Accounting, computer programming, sales, customer service and support

CONTACT: Human Resources Department; Phone (513) 872-8481.

COMMUNITY PSYCHIATRIC CENTERS
6600 WEST CHARLESTON, SUITE 118
LAS VEGAS, NEVADA 89102

OVERVIEW: Corporate office for different health facilities.

EXPERTISE/EDUCATION SOUGHT: Administration

CONTACT: Ms Sarah Spinharney, Assistant Vice President for Human Resources.

COMP USA
14951 NORTH DALLAS PARKWAY
DALLAS, TEXAS 75240-7570

OVERVIEW: Operates chain of computer products stores. Established: 1984.

KEY STATISTICS Annual Sales: $1.0 billion. Number of Employees: 5,086.

EXPERTISE/EDUCATION SOUGHT: Retail, computer science, management, accounting, merchandising

CONTACT: For individuals with previous experience: Ms Lisa Blunt, Recruiting Manager; Phone (214) 383-4606.

COMPAQ COMPUTER CORPORATION
20555 STATE HIGHWAY 249, PO BOX 692000
HOUSTON, TEXAS 77070

OVERVIEW: Manufactures personal computers, portable computers, and servers. Established: 1982.

KEY STATISTICS Number of Employees: 10,500.

EXPERTISE/EDUCATION SOUGHT: Electrical engineering, computer science, sales, marketing

CONTACTS: For college students and recent graduates: Human Resources Department; Phone (713) 374-2370. For individuals with previous experience: Ms Dee Ann Thompson, Manager of Recruitment and Human Resources Development, PO Box 692000, Mail Code 080111, Houston, TX, 77070-2000; Phone (713) 374-4395.

COMPUTER DATA SYSTEMS, INC.
1 CURIE COURT
ROCKVILLE, MARYLAND 20850-4389

OVERVIEW: Provides computer systems integration and consulting services. Established: 1968.

KEY STATISTICS Annual Sales: $181.0 million. Number of Employees: 3,400.

HIRING HISTORY Number of professional employees hired in 1993: 500.

EXPERTISE/EDUCATION SOUGHT: Computer programming, sales, marketing, accounting, finance, software engineering/development

CONTACTS: For college students and recent graduates: Ms Betty Kennedy, Director of Employment; Phone (301) 921-7000. For individuals with previous experience: Ms Susan Morales, Director Employment.

COMPUTERVISION CORPORATION
100 CROSBY DRIVE
BEDFORD, MASSACHUSETTS 01730-1480

OVERVIEW: Develops and sells computer aided design and computer aided manufacturing software. Established: 1972.

KEY STATISTICS Annual Sales: $827.0 million. Number of Employees: 3,800.

EXPERTISE/EDUCATION SOUGHT: Sales, product design and development, accounting, marketing, finance, software engineering/development, electrical engineering, mechanical engineering

CONTACT: Ms Sandy Arthur, Senior Human Resources Representative; Phone (617) 275-1800, ext. 2431.

CONAGRA GROCERY PRODUCTS COMPANIES
1645 WEST VALENCIA DRIVE
FULLERTON, CALIFORNIA 92633

OVERVIEW: Distributes brand name grocery products. Parent Company: ConAgra, Inc.

EXPERTISE/EDUCATION SOUGHT: Accounting, finance, auditing, line operations

CONTACT: For individuals with previous experience: Ms Enid Smith, Manager of Employment, 1645 West Valencia Drive, Fullerton, CA, 92633; Phone (714) 680-1000.

CONAGRA POULTRY COMPANY
422 NORTH WASHINGTON AVENUE
EL DORADO, ARKANSAS 71730-5616

OVERVIEW: Produces and processes poultry products. Established: 1965. Parent Company: ConAgra, Inc.

KEY STATISTICS Annual Sales: $1.0 billion. Number of Employees: 13,000.

EXPERTISE/EDUCATION SOUGHT: Marketing, finance, data processing, sales, accounting, computer programming

CONTACT: Mr Lester Clements, Vice President of Human Resources; Phone (501) 863-1600.

CONAGRA REFRIGERATED FOODS COMPANIES
2001 BUTTERFIELD ROAD
DOWNERS GROVE, ILLINOIS 60515

OVERVIEW: Distrubutes brand name frozen meats and grocery products. Parent Company: ConAgra, Inc.

EXPERTISE/EDUCATION SOUGHT: Accounting, finance, auditing, line operations

CONTACT: For individuals with previous experience: Mr Rick Ellspermann, Vice President Human Resources, 2001 Butterfield Rd., Downers Grove, IL, 60515; Phone (708) 512-1000.

CONAIR CORPORATION
1 CUMMINGS POINT ROAD
STAMFORD, CONNECTICUT 06904

OVERVIEW: Manufactures personal care products and small appliances. Established: 1959.

EXPERTISE/EDUCATION SOUGHT: Sales, marketing, accounting, management information systems

CONTACT: For individuals with previous experience: Human Resources.

CONDE-NAST
350 MADISON AVENUE
NEW YORK, NEW YORK 10017-3704

OVERVIEW: Publishes magazines. Established: 1922. Parent Company: Advance Publications, Inc.

KEY STATISTICS Annual Sales: $226.0 million. Number of Employees: 2,000.

EXPERTISE/EDUCATION SOUGHT: Journalism, communications

CONTACT: Ms Mary Macnab, Director of Personnel; Phone (212) 880-6885.

CONE MILLS CORPORATION
1201 MAPLE STREET
GREENSBORO, NORTH CAROLINA 27405-6910

OVERVIEW: Manufactures fabrics; operates textile mills.

KEY STATISTICS Number of Employees: 7,800.

EXPERTISE/EDUCATION SOUGHT: Textiles, accounting, chemistry, management

CONTACT: Mr Dan Minnis, Recruitment Manager.

CONNECTICUT MUTUAL LIFE INSURANCE COMPANY
140 GARDEN STREET
HARTFORD, CONNECTICUT 06154-0001

OVERVIEW: Provides life and disability insurance. Established: 1843.

KEY STATISTICS Number of Employees: 5,400.

EXPERTISE/EDUCATION SOUGHT: Actuarial

CONTACTS: For college students and recent graduates: Ms Martha Spada, Manager of Support Services; Phone (203) 987-2679. For individuals with previous experience: Ms Jo Ann Cephas, Assistant Vice President of Human Resources; Phone (203) 987-6500.

CONNER PERIPHERALS, INC.
3081 ZANKER ROAD
SAN JOSE, CALIFORNIA 95134-2128

OVERVIEW: Manufactures disk drives, computers, and computer components. Established: 1985.

KEY STATISTICS Annual Sales: $2.0 billion. Number of Employees: 9,100.

EXPERTISE/EDUCATION SOUGHT: Hardware engineering, mechanical engineering, accounting, finance, law, data processing

CONTACT: For individuals with previous experience: Ms Dianne Schlageter, Employment Manager; Phone (408) 456-4500.

CONSOLIDATED BISCUIT COMPANY
312 RADER ROAD
MCCOMB, OHIO 45858

OVERVIEW: Manufactures cookies and crackers.

KEY STATISTICS Annual Sales: $100.0 million. Number of Employees: 2,500.

EXPERTISE/EDUCATION SOUGHT: Production management, quality control, sales, marketing

CONTACT: For individuals with previous experience: Mr Rod Houchins, Vice President Human Resources; Phone (419) 293-2911.

CONSOLIDATED EDISON COMPANY OF NEW YORK
4 IRVING PLACE
NEW YORK, NEW YORK 10003-3598

OVERVIEW: Electric and gas utility. Established: 1884.

KEY STATISTICS Number of Employees: 17,586.

HIRING HISTORY Number of professional employees hired in 1994: 17. 1993: 24.

EXPERTISE/EDUCATION SOUGHT: Data processing

CONTACT: For individuals with previous experience: Mr Kevin Morgan, Manager of Professional Recruiting; Phone (212) 460-4600, ext. 2014.

CONSOLIDATED FREIGHTWAYS, INC.
3240 HILLVIEW AVENUE
PALO ALTO, CALIFORNIA 94304-1201

OVERVIEW: Provides truck and air freight services. Established: 1929.

KEY STATISTICS Number of Employees: 37,900.

EXPERTISE/EDUCATION SOUGHT: Accounting, management information systems, human resources, payroll, finance

CONTACT: For individuals with previous experience: Department of Human Resources; Phone (503) 499-2110.

CONSOLIDATED PAPERS, INC.
231 1ST AVENUE NORTH
WISCONSIN RAPID, WISCONSIN 54495-2774

OVERVIEW: Manufactures paper and cardboard. Established: 1894.

KEY STATISTICS Number of Employees: 4,946.

HIRING HISTORY Number of professional employees hired in 1993: 25.

EXPERTISE/EDUCATION SOUGHT: Accounting, marketing, finance, management information systems, sales

CONTACT: Ms Mary Polivka, Manager of Professional Employment; Phone (715) 422-3111, ext. 3283.

CONSUMERS POWER COMPANY
212 WEST MICHIGAN AVENUE
JACKSON, MICHIGAN 49201-2236

OVERVIEW: Electric and gas utility. Established: 1987. Parent Company: CMS Energy Corporation.

KEY STATISTICS Number of Employees: 9,700.

EXPERTISE/EDUCATION SOUGHT: Mechanical engineering, electrical engineering

CONTACT: For individuals with previous experience: Professional Placement Department; Phone (517) 788-0550.

CONTINENTAL CABLEVISION, INC.
THE PILOT HOUSE, LEWIS WHARF
BOSTON, MASSACHUSETTS 02110

OVERVIEW: Provides cable television services. Established: 1963.

KEY STATISTICS Annual Sales: $1.0 billion. Number of Employees: 7,000.

EXPERTISE/EDUCATION SOUGHT: Finance, communications, law, accounting, sales, marketing

CONTACT: For individuals with previous experience: Mr Andrew Dixon, Senior Vice President of Human Resources; Phone (617) 742-9500, ext. 3127.

CONTINENTAL CAN COMPANY, INC.
1 AERIAL WAY
SYOSSET, NEW YORK 11791-5501

OVERVIEW: Manufactures plastic film, plastic bottles, and food cans. Established: 1970.

KEY STATISTICS Annual Sales: $482.0 million. Number of Employees: 3,250.

EXPERTISE/EDUCATION SOUGHT: Accounting, finance, marketing, sales, management information systems

CONTACT: For individuals with previous experience: Mr Abdo Yazgi, Director of Human Resources; Phone (516) 822-4940.

CONTINENTAL CASUALTY COMPANY
333 SOUTH WOBUSH CNA PLAZA
CHICAGO, ILLINOIS 60685

OVERVIEW: Provides property and casualty insurance.

EXPERTISE/EDUCATION SOUGHT: Actuarial, mathematics, computer science, accounting, finance

CONTACTS: For college students and recent graduates: Ms. Victoria Thompson, Manager College Relations; Phone (312) 822-6934. For individuals with previous experience: Mr John McGinley, Director; Phone (312) 822-7801.

CONTINENTAL CIRCUITS CORPORATION
4830 SOUTH 36TH STREET
PHOENIX, ARIZONA 85040-3869

OVERVIEW: Manufactures multi-layer surface mounted PC boards. Established: 1972.

KEY STATISTICS Annual Sales: $77.0 million. Number of Employees: 860.

HIRING HISTORY Number of professional employees hired in 1993: 10.

EXPERTISE/EDUCATION SOUGHT: Management

CONTACT: Human Resources Department; Phone (602) 268-3461.

CONTINENTAL GENERAL TIRE, INC.
1 GENERAL STREET
AKRON, OHIO 44329-0002

OVERVIEW: Manufactures tires. Established: 1915.

KEY STATISTICS Annual Sales: $1.0 billion. Number of Employees: 7,600.

EXPERTISE/EDUCATION SOUGHT: Accounting, finance, data processing, sales, marketing

CONTACT: Mr Dave Mallory, Director of Human Resources Staffing and Development; Phone (216) 798-3000.

CONTINENTAL MEDICAL SYSTEMS
600 WILSON LANE
MECHANICSBURG, PENNSYLVANIA 17055-4440

OVERVIEW: Owns and operates rehabilitation hospitals.

KEY STATISTICS Annual Sales: $901.0 million. Number of Employees: 14,243.

EXPERTISE/EDUCATION SOUGHT: Accounting, health care, licensed practical nursing, computer programming, nursing, finance, design engineering, civil engineering, data processing

CONTACT: For individuals with previous experience: Ms Lorraine Snyder, Manager of Recruitment; Phone (717) 790-8300.

CONTRAN CORPORATION
5430 LBJ FREEWAY
DALLAS, TEXAS 75240

OVERVIEW: Manufactures sugar products.

EXPERTISE/EDUCATION SOUGHT: Accounting, business, finance

CONTACT: For individuals with previous experience: Ms Kathy Brownlee, Personnel Manager.

CON-WAY TRANSPORTATION SERVICES
2882 SANDHILL ROAD, SUITE 210
MENLO PARK, CALIFORNIA 94025-7056

OVERVIEW: Provides truck and transport services. Established: 1983. Parent Company: Consolidated Freightways, Inc.

KEY STATISTICS Annual Sales: $464.0 million. Number of Employees: 6,500.

HIRING HISTORY Number of professional employees hired in 1993: 400.

EXPERTISE/EDUCATION SOUGHT: Logistics, sales, distribution, transportation

CONTACT: Mr Robert Coon, Corporate Director of Human Resources; Phone (415) 854-7500.

COOKSON AMERICA, INC.
1 COOKSON PLACE
PROVIDENCE, RHODE ISLAND 02903

OVERVIEW: Metal refining and mineral products company. Established: 1979.

KEY STATISTICS Annual Sales: $1.0 billion. Number of Employees: 7,200.

EXPERTISE/EDUCATION SOUGHT: Accounting, computer programming, systems analysis, business administration, marketing, communications, law, environmental

CONTACT: For individuals with previous experience: Mr Robert Andreoni, Director of Administration; Phone (401) 521-1000.

COOPER AUTOMOTIVE
901 ROOSEVELT PARKWAY
CHESTERFIELD, MISSOURI 63017

OVERVIEW: Manufactures spark plugs. Parent Company: Cooper Industries.

EXPERTISE/EDUCATION SOUGHT: Finance, management information systems, production

CONTACT: For individuals with previous experience: Ms Trisha Drews, Director of Employment; Phone (314) 535-8160.

COOPER INDUSTRIES, INC.
1001 FANNIN STREET, SUITE 4000
HOUSTON, TEXAS 77002

OVERVIEW: Manufactures power systems, tools, hardware, and petroleum, industrial, electrical, and automotive products;.

EXPERTISE/EDUCATION SOUGHT: Human resources, management, recreation therapy, manufacturing

CONTACT: For individuals with previous experience: Ms Diane Easley, Recruitment Supervisor; Phone (713) 739-5400.

COOPER POWER SYSTEMS, INC.
2300 BADGER DRIVE
WAKEESHA, WISCONSIN 53188

OVERVIEW: Manufactures electrical equipment. Parent Company: Cooper Pacific Corporation.

KEY STATISTICS Number of Employees: 5,200.

EXPERTISE/EDUCATION SOUGHT: Marketing, sales, accounting, management information systems, computer programming, mechanical engineering, technical engineering, human resources

CONTACT: For individuals with previous experience: Ms Ruth Prince, Manager of Benefits and Salary Administration.

COOPERS AND LYBRAND
1251 AVENUE OF THE AMERICAS
NEW YORK, NEW YORK 10019

OVERVIEW: Provides auditing, consulting, and accounting services. Established: 1898.

KEY STATISTICS Annual Sales: $2.0 billion.

HIRING HISTORY Number of professional employees hired in 1994: 3,000. 1993: 3,000.

EXPERTISE/EDUCATION SOUGHT: Accounting, law, auditing, finance, business administration, auditing

CONTACT: For individuals with previous experience: Mr Andrew Safina, Manager of Recruitment.

COORS BREWING COMPANY
217 12TH FORD STREET
GOLDEN, COLORADO 80401-3118

OVERVIEW: Manufactures and distributes beer and other malt beverages. Established: 1873.

KEY STATISTICS Annual Sales: $2.0 billion. Number of Employees: 6,200.

HIRING HISTORY Number of professional employees hired in 1994: 127. 1993: 150.

EXPERTISE/EDUCATION SOUGHT: Accounting, marketing, sales, finance, food services, law, chemical engineering, mechanical engineering, packaging engineering

CONTACTS: For college students and recent graduates: Mr David Nielson, Director of Organizational Development and Personnel Training, Mail Stop BC217, Golden, CO, 80401; Phone (303) 277-7677. For individuals with previous experience: Mr Larry Moore, Manager of Placement.

COPELAND CORPORATION
1675 WEST CAMPBELL ROAD
SIDNEY, OHIO 45365-2493

OVERVIEW: Manufactures compressors. Established: 1921. Parent Company: Emerson Electric Company.

KEY STATISTICS Annual Sales: $1.0 billion. Number of Employees: 3,900.

HIRING HISTORY Number of professional employees hired in 1994: 70. 1993: 45.

EXPERTISE/EDUCATION SOUGHT: Marketing, sales

CONTACT: Ms Mary Cleveland, Corporate Recruiter; Phone (513) 498-3011.

CORAL INDUSTRIES, INC.
3010 RICE MINE ROAD NORTHEAST
TUSCALOOSA, ALABAMA 35406

OVERVIEW: Manufactures shower doors.

CONTACTS: For college students and recent graduates: Mr Duffy Van der Ford, Personnel Director. For individuals with previous experience: Mr Patrick Conner, Executive Vice President.

CORE INDUSTRIES, INC.
500 NORTH WOODWARD AVENUE
BLOOMFIELD HILLS, MICHIGAN 48304-2961

OVERVIEW: Manufactures specialty products for commercial and industrial use. Established: 1909.

KEY STATISTICS Annual Sales: $207.0 million. Number of Employees: 2,650.

EXPERTISE/EDUCATION SOUGHT: Accounting, finance, administration

CONTACT: Mr Tony Krull, Office Manager/Benefits Administration, PO Box 2000, Bloomfield Hills, MI, 48304-2000; Phone (810) 642-3400.

CORESTATES FINANCIAL CORPORATION
1500 MARKET STREET
PHILADELPHIA, PENNSYLVANIA 19101

OVERVIEW: Provides banking, discount brokerage, and related financial services. Established: 1803.

KEY STATISTICS Annual Sales: $2.0 billion. Number of Employees: 13,715.

EXPERTISE/EDUCATION SOUGHT: Accounting, finance, auditing, actuarial, computer programming

CONTACT: For individuals with previous experience: Ms Janice Walls, Assistant Vice President of Human Resources; Phone (215) 973-3100.

CORNING METPATH, INC.
1 MALCOLM AVENUE
TETERBORO, NEW JERSEY 07608

OVERVIEW: Operates medical laboratory. Parent Company: Corning, Inc.

KEY STATISTICS Annual Sales: $1.0 billion. Number of Employees: 15,000.

EXPERTISE/EDUCATION SOUGHT: Computer programming, laboratory chemistry, customer service and support, law, facilities management

CONTACT: For individuals with previous experience: Ms Maria Ciocco, Human Resources Manager; Phone (201) 393-5000.

CORNING, INC.
1 RIVERFRONT PLAZA
CORNING, NEW YORK 14831

OVERVIEW: Manufactures optical fiber and specialty materials; provides medical testing services. Established: 1851.

EXPERTISE/EDUCATION SOUGHT: Computer science, sales, finance, marketing, human resources, planning

CONTACTS: For college students and recent graduates: Mrs Andrea Miles, Staffing Director, Houghton Park C, Building 2-1, Corning, NY, 14831; Phone (607) 974-4678. For individuals with previous experience: Mr Richard Marks, Senior Vice President of Human Resources, Houghton Park C, Building 2-1, Corning, NY, 14831; Phone (607) 974-9000.

COSMAIR, INC.
575 5TH AVENUE, 34TH FLOOR
NEW YORK, NEW YORK 10017-1320

OVERVIEW: Manufactures and sells toiletries. Established: 1974.

KEY STATISTICS Annual Sales: $9.0 billion. Number of Employees: 3,500.

EXPERTISE/EDUCATION SOUGHT: Languages, human resources, marketing, sales, finance, computer programming, program analysis, accounting, law, chemistry

CONTACTS: For college students and recent graduates: Mr Michael Peece, Director of Human Resources; Phone (212) 818-1500. For individuals with previous experience: Mr Lou Gsabay, Assistant Vice President Human Resources, 575 5th Avenue 34th Floor, New York, NY, 10012.

COTTER AND COMPANY

2740 NORTH CLYBOURN AVENUE
CHICAGO, ILLINOIS 60614-1088

OVERVIEW: Distributes hardware products. Established: 1948.

KEY STATISTICS Annual Sales: $12.0 billion. Number of Employees: 4,300.

HIRING HISTORY Number of professional employees hired in 1994: 30. 1993: 30.

EXPERTISE/EDUCATION SOUGHT: Computer programming, accounting, sales, finance, marketing

CONTACT: Mr Pat Kelley, Manager of Human Resources; Phone (312) 975-2700.

COUNTRY INNS AND SUITES BY CARLSON

CARLSON PARKWAY-701 TOWER
MINNEAPOLIS, MINNESOTA 55459

OVERVIEW: Owns and operates hotels and resorts. Established: 1972. Parent Company: Carlson Companies, Inc.

KEY STATISTICS Annual Sales: $2.0 billion. Number of Employees: 6,000.

HIRING HISTORY Number of professional employees hired in 1993: 5.

EXPERTISE/EDUCATION SOUGHT: Marketing, finance, accounting, hospitality/hotel and restaurant management, business management, management information systems

CONTACT: Ms Suzanne Kincaid, Manager of Human Resources; Phone (612) 449-1900.

COUNTRYWIDE CREDIT INDUSTRIES

155 NORTH LAKE AVENUE
PASADENA, CALIFORNIA 91101-1857

OVERVIEW: Mortgage bank.

KEY STATISTICS Annual Sales: $756.0 million. Number of Employees: 3,000.

HIRING HISTORY Number of professional employees hired in 1994: 100.

EXPERTISE/EDUCATION SOUGHT: Underwriting, fund raising, finance

CONTACT: Ms Karen Simmons, Recruiter.

COUNTY SEAT STORES, INC.

17950 PRESTON ROAD, SUITE 1000
DALLAS, TEXAS 75252-5638

OVERVIEW: Operates chain of apparel stores. Established: 1973.

KEY STATISTICS Annual Sales: $503.0 million. Number of Employees: 5,700.

EXPERTISE/EDUCATION SOUGHT: Merchandising, distribution, financial analysis, real estate, marketing, retail management, leasing

CONTACT: For individuals with previous experience: Mr Tom Grissom, Corporate Human Resources Manager.

COURTAULDS COATINGS

400 SOUTH 13TH STREET
LOUISVILLE, FLORIDA 40203

OVERVIEW: Manufactures fibers, coatings, and packaging materials. Established: 1980.

KEY STATISTICS Annual Sales: $900.0 million. Number of Employees: 5,000.

EXPERTISE/EDUCATION SOUGHT: Sales, chemistry, accounting

CONTACT: For individuals with previous experience: Mr Ed Wilsmann, Personnel Manager; Phone (502) 588-9200.

COX ENTERPRISES, INC.

1400 LAKE HEARN DRIVE NORTHEAST
ATLANTA, GEORGIA 30319-1464

OVERVIEW: Publishes newspapers and magazines and operates radio and television stations. Established: 1968.

KEY STATISTICS Annual Sales: $2.0 billion. Number of Employees: 35,000.

EXPERTISE/EDUCATION SOUGHT: Communications, administration, sales, operations, marketing, electrical engineering, finance, mechanical engineering, accounting, telecommunications

CONTACTS: For college students and recent graduates: Ms Belinda Turner, Director of Training and Development; Phone (404) 843-5000. For individuals with previous experience: Ms Carol VerSteeg, Director Employee Relations.

CPC INTERNATIONAL, INC.

INTERNATIONAL PLAZA, 700 SYLVAN AVENUE
ENGLEWOOD CLIFFS, NEW JERSEY 07632

OVERVIEW: Produces processed foods. Established: 1906.

KEY STATISTICS Annual Sales: $7.0 billion. Number of Employees: 39,000.

EXPERTISE/EDUCATION SOUGHT: Accounting, auditing, marketing, finance, sales, management information systems

CONTACT: Mr Burt Belasco, Manager of Human Resources; Phone (201) 894-4000.

CRAWFORD AND COMPANY

5620 GLENRIDGE DRIVE NORTHEAST
ATLANTA, GEORGIA 30342-1399

OVERVIEW: Provides insurance and financial services.

KEY STATISTICS Annual Sales: $576.0 million. Number of Employees: 7,139.

EXPERTISE/EDUCATION SOUGHT: Finance, information systems, human resources

CONTACT: For individuals with previous experience: Ms Gloria Cunningham-Sneed, Assistant Vice President Director of Personnel Management, PO Box 5047, Atlanta, GA, 30302.

CRAY RESEARCH, INC.

655-A LONE OAK DRIVE
EAGAN, MINNESOTA 55121-1560

OVERVIEW: Manufactures supercomputers. Established: 1972.

KEY STATISTICS Annual Sales: $895.0 million. Number of Employees: 4,960.

EXPERTISE/EDUCATION SOUGHT: Electrical engineering, design engineering, computer engineering, computer science, mechanical engineering

CONTACT: For individuals with previous experience: Ms Judy Hoehn, Manager of Corporate Staffing, 1620 Olson Drive, Chippewa Falls, WI, 54729; Phone (715) 726-4369.

CREATIVE HAIR DRESSERS, INC.

2815 HARTLAND ROAD
FALLS CHURCH, VIRGINIA 22043-3536

OVERVIEW: Operates chain of beauty salons.

KEY STATISTICS Annual Sales: $100.0 million. Number of Employees: 6,000.

EXPERTISE/EDUCATION SOUGHT: Marketing, accounting, law, customer service and support

CONTACT: Human Resources Department; Phone (703) 698-7090.

CRESTAR FINANCIAL CORPORATION

919 EAST MAIN STREET
RICHMOND, VIRGINIA 23219

OVERVIEW: Provides commercial banking, mortgage, and investment services. Established: 1963.

EXPERTISE/EDUCATION SOUGHT: Finance, accounting, auditing, underwriting, investment

CONTACT: For individuals with previous experience: Ms Dawn Morris, Human Resources Department; Phone (804) 782-5000.

CROWLEY CARIBBEAN TRANSPORT

9487 REGENCY SQUARE
JACKSONVILLE, FLORIDA 32225-8198

OVERVIEW: Provides deep sea transportation services. Established: 1954. Parent Company: Crowley Maritime Corporation.

KEY STATISTICS Annual Sales: $775.0 million. Number of Employees: 2,568.

EXPERTISE/EDUCATION SOUGHT: Management information systems, accounting

CONTACT: For individuals with previous experience: Mr Lester Williams, Marine Personnel, 2801 Northwest 74th Avenue, Miami, FL, 33122-1423; Phone (305) 470-4000.

CROWLEY MARITIME CORPORATION

155 GRAND AVENUE
OAKLAND, CALIFORNIA 94612-3758

OVERVIEW: Provides marine shipping services. Established: 1892.

KEY STATISTICS Annual Sales: $1.0 billion. Number of Employees: 4,500.

EXPERTISE/EDUCATION SOUGHT: Management, management information systems, systems analysis, computer programming, personal computers

CONTACTS: For college students and recent graduates: Ms Donna Demott, Human Resources Representative; Phone (510) 251-7500. For individuals with previous experience: Ms Amy Sides, Human Resources Representative; Phone (510) 251-7690.

CRUM AND FORSTER INSURANCE

6 SYLVAN WAY
PARSIPPANY, NEW JERSEY 07054

OVERVIEW: Provides commercial insurance.

EXPERTISE/EDUCATION SOUGHT: Underwriting, accounting

CONTACT: Ms Patricia Vanesek, Senior Recruiter; Phone (201) 285-9300.

CS FIRST BOSTON GROUP, INC.

PARK AVENUE PLAZA
NEW YORK, NEW YORK 10055-0001

OVERVIEW: Provides investment banking services.

EXPERTISE/EDUCATION SOUGHT: Finance, management information systems, marketing, actuarial, real estate

CONTACTS: For college students and recent graduates: Ms Gabriele Greene, Vice President of Campus Recruitment. For individuals with previous experience: Ms Kerry Buckley, Human Resources; Phone (212) 322-7833.

CSC NETWORK/PRENTICE-HALL LEGAL AND FINANCIAL SERVICES

15 COLUMBUS CIRCLE
NEW YORK, NEW YORK 10023

OVERVIEW: Provides information retrieval services.

EXPERTISE/EDUCATION SOUGHT: Program analysis, computer programming, information services, software engineering/development

CONTACT: For individuals with previous experience: Ms Bobbi Gill, Senior Human Resources Generalist, 375 Hudson Street 11th Floor, New York, NY, 10014; Phone (212) 373-7500, ext. 4873.

CSX TRANSPORTATION

550 WATER STREET
JACKSONVILLE, FLORIDA 32202-5177

OVERVIEW: Provides railroad freight services. Established: 1987. Parent Company: CSX Corporation.

KEY STATISTICS Annual Sales: $258.0 million. Number of Employees: 780.

EXPERTISE/EDUCATION SOUGHT: Management information systems, transportation, administration, data processing

CONTACT: Ms Barbara Carter, Manager of Employee Relations; Phone (904) 359-3100, ext. 1078.

CUC INTERNATIONAL, INC.

707 SUMMER STREET
STAMFORD, CONNECTICUT 06901-1000

OVERVIEW: Provides membership based consumer services. Established: 1973.

KEY STATISTICS Annual Sales: $879.0 million. Number of Employees: 6,500.

EXPERTISE/EDUCATION SOUGHT: Accounting, finance, marketing, sales

CONTACT: Ms Claudia Vilas, Manager of Human Resources; Phone (203) 324-9261, ext. 8846.

CUMMINS ENGINE COMPANY

500 JACKSON STREET
COLUMBUS, INDIANA 47201-6258

OVERVIEW: Manufactures diesel engines for buses, trucks, and pickups. Established: 1919.

KEY STATISTICS Number of Employees: 23,600.

HIRING HISTORY Number of professional employees hired in 1993: 275.

EXPERTISE/EDUCATION SOUGHT: Electrical engineering, accounting, mechanical engineering, research and development, finance

CONTACT: Mr Doug Thomas, Manager of Corporate Human Resources; Phone (812) 377-5701.

CUNA MUTUAL INSURANCE SOCIETY

5910 MINERAL POINT ROAD
MADISON, WISCONSIN 53705

OVERVIEW: Provides life, health, property, and casualty insurance. Established: 1935.

EXPERTISE/EDUCATION SOUGHT: Law, accounting, computer programming, computer science

CONTACT: Mr Cal Lanzel, Human Resources Specialist; Phone (608) 238-5851.

CURTICE BURNS PRUFAC

90 LINDEN OAKS PLACE
ROCHESTER, NEW YORK 14610-3542

OVERVIEW: Distributes canned fruits and vegetables, sauces, and snack foods. Established: 1902.

KEY STATISTICS Annual Sales: $86.0 million. Number of Employees: 5,325.

EXPERTISE/EDUCATION SOUGHT: Finance, marketing, business management, accounting, manufacturing engineering, electrical engineering

CONTACT: Ms Lois Warlick-Jarvie, Vice President of Human Resources, PO Box 681, Rochester, NY, 14603; Phone (716) 383-1850.

CYPRUS AMAX MINERALS COMPANY

9100 EAST MINERAL CIRCLE
ENGLEWOOD, COLORADO 80112

OVERVIEW: Produces coal, oil, gas, aluminum and other metals.

KEY STATISTICS Annual Sales: $2.0 billion. Number of Employees: 10,750.

EXPERTISE/EDUCATION SOUGHT: Accounting, finance, data processing, computer programming, marketing

CONTACT: Mr Thomas LeBlanc, Manager of Corporate Human Resources; Phone (303) 643-5000.

COMMERCIAL CREDIT COMPANY

300 SAINT PAUL PLACE
BALTIMORE, MARYLAND 21202-2120

OVERVIEW: Provides financial services. Established: 1990.

KEY STATISTICS Number of Employees: 4,135.

EXPERTISE/EDUCATION SOUGHT: Sales, marketing, finance, business

CONTACT: For individuals with previous experience: Mr Aaron Blight, Human Resources Administrator; Phone (410) 332-3000.

DAIRY MART CONVENIENCE STORES

1 VISION DRIVE
ENFIELD, CONNECTICUT 06082

OVERVIEW: Operates chain of convenience stores. Parent Company: DM Associates, Ltd.

KEY STATISTICS Annual Sales: $591.0 million. Number of Employees: 5,000.

HIRING HISTORY Number of professional employees hired in 1994: 30.

EXPERTISE/EDUCATION SOUGHT: Accounting, law, business management, finance, marketing, real estate

CONTACT: Ms Kathy Schroder, Manager of Human Resources-Corporate; Phone (203) 741-3611.

DAN RIVER, INC.

2291 MEMORIAL DRIVE
DANVILLE, VIRGINIA 24541-4741

OVERVIEW: Operates textile mills and produces cotton fabrics.

KEY STATISTICS Annual Sales: $320.0 million. Number of Employees: 4,900.

EXPERTISE/EDUCATION SOUGHT: Industrial engineering, mechanical engineering, plant engineering, textiles, computer programming

CONTACT: Mr Edward Carroll, Vice President Industrial Relations.

DANA CORPORATION

4500 DORR STREET
TOLEDO, OHIO 43615-4040

OVERVIEW: Manufactures automotive parts, chassis, and transmissions. Established: 1904.

KEY STATISTICS Annual Sales: $5.0 billion. Number of Employees: 36,000.

EXPERTISE/EDUCATION SOUGHT: Finance, international finance, law, systems integration, human resources

CONTACT: For individuals with previous experience: Mr Patrick Gahagan, Manager of Human Resources; Phone (419) 535-4500.

DARCY MASIUS BENTON AND BOWLES

1675 BROADWAY
NEW YORK, NEW YORK 10019-5820

OVERVIEW: Advertising agency.

KEY STATISTICS Annual Sales: $5.0 billion. Number of Employees: 4,700.

EXPERTISE/EDUCATION SOUGHT: Accounting, marketing, finance, management, communications

CONTACT: For individuals with previous experience: Ms Judith Kemp, Personnel Director.

DARDEN RESTAURANTS

5900 LAKE ELLENOR DRIVE
ORLANDO, FLORIDA 32809-4639

OVERVIEW: Operates chain of seafood restaurants. Established: 1970. Parent Company: General Mills, Inc.

KEY STATISTICS Annual Sales: $3.0 billion. Number of Employees: 108,000.

HIRING HISTORY Number of professional employees hired in 1994: 80.

EXPERTISE/EDUCATION SOUGHT: Hospitality/hotel and restaurant management, finance, computer programming, accounting, auditing, marketing, program analysis

CONTACTS: For college students and recent graduates: Ms Karen Parker, Employment Representative; Phone (407) 245-4000. For individuals with previous experience: Ms Susan Lock, Management Recruiter; Phone (407) 245-4000.

DART GROUP CORPORATION

3300 75TH AVENUE
LANDOVER, MARYLAND 20785-1501

OVERVIEW: Owns and operates book, food, and auto parts stores. Established: 1954.

KEY STATISTICS Number of Employees: 10,000.

HIRING HISTORY Number of professional employees hired in 1993: 60.

EXPERTISE/EDUCATION SOUGHT: Management information systems, warehousing, finance, accounting, construction, computer science, marketing, data processing

CONTACT: Mr James Parker, Director of Personnel; Phone (301) 731-1200, ext. 562.

DATA GENERAL CORPORATION

4400 COMPUTER DRIVE
WESTBOROUGH, MASSACHUSETTS 01580-0002

OVERVIEW: Manufactures computers. Established: 1968.

KEY STATISTICS Annual Sales: $1.0 billion. Number of Employees: 6,500.

EXPERTISE/EDUCATION SOUGHT: Marketing, software engineering/development, hardware engineering

CONTACT: Mr Richard Maunder, Manager of College Relations; Phone (508) 898-5000.

DAY AND ZIMMERMANN, INC.

280 KING OF PRUSSIA ROAD
RADNOR, PENNSYLVANIA 19087-5172

OVERVIEW: Provides engineering, construction, and architectural services. Established: 1961.

KEY STATISTICS Number of Employees: 12,000.

EXPERTISE/EDUCATION SOUGHT: Electrical engineering, mechanical engineering, industrial engineering, civil engineering, accounting, finance, marketing, data processing

CONTACT: Mr Anthony Natale, Corporate Human Resources Vice President, 1818 Market Street, Philadelphia, PA, 19087; Phone (610) 975-6800.

DAYTON HUDSON CORPORATION

777 NICOLLET MALL
MINNEAPOLIS, MINNESOTA 55402-2055

OVERVIEW: Operates department stores and general merchandise discount stores. Established: 1902.

KEY STATISTICS Annual Sales: $19.0 billion. Number of Employees: 174,000.

EXPERTISE/EDUCATION SOUGHT: Accounting, finance, auditing

CONTACT: For college students and recent graduates: Ms Cindy Kivisto, Manager of Personnel Services; Phone (612) 370-6603.

DAYTON HUDSON MARSHALL FIELDS

111 NORTH STATE STREET
CHICAGO, ILLINOIS 60690

OVERVIEW: Operates chain of department stores. Parent Company: Dayton Hudson Corporation.

EXPERTISE/EDUCATION SOUGHT: Retail, retail management

CONTACT: For individuals with previous experience: Manager of Recruitment, 700 On the Mall, Box 862, Minneapolis, MN, 55402-2004; Phone (612) 375-2795.

THE DAYTON POWER AND LIGHT COMPANY

COURTHOUSE PLAZA SOUTH
DAYTON, OHIO 45402

OVERVIEW: Electric utility. Established: 1911.

KEY STATISTICS Number of Employees: 2,600.

HIRING HISTORY Number of professional employees hired in 1993: 145.

EXPERTISE/EDUCATION SOUGHT: Accounting, quality control, business administration, finance, auditing

CONTACT: Ms Patricia Swanke, Director of Employment, PO Box 1247, Dayton, OH, 45401-1247; Phone (513) 259-7148.

DEMOURAL SUPER MARKET

875 EAST STREET
TEWKSBURY, MASSACHUSETTS 01876

OVERVIEW: Operates food stores.

EXPERTISE/EDUCATION SOUGHT: Accounting, sales, marketing, computer programming

CONTACT: Mr William Marsden, Vice President of Operations; Phone (508) 851-8000.

DEAN FOODS COMPANY

3600 RIVER ROAD
FRANKLIN PARK, ILLINOIS 60131-2185

OVERVIEW: Manufactures dairy and non-dairy food products. Established: 1925.

KEY STATISTICS Annual Sales: $3.0 billion. Number of Employees: 10,500.

HIRING HISTORY Number of professional employees hired in 1994: 40.

EXPERTISE/EDUCATION SOUGHT: Research and development, sales, accounting, food science, marketing, auditing, purchasing

CONTACT: For individuals with previous experience: Ms Laurie Walsh, Coordinator of Human Resources.

DEBARTOLO, INC.

7620 MARKET STREET
YOUNGSTOWN, OHIO 44513

OVERVIEW: Provides shopping center development and property management services. Established: 1962.

EXPERTISE/EDUCATION SOUGHT: Accounting, finance, marketing, business management, data processing

CONTACT: Mr Irvin Kravitz, Vice President of Human Resources; Phone (216) 758-7292.

DEL MONTE CORPORATION

1 MARKET PLAZA
SAN FRANCISCO, CALIFORNIA 94105-1019

OVERVIEW: Manufactures food products. Established: 1916. Parent Company: Del Monte Foods Corporation.

KEY STATISTICS Annual Sales: $2.0 billion. Number of Employees: 17,000.

HIRING HISTORY Number of professional employees hired in 1994: 4.

EXPERTISE/EDUCATION SOUGHT: Marketing, finance, accounting

CONTACT: For individuals with previous experience: Ms Betty Lyle, Manager Corporate Employee Resources, PO Box 193575, San Francisco, CA, 94518.

DELCO ELECTRONICS CORPORATION

1 CORPORATE CENTER
KOKOMO, INDIANA 46902-4000

OVERVIEW: Manufactures automotive electronics products. Established: 1936. Parent Company: GM Hughes Electronics Corporation.

KEY STATISTICS Annual Sales: $3.0 billion. Number of Employees: 30,000.

EXPERTISE/EDUCATION SOUGHT: Mechanical engineering, engineering, electronics/electronics engineering, automotive engineering

CONTACT: Mr Michael Parker, Manager of Placement, PO Box 9005, Kokomo, IN, 46902; Phone (317) 451-0789.

DELL COMPUTER CORPORATION

2214 WEST BRAKER LANE, SUITE D
AUSTIN, TEXAS 78759-7299

OVERVIEW: Manufactures personal computers. Established: 1984.

KEY STATISTICS Annual Sales: $3.0 billion. Number of Employees: 4,980.

EXPERTISE/EDUCATION SOUGHT: Electrical engineering, computer engineering, manufacturing engineering, transportation, program analysis, sales, customer service and support, production, network analysis

CONTACT: Mr Sam Gassett, Director of Human Resources, 9505 Arboretum Boulevard, Austin, TX, 78759; Phone (512) 338-4400.

DELOITTE AND TOUCHE

10 WESTPORT ROAD
WILTON, CONNECTICUT 06897-0820

OVERVIEW: Provides accounting and business consulting services. Established: 1895.

EXPERTISE/EDUCATION SOUGHT: Accounting, information systems, systems integration, finance, law

CONTACTS: For college students and recent graduates: Mr Mark M Chain, National Director of Recruiting and University Relations. For individuals with previous experience: Mr Martin Schram, Director of Administration, PO Box 820, Wilton, CT, 06897-0820; Phone (203) 761-3000, ext. 3038.

DELTA AIR LINES, INC.

HARTSFIELD INTERNATIONAL AIRPORT
ATLANTA, GEORGIA 30320

OVERVIEW: Provides passenger airline services. Established: 1930.

KEY STATISTICS Number of Employees: 73,533.

EXPERTISE/EDUCATION SOUGHT: Computer programming, data processing, mechanical engineering, flight attendant, computer analysis

CONTACT: For individuals with previous experience: Mr Barry Nuggle, Personnel Specialist; Phone (404) 715-2600.

DELTA DENTAL PLAN OF CALIFORNIA

100 1ST STREET
SAN FRANCISCO, CALIFORNIA 94105-2634

OVERVIEW: Provides dental insurance. Established: 1955.

KEY STATISTICS Annual Sales: $2.0 billion. Number of Employees: 1,200.

EXPERTISE/EDUCATION SOUGHT: Accounting, finance, data processing, dentistry/dental hygiene, law, analysis, underwriting, actuarial, claims processing/management, and administration, human resources

CONTACT: For individuals with previous experience: Ms Lillian Tam, Manager of Employee Relations; Phone (415) 972-8300, ext. 8408.

DELUXE CORPORATION

1080 WEST COUNTRY ROAD SOUTH
SAINT PAUL, MINNESOTA 55126-2910

OVERVIEW: Prints checks and forms and provides electronic payment systems. Established: 1915.

KEY STATISTICS Annual Sales: $2.0 billion. Number of Employees: 17,748.

EXPERTISE/EDUCATION SOUGHT: Accounting, computer science, computer programming, marketing, sales

CONTACT: For individuals with previous experience: Ms Lorraine Fernandez, Employment Recruiter; Phone (612) 483-7111.

DEPARTMENT OF THE NAVY, NAVY COMPTROLLER PROGRAM

151 ELLYSON AVENUE, SUITE E
PENSACOLA, FLORIDA 32508-5114

OVERVIEW: Hires entry level budget analysts, to formulate and execute departmental budgets, for careers in the Department of the Navy.

EXPERTISE/EDUCATION SOUGHT: Business administration, accounting, economics, finance, federal government

Department of the Navy, Navy Comptroller Program (continued)

CONTACT: For college students and recent graduates: Mr Thomas W Steinbereg, Deputy Director; Phone (904) 452-3962; Fax (904) 452-3903.

CORPORATE PROFILE

I ndividuals who are looking for a challenge should consider a civilian career as a budget analyst for the Department of the Navy.

Planning and making career choices is indeed a challenge. Individuals may accept that challenge by choosing the Department of the Navy Centralized Financial Management Trainee Program (CFMTP)—a two-year, entry-level training program that prepares high-quality individuals for civilian careers as budget analysts.

Applicants must be college graduates in any major field of study (business, accounting, economics, liberal arts, social science, etc.) and have a minimum 3.45 GPA or be in the upper 10 percent of their graduating class.

Trainees enjoy the full benefits of federal service such as generous vacation time, a retirement plan with tax-deferred savings options, health and life insurance, and many others.

They also participate in rotational work assignments and academic training in all aspects of ancial management as part of their individual development plan.

Trainees are promoted at the end of the first and second year based on satisfactory performance, progressing from the GS-7 to the GS-11 pay grade. (Salaries increase more than $10,000 over the two-year period.)

Those who are eligible for the CFMTP and are looking for a challenge should contact the Navy Financial Management Career Center (NFMCC).

The application deadline is February 1 each year.

Applicants should send the following to the NFMCC address above: a comprehensive résumé and preliminary, unofficial college transcripts showing a minimum cumulative GPA of 3.45 or a letter from a college verifying that the applicant is in the upper 10 percent of the graduating class. U.S. citizenship is required.

The Department of the Navy is an equal opportunity employer.

DESERT PALACE, INC.
3570 LAS VEGAS BOULEVARD SOUTH
LAS VEGAS, NEVADA 89109-8924

OVERVIEW: Owns and operates hotels and casinos. Established: 1969. Parent Company: Caesar's Palace Corporation.

KEY STATISTICS Annual Sales: $575.0 million. Number of Employees: 6,500.

EXPERTISE/EDUCATION SOUGHT: Finance, marketing, sales, accounting, business

CONTACT: For individuals with previous experience: Mr Robert Eisen, Supervisor of Compensation and Employment.

DETROIT DIESEL CORPORATION
13400 OUTER DRIVE WEST
DETROIT, MICHIGAN 48239-5000

OVERVIEW: Designs, manufactures, sells, and services heavy duty diesel engines and engine parts. Established: 1938.

EXPERTISE/EDUCATION SOUGHT: Mechanical engineering, industrial engineering, electrical engineering, manufacturing engineering

CONTACT: Ms Joanne Fennicks, Corporate Manager of Personnel; Phone (313) 592-5000, ext. 7369.

DEVILBISS HEALTH CARE, INC.
1200 EAST MAIN STREET
SOMERSET, PENNSYLVANIA 15501-2100

OVERVIEW: Manufactures durable respiratory care equipment. Established: 1990. Parent Company: Sunrise Medical.

KEY STATISTICS Annual Sales: $95.0 million. Number of Employees: 600.

EXPERTISE/EDUCATION SOUGHT: Electrical engineering, manufacturing engineering, accounting, finance, data processing

CONTACT: Human Resources Department; Phone (814) 443-4881.

DEXTER CORPORATION
1 ELM STREET
WINDSOR LOCKS, CONNECTICUT 06096

OVERVIEW: Manufactures specialty nonwoven materials. Established: 1767.

KEY STATISTICS Annual Sales: $975.0 million.

EXPERTISE/EDUCATION SOUGHT: Sales, marketing, science, management information systems

CONTACT: For individuals with previous experience: Ms Michelle Virkler, Professional Recruiting; Phone (203) 627-9051.

DFS GROUP
655 MONTGOMERY STREET
SAN FRANCISCO, CALIFORNIA 94111-2633

OVERVIEW: Operates souvenir and gift shops.

KEY STATISTICS Annual Sales: $735.0 million. Number of Employees: 8,500.

EXPERTISE/EDUCATION SOUGHT: Retail, business management, merchandising, linguistics

CONTACT: Mr Dennis Franklin, Director of Human Resources; Phone (415) 397-5838; Fax (415) 627-3689.

DIAL CORPORATION
DIAL CORPORATE CENTER
PHOENIX, ARIZONA 85077

OVERVIEW: Manufactures soap and other consumer products. Established: 1914.

KEY STATISTICS Number of Employees: 25,000.

EXPERTISE/EDUCATION SOUGHT: Sales, computer programming, accounting, data processing, marketing, auditing, management information systems

CONTACT: For individuals with previous experience: Department of Human Resources; Phone (602) 207-5473.

DIAMON, INC.
512 BRIDGE STREET
DANVILLE, VIRGINIA 24545

OVERVIEW: Produces agricultural products and florist supplies. Established: 1873.

KEY STATISTICS Annual Sales: $1.0 billion. Number of Employees: 2,500.

EXPERTISE/EDUCATION SOUGHT: Finance, management

CONTACT: Ms Norma Lutz, Director of Human Resources; Phone (804) 792-7511.

DIAMOND SHAMROCK, INC.
9830 COLONNADE BOULEVARD
SAN ANTONIO, TEXAS 78230

OVERVIEW: Petroleum refining and marketing company.

KEY STATISTICS Annual Sales: $3.0 billion. Number of Employees: 6,000.

EXPERTISE/EDUCATION SOUGHT: Public relations, accounting, marketing, finance, data processing, computer programming, law

CONTACT: For individuals with previous experience: Ms Tara Ford, Human Resources Representative, PO Box 696000, San Antonio, TX, 78269; Phone (210) 641-6800.

DIAMOND-STAR MOTORS CORPORATION
100 NORTH DIAMOND STAR PARKWAY
NORMAL, ILLINOIS 61761-8000

OVERVIEW: Manufactures automobiles. Established: 1985. Parent Company: Mitsubishi Motor Corporation.

KEY STATISTICS Annual Sales: $23.0 billion. Number of Employees: 3,600.

HIRING HISTORY Number of professional employees hired in 1994: 31.

EXPERTISE/EDUCATION SOUGHT: Engineering, materials science, computer science, purchasing, human resources, finance, accounting, marketing, public relations, sales

CONTACT: Ms Jeana Leu, Personnel Representative; Phone (309) 888-8380.

DICTAPHONE CORPORATION
3191 BROADBRIDGE AVENUE
STRATFORD, CONNECTICUT 06497

OVERVIEW: Manufactures and markets dictation, voice processing, and communications equipment. Established: 1979. Parent Company: Pitney Bowes, Inc.

EXPERTISE/EDUCATION SOUGHT: Accounting, marketing, sales

CONTACT: Ms Sandra Almarayati, Senior Human Resources Representative; Phone (203) 381-7136.

DIEBOLD, INC.
818 MULBERRY ROAD SOUTHEAST
CANTON, OHIO 44707-3256

OVERVIEW: Manufactures electronic equipment such as ATMs and computer terminals.

KEY STATISTICS Number of Employees: 3,975.

EXPERTISE/EDUCATION SOUGHT: Electrical engineering, mechanical engineering, computer engineering, software engineering/ development, sales

CONTACT: For individuals with previous experience: Mr John Gotch, Manager of Human Resources, PO Box 8230, Canton, OH, 44711; Phone (216) 489-4000.

DIGITAL EQUIPMENT CORPORATION
111 POWDERMILL ROAD
MAYNARD, MASSACHUSETTS 01754-2504

OVERVIEW: Provides open client/server computing solutions from personal computers to integrated information systems. Established: 1957.

KEY STATISTICS Number of Employees: 65,600.

EXPERTISE/EDUCATION SOUGHT: Software engineering/development, manufacturing engineering, hardware engineering, product management, sales, technical sales

CONTACT: Ms Maejim Fields, Director of U.S. College Relations; Phone (508) 493-9154.

DILLARD DEPARTMENT STORES, INC.
1600 CANTRELL ROAD
LITTLE ROCK, ARKANSAS 72202-1110

OVERVIEW: Operates chain of retail department stores. Established: 1899.

KEY STATISTICS Number of Employees: 35,536.

HIRING HISTORY Number of professional employees hired in 1993: 75.

EXPERTISE/EDUCATION SOUGHT: Planning, business management, construction, data processing, finance, advertising, marketing

CONTACT: For individuals with previous experience: Ms Joyce Wisner, Manager of Personnel; Phone (501) 376-5200.

DILLON COMPANIES, INC.
700 EAST 30TH AVENUE
HUTCHINSON, KANSAS 67502-8435

OVERVIEW: Operates chain of retail stores. Established: 1983. Parent Company: The Kroger Company.

KEY STATISTICS Number of Employees: 44,000.

EXPERTISE/EDUCATION SOUGHT: Business management, retail, purchasing

CONTACT: For individuals with previous experience: Mr Harold Ryan, Vice President of Human Resources; Phone (316) 663-6801.

DISNEY STORE, INC.
101 NORTH BRAND BOULEVARD, SUITE 500
GLENDALE, CALIFORNIA 91203-2619

OVERVIEW: Operates chain of retail store specializing in Disney products. Established: 1987. Parent Company: Walt Disney Company, Inc.

KEY STATISTICS Annual Sales: $500.0 million. Number of Employees: 5,000.

EXPERTISE/EDUCATION SOUGHT: Retail, business management

CONTACT: For individuals with previous experience: Mr Robert Campbell, Manager Staffing and Development; Phone (818) 543-3505.

DOLLAR GENERAL CORPORATION
104 WOODMONT BOULEVARD
NASHVILLE, TENNESSEE 37205-2285

OVERVIEW: Operates chain of discount stores. Established: 1939.

KEY STATISTICS Number of Employees: 10,400.

HIRING HISTORY Number of professional employees hired in 1993: 80.

EXPERTISE/EDUCATION SOUGHT: Accounting, distribution, marketing, business management, warehousing, purchasing

CONTACT: For individuals with previous experience: Mr Jeff Rice, Manager of Human Resources; Phone (502) 237-5444, ext. 5269.

DOMINICK'S FINER FOODS
505 RAILROAD AVENUE
NORTH LAKE, ILLINOIS 60164-1604

OVERVIEW: Operates chain of food stores. Established: 1925.

KEY STATISTICS Annual Sales: $2.0 billion. Number of Employees: 18,000.

HIRING HISTORY Number of professional employees hired in 1993: 70.

EXPERTISE/EDUCATION SOUGHT: Management, management information systems, retail, accounting, distribution

CONTACT: Ms Laurie Canter, Employment Specialist; Phone (708) 562-1000, ext. 2041.

DONALDSON LUFKIN AND JENRETTE
140 BROADWAY
NEW YORK, NEW YORK 10005-1276

OVERVIEW: Investment bank. Established: 1959. Parent Company: Equitable Investment Corporation.

KEY STATISTICS Annual Sales: $2.0 billion. Number of Employees: 4,181.

EXPERTISE/EDUCATION SOUGHT: Finance, accounting, marketing

CONTACT: Ms Jane Kelly, Assistant Vice President; Phone (212) 504-3000.

R. R. DONNELLEY AND SONS COMPANY
77 WEST WACKER DRIVE
CHICAGO, ILLINOIS 60601-1696

OVERVIEW: Provides printing services to publishers and direct marketers. Established: 1864.

KEY STATISTICS Number of Employees: 34,000.

EXPERTISE/EDUCATION SOUGHT: Electrical engineering, computer science, environmental engineering, software engineering/development

CONTACT: Mr Larry Drummond, Supervisor of Human Resources.

DONNELLY CORPORATION
414 EAST 40TH STREET
HOLLAND, MICHIGAN 49423-5313

OVERVIEW: Manufactures automotive glass and plastic products. Established: 1905.

KEY STATISTICS Number of Employees: 2,650.

EXPERTISE/EDUCATION SOUGHT: Sales, accounting, marketing, languages

CONTACT: Mr James Wujkowski, Manager of Professional Recruitment; Phone (616) 786-6332.

DOVER ELEVATOR INTERNATIONAL
6750 POPLAR AVENUE, SUITE 419
MEMPHIS, TENNESSEE 38138-7416

OVERVIEW: Manufactures sells, installs, and services vertical transportation equipment. Established: 1958. Parent Company: Dover Corporation.

KEY STATISTICS Annual Sales: $800.0 million. Number of Employees: 7,600.

EXPERTISE/EDUCATION SOUGHT: Sales, marketing, finance, accounting, electrical engineering, mechanical engineering

CONTACT: For individuals with previous experience: Mr David Hey, Director of Human Resources Equal Employment Opportunity, PO Box 2177, Memphis, TN, 38101; Phone (601) 393-2110.

THE DOW CHEMICAL COMPANY
2030 WILLARD H. DOW CENTER
MIDLAND, MICHIGAN 48640

OVERVIEW: Manufactures chemical, plastic, and consumer products. Established: 1897.

EXPERTISE/EDUCATION SOUGHT: Marketing, finance, sales, human resources

CONTACT: For individuals with previous experience: Ms Paula Moses, Recruiter; Phone (517) 636-1000.

DOW CORNING CORPORATION
2200 WEST SALZBURG STREET
AUBURN, MICHIGAN 48611-8594

OVERVIEW: Manufactures silicone products and lubricants. Established: 1943.

KEY STATISTICS Number of Employees: 8,600.

HIRING HISTORY Number of professional employees hired in 1993: 11.

EXPERTISE/EDUCATION SOUGHT: Chemistry, chemical engineering, mechanical engineering, electrical engineering

CONTACTS: For college students and recent graduates: Ms Renee Connon, Manager of College Recruiting; Phone (517) 496-4000. For individuals with previous experience: Mr Doug Dawson, Director of Human Resources; Phone (517) 496-4000, ext. 6376.

DOW JONES AND COMPANY, INC.
200 LIBERTY STREET
NEW YORK, NEW YORK 10281

OVERVIEW: Provides on line and print news services. Established: 1882.

EXPERTISE/EDUCATION SOUGHT: Journalism, finance, computer programming, marketing, accounting, economics, printing, sales

CONTACT: For individuals with previous experience: Ms Charlene Watler, Director of Employee Relations; Phone (212) 416-2000.

DOWELANCO
9330 ZIONSVILLE ROAD
INDIANAPOLIS, INDIANA 46268-1054

OVERVIEW: Manufactures herbicides and pesticides.

KEY STATISTICS Annual Sales: $1.0 billion. Number of Employees: 3,100.

EXPERTISE/EDUCATION SOUGHT: Agricultural engineering, chemical engineering, accounting, environmental engineering, finance, chemistry, law, biological engineering, computer programming, biology

CONTACT: Human Resources; Phone (317) 337-4168.

DQE, INC.
1 OXFORD CENTER 301 GRANT STREET
PITTSBURGH, PENNSYLVANIA 15279

OVERVIEW: Electric utility. Established: 1880.

EXPERTISE/EDUCATION SOUGHT: Accounting, investment, electrical engineering, civil engineering, finance, credit/credit analysis, clinical nursing

CONTACT: Ms Sally Wade, Assistant Vice President of Human Resources; Phone (412) 393-6000, ext. 6440.

DR. PEPPER/SEVEN-UP COMPANIES
8144 WALNUT HILL LANE
DALLAS, TEXAS 75231

OVERVIEW: Produces soft drinks. Established: 1885.

EXPERTISE/EDUCATION SOUGHT: Sales, marketing

CONTACT: For individuals with previous experience: Human Resources Department; Phone (214) 360-7000.

DRESSER INDUSTRIES, INC.
2001 ROSS AVENUE
DALLAS, TEXAS 75201-8001

OVERVIEW: Provides equipment and services for the petroleum and mining industries. Established: 1880.

KEY STATISTICS Number of Employees: 25,926.

EXPERTISE/EDUCATION SOUGHT: Human resources, accounting, finance, data processing, computer programming, petroleum/petrochemical engineering, mechanical engineering, design engineering

CONTACT: For individuals with previous experience: Ms Veronica Thomson, Personnel Director; Phone (214) 740-6000.

DRESSER RAND COMPANY
BARON STEUBEN PLACE
CORNING, NEW YORK 14830

OVERVIEW: Manufactures compressors and turbines. Established: 1987.

EXPERTISE/EDUCATION SOUGHT: Petroleum/petrochemical engineering, mechanical engineering, design engineering, human resources, chemical engineering, accounting, drafting, finance, data processing, aeronautical engineering

CONTACT: For individuals with previous experience: Ms Caryl Lucardelli, Manager of Employee Relations; Phone (607) 937-4621.

DRUG EMPORIUM, INC.
155 HIDDEN RAVINES DRIVE
POWELL, OHIO 43065-8739

OVERVIEW: Operates chain of drug stores. Established: 1977.

KEY STATISTICS Annual Sales: $749.0 million. Number of Employees: 5,300.

EXPERTISE/EDUCATION SOUGHT: Sales, accounting, merchandising, data processing

CONTACT: Ms Laurie Stroman, Director of Human Resources; Phone (614) 548-7080.

DUKE POWER COMPANY
422 SOUTH CHURCH STREET
CHARLOTTE, NORTH CAROLINA 28242-0001

OVERVIEW: Electric and gas utility. Established: 1917.

KEY STATISTICS Number of Employees: 18,274.

EXPERTISE/EDUCATION SOUGHT: Nuclear engineering, mechanical engineering, electrical engineering, computer science, accounting

CONTACT: For individuals with previous experience: Mr Phillip Plott, Manager of Corporate Staffing; Phone (704) 373-4011.

DUN AND BRADSTREET CORPORATION
187 DANBURY ROAD
WILTON, CONNECTICUT 06897

OVERVIEW: Provides business, marketing, and credit information services. Established: 1841.

KEY STATISTICS Number of Employees: 52,000.

EXPERTISE/EDUCATION SOUGHT: Marketing, technology, finance, management

CONTACT: For individuals with previous experience: Ms Mary Pleasanton, Manager of Staffing Programs, 200 Nyala Farms, Westport, CT, 06880.

DUNLOP TIRE CORPORATION
200 JOHN JAMES AUDUBON PARK
AMHERST, NEW YORK 14228-1120

OVERVIEW: Manufactures tires. Established: 1923.

KEY STATISTICS Annual Sales: $605.0 million. Number of Employees: 3,300.

EXPERTISE/EDUCATION SOUGHT: Sales, marketing

CONTACT: Mr Roger Jones, Corporate Manager Human Resources, PO Box 1109, Buffalo, NY, 14240-1109; Phone (716) 639-5200, ext. 5552.

DUO-FAST CORPORATION
3702 RIVER ROAD
FRANKLIN PARK, ILLINOIS 60131-2121

OVERVIEW: Manufactures staplers, tackers, and nailers. Established: 1958.

KEY STATISTICS Annual Sales: $200.0 million. Number of Employees: 2,500.

EXPERTISE/EDUCATION SOUGHT: Sales, accounting, marketing

CONTACT: Ms Holly Roberts, Director of Human Resources; Phone (708) 678-0100, ext. 7451.

E. I. DUPONT DE NEMOURS AND COMPANY
1007 NORTH MARKET STREET
WILMINGTON, DELAWARE 19898

OVERVIEW: Discovers and manufactures industrial and agricultural chemicals, fibers, polymers, imaging systems, and energy products. Established: 1802.

EXPERTISE/EDUCATION SOUGHT: Chemical engineering, logistics, chemistry, electrical engineering, accounting, biology, biochemistry, computer science, mechanical engineering, management information systems

CONTACT: DuPont Human Resources N-12419; Phone (800) 774-2271; Fax (800) 631-2206.

DURACELL INTERNATIONAL, INC.
101 EAST RIDGE DRIVE, SUITE 104
BETHEL, CONNECTICUT 06801

OVERVIEW: Manufactures batteries. Established: 1916.

KEY STATISTICS Number of Employees: 7,700.

EXPERTISE/EDUCATION SOUGHT: Accounting, finance, computer programming, sales, marketing, design engineering, project engineering, mechanical engineering, electrical engineering

CONTACTS: For college students and recent graduates: Ms Judy Quinn, Human Resources Manager - USA Division. For individuals with previous experience: Ms Jean Larkin, Manager of Human Resources, Berkshire Corporate Park, Bethel, CT, 06801; Phone (203) 796-4000.

DURION COMPANY, INC.
3100 RESEARCH BOULEVARD
DAYTON, OHIO 45420-4005

OVERVIEW: Manufactures fluid control, filtration, and related industrial equipment. Established: 1912.

KEY STATISTICS Number of Employees: 2,450.

EXPERTISE/EDUCATION SOUGHT: Accounting, sales, marketing, management information systems

CONTACT: Ms Julie Tray, Director of Human Resources, PO Box 1145, Dayton, OH, 45401-8820; Phone (513) 476-6136.

DYNCORP
2000 EDMUND HALLEY DRIVE
RESTON, VIRGINIA 22091-3400

OVERVIEW: Provides construction and engineering services for industry and government. Established: 1946.

KEY STATISTICS Number of Employees: 21,800.

EXPERTISE/EDUCATION SOUGHT: Aerospace science, risk management, business management, law, accounting, human resources

CONTACT: For individuals with previous experience: Ms Beth Edwards, Personnel Specialist; Phone (703) 264-0330.

E ENTERTAINMENT TELEVISION
5670 WILSHIRE BOULEVARD
LOS ANGELES, CALIFORNIA 90036-5679

OVERVIEW: Provides cable television services. Established: 1984.

KEY STATISTICS Annual Sales: $30.0 million. Number of Employees: 300.

EXPERTISE/EDUCATION SOUGHT: Production, accounting, sales, marketing

CONTACT: For individuals with previous experience: Ms Lisa Kaye, Vice President of Human Resources; Phone (213) 954-2400.

E-SYSTEMS, INC.
6250 LBJ FREEWAY
DALLAS, TEXAS 75240-6388

OVERVIEW: Manufactures electronic systems used by government, military, and private industry. Established: 1964.

KEY STATISTICS Annual Sales: $2.0 billion. Number of Employees: 16,700.

EXPERTISE/EDUCATION SOUGHT: Electrical engineering, design engineering, aerospace engineering, computer programming, mathematics, physics, mechanical engineering, civil engineering, manufacturing engineering

CONTACT: Mr Jerry Shaver, Manager of Staffing and College Recruiting, PO Box 6602488, Dallas, TX, 75206-2488; Phone (214) 661-1000, ext. 4925.

EAGLE FOOD CENTERS, INC.
ROUTE 67 AND KNOXVILLE ROAD
MILAN, ILLINOIS 61264

OVERVIEW: Operates chain of food stores. Established: 1893. Parent Company: Odyssey Partners, LP.

KEY STATISTICS Annual Sales: $1.0 billion. Number of Employees: 9,007.

EXPERTISE/EDUCATION SOUGHT: Accounting, marketing, finance, management information systems, retail management

CONTACT: For individuals with previous experience: Ms Jan Wolf, Director of Human Resources; Phone (309) 787-7700.

EAGLE-PICHER INDUSTRIES, INC.
580 WALNUT STREET
CINCINNATI, OHIO 45202-3110

OVERVIEW: Manufactures rubber products, metals, plastics, chemicals, construction equipment, and automotive parts. Established: 1843.

KEY STATISTICS Number of Employees: 6,600.

EXPERTISE/EDUCATION SOUGHT: Law, finance, investor relations, electrical engineering, manufacturing engineering, electronics/electronics engineering, accounting

CONTACT: Mr Ernest Hirsh, Vice President of Employee Relations; Phone (513) 721-7010.

EASTERN MERCY HEALTH SYSTEM
100 MATSONFORD ROAD
RADNOR, PENNSYLVANIA 19087

OVERVIEW: Provides hospital consulting services.

KEY STATISTICS Annual Sales: $2.0 billion. Number of Employees: 18,973.

HIRING HISTORY Number of professional employees hired in 1993: 7.

EXPERTISE/EDUCATION SOUGHT: Business management, administration, finance, planning, risk management

CONTACTS: For college students and recent graduates: Ms Deborah Van DeGrift, Human Resources Manager; Phone (215) 971-9770. For individuals with previous experience: Mr James Wilson, Vice President of Human Resources; Phone (215) 971-9770, ext. 3449.

EASTMAN CHEMICAL COMPANY

PO BOX 1975
KINGSPORT, TENNESSEE 37662

OVERVIEW: Manufactures industrial chemicals, fibers, and plastics. Established: 1920.

KEY STATISTICS Annual Sales: $4.0 billion. Number of Employees: 18,000.

EXPERTISE/EDUCATION SOUGHT: Accounting, computer science, mechanical engineering, electrical engineering, industrial engineering, chemistry

CONTACTS: For college students and recent graduates: Ms Betty DeVinney, Employment Manager. For individuals with previous experience: Mr Hoyt Denton, Employment Manager; Phone (615) 229-2000.

EASTMAN KODAK COMPANY

343 STATE STREET
ROCHESTER, NEW YORK 14559-1613

OVERVIEW: Produces imaging systems and photographic equipment and accessories. Established: 1877.

KEY STATISTICS Annual Sales: $14.0 billion. Number of Employees: 96,300.

HIRING HISTORY Number of professional employees hired in 1994: 200. 1993: 200.

EXPERTISE/EDUCATION SOUGHT: Computer science, chemical engineering, electrical engineering, chemistry, systems engineering, software engineering/development

CONTACT: For individuals with previous experience: Staffing, Department DPEG; Phone (716) 724-4000.

EATON CORPORATION

EATON CENTER, 1111 SUPERIOR AVENUE
CLEVELAND, OHIO 44114-2584

OVERVIEW: Manufactures advanced technology products for industrial and transportation markets. Established: 1911.

KEY STATISTICS Annual Sales: $6.0 billion. Number of Employees: 51,000.

HIRING HISTORY Number of professional employees hired in 1993: 97.

EXPERTISE/EDUCATION SOUGHT: Industrial engineering, electrical engineering, metallurgical engineering, manufacturing engineering, accounting, human resources, finance

CONTACT: Ms Nancy J Carlson, Manager of Corporate Recruiting and Diversity; Phone (216) 523-4738; Fax (216) 479-7079.

EBSCO INDUSTRIES, INC.

5724 HIGHWAY 280
BIRMINGHAM, ALABAMA 35242-6818

OVERVIEW: Provides publication subscription, printing, and telemarketing services; manufactures metal and wire products. Established: 1948.

KEY STATISTICS Number of Employees: 3,500.

EXPERTISE/EDUCATION SOUGHT: Sales, management

CONTACT: For individuals with previous experience: Mr Leon Sizemore, Corporate Recruiter.

JACK ECKERD CORPORATION

8333 BRYAN DAIRY ROAD
LARGO, FLORIDA 34647-1230

OVERVIEW: Operates chain of drug stores. Established: 1952.

KEY STATISTICS Annual Sales: $4.0 billion. Number of Employees: 43,000.

EXPERTISE/EDUCATION SOUGHT: Marketing, sales, accounting, finance, merchandising, pharmaceutical

CONTACT: Ms Luisa Hollingworth, Manager of Human Resources; Phone (813) 399-6000.

ECOLAB CENTER

370 NORTH WABASHA STREET
SAINT PAUL, MINNESOTA 55102-1390

OVERVIEW: Provides equipment and services for housekeeping, nursing, and sanitizing. Established: 1923.

KEY STATISTICS Number of Employees: 7,600.

EXPERTISE/EDUCATION SOUGHT: Accounting, chemical engineering, financial analysis, sales, marketing

CONTACT: Ms Sue Metcalf, Director of Human Resources; Phone (612) 293-2089.

EDDIE BAUER, INC.

14850 NORTHEAST 36TH STREET
REDMOND, WASHINGTON 98052-5377

OVERVIEW: Provides private label retail and catalog sales services. Established: 1920. Parent Company: Spiegel, Inc.

KEY STATISTICS Annual Sales: $1.0 billion. Number of Employees: 3,000.

EXPERTISE/EDUCATION SOUGHT: Sales, marketing, finance, management information systems

CONTACT: Human Resource Department.

A.G. EDWARDS, INC.

1 NORTH JEFFERSON AVENUE
SAINT LOUIS, MISSOURI 63103

OVERVIEW: Provides brokerage and investment services.

EXPERTISE/EDUCATION SOUGHT: Accounting, finance, auditing

CONTACT: Mr William Snyder, Manager of Employment; Phone (314) 289-3000.

J. D. EDWARDS AND COMPANY, INC.

8055 EAST TUFTS AVENUE, SUITE 1331
DENVER, COLORADO 80237-2886

OVERVIEW: Provides business applications software services. Established: 1977.

KEY STATISTICS Annual Sales: $197.9 million. Number of Employees: 1,331.

EXPERTISE/EDUCATION SOUGHT: Consulting, quality control, program analysis, quality engineering, technical writing, computer programming, marketing, sales

CONTACT: For individuals with previous experience: Mr Tony Bengston, Recruitment Specialist; Phone (303) 488-4551.

EG&G ROCKY FLATS, INC.

PO BOX 464
GOLDEN, COLORADO 80402-0464

OVERVIEW: Provides environmental research and development services. Established: 1950.

KEY STATISTICS Annual Sales: $740.0 million. Number of Employees: 7,000.

EXPERTISE/EDUCATION SOUGHT: Sales, marketing, finance, accounting, mechanical engineering, chemical engineering, electrical engineering, civil engineering, industrial engineering, nuclear engineering

CONTACT: Ms Michelle Soule, Manager of Employment; Phone (303) 966-7000, ext. 2046; , ext. 4112.

EG&G, INC.

45 WILLIAM STREET
WELLSLEY, MASSACHUSETTS 02181

OVERVIEW: Provides technologically advanced products and services. Established: 1947.

EXPERTISE/EDUCATION SOUGHT: Finance, human resources, law

CONTACT: For individuals with previous experience: Ms Peter Murphy, Director of Corporate Training and Development; Phone (617) 237-5100, ext. 122.

EGGHEAD, INC.
22011 SOUTHEAST 51ST STREET
ISSAQUAH, WASHINGTON 98027-7249

OVERVIEW: Sells computer software through retail stores and mail order operations. Established: 1988.
KEY STATISTICS Annual Sales: $778.0 million. Number of Employees: 2,700.
EXPERTISE/EDUCATION SOUGHT: Management, retail, government regulation, sales, customer service and support
CONTACT: For individuals with previous experience: Ms Carol Kowalski, Professional Manager.

EICHLEAY CORPORATION
6585 PENNSYLVANIA AVENUE
PITTSBURGH, PENNSYLVANIA 15206-4483

OVERVIEW: Provides construction and engineering consulting services.
KEY STATISTICS Annual Sales: $81.0 million. Number of Employees: 7,500.
EXPERTISE/EDUCATION SOUGHT: Accounting, finance
CONTACT: For individuals with previous experience: Mr Tom Beggs, Manager Corporate Administration; Phone (412) 361-0200, ext. 3376.

ELDER-BEERMAN STORES CORPORATION
3155 ELBEE ROAD
DAYTON, OHIO 45439-1919

OVERVIEW: Operates department, shoe, and furniture stores. Established: 1962.
KEY STATISTICS Number of Employees: 8,500.
EXPERTISE/EDUCATION SOUGHT: Management, purchasing
CONTACT: Mr Jerry Ollman, Director of Recruiting; Phone (513) 296-2700.

ELECTROCOM AUTOMATION, INC.
2910 AVENUE F
ARLINGTON, TEXAS 76011-5214

OVERVIEW: Manufactures postal sorting machines. Established: 1983.
KEY STATISTICS Number of Employees: 1,100.
EXPERTISE/EDUCATION SOUGHT: Accounting, finance, business management, data processing, electrical engineering, mechanical engineering
CONTACT: For individuals with previous experience: Mr Leonard Cameron, Personnel Administrator; Phone (817) 640-5690.

ELECTROLUX CORPORATION
2300 WINDY RIDGE PARKWAY
ATLANTA, GEORGIA 30339-5202

OVERVIEW: Manufactures large appliances. Established: 1924.
KEY STATISTICS Annual Sales: $2.0 billion. Number of Employees: 15,000.
EXPERTISE/EDUCATION SOUGHT: Management
CONTACT: For individuals with previous experience: Ms Becky Garrigan, Manager Human Resources.

ELECTRONIC DATA SYSTEMS CORPORATION (EDS)
5400 LEGACY DRIVE
PLANO, TEXAS 75024-3199

OVERVIEW: Provides information technology services. Established: 1962. Parent Company: General Motors.

KEY STATISTICS Annual Sales: $10.0 billion. Number of Employees: 75,000.
EXPERTISE/EDUCATION SOUGHT: Information systems, accounting, computer science, finance, business administration, electrical engineering, management information systems, mechanical engineering
CONTACTS: For college students and recent graduates: EDS Staffing - Campus Relations Manager; Phone (214) 605-2700; Fax (214) 605-2643. For individuals with previous experience: EDS Staffing; Phone (214) 605-2700; Fax (214)605-2643.

For more information, see full corporate profile, pg. 208.

ELF ATOCHEM NORTH AMERICA, INC.
2000 MARKET STREET
PHILADELPHIA, PENNSYLVANIA 19103-3231

OVERVIEW: Manufactures industrial chemicals.
KEY STATISTICS Number of Employees: 4,500.
HIRING HISTORY Number of professional employees hired in 1994: 50.
EXPERTISE/EDUCATION SOUGHT: Chemical engineering, physics, chemistry, finance, computer programming
CONTACT: For individuals with previous experience: Mr Pat O'Neill, Manager of Employment; Phone (215) 419-7171.

ELI LILLY AND COMPANY
LILLY CORPORATE CENTER, DC 1811
INDIANAPOLIS, INDIANA 46285

OVERVIEW: Develops, manufactures, and markets pharmaceuticals and animal health products. Established: 1876.
KEY STATISTICS Annual Sales: $6.0 billion. Number of Employees: 30,100.
HIRING HISTORY Number of professional employees hired in 1994: 250. 1993: 300.
EXPERTISE/EDUCATION SOUGHT: Research and development, management information systems, marketing, sales, chemical engineering, finance
CONTACTS: For college students and recent graduates: Ms Joyce Foster, Senior Recruiting Assistant. For individuals with previous experience: Mr Ron L Anglea, Manager of Corporate Recruitment, Lilly Corporate Center, DC 1810, Indianapolis, IN, 46285; Phone (800) 428-4592.

EMERSON ELECTRIC COMPANY
8000 WEST FLORISSANT AVENUE
SAINT LOUIS, MISSOURI 63136-1415

OVERVIEW: Manufactures electrical and electronic products for industrial, commercial, and residential use. Established: 1890.
KEY STATISTICS Annual Sales: $8.0 billion. Number of Employees: 71,600.
EXPERTISE/EDUCATION SOUGHT: Business administration, electrical engineering, accounting, technical engineering, finance, mechanical engineering, law, auditing
CONTACT: For individuals with previous experience: Mr Mark Botterman, Director of Community Programs; Phone (314) 553-2000.

EMERSON POWER TRANSMISSION CORPORATION
620 SOUTH AURORA STREET
ITHACA, NEW YORK 14850-5726

OVERVIEW: Manufactures power transmissions. Established: 1983. Parent Company: Emerson Electric Company.
KEY STATISTICS Annual Sales: $409.0 million. Number of Employees: 4,000.
EXPERTISE/EDUCATION SOUGHT: Sales, business administration, management
CONTACTS: For college students and recent graduates: Mr Rick Hamilton, Director of Training; Phone (607) 274-6074. For individuals with previous experience: Mr Todd-Michael Balan, Director of Sales Training; Fax (607)224-6105.

EMERY WORLDWIDE
3350 WEST BAYSHORE ROAD
PALO ALTO, CALIFORNIA 94303-4236

OVERVIEW: Provides package delivery and courier services. Established: 1946. Parent Company: Consolidated Freightways, Inc.

KEY STATISTICS Number of Employees: 7,500.

EXPERTISE/EDUCATION SOUGHT: Sales, marketing, accounting, transportation

CONTACT: For individuals with previous experience: Mr Don Fausset, Director of Human Resoruces; Phone (800) 227-1981.

EMPIRE BLUE CROSS AND BLUE SHIELD
622 3RD AVENUE, 26TH FLOOR
NEW YORK, NEW YORK 10017-6758

OVERVIEW: Provides health insurance. Established: 1935.

KEY STATISTICS Annual Sales: $5.0 billion. Number of Employees: 9,678.

EXPERTISE/EDUCATION SOUGHT: Accounting, finance, data processing, computer programming, management information systems

CONTACT: Ms Lisa Engelson, Human Resources Recruiter; Phone (212) 476-1117.

EMPLOYERS HEALTH INSURANCE COMPANY
1100 EMPLOYERS BOULEVARD
GREEN BAY, WISCONSIN 54344

OVERVIEW: Provides health insurance. Parent Company: Lincoln National Corporation.

KEY STATISTICS Annual Sales: $1.3 billion. Number of Employees: 2,691.

EXPERTISE/EDUCATION SOUGHT: Accounting, finance, sales, management information systems

CONTACT: Ms Lynn Adamczak, Recruitment Manager; Phone (414) 337-7969, ext. 5366.

EMRO MARKETING COMPANY
500 SPEEDWAY DRIVE
ENON, OHIO 45323-1056

OVERVIEW: Operates convenience stores and gas stations. Established: 1975. Parent Company: Marathon Oil Company.

KEY STATISTICS Annual Sales: $3.0 billion. Number of Employees: 11,400.

EXPERTISE/EDUCATION SOUGHT: Retail, marketing

CONTACT: For individuals with previous experience: Mr Jerry Wagner, Manager of Human Resources; Phone (513) 864-3000, ext. 7867.

ENGELHARD CORPORATION
101 WOOD AVENUE SOUTH
ISELIN, NEW JERSEY 08830-2722

OVERVIEW: Manufactures chemicals and precious metals. Established: 1874.

KEY STATISTICS Annual Sales: $2.0 billion. Number of Employees: 5,750.

EXPERTISE/EDUCATION SOUGHT: Chemical engineering, chemistry, biochemistry

CONTACT: Mr William Dugle, Vice President of Human Resources; Phone (908) 205-6000.

ENRON CORPORATION
1400 SMITH STREET
HOUSTON, TEXAS 77002

OVERVIEW: Conducts oil and gas exploration, production, and pipeline transportation. Established: 1930.

EXPERTISE/EDUCATION SOUGHT: Civil engineering, petroleum/petrochemical engineering, finance, chemical engineering, accounting, computer programming, marketing

CONTACT: Ms Diane Johnson, Senior Human Resources Representative; Phone (713) 853-6161.

ENTERGY CORPORATION
639 LOYALA AVENUE
NEW ORLEANS, LOUISIANA 70115

OVERVIEW: Electric utility.

EXPERTISE/EDUCATION SOUGHT: Accounting, finance, data processing, sales, marketing

CONTACT: Mr Joe Hotard, Corporate Director of Employee Relations; Phone (504) 529-5262.

ENTERPRISE RENT-A-CAR
600 CORPORATE PARK DRIVE
SAINT LOUIS, MISSOURI 63105-2046

OVERVIEW: Provides automobile rental and leasing services. Established: 1957. Parent Company: Crawford Group, Inc.

KEY STATISTICS Annual Sales: $1.0 billion. Number of Employees: 18,000.

HIRING HISTORY Number of professional employees hired in 1993: 3,000.

EXPERTISE/EDUCATION SOUGHT: Sales, marketing, business management, information systems, business administration

CONTACT: Mr Craig A Marr, Corporate Human Resources Manager; Phone (314) 512-2320.

CORPORATE PROFILE

The Company. *Enterprise Rent-A-Car's phenomenal success has been driven by a fast-track approach to business, a philosophy that recognizes the importance of superlative customer service, and a professional staff comprised of entrepreneurial, enthusiastic, and highly motivated people.*

Job Opportunities/Career Development. *Enterprise Rent-A-Car is a people-driven company that is propelled by the highest standards of excellence. With the company's decentralized style of management, employees will be given every opportunity to grow to their fullest potential. Enterprise cultivates employees' stengths and helps them work on those areas that need attention.*

A management trainee's career begins with a thorough training program in how to provide the company's customers with a uniformly high level of personal service. The training covers everything from customer contact to administration, sales, and marketing. From the start, the trainee's goal will be to become a **branch manager.** *Depending upon initiative, adeptness at handling customers, and how quickly an individual trainee is able to grasp the fundamentals, advancement can be very fast.*

To qualify, applicants should have a demonstrated ability to organize and prioritize their goals. Strong leadership skills are essential, and applicants must be able to function effectively in a team setting.

Benefits. *Enterprise Rent-A-Car offers a competitive starting salary backed by a comprehensive benefits program that includes health, dental, life, and long-term disability insurance, profit sharing, 401(k) plan, sick days, sick leave, paid vacations, and personal days, as well as paid holidays. Upon reaching management, an individual can look forward to a base salary that's augmented by a percentage of the operation's profit.*

To obtain more information or arrange a personal interview, please contact the human resource supervisor or manager at the Enterprise Rent-A-Car office in your area, or send a résumé along with geographical preference to the address listed above. Internships are available.

Enterprise Rent-A-Car is an equal opportunity employer.

EQUIFAX, INC.
1600 PEACHTREE STREET NORTHWEST
ATLANTA, GEORGIA 30309-2468

OVERVIEW: Provides credit reports and consumer marketing information. Established: 1899.

KEY STATISTICS Annual Sales: $1.0 billion. Number of Employees: 12,800.

HIRING HISTORY Number of professional employees hired in 1994: 100.

EXPERTISE/EDUCATION SOUGHT: Marketing, health insurance, finance, actuarial, accounting, data processing, computer programming, law, auditing

CONTACTS: For college students and recent graduates: Job Line; Phone (404) 885-8550. For individuals with previous experience: Ms Betty Adams, Human Resources Recruiter; Phone (404) 885-8160.

EQUITABLE COMPANIES, INC.
787 7TH AVENUE
NEW YORK, NEW YORK 10019-6018

OVERVIEW: Provides insurance underwriting and investment advisory services.

KEY STATISTICS Assets: $6.0 billion. Number of Employees: 21,291.

EXPERTISE/EDUCATION SOUGHT: Accounting, finance, actuarial, real estate, law, health insurance, credit/credit analysis, collection, computer programming

CONTACTS: For college students and recent graduates: Mr John O'Hara, Vice President of Staffing and Placement; Phone (212) 554-2198. For individuals with previous experience: Ms Janet Friedman, Vice President of Human Resource Services; Phone (212) 554-1234.

ERICSSON, INC.
ONE TRIANGLE DRIVE
RESEARCH TRIANGLE PARK
NORTH CAROLINA 27709

OVERVIEW: Researches and developments wireless communications equipment. Established: 1957.

KEY STATISTICS Annual Sales: $342.0 million. Number of Employees: 4,000.

EXPERTISE/EDUCATION SOUGHT: Software engineering/development, radio frequency engineering, mechanical engineering, electronics/electronics engineering, research and development, digital technology

CONTACT: Mr Ernie Leskovec, Consultant; Phone (919) 990-7202.

ERNST AND YOUNG, LLP.
787 SEVENTH AVENUE
NEW YORK, NEW YORK 10172-0002

OVERVIEW: Provides accounting and consulting services. Established: 1894.

KEY STATISTICS Annual Sales: $2.0 billion. Number of Employees: 20,000.

EXPERTISE/EDUCATION SOUGHT: Accounting, tax, consulting, information systems, business administration, tax accounting, health care, finance

CONTACT: For individuals with previous experience: Mr Ed Brodie, Director of Recruitment.

ESAB WELDING AND CUTTING PRODUCTS, INC.
411 SOUTH EBENEZER ROAD
FLORENCE, SOUTH CAROLINA 29501

OVERVIEW: Manufactures welding equipment and supplies. Established: 1984. Parent Company: ESAB of Sweden, AB.

EXPERTISE/EDUCATION SOUGHT: Electrical engineering, electronics/electronics engineering, mechanical engineering, marketing, accounting, sales, data processing, computer science

CONTACT: For individuals with previous experience: Ms Phyllis Andrews, Manager of Human Resources; Phone (803) 664-4219.

ESTEE LAUDER, INC.
767 5TH AVENUE
NEW YORK, NEW YORK 10153-0002

OVERVIEW: Manufactures and sells cosmetics and fragrances. Established: 1946. Parent Company: EJL Corporation.

EXPERTISE/EDUCATION SOUGHT: Mechanical engineering, industrial engineering, accounting

CONTACT: For individuals with previous experience: Ms Marian Beatty, Vice President of Human Resources; Phone (212) 572-4200.

ETHYL CORPORATION
330 SOUTH 4TH STREET
RICHMOND, VIRGINIA 23217

OVERVIEW: Manufactures petrochemicals, industrial chemicals, and plastics. Established: 1887.

KEY STATISTICS Number of Employees: 1,750.

HIRING HISTORY Number of professional employees hired in 1994: 50. 1993: 60.

EXPERTISE/EDUCATION SOUGHT: Accounting, computer programming, finance, marketing, chemical engineering, physics

CONTACT: For individuals with previous experience: Mr Ernie Delia, Manager of Human Resources; Phone (804) 788-5674.

EVANGELICAL LUTHERAN GOOD SAMARITAN HOSPITAL
4860 WEST 57TH STREET
SIOUX FALLS, SOUTH DAKOTA 57106-1332

OVERVIEW: Provides long term health care and retirement living services. Established: 1922.

KEY STATISTICS Annual Sales: $404.0 million. Number of Employees: 16,600.

EXPERTISE/EDUCATION SOUGHT: Analog engineering, accounting, physical therapy, management

CONTACT: For individuals with previous experience: Ms Sonja Norine, Manager of Employment.

EVEREADY BATTERY COMPANY, INC.
PO BOX 450777
WESTLAKE, OHIO 44145

OVERVIEW: Manufactures batteries and battery chargers. Established: 1894. Parent Company: Ralston Purina Company.

KEY STATISTICS Annual Sales: $2.0 billion. Number of Employees: 16,400.

EXPERTISE/EDUCATION SOUGHT: Mechanical engineering, operations, quality engineering

CONTACT: Ms Gail E Holmes, Human Resources Administrator - Recruiting; Phone (216) 835-7826; Fax (216)835-7837.

EXCEL INDUSTRIES, INC.
1120 NORTH MAIN STREET
ELKHART, INDIANA 46514-3203

OVERVIEW: Manufactures automotive doors and windows. Established: 1928.

KEY STATISTICS Number of Employees: 3,500.

HIRING HISTORY Number of professional employees hired in 1994: 100.

EXPERTISE/EDUCATION SOUGHT: Finance, sales, marketing, engineering, design engineering, product engineering, manufacturing engineering, research and development

CONTACT: For individuals with previous experience: Mr Larry Knight, Corporate Manager of Recruitment; Phone (219) 264-2131, ext. 295.

EXPRESS, INC.
1 LIMITED PARKWAY
COLUMBUS, OHIO 43230

OVERVIEW: Operates chain of women's apparel stores.

KEY STATISTICS Annual Sales: $2.0 billion. Number of Employees: 15,000.

HIRING HISTORY Number of professional employees hired in 1994: 106.

EXPERTISE/EDUCATION SOUGHT: Merchandising, finance, management information systems

CONTACT: For individuals with previous experience: Mr Ed Jones, Director Executive Recruitment, PO Box 181000, Columbus, OH, 43218; Phone (614) 479-4000.

EXXON CORPORATION
225 EAST JOHN CARPENTER FREEWAY
IRVING, TEXAS 75062

OVERVIEW: Operates diversified oil business. Established: 1882.

EXPERTISE/EDUCATION SOUGHT: Treasury management, law, finance, economics

CONTACT: Mr Edward Price, Client Coordinator; Phone (214) 444-1887.

FABRI-CENTERS OF AMERICA, INC.
5555 DARROW ROAD
HUDSON, OHIO 44236-4011

OVERVIEW: Operates chain of fabric stores. Established: 1943.

KEY STATISTICS Number of Employees: 11,400.

EXPERTISE/EDUCATION SOUGHT: Retail, purchasing, warehousing, management information systems, computer programming

CONTACT: Ms Nyla Harrison, Director of Human Resources; Phone (216) 656-2600.

FAMILY RESTAURANTS, INC.
18831 VAN KARMAN AVENUE
IRVINE, CALIFORNIA 92715-1533

OVERVIEW: Owns and operates restaurants. Established: 1986.

KEY STATISTICS Annual Sales: $1.0 billion. Number of Employees: 56,200.

EXPERTISE/EDUCATION SOUGHT: Accounting, computer programming, marketing

CONTACT: For individuals with previous experience: Ms Julie Notley, Director of Admissions; Phone (714) 757-7900.

FAMOUS FOOTWEAR
208 EAST OLIN AVENUE
MADISON, WISCONSIN 53713

OVERVIEW: Operates chain of retail shoe stores. Established: 1961. Parent Company: Brown Group, Inc.

KEY STATISTICS Number of Employees: 7,500.

HIRING HISTORY Number of professional employees hired in 1994: 500.

EXPERTISE/EDUCATION SOUGHT: Accounting, sales, computer programming, information systems, merchandising

CONTACTS: For college students and recent graduates: Ms Annie Somermeyer, Recruitment and Training Manager; Phone (608) 284-6479; Fax (608) 284-6353. For individuals with previous experience: Ms Mary Kay Baldino, Employment Coordinator; Phone (608) 284-6479; Fax (608) 284-6353.

CORPORATE PROFILE

Background. *Famous Footwear, a division of Brown Group, Inc., is one of the fastest-growing brand name shoe retailers in America.*

The Famous Footwear story began in 1961 with the opening of the company's first store in Madison, Wisconsin. The company's motto then, "Quality Brand Name Shoes for Less," has stood the test of time and has fueled its rapid expansion.

Thirty-four years, 725+ stores coast to coast, the motto "Brand Name Shoes for Less. That's What Makes Us Famous" continue to fuel Famous Footwear's aggressive expansion plans, which include opening more than 100 stores a year. The company is coast to coast, making America famous.

Opportunities. *Famous Footwear offers professionals the promise of a challenging career and is committed to its customers and its employees.*

Employment opportunities begin at the store level. A new Famous Footwear assistant manager is taken through a competency-based training program. The company takes the time to teach a new assistant the successful balance between people, sales, expenses, and profits.

The next step, store manager, is achieved by those who are self-driven and motivated and who have proven their management abilities. Beyond store management, there are positions in field supervision—area, district, and regional sales management—as well as positions within the corporate structure.

Benefits. *The benefits of employment with Famous Footwear include a flexible schedule; medical, dental, and life insurance; vacation, holidays, and a wellness bonus; a 401(k) and stock purchase plan; a sales incentive program; an educational assistance program; and much more.*

FARAH USA, INC.
8889 GATEWAY BOULEVARD WEST
EL PASO, TEXAS 79985

OVERVIEW: Manufactures and markets clothing and apparel. Established: 1920.

EXPERTISE/EDUCATION SOUGHT: Chemistry, computer programming, computer science

CONTACT: Mr Frank Marroquin, Director of Human Resources; Phone (915) 593-4251.

FARMER JACK
18718 BORMAN STREET
DETROIT, MICHIGAN 48228-1112

OVERVIEW: Operates food stores and sells frozen desserts. Established: 1928. Parent Company: Great Atlantic and Pacific Tea Company, Inc.

KEY STATISTICS Number of Employees: 8,500.

EXPERTISE/EDUCATION SOUGHT: Marketing, finance, accounting, sales, merchandising, operations

CONTACT: For individuals with previous experience: Ms Mary Holden, Director of Personnel; Phone (313) 270-1354.

FARMER'S INSURANCE EXCHANGE
4680 WILSHIRE BOULEVARD
LOS ANGELES, CALIFORNIA 90010-3807

OVERVIEW: Provides automobile and life insurance. Established: 1928.

KEY STATISTICS Annual Sales: $4.0 billion. Number of Employees: 6,817.

HIRING HISTORY Number of professional employees hired in 1994: 800.

EXPERTISE/EDUCATION SOUGHT: Accounting, actuarial, underwriting, marketing, computer programming, finance, investment, claims adjustment/examination

CONTACT: Mr Steve Ladd, Assistant Vice President of Human Resources; Phone (213) 932-3591.

FARMLAND FOODS, INC.
10150 NORTH EXECUTIVE HILLS BOULEVARD
KANSAS CITY, MISSOURI 64153

OVERVIEW: Produces and sells processed meats. Established: 1966. Parent Company: Farmland Industries, Inc.

KEY STATISTICS Annual Sales: $854.2 million. Number of Employees: 4,000.

EXPERTISE/EDUCATION SOUGHT: Marketing, sales, accounting, finance

CONTACT: Ms Joyce Hurt, Human Resources Director; Phone (816) 891-1200.

FARMLAND INDUSTRIES, INC.
3315 NORTH OAK TRAFFICWAY
KANSAS CITY, MISSOURI 64116-2798

OVERVIEW: Manufactures and distributes feed, fertilizer, and chemicals; markets grain; processes beef and pork products. Established: 1929.

KEY STATISTICS Number of Employees: 12,700.

EXPERTISE/EDUCATION SOUGHT: Data processing, accounting, finance, sales, marketing, advertising, economics

CONTACT: For individuals with previous experience: Mr Levy Snow, Manager of Employment and Development; Phone (816) 459-6363.

FAY'S, INC.
7245 HENRY CLAY BOULEVARD
LIVERPOOL, NEW YORK 13088-3523

OVERVIEW: Operates chain of auto parts stores. Established: 1958.

KEY STATISTICS Annual Sales: $920.0 million. Number of Employees: 9,000.

HIRING HISTORY Number of professional employees hired in 1993: 50.

EXPERTISE/EDUCATION SOUGHT: Retail, distribution, accounting, human resources, finance, marketing, advertising

CONTACTS: For college students and recent graduates: Ms Cat Patterelli, Personnel Recruitor; Phone (315) 451-8000, ext. 2477. For individuals with previous experience: Mr Bill Scollion, Director of Human Resources, Wheels Division, 4577 Buckley Drive, Liverpool, NY, 13088; Phone (315) 652-7000, ext. 3219; Fax (315)652-3843.

FEDDERS CORPORATION
158 HIGHWAY 206
LIBERTY CORNER, NEW JERSEY 07938

OVERVIEW: Manufactures air conditioning equipment. Established: 1896.

KEY STATISTICS Annual Sales: $159.0 million. Number of Employees: 1,100.

EXPERTISE/EDUCATION SOUGHT: Law, accounting, finance, administration

CONTACT: For individuals with previous experience: Human Resources Department, Westgate Corporate Center, PO Box 813, Liberty Corner, NJ, 07938; Phone (908) 234-2100.

FEDERAL EMPLOYEES DISTRIBUTING COMPANY
9300 SANTA FE SPRINGS ROAD
SANTA FE SPRINGS, CALIFORNIA 90670-2621

OVERVIEW: Operates discount retail stores. Established: 1949.

KEY STATISTICS Number of Employees: 5,500.

EXPERTISE/EDUCATION SOUGHT: Warehousing, accounting, computer science, pharmacy, merchandising, finance, sales, optics

CONTACTS: For college students and recent graduates: Ms Vicki Jacobson, Manager of Human Resources; Phone (310) 946-2511. For individuals with previous experience: Mr Ron Biggs, Vice President of Human Resources.

FEDERAL HOME LOAN AND MORTGAGE CORPORATION
8200 JONES BRANCH DRIVE
MC LEAN, VIRGINIA 22102-3107

OVERVIEW: Provides mortgage services. Established: 1970.

KEY STATISTICS Annual Sales: $5.0 billion. Number of Employees: 2,929.

EXPERTISE/EDUCATION SOUGHT: Accounting, public relations, computer programming, risk management, communications, advertising, finance, sales, government affairs/relations

CONTACT: Ms Suzzane Withers, Director of Employment; Phone (703) 903-2850.

FEDERAL INSURANCE COMPANY
15 MOUNTAINVIEW ROAD
WARREN, NEW JERSEY 07059-6711

OVERVIEW: Provides property and casualty insurance. Established: 1967. Parent Company: Chubb Corporation.

KEY STATISTICS Number of Employees: 9,500.

EXPERTISE/EDUCATION SOUGHT: Computer programming, accounting, program analysis, network analysis, actuarial, systems analysis

CONTACT: For individuals with previous experience: Ms Judy Sullivan, Human Resources Representative, PO Box 1615, Warren, NJ, 07061; Phone (908) 903-2057.

FEDERAL MOGUL CORPORATION
26555 NORTHWESTERN HIGHWAY
SOUTHFIELD, MICHIGAN 48034-2199

OVERVIEW: Manufactures and distributes automotive parts. Established: 1900.

KEY STATISTICS Number of Employees: 14,400.

EXPERTISE/EDUCATION SOUGHT: Finance, sales, distribution, logistics

CONTACTS: For college students and recent graduates: Mr Reginald Brown, Manager of Human Resources; Phone (810) 354-7700, ext. 9856. For individuals with previous experience: Ms Jacqueline Coburn, Employment Supervisor; Phone (810) 354-2690.

FEDERAL NATIONAL MORTGAGE ASSOCIATION
3900 WISCONSIN AVENUE NORTHWEST
WASHINGTON, D.C. 20016-2892

OVERVIEW: Provides mortgage services. Established: 1938.

KEY STATISTICS Assets: $16.0 billion. Number of Employees: 3,400.

EXPERTISE/EDUCATION SOUGHT: Accounting, computer science, management information systems, finance, actuarial, auditing, underwriting

CONTACT: Ms Marion LeMaire, Director of Staffing; Phone (202) 752-7000.

FEDERAL PAPER BOARD COMPANY
75 CHESTNUT RIDGE ROAD
MONTVALE, NEW JERSEY 07645

OVERVIEW: Manufactures pulp, paper, and wood products. Established: 1916.

EXPERTISE/EDUCATION SOUGHT: Electrical engineering, mechanical engineering

CONTACT: Mr Barry Smedstad, Manager of Human Resources, PO Box 357, Montvale, NJ, 07643; Phone (201) 391-1776.

FEDERAL RESERVE BANK OF NEW YORK
33 LIBERTY STREET
NEW YORK, NEW YORK 10045-0001

OVERVIEW: Federal Reserve bank. Established: 1913.

EXPERTISE/EDUCATION SOUGHT: Economics, finance, accounting, computer programming, network analysis

CONTACTS: For college students and recent graduates: Ms Lisa Gasperini, Director of College Relations; Phone (212) 720-6557. For individuals with previous experience: Ms Patricia Cabello, Staffing Director; Phone (212) 720-5000.

FEDERAL RESERVE BANK OF RICHMOND
701 EAST BYRD STREET
RICHMOND, VIRGINIA 23219-4528

OVERVIEW: Federal Reserve bank. Established: 1914.

KEY STATISTICS Number of Employees: 2,434.

EXPERTISE/EDUCATION SOUGHT: Finance, accounting, business administration, economics

CONTACT: For individuals with previous experience: Ms Hattie Barley, Personnel Manager; Phone (804) 697-8000.

FEDERATED DEPARTMENT STORES
7 WEST 7TH STREET
CINCINNATI, OHIO 45202

OVERVIEW: Owns and operates retail department stores. Established: 1929.

EXPERTISE/EDUCATION SOUGHT: Sales, marketing, accounting, computer programming, program analysis, project management, law, auditing

CONTACT: For individuals with previous experience: Ms Mary Bennett, Manager Human Resources; Phone (513) 579-7253.

FEDEX CORPORATION
3035 DIRECTORS ROAD
MEMPHIS, TENNESSEE 38132-1796

OVERVIEW: Provides package delivery and courier services. Established: 1971.

KEY STATISTICS Annual Sales: $8.0 billion. Number of Employees: 101,000.

EXPERTISE/EDUCATION SOUGHT: Marketing, data processing, accounting, computer programming, finance, law, mechanical engineering, electrical engineering

CONTACT: Ms Linda Pappas, Manager of Corporate Employment; Phone (901) 397-4300.

FEL-PRO, INC.
7450 NORTH MCCORMICK BOULEVARD, PO BOX 1103
SKOKIE, ILLINOIS 60076

OVERVIEW: Manufactures automotive gasket and chemical products. Established: 1918.

EXPERTISE/EDUCATION SOUGHT: Accounting

CONTACT: Ms Kelly Kane, Recruitment and Employment Manager; Phone (208) 568-2595.

FERGUSON ENTERPRISES, INC.
618 BLAND AVENUE
NEWPORT NEWS, VIRGINIA 23602

OVERVIEW: Distributes industrial supplies. Established: 1953.

KEY STATISTICS Number of Employees: 3,500.

EXPERTISE/EDUCATION SOUGHT: Sales, management, purchasing

CONTACT: Ms Audry Clegg, Manager of Recruiting; Phone (804) 874-7795.

FERRO CORPORATION
1000 LAKESIDE AVENUE EAST
CLEVELAND, OHIO 44114-1147

OVERVIEW: Manufactures pigments, coatings, glass, composites, and compounds. Established: 1919.

KEY STATISTICS Number of Employees: 6,535.

EXPERTISE/EDUCATION SOUGHT: Accounting, purchasing

CONTACTS: For college students and recent graduates: Mr Paul Richard, Director of Human Resources; Phone (216) 641-8580. For individuals with previous experience: Ms Judy Miller, Corporate Manager of Employment.

FHP, INC.
9900 TALBERT AVENUE
FOUNTAIN VALLEY, CALIFORNIA 92708-5153

OVERVIEW: Health maintenance organization. Established: 1971. Parent Company: FHP International Corporation.

KEY STATISTICS Number of Employees: 11,500.

EXPERTISE/EDUCATION SOUGHT: Computer programming, marketing, sales, finance, accounting, data processing

CONTACT: Mr Peter Chart, Director of Corporate Executive Staffing; Phone (714) 963-3965; Fax (714)964-6075.

FHP TAKECARE
2300 CLAYTON ROAD, SUITE 100
CONCORD, CALIFORNIA 94520

OVERVIEW: Provides insurance and operates HMO. Established: 1978.

EXPERTISE/EDUCATION SOUGHT: Registered nursing, accounting, underwriting

CONTACT: For individuals with previous experience: Mr Crage Hurty, Manager of Human Resources, 2300 Clayton Road, Suite 1000, Concord, CA, 94520; Phone (510) 246-1300.

FIDELITY AND DEPOSIT COMPANY
300 SAINT PAUL PLACE
BALTIMORE, MARYLAND 21202

OVERVIEW: Insurance and bonding company. Established: 1890.

KEY STATISTICS Number of Employees: 1,229.

EXPERTISE/EDUCATION SOUGHT: Actuarial, underwriting, business

CONTACTS: For college students and recent graduates: Human Resources Services; Phone (410) 528-2516. For individuals with previous experience: Ms Joan Meyers, Employment Supervisor.

FIDELITY INVESTMENT
82 DEVONSHIRE STREET
BOSTON, MASSACHUSETTS 02109

OVERVIEW: Investment advisory firm.

EXPERTISE/EDUCATION SOUGHT: Management information systems, finance, accounting

CONTACT: Ms Anne E Spangher, College Relations Manager; Phone (617) 720-3691.

FIELD CONTAINER COMPANY, LP.
1500 NICHOLAS BOULEVARD
ELK GROVE VILLAGE, ILLINOIS 60007-5516

OVERVIEW: Manufactures paperboard products and ink.

KEY STATISTICS Annual Sales: $400.0 million. Number of Employees: 2,500.

EXPERTISE/EDUCATION SOUGHT: Training and development

CONTACT: For individuals with previous experience: Mr Rich Johnson, Human Resources Associate; Phone (208) 956-3224.

FIELDCREST CANNON, INC.
326 EAST STADIUM DRIVE
EDEN, NORTH CAROLINA 27288-3523

OVERVIEW: Manufactures sheets, bedding, and towels. Established: 1953. Parent Company: Downeast Securities Corporation.

KEY STATISTICS Number of Employees: 14,090.

EXPERTISE/EDUCATION SOUGHT: Business management, chemical analysis, product management, marketing, finance, textiles

CONTACT: For individuals with previous experience: Dr Brian Bergman, Director of Human Resources Development; Phone (910) 627-3048.

FIESTA MART, INC.
5235 KATY FREEWAY
HOUSTON, TEXAS 77007-2210

OVERVIEW: Operates chain of food stores. Established: 1972.

KEY STATISTICS Annual Sales: $578.6 million. Number of Employees: 6,200.

EXPERTISE/EDUCATION SOUGHT: Accounting, finance, computer programming, retail management

CONTACT: Ms Debra Van Matre, Employment Manager.

FIFTH THIRD BANCORP
38 FOUNTAIN SQUARE PLAZA
CINCINNATI, OHIO 45263

OVERVIEW: Commercial bank. Established: 1975.

KEY STATISTICS Number of Employees: 4,938.

HIRING HISTORY Number of professional employees hired in 1994: 145. 1993: 120.

EXPERTISE/EDUCATION SOUGHT: Accounting, computer programming, finance, marketing, auditing, sales, retail

CONTACTS: For college students and recent graduates: Ms Janine LaFica, College Recruiting and Associate Program Manager; Phone (513) 744-8983. For individuals with previous experience: Mr Mark Brandt, Manager of Human Resources; Phone (513) 579-5300.

50-OFF STORES, INC.
8750 TESORO DRIVE
SAN ANTONIO, TEXAS 78217-6221

OVERVIEW: Operates chain of apparel, housewares, gift, stationary, and hobby shops. Established: 1986.

KEY STATISTICS Annual Sales: $199.6 million. Number of Employees: 3,008.

EXPERTISE/EDUCATION SOUGHT: Retail management, merchandising

CONTACT: Mr Cliff Gillette, Human Resource Manager; Phone (210) 805-9300.

FIGGIE INTERNATIONAL, INC.
4420 SHERWIN ROAD
WILLOUGHBY, OHIO 44094-7938

OVERVIEW: Manufactures fire fighting and protection equipment. Established: 1910.

KEY STATISTICS Annual Sales: $769.0 million. Number of Employees: 12,600.

EXPERTISE/EDUCATION SOUGHT: Electrical engineering, mechanical engineering, manufacturing engineering, production, design engineering, accounting, quality control, finance

CONTACT: For individuals with previous experience: Mr William Sickman, Director of Manpower Development; Phone (216) 953-2700.

FINA OIL AND PETROLEUM, INC.
PO BOX 2159
DALLAS, TEXAS 75221

OVERVIEW: Produces and distributes petroleum, gas, and chemical products. Established: 1956.

EXPERTISE/EDUCATION SOUGHT: Chemical engineering, sales, mechanical engineering, law, petroleum/petrochemical engineering, marketing, accounting

CONTACT: Ms Karen Rupple, Senior Staff Human Resources Representative; Phone (214) 750-2400.

FINANCIAL INSTITUTIONS, INC.
55 NORTH MAIN STREET
WARSAW, NEW YORK 14569-1325

OVERVIEW: Commercial bank. Established: 1931.

KEY STATISTICS Annual Sales: $43.0 million. Number of Employees: 427.

EXPERTISE/EDUCATION SOUGHT: Finance, accounting, real estate

CONTACT: For individuals with previous experience: Ms Regina Colegrove, Manager of Human Resources; Phone (716) 786-3131.

FINGERHUT CORPORATION
4400 BAKER ROAD
MINNETONKA, MINNESOTA 55343-8699

OVERVIEW: Provides catalog and mail order services. Established: 1948. Parent Company: Fingerhut Companies, Inc.

KEY STATISTICS Annual Sales: $1.0 billion. Number of Employees: 6,500.

HIRING HISTORY Number of professional employees hired in 1993: 400.

EXPERTISE/EDUCATION SOUGHT: Marketing, information systems, merchandising, finance

CONTACT: Mr Robert Cocker, Director of Human Resources; Phone (612) 932-3100, ext. 3410.

FINLAY ENTERPRISES, INC.
521 5TH AVENUE
NEW YORK, NEW YORK 10175-0003

OVERVIEW: Sells jewelry, watches, and precious stones.

KEY STATISTICS Annual Sales: $506.0 million. Number of Employees: 6,000.

EXPERTISE/EDUCATION SOUGHT: Retail management, merchandising

CONTACT: For individuals with previous experience: Ms Ilana Brajer, Director of Executive Recruitment and Development; Phone (212) 808-2069.

FIREMAN'S FUND INSURANCE COMPANY
777 SAN MARIN DRIVE
NOVATO, CALIFORNIA 94998-0001

OVERVIEW: Provides property and casualty insurance to businesses and individuals. Established: 1863. Parent Company: Allianz of America, Inc.

KEY STATISTICS Assets: $3.3 billion. Number of Employees: 8,200.

EXPERTISE/EDUCATION SOUGHT: Accounting, auditing, actuarial, finance, law, real estate, product design and development, underwriting, claims adjustment/examination, human resources

CONTACTS: For college students and recent graduates: Mr Dave Howitt, Assistant Vice President Human Resources. For individuals with previous experience: Mr Larry Kotch, Vice President of Human Resources; Phone (415) 899-3255.

FIRST ALABAMA BANK
417 20TH STREET NORTH
BIRMINGHAM, ALABAMA 35203-3203

OVERVIEW: Provides commercial banking services. Parent Company: Regions Financial Corporation.

KEY STATISTICS Annual Sales: $556.0 million. Number of Employees: 5,420.

EXPERTISE/EDUCATION SOUGHT: Customer service and support, finance, financial analysis, accounting, credit/credit analysis

CONTACT: For individuals with previous experience: Ms Michelle Roth, Employment Manager; Phone (205) 326-7251.

FIRST AMERICA HEALTHCARE, INC.
3528 DARIEN HIGHWAY
BRUNSWICK, GEORGIA 31525-2401

OVERVIEW: Provides home healthcare services.

KEY STATISTICS Annual Sales: $500.0 million. Number of Employees: 8,000.

EXPERTISE/EDUCATION SOUGHT: Program analysis, computer programming, accounting, marketing

CONTACT: For individuals with previous experience: Mr Ernest Streicher, Manager of Recruitment and Employment; Phone (912) 264-1940.

FIRST BANK SYSTEM, INC.
601 SECOND AVENUE SOUTH, PO BOX A512
MINNEAPOLIS, MINNESOTA 55402-4303

OVERVIEW: Bank holding company. Established: 1929.

KEY STATISTICS Number of Employees: 12,300.

EXPERTISE/EDUCATION SOUGHT: Accounting, computer programming, finance, marketing, actuarial, business management

CONTACTS: For college students and recent graduates: Ms Stephanie Saffold, Senior Human Resources Counsel; Phone (612) 973-1111. For individuals with previous experience: Ms Cynthia Haugh, Human Resources Recruiter; Phone (612) 973-2425.

FIRST BRANDS CORPORATION
83 WOOSTER HEIGHTS
DANBURY, CONNECTICUT 06813-1911

OVERVIEW: Manufactures and markets consumer, household, and automotive products.

KEY STATISTICS Annual Sales: $1.0 billion. Number of Employees: 3,750.

EXPERTISE/EDUCATION SOUGHT: Chemical engineering, computer programming, mechanical engineering, electrical engineering, sales, industrial engineering, accounting

First Brands Corporation (continued)

Contact: Mr Doug Bobay, Manager of Recruiting; Phone (203) 731-2091.

FIRST CHICAGO CORPORATION
1 FIRST NATIONAL PLAZA
CHICAGO, ILLINOIS 60670

Overview: Provides diversified financial services. Established: 1969. Parent Company: First Chicago Corporation.

Key Statistics Assets: $1.0 billion. Number of Employees: 12,775.

Expertise/Education Sought: Auditing, management information systems, finance, business management, credit/credit analysis, financial analysis

Contact: For individuals with previous experience: Mr Robert Chrismer, Vice President of Development and Training; Phone (312) 407-3139.

FIRST DATA CORPORATION
401 HACKENSACK AVENUE
HACKENSACK, NEW JERSEY 07601-6411

Overview: Provides information processing services. Established: 1989. Parent Company: American Express Company.

Key Statistics Annual Sales: $1.0 billion. Number of Employees: 21,800.

Expertise/Education Sought: Computer programming, customer service and support, information systems, software engineering/development, sales, marketing, accounting, finance

Contacts: For college students and recent graduates: Mr Steve Luha, Director Professional Recruitment, 1178 Nicholas Street, Omaha, NE, 68154; Phone (402) 222-3170. For individuals with previous experience: Mr Donald Crowley, Senior Vice President Human Resources.

FIRST FIDELITY BANK CORPORATION
550 BROAD STREET
NEWARK, NEW JERSEY 07102

Overview: Commercial bank holding company. Established: 1969.

Key Statistics Assets: $2.0 billion. Number of Employees: 12,000.

Expertise/Education Sought: Accounting, finance, law, auditing, real estate

Contact: Mr Charles Schwenk, Senior Vice President and Deputy Director of Human Resources; Phone (201) 565-5775.

FIRST FINANCIAL MANAGEMENT CORPORATION
3 CORPORATE SQUARE NORTHEAST
ATLANTA, GEORGIA 30329-2013

Overview: Provides credit card authorization and check processing services. Established: 1971.

Key Statistics Annual Sales: $2.0 billion. Number of Employees: 11,500.

Hiring History Number of professional employees hired in 1993: 12.

Expertise/Education Sought: Systems analysis, computer programming, accounting, finance

Contact: For individuals with previous experience: Mr Frank Malone, Director of Human Resources; Phone (404) 321-0120.

FIRST INTERSTATE BANCORP
707 WILSHIRE BOULEVARD
LOS ANGELES, CALIFORNIA 90071-2005

Overview: Commercial bank holding company. Established: 1859.

Key Statistics Number of Employees: 26,589.

Expertise/Education Sought: Accounting, finance, auditing, real estate, mortgage, credit/credit analysis

Contacts: For college students and recent graduates: Ms Becky Johns, Corporate Recruiter; Phone (213) 614-7743. For individuals with

previous experience: Mr Ken Bertok, Vice President of Human Resources, 707 Wilshire Blvd W25-23, Los Angeles, CA, 90017; Phone (213) 641-7743.

FIRST INVESTORS CORPORATION
95 WALL STREET
NEW YORK, NEW YORK 10005-4297

Overview: Investment and life insurance firm. Established: 1930.

Key Statistics Assets: $4.0 billion. Number of Employees: 1,500.

Expertise/Education Sought: Finance, general insurance, marketing, sales, management, computer programming

Contact: Mr Thomas P Barden, National Recruiting Director, 570 Taxter Road, Department - JO96, Elmsford, NY, 10523; Phone (914) 592-0100.

THE FIRST NATIONAL BANK OF BOSTON
100 FEDERAL STREET
BOSTON, MASSACHUSETTS 02110-1802

Overview: Commercial bank. Established: 1784. Parent Company: Bank of Boston Corporation.

Key Statistics Number of Employees: 18,618.

Expertise/Education Sought: Administration, finance, credit/credit analysis

Contact: For individuals with previous experience: Mr Patrick McBride, Director of Employment, 100 Federal Street 15th Floor, Boston, MA, 02110; Phone (617) 434-2200.

FIRST NATIONAL BANK OF OHIO
106 SOUTH MAIN STREET
AKRON, OHIO 44308

Overview: Commercial bank and savings and loan institution. Established: 1890.

Key Statistics Assets: $4.0 billion. Number of Employees: 2,600.

Expertise/Education Sought: Banking

Contact: Ms Sherry Voss, Assistant Vice President of Human Resources; Phone (216) 384-8000.

FIRST OF AMERICA BANK CORPORATION
225 NORTH ROSE STREET
KALAMAZOO, MICHIGAN 49007

Overview: Bank holding company. Established: 1971.

Expertise/Education Sought: Program analysis, computer programming, systems analysis, finance, banking

Contacts: For college students and recent graduates: Ms Jennifer Crayner, Human Resources Assistant. For individuals with previous experience: Ms Cydney Kildupp, Employment and Recruiting Manager; Phone (616) 376-7689.

FIRST SUPERMARKETS
1700 ROCKSIDE ROAD
MAPLE HEIGHTS, OHIO 44137

Overview: Operates chain of food stores. Established: 1978. Parent Company: Royal Ahold (Netherlands).

Key Statistics Annual Sales: $1.0 billion. Number of Employees: 7,500.

Expertise/Education Sought: Retail management, pharmacy

Contact: Ms Patricia A Drosz, Manager of Recruitment; Phone (216) 587-7100, ext. 6750.

FIRST TENNESSEE NATIONAL CORPORATION
165 MADISON AVENUE
MEMPHIS, TENNESSEE 38103-2723

Overview: Commercial bank. Established: 1864.

Key Statistics Annual Sales: $857.0 million. Number of Employees: 6,664.

Expertise/Education Sought: Accounting, finance, investment, treasury management, credit/credit analysis, auditing

CONTACTS: For college students and recent graduates: Ms. Jennifer Scherer, Manager of College Relations, PO Box 84, Memphis, TN, 38101-8465. For individuals with previous experience: Ms Martha Seiweirt, Personnel Specialist, PO Box 84, Memphis, TN, 38101-8465; Phone (901) 523-5882.

FIRST UNION CORPORATION
1400 ONE FIRST UNION CENTER
CHARLOTTE, NORTH CAROLINA 28288-0953

OVERVIEW: Provides commercial, mortgage, and investment banking services. Established: 1967.

EXPERTISE/EDUCATION SOUGHT: Management

CONTACT: For college students and recent graduates: Ms Betsy Williams, Manager of College Recruitment; Phone (704) 374-3437.

FIRST UNION NATIONAL BANK OF FLORIDA
225 WATER STREET
JACKSONVILLE, FLORIDA 32202-5185

OVERVIEW: Commercial bank. Established: 1903. Parent Company: First Union Corporation of Florida.

KEY STATISTICS Assets: $2.0 billion. Number of Employees: 9,940.

EXPERTISE/EDUCATION SOUGHT: Telecommunications, real estate, sales, production control, actuarial, management

CONTACT: Ms Mary Carol Dickson, Manager of College Recruiting, PO Box 2080, Jacksonville, FL, 32231; Phone (904) 361-2265.

FIRST UNION NATIONAL BANK OF NORTH CAROLINA
14TH FLOOR, 301 SOUTH COLLEGE STREET
CHARLOTTE, NORTH CAROLINA 28288

OVERVIEW: Commercial bank. Established: 1968. Parent Company: First Union Corporation.

KEY STATISTICS Number of Employees: 9,135.

EXPERTISE/EDUCATION SOUGHT: Marketing, treasury management, auditing, finance, accounting, investment, automation, management, credit/credit analysis

CONTACT: Ms Kim Barnhart, Staffing Coordinator, 301 South College Street, 14th Floor, Charlotte, NC, 28288; Phone (704) 324-4683.

FISHER-PRICE, INC.
636 GIRARD AVENUE
EAST AURORA, NEW YORK 14052-1885

OVERVIEW: Manufactures and distributes toys. Established: 1936.

KEY STATISTICS Annual Sales: $700.0 million. Number of Employees: 5,600.

EXPERTISE/EDUCATION SOUGHT: Marketing, mechanical engineering, sales, accounting

CONTACT: Ms Mary MacIntoch, Manager of Employment; Phone (716) 687-3000, ext. 3681.

FKI INDUSTRIES
425 POST ROAD
FAIRFIELD, CONNECTICUT 06430

OVERVIEW: Manufactures automotive and heavy industrial equipment. Established: 1975. Parent Company: FKI Holdings, Inc.

EXPERTISE/EDUCATION SOUGHT: Accounting, finance, marketing, sales

CONTACT: Mr Bob Miller, Director of Human Resources.

FLEET FINANCIAL GROUP
50 KENNEDY PLAZA
PROVIDENCE, RHODE ISLAND 02903-2393

OVERVIEW: Commercial banking, consumer finance, and investment banking. Established: 1791.

KEY STATISTICS Annual Sales: $5.0 billion. Number of Employees: 26,000.

EXPERTISE/EDUCATION SOUGHT: Banking, finance, law, accounting

CONTACTS: For college students and recent graduates: Mr Michael L DeVaughn, Vice President of Corporate College Relations, 111 Westminster Street, Providence, RI, 02903; Phone (401) 278-5128. For individuals with previous experience: Mr Domenick Cana, Senior Vice President of Human Resources; Phone (401) 278-5800.

FLEET SERVICES CORPORATION
111 WESTMINSTER STREET
PROVIDENCE, RHODE ISLAND 02903-2305

OVERVIEW: Provides data processing services. Established: 1988. Parent Company: Fleet Financial Group, Inc.

KEY STATISTICS Annual Sales: $383.0 million. Number of Employees: 6,000.

EXPERTISE/EDUCATION SOUGHT: Network analysis, systems analysis, management information systems, program analysis, accounting, finance

CONTACT: Ms Caroline Scoenecker, Human Resources Manager, PO Box 366, Providence, RI, 02907; Phone (401) 278-6282.

FLEETGUARD, INC.
402 BNA DRIVE, SUITE 500
NASHVILLE, TENNESSEE 37217-2526

OVERVIEW: Manufactures heavy duty filters. Established: 1974. Parent Company: Cummins Engine Company, Inc.

KEY STATISTICS Annual Sales: $196.0 million. Number of Employees: 2,100.

EXPERTISE/EDUCATION SOUGHT: Computer programming, data processing, finance, sales, marketing

CONTACT: For individuals with previous experience: Ms Darnella Mosley, Manager of Human Resources; Phone (615) 367-0040.

FLEETWOOD ENTERPRISES, INC.
3125 MYERS STREET
RIVERSIDE, CALIFORNIA 92503-7638

OVERVIEW: Manufactures recreational vehicles and houses. Established: 1950.

KEY STATISTICS Number of Employees: 16,000.

HIRING HISTORY Number of professional employees hired in 1994: 94.

EXPERTISE/EDUCATION SOUGHT: Accounting, finance, marketing, computer programming, purchasing

CONTACT: Mr Louis Botka, Human Resources Director; Phone (909) 351-3500; Fax (714)351-3312.

FLEMING COMPANIES, INC.
6301 WATERFORD BOULEVARD
OKLAHOMA CITY, OKLAHOMA 73118-1103

OVERVIEW: Distributes wholesale food. Established: 1915.

KEY STATISTICS Annual Sales: $13.0 billion. Number of Employees: 43,300.

EXPERTISE/EDUCATION SOUGHT: Finance, accounting, computer science, program analysis, computer programming, management information systems

CONTACT: Ms Judy Stranczek, Manager Human Resources; Phone (405) 840-7200.

FLEXIBLE PRODUCTS COMPANY
1007 INDUSTRIAL PARK DRIVE
MARIETTA, GEORGIA 30062-2463

OVERVIEW: Manufactures ink used for logos and t-shirts.

KEY STATISTICS Number of Employees: 370.

EXPERTISE/EDUCATION SOUGHT: Business, finance, accounting, data processing, chemistry, sales

CONTACT: For individuals with previous experience: Mr J P Hinson, President; Phone (404) 428-2684.

FLINT INDUSTRIES, INC.
1624 WEST 21ST STREET
TULSA, OKLAHOMA 74107

OVERVIEW: Provides industrial and commercial construction services. Established: 1907.

EXPERTISE/EDUCATION SOUGHT: Accounting, finance, sales

CONTACT: Ms Karen Hall, Director of Human Resources, PO Box 490, Tulsa, OK, 74101-0490; Phone (918) 587-8451, ext. 441.

FLORIDA HOSPITAL MEDICAL CENTER
601 EAST ROLLINS STREET
ORLANDO, FLORIDA 32803

OVERVIEW: Owns and operates hospitals and medical centers. Established: 1908.

KEY STATISTICS Annual Sales: $736.0 million. Number of Employees: 8,500.

EXPERTISE/EDUCATION SOUGHT: Nursing, occupational therapy, physical therapy, critical care nursing, pharmacy

CONTACTS: For college students and recent graduates: Ms Smitty Hagopian, Human Resources Specialist; Phone (407) 897-1998. For individuals with previous experience: Ms Judy Bond, Manager of Employment.

FLORIDA POWER AND LIGHT COMPANY
700 UNIVERSE BOULEVARD
JUNO BEACH, FLORIDA 33408-2683

OVERVIEW: Electric utility. Established: 1984. Parent Company: FPL Group, Inc.

KEY STATISTICS Number of Employees: 12,000.

EXPERTISE/EDUCATION SOUGHT: Electrical engineering, accounting, marketing

CONTACT: Mr James King, Manager of Professional Placement, PO Box 29100, Miami, FL, 33102-9100; Phone (305) 552-4060.

FLORIDA POWER CORPORATION
3201 34TH STREET SOUTH
SAINT PETERSBURG, FLORIDA 33711-4042

OVERVIEW: Electric utility. Established: 1899. Parent Company: Florida Progress Corporation.

KEY STATISTICS Number of Employees: 6,530.

HIRING HISTORY Number of professional employees hired in 1993: 15.

EXPERTISE/EDUCATION SOUGHT: Program analysis, auditing, law, accounting, environmental

CONTACTS: For college students and recent graduates: Ms Clarrisa Surls, College Relations Coordinator; Phone (813) 866-4004. For individuals with previous experience: Dr Kathleen McNelis, PhD, Manager Human Resources Development, PO Box 14042, Saint Petersburg, FL, 33733-8042; Phone (813) 866-5151.

FLUOR DANIEL, INC.
3333 MICHELSON DRIVE
IRVINE, CALIFORNIA 92730-0625

OVERVIEW: Engineering and construction firm serving the petroleum and other process based industries. Established: 1912.

KEY STATISTICS Number of Employees: 38,532.

EXPERTISE/EDUCATION SOUGHT: Financial analysis, accounting

CONTACTS: For college students and recent graduates: Job Hotline; Phone (714) 975-5253. For individuals with previous experience: Ms Kristen Speer, Manager of Human Resources; Phone (714) 975-2000, ext. 2130.

FOLLETT COLLEGE STORES CORPORATION
2233 WEST STREET
RIVER GROVE, ILLINOIS 60171

OVERVIEW: Operates chain of college bookstores. Established: 1876.

KEY STATISTICS Annual Sales: $458.0 million. Number of Employees: 3,500.

HIRING HISTORY Number of professional employees hired in 1994: 25.

EXPERTISE/EDUCATION SOUGHT: Auditing, accounting, treasury management, payroll

CONTACT: For individuals with previous experience: Mr Lou Monoscalco, Manager/Employee Relations; Phone (708) 583-2000.

FOOD 4 LESS SUPERMARKETS, INC.
777 SOUTH HARBOR BOULEVARD
LA HABRA, CALIFORNIA 90631

OVERVIEW: Operates chain of food stores.

EXPERTISE/EDUCATION SOUGHT: Marketing, sales, business management, purchasing

CONTACT: Mr Don Ropele, Vice President of Human Resources; Phone (714) 738-2000, ext. 2315.

FOOD LION, INC.
2110 EXECUTIVE DRIVE
SALISBURY, NORTH CAROLINA 28147-9047

OVERVIEW: Operates chain of food stores. Established: 1976.

KEY STATISTICS Number of Employees: 65,494.

EXPERTISE/EDUCATION SOUGHT: Management information systems

CONTACT: For individuals with previous experience: Mr Kay Wagoner, Recruitment and Education Administrator, PO Box 1330, Salisbury, NC, 28145-9047; Phone (704) 633-8250.

FOODMAKER, INC.
9330 BALBOA AVENUE
SAN DIEGO, CALIFORNIA 92123-1516

OVERVIEW: Operates chain of fast food restaurants. Established: 1971.

KEY STATISTICS Annual Sales: $1.0 billion. Number of Employees: 23,115.

EXPERTISE/EDUCATION SOUGHT: Sales, data processing, business administration, systems integration, finance, accounting, computer programming

CONTACT: Ms Robin Jones, Manager of Human Resources; Phone (619) 571-2121; Fax (619)571-2101.

J. P. FOODSERVICE, INC.
9830 PATUXENT WOODS DRIVE
COLUMBIA, MARYLAND 21046-1561

OVERVIEW: Distributes food products.

KEY STATISTICS Annual Sales: $1.0 billion. Number of Employees: 2,500.

EXPERTISE/EDUCATION SOUGHT: Accounting, purchasing, finance, computer programming

CONTACT: Ms Janet Cathey, Manager of Human Resources; Phone (410) 312-7100.

FOODTOWN, INC.
1020 FORT STREET
MAUMEE, OHIO 43537

OVERVIEW: Operates chain of food stores.

EXPERTISE/EDUCATION SOUGHT: Sales, marketing, management

CONTACT: For individuals with previous experience: Mr Chuck North, Director of Human Resources; Phone (419) 893-9401.

FORD MOTOR COMPANY
AMERICAN ROAD
DEARBORN, MICHIGAN 48121-0890

OVERVIEW: Manufactures automobiles and trucks. Established: 1903.

KEY STATISTICS Annual Sales: $128.0 billion. Number of Employees: 337,800.

EXPERTISE/EDUCATION SOUGHT: Accounting, business administration, chemical engineering, electrical engineering, computer science, finance, human resources, management information systems, marketing, logistics

CONTACTS: For college students and recent graduates: Manager of College Relations, PO 890, Dearborn, MI, 48121-0890. For individuals with previous experience: Corporate Recruiting Office, PO Box 890, Dearborn, MI, 48121-0890.

FORT HOWARD CORPORATION
1919 SOUTH BROADWAY
GREEN BAY, WISCONSIN 54304-1919

OVERVIEW: Manufactures paper napkins, towels, and tissues. Established: 1919.

KEY STATISTICS Number of Employees: 6,800.

EXPERTISE/EDUCATION SOUGHT: Marketing, production, accounting, finance, transportation, mechanical engineering, sales

CONTACT: Ms Susan Powers, Recruiting Manager; Phone (414) 435-8821.

FOSTER WHEELER CORPORATION
PERRYVILLE CORPORATE PARK
CLINTON, NEW JERSEY 08809-4000

OVERVIEW: Provides industrial engineering and construction services. Established: 1900.

EXPERTISE/EDUCATION SOUGHT: Accounting, finance, computer programming, marketing, mechanical engineering, electrical engineering, structural engineering, environmental engineering, chemical engineering

CONTACT: Mr Paul Mahnion, Manager of Recruitment.

FOX, INC.
10201 WEST PICO BOULEVARD
LOS ANGELES, CALIFORNIA 90035

OVERVIEW: Provides network broadcasting services.

EXPERTISE/EDUCATION SOUGHT: Sales, marketing, accounting, law, finance

CONTACT: For individuals with previous experience: Human Resources Department, PO Box 900, Beverly Hills, CA, 90213; Phone (310) 277-2211.

THE FOXBORO COMPANY
33 COMMERCIAL STREET
FOXBORO, MASSACHUSETTS 02035-2525

OVERVIEW: Manufactures industrial process control equipment. Established: 1908.

KEY STATISTICS Annual Sales: $2.0 billion. Number of Employees: 6,000.

HIRING HISTORY Number of professional employees hired in 1994: 250.

EXPERTISE/EDUCATION SOUGHT: Mechanical engineering, electrical engineering, chemical engineering, computer science

CONTACT: Corporate Staffing; Fax (508)549-4486.

FOXMEYER CORPORATION
1220 SENLAC DRIVE
CAROLLTON, TEXAS 75006

OVERVIEW: Distributes pharmaceuticals and health care products.

EXPERTISE/EDUCATION SOUGHT: Business administration, finance, accounting, law, management information systems, medical technology, pharmaceutical chemistry, customer service and support, program analysis

CONTACTS: For college students and recent graduates: Ms Kathleen Smith, Senior Human Resources Representative; Phone (214) 446-4800; Fax (214) 446-4667. For individuals with previous experience: Mr Douglas Ortega, Senior Human Resources Representative; Phone (214) 446-4800.

FOXWOODS RESORT AND CASINO
39 NORWICH WESTERLY ROAD
LEDYARD, CONNECTICUT 06339-9801

OVERVIEW: Owns and operates resort hotel and casino.

KEY STATISTICS Annual Sales: $303.0 million. Number of Employees: 9,000.

EXPERTISE/EDUCATION SOUGHT: Hospitality/hotel and restaurant management

CONTACT: For individuals with previous experience: Mr Al Prudenti, Director of Human Resources, PO Box 410, Ledyard, CT, 06339; Phone (203) 887-4170.

FRANCISCAN HEALTH SYSTEM, INC.
1 MACINTYRE DRIVE
ASTON, PENNSYLVANIA 19014-1144

OVERVIEW: Provides hospital management services. Established: 1981.

KEY STATISTICS Annual Sales: $1.0 billion. Number of Employees: 12,307.

EXPERTISE/EDUCATION SOUGHT: Accounting, marketing, finance, management information systems, business management

CONTACT: For individuals with previous experience: Ms Mary Beth Grubb-Oberg, Director of Human Resources; Phone (215) 358-3950.

FRED MEYER, INC.
3800 SOUTHEAST 22ND AVENUE
PORTLAND, OREGON 97202-2999

OVERVIEW: Operates food, general merchandise, and specialty stores. Parent Company: FMI Associates, Ltd.

KEY STATISTICS Number of Employees: 25,000.

EXPERTISE/EDUCATION SOUGHT: Management

CONTACTS: For college students and recent graduates: Ms Christi Grossman, Recruiter; Phone (503) 232-8844. For individuals with previous experience: Mr Peter Gilmore, Corporate Rercruiter Director; Phone (503) 232-8844.

FREEPORT-MCMORAN, INC.
1615 POYDRAS STREET
NEW ORLEANS, LOUISIANA 70112

OVERVIEW: Provides diversified mining and petroleum exploration and production services. Established: 1981.

EXPERTISE/EDUCATION SOUGHT: Marketing, finance, sales, accounting

CONTACTS: For college students and recent graduates: Mr Todd Graver, Employment Specialist; Phone (504) 582-4000. For individuals with previous experience: Human Resources Department; Phone (504) 582-4000.

FRIENDLY'S ICE CREAM CORPORATION
1855 BOSTON ROAD
WILBRAHAM, MASSACHUSETTS 01095

OVERVIEW: Operates chain of ice cream stores and restaurants. Established: 1935.

EXPERTISE/EDUCATION SOUGHT: Marketing, management information systems, accounting, public affairs, public relations, human resources, research and development, real estate, food services, finance

CONTACTS: For college students and recent graduates: Mr Steve Davidson, Field Manager of Human Resources; Phone (413) 543-2400, ext. 2732. For individuals with previous experience: Ms Kathleen Danahy, Director of Corporate Human Resources; Phone (413) 543-2400.

FRITO-LAY, INC.

PO BOX 225458
DALLAS, TEXAS 75222-5458

OVERVIEW: Manufactures and distributes snack foods. Established: 1965. Parent Company: Pepsico, Inc.

KEY STATISTICS Number of Employees: 27,400.

EXPERTISE/EDUCATION SOUGHT: Manufacturing engineering, marketing, sales, finance

CONTACT: Staffing Department.

FRITZ COMPANIES, INC.

706 MISSION STREET, SUITE 900
SAN FRANCISCO, CALIFORNIA 94103-3113

OVERVIEW: Provides door-to-door transportation services (shipping, customs clearance, and warehousing) for exporters.

KEY STATISTICS Annual Sales: $342.0 million. Number of Employees: 3,140.

EXPERTISE/EDUCATION SOUGHT: Marketing, accounting, human resources, computer programming, importing/exporting

CONTACT: For individuals with previous experience: Ms Martha Clark, Director Human Resources; Phone (415) 904-8202.

FRONTIER CORPORATION

180 SOUTH CLINTON AVENUE
ROCHESTER, NEW YORK 14646-0002

OVERVIEW: Provides telephone and telecommunications services. Established: 1921.

KEY STATISTICS Number of Employees: 4,381.

EXPERTISE/EDUCATION SOUGHT: Accounting, computer programming, sales, finance, electrical engineering, information systems

CONTACT: Mr Christopher Carey, Corporate Staffing Manager; Phone (716) 777-1000.

FRUEHAUF TRAILER CORPORATION

111 MONUMENT CIRCLE, SUITE 3200
INDIANAPOLIS, INDIANA 42204

OVERVIEW: Manufactures truck trailers. Established: 1926. Parent Company: Terex Corporation.

KEY STATISTICS Annual Sales: $263.0 million. Number of Employees: 1,979.

EXPERTISE/EDUCATION SOUGHT: Mechanical engineering, electrical engineering, marketing, law, human resources, finance

CONTACT: For individuals with previous experience: Ms Cindy Doxstater, Manager of Human Resources, PO Box 44913, Indianapolis, IN, 42644-0913; Phone (313) 948-1300.

FRUIT OF THE LOOM, INC.

1 FRUIT OF THE LOOM DRIVE
BOWLING GREEN, KENTUCKY 42103-6401

OVERVIEW: Manufactures basic family apparel. Established: 1926.

KEY STATISTICS Annual Sales: $2.0 billion. Number of Employees: 35,000.

EXPERTISE/EDUCATION SOUGHT: Customer service and support, sales, accounting

CONTACT: Personnel Department/Corporate Recruiting, PO Box 90015, Bowling Green, KY, 42102; Phone (502) 781-6400.

FUJI PHOTO FILM, INC.

211 PUCKETT FERRY ROAD
GREENWOOD, SOUTH CAROLINA 29649-8739

OVERVIEW: Manufactures film and printing equipment. Established: 1966. Parent Company: Fujifilm America, Inc.

KEY STATISTICS Annual Sales: $65.0 million. Number of Employees: 430.

EXPERTISE/EDUCATION SOUGHT: Mechanical engineering, chemistry, industrial engineering, electrical engineering, accounting, marketing, management information systems

CONTACTS: For college students and recent graduates: Ms Rene Griswold, Administrative Service Specialist; Phone (803) 223-2888; Fax (803) 223-8171. For individuals with previous experience: Ms Nancy Houston, Administrative Manager; Phone (803) 223-2888.

FUJITSU AMERICA, INC.

3055 ORCHARD DRIVE
SAN JOSE, CALIFORNIA 95134-2005

OVERVIEW: Manufactures computer equipment and software. Established: 1968.

KEY STATISTICS Annual Sales: $2.0 billion. Number of Employees: 4,000.

EXPERTISE/EDUCATION SOUGHT: Software engineering/development, design engineering, computer programming, marketing, sales, administration

CONTACT: Ms Lela Chavez, Manager of Human Resources; Phone (408) 432-1300.

FUJITSU MICROELECTRONICS, INC.

3545 NORTH 1ST STREET
SAN JOSE, CALIFORNIA 95134-1804

OVERVIEW: Manufactures semiconductors. Established: 1979.

KEY STATISTICS Annual Sales: $100.0 million. Number of Employees: 1,300.

EXPERTISE/EDUCATION SOUGHT: Management, marketing, sales

CONTACT: For individuals with previous experience: Mr Don Scettrini, Human Resources Representative; Phone (408) 922-9069.

FULCRUM II, LP.

600 MADISON AVENUE
NEW YORK, NEW YORK 10022-1615

OVERVIEW: Investment bank.

KEY STATISTICS Assets: $937.0 million. Number of Employees: 9,500.

EXPERTISE/EDUCATION SOUGHT: Finance, accounting, banking, investment

CONTACT: For individuals with previous experience: Mr Todd Goodwin, General Partner; Phone (212) 832-2400.

H. B. FULLER

2400 ENERGY PARK DRIVE
SAINT PAUL, MINNESOTA 55108

OVERVIEW: Manufactures adhesives, brushes, chemicals, and cleaning products. Established: 1887.

KEY STATISTICS Annual Sales: $934.0 million. Number of Employees: 5,800.

EXPERTISE/EDUCATION SOUGHT: Chemical engineering, chemistry, computer programming, sales, accounting, marketing, facilities management

CONTACT: Mr Leo Johnson, Director Development and Employment, 1200 County Road "E" West, Arden Hills, MN, 55112; Phone (612) 481-4610.

GABRIEL, INC.

1500 EXECUTIVE DRIVE
ELGIN, ILLINOIS 60123-9311

OVERVIEW: Manufactures communications equipment. Established: 1986.

KEY STATISTICS Annual Sales: $57.0 million. Number of Employees: 810.

CONTACT: For individuals with previous experience: Ms Chris Jacobson, Assistant to Chairman; Phone (708) 888-7259.

GAF CORPORATION

136 ALPS ROAD
WAYNE, NEW JERSEY 07470

OVERVIEW: Manufactures specialty chemicals and building materials. Established: 1930.

Expertise/Education Sought: Chemical engineering, computer programming, accounting, law, marketing, sales, research

Contact: For individuals with previous experience: Mr Gary Schneid, Director of Employment; Phone (201) 628-3000.

ARTHUR J GALLAGHER AND COMPANY
2 PIERCE PLACE
ITASCA, ILLINOIS 60143-1203

Overview: Provides insurance brokerage services. Established: 1927.

Key Statistics Annual Sales: $318.0 million. Number of Employees: 3,000.

Expertise/Education Sought: Claims adjustment/examination, business development, risk management

Contact: For individuals with previous experience: Mr Chris Neigel, Manager of Human Resources.

GANNETT COMPANY, INC.
1100 WILSON BOULEVARD
ARLINGTON, VIRGINIA 22234-0001

Overview: Publishes newspapers and directories and operates radio and television stations. Established: 1906.

Key Statistics Annual Sales: $4.0 billion. Number of Employees: 36,500.

Expertise/Education Sought: Systems analysis, radio broadcasting, advertising, finance, computer programming, data processing, marketing, editing, graphic arts, accounting

Contact: For individuals with previous experience: Ms Karen Van Lair, Personnel Administrator; Phone (703) 284-6000, ext. 6739.

THE GAP, INC.
900 CHERRY AVENUE
SAN BRUNO, CALIFORNIA 94066-1602

Overview: Operates chain of retail clothing stores. Established: 1969.

Key Statistics Annual Sales: $3.0 billion. Number of Employees: 44,000.

Expertise/Education Sought: Architecture, real estate, drafting, finance, structural engineering, electrical engineering, mechanical engineering, data processing, computer programming, design

Contacts: For college students and recent graduates: Mr Bob Andrews, Manager of Nonexempt Recruitment; Phone (415) 737-4665; Fax (415) 543-3186. For individuals with previous experience: Ms Christine Casey, Manager of Corporate Employment, 1 Harrison Street, San Francisco, CA, 94105; Phone (415) 737-4665.

GATES CORPORATION
900 SOUTH BROADWAY
DENVER, COLORADO 80209

Overview: Manufactures belts and hoses. Established: 1911.

Key Statistics Annual Sales: $1.0 billion. Number of Employees: 15,700.

Expertise/Education Sought: Mechanical engineering, quality control, public relations, industrial engineering, business, manufacturing engineering, electrical engineering, marketing, sales, finance

Contact: Ms Sandra Skuball, Manager of Employment Services; Phone (303) 744-5778.

GATEWAY APPAREL, INC.
8500 VALCOUR AVENUE
SAINT LOUIS, MISSOURI 63123-2299

Overview: Operates chain of women's and children's clothing stores. Established: 1970.

Key Statistics Annual Sales: $252.3 million. Number of Employees: 4,500.

Expertise/Education Sought: Retail management

Contact: For individuals with previous experience: Ms Carla Lucz, Employment Supervisor; Phone (314) 822-1550, ext. 2651.

GATEWAY FOODS, INC.
1637 SAINT JAMES STREET
LA CROSSE, WISCONSIN 54601-3521

Overview: Distributes wholesale foods. Established: 1922. Parent Company: Scrivner Food Holdings, Inc.

Key Statistics Number of Employees: 8,700.

Expertise/Education Sought: Marketing, accounting, data processing, sales

Contact: For individuals with previous experience: Mr Lyell Montgomery, Director of Human Resources; Phone (608) 785-1330.

GATEWAY 2000
610 GATEWAY DRIVE
NORTH SIOUX CITY, SOUTH DAKOTA 57049

Overview: Manufactures computer and communications equipment. Established: 1985.

Key Statistics Annual Sales: $2.0 billion. Number of Employees: 3,018.

Expertise/Education Sought: Customer service and support, sales, technical, product design and development

Contacts: For college students and recent graduates: Mr Earle Grueskin, Facilities Director; Phone (605) 232-2000; Fax (605) 232-2023. For individuals with previous experience: Mr DeWayne Rideout, Director of Human Resources; Phone (605) 232-2000.

GATX CORPORATION
500 WEST MONROE STREET
CHICAGO, ILLINOIS 60661-3630

Overview: Provides industry with transportation equipment. Established: 1898.

Key Statistics Number of Employees: 5,500.

Expertise/Education Sought: Finance, treasury management, law, human resources, accounting, auditing, broadcast engineering, general insurance, information systems

Contact: For individuals with previous experience: Mr Bruce Handler, Human Resources Manager; Phone (312) 621-6200.

CJ GAYFER COMPANY, INC.
3250 AIRPORT BOULEVARD
MOBILE, ALABAMA 36606-3803

Overview: Operates regional chain of department stores. Established: 1950. Parent Company: Mercantile Stores Company, Inc.

Key Statistics Annual Sales: $730.0 million. Number of Employees: 5,000.

Hiring History Number of professional employees hired in 1993: 100.

Expertise/Education Sought: Management, merchandising, marketing, retail, human resources, management, merchandising

Contact: For individuals with previous experience: Mr Ron Parrish, Director of Human Resources; Phone (205) 471-6000, ext. 605.

GAYLORD CONTAINER CORPORATION
500 LAKE COOK ROAD, SUITE 400
DEERFIELD, ILLINOIS 60015-5269

Overview: Manufactures containers and packaging materials.

Key Statistics Annual Sales: $734.0 million. Number of Employees: 4,300.

Expertise/Education Sought: Packaging engineering, mechanical engineering, computer programming

Contact: Ms Sue Damon, Manager of Human Resources; Phone (708) 405-5500.

GAYLORD ENTERTAINMENT COMPANY
1 GAYLORD DRIVE
NASHVILLE, TENNESSEE 37214-1200

Overview: Diversified company with operations in entertainment, cable television, and broadcasting. Established: 1925.

Gaylord Entertainment Company (continued)

KEY STATISTICS Number of Employees: 5,500.

EXPERTISE/EDUCATION SOUGHT: Electrical engineering, mechanical engineering, sales, marketing, computer programming, data processing

CONTACT: For individuals with previous experience: Mr Tom Coles, Manager of Employment, 2802 Opryland Drive, Nashville, TN, 37214-1296; Phone (615) 871-7775.

GE
3135 EASTON TURNPIKE
FAIRLFIELD, CONNECTICUT 06431

OVERVIEW: Diversified company that includes high technology, service, and manufacturing businesses. Established: 1892.

KEY STATISTICS Annual Sales: $60.0 billion. Number of Employees: 221,000.

EXPERTISE/EDUCATION SOUGHT: Business administration, computer science, accounting, finance, engineering, human resources, management, manufacturing, marketing, statistics

CONTACT: Manager of Recruiting Support Services, Department PG; Phone (203) 373-3123.

CORPORATE STATEMENT

Organization. *Major businesses include aircraft engines, broadcasting (NBC), electrical distribution equipment, motors and industrial systems, capital services, power systems, information services, lighting, transportation systems, major appliances, medical systems, and plastics.*

Opportunities and Requirements. *Training programs exist in fields such as finance, information systems, engineering, manufacturing, technical sales, and human resources. Strong academic credentials, leadership ability, and relevant experience are required.*

GE CAPITAL/MONOGRAM RETAILER CREDIT SERVICES
9510 WEST 67TH STREET
MERRIAM, KANSAS 66203

OVERVIEW: Provides credit card services. Parent Company: GE Capital.

KEY STATISTICS Number of Employees: 2,000.

HIRING HISTORY Number of professional employees hired in 1994: 5.

EXPERTISE/EDUCATION SOUGHT: Customer service and support

CONTACT: Ms Pam Witt, Recruiter; Phone (913) 676-4373; Fax (913)676-4376.

GEICO CORPORATION
1 GEICO PLAZA
WASHINGTON, D.C. 20076

OVERVIEW: Provides property and casualty insurance. Established: 1936.

KEY STATISTICS Assets: $3.0 billion. Number of Employees: 7,314.

EXPERTISE/EDUCATION SOUGHT: Claims adjustment/examination, mathematics, actuarial, computer programming, marketing, accounting

CONTACTS: For college students and recent graduates: Ms Debra Lipsey, College Relations Recruiting Specialist; Phone (301) 986-2954. For individuals with previous experience: Ms Margie Robertson, Senior Employment Specialist.

GENCORP, INC.
175 GANNETT ROAD
FAIRLAWN, OHIO 44333-3300

OVERVIEW: Manufactures aerospace, automotive, and polymer products. Established: 1915.

EXPERTISE/EDUCATION SOUGHT: Mechanical engineering, finance, accounting, polymers

CONTACT: Ms Peggy Parson, Human Resources Representative and College Recruiter; Phone (216) 869-4200, ext. 4353.

GENERAL ACCIDENT CORPORATION OF AMERICA
436 WALNUT STREET
PHILADELPHIA, PENNSYLVANIA 19106

OVERVIEW: Provides personal and casualty insurance. Established: 1899.

EXPERTISE/EDUCATION SOUGHT: Accounting, finance, actuarial, underwriting, claims adjustment/examination, management information systems

CONTACTS: For college students and recent graduates: Ms Maria Paffas, Employment Specialist; Phone (215) 625-1000. For individuals with previous experience: Ms Pat Comfort, Manager of Employment and Employee Relations; Phone (215) 625-1000.

GENERAL BINDING CORPORATION
1 GBC PLAZA
NORTHBROOK, ILLINOIS 60062-4195

OVERVIEW: Manufactures and distributes binding, shredding, and printing equipment. Established: 1968. Parent Company: Lane Industries, Inc.

KEY STATISTICS Number of Employees: 3,363.

EXPERTISE/EDUCATION SOUGHT: Management information systems, accounting, sales, marketing, finance, manufacturing engineering

CONTACTS: For college students and recent graduates: Ms Shawn Dannely, Human Resources Representative; Phone (708) 272-3700. For individuals with previous experience: Mr Kris Leonard, Employment Manager; Phone (708) 272-3700.

GENERAL CABLE CORPORATION
4 TESSENEER DRIVE
HIGHLAND HEIGHTS, KENTUCKY 41076

OVERVIEW: Manufactures wire and cable, and industrial machinery.

EXPERTISE/EDUCATION SOUGHT: Finance, accounting, computer programming, mechanical engineering, electrical engineering, industrial engineering, process engineering, manufacturing engineering, sales, marketing

CONTACT: For individuals with previous experience: Ms Gina Ennis, Compensation Assistant; Phone (606) 572-8923.

GENERAL DYNAMICS CORPORATION
3190 FAIRVIEW PARK DRIVE
FALLS CHURCH, VIRGINIA 22042

OVERVIEW: Manufactures nuclear submarines and land systems.

KEY STATISTICS Number of Employees: 23,000.

EXPERTISE/EDUCATION SOUGHT: Mechanical engineering, electrical engineering, nuclear engineering, design engineering

CONTACT: For individuals with previous experience: Mr Kenneth A Hill, Vice President of Personnel Relations.

GENERAL DYNAMICS LAND SYSTEMS
38500 MOUND ROAD
STERLING HEIGHT, MICHIGAN 48310-3260

OVERVIEW: Manufactures military vehicles. Established: 1941. Parent Company: General Dynamics Corporation.

KEY STATISTICS Annual Sales: $1.0 billion. Number of Employees: 6,518.

EXPERTISE/EDUCATION SOUGHT: Marketing, accounting, finance, sales, computer programming, software engineering/development, electrical engineering, electronics/electronics engineering

CONTACT: For individuals with previous experience: Mr Jack Boyce, Manager of Staffing; Phone (313) 825-4000.

GENERAL HOST CORPORATION
PO BOX 10045
STAMFORD, CONNECTICUT 06904

OVERVIEW: Owns and operates retail nursery and craft stores. Established: 1911.

EXPERTISE/EDUCATION SOUGHT: Accounting, finance, data processing, marketing

CONTACT: Mr Robert Smith, Manager of Human Resources Frank's Nursery and Crafts, 6501 East Nevada, Detroit, MI, 48234; Phone (313) 564-2255.

GENERAL INSTRUMENT CORPORATION
181 WEST MADISON STREET
CHICAGO, ILLINOIS 60602-4510

OVERVIEW: Manufactures communication and electronics equipment. Established: 1923.

KEY STATISTICS Number of Employees: 10,100.

EXPERTISE/EDUCATION SOUGHT: Communications, law, business administration, electronics/electronics engineering, technical engineering, manufacturing engineering

CONTACT: Mr Lee R Keenan, Vice President of Human Resources; Phone (312) 541-5000.

GENERAL MILLS, INC.
ONE GENERAL MILLS BOULEVARD
MINNEAPOLIS, MINNESOTA 55426

OVERVIEW: Manufactures and distributes cereals and other food products. Established: 1928.

KEY STATISTICS Number of Employees: 125,670.

EXPERTISE/EDUCATION SOUGHT: Finance, information systems, marketing, manufacturing engineering, research and development, logistics, advertising

CONTACT: Mr William Dittmore, Director of Recruiting and College Relations, PO Box 1113, Minneapolis, MN, 55440-1113; Phone (612) 540-2311; Fax (612) 540-2445.

GENERAL MOTORS CORPORATION
3044 WEST GRAND BOULEVARD
DETROIT, MICHIGAN 48202-3080

OVERVIEW: Manufactures cars, trucks, and automotive parts. Established: 1908.

KEY STATISTICS Number of Employees: 694,000.

EXPERTISE/EDUCATION SOUGHT: Accounting, finance, computer programming, computer science, sales

CONTACT: Ms Betty Anderson, Director of Education Relations; Phone (313) 556-3569.

GENERAL NUTRITION, INC.
921 PENN AVENUE
PITTSBURGH, PENNSYLVANIA 15222-3814

OVERVIEW: Retail chain selling vitamins and health foods. Established: 1935.

KEY STATISTICS Number of Employees: 6,402.

HIRING HISTORY Number of professional employees hired in 1993: 1,000.

EXPERTISE/EDUCATION SOUGHT: Marketing, quality control, franchising, sales, accounting

CONTACTS: For college students and recent graduates: Ms Marilyn Ramkey, Employment Manager; Phone (412) 288-4705. For individuals with previous experience: Ms Eileen Scott, Director of Human Resources; Phone (412) 288-4705.

GENERAL PUBLIC UTILITIES CORPORATION
100 INTERPACE PARKWAY
PARSIPPANY, NEW JERSEY 07054-1149

OVERVIEW: Public utility. Established: 1906.

KEY STATISTICS Number of Employees: 10,000.

EXPERTISE/EDUCATION SOUGHT: Nuclear engineering, mechanical engineering, electrical engineering, accounting, management information systems, human resources

CONTACT: Ms Ann Meagan, Manager of Recruitment, 1 Upper Ponds Road, Parsipanny, NJ, 07054; Phone (201) 263-6500.

GENERAL REINSURANCE
695 EAST MAIN STREET
STAMFORD, CONNECTICUT 06904

OVERVIEW: Provides insurance protection by obtaining insurance from a second insurer. Parent Company: General Re Corporation.

KEY STATISTICS Annual Sales: $13.0 billion. Number of Employees: 2,400.

EXPERTISE/EDUCATION SOUGHT: Health insurance, management

CONTACT: For individuals with previous experience: Mr Matthew Pearlman, Manager Professional Recruitment; Phone (203) 328-5000.

GENERAL SIGNAL CORPORATION
1 HIGH RIDGE PARK
STAMFORD, CONNECTICUT 06904

OVERVIEW: Manufactures process control, electrical, electronic, and communications equipment. Established: 1904.

KEY STATISTICS Annual Sales: $2.0 billion. Number of Employees: 12,900.

EXPERTISE/EDUCATION SOUGHT: Marketing, finance, manufacturing engineering

CONTACT: For individuals with previous experience: Mr Kenneth Jones, Human Resources Manager, PO Box 10010, Stamford, CT, 06904-2010.

GENUINE PARTS COMPANY
2999 CIRCLE 75 PARKWAY NORTHWEST
ATLANTA, GEORGIA 30339-3073

OVERVIEW: Distributes automotive replacement parts, industrial replacement parts, and office supplies. Established: 1928.

KEY STATISTICS Number of Employees: 20,500.

EXPERTISE/EDUCATION SOUGHT: Management

CONTACT: Mr William Evans, Director of Personnel Services; Phone (404) 953-1700.

GEORGIA GULF CORPORATION
400 PERIMETER CENTER TERRACE, SUITE 595
ATLANTA, GEORGIA 30346-1264

OVERVIEW: Manufactures chemicals and petroleum products. Established: 1971.

KEY STATISTICS Annual Sales: $769.0 million. Number of Employees: 1,124.

HIRING HISTORY Number of professional employees hired in 1994: 30.

EXPERTISE/EDUCATION SOUGHT: Chemical engineering, chemistry, accounting

CONTACT: For individuals with previous experience: Mr John Hager, Corporate Personnel Manager; Phone (404) 395-4500.

GEORGIA POWER COMPANY
333 PIEDMONT AVENUE NORTHEAST
ATLANTA, GEORGIA 30308-3308

OVERVIEW: Electric utility. Established: 1945. Parent Company: Southern Company, Inc.

KEY STATISTICS Number of Employees: 12,558.

EXPERTISE/EDUCATION SOUGHT: Electrical engineering, mechanical engineering, industrial engineering, civil engineering

CONTACT: For individuals with previous experience: Ms Gracie Horton, Personnel Representative; Phone (404) 526-7660.

GERBER PRODUCTS COMPANY
445 STATE STREET
FREMONT, MICHIGAN 49413-1056

OVERVIEW: Produces processed baby foods, children's apparel, and child care products. Established: 1901.

KEY STATISTICS Number of Employees: 8,679.

EXPERTISE/EDUCATION SOUGHT: Accounting, data processing, finance, sales, marketing, law, computer programming, business administration

CONTACT: Ms Melissa Redinger, Senior Consultant Employee Relations; Phone (616) 928-2213, ext. 2299.

G. F. INDUSTRIES, INC.
930 98TH AVENUE
OAKLAND, CALIFORNIA 94603

OVERVIEW: Produces snack foods. Established: 1980.

EXPERTISE/EDUCATION SOUGHT: Marketing, advertising, accounting, sales, finance

CONTACT: For individuals with previous experience: Ms Shirley Stapp, Manager of Industrial Relations; Phone (510) 635-5400.

GI COMMUNICATIONS
2200 BYBERRY ROAD
HATBORO, PENNSYLVANIA 19040

OVERVIEW: Manufactures broad band communications equipment including cable television, audio, voice, and data. Established: 1948. Parent Company: General Instrument Corporation.

KEY STATISTICS Annual Sales: $1.0 billion. Number of Employees: 1,800.

HIRING HISTORY Number of professional employees hired in 1994: 300. 1993: 100.

EXPERTISE/EDUCATION SOUGHT: Engineering, digital technology, communications, marketing, software engineering/development, sales

CONTACT: Mr Edward M Zakrzewski, Director of Recruiting; Phone (215) 956-6414.

GIANT FOOD, INC.
6300 SHERIFF ROAD
LANDOVER, MARYLAND 20785-4392

OVERVIEW: Operates chain of food stores. Established: 1935.

KEY STATISTICS Number of Employees: 23,700.

HIRING HISTORY Number of professional employees hired in 1993: 100.

EXPERTISE/EDUCATION SOUGHT: Accounting, retail, management information systems

CONTACT: Ms Ricki Creszenci, Employment Manager, PO Box 1804, Washington, DC, 20013; Phone (301) 341-4267.

THE GILLETTE COMPANY
PRUDENTIAL TOWER
BOSTON, MASSACHUSETTS 02199

OVERVIEW: Manufactures razors and blades, toiletries, dental products, stationery products, and small appliances. Established: 1901.

EXPERTISE/EDUCATION SOUGHT: Accounting, business administration, law, marketing, sales

CONTACT: Ms Patricia Griffin, Senior Recruiter; Phone (617) 421-7658.

GKN NORTH AMERICA, INC.
601 SOUTH DUDLEY STREET
MEMPHIS, TENNESSEE 38104-4408

OVERVIEW: Manufactures automotive parts and supplies. Established: 1981.

KEY STATISTICS Annual Sales: $616.0 million. Number of Employees: 5,000.

EXPERTISE/EDUCATION SOUGHT: Data processing, program analysis, marketing, finance, accounting

CONTACT: For individuals with previous experience: Ms Beth Lemke, Employee Relations Manager; Phone (901) 523-7711, ext. 309.

GKN UNIVERSAL TRANSMISSIONS
3300 UNIVERSITY DRIVE
AUBURN, MICHIGAN 48326

OVERVIEW: Distributes automotive parts and components. Established: 1981.

EXPERTISE/EDUCATION SOUGHT: Mechanical engineering, business, finance

CONTACT: For individuals with previous experience: Ms Mary Rastigue, Human Resources Associate; Phone (810) 377-1200.

GLAXO, INC.
5 MOORE DRIVE
RESEARCH TRIANGLE PARK
NORTH CAROLINA 27709-4613

OVERVIEW: Manufactures pharmaceutical products. Established: 1972.

KEY STATISTICS Annual Sales: $707.0 million. Number of Employees: 5,500.

EXPERTISE/EDUCATION SOUGHT: Chemistry, biology, chemical engineering, accounting, biochemistry, finance

CONTACT: Mr Steve Sons, Director of Human Resources; Phone (919) 248-2100.

GLENDALE FEDERAL BANK
201 WEST LEXINGTON DRIVE
GLENDALE, CALIFORNIA 91203

OVERVIEW: Savings and loan institution. Established: 1934.

EXPERTISE/EDUCATION SOUGHT: Treasury management, accounting, credit/credit analysis, marketing, systems analysis, finance, law, sales, customer service and support

CONTACT: Mr James Hose, Corporate and Technical Recruiter, PO Box 1709, Glendale, CA, 91209; Phone (818) 500-2000, ext. 2638.

THE GLIDDEN COMPANY
925 EUCLID AVENUE
CLEVELAND, OHIO 44115-1408

OVERVIEW: Manufactures paints and coatings. Established: 1873. Parent Company: ICI America Holdings, Inc.

KEY STATISTICS Annual Sales: $876.0 million. Number of Employees: 4,302.

EXPERTISE/EDUCATION SOUGHT: Accounting, computer programming, sales, industrial engineering

CONTACTS: For college students and recent graduates: Ms Connie Mayse, Personnel Assistant. For individuals with previous experience: Ms Sue Whitman, Manager of Employment; Phone (216) 344-8000.

GNB, INC.
375 NORTHRIDGE ROAD
ATLANTA, GEORGIA 30350-3290

OVERVIEW: Manufactures storage batteries and inorganic pigments. Established: 1983. Parent Company: Pacific Dunlop GNB Corporation.

KEY STATISTICS Annual Sales: $400.0 million. Number of Employees: 4,000.

EXPERTISE/EDUCATION SOUGHT: Accounting, finance, marketing, sales, data processing, manufacturing engineering, industrial engineering, design engineering

CONTACT: For individuals with previous experience: Mr Andy Savage, Vice President of Human Resources, PO Box 64100, Atlanta, GA, 30350; Phone (404) 551-0300.

GOLD KIST, INC.
244 PERIMETER CENTER PARKWAY
ATLANTA, GEORGIA 30346-2302

OVERVIEW: Manages agribusiness and processes poultry. Established: 1933.

KEY STATISTICS Annual Sales: $1.0 billion. Number of Employees: 15,000.

HIRING HISTORY Number of professional employees hired in 1994: 25. 1993: 35.

EXPERTISE/EDUCATION SOUGHT: Animal sciences, business administration, human resources, management information systems

CONTACT: For individuals with previous experience: Mr George Crawford, Corporate Employment Director, PO Box 2210, Atlanta, GA, 30301; Phone (404) 393-5000, ext. 5249.

GOLDEN ALUMINUM COMPANY
1600 JACKSON STREET
GOLDEN, COLORADO 80401-1958

OVERVIEW: Provides recycling services. Established: 1992. Parent Company: ACX Technologies, Inc.

KEY STATISTICS Annual Sales: $150.0 million. Number of Employees: 604.

EXPERTISE/EDUCATION SOUGHT: Accounting, finance, data processing, metallurgical engineering, chemical engineering

CONTACT: Ms Toni Shotwell, Human Resources Administrator; Phone (303) 277-7500.

GOLDEN WEST FINANCIAL CORPORATION
1901 HARRISON STREET
OAKLAND, CALIFORNIA 94612-3588

OVERVIEW: Provides home loans and checking/savings services. Established: 1959.

KEY STATISTICS Annual Sales: $2.0 billion. Number of Employees: 3,261.

EXPERTISE/EDUCATION SOUGHT: Accounting, project management, finance, auditing, investment, systems analysis

CONTACTS: For college students and recent graduates: Ms Susan Almquist, Manager of Human Resources; Phone (510) 446-3068. For individuals with previous experience: Ms Susan Lennox, Senior Vice President Human Resources.

THE GOLLUB CORPORATION
501 DUANESBURG ROAD
SCHENECTADY, NEW YORK 12306-1014

OVERVIEW: Operates chain of food stores stores. Established: 1937. Parent Company: Golub Corporation.

KEY STATISTICS Number of Employees: 8,500.

HIRING HISTORY Number of professional employees hired in 1994: 20.

EXPERTISE/EDUCATION SOUGHT: Marketing, advertising, sales, computer programming

CONTACT: Mr Wes Holloway, Manager of Corporate Diversity Initiatives.

B. F. GOODRICH
3925 EMBASSY PARKWAY
AKRON, OHIO 44333

OVERVIEW: Manufactures and markets chemical and aerospace products. Established: 1870.

KEY STATISTICS Annual Sales: $2.0 billion. Number of Employees: 13,416.

EXPERTISE/EDUCATION SOUGHT: Aeronautical engineering, mechanical engineering, electrical engineering, chemical engineering

CONTACT: Mr Harold W Mason, Director of Human Resources; Phone (216) 374-3549.

THE GOODYEAR TIRE AND RUBBER COMPANY
1144 EAST MARKET STREET
AKRON, OHIO 44316-0001

OVERVIEW: Manufactures tires, rubber products, and chemicals. Established: 1898.

KEY STATISTICS Number of Employees: 90,384.

EXPERTISE/EDUCATION SOUGHT: Mechanical engineering, finance, chemical engineering, systems analysis, electrical engineering, plastics engineering, civil engineering, accounting, polymers, business administration

CONTACTS: For college students and recent graduates: Mr David Jones, Manager of College Recruiting; Phone (216) 796-2121. For individuals with previous experience: Mr Mike Burns, Vice President of Human Resources; Phone (216) 796-2121.

GOULD'S PUMPS, INC.
240 FALL STREET
SENECA FALLS, NEW YORK 13148-1590

OVERVIEW: Manufactures pumps and motors for commercial and consumer use. Established: 1844.

KEY STATISTICS Number of Employees: 4,100.

EXPERTISE/EDUCATION SOUGHT: Computer programming, data processing, sales, marketing, mechanical engineering, electrical engineering, design engineering

CONTACT: For individuals with previous experience: Ms Tracey Dow, Human Resources Representative.

GPM
1300 POST OAK BOULEVARD
HOUSTON, TEXAS 77056-3010

OVERVIEW: Produces petroleum. Established: 1986. Parent Company: Phillips Petroleum Company.

KEY STATISTICS Annual Sales: $1.0 billion. Number of Employees: 1,800.

EXPERTISE/EDUCATION SOUGHT: Accounting, finance, law, petroleum/petrochemical engineering, chemical engineering, mechanical engineering

CONTACT: For individuals with previous experience: Ms Elaine Redus, Human Resources Associate; Phone (713) 297-6066.

W. R. GRACE AND COMPANY, INC.
1 TOWN CENTER ROAD
BOCA RATON, FLORIDA 33486

OVERVIEW: Manufactures chemicals, building materials, and medical supplies. Established: 1854.

KEY STATISTICS Number of Employees: 450.

EXPERTISE/EDUCATION SOUGHT: Accounting, law, chemical engineering, manufacturing engineering, technical engineering

CONTACT: For individuals with previous experience: Ms Sarah Morales, Personnel Representative; Phone (407) 362-2000, ext. 2309.

W.W. GRAINGER, INC.
5500 HOWARD STREET
SKOKIE, ILLINOIS 60077-2699

OVERVIEW: Distributes industrial and commercial equipment and supplies. Established: 1927.

KEY STATISTICS Number of Employees: 10,219.

EXPERTISE/EDUCATION SOUGHT: Accounting, systems integration, law, human resources, industrial engineering, chemical engineering

CONTACT: For individuals with previous experience: Ms Sue Valentino, Manager of Personnel; Phone (708) 982-9000.

GRANCARE, INC.
1 RAVINIA DRIVE, SUITE 1500
ATLANTA, GEORGIA 30346-2103

OVERVIEW: Operates chain of nursing homes in addition to rehabilitation centers, pharmacies, and a home health care division. Established: 1988.

KEY STATISTICS Annual Sales: $506.0 million. Number of Employees: 11,000.

HIRING HISTORY Number of professional employees hired in 1993: 300.

EXPERTISE/EDUCATION SOUGHT: Licensed practical nursing, pharmacy, therapy, hospital administration, registered nursing

CONTACT: For individuals with previous experience: Mr Mark Rubenstein, Vice President of Human Resources, 1051 Ogden Avenue, Suite 200, Milwaukee, WI, 53202; Phone (414) 273-1212.

THE GRAND UNION COMPANY
201 WILLOWBROOK BOULEVARD
WAYNE, NEW JERSEY 07470-7031

OVERVIEW: Operates chain of food stores. Established: 1872. Parent Company: Grand Union Capital Corporation.

KEY STATISTICS Annual Sales: $2.0 billion. Number of Employees: 17,000.

EXPERTISE/EDUCATION SOUGHT: Retail, electrical engineering, drafting, business management, marketing, finance, accounting

CONTACT: Ms Donna Desena, Employment Benefits Coordinator; Phone (201) 890-6000.

GRANITE BROADCASTING CORPORATION
767 3RD AVENUE FLOOR 28
NEW YORK, NEW YORK 10017-2023

OVERVIEW: Operates television broadcasting stations. Established: 1988.

KEY STATISTICS Annual Sales: $37.5 million. Number of Employees: 540.

EXPERTISE/EDUCATION SOUGHT: Accounting, computer programming, finance

CONTACT: For individuals with previous experience: Ms Ellen McClain, Vice President of Corporate Development and Treasurer; Phone (212) 826-2530.

GRAYBAR ELECTRIC COMPANY, INC.
34 NORTH MERAMEC AVENUE
SAINT LOUIS, MISSOURI 63105

OVERVIEW: Distributes wholesale electrical and communication products. Established: 1926.

KEY STATISTICS Annual Sales: $2.0 billion. Number of Employees: 5,400.

EXPERTISE/EDUCATION SOUGHT: Computer programming, finance, computer science

CONTACT: For individuals with previous experience: Ms Rosemary Evans, Personnel Specialist; Phone (314) 727-3900, ext. 223.

GREAT AMERICAN INSURANCE COMPANY
580 WALNUT STREET
CINCINNATI, OHIO 45202-3139

OVERVIEW: Provides property, life, and automobile insurance. Established: 1973.

KEY STATISTICS Assets: $1.0 billion. Number of Employees: 4,000.

HIRING HISTORY Number of professional employees hired in 1994: 350. 1993: 300.

EXPERTISE/EDUCATION SOUGHT: Accounting, finance, actuarial, underwriting, marketing

CONTACT: Ms Rene Haven, Employment Services Manager; Phone (513) 369-5000, ext. 5653.

THE GREAT ATLANTIC AND PACIFIC TEA COMPANY, INC.
2 PARAGON DRIVE
MONTVALE, NEW JERSEY 07645

OVERVIEW: Operates chain of food stores. Established: 1859.

KEY STATISTICS Number of Employees: 650.

EXPERTISE/EDUCATION SOUGHT: Computer science, accounting, finance, retail

CONTACT: For individuals with previous experience: Ms Corine Blake, Director of Personnel and Building Services, PO Box 418, Montvale, NJ, 07645; Phone (201) 930-4416.

GREAT LAKES CHEMICAL CORPORATION
1 GREAT LAKES BOULEVARD
WEST LAFAYETTE, INDIANA 47906

OVERVIEW: Manufactures specialty chemicals. Established: 1933.

KEY STATISTICS Number of Employees: 7,000.

HIRING HISTORY Number of professional employees hired in 1993: 30.

EXPERTISE/EDUCATION SOUGHT: Chemistry, chemical engineering, accounting, information services

CONTACT: Ms Diane M Foster, Human Resources Specialist; Phone (317) 497-6253.

GREAT WESTERN FINANCIAL CORPORATION
9200 OAKDALE AVENUE
CHATSWORTH, CALIFORNIA 91311-6519

OVERVIEW: Provides consumer finance and retail banking services. Established: 1955.

KEY STATISTICS Number of Employees: 17,029.

EXPERTISE/EDUCATION SOUGHT: Finance, information systems, real estate, banking

CONTACT: Ms Robin McNeill, Vice President Staffing; Phone (818) 775-4260.

GREENWOOD MILLS, INC.
104 MAXWELL AVENUE
GREENWOOD, SOUTH CAROLINA 29646-2641

OVERVIEW: Manufactures textiles. Established: 1889.

KEY STATISTICS Annual Sales: $520.0 million. Number of Employees: 7,000.

HIRING HISTORY Number of professional employees hired in 1994: 15. 1993: 20.

EXPERTISE/EDUCATION SOUGHT: Accounting, customer service and support, auditing, plant management, quality control, finance, purchasing, human resources, data processing

CONTACT: For individuals with previous experience: Mr J R Smith, Group Manager of Personnel Services, PO Box 1017, Greenwood, SC, 29648-1017; Phone (803) 229-2571.

GREIF BROTHERS CORPORATION
621 PENNSYLVANIA AVENUE
DELAWARE, OHIO 43015-1524

OVERVIEW: Manufactures metal, wood, paper, and plastic containers.

KEY STATISTICS Number of Employees: 4,000.

EXPERTISE/EDUCATION SOUGHT: Administration

CONTACT: Mr John Dieker, Controller.

GREY ADVERTISING
777 3RD AVENUE
NEW YORK, NEW YORK 10017-1379

OVERVIEW: Advertising agency. Established: 1917.

KEY STATISTICS Number of Employees: 7,295.

HIRING HISTORY Number of professional employees hired in 1994: 60. 1993: 100.

EXPERTISE/EDUCATION SOUGHT: Sales, marketing, customer service and support, advertising, communications

CONTACT: For individuals with previous experience: Ms Jeanmarie Cabany, Assistant Human Resources Manager; Phone (212) 546-2000.

GREYHOUND LINES, INC.

15110 DALLAS PARKWAY STREET
DALLAS, TEXAS 75248-4665

OVERVIEW: Provides bus transportation services. Established: 1914.

KEY STATISTICS Annual Sales: $666.0 million. Number of Employees: 11,500.

HIRING HISTORY Number of professional employees hired in 1994: 17.

EXPERTISE/EDUCATION SOUGHT: Law, accounting, finance, tax, auditing, telecommunications, computer programming

CONTACT: For individuals with previous experience: Mr Jeff Matthews, Manager of Human Resources; Phone (214) 777-8055.

GRINNELL CORPORATION

3 TYCO PARK
EXETER, NEW HAMPSHIRE 03833

OVERVIEW: Manufactures fire protection systems. Established: 1976. Parent Company: Tyco International, Ltd.

KEY STATISTICS Annual Sales: $1.0 billion. Number of Employees: 12,000.

EXPERTISE/EDUCATION SOUGHT: Finance, marketing, accounting, business management, data processing

CONTACT: Mr John Helfrich, Vice President of Human Resources; Phone (603) 778-9200.

GROLIER, INC.

SHERMAN TURNPIKE
DANBURY, CONNECTICUT 06016

OVERVIEW: Publishing company. Established: 1936.

EXPERTISE/EDUCATION SOUGHT: Publishing, marketing

CONTACT: For individuals with previous experience: Ms Joan Papp, Human Resources Recruiter.

GROUP HEALTH COOPERATIVE OF PUGET SOUND

521 WALL STREET
SEATTLE, WASHINGTON 98121-1524

OVERVIEW: Provides health maintenance services. Established: 1945.

KEY STATISTICS Annual Sales: $934.0 million. Number of Employees: 6,670.

EXPERTISE/EDUCATION SOUGHT: Nursing, pharmacy, data processing, physics, chemistry, physical therapy

CONTACT: For individuals with previous experience: Ms Denise Rubin, Manager of Employment; Phone (206) 448-2748; Fax (206)448-5963.

GROUP HEALTH, INC.

441 9TH AVENUE, 1ST FLOOR
NEW YORK, NEW YORK 10001-6902

OVERVIEW: Provides health care services. Established: 1939.

KEY STATISTICS Annual Sales: $1.1 billion. Number of Employees: 2,100.

EXPERTISE/EDUCATION SOUGHT: Registered nursing, licensed practical nursing, law, accounting, finance, data processing

CONTACT: For individuals with previous experience: Mr Perry Pascasio, Manager of Employment; Phone (212) 615-4826.

GTE CALIFORNIA, INC.

ONE GTE PLACE
THOUSAND OAKS, CALIFORNIA 91362-3811

OVERVIEW: Provides sales and dial tone services. Established: 1939. Parent Company: GTE Corporation.

KEY STATISTICS Number of Employees: 13,536.

EXPERTISE/EDUCATION SOUGHT: Finance, management, computer science, sales, electrical engineering

CONTACT: Mr Dan Long, Recruiting Coordinator for Education,Training, and Development; Phone (805) 372-6000.

GTE DATA SERVICES, INC.

1 EAST TELECOM PARKWAY
TEMPLE TERRACE, FLORIDA 33637-0902

OVERVIEW: Provides software development and information processing services. Established: 1967. Parent Company: GTE Corporation.

KEY STATISTICS Annual Sales: $750.0 million. Number of Employees: 3,500.

EXPERTISE/EDUCATION SOUGHT: Systems analysis, computer programming, software engineering/development, database management, network management systems, business information analysts, networking

CONTACT: Ms Kathy Costenbaden, Staff Administrator-Professional Recruitment, PO Box 110, Temple Terrace, FL, 33601; Phone (813) 978-4925.

GTE DIRECTORIES CORPORATION

DALLAS/FORT WORTH AIRPORT
DALLAS, TEXAS 75261

OVERVIEW: Publishes telephone books and Yellow Page directories. Established: 1936. Parent Company: GTE Corporation.

KEY STATISTICS Number of Employees: 5,114.

HIRING HISTORY Number of professional employees hired in 1994: 200. 1993: 250.

EXPERTISE/EDUCATION SOUGHT: Computer programming, systems analysis, telecommunications, accounting, sales, customer service and support, quality control, management information systems, planning, operations

CONTACT: For individuals with previous experience: Ms Nancy Zorn, Director Staffing and Development, GTE Place at West Airfield Drive, Dallas/Fort Worth Airport, Dallas, TX, 75261; Phone (214) 453-7000.

GTE HAWAIIAN TELEPHONE COMPANY, INC.

PO BOX 2200
HONOLULU, HAWAII 96041-2808

OVERVIEW: Provides local telecommunications services. Established: 1883.

KEY STATISTICS Number of Employees: 3,187.

EXPERTISE/EDUCATION SOUGHT: Electrical engineering, sales

CONTACT: For individuals with previous experience: Ms Terri Bowen, Senior Administrator; Phone (808) 546-2014.

GTE SERVICE

1 STAMFORD FORUM
STAMFORD, CONNECTICUT 06904

OVERVIEW: Provides telecommunications services. Established: 1926. Parent Company: GTE Products of Connecticut.

KEY STATISTICS Number of Employees: 5,022.

HIRING HISTORY Number of professional employees hired in 1994: 260. 1993: 200.

EXPERTISE/EDUCATION SOUGHT: Computer programming, management information systems, telecommunications, sales, customer service and support, electrical engineering, computer science, finance, accounting, human resources

CONTACTS: For college students and recent graduates: Ms Penny Smith, Manager of College Relations; Phone (203) 965-2000. For individuals with previous experience: Mr William MacAuley, Director of Staffing and Development; Phone (203) 965-2000, ext. 3511.

G-TECH CORPORATION
55 TECHNOLOGY WAY
WEST GREENWICH, RHODE ISLAND 02817-1711

OVERVIEW: Supplies and operates on line lottery systems and government benefits delivery systems. Established: 1980.

KEY STATISTICS Annual Sales: $633.0 million. Number of Employees: 4,000.

EXPERTISE/EDUCATION SOUGHT: Software engineering/development, electrical engineering, hardware engineering, marketing, finance, administration

CONTACT: For individuals with previous experience: Mr Rick Bates, Recruiter; Phone (401) 392-1000.

GUARDIAN LIFE INSURANCE COMPANY OF AMERICA
201 PARK AVENUE SOUTH
NEW YORK, NEW YORK 10003

OVERVIEW: Provides life, health, and disability insurance. Established: 1860.

EXPERTISE/EDUCATION SOUGHT: Marketing, sales, finance, actuarial, accounting, underwriting, computer programming, law, industrial engineering

CONTACT: For individuals with previous experience: Ms Alix Kane, Director of Human Resources.

GUARDSMARK, INC.
22 SOUTH 2ND STREET
MEMPHIS, TENNESSEE 38103-2695

OVERVIEW: Provides security and investigative services.

KEY STATISTICS Number of Employees: 9,000.

HIRING HISTORY Number of professional employees hired in 1994: 50.

EXPERTISE/EDUCATION SOUGHT: Management, accounting, security

CONTACT: For individuals with previous experience: Mr Brandon Cox, Recrutiing Manager; Phone (901) 522-6000.

HALLIBURTON COMPANY
3600 LINCOLN PLAZA
DALLAS, TEXAS 75201

OVERVIEW: Provides oil field, construction and engineering services. Established: 1924.

KEY STATISTICS Annual Sales: $7.0 billion. Number of Employees: 69,000.

HIRING HISTORY Number of professional employees hired in 1994: 10.

EXPERTISE/EDUCATION SOUGHT: Accounting, finance

CONTACT: For individuals with previous experience: Human Resources Department; Phone (214) 978-2600.

HALLIBURTON ENERGY SERVICES COMPANY
5151 SAN FELIPE
HOUSTON, TEXAS 75201-3391

OVERVIEW: Provides oil field and construction services. Established: 1919. Parent Company: Halliburton Energy Services Company.

KEY STATISTICS Annual Sales: $6.0 billion. Number of Employees: 64,700.

EXPERTISE/EDUCATION SOUGHT: Accounting, tax accounting, investor relations, operations, engineering, petroleum/petrochemical engineering, civil engineering, industrial engineering, business management, finance

CONTACT: For individuals with previous experience: Mr Don King, Director of Human Resources; Phone (214) 978-2618.

HALLIBURTON NUS ENVIRONMENTAL CORPORATION
910 CLOPPER ROAD
GAITHESBERG, MARYLAND 20878-1399

OVERVIEW: Provides environmental services. Established: 1978. Parent Company: Halliburton Company.

KEY STATISTICS Number of Employees: 2,400.

EXPERTISE/EDUCATION SOUGHT: Sales, marketing, accounting, finance, environmental engineering

CONTACT: Ms Susan Young, Manager of Employment; Phone (301) 258-6000, ext. 1898.

HALLMARK CARDS, INC.
2501 MCGEE STREET
KANSAS CITY, MISSOURI 64108-2615

OVERVIEW: Manufactures greeting cards, gift wrap, and other personal communications products. Established: 1910.

KEY STATISTICS Number of Employees: 21,500.

EXPERTISE/EDUCATION SOUGHT: Marketing, production engineering, information systems, finance, sales, production management, materials management, human resources, graphic arts, research and development

CONTACT: Mr Tim Moran, Manager of Corporate Staffing; Phone (816) 274-4062.

HAMILTON BEACH/PROCTOR-SILEX
4421 WATERFRONT DRIVE
GLEN ALLEN, VIRGINIA 23060-3375

OVERVIEW: Manufactures household appliances. Established: 1901.

KEY STATISTICS Annual Sales: $359.0 million. Number of Employees: 3,500.

EXPERTISE/EDUCATION SOUGHT: Mechanical engineering, electrical engineering, industrial engineering, quality control, marketing

CONTACT: For individuals with previous experience: Ms Susan Wall, Human Resources Administrator; Phone (804) 273-9777, ext. 290.

HANDLEMAN COMPANY
500 KIRTS BOULEVARD
TROY, MICHIGAN 48084-4142

OVERVIEW: Distributes wholesale books, records, tapes, software, and videocassettes. Established: 1934.

KEY STATISTICS Annual Sales: $1.0 billion. Number of Employees: 4,000.

EXPERTISE/EDUCATION SOUGHT: Advertising, marketing, business, sales, data processing, customer service and support, accounting, finance

CONTACT: Ms Cynthia Oparka, Human Resources Manager; Phone (810) 362-4400, ext. 716.

J.E. HANGER, INC.
5010 MCGINNIS FERRY ROAD
ALPHARETTA, GEORGIA 30202-3919

OVERVIEW: Manufactures prostheses. Established: 1942.

KEY STATISTICS Number of Employees: 400.

EXPERTISE/EDUCATION SOUGHT: Accounting, finance, marketing, human resources

CONTACT: Ms Sue Katz, Director of Human Resources; Phone (404) 667-9013.

M. A. HANNA COMPANY
200 PUBLIC SQUARE, SUITE 36-5000
CLEVELAND, OHIO 44114-2304

OVERVIEW: Manufactures specialty chemicals, plastics, and polymers. Established: 1885.

KEY STATISTICS Number of Employees: 6,334.

EXPERTISE/EDUCATION SOUGHT: Chemical engineering, chemistry, data processing, accounting, marketing

CONTACT: Human Resources Department; Phone (216) 589-4000.

HANNAFORD BROTHERS COMPANY
145 PLEASANT HILL ROAD
SCARBOROUGH, MAINE 04074-8768

OVERVIEW: Operates chain of food stores. Established: 1883.

KEY STATISTICS Annual Sales: $3.0 billion. Number of Employees: 17,000.

EXPERTISE/EDUCATION SOUGHT: Management, accounting, data processing, management

CONTACT: Ms Pat Pelletier, Employment Administrator; Phone (207) 883-2911, ext. 2281.

HARCOURT BRACE AND COMPANY, INC.
6277 SEA HARBOR DRIVE
ORLANDO, FLORIDA 32887

OVERVIEW: Publishing company. Parent Company: Harcourt General, Inc.

EXPERTISE/EDUCATION SOUGHT: Accounting, computer science, business, computer programming

CONTACT: For individuals with previous experience: Ms Shannon Green, Professional Recruiter; Phone (407) 345-3176.

HARCOURT GENERAL
1280 BOYLSTON STREET
CHESTNUT HILL, MASSACHUSETTS 02167-1719

OVERVIEW: Operates movie theaters, department and specialty stores, publishing businesses, and insurance companies. Established: 1922.

KEY STATISTICS Number of Employees: 23,120.

HIRING HISTORY Number of professional employees hired in 1994: 20.

EXPERTISE/EDUCATION SOUGHT: Information systems, finance

CONTACT: For individuals with previous experience: Mr Nick Figarelli, Director of Human Resources; Phone (617) 264-9108.

HARDEE'S FOOD SYSTEMS, INC.
1233 HARDEES BOULEVARD
ROCKY MOUNT, NORTH CAROLINA 27804-2036

OVERVIEW: Operates chain of family and fast food restaurants. Parent Company: Imasco Holdings, Inc.

KEY STATISTICS Annual Sales: $2.0 billion. Number of Employees: 48,000.

HIRING HISTORY Number of professional employees hired in 1993: 41.

EXPERTISE/EDUCATION SOUGHT: Research and development, chemistry, biology, marketing, finance

CONTACT: For individuals with previous experience: Ms Carolyn McCrorey, Director of Corporate Human Resources; Phone (919) 977-2000.

JOHN H. HARLAND COMPANY
2939 MILLER ROAD
DECATUR, GEORGIA 30035-4038

OVERVIEW: Prints checks and business forms. Established: 1923.

KEY STATISTICS Number of Employees: 7,300.

HIRING HISTORY Number of professional employees hired in 1993: 85.

EXPERTISE/EDUCATION SOUGHT: Production management, sales, management information systems, network analysis

CONTACTS: For college students and recent graduates: Ms Schwell Stahl, Senior Recruiter. For individuals with previous experience: Ms Carol Patty, Director of Employee Services; Phone (404) 455-9460.

HARLEY-DAVIDSON, INC.
3700 WEST JUNEAU AVENUE
MILWAUKEE, WISCONSIN 53208-2865

OVERVIEW: Manufactures motorcycles and related products. Established: 1903.

KEY STATISTICS Annual Sales: $1.0 billion. Number of Employees: 6,000.

EXPERTISE/EDUCATION SOUGHT: Business, engineering

CONTACT: Ms Cynthia Bathey, Human Resources Representative, PO Box 653, Milwaukee, WI, 53201-0653; Phone (414) 935-4045.

HARMAN INTERNATIONAL INDUSTRIES, INC.
1101 PENNSYLVANIA AVENUE NORTHWEST
WASHINGTON, D.C. 20004-2514

OVERVIEW: Manufactures and distributes audio and video equipment. Established: 1953.

KEY STATISTICS Annual Sales: $862.0 million. Number of Employees: 6,849.

EXPERTISE/EDUCATION SOUGHT: Sales, manufacturing engineering, electrical engineering, marketing, finance, accounting, auditing, research and development, acoustic engineering

CONTACT: Ms Kay Dega, Manager of Compensation and Benefits, 8500 Balboa Boulevard, Northridge, CA, 91329; Phone (818) 893-8411.

HARNISCHFEGER INDUSTRIES, INC.
4400 WEST NATIONAL AVENUE
MILWAUKEE, WISCONSIN 53214

OVERVIEW: Manufactures paper making machinery and other industrial equipment. Established: 1885.

KEY STATISTICS Number of Employees: 2,800.

EXPERTISE/EDUCATION SOUGHT: Engineering, electrical engineering, mechanical engineering, accounting, finance, production control, systems analysis

CONTACT: For individuals with previous experience: Human Resource Department; Phone (414) 671-7528.

HARPER COLLINS PUBLISHERS, INC.
10 EAST 53RD STREET
NEW YORK, NEW YORK 10022

OVERVIEW: Publishing company. Established: 1817. Parent Company: The News Corporation, Ltd.

KEY STATISTICS Annual Sales: $750.0 million.

HIRING HISTORY Number of professional employees hired in 1994: 247.

EXPERTISE/EDUCATION SOUGHT: Sales, administration, computer programming, marketing, editing, production, inventory control, law, finance, accounting

CONTACT: Ms Linda Kira, Recruiter; Phone (212) 207-7471.

HARRAH'S ENTERTAINMENT, INC.
1023 CHERRY ROAD
MEMPHIS, TENNESSEE 38117

OVERVIEW: Operates casinos and hotels. Established: 1952.

KEY STATISTICS Annual Sales: $1.0 billion. Number of Employees: 22,000.

EXPERTISE/EDUCATION SOUGHT: Marketing, advertising, finance, accounting, hospitality/hotel and restaurant management

CONTACT: Ms Lisa Edenton, Director of College Relations; Phone (901) 762-8600.

HARRIS CORPORATION
1025 WEST NASA BOULEVARD
MELBOURNE, FLORIDA 32919-1821

OVERVIEW: Manufactures electronic systems, semiconductors, communications systems, and office equipment. Established: 1895.

KEY STATISTICS Annual Sales: $3.0 billion. Number of Employees: 28,000.

EXPERTISE/EDUCATION SOUGHT: Electrical engineering, computer engineering, computer science, software engineering/development, business administration

CONTACT: For individuals with previous experience: College Relations Department; Phone (305) 974-1700.

HARRIS COUNTY HOSPITAL DISTRICT
2525 HOLLY HALL STREET
HOUSTON, TEXAS 77054-4124

OVERVIEW: Public hospital. Established: 1965.

Harris County Hospital District (continued)

KEY STATISTICS Annual Sales: $533.0 million. Number of Employees: 5,232.

EXPERTISE/EDUCATION SOUGHT: Registered nursing, medical technology, physical therapy, occupational therapy

CONTACT: Ms Jennie Carmouche, Director of Employment; Phone (713) 746-6495.

HARRIS METHODIST HEALTH SYSTEM

1325 PENNSYLVANIA AVENUE
FORT WORTH, TEXAS 76104-2196

OVERVIEW: Owns and operates hospitals and related facilities.

KEY STATISTICS Annual Sales: $604.0 million. Number of Employees: 7,000.

EXPERTISE/EDUCATION SOUGHT: Marketing, sales, data processing, health insurance, computer programming, finance, occupational therapy, physical therapy, registered nursing

CONTACTS: For college students and recent graduates: Job Line; Phone (800) 477-7876. For individuals with previous experience: Ms Louise Harris, Senior Recruiter and Manager; Phone (817) 462-6132.

HARRIS TEETER, INC.

701 CRESTDALE ROAD
MATTHEWS, NORTH CAROLINA 28105-1700

OVERVIEW: Operates chain of food stores. Established: 1969. Parent Company: Ruddick Corporation.

KEY STATISTICS Annual Sales: $1.4 billion. Number of Employees: 14,500.

EXPERTISE/EDUCATION SOUGHT: Retail, warehousing, food science

CONTACT: Mr Jerry Allen, Corporate Recruiter; Phone (704) 845-3100.

HARRIS TRUST AND SAVINGS BANK

111 WEST MONROE STREET
CHICAGO, ILLINOIS 60603-4095

OVERVIEW: Commercial bank. Established: 1971. Parent Company: Bankmont Financial Corporation.

KEY STATISTICS Assets: $1.0 billion. Number of Employees: 5,792.

HIRING HISTORY Number of professional employees hired in 1993: 250.

EXPERTISE/EDUCATION SOUGHT: Accounting, finance, actuarial, marketing, data processing

CONTACT: Ms Karen Stoeller, Vice President of Human Resources, PO Box 755, Chicago, IL, 60690; Phone (312) 461-6990, ext. 7778.

HARSCO CORPORATION

350 POPLAR CHURCH ROAD
CAMP HILL, PENNSYLVANIA 17011-2599

OVERVIEW: Manufactures and services industrial equipment. Established: 1850.

KEY STATISTICS Number of Employees: 13,000.

HIRING HISTORY Number of professional employees hired in 1993: 94.

EXPERTISE/EDUCATION SOUGHT: Accounting, finance, operations

CONTACT: For individuals with previous experience: Mr Richard C Hawkins, Vice President of Human Resources; Phone (717) 763-7064.

HARTMARX CORPORATION

101 WACKER DRIVE
CHICAGO, ILLINOIS 60606

OVERVIEW: Manufactures apparel. Established: 1887.

EXPERTISE/EDUCATION SOUGHT: Quality control, marketing, merchandising, sales, management

CONTACT: For individuals with previous experience: Ms Susan Klawitter, Director of Human Resources Administration; Phone (312) 357-5692.

HARTZ MOUNTAIN CORPORATION

700 FRANK RODGERS BOULEVARD SOUTH
HARRISON, NEW JERSEY 07029-2307

OVERVIEW: Manufactures and distributes pet food and related products. Established: 1926. Parent Company: Hartz Group, Inc.

KEY STATISTICS Annual Sales: $720.0 million. Number of Employees: 3,100.

EXPERTISE/EDUCATION SOUGHT: Accounting, marketing

CONTACT: Ms Debora Walker, Human Resources Assistant, 600 South 4th Street, Harrison, NJ, 07029-2305; Phone (201) 485-5300.

HARVARD COMMUNITY HEALTH PLAN

10 BROOKLINE PLACE WEST
BROOKLINE, MASSACHUSETTS 02146-7215

OVERVIEW: Provides health insurance and health care services. Established: 1968.

KEY STATISTICS Annual Sales: $904.0 million. Number of Employees: 6,000.

EXPERTISE/EDUCATION SOUGHT: Health insurance, customer service and support, marketing, information systems, finance, hospital administration, real estate, accounting, human resources, law

CONTACT: For individuals with previous experience: Ms Anne Smith, Human Resource Director; Phone (617) 731-7300.

HARVARD INDUSTRIES, INC.

CENTRAL AVENUE
UNION, NEW JERSEY 07083-5038

OVERVIEW: Manufactures office and commercial furnishings and fixtures. Established: 1932. Parent Company: FEL Corporation.

KEY STATISTICS Number of Employees: 5,600.

EXPERTISE/EDUCATION SOUGHT: Accounting, finance, data processing, manufacturing engineering, technical engineering, electronics/electronics engineering, government affairs/relations

CONTACT: For individuals with previous experience: Mr Brad Byers, Director of Human Resources; Phone (908) 686-6000.

HASBRO, INC.

1027 NEWPORT AVENUE
PAWTUCKET, RHODE ISLAND 02862

OVERVIEW: Manufactures toys. Established: 1912.

EXPERTISE/EDUCATION SOUGHT: Sales, marketing, finance, accounting, economics, product design and development

CONTACT: Mr James Kershner, Corporate Director of Staffing; Phone (401) 431-8697.

HAWAII MEDICAL SERVICE ASSOCIATION

818 KEEAUMOKU STREET
HONOLULU, HAWAII 96814-2365

OVERVIEW: Provides health insurance. Established: 1938.

KEY STATISTICS Annual Sales: $924.0 million. Number of Employees: 1,500.

HIRING HISTORY Number of professional employees hired in 1994: 50.

EXPERTISE/EDUCATION SOUGHT: Actuarial, accounting, finance, data processing, marketing, systems analysis, nursing

CONTACT: For individuals with previous experience: Ms Jennie Roberts, Manager Employment and Training; Phone (808) 944-2110; Fax (808) 941-9978.

HAWAIIAN ELECTRIC COMPANIES

900 RICHARDS STREET
HONOLULU, HAWAII 96813-2919

OVERVIEW: Electric utility. Established: 1981.

KEY STATISTICS Annual Sales: $1.0 billion. Number of Employees: 3,000.

EXPERTISE/EDUCATION SOUGHT: Electronics/electronics engineering, mechanical engineering, civil engineering

CONTACT: Mr Jeff Johnston, Director of Employment and Equal Employment Opportunity, PO Box 2750, Honolulu, HI, 96840; Phone (808) 543-5662, ext. 4685.

HAWORTH®

HAWORTH, INC.
ONE HAWORTH CENTER
HOLLAND, MICHIGAN 49423

OVERVIEW: Manufactures office furniture. Established: 1948.

KEY STATISTICS Annual Sales: $1.0 billion. Number of Employees: 7,000.

HIRING HISTORY Number of professional employees hired in 1994: 83.

EXPERTISE/EDUCATION SOUGHT: Mechanical engineering, industrial engineering, information systems, marketing, drafting

CONTACT: Ms Linda Farr, Recruiter; Phone (616) 393-1608; Fax (616)393-1551.

CORPORATE STATEMENT

Organization. *Haworth, Inc. is a quality-oriented organization voted one of the "100 Best Companies to Work For." It is a worldwide manufacturer of office furniture and is experiencing tremendous growth with customers in 72 countries around the globe.*

Opportunities and Requirements. *Haworth seeks individuals with strong engineering, technical, information systems, finance, or marketing skills who thrive on challenges.*

HAYES-WHEELS CORPORATION, INTERNATIONAL
11878 HUBBARD STREET
LIVONIA, MICHIGAN 48150

OVERVIEW: Manufactures wheels and brakes. Established: 1908. Parent Company: Massey-Ferguson.

EXPERTISE/EDUCATION SOUGHT: Product design and development

CONTACT: Mr Tom Noteman, Director of Human Resources, 38481 Huron River Drive, Romulus, MI, 48174-1158; Phone (313) 942-8172, ext. 8781.

HEALTH CARE RETIREMENT CORPORATION OF AMERICA
1 SEAGATE
TOLDEO, OHIO 43666-1558

OVERVIEW: Owns and manages 130 long term care facilities throughout the United States. Established: 1991. Parent Company: HCRC, Inc.

KEY STATISTICS Number of Employees: 16,500.

EXPERTISE/EDUCATION SOUGHT: Business administration, accounting, finance, marketing, information systems

CONTACT: For individuals with previous experience: Mr Wade O' Brian, Vice President of Human Resources; Phone (419) 252-5500, ext. 1099.

HEALTH CONSULTANTS
9030 MONROE ROAD
HOUSTON, TEXAS 77061

OVERVIEW: Gas and water leak consultants. Established: 1933.

HIRING HISTORY Number of professional employees hired in 1994: 140.

EXPERTISE/EDUCATION SOUGHT: Sales, pollution control

CONTACT: For individuals with previous experience: Mr Taren Hollister, Manager of Administration - Human Resources; Phone (713) 947-9292.

HEALTH MIDWEST
2304 EAST MEYER BOULEVARD
KANSAS CITY, MISSOURI 64132-4104

OVERVIEW: Owns several hospitals in the Kansas City area. Established: 1990.

KEY STATISTICS Annual Sales: $472.0 million. Number of Employees: 10,000.

EXPERTISE/EDUCATION SOUGHT: Dietetics, data processing, food services, hospital administration, medical records, pharmacy, registered nursing, licensed practical nursing

CONTACT: Ms Karen Lowe, Human Resources Specialist; Phone (816) 276-9111.

HEALTH-O-METER, INC.
24700 MILES ROAD
BEDFORD HEIGHTS, OHIO 44146

OVERVIEW: Manufactures electric coffee makers for the consumer market. Established: 1970.

EXPERTISE/EDUCATION SOUGHT: Sales, marketing, accounting, law

CONTACT: For individuals with previous experience: Ms Shiela Hanshaw, Affirmative Action Coordinator; Phone (216) 464-4000.

HEALTHCARE SERVICES GROUP, INC.
2643 HUNTINGDON PIKE
HUNTINGDON VALLEY, PENNSYLVANIA 19006-5197

OVERVIEW: Provides laundry service to hospitals, and nursing homes. Established: 1976.

KEY STATISTICS Annual Sales: $114.3 million. Number of Employees: 6,200.

EXPERTISE/EDUCATION SOUGHT: Business management, data processing, accounting, finance, industrial hygiene, human resources

CONTACT: For individuals with previous experience: Department of Human Resources; Phone (215) 938-1661.

HEARST CORPORATION
959 8TH AVENUE
NEW YORK, NEW YORK 10019

OVERVIEW: Publishing company. Established: 1887.

EXPERTISE/EDUCATION SOUGHT: Marketing, finance, journalism, business administration

CONTACT: Mr Kenneth Feldman, Vice President of Human Resources, 224 West 57th Street, New York, NY, 10019; Phone (212) 649-2000.

HEATCRAFT, INC.
3984 HIGHWAY 51 SOUTH
GRENADA, MISSISSIPPI 38901

OVERVIEW: Manufactures heating and air conditioning systems. Established: 1986. Parent Company: Lennox International, Inc.

KEY STATISTICS Annual Sales: $209.0 million. Number of Employees: 3,000.

EXPERTISE/EDUCATION SOUGHT: Accounting, computer programming, finance, sales, marketing, mechanical engineering, electrical engineering, design engineering, distribution, purchasing

CONTACT: For individuals with previous experience: Mr Steven Wolfe, Manager Employment Services, PO Box 799900, Dallas, TX, 75379; Phone (214) 497-5270.

HECHINGER COMPANY
1801 MCCORMICK DRIVE
LANDOVER, MARYLAND 20785-1684

OVERVIEW: Operates chain of home improvement stores. Established: 1911.

KEY STATISTICS Annual Sales: $2.0 billion. Number of Employees: 17,000.

EXPERTISE/EDUCATION SOUGHT: Business administration

CONTACT: Ms Arletta Nicholl, Corporate Recruiter; Phone (301) 341-1000.

H. J. HEINZ COMPANY
600 GRANT STREET
PITTSBURGH, PENNSYLVANIA 15219-2857

OVERVIEW: Produces condiments, prepared foods, and pet food. Established: 1869.

KEY STATISTICS Number of Employees: 37,700.

EXPERTISE/EDUCATION SOUGHT: Accounting, finance, marketing, sales, law

CONTACTS: For college students and recent graduates: Mr Ross Craig, General Manager of Human Resources. For individuals with previous experience: Ms Cathy McGill, Manager of Recruitment Services; Phone (412) 456-5700.

HELENE CURTIS, INC.
325 NORTH WELLS STREET
CHICAGO, ILLINOIS 60610-4791

OVERVIEW: Manufactures and distributes cosmetics and fragrances. Established: 1927.

KEY STATISTICS Number of Employees: 3,500.

EXPERTISE/EDUCATION SOUGHT: Marketing, operations, finance, research and development, sales, accounting, auditing

CONTACT: Ms Mary Wilson, Human Resources Specialist; Phone (312) 661-0222.

HELMSLEY-SPEAR, INC.
60 EAST 42ND STREET
NEW YORK, NEW YORK 10165

OVERVIEW: Operates hotels and manages real estate.

EXPERTISE/EDUCATION SOUGHT: Accounting, real estate, finance, business management, actuarial, underwriting

CONTACTS: For college students and recent graduates: Ms Helen Coppola, Assistant Manager of Human Resources; Phone (212) 687-6400. For individuals with previous experience: Ms Jenny Voscina, Manager of Personnel; Phone (212) 687-6400.

HENRY FORD HEALTH SYSTEM
1 FORD PLACE
DETROIT, MICHIGAN 48202-3039

OVERVIEW: General hospital.

KEY STATISTICS Annual Sales: $1.0 billion. Number of Employees: 16,300.

EXPERTISE/EDUCATION SOUGHT: Medical technology, registered nursing, licensed practical nursing, occupational therapy, physical therapy, accounting, finance, marketing, data processing, computer programming

CONTACTS: For college students and recent graduates: Ms Brenda Hunt, Senior Employment Representative; Phone (313) 876-2600. For individuals with previous experience: Ms Dolores Hunt, Director of Employment; Phone (313) 876-8450.

GR HERBERGERS, INC.
600 MALL GERMAIN
SAINT CLOUD, MINNESOTA 56302

OVERVIEW: Operates chain of department stores. Established: 1927.

KEY STATISTICS Number of Employees: 4,600.

HIRING HISTORY Number of professional employees hired in 1994: 25.

EXPERTISE/EDUCATION SOUGHT: Management

CONTACT: For individuals with previous experience: Mr Neal Engelman, Director of Stores; Phone (612) 251-5351.

HERCULES, INC.
1313 NORTH MARKET STREET
WILMINGTON, DELAWARE 19894

OVERVIEW: Manufactures specialty chemicals. Established: 1912.

KEY STATISTICS Annual Sales: $3.0 billion.

EXPERTISE/EDUCATION SOUGHT: Accounting, finance, data processing, chemistry, environmental engineering

CONTACTS: For college students and recent graduates: Mr Fred J Laquinta, Director of Human Resources; Phone (302) 594-5000. For individuals with previous experience: Ms Claire Cary, Director of Staffing; Phone (302) 594-5000.

HERITAGE MEDIA CORPORATION
13355 NOEL ROAD, SUITE 500
DALLAS, TEXAS 75240-6650

OVERVIEW: Provides television, radio, and in-store marketing services.

KEY STATISTICS Annual Sales: $291.0 million. Number of Employees: 16,300.

EXPERTISE/EDUCATION SOUGHT: Accounting

CONTACT: For individuals with previous experience: Ms Amy Kruckemeyer, Human Resources Manager.

HERMAN MILLER, INC.
855 EAST MAIN STREET
ZEELAND, MICHIGAN 49464-1372

OVERVIEW: Manufactures and distributes office furniture. Established: 1905.

KEY STATISTICS Annual Sales: $32.0 million. Number of Employees: 6,005.

EXPERTISE/EDUCATION SOUGHT: Interior design, industrial engineering, mechanical engineering, accounting, data processing, finance, materials management, logistics

CONTACT: For individuals with previous experience: Mr Eric Heiberg, Senior Staffing Representative; Phone (616) 772-3300.

HERMANS SPORTING GOODS, INC.
2 GERMAK DRIVE
CARTERET, NEW JERSEY 07008-1217

OVERVIEW: Sells sporting goods. Established: 1986. Parent Company: HSG Holdings, Inc.

KEY STATISTICS Annual Sales: $300.0 million. Number of Employees: 3,000.

EXPERTISE/EDUCATION SOUGHT: Management, retail management

CONTACT: For individuals with previous experience: Mr Mike Murray, Director of Human Resources; Phone (908) 969-4227; Fax (908) 969-4767.

HERSHEY FOODS CORPORATION
100 CRYSTAL DRIVE
HERSHEY, PENNSYLVANIA 17033

OVERVIEW: Manufactures candy and other food products. Established: 1893.

KEY STATISTICS Number of Employees: 15,900.

EXPERTISE/EDUCATION SOUGHT: Human resources, chemical engineering, customer service and support, electrical engineering, sales, microbiology, food science, finance

CONTACT: Ms Pam Zerphy, Manager of Employee Relations; Phone (717) 534-7686.

HERTZ CORPORATION
225 BRAE BOULEVARD
PARK RIDGE, NEW JERSEY 07656

OVERVIEW: Provides car rental services.

KEY STATISTICS Annual Sales: $3.0 billion. Number of Employees: 18,000.

EXPERTISE/EDUCATION SOUGHT: Management, customer service and support

CONTACT: For individuals with previous experience: Human Resources Department; Phone (201) 307-2000.

HEUBLEIN, INC.
16 MUNSON ROAD
FARMINGTON, CONNECTICUT 06034

OVERVIEW: Produces and markets beverage alcohol. Established: 1873.

EXPERTISE/EDUCATION SOUGHT: Sales, marketing

CONTACT: For individuals with previous experience: Ms Anne Marie Schroeder, Manager of Sales Recruitment; Phone (203) 231-5000.

HEWITT ASSOCIATES, LLC.
100 HALF DAY ROAD
LINCOLNSHIRE, ILLINOIS 60069-3242

OVERVIEW: Provides business consulting services.

KEY STATISTICS Annual Sales: $333.0 million. Number of Employees: 4,000.

EXPERTISE/EDUCATION SOUGHT: Marketing, accounting, marketing, actuarial, human resources

CONTACT: For individuals with previous experience: Mr Ed Santimauro, Head of Recruiting; Phone (708) 295-5000.

HILLENBRAND INDUSTRIES, INC.
STATE ROUTE 46
BATESVILLE, INDIANA 47006-8835

OVERVIEW: Manufactures hospital equipment, luggage, locks, and burial caskets. Established: 1891.

KEY STATISTICS Annual Sales: $1.0 billion. Number of Employees: 9,800.

HIRING HISTORY Number of professional employees hired in 1993: 10.

EXPERTISE/EDUCATION SOUGHT: Administration, finance

CONTACT: Mr Tim Dietz, Manager of Human Resources; Phone (812) 934-7000, ext. 7771.

HILLHAVEN CORPORATION
1148 BROADWAY
TACOMA, WASHINGTON 98402-3513

OVERVIEW: Provides convalescent care. Established: 1946.

KEY STATISTICS Annual Sales: $1.0 billion. Number of Employees: 38,100.

EXPERTISE/EDUCATION SOUGHT: Human resources, data processing, finance, accounting, risk management, marketing

CONTACT: For individuals with previous experience: Ms Patricia Holterman, Manager Rehabilitation Recruiting; Phone (206) 756-4875.

HILL'S DEPARTMENT STORES
15 DAN ROAD
CANTON, MASSACHUSETTS 02021-2847

OVERVIEW: Operates chain of retail department stores. Established: 1957.

KEY STATISTICS Number of Employees: 17,775.

EXPERTISE/EDUCATION SOUGHT: Accounting, marketing, finance, retail, business management

CONTACT: For individuals with previous experience: Ms Julie Hagearty, Senior Supervisor of Recruiting; Phone (617) 821-1000.

HILTON HOTELS CORPORATION
9336 CIVIC CENTER DRIVE
BEVERLY HILLS, CALIFORNIA 90210-3604

OVERVIEW: Owns and operates hotels and casinos. Established: 1946.

KEY STATISTICS Number of Employees: 43,000.

EXPERTISE/EDUCATION SOUGHT: Marketing, finance, accounting, business management

CONTACT: For individuals with previous experience: Ms Julia Peter, Director of Human Resources; Phone (310) 278-4321.

HITACHI AMERICA, LTD.
50 PROSPECT AVENUE
TARRYTOWN, NEW YORK 10591-4625

OVERVIEW: Manufactures electronics components, computers, and automotive supplies. Established: 1959.

KEY STATISTICS Annual Sales: $3.0 billion. Number of Employees: 2,610.

EXPERTISE/EDUCATION SOUGHT: Accounting, marketing, sales, electronics/electronics engineering, computer engineering, automotive engineering

CONTACT: Mr Phil Kozlowski, Manager of Employment; Phone (914) 332-5800, ext. 301.

HITACHI DATA SYSTEMS CORPORATION
750 CENTRAL EXPRESSWAY
SANTA CLARA, CALIFORNIA 95050-2627

OVERVIEW: Manufactures and sells mainframe computers and other computer products.

KEY STATISTICS Annual Sales: $2.0 billion. Number of Employees: 2,500.

EXPERTISE/EDUCATION SOUGHT: Accounting, marketing, finance, law, sales

CONTACT: For individuals with previous experience: Ms Cathy Block, Director of Human Resources; Phone (408) 970-1000.

HITACHI METALS AMERICA, LTD.
2400 WESTCHESTER AVENUE
PURCHASE, NEW YORK 10577-2514

OVERVIEW: Manufactures metal products. Established: 1965.

KEY STATISTICS Annual Sales: $336.0 million. Number of Employees: 1,700.

EXPERTISE/EDUCATION SOUGHT: Manufacturing engineering, electrical engineering, ceramic engineering, marketing, accounting, finance

CONTACT: Mr James P Jones, Vice President of Human Resources; Phone (914) 694-9200, ext. 1265.

HM ANGLO-AMERICAN, LTD.
410 PARK AVENUE
NEW YORK, NEW YORK 10022-4407

OVERVIEW: Manufactures pigments, lighting fixtures, industrial cranes, and stainless steel ware.

KEY STATISTICS Annual Sales: $9.0 billion. Number of Employees: 80,000.

EXPERTISE/EDUCATION SOUGHT: Marketing, sales, computer programming

CONTACT: For individuals with previous experience: Mr Michael Keating, Vice President Human Resources, 99 Wood Avenue South, Iselin, NJ, 08830; Phone (908) 603-6600.

HOECHST CELANESE CORPORATION
ROUTE 202-206 NORTH
BRIDGEWATER, NEW JERSEY 08807

OVERVIEW: Manufactures chemicals, fibers, plastics, and pharmaceuticals. Established: 1918.

EXPERTISE/EDUCATION SOUGHT: Finance, accounting, law, data processing, marketing, sales

CONTACT: Ms Jill Sia, Director of University Recruiting; Phone (908) 231-2000.

HOFFMANN-LA ROCHE, INC.
340 KINGSLAND STREET
NUTLEY, NEW JERSEY 07110-1199

OVERVIEW: Manufactures pharmaceutical products. Established: 1905.

KEY STATISTICS Number of Employees: 18,000.

EXPERTISE/EDUCATION SOUGHT: Accounting, finance, marketing, data processing, computer science, business administration, pharmacy, pharmaceutical, biochemistry, chemistry

CONTACT: Mr Alvin L Vinson, Director of Human Resources; Phone (201) 235-5000.

HOLIDAY INNS, INC.
1100 ASHWOOD PARKWAY, SUITE 200
ATLANTA, GEORGIA 30346-2149

OVERVIEW: Owns and operates hotels.

KEY STATISTICS Number of Employees: 15,000.

EXPERTISE/EDUCATION SOUGHT: Marketing, finance, management information systems, accounting, real estate, law, business management, investor relations, administration

CONTACT: Ms Debbie Shaw, Manager of Employment; Phone (404) 604-2000.

HOLNAM, INC.
6211 NORTH ANN ARBOR ROAD
DUNDEE, MICHIGAN 48131

OVERVIEW: Develops land, operates mines, and produces cement. Established: 1981.

EXPERTISE/EDUCATION SOUGHT: Mechanical engineering, industrial engineering, environmental engineering, accounting, law, sales, computer programming

CONTACT: For individuals with previous experience: Mr Don Hammerstrom, Manager Employee Relations.

HOLY CROSS HEALTH SYSTEM CORPORATION
3606 EAST JEFFERSON BOULEVARD
SOUTH BEND, INDIANA 46615-3036

OVERVIEW: Provides health care. Established: 1978.

KEY STATISTICS Annual Sales: $24.7 million. Number of Employees: 18,360.

EXPERTISE/EDUCATION SOUGHT: Communications, accounting, finance, marketing, data processing

CONTACT: Mr Jeff Bernard, Director of Human Resources; Phone (219) 233-8558, ext. 231.

HOME DEPOT, INC.
3030 NORTH ROCKY POINT DRIVE
TAMPA, FLORIDA 33607-4089

OVERVIEW: Operates chain of home improvement stores. Established: 1978.

KEY STATISTICS Annual Sales: $9.0 billion. Number of Employees: 50,700.

EXPERTISE/EDUCATION SOUGHT: Sales, marketing, accounting, computer programming

CONTACT: For individuals with previous experience: Mr David Bloom, Staffing Manager; Phone (813) 289-0040.

HOME LIFE INSURANCE COMPANY
1 AMERICAN ROW
HARTFORD, CONNECTICUT 06103-5056

OVERVIEW: Provides life insurance.

EXPERTISE/EDUCATION SOUGHT: Accounting, finance, real estate, credit/credit analysis, computer programming, auditing, underwriting, health insurance, sales, marketing

CONTACT: For individuals with previous experience: Ms Wyrot Ward, Director of Human Resources; Phone (203) 253-1000.

HOME QUARTERS WAREHOUSE, INC.
575 LYNNHAVEN PARKWAY
VIRGINIA BEACH, VIRGINIA 23452-7311

OVERVIEW: Operates chain of home improvement warehouses. Parent Company: Hechinger Company.

KEY STATISTICS Annual Sales: $1.0 billion. Number of Employees: 8,500.

EXPERTISE/EDUCATION SOUGHT: Warehousing

CONTACT: For individuals with previous experience: Mr Alan Noel, Senior Vice President of Human Resources; Phone (804) 498-7100.

HOME SHOPPING NETWORK, INC.
2501 118TH AVENUE NORTH
SAINT PETERSBURG, FLORIDA 33716-1900

OVERVIEW: Home shopping service and cable television network. Established: 1982.

KEY STATISTICS Annual Sales: $1.0 billion. Number of Employees: 5,018.

HIRING HISTORY Number of professional employees hired in 1993: 300.

EXPERTISE/EDUCATION SOUGHT: Merchandising, business administration, auditing, graphic arts, software engineering/development, hardware engineering, telecommunications, television broadcasting

CONTACT: Mr Daryl Baker, Director of Employment, PO Box 9090, Clearwater, FL, 34618; Phone (813) 572-8585.

HOMEDCO GROUP, INC.
17650 NEWHOPE STREET
FOUNTAIN VALLEY, CALIFORNIA 92708-4220

OVERVIEW: Provides home health care.

KEY STATISTICS Annual Sales: $470.0 million. Number of Employees: 4,501.

EXPERTISE/EDUCATION SOUGHT: Management information systems, finance, human resources, accounting, registered nursing, operations, respiratory therapy, pharmacy

CONTACT: For individuals with previous experience: Ms Sandy Northcutt, Professional Staffing; Phone (714) 755-5600.

HOMELAND STORES, INC.
400 NORTHEAST 36TH STREET
OKLAHOMA CITY, OKLAHOMA 73105

OVERVIEW: Operates chain of food stores. Established: 1988.

EXPERTISE/EDUCATION SOUGHT: Management information systems

CONTACT: Ms Joanne Pace, Supervisor of Human Resources; Phone (405) 557-5500.

HON INDUSTRIES, INC.
414 EAST 3RD STREET
MUSCATINE, IOWA 52761-4199

OVERVIEW: Manufactures office furniture and office products. Established: 1944.

KEY STATISTICS Number of Employees: 6,257.

HIRING HISTORY Number of professional employees hired in 1993: 35.

EXPERTISE/EDUCATION SOUGHT: Advertising, marketing, finance, accounting, manufacturing engineering, business management, human resources, design engineering

CONTACT: Mr John Wojtecki, Manager of Human Resources; Phone (319) 264-7400.

HONDA OF AMERICA MANUFACTURING, INC.
24000 HONDA PARKWAY
MARYSVILLE, OHIO 43040

OVERVIEW: Manufactures cars and motorcycles. Established: 1978. Parent Company: American Honda Motor Company, Inc.

KEY STATISTICS Annual Sales: $6.0 billion. Number of Employees: 10,200.

EXPERTISE/EDUCATION SOUGHT: Engineering, computer engineering, information systems, electrical engineering, mechanical engineering, computer analysis

CONTACT: Ms Diane Ross, Recruiter; Phone (513) 642-5000.

HONEYWELL TECHNOLOGY CENTER
3660 TECHNOLOGY DRIVE
MINNEAPOLIS, MINNESOTA 55418

OVERVIEW: Researches and develops advanced technologies and products. Established: 1885.

KEY STATISTICS Annual Sales: $6.0 billion. Number of Employees: 475.

EXPERTISE/EDUCATION SOUGHT: Design engineering, product design and development, software engineering/development, manufacturing engineering, sales

CONTACT: For individuals with previous experience: Mr Ernie Von Heinberg, Manager of Corporate Staffing.

HOOPER HOLMES, INC.
170 MOUNT AIRY ROAD
BASKING RIDGE, NEW JERSEY 07920-2016

OVERVIEW: Provides supply services to nursing homes. Established: 1899.

KEY STATISTICS Annual Sales: $187.4 million. Number of Employees: 11,600.

EXPERTISE/EDUCATION SOUGHT: Management information systems, data processing

CONTACTS: For college students and recent graduates: Ms Jennifer Ferluga, Personnel Coordinator; Phone (908) 766-5000. For individuals with previous experience: Mr Richard D'Alesandro, Manager of Human Resources; Phone (908) 766-5000.

HOOVER COMPANY, INC.
101 EAST MAPLE STREET
CANTON, OHIO 44720-2597

OVERVIEW: Manufactures vacuum cleaners and electric floor washers and polishers. Established: 1908.

KEY STATISTICS Annual Sales: $500.0 million. Number of Employees: 4,000.

EXPERTISE/EDUCATION SOUGHT: Electrical engineering, mechanical engineering, plastics engineering

CONTACT: For individuals with previous experience: Ms Norma Feim, Human Resources Manager.

HORIZON HEALTHCARE CORPORATION
6001 INDIAN SCHOOL ROAD NORTHEAST
ALBUQUERQUE, NEW MEXICO 87110-4152

OVERVIEW: Owns and operates nursing homes. Established: 1986.

KEY STATISTICS Annual Sales: $367.9 million. Number of Employees: 15,700.

EXPERTISE/EDUCATION SOUGHT: Administration, nursing, physical therapy, occupational therapy, speech therapy, nursing management and administration

CONTACT: For individuals with previous experience: Ms Peggy Cave, Recruiter; Phone (505) 881-4961.

HORMEL FOODS CORPORATION
1 HORMEL PLACE
AUSTIN, MINNESOTA 55912-3680

OVERVIEW: Manufactures food. Established: 1891.

KEY STATISTICS Annual Sales: $3.0 billion. Number of Employees: 9,500.

HIRING HISTORY Number of professional employees hired in 1994: 130.

EXPERTISE/EDUCATION SOUGHT: Sales, business management, accounting, business administration, marketing

CONTACT: Ms Lynette M VanHyfte, Professional Employment Representative, Suite 981, 1 Hormel Place, Austin, MN, 55912-3680; Phone (507) 437-5623.

CORPORATE PROFILE

Company Overview. *Hormel Foods is a Fortune 500 company with the ability to move aggressively into new areas of opportunity, domestic or international. It was founded in 1891 in Austin, Minnesota. Hormel Foods and its family of subsidiaries manufacture, market, and distribute thousands of processed food products worldwide that are known and respected by consumers, retail grocers, food service operators, and industrial customers. Some of the company's well-established trademarks are as follows: Dinty Moore, Chi Chi's, House of Tsang, Cure 81, Black Label, and Light & Lean.*

The company's mission is clear: "To be a leader in the food field with highly differentiated quality products that attain optimum share of market while meeting established profit objectives."

Fiscal 1994 was a record-breaking year for Hormel. Dollar sales passed the $3 billion mark. Net earnings also reached an all-time high at $118 million. Cash dividends rose 14 percent, making this the 28th consecutive year in which dividends on common stock have increased. In fiscal 1994, the company spent $65 million to ensure that Hormel Foods continues to operate efficiently.

Entry-Level Opportunities—Sales, Production Management, and More. *Hormel Foods Corporation offers opportunities to college graduates who have enjoyed leading and influencing others. People who find it rewarding to give a little more to a task than just what was required are welcomed to the company. The company is particularly interested in people who have a history of accomplishments that reflect initiative and problem-solving abilities.*

Sales positions exist throughout the United States. The rewards and recognition are abundant in this highly competitive industry as a sales representative strives to increase business with existing customers in an established territory.

Production management positions are primarily in the Midwest. Providing leadership to a highly skilled workforce, coordinating department functions with peers, and anticipating needs gives these managers a great sense of accomplishment.

Other entry-level positions include staff accountant, computer analyst, quality and process control engineer, industrial engineer, and associate maintenance engineer.

Career Advancement. *In this promote-from-within environment, employees begin their careers at entry level. Aggressive high achievers will succeed and be recognized for their contributions. Career paths show no boundaries, as many employees early in their careers attain positions of great responsibility either within their entry-level division or by crossing over into another function. Promotions typically involve relocation.*

HOSPITAL SISTERS HEALTH SYSTEM
SANGAMON AVENUE ROAD, PO BOX 19431
SPRINGFIELD, ILLINOIS 62794-9431

OVERVIEW: Owns and operates hospitals and medical centers. Established: 1979.

KEY STATISTICS Annual Sales: $420.0 million. Number of Employees: 12,500.

HIRING HISTORY Number of professional employees hired in 1994: 12. 1993: 5.

EXPERTISE/EDUCATION SOUGHT: Finance, management information systems, accounting, auditing, computer programming, systems analysis

CONTACTS: For college students and recent graduates: Ms Billie Johnston, Manager of Personnel; Phone (217) 522-6969. For individuals with previous experience: Mr Charles Moe, Vice President of Human Resources; Phone (217) 522-6969.

HOST MARRIOTT, INC.
10400 FERNWOOD ROAD
BETHESDA, MARYLAND 20817-1109

OVERVIEW: Owns and operates hotels and resorts.

KEY STATISTICS Number of Employees: 12,000.

HIRING HISTORY Number of professional employees hired in 1993: 10.

EXPERTISE/EDUCATION SOUGHT: Human resources, business management, law, information systems, quality control, administration, marketing, finance, accounting, investment

CONTACT: Ms Cathy Giacolone, Director of Recruiting.

HOUSEHOLD FINANCE CORPORATION
2700 SANDERS ROAD
PROSPECT HEIGHTS, ILLINOIS 60070-2799

OVERVIEW: Provides consumer loan and financing services. Established: 1981. Parent Company: Household International, Inc.

KEY STATISTICS Number of Employees: 5,300.

EXPERTISE/EDUCATION SOUGHT: Finance, accounting, marketing, auditing, underwriting

CONTACT: For individuals with previous experience: Ms Jeanne Gruner, Director of Human Resources; Phone (708) 564-7359.

HOUSTON INDUSTRIES, INC.
4400 POST OAK PARKWAY
HOUSTON, TEXAS 77027

OVERVIEW: Electric utility. Established: 1976.

KEY STATISTICS Annual Sales: $4.0 billion. Number of Employees: 11,350.

EXPERTISE/EDUCATION SOUGHT: Auditing, finance, accounting, systems integration, treasury management, public affairs, electrical engineering

CONTACT: For individuals with previous experience: Ms Diane Thompson, Administrator of Corporate Personnel, PO Box 4567, Houston, TX, 77027; Phone (713) 629-3000.

HOVNANIAN ENTERPRISES, INC.
10 STATE HIGHWAY 35
RED BANK, NEW JERSEY 07701-5902

OVERVIEW: Develops real estate. Established: 1967.

KEY STATISTICS Annual Sales: $587.0 million. Number of Employees: 1,070.

EXPERTISE/EDUCATION SOUGHT: Administration, architecture

CONTACT: For individuals with previous experience: Ms Sydney Koerner, Director of Human Resources.

HOWMET CORPORATION
475 STEAMBOAT ROAD
GREENWICH, CONNECTICUT 06830-7144

OVERVIEW: Manufactures turbines and electrical supplies. Established: 1970.

KEY STATISTICS Annual Sales: $11.0 billion. Number of Employees: 26,000.

EXPERTISE/EDUCATION SOUGHT: Mechanical engineering, metallurgical engineering, ceramic engineering, materials science

CONTACT: Ms Cheryl Matteis-Busby, Director of Human Resources; Phone (203) 661-4600.

HUBBELL, INC.
584 DERBY MILFORD ROAD
ORANGE, CONNECTICUT 06477

OVERVIEW: Manufactures wiring, cable, lighting, electronics, and industrial control equipment. Established: 1888.

EXPERTISE/EDUCATION SOUGHT: Finance, auditing

CONTACT: Mr George Zurman, Director of Human Resources, PO Box 549, Orange, CT, 06477-4024; Phone (203) 799-4100, ext. 255.

HUDSON FOODS, INC.
HUDSON ROAD AND 13TH STREET
ROGERS, ARKANSAS 72756-2396

OVERVIEW: Produces poultry products and processed meats. Established: 1972.

KEY STATISTICS Annual Sales: $921.0 million. Number of Employees: 8,554.

HIRING HISTORY Number of professional employees hired in 1994: 75. 1993: 100.

EXPERTISE/EDUCATION SOUGHT: Accounting, chemistry, computer programming, food science, marketing, sales

CONTACT: For individuals with previous experience: Mr Michael Needham, Corporate Human Resources Representative, PO Box 777, Rogers, AR, 72757; Phone (501) 636-1100.

HUFFY CORPORATION
225 BYERS ROAD
MIAMISBURG, OHIO 45342-3657

OVERVIEW: Manufactures bicycles and sporting goods. Established: 1924.

KEY STATISTICS Number of Employees: 5,854.

HIRING HISTORY Number of professional employees hired in 1993: 3.

EXPERTISE/EDUCATION SOUGHT: Marketing, finance, human resources, accounting, computer programming

CONTACT: Mr Donald Scheick, Director of Human Resources, 7701 Byers Road, Miamisburg, OH, 45342-3657; Phone (513) 866-6251.

HUGHES ELECTRONICS
7200 HUGHESTERRACE
LOS ANGELES, CALIFORNIA 90045

OVERVIEW: Manufactures microelectronic components. Established: 1985.

EXPERTISE/EDUCATION SOUGHT: Electrical engineering, electronics/electronics engineering, mechanical engineering, computer science, physics

CONTACT: Ms Ruby Quallsgray, Manager of Staffing and College Programs, PO Box 28, Mailstop/C128, Los Angeles, CA, 90080-0028; Phone (310) 568-7187.

HUGHES MISSILE SYSTEMS INTERNATIONAL COMPANY
PO BOX 45066
LOS ANGELES, CALIFORNIA 90045-0066

OVERVIEW: Manufactures military hardware and weapon systems.

EXPERTISE/EDUCATION SOUGHT: Electrical engineering, optics

CONTACTS: For college students and recent graduates: Staffing and College Programs Office, "Fellowship Programs", Los Angeles, CA, 90080-0028; Phone (310) 568-6711. For individuals with previous experience: Mr Richard E Battle, Director Human Resources-International; Phone (310) 560-7775.

HUMANA, INC.
500 WEST MAIN STREET
LOUISVILLE, KENTUCKY 40202-4268

OVERVIEW: Provides health insurance. Established: 1961.

KEY STATISTICS Annual Sales: $3.0 billion. Number of Employees: 8,800.

EXPERTISE/EDUCATION SOUGHT: Accounting, finance, actuarial, economics, sales

CONTACT: Ms Ann Spalding, Senior Recruiting Coordinator; Phone (502) 580-1000, ext. 2060.

J. B. HUNT TRANSPORT SERVICES, INC.
615 J.B. HUNT CORPORATE DRIVE
LOWELL, ARKANSAS 72745

OVERVIEW: Provides truck and intermodal shipping services. Established: 1961.

KEY STATISTICS Number of Employees: 10,520.

EXPERTISE/EDUCATION SOUGHT: Data processing, management, logistics

CONTACTS: For college students and recent graduates: Ms Amy McDonald, Personnel Assistant; Phone (501) 820-8246. For individuals with previous experience: Ms Sherry Moncrief, Personnel Manager; Phone (501) 820-0000.

HUNT-WESSON, INC.
1645 WEST VALENCIA DRIVE
FULLERTON, CALIFORNIA 92633-3860

OVERVIEW: Produces canned fruits and vegetables and cooking oils. Established: 1890. Parent Company: Norton Simon, Inc.

KEY STATISTICS Annual Sales: $1.0 billion. Number of Employees: 7,000.

EXPERTISE/EDUCATION SOUGHT: Marketing, data processing, finance, research, accounting, sales, business administration, business management

CONTACT: Ms Enid Smith, Manager of Employment; Phone (714) 680-1000.

HUNTINGTON BANK
41 SOUTH HIGH STREET
COLUMBUS, OHIO 43287

OVERVIEW: Commercial bank. Established: 1866.

KEY STATISTICS Assets: $2.0 billion. Number of Employees: 8,395.

HIRING HISTORY Number of professional employees hired in 1994: 40.

EXPERTISE/EDUCATION SOUGHT: Computer programming, systems analysis, accounting, finance

CONTACT: Mr Joseph D'Andrea, Senior Vice President of Executive Recruitment; Phone (614) 476-8300.

HUSSMANN CORPORATION
12999 SAINT CHARLES ROCK ROAD
BRIDGETON, MISSOURI 63044-2419

OVERVIEW: Manufactures refrigerators and displays for food stores. Established: 1978. Parent Company: Whitman Corporation.

KEY STATISTICS Number of Employees: 6,900.

HIRING HISTORY Number of professional employees hired in 1994: 200. 1993: 100.

EXPERTISE/EDUCATION SOUGHT: Manufacturing engineering, mechanical engineering, international finance

CONTACT: For individuals with previous experience: Mr Jean Evans, Corporate Vice President of Human Resources; Phone (314) 291-2000, ext. 6534.

HY-VEE FOOD STORES, INC.
1801 OSCEOLA AVENUE
CHARITON, IOWA 50049-1503

OVERVIEW: Operates chain of food stores. Established: 1930.

KEY STATISTICS Number of Employees: 28,537.

EXPERTISE/EDUCATION SOUGHT: Retail, sales, business administration

CONTACT: For individuals with previous experience: Mr Jerry Willis, Manager of Human Resources; Phone (515) 774-2121.

HYATT CORPORATION
200 WEST MADISON STREET
CHICAGO, ILLINOIS 60606-3414

OVERVIEW: Owns and operates hotels and resorts. Established: 1979.

KEY STATISTICS Number of Employees: 24,000.

EXPERTISE/EDUCATION SOUGHT: Sales, public relations, hospitality/hotel and restaurant management, finance, accounting, advertising

CONTACT: Mr Gene Monteagudo, Manager of College Relations; Phone (312) 750-1234, ext. 8234.

HYGRADE FOOD PRODUCTS ASSOCIATION
40 OAK HOLLOW STREET, SUITE 355
SOUTHFIELD, MICHIGAN 48034-7452

OVERVIEW: Manufactures meat products. Established: 1927.

KEY STATISTICS Annual Sales: $295.0 million. Number of Employees: 4,000.

EXPERTISE/EDUCATION SOUGHT: Sales, production management

CONTACT: For individuals with previous experience: Mr Mark Nevio, Vice President Human Resources.

IBP, INC.
HIGHWAY 35, PO BOX 515
DAKOTA CITY, NEBRASKA 68731-0513

OVERVIEW: Owns and operates beef and pork processing plants. Established: 1960.

KEY STATISTICS Annual Sales: $12.0 billion. Number of Employees: 29,200.

EXPERTISE/EDUCATION SOUGHT: Accounting, finance, data processing, law, economics

CONTACT: Ms Louise Norris, Corporate Recruiter; Phone (402) 494-2061.

ICI AMERICAS, INC.
3411 SILVERSIDE ROAD
WILMINGTON, DELAWARE 19850-5391

OVERVIEW: Manages operations in pharmaceuticals, paints, fibers, and financial services. Established: 1912. Parent Company: ICI American Holdings, Inc.

KEY STATISTICS Annual Sales: $3.0 billion. Number of Employees: 9,500.

EXPERTISE/EDUCATION SOUGHT: Chemical engineering, mechanical engineering, chemistry

CONTACTS: For college students and recent graduates: College Relations - Human Resources. For individuals with previous experience: Manager of Wilmington Human Resources Services, PO Box 15391, Wilmington, DE, 19850-5391.

ICN PHARMACEUTICALS, INC.
3300 HYLAND AVENUE
COSTA MESA, CALIFORNIA 92626-1482

OVERVIEW: Distributes pharmaceutical products. Established: 1960.

KEY STATISTICS Annual Sales: $63.0 million. Number of Employees: 549.

EXPERTISE/EDUCATION SOUGHT: Pharmaceutical

CONTACT: Ms Christine Schumacher, Manager of Recruiting; Phone (714) 545-0100, ext. 3087.

IDAHO POWER COMPANY
1221 WEST IDAHO STREET
BOISE, IDAHO 83702-5610

OVERVIEW: Electric utility. Established: 1915.

KEY STATISTICS Number of Employees: 1,654.

EXPERTISE/EDUCATION SOUGHT: Marketing, accounting, information systems

CONTACT: For individuals with previous experience: Mr Dan Miner, Manager of Employment and Compensation; Phone (208) 383-2883.

IDEX CORPORATION
630 DUNDEE ROAD, SUITE 400
NORTHBROOK, ILLINOIS 60062-2745

OVERVIEW: Manufactures fluid handling and industrial products.

KEY STATISTICS Annual Sales: $309.0 million. Number of Employees: 19.

HIRING HISTORY Number of professional employees hired in 1993: 4.

EXPERTISE/EDUCATION SOUGHT: Human resources, administration, accounting

Idex Corporation (continued)

Contact: For individuals with previous experience: Mr Jerry Derck, Vice President of Human Resources; Phone (708) 498-7070.

IHC HOSPITALS, INC.
36 SOUTH STATE STREET
SALT LAKE CITY, UTAH 84111

Overview: Owns and operates hospitals and medical centers.

Expertise/Education Sought: Accounting, finance, marketing, data processing

Contacts: For college students and recent graduates: Ms Pam Alder, Human Resources Generalist; Phone (801) 533-8282. For individuals with previous experience: Ms Ruth Strong, Human Resources Generalist; Phone (801) 533-8282.

ILLINOIS POWER COMPANY
500 SOUTH 27TH STREET
DECATUR, ILLINOIS 62525

Overview: Electric utility. Established: 1923.

Key Statistics Number of Employees: 4,540.

Expertise/Education Sought: Computer science, marketing

Contact: For individuals with previous experience: Ms Veta Rudolph, Professional Recruiting Specialist.

IMC GLOBAL, INC.
2100 SANDERS ROAD
NORTHBROOK, ILLINOIS 60062-6146

Overview: Manufactures fertilizer. Established: 1909.

Key Statistics Annual Sales: $897.0 million. Number of Employees: 5,200.

Expertise/Education Sought: Data processing, accounting, finance, marketing, law

Contact: Human Resources Department; Phone (708) 272-9200.

IMI CORNELIUS, INC.
1 CORNELIUS PLACE
ANOKA, MINNESOTA 55303-1583

Overview: Manufactures beverage dispensing equipment. Established: 1981.

Key Statistics Annual Sales: $450.0 million. Number of Employees: 3,500.

Expertise/Education Sought: Accounting, marketing, finance, sales, electronics/electronics engineering, hardware engineering, mechanical engineering, design engineering

Contact: Staffing Administrator; Phone (612) 422-3650.

IN HOME HEALTH, INC.
601 LAKESHORE PARKWAY, SUITE 500
MINNETONKA, MINNESOTA 55305-5214

Overview: Provides home health care services. Established: 1977.

Key Statistics Annual Sales: $104.0 million. Number of Employees: 5,150.

Expertise/Education Sought: Accounting, nursing

Contact: For individuals with previous experience: Mr Mike Murphy, Human Resources Coordinator.

INDEPENDENCE BLUE CROSS
1901 MARKET STREET
PHILADELPHIA, PENNSYLVANIA 19103

Overview: Provides health insurance. Established: 1938.

Expertise/Education Sought: CAT/MRI technology, customer service and support, information systems

Contact: Mr Ronald Gilg, Manager of Staffing; Phone (215) 241-3210.

INDEPENDENCE BROADCASTING CORPORATION
199 ETHAN ALLEN HIGHWAY
RIDGEFIELD, CONNECTICUT 06877

Overview: Radio broadcasting stations.

Expertise/Education Sought: Accounting, data processing

Contact: For individuals with previous experience: Ms Beth Rudd, Assistant to the President; Phone (203) 431-6877.

INDEPENDENT LIFE AND ACCIDENT INSURANCE COMPANY
1 INDEPENDENT DRIVE
JACKSONVILLE, FLORIDA 32276-0001

Overview: Provides life, health, accident, property, and casualty insurance. Established: 1920.

Key Statistics Annual Sales: $472.0 million. Number of Employees: 4,300.

Expertise/Education Sought: Marketing, accounting, finance, underwriting, auditing

Contact: Ms Marian Evans, Recruiter; Phone (904) 358-5151.

INDIANA MICHIGAN POWER COMPANY
1 SUMMIT SQUARE
FORT WAYNE, INDIANA 46801

Overview: Electric and gas utility. Established: 1925. Parent Company: American Electric Power Company.

Key Statistics Number of Employees: 3,500.

Hiring History Number of professional employees hired in 1993: 100.

Expertise/Education Sought: Physics, accounting, purchasing, finance, marketing, sales, computer programming, law

Contacts: For college students and recent graduates: Mr Robert Handle, Training Supervisor; Phone (219) 425-2151. For individuals with previous experience: Ms Sheryl Edwards, Personnel Service Manager; Phone (219) 425-2143.

INDIANAPOLIS POWER AND LIGHT COMPANY
25 MONUMENT CIRCLE
INDIANAPOLIS, INDIANA 46206-2936

Overview: Electric utility.

Expertise/Education Sought: Accounting, computer programming, finance, electrical engineering, mechanical engineering, civil engineering

Contact: For individuals with previous experience: Ms Celia Hawkens, Supervisor of Employees, PO Box 1595, Indianapolis, IN, 46206-1595; Phone (317) 261-8261; Fax (317) 261-8026.

ING AMERICA LIFE
5780 POWERS FERRY ROAD
ATLANTA, GEORGIA 30327-4349

Overview: Provides life and health insurance.

Key Statistics Annual Sales: $650.0 million. Number of Employees: 4,125.

Expertise/Education Sought: Administration, health insurance

Contact: For individuals with previous experience: Mr John Krawietz, Human Resources Offices; Phone (404) 980-5710.

INGALLS SHIPBUILDING, INC.
1000 ACCESS ROAD
PASCAGOULA, MISSISSIPPI 39567

Overview: Constructs ships. Established: 1968. Parent Company: Litton Industries, Inc.

Key Statistics Annual Sales: $1.0 billion. Number of Employees: 15,000.

Hiring History Number of professional employees hired in 1993: 24.

EXPERTISE/EDUCATION SOUGHT: Mechanical engineering, electrical engineering, design engineering, industrial engineering, accounting

CONTACT: For college students and recent graduates: Mr George Canaga, Director of Employment; Phone (601) 935-3594.

INGERSOLL-RAND

INGERSOLL-RAND COMPANY
200 CHESTNUT RIDGE ROAD
WOODCLIFF LAKE, NEW JERSEY 07675

OVERVIEW: Manufactures industrial machinery and equipment. Established: 1871.

KEY STATISTICS Annual Sales: $5.0 billion. Number of Employees: 35,000.

HIRING HISTORY Number of professional employees hired in 1993: 97.

EXPERTISE/EDUCATION SOUGHT: Sales, accounting, human resources, finance, mechanical engineering, industrial engineering

CONTACT: For college students and recent graduates: Manager of College Relations.

CORPORATE PROFILE

Ingersoll-Rand is a leading worldwide manufacturer of industrial machinery, construction equipment, pumps, tools, bearings, and door hardware. Through joint ventures, it is a leading supplier of hydrocarbon processing equipment and services. Ingersoll-Rand has 93 manufacturing plants, 45 of which are outside the United States.

Corporate Profile. Ingersoll-Rand is one of the most experienced and trusted suppliers of machinery, equipment, and services to worldwide manufacturing, assembly, process, construction, and mining industries. Through its Torrington Company subsidiary, the company supplies a broad line of bearings and precision components to the automotive industry and bearings used in general industry. Through its Schlage Lock subsidiary and related businesses, the company provides commercial, institutional, and residential buildings with a variety of door hardware and security products.

Expertise Needed. Ingersoll-Rand's products are designed to enhance the efficiency and productivity of customer operations or products. As a result, emphasis is placed upon hiring individuals with strong engineering skills who can help develop new or improve existing products. Also, opportunities exist for individuals who can apply technical knowledge in a sales capacity, especially those who can find appropriate solutions to customer needs. Because of Ingersoll-Rand's high-quality standards, individuals skilled in design and manufacturing engineering are required to continually improve the way products are developed and built.

INGRAM MICRO, INC.
1600 EAST SAINT ANDREW PLACE
SANTA ANA, CALIFORNIA 92705

OVERVIEW: Distributes personal computer products and software. Established: 1979.

KEY STATISTICS Annual Sales: $5.0 billion. Number of Employees: 2,100.

HIRING HISTORY Number of professional employees hired in 1994: 700. 1993: 500.

EXPERTISE/EDUCATION SOUGHT: Sales, marketing, purchasing, customer service and support

CONTACTS: For college students and recent graduates: Ms Cynthia Baker, Manager of Human Resources. For individuals with previous experience: Mr Joe Hart, Senior Manager Staffing; Phone (714) 566-1000.

INLAND CONTAINER CORPORATION
4030 VINCENNES ROAD
INDIANAPOLIS, INDIANA 46268

OVERVIEW: Manufactures corrugated and folding boxes. Established: 1925. Parent Company: Temple-Inland, Inc.

KEY STATISTICS Number of Employees: 8,000.

EXPERTISE/EDUCATION SOUGHT: Accounting, computer programming, business management, production management

CONTACT: For individuals with previous experience: Mr Jack Leon, Corporate Manager; Phone (317) 879-4521.

INLAND MATERIALS DISTRIBUTING
4400 PEACHTREE INDUSTRIAL BOULEVARD
NORCROSS, GEORGIA 30071

OVERVIEW: Distributes metals and industrial plastics.

HIRING HISTORY Number of professional employees hired in 1994: 3.

EXPERTISE/EDUCATION SOUGHT: Accounting, finance, marketing, warehousing, business management, sales

CONTACT: Ms Lora Smith, Manager of Human Resources; Phone (404) 368-4311.

INSILCO CORPORATION
425 METRO PLACE NORTH
DUBLIN, OHIO 43017

OVERVIEW: Manages operations in the automotive, electronics, defense, and consumer products industries. Established: 1898. Parent Company: INR Partners.

EXPERTISE/EDUCATION SOUGHT: Accounting, finance, logistics, purchasing

CONTACT: For individuals with previous experience: Mr Les Jacob, Vice President of Human Resources; Phone (915) 684-4411.

INSTEEL INDUSTRIES, INC.
1373 BOGGS DRIVE
MOUNT AIRY, NORTH CAROLINA 27030-2145

OVERVIEW: Manufactures wire and wire products. Established: 1958.

KEY STATISTICS Number of Employees: 1,050.

HIRING HISTORY Number of professional employees hired in 1993: 5.

EXPERTISE/EDUCATION SOUGHT: Data processing, finance, marketing

CONTACT: Mr Richard Starr, Director of Human Resources; Phone (910) 786-2141.

INTEGRA FINANCIAL CORPORATION
4 PPG PLACE
PITTSBURGH, PENNSYLVANIA 15222-5408

OVERVIEW: National commercial bank. Established: 1989.

KEY STATISTICS Annual Sales: $978.0 million. Number of Employees: 5,047.

EXPERTISE/EDUCATION SOUGHT: Accounting, finance, marketing

CONTACT: Mr Robert Price, Manager of Personnel Services; Phone (412) 644-7974.

INTEL CORPORATION
2200 MISSION COLLEGE BOULEVARD
SANTA CLARA, CALIFORNIA 95054-1537

OVERVIEW: Manufactures microprocessors and computer memory products. Established: 1968.

KEY STATISTICS Annual Sales: $9.0 billion. Number of Employees: 25,800.

EXPERTISE/EDUCATION SOUGHT: Electrical engineering, mechanical engineering

CONTACT: For individuals with previous experience: Ms Barbara Maxey, Human Resources-Site Services Manager; Phone (408) 765-3735.

INTELLIGENT ELECTRONICS, INC.
411 EAGLEVIEW BOULEVARD
EXTON, PENNSYLVANIA 19341

OVERVIEW: Sells computer and office equipment through wholesale and retail outlets. Established: 1982.

KEY STATISTICS Annual Sales: $2.0 billion. Number of Employees: 520.

EXPERTISE/EDUCATION SOUGHT: Management, sales, marketing

Intelligent Electronics, Inc. (continued)

CONTACT: For individuals with previous experience: Human Resources Department; Phone (610) 458-5500.

INTER-CITY PRODUCTS CORPORATION

1136 HEIL QUAKER BOULEVARD
LA VERGNE, TENNESSEE 37086

OVERVIEW: Manufactures refrigeration and heating equipment.

KEY STATISTICS Number of Employees: 3,000.

HIRING HISTORY Number of professional employees hired in 1993: 32.

EXPERTISE/EDUCATION SOUGHT: Accounting, computer programming, marketing, sales, industrial engineering, design engineering

CONTACT: For individuals with previous experience: Ms Lee Anne Allen, Manager of Training and Recruitment, PO Box 3005, LaVergne, TN, 37086; Phone (615) 793-0450.

INTERGRAPH CORPORATION

1 MADISON INDUSTRIAL PARK
HUNTSVILLE, ALABAMA 35894-1112

OVERVIEW: Manufactures computers and software for industrial use. Established: 1969.

KEY STATISTICS Annual Sales: $1.0 billion. Number of Employees: 9,500.

EXPERTISE/EDUCATION SOUGHT: Electrical engineering, computer engineering, design engineering, computer-aided design

CONTACTS: For college students and recent graduates: Mr John Richards, Senior Supervisor of Staffing; Phone (205) 730-2000. For individuals with previous experience: Mr David Nawrocki, Executive Manager of Professional Employment; Phone (205) 730-7867.

THE INTERLAKE CORPORATION

550 WARRENVILLE ROAD
LISLE, ILLINOIS 60532

OVERVIEW: Multinational corporation engaged in the design, manufacture, and sale of products for the automotive, aerospace, material handling and packaging industries. Established: 1905.

EXPERTISE/EDUCATION SOUGHT: Auditing, sales, finance, accounting, law, computer programming, human resources, chemical engineering

CONTACT: Mr Craig Grant, Vice President of Human Resources; Phone (708) 852-8800.

INTERLEAF, INC.

9 HILLSIDE AVENUE
WALTHAM, MASSACHUSETTS 02154-7556

OVERVIEW: Develops document software. Established: 1981.

KEY STATISTICS Annual Sales: $111.0 million. Number of Employees: 895.

EXPERTISE/EDUCATION SOUGHT: Administration, management

CONTACT: Ms Gloria Dumas, Vice President of Human Resources; Phone (617) 290-0710.

INTERMEDICS, INC.

4000 TECHNOLOGY ROAD
ANGLETON, TEXAS 77515-2523

OVERVIEW: Manufactures surgical supplies, electromedical equipment, and cardiac rhythm instrumentation. Established: 1973. Parent Company: Sulzer Brothers, Inc.

KEY STATISTICS Annual Sales: $303.0 million. Number of Employees: 3,020.

EXPERTISE/EDUCATION SOUGHT: Accounting, computer programming, marketing, finance, electrical engineering, mechanical engineering, biomedical engineering, data processing

CONTACT: For individuals with previous experience: Ms Terri White, Technical Recruiter.

INTERMOUNTAIN HEALTH CARE, INC.

36 SOUTH STATE STREET, SUITE 220
SALT LAKE CITY, UTAH 84111-1453

OVERVIEW: Owns and operates hospitals and health care facilities. Established: 1975.

KEY STATISTICS Annual Sales: $980.0 million. Number of Employees: 19,000.

EXPERTISE/EDUCATION SOUGHT: Accounting, systems engineering, computer programming, finance, economics, data processing

CONTACT: For individuals with previous experience: Ms Ruth Strong, Human Resources Generalist; Phone (801) 530-3333; Fax (801)530-3327.

INTERNATIONAL BUSINESS MACHINES CORPORATION

OLD ORCHARD ROAD
ARMONK, NEW YORK 10504

OVERVIEW: Provides information technology and processing services and manufactures computers. Established: 1911.

KEY STATISTICS Annual Sales: $63.0 billion. Number of Employees: 256,000.

EXPERTISE/EDUCATION SOUGHT: Computer science, computer engineering, electrical engineering, finance, sales, marketing, accounting

CONTACT: For individuals with previous experience: Nearest IBM Location; Phone (914) 765-1900.

CORPORATE PROFILE

Dynamic and demanding, with challenges in all areas of advanced technology, IBM is changing dramatically. It is answering the needs of business, government, science, space exploration, education, and medicine. A company more vigorous and flexible than ever, today's IBM is best known not only for its computers but also for its consumer products, new methods of distribution, and business units with a great deal of autonomy coupled with a spirit of entrepreneurship.

Computers and communications are changing the way IBM does business, making it easier for people to gather, process, and distribute information. And IBM is at the center of all these developments. Its systems are used around the world to help conserve power, maintain inventories, diagnose illnesses, forecast weather, monitor space flights, grow healthier crops, teach new subjects, manufacture products—and for hundreds of other applications.

At IBM, employees find meaningful marketing and sales challenges. As part of a top-notch sales force, they receive the responsibility, stimulation, and encouragement to exceed their own expectations. Working with some of today's most exciting product breakthroughs, employees meet with clients and customers to analyze their needs and recommend the products and systems that will best solve their unique business problems. Graduates can apply their business degree in areas of finance and accounting, or an M.B.A. holder may be involved in a variety of business and marketing activities, such as planning, analysis, and sales.

As employees develop their knowledge and expertise, they are able to specialize and even move from one area to another. This means that they can be marketers, programmers, or financial analysts, all within IBM. To find out how to merge their talents with IBM's exciting future, students should contact their placement office or the nearest IBM location.

IBM is an equal opportunity employer.

INTERNATIONAL FLAVORS AND FRAGRANCES

521 WEST 57TH STREET
NEW YORK, NEW YORK 10019

OVERVIEW: Manufactures synthetic flavors and fragrances for commercial products. Established: 1909.

EXPERTISE/EDUCATION SOUGHT: Finance, marketing, law, sales, chemical engineering, chemistry, chemical analysis, manufacturing engineering, product design and development, product design engineering

CONTACT: For individuals with previous experience: Ms Kashmira Palkhivala, Employee Relations Manager; Phone (212) 765-5500.

INTERNATIONAL JENSEN, INC.

25 TRI STATE INTERNATIONAL, SUITE 400
LINCOLNSHIRE, ILLINOIS 60069

OVERVIEW: Manufactures stereo equipment. Established: 1988.

KEY STATISTICS Number of Employees: 2,000.

EXPERTISE/EDUCATION SOUGHT: Computer-aided design, accounting, marketing, finance, sales, computer programming

CONTACT: Ms Eileen Hoban, Human Resources Supervisor; Phone (708) 317-3700.

INTERNATIONAL MONETARY FUND

700 19TH STREET NORTHWEST
WASHINGTON, D.C. 20431-0001

OVERVIEW: Specialized agency associated with the United Nations that makes financing available to member nations. Established: 1944.

KEY STATISTICS Number of Employees: 2,700.

EXPERTISE/EDUCATION SOUGHT: Economics

CONTACT: For individuals with previous experience: Mr Christer Ahl, Division Chief of Recruitment; Phone (202) 623-7422.

INTERNATIONAL PAPER

6400 POPLAR AVENUE, COLLEGE RECRUITING
DEPARTMENT/PJO
MEMPHIS, TENNESSEE 38197

OVERVIEW: Manufactures paper and wood products and specialty products. Established: 1898.

KEY STATISTICS Annual Sales: $15.0 billion.

EXPERTISE/EDUCATION SOUGHT: Accounting, sales, human resources, marketing, management information systems

CONTACT: For individuals with previous experience: Ms Kitty Moore, Recruiting Analyst, 6400 Poplar Avenue, Dept PJO, Memphis, TN, 38197; Phone (901) 763-6000.

INTERNATIONAL RECTIFIER CORPORATION

233 KANSAS STREET
EL SEGUNDO, CALIFORNIA 90245-4316

OVERVIEW: Manufactures power semiconductors. Established: 1947.

KEY STATISTICS Annual Sales: $282.0 million. Number of Employees: 2,970.

EXPERTISE/EDUCATION SOUGHT: Marketing, sales, finance, electrical engineering, chemical engineering, design engineering

CONTACT: Ms Linda Redgrift, Manager of Human Resources; Phone (310) 322-3331.

INTERNATIONAL TELECOMMUNICATIONS SATELLITE ORGANIZATION

3400 INTERNATIONAL DRIVE NORTHWEST
WASHINGTON, D.C. 20008-3006

OVERVIEW: International consortium for communications satellite operations. Established: 1964.

KEY STATISTICS Annual Sales: $658.2 million. Number of Employees: 775.

EXPERTISE/EDUCATION SOUGHT: Sales, marketing, accounting, finance, human resources

CONTACT: For individuals with previous experience: Ms Jill Wilkinson, Senior Employment Specialist; Phone (202) 944-7895.

INTERNATIONAL TOTAL SERVICES

5005 ROCKSIDE ROAD, SUITE 1200
CLEVELAND, OHIO 44131-6808

OVERVIEW: Provides security systems and security services for airports.

KEY STATISTICS Annual Sales: $68.8 million. Number of Employees: 7,000.

EXPERTISE/EDUCATION SOUGHT: Accounting, management information systems, human resources

CONTACT: For individuals with previous experience: Ms Sonya Boardman, Human Resources Manager.

INTERTECH GROUP, INC.

4838 JENKINS AVENUE
NORTH CHARLES, SOUTH CAROLINA 29405-4816

OVERVIEW: Manufactures polymers and elastimers.

KEY STATISTICS Annual Sales: $866.0 million. Number of Employees: 6,010.

EXPERTISE/EDUCATION SOUGHT: Accounting, finance, marketing, chemistry, chemical engineering, extrusion

CONTACT: Mr Al Tiedman, Senior Vice President of Human Resources; Phone (803) 744-5174, ext. 235.

INTESYS TECHNOLOGIES, INC.

1300 NORTH FIESTA BOULEVARD
GILBERT, ARIZONA 85233-1605

OVERVIEW: Manufactures plastic moldings for computers and cars. Established: 1992.

KEY STATISTICS Annual Sales: $125.0 million. Number of Employees: 1,000.

HIRING HISTORY Number of professional employees hired in 1994: 50. 1993: 50.

EXPERTISE/EDUCATION SOUGHT: Data processing, accounting, finance

CONTACT: For individuals with previous experience: Mr Nick Smeed, Vice President of Administration; Phone (602) 497-1401.

IONICS, INC.

65 GROVE STREET
WATERTOWN, MASSACHUSETTS 02172

OVERVIEW: Provides water purification and desalination services. Established: 1948.

EXPERTISE/EDUCATION SOUGHT: Accounting, sales

CONTACT: Ms Marianne Winsser, Director of Human Resources, PO Box 9131, Watertown, MA, 02272-2882; Phone (617) 926-2500.

ISS INTERNATIONAL SERVICE SYSTEMS, INC.

375 HUDSON STREET
NEW YORK, NEW YORK 10014

OVERVIEW: Provides building maintenance and cleaning services. Established: 1964.

EXPERTISE/EDUCATION SOUGHT: Finance, marketing

CONTACT: For individuals with previous experience: Mr Lou Gadime, Supervisor of Personnel; Phone (212) 229-4000.

ITI MARKETING SERVICES, INC.

909 NORTH 91ST PLAZA
OMAHA, NEBRASKA 68114-2411

OVERVIEW: Provides telemarketing services.

KEY STATISTICS Annual Sales: $81.7 million. Number of Employees: 5,400.

EXPERTISE/EDUCATION SOUGHT: Telemarketing

CONTACT: For individuals with previous experience: Ms Denise Robertson, Director of Human Relations; Phone (402) 393-5730.

ITOCHU INTERNATIONAL, INC.
335 MADISON AVENUE
NEW YORK, NEW YORK 10017

OVERVIEW: Diversified international trading company. Established: 1889. Parent Company: ITOCHU Corporation, Japan.

KEY STATISTICS Number of Employees: 3,100.

EXPERTISE/EDUCATION SOUGHT: Accounting, finance

CONTACT: For individuals with previous experience: Mr Neil Hobart, Assistant General Manager of Human Resource Strategy.

ITT CORPORATION
1330 AVENUE OF THE AMERICAS
NEW YORK, NEW YORK 10019

OVERVIEW: Diversified company with manufacturing, hospitality, and insurance and financial services businesses. Established: 1920.

EXPERTISE/EDUCATION SOUGHT: Accounting, finance, marketing, data processing

CONTACT: For individuals with previous experience: Ms Barbara Fierro, Manager of Headquarters Personnel; Phone (212) 258-1500.

ITT DEFENSE AND ELECTRONICS
1650 TYSONS BOULEVARD, SUITE 1700
MCLEAN, VIRGINIA 22102-3901

OVERVIEW: Produces electronic defense systems for government and military uses. Established: 1992. Parent Company: ITT Corporation.

KEY STATISTICS Annual Sales: $987.0 million. Number of Employees: 15,000.

HIRING HISTORY Number of professional employees hired in 1994: 50.

EXPERTISE/EDUCATION SOUGHT: Electrical engineering, mechanical engineering, design engineering, aerospace engineering

CONTACT: For individuals with previous experience: Ms Elizabeth Gray, Director of Personnel, 1650 Tysons Boulevard Suite 1700, McLean, VA, 22102-3901; Phone (703) 790-6300.

ITT HARTFORD
690 ASYLUM AVENUE
HARTFORD, CONNECTICUT 06115

OVERVIEW: Provides life insurance.

EXPERTISE/EDUCATION SOUGHT: Accounting, finance, actuarial, health insurance, underwriting

CONTACTS: For college students and recent graduates: Ms Janet Gemmiti, Manager of College Relations; Phone (203) 547-5000, ext. 2776. For individuals with previous experience: Mr Thomas Thayer, Assiatant Vice President of Human Resources; Phone (203) 547-5000.

ITT WORLD DIRECTORIES
100 PLAZA DRIVE
SECAUCUS, NEW JERSEY 07096-0002

OVERVIEW: Publishes telephone and other directories.

KEY STATISTICS Annual Sales: $303.0 million. Number of Employees: 4,000.

EXPERTISE/EDUCATION SOUGHT: Business development, administration

CONTACT: For individuals with previous experience: Mr Jim Malone, Senior Vice President-Director Human Resources; Phone (201) 601-4290.

IVAC CORPORATION
10300 CAMPUS POINT DRIVE
SAN DIEGO, CALIFORNIA 92121-1511

OVERVIEW: Manufactures medical instruments and equipment. Established: 1968.

KEY STATISTICS Annual Sales: $200.0 million. Number of Employees: 1,400.

EXPERTISE/EDUCATION SOUGHT: Accounting, finance, marketing, management information systems

CONTACT: For individuals with previous experience: Mr Curt Lindvedt, Vice President Human Resources.

IVAX CORPORATION
8800 NORTHWEST 36TH STREET
MIAMI, FLORIDA 33178-2433

OVERVIEW: Manufactures pharmaceutical products. Established: 1972.

KEY STATISTICS Annual Sales: $645.0 million. Number of Employees: 2,900.

EXPERTISE/EDUCATION SOUGHT: Chemical engineering, computer programming, accounting, sales

CONTACT: For individuals with previous experience: Ms Marcia Bucknor, Manager of Human Resources; Phone (305) 590-2200.

JACOBS ENGINEERING GROUP, INC.
251 SOUTH LAKE AVENUE
PASADENA, CALIFORNIA 91101-3063

OVERVIEW: Provides engineering, consulting, and construction management services. Established: 1947.

KEY STATISTICS Annual Sales: $1.0 billion. Number of Employees: 5,300.

EXPERTISE/EDUCATION SOUGHT: Mechanical engineering, civil engineering, computer graphics, design engineering, environmental engineering, electrical engineering, petroleum/petrochemical engineering, computer-aided design, industrial engineering

CONTACT: For individuals with previous experience: Ms Maryanne Willetts, Manager of Personnel; Phone (818) 449-2171; Fax (818)578-6914.

JAMES RIVER CORPORATION
120 TREDEGAR STREET
RICHMOND, VIRGINIA 23219-4306

OVERVIEW: Manufactures paper products for consumers, packaging, and industry. Established: 1969.

KEY STATISTICS Annual Sales: $5.0 billion. Number of Employees: 35,000.

EXPERTISE/EDUCATION SOUGHT: Mechanical engineering, electrical engineering, management information systems, accounting, finance

CONTACT: Ms Barbara Lanier, Manager of Recruiting; Phone (804) 644-5411.

JAMESWAY CORPORATION
40 HARTZ WAY
SECAUCUS, NEW JERSEY 07096-2479

OVERVIEW: Discount merchandise chain. Established: 1958.

KEY STATISTICS Number of Employees: 6,300.

EXPERTISE/EDUCATION SOUGHT: Business management, retail, marketing, finance, accounting, sales

CONTACT: Ms Thomas Corcoran, Assistant Vice President of Human Resources; Phone (201) 330-6000.

JCPenney

JCPENNEY COMPANY, INC.
BOX 10001
PLANO, TEXAS 75801-8115

OVERVIEW: Operates national chain of department stores. Established: 1902.

KEY STATISTICS Annual Sales: $21.0 billion. Number of Employees: 200,000.

HIRING HISTORY Number of professional employees hired in 1994: 800. 1993: 700.

EXPERTISE/EDUCATION SOUGHT: Marketing, merchandising, accounting, information systems, business administration

CONTACT: For college students and recent graduates: Ms. Linda Goodale, College Relations Manager; Phone (214) 431-2316.

CORPORATE STATEMENT

Overview. *JCPenney provides merchandise and services to consumers through department stores that include catalog departments.*

Opportunities and Requirements. *JCPenney seeks candidates with a background in business, accounting, finance, computer science, or fashion merchandising. Candidates with work experience are preferred.*

JEFFERSON PILOT CORPORATION
100 NORTH GREEN STREET
GREENSBORO, NORTH CAROLINA 27401

OVERVIEW: Provides life insurance.

KEY STATISTICS Number of Employees: 1,250.

HIRING HISTORY Number of professional employees hired in 1994: 55.

EXPERTISE/EDUCATION SOUGHT: Accounting, actuarial, underwriting, finance, health insurance, information systems

CONTACT: Mr Ron Pittman, Second Vice President of Human Resources; Phone (910) 691-3000.

JEFFERSON SMURFIT CORPORATION
8182 MARYLAND AVENUE
SAINT LOUIS, MISSOURI 63105

OVERVIEW: Manufactures paper packaging. Established: 1926. Parent Company: Jefferson Smurfit Corporation (Ireland).

KEY STATISTICS Annual Sales: $3.0 billion. Number of Employees: 16,600.

EXPERTISE/EDUCATION SOUGHT: Management, sales, accounting, computer programming, human resources, law

CONTACT: For individuals with previous experience: Manager of Human Resources; Phone (314) 746-1100.

THOMAS JEFFERSON UNIVERSITY HOSPITAL
201 SOUTH 11TH STREET
PHILADELPHIA, PENNSYLVANIA 19107-5567

OVERVIEW: Public hospital. Established: 1824.

KEY STATISTICS Annual Sales: $765.0 million. Number of Employees: 7,537.

EXPERTISE/EDUCATION SOUGHT: Registered nursing, accounting, finance, data processing, medical technology, radiology, physician assistant, physical therapy, occupational therapy, respiratory therapy

CONTACT: For individuals with previous experience: Ms Linda Mitchell, Manager of Employee Selection and Placement; Phone (215) 955-7700; Fax (215)955-2183.

JENNY CRAIG INTERNATIONAL, INC.
445 MARINEVIEW AVENUE, SUITE 300
DELMAR, CALIFORNIA 92014

OVERVIEW: Operates chain of weight loss centers.

EXPERTISE/EDUCATION SOUGHT: Accounting, finance, information systems, marketing

CONTACT: For individuals with previous experience: Ms Nancy French, Corporate Staffing Manager.

JEWEL FOOD STORES, INC.
709 EAST SOUTH TEMPLE
SALT LAKE CITY, UTAH 84102-1205

OVERVIEW: Operates chain of food and drug stores. Established: 1917. Parent Company: Jewel Holdings, Inc.

KEY STATISTICS Number of Employees: 32,000.

EXPERTISE/EDUCATION SOUGHT: Accounting, marketing, finance, data processing

CONTACT: For individuals with previous experience: Mr Curt Rosentreter, Director of Personnel Admin; Phone (801) 320-5556.

JEWELL COMPANIES, INC.
1955 WEST NORTH AVENUE
MELROSE PARK, ILLINOIS 60160

OVERVIEW: Operates chain of food and drug stores.

EXPERTISE/EDUCATION SOUGHT: Accounting, finance

CONTACT: For individuals with previous experience: Mr David Stailey, Manager of Office Personnel; Phone (708) 531-6000.

JMB REALTY CORPORATION
900 NORTH MICHIGAN AVENUE 1900
CHICAGO, ILLINOIS 60611

OVERVIEW: Real estate investment, syndication, and development firm. Established: 1968.

EXPERTISE/EDUCATION SOUGHT: Law, accounting, management information systems, computer programming, real estate

CONTACTS: For college students and recent graduates: Ms Elizabeth Yowell, Personnel Assistant; Phone (312) 440-4800. For individuals with previous experience: Ms Alice Anson, Manager of Staffing; Phone (312) 915-1740.

JOHNSON AND HIGGINS
125 BROAD STREET
NEW YORK, NEW YORK 10004-2400

OVERVIEW: Provides insurance brokerage services. Established: 1957.

KEY STATISTICS Annual Sales: $970.0 million. Number of Employees: 8,600.

EXPERTISE/EDUCATION SOUGHT: Health insurance, credit/credit analysis, computer programming, collection, accounting, finance, actuarial, underwriting, law, data processing

CONTACT: For individuals with previous experience: Mr James Reardon, Vice President of Human Resources; Phone (212) 574-7000.

JOHNSON & JOHNSON
1 JOHNSON AND JOHNSON PLAZA
NEW BRUNSWICK, NEW JERSEY 08933

OVERVIEW: Manufactures pharmaceuticals, medical supplies, and healthcare products. Established: 1887.

EXPERTISE/EDUCATION SOUGHT: Accounting, marketing, finance, management information systems, sales, law

CONTACTS: For college students and recent graduates: Mr Bruce Gable, Director Shared Services/Recruitment; Phone (908) 524-0400. For individuals with previous experience: Mr Richard Kroon, Manager of Human Resources; Phone (908) 524-3238.

JOHNSON CONTROLS, INC.
49200 HALYARD DRIVE
PLYMOUTH, MICHIGAN 48170-2481

OVERVIEW: Manufactures batteries, automotive seats, building and industrial controls, and plastics. Established: 1885.

KEY STATISTICS Number of Employees: 16,761.

EXPERTISE/EDUCATION SOUGHT: Electrical engineering, mechanical engineering, chemical engineering, marketing, law, technical writing, management information systems, accounting, strategic planning, auditing

CONTACTS: For college students and recent graduates: Ms Susan Davis, Vice President of Human Resources. For individuals with previous experience: Recruitment Department, PO Box 8010, Plymouth, MI, 48170; Phone (313) 454-5000.

JOHNSON CONTROLS, INC.
5757 NORTH GREEN BAY AVENUE
MILWAUKEE, WISCONSIN 53209-4408

OVERVIEW: Manufactures control systems and products, batteries, plastics, and automotive seats. Established: 1885.

KEY STATISTICS Number of Employees: 50,100.

EXPERTISE/EDUCATION SOUGHT: Mechanical engineering, electrical engineering, accounting, finance, data processing, marketing, sales

CONTACT: For individuals with previous experience: Ms Beverly Edwards, Manager of Staffing and Equal Employment Opportunity Administration; Phone (414) 228-1200.

SC JOHNSON WAX
1525 HOWE STREET
RACINE, WISCONSIN 53403-2237

OVERVIEW: Manufactures and markets home care and personal care products and insecticides. Established: 1886.

KEY STATISTICS Annual Sales: $1.4 billion. Number of Employees: 13,400.

EXPERTISE/EDUCATION SOUGHT: Manufacturing engineering, marketing, electrical engineering, research and development, chemical engineering, finance, mechanical engineering, management information systems, industrial engineering

CONTACT: Mr Steve Price, Director of Human Resources; Phone (414) 631-2000, ext. 4156.

JOHNSTON COCA-COLA BOTTLING GROUP
HIGHWAY 64 BYPASS & REFRESHMENT LANE
ATLANTA, GEORGIA 30313

OVERVIEW: Produces soft drinks. Established: 1919. Parent Company: Coca-Cola Enterprises, Inc.

KEY STATISTICS Annual Sales: $838.0 million. Number of Employees: 5,500.

EXPERTISE/EDUCATION SOUGHT: Administration, warehousing

CONTACT: For individuals with previous experience: Human Resources Department; Phone (404) 676-2100.

EDWARD D. JONES AND COMPANY
201 PROGRESS PARKWAY
MARYLAND HEIGHTS, MISSOURI 63043-3003

OVERVIEW: Security brokers. Established: 1985.

KEY STATISTICS Annual Sales: $650.0 million. Number of Employees: 8,086.

EXPERTISE/EDUCATION SOUGHT: Information systems, finance, marketing, brokerage, training and development

CONTACTS: For college students and recent graduates: Ms Nadine Smith, Recruiter; Phone (800) 440-3040. For individuals with previous experience: Recruiting Specialist; Phone (800) 999-5650.

JONES GROUP, INC.
6060 J A JONES DRIVE
CHARLOTTE, NORTH CAROLINA 28287-0001

OVERVIEW: Commercial, energy, process, industrial, heavy, and marine construction company. Established: 1890. Parent Company: Philipp Holzmann USA, Inc.

KEY STATISTICS Number of Employees: 5,000.

EXPERTISE/EDUCATION SOUGHT: Civil engineering, mechanical engineering, construction engineering, project management

CONTACT: For individuals with previous experience: Mr Gerald O Vaughn, Manager of Professional Placement; Phone (704) 553-3000, ext. 3180.

JONES INTERNATIONAL, LTD.
9697 EAST MINERAL AVENUE
ENGLEWOOD, COLORADO 80112

OVERVIEW: Provides cable television and brokerage services.

EXPERTISE/EDUCATION SOUGHT: Accounting, finance, business management, data processing, electrical engineering, mechanical engineering

CONTACT: Human Resources Department.

JOSTEN'S, INC.
5501 NORMAN CENTER DRIVE
MINNEAPOLIS, MINNESOTA 55437-1088

OVERVIEW: Manufactures toys and games. Established: 1897.

KEY STATISTICS Annual Sales: $827.0 million. Number of Employees: 8,000.

EXPERTISE/EDUCATION SOUGHT: Communications, sales, management, customer service and support, accounting, finance, data processing, law, computer programming

CONTACT: Ms Diane Johnson, Staffing Specialist; Phone (612) 830-3300.

JVC MAGNETICS COMPANY
1 JVC ROAD
TUSCALOOSA, ALABAMA 35405-3548

OVERVIEW: Manufactures floppy disks, VCR tapes, and compact disks. Established: 1986. Parent Company: JVC America, Inc.

KEY STATISTICS Annual Sales: $160.0 million. Number of Employees: 600.

EXPERTISE/EDUCATION SOUGHT: Marketing, sales

CONTACT: For individuals with previous experience: Ms Mary Nye, Personnel Specialist; Phone (205) 556-7111.

ALBERT KAHN ASSOCIATES, INC.
ALBERT KAHN BUILDING, 7430 SECOND AVENUE
DETROIT, MICHIGAN 48202-2798

OVERVIEW: Provides architectural and engineering services. Established: 1895.

KEY STATISTICS Annual Sales: $22.0 million. Number of Employees: 270.

HIRING HISTORY Number of professional employees hired in 1994: 20. 1993: 25.

EXPERTISE/EDUCATION SOUGHT: Civil engineering, mechanical engineering, electrical engineering, structural engineering

CONTACT: Mr Charles T Robinson, PE, Vice President; Phone (313) 871-8500; Fax (313)871-8539.

KAISER ALUMINUM CORPORATION
5847 SAN FELIPE STREET
HOUSTON, TEXAS 77057-3010

OVERVIEW: Produces aluminum and aluminum products. Established: 1940.

KEY STATISTICS Annual Sales: $2.0 billion. Number of Employees: 10,000.

HIRING HISTORY Number of professional employees hired in 1994: 12.

EXPERTISE/EDUCATION SOUGHT: Tax, accounting, auditing

CONTACT: For individuals with previous experience: Ms Marilyn Gentry, Personnel Coordinator; Phone (713) 267-3777.

KAISER FOUNDATION HEALTH OF THE NORTHWEST
500 NORTHEAST MULTINOMAH STREET
PORTLAND, OREGON 97232

OVERVIEW: Provides HMO and managed care services. Established: 1945. Parent Company: Kaiser Foundation Health Plan.

KEY STATISTICS Annual Sales: $3.0 billion.

EXPERTISE/EDUCATION SOUGHT: Nursing, allied health, physical therapy, occupational therapy, physicians, pharmacy, managed health care, claims processing/management, and administration

CONTACT: Human Resources Department; Phone (510) 271-5910.

KAISER FOUNDATION HEALTH PLAN

1 KAISER PLAZA
OAKLAND, CALIFORNIA 94612

OVERVIEW: Provides HMO and managed care services. Established: 1945.

EXPERTISE/EDUCATION SOUGHT: Nursing, radiology, pathology, anesthesiology, dialysis, emergency services, health care, intensive care, licensed practical nursing, medical records

CONTACT: For individuals with previous experience: Human Resources Department; Phone (510) 271-5833.

KAISER FOUNDATION HEALTH PLAN OF COLORADO, INC.

2500 SOUTH HAVANA
AURORA, COLORADO 80014

OVERVIEW: Provides health care services. Established: 1969. Parent Company: Kaiser Foundation Health Plan.

KEY STATISTICS Annual Sales: $500.0 million. Number of Employees: 2,900.

EXPERTISE/EDUCATION SOUGHT: Sales, accounting, administration, health insurance, planning, nursing, clinical services, physicians, radiology, optometry

CONTACT: Ms Melanie Kaskaske, Director of Personnel Services; Phone (303) 338-3900; Fax (303) 338-3900.

KAISER FOUNDATION HEALTH PLAN OF TEXAS

12720 HILLCREST ROAD, SUITE 600
DALLAS, TEXAS 75230-2035

OVERVIEW: Manages health care centers. Established: 1982. Parent Company: Kaiser Foundation Health Plan.

KEY STATISTICS Annual Sales: $230.0 million. Number of Employees: 1,065.

HIRING HISTORY Number of professional employees hired in 1993: 270.

EXPERTISE/EDUCATION SOUGHT: Accounting, physical therapy, nursing, medical technology, radiation technology

CONTACT: For individuals with previous experience: Ms Linda Fonteneaux, Director of Human Resources Planning; Phone (214) 458-5050.

KAMAN CORPORATION

1322 BLUE HILLS AVENUE
BLOOMFIELD, CONNECTICUT 06002

OVERVIEW: Manufacturing aerospace and aircraft equipment, measurement devices, musical instruments, and industrial supplies. Established: 1945.

EXPERTISE/EDUCATION SOUGHT: Human resources

CONTACT: Ms Wendy Cantliffe, Manager of Corporate Payroll; Phone (203) 243-7934.

KANSAS CITY POWER AND LIGHT COMPANY

1201 WALNUT STREET
KANSAS CITY, MISSOURI 64106-2117

OVERVIEW: Electric utility. Established: 1882.

KEY STATISTICS Number of Employees: 2,735.

EXPERTISE/EDUCATION SOUGHT: Business management, data processing, marketing, accounting, finance, computer science, electrical engineering

CONTACT: Ms Joe Ann Alexander, Manager of Employment Services.

KANSAS CITY SOUTHERN INDUSTRIES, INC.

114 WEST 11TH STREET
KANSAS CITY, MISSOURI 64105-1804

OVERVIEW: Provides railroad transportation and financial services. Established: 1900.

KEY STATISTICS Number of Employees: 6,071.

EXPERTISE/EDUCATION SOUGHT: Accounting, finance, law, computer programming, marketing

CONTACT: Mr Rich Venditti, Human Resources Manager.

KANSAS POWER AND LIGHT COMPANY, INC.

818 SOUTH KANSAS AVENUE
TOPEKA, KANSAS 66612-1217

OVERVIEW: Electric utility. Established: 1924.

KEY STATISTICS Number of Employees: 4,192.

EXPERTISE/EDUCATION SOUGHT: Accounting, finance, marketing, electrical engineering, mechanical engineering

CONTACT: Ms Vicki Pritchard, Employment Specialist; Phone (913) 575-6317.

KANTUS CORPORATION

201 GARRET PARKWAY
LEWISBURG, TENNESSEE 37091-3557

OVERVIEW: Manufactures motor vehicle parts and accessories. Established: 1984.

KEY STATISTICS Annual Sales: $180.0 million. Number of Employees: 800.

EXPERTISE/EDUCATION SOUGHT: Mechanical engineering, electrical engineering, industrial engineering, data processing, accounting, marketing, finance

CONTACT: For individuals with previous experience: Mr Shel Dickens, Director of Human Resources.

KAY-BEE TOY AND HOBBY SHOPS, INC.

100 WEST STREET
PITTSFIELD, MASSACHUSETTS 01201-5702

OVERVIEW: Operates chain of toy stores. Established: 1945. Parent Company: Melville Corporation.

KEY STATISTICS Number of Employees: 13,000.

HIRING HISTORY Number of professional employees hired in 1993: 30.

EXPERTISE/EDUCATION SOUGHT: Purchasing, accounting, finance, data processing

CONTACT: Ms Patti Ippoliti, Vice President of Human Resources.

KEEBLER COMPANY

1 HOLLOW TREE LANE
ELMHURST, ILLINOIS 60126

OVERVIEW: Manufactures cookies, crackers, and other snack foods. Established: 1974.

EXPERTISE/EDUCATION SOUGHT: Management information systems, food science

CONTACT: Ms Nancy Doyle, Manager of Corporate Staffing; Phone (708) 833-2900.

KELLOGG COMPANY

1 KELLOGG SQUARE
BATTLE CREEK, MICHIGAN 49017-3599

OVERVIEW: Manufactures cereal products and processed foods. Established: 1906.

KEY STATISTICS Number of Employees: 16,150.

EXPERTISE/EDUCATION SOUGHT: Manufacturing engineering, packaging engineering, chemical engineering, technical engineering, sales

CONTACT: Mr William Steele, Director of Employee Services; Phone (616) 961-2000.

KELLY SERVICES, INC.

999 WEST BIG BEAVER ROAD
TROY, MICHIGAN 48084-4782

OVERVIEW: Provides temporary personnel services. Established: 1946.

KEY STATISTICS Number of Employees: 634,300.

Kelly Services, Inc. (continued)

EXPERTISE/EDUCATION SOUGHT: Sales, finance, purchasing, management information systems, human resources

CONTACT: Ms Maureen Goodin, Manager of Human Resources; Phone (810) 362-4444.

THE KELLY-SPRINGFIELD TIRE COMPANY
12501 WILLOWBROOK ROAD SOUTHEAST
CUMBERLAND, MARYLAND 21502-2554

OVERVIEW: Manufactures tires. Established: 1935. Parent Company: The Goodyear Tire and Rubber Company.

KEY STATISTICS Number of Employees: 6,874.

HIRING HISTORY Number of professional employees hired in 1993: 30.

EXPERTISE/EDUCATION SOUGHT: Chemical engineering, industrial engineering, engineering science, drafting, physics, computer programming, mechanical engineering

CONTACT: Ms Ruth Chaney, Director of Salaried Personnel and Benefits; Phone (301) 777-6690.

KELSEY-HAYES COMPANY
38481 WEST HURON RIVER DRIVE
ROMULUS, MICHIGAN 48174-1158

OVERVIEW: Manufactures wheels and brakes for the automotive aftermarket. Established: 1909.

KEY STATISTICS Number of Employees: 2,710.

EXPERTISE/EDUCATION SOUGHT: Manufacturing engineering, design engineering, electrical engineering, mechanical engineering

CONTACT: Mr James Maniatis, Vice President of Human Resources-Foundation Brakes Division, 1200 Tech Center Drive, Livonia, MI, 48150; Phone (313) 513-4524.

KEMPER NATIONAL INSURANCE COMPANIES
1 KEMPER DRIVE
LONG GROVE, ILLINOIS 60047-9108

OVERVIEW: Provides property and casualty insurance provider. Established: 1905.

KEY STATISTICS Assets: $2.0 billion. Number of Employees: 6,300.

EXPERTISE/EDUCATION SOUGHT: Computer programming, actuarial, claims adjustment/examination, finance, accounting, law, real estate, underwriting

CONTACT: Mr Gary Slettum, Manager of Employment; Phone (708) 320-2000.

THE KENDALL COMPANY
15 HAMPSHIRE STREET
MANSFIELD, MASSACHUSETTS 02048

OVERVIEW: Manufactures medical and health care products and supplies. Established: 1904.

EXPERTISE/EDUCATION SOUGHT: Marketing, data processing, health care, economics, finance, sales, accounting, auditing, engineering, chemistry

CONTACT: Mr Roger Sturtevant, Manager of Employment.

KENNECOTT
PO BOX 11248
SALT LAKE CITY, UTAH 84147

OVERVIEW: Mines coal and processes coke. Established: 1989.

KEY STATISTICS Annual Sales: $555.0 million. Number of Employees: 5,500.

EXPERTISE/EDUCATION SOUGHT: Metallurgy, mining engineering, metallurgical engineering, environmental engineering, mechanical engineering, geotechnical engineering, geology, health and safety

CONTACT: For individuals with previous experience: Mr Al Bakke, Manager Corporate Employment; Phone (801) 322-7311.

KERR-MCGEE CORPORATION
KERR-MCGEE CENTER
OKLAHOMA CITY, OKLAHOMA 73125

OVERVIEW: Produces and distributes petroleum and chemical products.

KEY STATISTICS Annual Sales: $3.0 billion. Number of Employees: 5,800.

EXPERTISE/EDUCATION SOUGHT: Petroleum/petrochemical engineering, chemical engineering

CONTACT: For individuals with previous experience: Human Resources Department, PO Box 25861, Oklahoma City, OK, 73125; Phone (405) 270-1313.

KERR-MCGEE REFINING CORPORATION
2211 NORFOLK STREET, SUITE 1100
HOUSTON, TEXAS 77098

OVERVIEW: Refines petroleum.

KEY STATISTICS Annual Sales: $2.1 billion. Number of Employees: 1,500.

CONTACT: For individuals with previous experience: Ms Linda Jeter, Manager Personnel; Phone (713) 638-4700.

KEY BANK OF NEW YORK
66 SOUTH PEARL STREET
ALBANY, NEW YORK 12207-1501

OVERVIEW: Commercial bank. Established: 1825.

KEY STATISTICS Assets: $1.0 billion. Number of Employees: 4,790.

EXPERTISE/EDUCATION SOUGHT: Data processing, leasing, sales, credit/credit analysis, management, finance, computer programming, operations, network analysis

CONTACT: Human Resources Department; Phone (518) 486-8500.

KEY CORPORATION MANAGEMENT COMPANY
1 KEY CORP PLAZA
ALBANY, NEW YORK 12207

OVERVIEW: Commercial bank. Parent Company: KeyCorp.

KEY STATISTICS Assets: $704.0 million. Number of Employees: 5,500.

EXPERTISE/EDUCATION SOUGHT: Accounting, finance, underwriting, retail, credit/credit analysis, data processing, computer programming

CONTACT: Ms Evelyn Morris, Director of Human Resources, PO Box 88, Albany, NY, 12201-088; Phone (518) 391-1424.

KEYCORP
127 PUBLIC SQUARE
CLEVELAND, OHIO 44114

OVERVIEW: Provides banking and financial services. Established: 1970.

KEY STATISTICS Assets: $67.0 billion. Number of Employees: 30,000.

EXPERTISE/EDUCATION SOUGHT: Accounting, finance, marketing

CONTACT: For individuals with previous experience: Mr Grogory S Thomas, Manager, College Relations and Recruiting; Phone (216) 689-3428.

CORPORATE PROFILE

K eyCorp (NYSE:KEY) is one of the largest bank holding companies in the United States, with assets of $66.8 billion and total shareholders' equity of $4.7 billion. Headquartered in Cleveland, the company is comprised of full-service commercial banks and related financial services companies with more than 1,300 branch and affiliate offices in more than twenty states. Its related financial services companies provide *such services as investment management and trust, mortgage banking, and securities brokerage to the existing banking franchise and other selected markets.*

KeyCorp offers management training programs in commercial and retail banking, investment management and trust services, information technology, and operations services.

KEYSTONE FOODS CORPORATION
401 EAST CITY AVENUE, SUITE 800
BALA CYNWYD, PENNSYLVANIA 19004-1122

Overview: Manufactures and distributes meat and meat products.

Key Statistics Annual Sales: $1.0 billion. Number of Employees: 1,875.

Expertise/Education Sought: Accounting, management information systems, budgeting, utilization review, research

Contact: For individuals with previous experience: Mr Sim Blahut, Manager Compensation and Employment; Phone (610) 667-6700.

KEYSTONE HEALTH PLAN EAST, INC.
1901 MARKET STREET
PHILADELPHIA, PENNSYLVANIA 19103-1400

Overview: Provides health care insurance. Parent Company: Medical Service Association of Pennsylvania.

Key Statistics Annual Sales: $831.5 million. Number of Employees: 571.

Expertise/Education Sought: Claims adjustment/examination, accounting, customer service and support

Contact: For individuals with previous experience: Ms Kate Smith, Director of Human Resources; Phone (215) 241-2299.

KFC CORPORATION
1441 GARDINER LANE
LOUISVILLE, KENTUCKY 40213-1914

Overview: Operates chain of fast food restaurants. Parent Company: Pepsico.

Key Statistics Annual Sales: $4.0 billion. Number of Employees: 24,000.

Expertise/Education Sought: Finance, accounting, research and development, information systems, marketing

Contact: For individuals with previous experience: Ms Sandy Hiob, Manager of Employment Relations; Phone (502) 456-8300.

KIEWIT CONSTRUCTION GROUP, INC.
1000 KIEWIT PLAZA
OMAHA, NEBRASKA 68131

Overview: Provides general heavy construction contracting services. Established: 1884. Parent Company: Peter Kiewit and Sons, Inc.

Expertise/Education Sought: Accounting, finance, marketing, civil engineering, mechanical engineering

Contact: Ms Dee White, Human Resources Generalist; Phone (402) 342-2052.

K-III COMMUNICATIONS CORPORATION
745 5TH AVENUE, 21ST FLOOR
NEW YORK, NEW YORK 10151

Overview: Publishes magazines, books, and directories.

Expertise/Education Sought: Publishing

Contact: For individuals with previous experience: Ms Rebecca Albrecht, Human Resources Director.

KIMBALL INTERNATIONAL, INC.
1600 ROYAL STREET
JASPER, INDIANA 47549-1001

Overview: Manufactures furniture and musical instruments. Established: 1939.

Key Statistics Number of Employees: 7,730.

Hiring History Number of professional employees hired in 1993: 75.

Expertise/Education Sought: Information systems, industrial engineering, electrical engineering, mechanical engineering, accounting, finance

Contact: Mr Thomas Heake, Manager of Recruiting; Phone (812) 482-1600.

KIMBERLY-CLARK CORPORATION
545 CARPENTER FREEWAY, SUITE 1300
IRVING, TEXAS 75062

Overview: Manufactures paper and fiber products for consumer, health care, and industrial use. Established: 1872.

Key Statistics Number of Employees: 42,131.

Expertise/Education Sought: Research, operations, engineering, logistics, finance

Contact: Recruiting Department, 2100 Winchester Road, Neenah, WI, 54956; Phone (414) 721-6965.

KINDER-CARE LEARNING CENTERS
2400 PRESIDENTS DRIVE
MONTGOMERY, ALABAMA 36116-1616

Overview: Owns and operates a chain of child care centers. Established: 1969.

Key Statistics Annual Sales: $489.0 million. Number of Employees: 21,000.

Expertise/Education Sought: Education, psychology, accounting, finance, business, auditing, management information systems, business management, computer science, data processing

Contact: Ms Lisa Castleman, Field Employee Relations Administrator; Phone (334) 227-5090.

KING COUNTY MEDICAL BLUE SHIELD COMBINED SERVICES NORTHWEST
1800 9TH AVENUE
SEATTLE, WASHINGTON 98101-1322

Overview: Provides health insurance. Established: 1933.

Key Statistics Annual Sales: $953.0 million. Number of Employees: 1,400.

Expertise/Education Sought: Actuarial, claims adjustment/examination

Contact: For individuals with previous experience: Mr Ray Olitt, Manager of Training and Development; Phone (206) 464-3600, ext. 5552; Fax (206) 343-0848.

KINNEY SHOE CORPORATION
233 BROADWAY
NEW YORK, NEW YORK 10279

Overview: Manufactures shoes and accessories. Established: 1963. Parent Company: Woolworth Corporation.

Expertise/Education Sought: Sales, marketing, finance, accounting, auditing

Contact: Ms Sharon Orloop, Vice President and Director of Fair Employment; Phone (212) 720-3700.

KLOSTER CRUISE, LTD.
95 MERRICK WAY, 6TH FLOOR
CORAL GABLES, FLORIDA 33134-5312

Overview: Operates cruise ships. Established: 1906.

Key Statistics Annual Sales: $918.0 million. Number of Employees: 6,531.

Expertise/Education Sought: Accounting, marketing, data processing, computer programming

Contact: Ms Judith Collins, Director of Human Resources; Phone (305) 447-9660.

KNIGHT-RIDDER, INC.
1 HERALD PLAZA
MIAMI, FLORIDA 33132-1609

OVERVIEW: Publishes newspapers and provides electronic information services. Established: 1892.

KEY STATISTICS Number of Employees: 20,000.

EXPERTISE/EDUCATION SOUGHT: Production, auditing, journalism, data processing, marketing, finance

CONTACT: Ms Rebecca Baybrook-Heckenbach, Assistant Vice President of Employment; Phone (305) 376-3940.

KOCH ENGINEERING COMPANY, INC.
4111 EAST 37TH STREET NORTH
WICHITA, KANSAS 67220-3298

OVERVIEW: Provides engineering services to the oil and gas industries. Established: 1945. Parent Company: Koch Industries, Inc.

KEY STATISTICS Number of Employees: 2,500.

EXPERTISE/EDUCATION SOUGHT: Chemical engineering, mechanical engineering, electrical engineering, accounting, finance, marketing, computer programming

CONTACTS: For college students and recent graduates: Ms Patricia Calvert, Coordinator of College Recruitment; Phone (316) 832-5500. For individuals with previous experience: Mr Chip Davis, Manager of Employee Relations; Phone (316) 832-5110, ext. 5902.

KOHLER COMPANY
444 HIGHLAND DRIVE
KOHLER, WISCONSIN 53044-1515

OVERVIEW: Manufactures plumbing fixtures, engines, and generators. Established: 1873.

KEY STATISTICS Number of Employees: 14,000.

HIRING HISTORY Number of professional employees hired in 1993: 150.

EXPERTISE/EDUCATION SOUGHT: Mechanical engineering, accounting, marketing

CONTACTS: For college students and recent graduates: Mr Bernie Williams, Senior Technical Recruiter; Phone (414) 457-4441, ext. 7066. For individuals with previous experience: Mr Rick Hamiston, Director of Personnel; Phone (414) 457-4441.

KOHL'S DEPARTMENT STORES, INC.
13600 WOODALE DRIVE
MENOMONEE FALLS, WISCONSIN 53051-7026

OVERVIEW: Operates chain of department stores. Established: 1962. Parent Company: Kohl's Corporation.

KEY STATISTICS Annual Sales: $1.0 billion. Number of Employees: 14,900.

EXPERTISE/EDUCATION SOUGHT: Management, merchandising, management information systems, finance, advertising, human resources, operations, distribution

CONTACTS: For college students and recent graduates: Mr Telvin Jefferies, Manager of College Relations and Recruitment; Phone (414) 783-5800. For individuals with previous experience: Ms Diane Seal, Manager of Human Resources; Phone (414) 783-5800.

KPMG PEAT MARWICK
767 5TH AVENUE 47TH FLOOR
NEW YORK, NEW YORK 10153

OVERVIEW: Provides accounting and financial services. Established: 1897.

EXPERTISE/EDUCATION SOUGHT: Underwriting, accounting, actuarial

CONTACT: Mr Bernard Milano, Partner in Charge of Recruiting, 3 Chestnut Road, Montvale, NJ, 10153-0001; Phone (201) 307-7000, ext. 7762.

KRAFT FOOD INGREDIENTS CORPORATION
6410 POPLAR
MEMPHIS, TENNESSEE 38119-4844

OVERVIEW: Produces and distributes food ingredients and specialty foods. Established: 1965. Parent Company: Kraft General Foods, Inc.

KEY STATISTICS Annual Sales: $800.0 million. Number of Employees: 1,800.

EXPERTISE/EDUCATION SOUGHT: Marketing, food science, program analysis, computer programming, sales, accounting

CONTACT: Ms Jan Reynolds, Human Resources Associate; Phone (901) 766-2606.

KRAFT FOOD SERVICE
1 PARKWAY NORTH
DEERFIELD, ILLINOIS 60015-2532

OVERVIEW: Provides food service products to hospitals and restaurants. Parent Company: Kraft General Foods, Inc.

KEY STATISTICS Annual Sales: $100.0 million. Number of Employees: 8,600.

EXPERTISE/EDUCATION SOUGHT: Finance, marketing

CONTACT: Mr Brian Glancy, Director of Human Services; Phone (708) 405-8827.

KRAFT FOODS BAKERY
55 PARADISE LANE
BAY SHORE, NEW YORK 11706-2224

OVERVIEW: Produces and distributes specialty baked products. Parent Company: Kraft General Foods, Inc.

KEY STATISTICS Annual Sales: $699.0 million. Number of Employees: 9,000.

EXPERTISE/EDUCATION SOUGHT: Finance, sales, administration

CONTACT: For individuals with previous experience: Ms Lori Browning, Recruiter, 5th Avenue, Bay Shore, NY, 11706; Phone (516) 273-6000.

THE KROGER COMPANY
1014 VINE STREET
CINCINNATI, OHIO 45202-1119

OVERVIEW: Operates chain of food stores. Established: 1883.

KEY STATISTICS Number of Employees: 190,000.

EXPERTISE/EDUCATION SOUGHT: Law, sales, marketing, advertising, accounting, business management, retail, finance, economics

CONTACT: Ms Terry Kuhl, Manager of Human Resources; Phone (513) 762-4000.

L. A. GEAR, INC.
2850 OCEAN PARK BOULEVARD
SANTA MONICA, CALIFORNIA 90405

OVERVIEW: Markets and sells athletic and casual footwear and apparel.

KEY STATISTICS Annual Sales: $430.0 million. Number of Employees: 750.

EXPERTISE/EDUCATION SOUGHT: Management, marketing, sales

CONTACT: For individuals with previous experience: Mr Richard Delson, Director Human Resources.

LA QUINTA INNS, INC.
112 EAST PECAN STREET
SAN ANTONIO, TEXAS 78205-1512

OVERVIEW: Operates chain of motels. Established: 1978.

KEY STATISTICS Annual Sales: $272.0 million. Number of Employees: 6,100.

EXPERTISE/EDUCATION SOUGHT: Hospitality/hotel and restaurant management

CONTACT: For individuals with previous experience: Ms. Monica Lanum, Senior Human Resources Representative, PO Box 2636, San Antonio, TX, 78299.

LA-Z-BOY CHAIR COMPANY
1284 NORTH TELEGRAPH ROAD
MONROE, MICHIGAN 48161-3390

OVERVIEW: Manufactures chairs, sofas, and other furniture. Established: 1929.

KEY STATISTICS Number of Employees: 8,724.

EXPERTISE/EDUCATION SOUGHT: Mechanical engineering, manufacturing engineering, marketing, finance, sales

CONTACT: For individuals with previous experience: Mr Mark Lohman, Manager of Human Resources; Phone (810) 242-1444.

LACLEDE GAS COMPANY
720 OLIVE STREET
SAINT LOUIS, MISSOURI 63101-2329

OVERVIEW: Natural gas production, storage, and distribution public utility. Established: 1911.

KEY STATISTICS Annual Sales: $524.0 million. Number of Employees: 2,000.

EXPERTISE/EDUCATION SOUGHT: Accounting, mechanical engineering, electrical engineering

CONTACT: For individuals with previous experience: Ms Donna K Krutzman, Manager of Employment; Phone (314) 342-0646.

LAFARGE CORPORATION
11130 SUNRISE VALLEY DRIVE
RESTON, VIRGINIA 22091-4393

OVERVIEW: Manufactures cement, concrete, and construction materials. Established: 1977.

KEY STATISTICS Annual Sales: $1.0 billion. Number of Employees: 7,400.

EXPERTISE/EDUCATION SOUGHT: Marketing, finance, accounting, human resources, mechanical engineering, industrial engineering, electrical engineering, metallurgical engineering

CONTACT: Mr Thomas Tatum, Senior Vice President of Human Resources; Phone (703) 264-3600.

LAIDLAW WASTE SYSTEMS, INC.
669 AIRPORT FREEWAY
FORT WORTH, TEXAS 76053

OVERVIEW: Provides waste collection and disposal services.

KEY STATISTICS Annual Sales: $756.0 million. Number of Employees: 6,070.

EXPERTISE/EDUCATION SOUGHT: Computer programming, accounting, collection, marketing, sales, credit/credit analysis

CONTACT: Ms Jill Anderson, Director of Human Resources; Phone (817) 485-9950, ext. 246.

LANCASTER COLONY CORPORATION
37 WEST BROAD STREET
COLUMBIS, OHIO 43215-4132

OVERVIEW: Manufactures automotive after market products, housewares, and specialty foods. Established: 1961.

EXPERTISE/EDUCATION SOUGHT: Accounting, business administration, law, health insurance, finance

CONTACT: Mr John B Gerlach, Chairman and Chief Executive Officer; Phone (614) 224-7141.

LAND O'LAKES, INC.
4001 LEXINGTON AVENUE NORTH
SAINT PAUL, MINNESOTA 55126

OVERVIEW: Manufactures and distributes dairy products. Established: 1921.

KEY STATISTICS Number of Employees: 5,500.

EXPERTISE/EDUCATION SOUGHT: Marketing, finance, sales, accounting, merchandising

CONTACT: For individuals with previous experience: Mr Jack Martin, Vice President of Human Resources, PO Box 116, Minneapolis, MN, 55440-0116; Phone (612) 481-2222.

LANIER WORLDWIDE, INC.
2300 PARKLAKE DRIVE NORTHEAST
ATLANTA, GEORGIA 30345-2814

OVERVIEW: Distributes copiers, facsimile machines, dictation equipment, and other office equipment. Established: 1934. Parent Company: Harris Corporation.

KEY STATISTICS Annual Sales: $922.0 million. Number of Employees: 7,000.

EXPERTISE/EDUCATION SOUGHT: Marketing, accounting, finance, electrical engineering, mechanical engineering, computer science

CONTACT: For individuals with previous experience: Ms Clara Wallington, Senior Human Resources Representative; Phone (404) 621-1409.

LAWRENCE LIVERMORE NATIONAL LABORATORY
7000 EAST AVENUE
LIVERMORE, CALIFORNIA 94550

OVERVIEW: Conducts research in applied science and engineering. Established: 1952.

KEY STATISTICS Annual Sales: $930.0 million. Number of Employees: 8,000.

HIRING HISTORY Number of professional employees hired in 1993: 85.

EXPERTISE/EDUCATION SOUGHT: Mathematics, biology, biotechnology, physical science, environmental science, mechanical engineering, civil engineering, electrical engineering, chemical engineering, compliance

CONTACTS: For college students and recent graduates: Mr Arthur Wong, Division Leader/Recruiting; Phone (510) 422-1100. For individuals with previous experience: Ms Gay Spivey, Recruiting and Advertising Coordinator; Phone (510) 422-9367.

LDI CORPORATION
4770 HINCKLEY INDUSTRIAL PARKWAY
CLEVELAND, OHIO 44109-1724

OVERVIEW: Rents and leases computer equipment. Established: 1972.

KEY STATISTICS Annual Sales: $272.0 million. Number of Employees: 751.

EXPERTISE/EDUCATION SOUGHT: Accounting, data processing, computer engineering, sales, marketing, finance

CONTACT: Ms Barbara Gallo, Director of Human Resources; Phone (216) 661-5400.

LEAR SEATING CORPORATION
21557 TELEGRAPH ROAD
SOUTHFIELD, MICHIGAN 48034-6817

OVERVIEW: Manufactures automotive seating. Established: 1987.

KEY STATISTICS Annual Sales: $2.0 billion. Number of Employees: 18,500.

EXPERTISE/EDUCATION SOUGHT: Mechanical engineering

CONTACT: Ms Kelli Sison, Recruiter; Phone (313) 746-1747.

THE LEE APPAREL COMPANY, INC.
9001 WEST 67TH STREET
MERRIAM, KANSAS 66202-3632

OVERVIEW: Manufactures clothing and apparel. Established: 1889. Parent Company: VF Corporation.

KEY STATISTICS Number of Employees: 10,300.

EXPERTISE/EDUCATION SOUGHT: Industrial engineering, manufacturing, computer engineering, distribution, finance

CONTACT: Ms Carol Eubank, Manager of Human Resources; Phone (913) 384-4000.

LEGGETT AND PLATT, INC.
1 LEGGETT ROAD
CARTHAGE, MISSOURI 64836

OVERVIEW: Manufactures and markets furniture and carpet. Established: 1883.

KEY STATISTICS Number of Employees: 13,000.

EXPERTISE/EDUCATION SOUGHT: Accounting, mechanical engineering, industrial engineering, marketing, law, computer programming, data processing

CONTACT: Ms Valerie Glaze, Employment Coordinator; Phone (417) 358-8131, ext. 3002.

LENSCRAFTERS, INC.
8650 GOVERNORS HILL DRIVE
CINCINNATI, OHIO 45249-1386

OVERVIEW: Operates chain of eyeglass stores. Parent Company: United States Shoe Corporation.

KEY STATISTICS Annual Sales: $698.0 million. Number of Employees: 10,000.

EXPERTISE/EDUCATION SOUGHT: Marketing, information systems, merchandising, accounting, finance, human resources, operations

CONTACTS: For college students and recent graduates: Mr Paul Stewart, Recruiting Manager; Phone (513) 583-6000. For individuals with previous experience: Ms Carolyn Slager, Director of Human Resources; Phone (513) 583-6000.

LERNER NEW YORK, INC.
460 WEST 33RD STREET, 5TH FLOOR
NEW YORK, NEW YORK 10001-2606

OVERVIEW: Operates chain of women's specialty apparel stores. Established: 1918. Parent Company: Limited, Inc.

KEY STATISTICS Number of Employees: 11,500.

HIRING HISTORY Number of professional employees hired in 1993: 80.

EXPERTISE/EDUCATION SOUGHT: Merchandising, management, human resources, marketing, sales, finance, accounting, management information systems, product design and development, planning

CONTACT: For individuals with previous experience: Ms Ruth Stearns, Staffing Administrator; Phone (212) 736-1222.

LEVI STRAUSS ASSOCIATES, INC.
1155 BATTERY STREET
SAN FRANCISCO, CALIFORNIA 94111

OVERVIEW: Manufactures apparel. Established: 1850.

EXPERTISE/EDUCATION SOUGHT: Sales, marketing, finance, product engineering, human resources

CONTACT: Director of Employment; Phone (415) 544-6000.

LEVITZ FURNITURE CORPORATION
6111 NORTHWEST BROKEN SOUND PARKWAY
BOCA RATON, FLORIDA 33487-2745

OVERVIEW: Operates chain of home furnishings stores. Established: 1910.

KEY STATISTICS Annual Sales: $984.0 million. Number of Employees: 6,000.

EXPERTISE/EDUCATION SOUGHT: Law, operations, computer programming, advertising, graphic arts, human resources

CONTACT: Mr Greg Duckworth, Personnel Administration Manager; Phone (407) 994-6006.

LIBBEY GLASS, INC.
940 ASH STREET
TOLEDO, OHIO 43611-1209

OVERVIEW: Manufactures glassware. Established: 1987. Parent Company: Libbey, Inc.

KEY STATISTICS Annual Sales: $281.0 million. Number of Employees: 2,900.

EXPERTISE/EDUCATION SOUGHT: Electrical engineering, mechanical engineering, design engineering, industrial engineering, accounting, marketing, finance, computer programming

CONTACT: For individuals with previous experience: Mr Bob Ellithorpe, Human Resources Manager; Phone (419) 727-2401.

LIBBEY-OWENS-FORD COMPANY
811 MADISON AVENUE
TOLEDO, OHIO 43624-1626

OVERVIEW: Manufactures glass and glass products. Established: 1930. Parent Company: Pilkington Holdings, Inc.

KEY STATISTICS Annual Sales: $982.0 million. Number of Employees: 7,496.

HIRING HISTORY Number of professional employees hired in 1993: 100.

EXPERTISE/EDUCATION SOUGHT: Accounting, finance, marketing, auditing, engineering

CONTACT: For individuals with previous experience: Ms Jan Sterling, Supervisor of Personnel Services; Phone (419) 247-4887.

LIBERTY MUTUAL INSURANCE COMPANY
175 BERKELEY STREET
BOSTON, MASSACHUSETTS 02117-5066

OVERVIEW: Provides life, health, and casualty insurance. Established: 1912.

KEY STATISTICS Assets: $5.6 billion. Number of Employees: 20,000.

EXPERTISE/EDUCATION SOUGHT: Actuarial, accounting, insurance brokerage

CONTACT: For individuals with previous experience: Ms Helen Sayles, Vice President-Manager Human Resources; Phone (617) 357-9500.

LIBERTY NATIONAL LIFE INSURANCE COMPANY
2001 3RD AVENUE SOUTH
BIRMINGHAM, ALABAMA 35233-2101

OVERVIEW: Provides life, accident, and health insurance. Established: 1929.

KEY STATISTICS Number of Employees: 3,909.

EXPERTISE/EDUCATION SOUGHT: Actuarial, computer science, law

CONTACT: For individuals with previous experience: Mr George Thompson, Second Vice President-Personnel.

LIFE TECHNOLOGIES, INC.
8400 HELGERMAN COURT
GAITHERSBURG, MARYLAND 20884-9780

OVERVIEW: Manufactures products for the biotechnology industry. Established: 1983.

KEY STATISTICS Annual Sales: $235.0 million. Number of Employees: 1,400.

HIRING HISTORY Number of professional employees hired in 1994: 100.

EXPERTISE/EDUCATION SOUGHT: Biochemistry, biology, chemical engineering, molecular biology, microbiology

CONTACT: Ms J Clancy Kress, Manager of Staffing and College Relations; Phone (301) 840-4078; Fax (301) 921-2215.

LIFETIME TV
309 WEST 49TH STREET
NEW YORK, NEW YORK 10019

OVERVIEW: Television broadcasting company. Established: 1983.

KEY STATISTICS Annual Sales: $47.0 million. Number of Employees: 350.

EXPERTISE/EDUCATION SOUGHT: Data processing, finance, electrical engineering, television broadcasting, communications, accounting, marketing, computer programming

CONTACT: For individuals with previous experience: Ms Debra Henderson, Director of Human Resources; Phone (212) 424-7000.

THE LIMITED STORES, INC.
3 LIMITED PARKWAY
COLUMBUS, OHIO 43230

OVERVIEW: Operates chain of women's apparel stores. Established: 1963. Parent Company: Limited, Inc.

KEY STATISTICS Annual Sales: $984.0 million. Number of Employees: 18,000.

EXPERTISE/EDUCATION SOUGHT: Marketing, product design and development, warehousing, information systems, sales, planning, finance, merchandising

CONTACT: For individuals with previous experience: Mr Fred Lamster, Director of Staffing, PO Box 16528, Columbus, OH, 43216-6528; Phone (614) 479-2000.

LIN BROADCASTING CORPORATION
5295 CARILLON POINT
KIRKLAND, WASHINGTON 98033-7356

OVERVIEW: Operates TV stations and publishes magazines.

KEY STATISTICS Annual Sales: $705.0 million. Number of Employees: 1,200.

EXPERTISE/EDUCATION SOUGHT: Computer science, computer engineering, software engineering/development, cellular engineering, administration, sales, marketing

CONTACT: For individuals with previous experience: Mr Kerry Larson, Senior Vice President Human Resources.

THE LINCOLN ELECTRIC COMPANY
22801 SAINT CLAIR AVENUE
CLEVELAND, OHIO 44117-2524

OVERVIEW: Manufactures motors, welders, and electrical equipment. Established: 1895.

KEY STATISTICS Number of Employees: 6,036.

EXPERTISE/EDUCATION SOUGHT: Electrical engineering, mechanical engineering, accounting, finance, data processing

CONTACT: Ms Akita Wrench, Manager of Recruitment and Training; Phone (216) 481-8100, ext. 2655.

LINCOLN NATIONAL CORPORATION
1300 SOUTH CLINTON STREET
FT. WAYNE, INDIANA 46802

OVERVIEW: Provides life insurance and financial services.

HIRING HISTORY Number of professional employees hired in 1994: 75.

EXPERTISE/EDUCATION SOUGHT: Accounting, underwriting, financial analysis, actuarial, law, data processing, auditing, investment

CONTACT: Ms Tanya Flightner, Manager of Recruitment; Phone (219) 455-2000, ext. 3011.

LINCOLN PROPERTY COMPANY
500 NORTH AKARD STREET, SUITE 3300
DALLAS, TEXAS 75201-3320

OVERVIEW: Provides construction and real estate. Established: 1965.

KEY STATISTICS Annual Sales: $1.0 billion. Number of Employees: 4,400.

EXPERTISE/EDUCATION SOUGHT: Finance, mechanical engineering, electrical engineering, construction engineering, civil engineering, information systems

CONTACT: For individuals with previous experience: Human Resources Department; Phone (214) 740-3300.

LIQUID CARBONIC INDUSTRIAL CORPORATION
810 JORIE BOULEVARD
OAK BROOK, ILLINOIS 60521-2254

OVERVIEW: Manufactures industrial gases. Established: 1888. Parent Company: CBI Industries, Inc.

KEY STATISTICS Annual Sales: $826.0 million. Number of Employees: 6,600.

EXPERTISE/EDUCATION SOUGHT: Marketing, auditing, finance, accounting, chemical engineering, data processing

CONTACT: Mr James Morgan, Manager of Staffing/Equal Employment Opportunity; Phone (708) 572-7500.

LITTON INDUSTRIES, INC.
21240 BURBANK BOULEVARD
WOODLAND HILLS, CALIFORNIA 91367-6675

OVERVIEW: Provides electronics, defense, and industrial automation products. Established: 1953.

EXPERTISE/EDUCATION SOUGHT: Accounting, law, finance, real estate, data processing, health insurance, economics

CONTACT: For individuals with previous experience: Ms Nancy Thacker, Director of Personnel; Phone (310) 859-5000.

LIVING CENTER OF AMERICA, INC.
15415 KATY FREEWAY, SUITE 800
HOUSTON, TEXAS 77094-1815

OVERVIEW: Operates residential communities for the elderly. Established: 1984. Parent Company: ARA Group, Inc.

KEY STATISTICS Annual Sales: $389.0 million. Number of Employees: 17,500.

HIRING HISTORY Number of professional employees hired in 1993: 200.

EXPERTISE/EDUCATION SOUGHT: Accounting, management, information systems, computer programming, law, claims adjustment/examination, program analysis

CONTACT: Ms Theresa Tucker, Director of Recruiting; Phone (713) 578-4760.

LIZ CLAIBORNE, INC.
1441 BROADWAY
NEW YORK, NEW YORK 10018-2002

OVERVIEW: Manufactures and markets clothing, accessories, and cosmetics. Established: 1976.

KEY STATISTICS Annual Sales: $2.0 billion. Number of Employees: 7,900.

EXPERTISE/EDUCATION SOUGHT: Marketing, public relations, finance, sales, merchandising, accounting

CONTACT: Human Resources Department; Phone (212) 354-4900.

LOCKHEED MARTIN
6801 ROCKLEDGE DRIVE
BETHESDA, MARYLAND 20817

OVERVIEW: Manufactures aircraft, defense systems, and electronic systems. Established: 1909.

EXPERTISE/EDUCATION SOUGHT: Finance, accounting, human resources

CONTACT: For individuals with previous experience: Human Resources; Phone (301) 897-6000.

LOCKHEED SANDERS, INC.
65 SPIT BROOK ROAD
NASHUA, NEW HAMPSHIRE 03060

OVERVIEW: Manufactures electronic defense systems and related products. Established: 1951. Parent Company: Lockheed Martin Corporation.

EXPERTISE/EDUCATION SOUGHT: Electrical engineering, mechanical engineering, software engineering/development

CONTACT: Ms Kelly Dunn, Coordinator of College Recruiting; Phone (603) 885-4321.

LOCKHEED/MARTIN SERVICES GROUP
2131 RYE ROAD, ROUTE 38
CHERRY HILL, NEW JERSEY 08002-2045

OVERVIEW: Provides engineering and technical development services. Parent Company: Lockheed Martin Corporation.

KEY STATISTICS Annual Sales: $500.0 million. Number of Employees: 7,000.

EXPERTISE/EDUCATION SOUGHT: Manufacturing engineering, chemical engineering, industrial engineering, electronics/electronics engineering, engineering science

CONTACT: For individuals with previous experience: Ms Ronnie Rauff, Employment Department; Phone (609) 486-5207, ext. 3.

LOCTITE CORPORATION
1001 TROUT BROOK CROSSING
ROCKY HILL, CONNECTICUT 06067-3910

OVERVIEW: Manufactures sealants and adhesives. Established: 1953.

EXPERTISE/EDUCATION SOUGHT: Marketing, finance, sales, accounting, chemistry

CONTACT: For individuals with previous experience: Mr Bill Mastrianna, Manager of Employment, 705 North Mountain Road, Newington, CT, 06111; Phone (800) 243-4874.

LOEWS CORPORATION
667 MADISON AVENUE
NEW YORK, NEW YORK 10021-8087

OVERVIEW: Manages operations in the financial and hotel industries. Established: 1955.

KEY STATISTICS Number of Employees: 26,700.

EXPERTISE/EDUCATION SOUGHT: Accounting, marketing, finance, management information systems, hospitality/hotel and restaurant management

CONTACT: For individuals with previous experience: Ms Linda Dominguez, Manager of Employment, 1 Park Avenue, New York, NY, 10016; Phone (212) 545-2000.

LOJACK CORPORATION
333 ELM STREET
DEDHAM, MASSACHUSETTS 02026-4530

OVERVIEW: Develops computer tracking devices to locate stolen vehicles. Established: 1978.

KEY STATISTICS Annual Sales: $30.2 million. Number of Employees: 240.

EXPERTISE/EDUCATION SOUGHT: Sales, marketing, accounting

CONTACT: For individuals with previous experience: Ms Cindy Hood, Office Manager; Phone (617) 326-4700.

LONE STAR TECHNOLOGIES, INC.
5501 LBJ FREEWAY
DALLAS, TEXAS 75240-2313

OVERVIEW: Manufactures steel pipes and tubes.

KEY STATISTICS Number of Employees: 1,800.

EXPERTISE/EDUCATION SOUGHT: Management, electrical engineering, electronics/electronics engineering, test engineering

CONTACT: For individuals with previous experience: Ms Billie Sifton, Personnel Administrator; Phone (214) 386-3981.

LONG ISLAND LIGHTING COMPANY
175 EAST OLD COUNTRY ROAD
HICKSVILLE, NEW YORK 11801-4257

OVERVIEW: Electric utility. Established: 1910.

KEY STATISTICS Annual Sales: $3.0 billion. Number of Employees: 6,300.

HIRING HISTORY Number of professional employees hired in 1993: 150.

EXPERTISE/EDUCATION SOUGHT: Information systems, management information systems

CONTACT: Ms Nancy Jacob, Employment Services Administrator; Phone (516) 937-3153.

THE LONG ISLAND RAILROAD COMPANY
JAMAICA STATION
JAMAICA, NEW YORK 11435

OVERVIEW: Operates railroad. Established: 1834.

KEY STATISTICS Number of Employees: 6,430.

EXPERTISE/EDUCATION SOUGHT: Finance, accounting, auditing, transportation

CONTACT: For individuals with previous experience: Employment Office; Phone (718) 558-7400.

LONG JOHN SILVERS RESTAURANT
101 JERRICO DRIVE
LEXINGTON, KENTUCKY 40509-1809

OVERVIEW: Operates chain of seafood restaurants. Established: 1969.

KEY STATISTICS Annual Sales: $700.0 million. Number of Employees: 19,000.

EXPERTISE/EDUCATION SOUGHT: Accounting, finance, information systems, marketing

CONTACT: Ms Carol Caskey, Director of Corporate Human Resources; Phone (606) 263-6000.

LONG'S DRUG STORES CORPORATION
141 NORTH CIVIC DRIVE
WALNUT CREEK, CALIFORNIA 94596-3815

OVERVIEW: Operates chain of drug stores. Established: 1938.

KEY STATISTICS Annual Sales: $2.0 billion. Number of Employees: 15,200.

EXPERTISE/EDUCATION SOUGHT: Computer programming, business administration, finance, accounting, pharmacy

CONTACT: For individuals with previous experience: Ms Karen Cole, Supervisor of Employment; Phone (510) 937-1170.

LORAL AEROSPACE CORPORATION
29947 AVENDA DE LOS BANDERAS
RANCHO SANTA MARITA, CALIFORNIA 92688-2964

OVERVIEW: Manufactures electronics and communications equipment for the aerospace industry.

KEY STATISTICS Annual Sales: $990.0 million. Number of Employees: 11,585.

EXPERTISE/EDUCATION SOUGHT: Electrical engineering, systems engineering, communications, software engineering/development

CONTACT: For individuals with previous experience: Mr Randy Takahashi, Director of Human Resources; Phone (714) 459-3300.

LORAL CORPORATION
600 3RD AVENUE
NEW YORK, NEW YORK 10016

OVERVIEW: Manufactures electronic defense systems and telecommunications and weather satellites. Established: 1948.

EXPERTISE/EDUCATION SOUGHT: Administration, accounting, communications, electrical engineering, systems engineering, software engineering/development

CONTACT: For individuals with previous experience: Ms Cindy Simon, Manager of Corporate Personnel; Phone (212) 697-1105.

LORILLARD TOBACCO COMPANY
1 PARK AVENUE
NEW YORK, NEW YORK 10016

OVERVIEW: Manufactures and distributes tobacco products and cigarettes. Parent Company: Loews Corporation.

EXPERTISE/EDUCATION SOUGHT: Sales, marketing, finance, accounting, auditing, management information systems

CONTACTS: For college students and recent graduates: Mr Kenneth Abraham, Vice President of Human Resources; Phone (212) 545-2500. For individuals with previous experience: Ms Linda Dominquez, Employment Manager; Phone (212) 545-2523.

LOUISIANA-PACIFIC CORPORATION
111 SOUTH WEST 5TH AVENUE
PORTLAND, OREGON 92204

OVERVIEW: Manufactures wood and timber products.

EXPERTISE/EDUCATION SOUGHT: Marketing, finance, accounting, computer programming, data processing

CONTACT: Mr Gary Maffei, Director of Personnel, 111Southwest 5th Avenue, 42nd Floor, Portland, OR, 97204; Phone (503) 221-0800.

LOUISIANA POWER AND LIGHT COMPANY
225 BARONNE STREET
NEW ORLEANS, LOUISIANA 70113-3125

OVERVIEW: Electric utility. Established: 1949. Parent Company: Energy Corporation.

KEY STATISTICS Annual Sales: $2.0 billion. Number of Employees: 2,000.

HIRING HISTORY Number of professional employees hired in 1993: 5.

EXPERTISE/EDUCATION SOUGHT: Management information systems, finance, electrical engineering

CONTACT: Mr Joseph Hotard, Manager of Human Resources; Phone (504) 569-4953.

LOWE'S COMPANIES, INC.
HIGHWAY 268 EAST
NORTH WILKESBORO, NORTH CAROLINA 28659

OVERVIEW: Operates chain of home improvement stores. Established: 1921.

KEY STATISTICS Number of Employees: 28,843.

EXPERTISE/EDUCATION SOUGHT: Accounting, marketing, sales, management information systems

CONTACT: For individuals with previous experience: Employment Services, PO Box 111, North Wilkesboro, NC, 28656.

LTV CORPORATION
25 WEST PROSPECT AVENUE
CLEVELAND, OHIO 44115-1000

OVERVIEW: Manufactures steel and oil field drilling equipment. Established: 1953.

KEY STATISTICS Number of Employees: 17,000.

EXPERTISE/EDUCATION SOUGHT: Accounting, finance, marketing, law, data processing

CONTACT: Mr Charles Butters, Director of Employee Development and Recruiting; Phone (216) 622-5234.

LUBRIZOL CORPORATION
29400 LAKELAND BOULEVARD
WICKLIFFE, OHIO 44092-2298

OVERVIEW: Manufactures plant genetics products and provides services for the agricultural industry. Established: 1928.

KEY STATISTICS Number of Employees: 4,609.

HIRING HISTORY Number of professional employees hired in 1993: 15.

EXPERTISE/EDUCATION SOUGHT: Mechanical engineering, chemical engineering, chemistry

CONTACTS: For college students and recent graduates: Ms Natalie Wochkovich, Employment Manager; Phone (216) 943-4200. For individuals with previous experience: Ms Liz Martin, Manager of Staffing and Recruiting; Phone (216) 943-4200.

LUCKY STORES, INC.
1701 MARINA BOULEVARD
SAN LEANDRO, CALIFORNIA 94577

OVERVIEW: Operates chain of food stores. Established: 1931. Parent Company: American Stores Company.

KEY STATISTICS Number of Employees: 45,000.

EXPERTISE/EDUCATION SOUGHT: Sales, marketing, business management, accounting, law

CONTACT: Ms Jeanine Schreiber, Vice President of Human Resources; Phone (510) 678-4200; Fax (510)833-6234.

LUTHERAN HEALTH SYSTEMS
4310 17TH AVENUE SOUTHWEST
FARGO, NORTH DAKOTA 58103-3339

OVERVIEW: Operates general hospital, children's hospital, and school for the physically handicapped.

KEY STATISTICS Annual Sales: $452.1 million. Number of Employees: 10,000.

EXPERTISE/EDUCATION SOUGHT: Physical therapy, occupational therapy, licensed practical nursing, registered nursing

CONTACT: For individuals with previous experience: Ms Jerrie Tooney, Director Human Resources; Phone (701) 277-7500.

LYONDELL PETROCHEMICAL COMPANY
1221 MCKINNEY STREET, SUITE 1600
HOUSTON, TEXAS 77010

OVERVIEW: Manufactures and processes petroleum products and chemicals.

KEY STATISTICS Annual Sales: $5.0 billion. Number of Employees: 2,300.

HIRING HISTORY Number of professional employees hired in 1994: 30.

EXPERTISE/EDUCATION SOUGHT: Chemical engineering, petroleum/petrochemical engineering, technical engineering

CONTACT: For individuals with previous experience: Human Resources Department, PO Box 3646, Houston, TX, 77253; Phone (713) 652-7200.

M&M/MARS, INC.
HIGH STREET
HACKETTSTOWN, NEW JERSEY 07840

OVERVIEW: Manufactures candy, pet foods, and rice products.

EXPERTISE/EDUCATION SOUGHT: Sales, mechanical engineering, computer science, accounting, marketing, packaging engineering, electrical engineering, business, industrial engineering

CONTACTS: For college students and recent graduates: Ms Karen Green, Personnel Specialist. For individuals with previous experience: Ms Marilyn Stetar, Personnel and Organizational Manager; Phone (908) 852-1000.

MACFRUGAL'S BARGAINS, INC.
2430 EAST DEL AMO BOULEVARD
COMPTON, CALIFORNIA 90220

OVERVIEW: Operates chain of discount stores.

EXPERTISE/EDUCATION SOUGHT: Accounting, marketing, information systems, management, purchasing

CONTACT: Mr Frank Bianchi, Vice President of Human Resources; Phone (310) 537-9220, ext. 4380.

MACK TRUCKS, INC.
2100 MACK BOULEVARD
ALLENTOWN, PENNSYLVANIA 18103-5622

OVERVIEW: Manufactures trucks. Established: 1900.

KEY STATISTICS Annual Sales: $1.0 billion. Number of Employees: 5,500.

HIRING HISTORY Number of professional employees hired in 1993: 65.

EXPERTISE/EDUCATION SOUGHT: Mechanical engineering, electrical engineering, accounting, administration, quality control, purchasing

CONTACT: For individuals with previous experience: Mr Frank P Romao, Human Resources Administrator; Phone (610) 709-3011.

MACY'S CALIFORNIA, INC.
170 O'FARRELL STREET
SAN FRANCISCO, CALIFORNIA 94108-5808

OVERVIEW: Operates chain of department stores. Established: 1976. Parent Company: R. H. Macy & Company, Inc.

Macy's California, Inc. (continued)

KEY STATISTICS Annual Sales: $653.0 million.

EXPERTISE/EDUCATION SOUGHT: Sales, marketing, accounting, computer programming, law, program analysis, management, auditing

CONTACT: For individuals with previous experience: Recruitment Department; Phone (415) 954-6000.

MACY'S WEST BULLOCK
PO BOX 7888
SAN FRANCISCO, CALIFORNIA 94120

OVERVIEW: Operates chain of retail stores.

EXPERTISE/EDUCATION SOUGHT: Retail

CONTACT: Mr Gene Ross, Manager of College Relations; Phone (415) 954-6000.

MAGNECOMP CORPORATION
471 ATLAS STREET
BREA, CALIFORNIA 92621

OVERVIEW: Manufactures spring assemblies for computer disk drives.

CONTACT: For individuals with previous experience: Ms Nancy Guardado, Personnel Coordinator; Phone (714) 990-3874.

MAGNETEK, INC.
11126 CENTURY BOULEVARD
NASHVILLE, TENNESSEE 37229

OVERVIEW: Manufactures electrical equipment and components. Established: 1970.

KEY STATISTICS Annual Sales: $2.0 billion. Number of Employees: 17,600.

EXPERTISE/EDUCATION SOUGHT: Mechanical engineering, electrical engineering, design engineering, manufacturing engineering

CONTACT: For individuals with previous experience: Ms Beckie Trudeau, Human Resources Specialist, PO Box 290159, Nashville, TN, 37229; Phone (615) 316-5100.

MALLINCKRODT MEDICAL
675 MCDONNELL BOULEVARD
HAZELWOOD, MISSOURI 63042-2301

OVERVIEW: Manufactures medical devices. Established: 1867. Parent Company: .

KEY STATISTICS Number of Employees: 7,000.

EXPERTISE/EDUCATION SOUGHT: Accounting, engineering, sales, marketing, radiology, human resources, chemistry

CONTACT: For individuals with previous experience: Ms Mary Monnet, Vice President of Human Resources-Mallinckrodt Medical, PO Box 5840, Hazelwood, MO, 63134.

MANOR CARE, INC.
10750 COLUMBIA PIKE
SILVER SPRING, MARYLAND 20901-4493

OVERVIEW: Owns and operates nursing homes. Established: 1968.

KEY STATISTICS Annual Sales: $1.0 billion. Number of Employees: 25,500.

HIRING HISTORY Number of professional employees hired in 1993: 200.

EXPERTISE/EDUCATION SOUGHT: Finance, auditing, budgeting, computer programming, systems analysis, management information systems, accounting, administration

CONTACT: Ms Tracy Henshaw, Manager of Corporate Employment; Phone (301) 681-9400.

MANPOWER INTERNATIONAL, INC.
5301 NORTH IRONWOOD ROAD
MILWAUKEE, WISCONSIN 53217-4910

OVERVIEW: Temporary personnel services. Parent Company: BAS Holdings Corporation.

KEY STATISTICS Number of Employees: 1,200,000.

EXPERTISE/EDUCATION SOUGHT: Human resources, marketing, finance, accounting, computer programming

CONTACT: For individuals with previous experience: Ms Sharon Rooney, Manager of Employee Services and Human Resources; Phone (414) 961-1000.

MARC GLASSMAN, INC.
5841 WEST 130TH STREET
CLEVELAND, OHIO 44130-3608

OVERVIEW: Operates chain of drug stores.

KEY STATISTICS Annual Sales: $500.0 million. Number of Employees: 5,500.

EXPERTISE/EDUCATION SOUGHT: Management

CONTACT: For individuals with previous experience: Mr Kevin Yaugher, Vice President Corporate Operations.

MARINE MIDLAND BANKS, INC.
1 MARINE MIDLAND CENTER
BUFFALO, NEW YORK 14203-2885

OVERVIEW: Commercial bank.

EXPERTISE/EDUCATION SOUGHT: Business, finance, accounting, banking, mortgage

CONTACT: Mr Patrick O'Leary, Vice President, Officer of Staffing; Phone (716) 841-5849.

MARION MERRELL DOW, INC.
9300 WARD PARKWAY
KANSAS CITY, MISSOURI 64114-3321

OVERVIEW: Produces prescription drugs and consumer health care products. Established: 1952. Parent Company: The Dow Chemical Company.

KEY STATISTICS Number of Employees: 9,827.

EXPERTISE/EDUCATION SOUGHT: Pharmacy, packaging engineering, quality control, chemical engineering, mechanical engineering, industrial engineering, biology, physics

CONTACT: For individuals with previous experience: Mr Jack Major, Manager of Recruiting and Relocation; Phone (816) 966-4000.

MARITZ, INC.
1375 NORTH HIGHWAY DRIVE
FENTON, MISSOURI 63099-0001

OVERVIEW: Provides research and management consulting services. Established: 1923.

KEY STATISTICS Number of Employees: 10,966.

EXPERTISE/EDUCATION SOUGHT: Marketing, sales, accounting, finance, auditing, computer programming, tax, marketing, market research, latex/rubber engineering

CONTACT: For individuals with previous experience: Mr Terry Goring, Senior Vice President of Human Resources; Phone (314) 827-4000.

MARRIOTT MANAGEMENT SERVICES
10400 FERNWOOD ROAD
BETHESDA, MARYLAND 20817

OVERVIEW: Provides food and facilities management services.

EXPERTISE/EDUCATION SOUGHT: Finance, business, hospitality/hotel and restaurant management, accounting

CONTACT: Mr James A Mueller, Director, Staffing and Placement, Marriot Drive, Washington, DC, 20058; Phone (301) 380-1089.

MARSH AND MCLENNAN, INC.
1166 AVENUE OF THE AMERICAS
NEW YORK, NEW YORK 10036

OVERVIEW: Provides insurance and business and insurance consulting services.

CONTACT: Ms Gina Marrella, Director of Human Resources; Phone (212) 345-6785.

MARSH SUPERMARKETS, INC.
9800 CROSS POINT BOULEVARD
INDIANAPOLIS, INDIANA 46256-3350

OVERVIEW: Operates chain of food stores. Established: 1931.

KEY STATISTICS Number of Employees: 11,000.

EXPERTISE/EDUCATION SOUGHT: Sales, retail, business

CONTACT: Mr Bruce Bain, Vice President of Human Resources; Phone (317) 594-2100.

MARSHALL'S, INC.
200 BRICKSTONE SQUARE
ANDOVER, MASSACHUSETTS 01810-1429

OVERVIEW: Operates chain of department stores. Established: 1976. Parent Company: Melville Corporation.

KEY STATISTICS Annual Sales: $3.0 billion. Number of Employees: 19,000.

EXPERTISE/EDUCATION SOUGHT: Marketing, sales, business management, finance, accounting

CONTACTS: For college students and recent graduates: Ms Jane O'Reilly, Manager of Human Resources; Phone (508) 474-7154. For individuals with previous experience: Mr Paul Mantell, Manager of Corporate Staffing; Phone (508) 474-7000, ext. 7269.

THE MARTIN BROWER COMPANY
1020 WEST 31ST STREET
DOWNERS GROVE, ILLINOIS 60515-5508

OVERVIEW: Distributes foods and supplies to restaurants. Established: 1962.

KEY STATISTICS Number of Employees: 3,800.

EXPERTISE/EDUCATION SOUGHT: Marketing, accounting, sales, data processing, computer programming

CONTACT: Ms Denise Wydra, Human Resources Coordinator.

MARTIN MARIETTA ENERGY SYSTEMS
241 WEST TYRONE ROAD
OAK RIDGE, TENNESSEE 37831

OVERVIEW: Provides research in the areas of nuclear power and resource/energy recovery. Parent Company: Lockheed Martin Corporation.

KEY STATISTICS Annual Sales: $1.0 billion. Number of Employees: 20,876.

EXPERTISE/EDUCATION SOUGHT: Engineering science, environmental engineering, nuclear engineering, civil engineering, chemical engineering

CONTACT: Mr Michael Willard, Director of Staffing, PO Box 2002, Oak Ridge, TN, 37831-6501; Phone (615) 576-1389.

MARUBENI AMERICA CORPORATION
450 LEXINGTON AVENUE
NEW YORK, NEW YORK 10017

OVERVIEW: Provide import, export, and trading services. Established: 1951. Parent Company: Marubeni Corporation of Japan.

KEY STATISTICS Annual Sales: $18.0 billion. Number of Employees: 500.

EXPERTISE/EDUCATION SOUGHT: Marketing, finance, accounting, sales, data processing, computer programming

CONTACT: Mr Joe Van Dorn, Senior Vice President of Human Resources, 200 Park Avenue, New York, NY, 10166; Phone (212) 450-0100.

MASCO CORPORATION
21001 VAN BORN ROAD
TAYLOR, MICHIGAN 48180

OVERVIEW: Manufactures automotive parts, plumbing fixtures, hardware, and furnishings. Established: 1929.

KEY STATISTICS Annual Sales: $5.0 billion. Number of Employees: 53,100.

HIRING HISTORY Number of professional employees hired in 1993: 125.

EXPERTISE/EDUCATION SOUGHT: Operations, finance, product engineering, manufacturing engineering, sales, marketing, design engineering, automotive engineering

CONTACT: For individuals with previous experience: Mr Dave Kinsella, Director of Executive Recruitment; Phone (313) 274-7400, ext. 411; Fax (313) 374-6657.

MASONITE CORPORATION
1 SOUTH WACKER DRIVE, 36TH FLOOR
CHICAGO, ILLINOIS 60606-4614

OVERVIEW: Manufactures building materials and home improvement products. Established: 1925. Parent Company: International Paper Company.

KEY STATISTICS Number of Employees: 5,500.

EXPERTISE/EDUCATION SOUGHT: Mechanical engineering, mathematics, electrical engineering, environmental engineering, research and development, physics

CONTACT: For individuals with previous experience: Ms Stephanie Jones, Manager of Communications Development and Administration.

MASSACHUSETTS GENERAL HOSPITAL CORPORATION
55 FRUIT STREET
BOSTON, MASSACHUSETTS 02114-2621

OVERVIEW: General surgical hospital. Established: 1811.

KEY STATISTICS Annual Sales: $733.0 million. Number of Employees: 10,156.

EXPERTISE/EDUCATION SOUGHT: Accounting, finance, marketing, data processing, auditing

CONTACT: Ms Mary French, Manager of Employee Relations and Recruiting; Phone (617) 726-2000, ext. 5483.

MASSACHUSETTS MUTUAL LIFE INSURANCE
1295 STATE STREET
SPRINGFIELD, MASSACHUSETTS 01111-0001

OVERVIEW: Provides life insurance. Established: 1851.

KEY STATISTICS Assets: $32.0 billion. Number of Employees: 9,049.

EXPERTISE/EDUCATION SOUGHT: Underwriting, finance, marketing, sales, accounting, management information systems, health insurance, management

CONTACTS: For college students and recent graduates: Human Resources Department; Phone (413) 788-8411. For individuals with previous experience: Mr Kenneth Blanchard, Director of Staffing; Phone (413) 788-8411, ext. 3785.

MATTEL, INC.
333 CONTINENTAL BOULEVARD
EL SEGUNDO, CALIFORNIA 90245

OVERVIEW: Manufactures and markets toys and games.

KEY STATISTICS Annual Sales: $2.0 billion. Number of Employees: 15,000.

EXPERTISE/EDUCATION SOUGHT: Management, marketing, advertising

CONTACT: For individuals with previous experience: Human Resources Department; Phone (310) 252-3532.

MAXTOR CORPORATION
251 RIVER OAKS PARKWAY
SAN JOSE, CALIFORNIA 95134-1913

OVERVIEW: Manufactures magnetic disk drives.

KEY STATISTICS Annual Sales: $1.0 billion. Number of Employees: 6,200.

EXPERTISE/EDUCATION SOUGHT: Accounting, manufacturing engineering, finance, marketing, software engineering/development, electrical engineering

CONTACT: For individuals with previous experience: Ms Sandy Taylor, Senior Human Resources Representative; Phone (408) 432-4343.

MAXXAM GROUP, INC.
5847 SAN FELIPE STREET, SUITE 2600
HOUSTON, TEXAS 77257

OVERVIEW: Manufactures aluminum products.

EXPERTISE/EDUCATION SOUGHT: Accounting, tax

CONTACT: For individuals with previous experience: Ms Marilyn Gentry, Personnel Coordinator; Phone (713) 975-7600.

THE MAY DEPARTMENT STORES COMPANY
611 OLIVE STREET
SAINT LOUIS, MISSOURI 63101-1721

OVERVIEW: Operates chain of department stores. Established: 1877.

KEY STATISTICS Number of Employees: 113,000.

EXPERTISE/EDUCATION SOUGHT: Finance, merchandising

CONTACT: For individuals with previous experience: Ms Colleen Lee, Director of Executive Recruitment; Phone (314) 342-6778.

MAYFLOWER LAIDLAW CONTRACT SERVICES
5360 COLLEGE BOULEVARD
OVERLAND PARK, KANSAS 66211-1641

OVERVIEW: Operates school buses and other bus lines.

KEY STATISTICS Annual Sales: $240.0 million. Number of Employees: 30,000.

HIRING HISTORY Number of professional employees hired in 1994: 750.

EXPERTISE/EDUCATION SOUGHT: Logistics, management

CONTACT: For individuals with previous experience: Ms Joanne Gastin, Vice President of Human Resources; Phone (913) 345-1986.

MAYFLOWER TRANSIT, INC.
9998 NORTH MICHIGAN ROAD
CARMEL, INDIANA 46032

OVERVIEW: Provides moving services.

EXPERTISE/EDUCATION SOUGHT: Customer service and support, accounting, law, sales, marketing, transportation, information systems

CONTACT: Mr Ron Diehm, Director of Employee Relations; Phone (317) 875-1000, ext. 1435.

MAYO FOUNDATION
200 1ST STREET SOUTHWEST
ROCHESTER, MINNESOTA 55905-0001

OVERVIEW: Diagnostic medical center. Established: 1863.

KEY STATISTICS Number of Employees: 20,615.

EXPERTISE/EDUCATION SOUGHT: Chemistry, biology, microbiology, licensed practical nursing, registered nursing, nuclear medicine, medical technology

CONTACT: Ms Cindy Nelson, College Recruiter; Phone (507) 284-2511.

MAYTAG CORPORATION
1 DEPENDABILITY SQUARE
NEWTON, IOWA 50208

OVERVIEW: Manufactures consumer appliances. Established: 1893.

KEY STATISTICS Number of Employees: 19,750.

EXPERTISE/EDUCATION SOUGHT: Sales, marketing, computer science

CONTACT: Ms Mindy Kehoe, Employment Representative; Phone (515) 792-8000; Fax (515) 791-8244.

MBNA CORPORATION
400 CHRISTIANA ROAD
NEWARK, DELAWARE 19713

OVERVIEW: Commercial bank.

EXPERTISE/EDUCATION SOUGHT: Accounting, finance, auditing, underwriting, marketing, sales

CONTACT: Mr Godfrey Streat, First Vice President of Employment.

MCDERMOTT INTERNATIONAL, INC.
1450 POYDRAS
NEW ORLEANS, LOUISIANA 70112

OVERVIEW: Provides marine construction services and power generation systems.

HIRING HISTORY Number of professional employees hired in 1994: 15.

EXPERTISE/EDUCATION SOUGHT: Finance, accounting, chemical engineering, structural engineering, systems integration, civil engineering, construction engineering, data processing

CONTACTS: For college students and recent graduates: Mr Robert Youngblood, Manager of College Recruitment; Phone (504) 587-5400. For individuals with previous experience: Mr Kevin Blasini, Corporate Employment Assistant; Phone (504) 587-5400.

MCCANN-ERICKSON USA, INC.
750 3RD AVENUE
NEW YORK, NEW YORK 10017-2703

OVERVIEW: Advertising agency. Established: 1964. Parent Company: Interpublic Group Companies, Inc.

KEY STATISTICS Annual Sales: $4.0 billion.

EXPERTISE/EDUCATION SOUGHT: Marketing, advertising, graphic arts, computer programming, market research, account management, audiovisual technology

CONTACT: For individuals with previous experience: Ms Kathy Yuill, Supervisor of Employment; Phone (212) 697-6000.

MCCAW CELLULAR COMMUNICATIONS
5400 CARILLON POINT
KIRKLAND, WASHINGTON 98033-7356

OVERVIEW: Provides cellular communications, broadcasting, and publishing services. Established: 1982. Parent Company: AT&T.

KEY STATISTICS Number of Employees: 5,800.

EXPERTISE/EDUCATION SOUGHT: Management information systems, software engineering/development, architecture, electrical engineering, electronics/electronics engineering, design engineering

CONTACT: For individuals with previous experience: Ms Nancy Rounds, Manager of Corporate Staffing; Phone (206) 827-4500.

MCCORMICK AND COMPANY, INC.
18 LOVETON CIRCLE
SPARKS, MARYLAND 21152-9202

OVERVIEW: Manufactures spices and seasonings. Established: 1889.

KEY STATISTICS Annual Sales: $2.0 billion. Number of Employees: 8,600.

EXPERTISE/EDUCATION SOUGHT: Marketing, accounting, finance, sales, research and development, management information systems

CONTACT: Mr Michael Treske, Director of Organization Development; Phone (410) 771-6000.

MCCRORY STORES
2955 EAST MARKET STREET
YORK, PENNSYLVANIA 17402

OVERVIEW: Operates chain of discount department stores.

EXPERTISE/EDUCATION SOUGHT: Retail management, marketing, management information systems

CONTACTS: For college students and recent graduates: Mr Doug Reeder, Manager of Human Resources; Phone (717) 757-8700. For individuals with previous experience: Mr Thomas Russell, Senior Vice President of Personnel; Phone (717) 757-8400.

MCDONALD'S CORPORATION
MCDONALD'S PLAZA
OAK BROOK, ILLINOIS 60521

OVERVIEW: Operates chain of fast food restaurants. Established: 1955.

EXPERTISE/EDUCATION SOUGHT: Food science, business management, finance, accounting, marketing, sales, product design and development, electrical engineering, nutrition, quality control

CONTACT: Employment Staffing; Phone (708) 575-5490.

MCDONNELL DOUGLAS CORPORATION
AIRPORT ROAD AND MCDONNELL BOULEVARD
SAINT LOUIS, MISSOURI 63134

OVERVIEW: Manufactures commercial airplanes, military aircraft, and defense systems. Established: 1939.

KEY STATISTICS Annual Sales: $14.0 billion. Number of Employees: 67,751.

EXPERTISE/EDUCATION SOUGHT: Computer science, electrical engineering, manufacturing engineering

CONTACT: Mr Andy Minor, Group Manager for College Relations; Phone (314) 232-0232.

MCGRAW-HILL, INC.
1221 AVENUE OF THE AMERICAS
NEW YORK, NEW YORK 10020

OVERVIEW: Multimedia publishing and information services company. Established: 1888.

EXPERTISE/EDUCATION SOUGHT: Law, finance, accounting, marketing

CONTACTS: For college students and recent graduates: Mr James Angeloni, Human Resources Associate; Phone (212) 512-2000. For individuals with previous experience: Mr Frank Durante, Manager of Staffing and Equal Opportunity Employment; Phone (212) 512-2018.

MCI COMMUNICATIONS CORPORATION
1801 PENNSYLVANIA AVENUE NORTHWEST
WASHINGTON, D.C. 20006-3606

OVERVIEW: Provides telecommunications services. Established: 1968.

KEY STATISTICS Annual Sales: $12.0 billion. Number of Employees: 36,000.

EXPERTISE/EDUCATION SOUGHT: Accounting, finance, marketing, sales, management information systems, management, computer science, telecommunications, electronics/electronics engineering

CONTACT: For individuals with previous experience: Ms Mary T Hayes, Senior Staffing Specialist.

MCKESSON CORPORATION
1 POST STREET
SAN FRANCISCO, CALIFORNIA 94104

OVERVIEW: Distributes drug and toiletry products. Established: 1832.

KEY STATISTICS Annual Sales: $12.0 billion. Number of Employees: 13,000.

EXPERTISE/EDUCATION SOUGHT: Pharmacy, systems analysis, marketing, accounting, finance, human resources, logistics, information systems

CONTACTS: For college students and recent graduates: Employment Hotline; Phone (415) 983-8409. For individuals with previous experience: Ms Kelly Barrington, Manager of Employment and Staffing; Phone (415) 983-8300.

MCKINSEY AND COMPANY, INC.
55 EAST 52ND STREET
NEW YORK, NEW YORK 10022

OVERVIEW: Provides management consulting services. Established: 1926.

KEY STATISTICS Annual Sales: $1.0 billion. Number of Employees: 5,500.

EXPERTISE/EDUCATION SOUGHT: Business development, management, financial analysis

CONTACT: For individuals with previous experience: Human Resources Department; Phone (212) 446-7000.

MEAD CORPORATION
COURTHOUSE PLAZA NORTHEAST
DAYTON, OHIO 45463

OVERVIEW: Manufactures paper, office supplies and packaging; provides on line database services. Established: 1846.

KEY STATISTICS Annual Sales: $5.0 billion. Number of Employees: 19,600.

HIRING HISTORY Number of professional employees hired in 1994: 100.

EXPERTISE/EDUCATION SOUGHT: Finance, human resources, information services

CONTACT: For individuals with previous experience: Ms Donna Chapman, Director of Recruiting and Staffing; Phone (513) 495-3923; Fax (513) 495-3208.

MEAD DATA CENTRAL, INC.
9393 SPRINGBORO PIKE
MAIMISBURG, OHIO 45542

OVERVIEW: Provides electronic information and publishing services. Established: 1970.

EXPERTISE/EDUCATION SOUGHT: Sales, marketing, computer science, computer programming, data processing

CONTACT: Carletta Railey-Worthy, Human Resources; Phone (513) 865-6800.

MEAD JOHNSON AND COMPANY
2400 WEST LLOYD EXPRESSWAY
EVANSVILLE, INDIANA 47721-0001

OVERVIEW: Manufactures nutritional and pharmaceutical products. Established: 1967. Parent Company: Bristol-Myers Squibb Company.

EXPERTISE/EDUCATION SOUGHT: Sales, marketing, finance, accounting, engineering

CONTACT: Mr Pat Aquart, Director of Human Resources; Phone (812) 429-7150.

MEDCO CONTAINMENT SERVICES, INC.
100 SUMMIT AVENUE
MONTVALE, NEW JERSEY 07645-1712

OVERVIEW: Designs and manages prescription drug benefit plans. Established: 1970. Parent Company: Merck and Company, Inc.

KEY STATISTICS Annual Sales: $3.0 billion. Number of Employees: 4,400.

EXPERTISE/EDUCATION SOUGHT: Accounting, mechanical engineering, packaging engineering, design engineering, sales, computer programming, systems analysis, pharmacy

CONTACT: Manager of Employment; Phone (201) 358-3400, ext. 5702.

MEDTRONIC, INC.
7000 CENTRAL AVENUE NORTHEAST
MINNEAPOLIS, MINNESOTA 55432-3568

OVERVIEW: Manufactures cardiovascular and neurological implants. Established: 1949.

KEY STATISTICS Number of Employees: 9,800.

EXPERTISE/EDUCATION SOUGHT: Finance, marketing, materials science, biomedical engineering, electrical engineering, chemical engineering, mechanical engineering, project engineering, software engineering/development, biological sciences

Medtronic, Inc. (continued)

CONTACTS: For college students and recent graduates: Job Hotline; Phone (612) 586-7724. For individuals with previous experience: Ms Diane Anderson, Employment Coordinator; Phone (612) 574-4780; Fax (612)574-6190.

MEIJER, INC.
2929 WALKER AVENUE NORTHWEST
GRAND RAPIDS, MICHIGAN 49504-9424

OVERVIEW: Operates food and general merchandise stores. Established: 1934.

KEY STATISTICS Number of Employees: 55,000.

EXPERTISE/EDUCATION SOUGHT: Computer programming, retail, management

CONTACTS: For college students and recent graduates: Mr Mike Guir, Employment Manager; Phone (616) 453-6711, ext. 5210. For individuals with previous experience: Mr Brian Michmerhuizen, Vice President of Human Resources; Phone (616) 453-6711.

MELLON BANK CORPORATION
1 MELLON BANK CENTER, 500 GRANT STREET
PITTSBURGH, PENNSYLVANIA 15258-0001

OVERVIEW: Provides commercial, retail, and investment banking services. Established: 1869.

KEY STATISTICS Assets: $3.0 billion. Number of Employees: 21,400.

EXPERTISE/EDUCATION SOUGHT: Finance, computer programming, network analysis, banking, government affairs/relations, systems analysis

CONTACT: For individuals with previous experience: Ms Elizabeth Knobloch, Vice President of Corporate Staffing, 1 Mellon Bank Center, Room 170, Pittsburgh, PA, 15258-0001; Phone (412) 236-0892.

MELVILLE CORPORATION
1 THEALL ROAD
RYE, NEW YORK 10583

OVERVIEW: Operates chains of specialty stores. Established: 1914.

KEY STATISTICS Annual Sales: $11.0 billion.

EXPERTISE/EDUCATION SOUGHT: Accounting, finance, marketing, data processing

CONTACT: For individuals with previous experience: Ms Peggy Kehston, Vice President of Executive Development; Phone (918) 925-4000.

MEMOREX TELEX CORPORATION
545 EAST JOHN CARPENTER FREEWAY
IRVING, TEXAS 75062-3931

OVERVIEW: Manufactures magnetic tape, diskettes, computer supplies; provides network and storage solutions and services. Established: 1963.

KEY STATISTICS Number of Employees: 2,740.

EXPERTISE/EDUCATION SOUGHT: Business, computer science, marketing, accounting, finance, sales, engineering, systems engineering

CONTACT: For individuals with previous experience: Mr Jimmy Webster, Manager of Recruiting; Phone (214) 444-3500.

MENARD, INC.
4777 MENARD DRIVE
EAU CLAIRE, WISCONSIN 54703-9625

OVERVIEW: Operates chain of home improvement stores. Established: 1960.

KEY STATISTICS Number of Employees: 7,500.

EXPERTISE/EDUCATION SOUGHT: Business management, finance, computer programming, computer science, manufacturing engineering, accounting, management, management information systems, information systems

CONTACT: For individuals with previous experience: Mr Ron Mehr, Operations Personnel Director; Phone (715) 874-5911.

MENASHA CORPORATION
1645 BERGSTROM ROAD
NEENAH, WISCONSIN 54956

OVERVIEW: Manufactures corrugated containers and plastics. Established: 1849.

KEY STATISTICS Number of Employees: 4,100.

EXPERTISE/EDUCATION SOUGHT: Marketing, finance, sales, accounting, business management, law, management information systems, product management

CONTACTS: For college students and recent graduates: Mr Steve Kromholz, Staffing Manager; Phone (414) 751-1000. For individuals with previous experience: Mr David Rust, Vice President of Human Resources; Phone (414) 751-1000.

MERCANTILE STORES COMPANY, INC.
9450 SEWARD ROAD
FAIRFIELD, OHIO 45014-5412

OVERVIEW: Operates chain of department stores. Established: 1919.

KEY STATISTICS Number of Employees: 32,000.

EXPERTISE/EDUCATION SOUGHT: Product design and development, accounting, merchandising, marketing, management information systems, management

CONTACT: Ms Alice Wilson, Manager of Employment; Phone (513) 881-8000.

MERCEDES-BENZ NORTH AMERICA, INC.
1 MERCEDES DRIVE
MONTVALE, NEW JERSEY 07645

OVERVIEW: Manufactures automobiles. Established: 1965. Parent Company: Daimler-Benz North America Corporation.

KEY STATISTICS Number of Employees: 1,500.

HIRING HISTORY Number of professional employees hired in 1994: 30.

EXPERTISE/EDUCATION SOUGHT: Marketing, finance, accounting

CONTACT: Ms Janice Simonson, Employee Relations Specialist; Phone (201) 573-2532.

MERCK AND COMPANY, INC.
1 MERCK DRIVE, PO BOX 100
WHITEHOUSE STATION, NEW JERSEY 08889-0100

OVERVIEW: Manufactures specialty chemicals, pharmaceuticals, and animal health products. Established: 1891.

KEY STATISTICS Annual Sales: $15.0 billion. Number of Employees: 47,500.

HIRING HISTORY Number of professional employees hired in 1994: 400.

EXPERTISE/EDUCATION SOUGHT: Computer science, sales, marketing, finance, human resources

CONTACT: Ms Diane Dalinsky, Manager of College Relations; Phone (908) 423-6221.

MERCY HEALTH SERVICES
34605 WEST 12 MILE ROAD
FARMINGTON HILLS, MICHIGAN 48331-3263

OVERVIEW: Provides health care. Established: 1976.

KEY STATISTICS Annual Sales: $2.0 billion. Number of Employees: 22,106.

EXPERTISE/EDUCATION SOUGHT: Accounting, finance, marketing, information systems, computer programming, data processing, law

CONTACTS: For college students and recent graduates: Ms Paula Huot, Director of Operations; Phone (810) 489-6000. For individuals with previous experience: Ms Teri Skibowski, Human Resource Specialist; Phone (810) 489-6840.

MERCY HEALTH SYSTEM

2335 GRANDVIEW AVENUE
CINCINNATI, OHIO 45206-2219

OVERVIEW: Provides hospital administration services.

KEY STATISTICS Number of Employees: 18,400.

EXPERTISE/EDUCATION SOUGHT: Accounting, finance, human resources

CONTACT: For individuals with previous experience: Ms Elizabeth Baldock, Director of Management, Development and Recruitment; Phone (513) 221-2736.

MERIDIAN BANCORP, INC.

1 MERIDIAN BOULEVARD
WYOMISSING, PENNSYLVANIA 19601-3539

OVERVIEW: Commercial bank. Established: 1983.

KEY STATISTICS Assets: $1.0 billion. Number of Employees: 5,000.

EXPERTISE/EDUCATION SOUGHT: Accounting, marketing, finance, management information systems, computer science, retail, management

CONTACT: Mr Christopher Cardarelli, Human Resources Officer, PO Box 1102, Reading, PA, 19601; Phone (610) 655-2000.

MERRY-GO-ROUND ENTERPRISES

3300 FASHION WAY
JOPPA, MARYLAND 21085-3206

OVERVIEW: Operates retail clothing stores. Established: 1968.

KEY STATISTICS Annual Sales: $960.0 million. Number of Employees: 14,970.

EXPERTISE/EDUCATION SOUGHT: Management information systems, marketing, management, finance, accounting

CONTACT: For individuals with previous experience: Mr Jonathan Jusie, Field Recruitment Manager.

METHODIST HOSPITAL OF LUBBOCK TEXAS

3615 19TH STREET
LUBBOCK, TEXAS 79410-1203

OVERVIEW: Public hospital. Established: 1918.

KEY STATISTICS Annual Sales: $502.0 million. Number of Employees: 8,450.

EXPERTISE/EDUCATION SOUGHT: Nursing, physical therapy, radiology

CONTACTS: For college students and recent graduates: Ms Susie Luker, Nursing Recruiter; Phone (806) 792-1011. For individuals with previous experience: Mr Larry Calvert, Personnel Director; Phone (806) 792-1011.

METROCEL CELLULAR TELEPHONE COMPANY

17300 NORTH DALLAS PARKWAY, SUITE 1000
DALLAS, TEXAS 75248

OVERVIEW: Provides cellular telephone service. Established: 1985.

EXPERTISE/EDUCATION SOUGHT: Accounting, finance, data processing, electrical engineering, software engineering/development

CONTACT: For individuals with previous experience: Ms Karen Bailey, Vice President of Human Resources; Phone (214) 407-6100.

METROPOLITAN LIFE INSURANCE COMPANY

1 MADISON AVENUE
NEW YORK, NEW YORK 10010-3603

OVERVIEW: Provides life insurance. Established: 1868.

EXPERTISE/EDUCATION SOUGHT: Health insurance, credit/credit analysis, computer programming, sales, law, advertising, marketing, actuarial, auditing

CONTACT: For individuals with previous experience: Ms Lorna Simon, Director of Career Development and Staffing; Phone (212) 578-2211.

METROPOLITAN TRANSPORTATION AUTHORITY

347 MADISON AVENUE
NEW YORK, NEW YORK 10017-3706

OVERVIEW: Provides local transit services. Established: 1965.

KEY STATISTICS Number of Employees: 64,838.

EXPERTISE/EDUCATION SOUGHT: Accounting, finance, law, data processing, public relations

CONTACT: Mr Sheldon Dixon, Manager of Recruitment; Phone (212) 878-7000.

M AND I DATA SERVICES, INC.

4900 WEST BROWN DEER ROAD
BROWN DEER, WISCONSIN 53223-2422

OVERVIEW: Provides data processing services. Established: 1985. Parent Company: Marshall and Ilsley Corporation.

KEY STATISTICS Annual Sales: $114.0 million.

EXPERTISE/EDUCATION SOUGHT: Computer science, banking

CONTACT: Ms Michelle Wingo, Employment Representative; Phone (800) 236-3282, ext. 42554.

MICHELIN TIRE CORPORATION

1 PARKWAY SOUTH, PO BOX 19001
GREENVILLE, SOUTH CAROLINA 29602-9001

OVERVIEW: Manufactures tires. Established: 1950. Parent Company: Michelin Corporation.

KEY STATISTICS Annual Sales: $4.0 billion. Number of Employees: 25,000.

HIRING HISTORY Number of professional employees hired in 1994: 100.

EXPERTISE/EDUCATION SOUGHT: Accounting, management information systems, computer programming, marketing, finance

CONTACT: For individuals with previous experience: Mr Steve Avery, Director of Recruiting, PO Box 19001, Greenville, SC, 29602-9001; Phone (803) 458-5000.

MICHIGAN NATIONAL CORPORATION

27777 INSKTER ROAD
FARMINGTON HILLS, MICHIGAN 48334

OVERVIEW: Commercial bank. Established: 1970.

EXPERTISE/EDUCATION SOUGHT: Health insurance, finance, law, actuarial, real estate

CONTACTS: For college students and recent graduates: Ms Velda Strong-Glenn, Director of Staffing; Phone (313) 473-3000. For individuals with previous experience: Mr Thomas Kimbo, Director of Human Resources; Phone (313) 473-3000.

MICRO WAREHOUSE, INC.

535 CONNECTICUT AVENUE
NORWALK, CONNECTICUT 06854-3010

OVERVIEW: Computer catalog and mail order company. Established: 1987.

KEY STATISTICS Annual Sales: $776.0 million. Number of Employees: 2,000.

EXPERTISE/EDUCATION SOUGHT: Marketing, sales, production, publishing, systems analysis, purchasing

CONTACT: Angela Mizak, Director of Human Resources; Phone (203) 899-4000.

MICROBILT CORPORATION

6190 POWERS FERRY ROAD NORTHWEST
ATLANTA, GEORGIA 30339-2917

OVERVIEW: Provides data processing services. Established: 1989. Parent Company: First Financial Management Corporation.

KEY STATISTICS Annual Sales: $150.0 million. Number of Employees: 675.

EXPERTISE/EDUCATION SOUGHT: Sales, accounting, marketing, finance, electrical engineering, mechanical engineering

CONTACT: For individuals with previous experience: Corporate Recruiter; Phone (404) 955-0313.

MICRON TECHNOLOGY, INC.
2805 EAST COLUMBIA ROAD
BOISE, IDAHO 83706

OVERVIEW: Manufactures computer chips. Established: 1978.

KEY STATISTICS Annual Sales: $828.0 million. Number of Employees: 5,400.

EXPERTISE/EDUCATION SOUGHT: Electrical engineering, chemical engineering, design engineering

CONTACT: For individuals with previous experience: Mr Brad Mabe, Personnel Specialist, PO Box 6, Boise, ID, 83707-0006; Phone (208) 368-4329.

MICROSEMI CORPORATION
2830 SOUTH FAIRVIEW STREET
SANTA ANA, CALIFORNIA 92704-7700

OVERVIEW: Designs and manufactures semiconductor assemblies and other power conditioning products. Established: 1960.

KEY STATISTICS Annual Sales: $124.0 million. Number of Employees: 1,520.

EXPERTISE/EDUCATION SOUGHT: Accounting, finance, sales, marketing, computer science, data processing, business management

CONTACTS: For college students and recent graduates: Ms Maria Casas, Human Resources Assistant. For individuals with previous experience: Mr James Thomas, Vice President of Human Resources; Phone (714) 979-8220.

MICROSOFT CORPORATION
1 MICROSOFT WAY
REDMOND, WASHINGTON 98052-6399

OVERVIEW: Develops and markets software and products for personal computers. Established: 1975.

KEY STATISTICS Annual Sales: $5.0 billion. Number of Employees: 15,000.

EXPERTISE/EDUCATION SOUGHT: Computer science, software engineering/development, computer engineering, computer programming, electrical engineering

CONTACT: For individuals with previous experience: Ms Lorie Swift, Technical Recruiting Coordinator/Intern Program Coordinator; Phone (206) 936-3555; Fax (206)936-8529.

MIDCON CORPORATION
701 EAST 22ND STREET
LOMBARD, ILLINOIS 60148-5009

OVERVIEW: Distributes natural gas. Established: 1981. Parent Company: Occidental Petroleum Corporation.

KEY STATISTICS Annual Sales: $2.0 billion. Number of Employees: 2,342.

EXPERTISE/EDUCATION SOUGHT: Management information systems, computer programming, accounting, mechanical engineering, petroleum/petrochemical engineering

CONTACT: For individuals with previous experience: Ms Karen Brown, Human Resources Representative; Phone (708) 691-3419.

MIDATLANTIC CORPORATION
499 THORNALL STREET
EDISON, NEW JERSEY 08837

OVERVIEW: Provides commercial and retail banking and related financial services. Established: 1804.

KEY STATISTICS Annual Sales: $1.0 billion. Number of Employees: 6,000.

EXPERTISE/EDUCATION SOUGHT: Accounting, finance, actuarial, underwriting, marketing, real estate

CONTACT: For individuals with previous experience: Human Resource Department; Phone (908) 321-8000.

MIDWEST RESOURCES AND IOWA PUBLIC SERVICES
666 GRAND AVENUE
DES MOINES, IOWA 50309

OVERVIEW: Public utility.

KEY STATISTICS Annual Sales: $1.0 billion. Number of Employees: 3,100.

EXPERTISE/EDUCATION SOUGHT: Electrical engineering, mechanical engineering, accounting

CONTACT: Mr Steven Saunders, Manager of Organizational Development; Phone (515) 242-4300, ext. 7622.

MILLBROOK DISTRIBUTION SERVICES
401 HIGHWAY 43 EAST
HARRISON, ARKANSAS 72601

OVERVIEW: Manufactures specialty foods and aspirin. Established: 1933. Parent Company: McKesson Corporation.

KEY STATISTICS Annual Sales: $564.0 million. Number of Employees: 3,000.

EXPERTISE/EDUCATION SOUGHT: Finance, accounting, purchasing, computer programming

CONTACT: For individuals with previous experience: Ms Kendra Pry, Human Resources Specialist; Phone (501) 741-3425.

MILLER BREWING COMPANY
3939 WEST HIGHLAND BOULEVARD
MILWAUKEE, WISCONSIN 53208-2866

OVERVIEW: Manufactures and distributes beer. Established: 1855. Parent Company: Philip Morris Companies, Inc.

KEY STATISTICS Number of Employees: 9,800.

EXPERTISE/EDUCATION SOUGHT: Sales, marketing, finance, accounting, law, human resources, retail, purchasing, management information systems

CONTACT: Mr Jeff Garden, Corporate Staffing Manager; Phone (414) 931-2000.

MILLIPORE CORPORATION
80 ASHBY ROAD
BEDFORD, MASSACHUSETTS 01730

OVERVIEW: Manufactures specialty application filters. Established: 1954.

KEY STATISTICS Annual Sales: $497.0 million. Number of Employees: 3,100.

HIRING HISTORY Number of professional employees hired in 1994: 75.

EXPERTISE/EDUCATION SOUGHT: Data processing, business administration, chemistry, accounting, finance, microbiology

CONTACT: Mr Jeff Smith, Manager of Employment; Phone (617) 533-2813.

MINE SAFETY APPLIANCES COMPANY
121 GAMMA DRIVE
PITTSBURGH, PENNSYLVANIA 15238

OVERVIEW: Manufactures and distributes mine safety appliances. Established: 1914.

KEY STATISTICS Annual Sales: $460.0 million. Number of Employees: 5,000.

HIRING HISTORY Number of professional employees hired in 1994: 25. 1993: 25.

EXPERTISE/EDUCATION SOUGHT: Finance, accounting, manufacturing engineering, industrial engineering, sales, marketing

CONTACT: Mr Kenneth Krall, Corporate Human Resources Manager, PO Box 426, Pittsburgh, PA, 15230; Phone (412) 967-3000.

MINNESOTA MINING AND MANUFACTURING COMPANY

3M CENTER
SAINT PAUL, MINNESOTA 55144-1000

Overview: Manufactures adhesives, polymers, coatings, surgical supplies, and digital information and imaging products. Established: 1902.

Key Statistics Number of Employees: 86,168.

Expertise/Education Sought: Accounting, finance, economics, computer science, management information systems

Contact: Mr Marty Hanson, College Relations Director; Phone (612) 723-1755.

MINOLTA BUSINESS SYSTEMS, INC.

500 NORTH FRANKLIN TURNPIKE
RAMSEY, NEW JERSEY 07446-2820

Overview: Manufactures photocopying and fax machines.

Key Statistics Annual Sales: $135.0 million. Number of Employees: 60.

Expertise/Education Sought: Administration

Contact: For individuals with previous experience: Ms Carol Ceralli, Human Resources Manager; Phone (201) 825-8600, ext. 567.

MINOLTA CORPORATION

101 WILLIAMS DRIVE
RAMSEY, NEW JERSEY 07446

Overview: Manufactures photocopying machines and photographic equipment and supplies. Established: 1959.

Key Statistics Annual Sales: $900.0 million.

Expertise/Education Sought: Sales, accounting, marketing, software engineering/development, credit management

Contact: Ms Linda Loveland, Employment and Compensation Manager; Phone (201) 934-5251.

THE MIRAGE HOTEL CASINO

3400 LAS VEGAS BOULEVARD SOUTH
LAS VEGAS, NEVADA 89109

Overview: Operates hotels and casinos. Established: 1989.

Expertise/Education Sought: Management, finance, food services, security, accounting

Contacts: For college students and recent graduates: Ms Heather Powell, Director of Training and Development; Phone (702) 791-7111. For individuals with previous experience: Mr Sandy McHenry, Employment Manager; Phone (702) 741-7506.

MIRAGE RESORTS, INC.

3400 LAS VEGAS BOULEVARD SOUTH
LAS VEGAS, NEVADA 89109-8923

Overview: Owns and operates hotels and casinos. Established: 1946.

Key Statistics Number of Employees: 17,000.

Expertise/Education Sought: Languages, hospitality/hotel and restaurant management, marketing, customer service and support, accounting, computer programming, security, food services, finance, accounting

Contact: For individuals with previous experience: Mr Arthur Nathan, Vice President of Human Resources, PO Box 7777, Las Vegas, NV, 89177; Phone (702) 791-7500; Fax (702) 792-7730.

MITCHELL ENERGY AND DEVELOPMENT CORPORATION

2001 TIMBERLOCH PLACE
THE WOODLANDS, TEXAS 77380-1182

Overview: Oil and gas exploration and production company. Established: 1946.

Key Statistics Number of Employees: 2,900.

Hiring History Number of professional employees hired in 1994: 10.

Expertise/Education Sought: Accounting, marketing, geology, environmental, environmental planning, petroleum/petrochemical engineering

Contact: For individuals with previous experience: Employee Relations, PO Box 4000, The Woodlands, TX, 77387-4000; Phone (713) 377-5500.

THE MITRE CORPORATION

BURLINGTON ROAD
BEDFORD, MASSACHUSETTS 01730

Overview: Technical adviser to the Air Force, other branches of the Department of Defense, the FAA, and NASA. Established: 1958.

Key Statistics Annual Sales: $600.0 million. Number of Employees: 6,000.

Hiring History Number of professional employees hired in 1993: 200.

Expertise/Education Sought: Computer science, software engineering/development, electrical engineering, physics, mathematics, telecommunications

Contact: For individuals with previous experience: Corporate Recruitment; Phone (617) 271-2000.

MITSUBISHI CHEMICAL AMERICA, INC.

81 MAIN STREET
WHITE PLAINS, NEW YORK 10601-1711

Overview: Manufactures chemicals and pharmaceutical products. Established: 1981.

Key Statistics Annual Sales: $623.0 million. Number of Employees: 3,000.

Expertise/Education Sought: Accounting, finance, marketing, sales, pharmacology

Contact: Ms Vera Hunter, Manager of Personnel; Phone (914) 286-3614.

MITSUBISHI ELECTRIC AMERICA

5665 PLAZA DRIVE
CYPRESS, CALIFORNIA 90630-5023

Overview: Manufactures and distributes electrical and electronics products. Established: 1973.

Key Statistics Annual Sales: $1.0 billion. Number of Employees: 4,400.

Expertise/Education Sought: Sales, marketing

Contact: Ms Debbie Fudge, Manager of Employment Relations, 5757 Plaza Drive, Cypress, CA, 90630-5029; Phone (714) 220-4613; Fax (714) 229-3898.

MOBIL CORPORATION

3225 GALLOWS ROAD
FAIRFAX, VIRGINIA 22037-0001

Overview: Produces and distributes oil, gas, and petroleum based products.

Expertise/Education Sought: Petroleum/petrochemical engineering, chemical engineering, mechanical engineering, geology

Contact: For individuals with previous experience: Mr Dan Smith, Recruitment; Phone (703) 846-3000.

MODINE MANUFACTURING COMPANY

1500 DE KOVEN AVENUE
RACINE, WISCONSIN 53403-2552

Overview: Manufactures heat transfer equipment. Established: 1916.

Key Statistics Number of Employees: 7,157.

Hiring History Number of professional employees hired in 1994: 70.

Expertise/Education Sought: Manufacturing engineering, design engineering, mechanical engineering, industrial engineering, accounting

Contact: Mr A O Bixler, Manager of Recruiting and College Relations; Phone (414) 636-1246.

MOHON INTERNATIONAL, INC.
1865 NORTH MARKET STREET
PARIS, TENNESSEE 38242

OVERVIEW: Manufactures laboratory furniture for schools. Established: 1976.

KEY STATISTICS Annual Sales: $28.0 million. Number of Employees: 325.

EXPERTISE/EDUCATION SOUGHT: Marketing, accounting, drafting

CONTACT: For individuals with previous experience: Mr Riley Mohon, President; Phone (901) 642-4251.

MOLEX, INC.
2222 WELLINGTON COURT
LISLE, ILLINOIS 60532-1682

OVERVIEW: Manufactures electronic components. Established: 1938.

KEY STATISTICS Number of Employees: 7,985.

EXPERTISE/EDUCATION SOUGHT: Finance, marketing

CONTACT: For individuals with previous experience: Mr Herb Gosewisch, Manager of Employment; Phone (708) 969-4550.

MONFORT, INC.
1918 AA STREET
GREELEY, COLORADO 80631-9663

OVERVIEW: Produces meat products and prepared foods. Established: 1969. Parent Company: ConAgra, Inc.

KEY STATISTICS Annual Sales: $6.0 billion. Number of Employees: 14,000.

EXPERTISE/EDUCATION SOUGHT: Laboratory technology, law, microbiology, chemistry, electrical engineering, accounting, mechanical engineering, finance

CONTACTS: For college students and recent graduates: Ms Mary Anne Rakke, Administrative Assistant; Phone (303) 353-8177. For individuals with previous experience: Ms Sue Vanderberg, Manager of Employee Relations Manager of Employee Relations.

MONIER ROOF TILE, INC.
1 PARK PLACE, SUITE 900
IRVINE, CALIFORNIA 92714

OVERVIEW: Manufactures concrete and clay roofing materials. Established: 1987. Parent Company: Redland America Corporation.

KEY STATISTICS Annual Sales: $77.0 million. Number of Employees: 766.

EXPERTISE/EDUCATION SOUGHT: Accounting, finance, data processing, product engineering, mechanical engineering, electrical engineering

CONTACT: For individuals with previous experience: Ms Marueene Action, Director of Human Resources, PO Box 19792, Irvine, CA, 92713; Phone (714) 756-1605.

MONSANTO COMPANY
800 NORTH LINDBERGH BOULEVARD
SAINT LOUIS, MISSOURI 63167-0001

OVERVIEW: Manufactures chemicals, pharmaceuticals, agricultural products, fibers, and plastics. Established: 1901.

KEY STATISTICS Number of Employees: 30,000.

EXPERTISE/EDUCATION SOUGHT: Biological sciences, public affairs, finance, law, human resources, agricultural science, chemistry, biotechnology, public relations, logistics

CONTACT: For individuals with previous experience: Ms Gwen Wesley, Staffing Team Leader; Phone (314) 694-1000.

MONTEFIORE MEDICAL CENTER
111 EAST 210TH STREET
BRONX, NEW YORK 10467-2490

OVERVIEW: Hospital. Established: 1884.

KEY STATISTICS Annual Sales: $656.0 million. Number of Employees: 9,500.

HIRING HISTORY Number of professional employees hired in 1994: 100.

EXPERTISE/EDUCATION SOUGHT: Radiology, cardiology, physicians, oncology

CONTACT: Ms Maria Alport, Director of Human Resources; Phone (718) 920-4321.

MONTGOMERY WARD AND COMPANY, INC.
1 MONTGOMERY WARD PLAZA
CHICAGO, ILLINOIS 60671-0002

OVERVIEW: Operates chain of department and specialty stores. Established: 1872.

KEY STATISTICS Number of Employees: 51,350.

EXPERTISE/EDUCATION SOUGHT: Marketing, merchandising, retail, accounting, finance, advertising

CONTACT: For individuals with previous experience: Ms Judy Gustafson, Director of Human Resources Operations, Training and Development; Phone (312) 467-2000.

MOORE BUSINESS FORMS AND SYSTEMS DIVISION
275 NORTH FIELD DRIVE
LAKE FOREST, ILLINOIS 60045-2592

OVERVIEW: Manufactures and markets business forms and supplies. Established: 1882.

KEY STATISTICS Annual Sales: $240.0 million. Number of Employees: 19,890.

EXPERTISE/EDUCATION SOUGHT: Accounting, marketing, sales

CONTACT: For individuals with previous experience: Mr Ron Troline, Employment Coordinator; Phone (708) 615-6000.

MOORMAN, INC.
1000 NORTH 30TH STREET
QUINCY, ILLINOIS 63205-3428

OVERVIEW: Manufactures livestock feed, and agricultural equipment. Established: 1885.

EXPERTISE/EDUCATION SOUGHT: Marketing, sales, research

CONTACT: For individuals with previous experience: Mr John Jones, Personnel Manager; Phone (217) 222-7100, ext. 2418.

MORGAN GUARANTY TRUST COMPANY OF NEW YORK
60 WALL STREET
NEW YORK, NEW YORK 10260-0060

OVERVIEW: Commercial bank. Parent Company: J. P. Morgan and Company, Inc.

KEY STATISTICS Number of Employees: 12,968.

EXPERTISE/EDUCATION SOUGHT: Credit/credit analysis, finance, computer programming, management, program analysis, accounting

CONTACT: For individuals with previous experience: Ms Kimberly Kale, Vice President Corporate Recruiting; Phone (212) 483-2323.

J. P. MORGAN AND COMPANY, INC.
60 WALL STREET
NEW YORK, NEW YORK 10260-0060

OVERVIEW: Provides corporate finance, investment, and related financial services. Established: 1838.

KEY STATISTICS Annual Sales: $12.0 billion. Number of Employees: 15,745.

EXPERTISE/EDUCATION SOUGHT: Accounting, economics, business administration, finance, marketing

CONTACT: Ms Patricia A Northey, Associate Staffing and Employment, 500 Stanton Christiana, Newark, DE, 19713; Phone (302) 634-4114.

MORGAN STANLEY AND COMPANY, INC.
1251 AVENUE OF THE AMERICAS
NEW YORK, NEW YORK 10020-1104

OVERVIEW: Investment bank. Parent Company: Morgan Stanley Group, Inc.

KEY STATISTICS Number of Employees: 9,300.

EXPERTISE/EDUCATION SOUGHT: Investment, financial analysis, credit/credit analysis, brokerage, information systems

CONTACT: Recruiting Manager.

JOHN MORRELL AND COMPANY, INC.
1400 NORTH WEBER AVENUE
SIOUX FALLS, SOUTH DAKOTA 57104

OVERVIEW: Packages meat. Established: 1927. Parent Company: Chiquita Brands International.

KEY STATISTICS Annual Sales: $1.0 billion. Number of Employees: 6,000.

EXPERTISE/EDUCATION SOUGHT: Marketing, computer science, finance, sales

CONTACT: Ms Aggie Carlson, Supervisor of Human Resources; Phone (605) 330-3333; Fax (605)330-3154.

MORRISON, INC.
4721 MORRISON DRIVE
MOBILE, ALABAMA 36609-3350

OVERVIEW: Owns and operates cafeterias, food service businesses, and restaurants. Established: 1920.

KEY STATISTICS Annual Sales: $1.0 billion. Number of Employees: 35,000.

EXPERTISE/EDUCATION SOUGHT: Management, food services, health care

CONTACT: Mr Ron Vilord, Senior Vice President of Human Resources; Phone (334) 344-3000; Fax (334)344-9513.

MORRISON KNUDSEN CORPORATION
MORRISON KNUDSEN PLAZA
BOISE, IDAHO 83729

OVERVIEW: Provides international engineering, design, and construction services. Established: 1912.

KEY STATISTICS Annual Sales: $3.0 billion. Number of Employees: 11,910.

EXPERTISE/EDUCATION SOUGHT: Marketing, finance, accounting, data processing, computer programming, electrical engineering, environmental engineering, chemical engineering

CONTACT: Ms Alvia Henderson, Vice President of Human Resources; Phone (208) 386-5000.

MORTON INTERNATIONAL, INC.
100 NORTH RIVERSIDE PLAZA
CHICAGO, ILLINOIS 60606-1518

OVERVIEW: Manufactures salt, specialty chemicals, and automotive air bags. Established: 1848.

KEY STATISTICS Annual Sales: $3.0 billion. Number of Employees: 11,900.

HIRING HISTORY Number of professional employees hired in 1994: 12.

EXPERTISE/EDUCATION SOUGHT: Chemical engineering, chemistry, accounting, marketing, data processing, sales

CONTACT: Human Resources Department; Phone (312) 807-2000.

MOTEL 6
14651 DALLAS PARKWAY, SUITE 500
DALLAS, TEXAS 75240-8897

OVERVIEW: Operates chain of motels. Established: 1962.

KEY STATISTICS Annual Sales: $650.0 million. Number of Employees: 17,500.

EXPERTISE/EDUCATION SOUGHT: Hospitality/hotel and restaurant management, business, finance

CONTACT: Mr Joseph Eulberg, Vice President of Human Resources; Phone (214) 386-6161.

MOTOROLA, INC.
1301 EAST ALGONQUIN ROAD
SCHAUMBERG, ILLINOIS 60196

OVERVIEW: Manufactures and markets wireless communications, semiconductors, and advanced electronics. Established: 1928.

KEY STATISTICS Annual Sales: $2.0 billion. Number of Employees: 132,000.

EXPERTISE/EDUCATION SOUGHT: Electrical engineering, civil engineering, manufacturing engineering, mechanical engineering, software engineering/development, chemical engineering, physics, mathematics, computer science, management information syste

CONTACT: For college students and recent graduates: University Relations; Phone (708) 576-5000.

MOUNT SINAI HOSPITAL, INC.
1 GUSTAVE L LEVY PLACE
NEW YORK, NEW YORK 10029-6504

OVERVIEW: General hospital. Established: 1852.

KEY STATISTICS Annual Sales: $708.0 million. Number of Employees: 7,685.

EXPERTISE/EDUCATION SOUGHT: Cardiology, nursing, oncology, pediatric care, rehabilitation

CONTACT: For individuals with previous experience: Ms Naomi K Secklon, Manager of Recruitment and Placement; Phone (212) 241-6500.

MTD PRODUCTS, INC.
5965 GRAFTON ROAD
CLEVELAND, OHIO 44136

OVERVIEW: Manufactures lawnmowers and garden equipment. Established: 1932.

KEY STATISTICS Annual Sales: $500.0 million. Number of Employees: 6,000.

HIRING HISTORY Number of professional employees hired in 1994: 50.

EXPERTISE/EDUCATION SOUGHT: Accounting, finance, sales, marketing, data processing

CONTACT: Ms Fran Walsh, Manager of Personnel, PO Box 368022, Cleveland, OH, 44136; Phone (216) 225-2600.

THE MULTICARE COMPANIES, INC.
411 HACKENSACK AVENUE
HACKENSACK, NEW JERSEY 07601-6328

OVERVIEW: Provides long term and specialized health care and pharmacy services.

KEY STATISTICS Annual Sales: $162.0 million. Number of Employees: 7,000.

EXPERTISE/EDUCATION SOUGHT: Accounting, nursing

CONTACT: For individuals with previous experience: Ms Alice Osur, Recruitment Manager.

MULTIFOODS
MULTIFOODS TOWER, PO BOX 2942
MINNEAPOLIS, MINNESOTA 55402-3601

OVERVIEW: Manufactures food. Established: 1892.

KEY STATISTICS Number of Employees: 8,341.

EXPERTISE/EDUCATION SOUGHT: Marketing, computer programming, sales, data processing, accounting, auditing

CONTACT: For individuals with previous experience: Ms Terri Nelson, Corporate Recruiter; Phone (612) 340-3300.

MURPHY OIL CORPORATION
200 PEACH STREET
EL DORADO, ARKANSAS 71730

Overview: Oil drilling, refining, and petroleum products company. Established: 1950.

Expertise/Education Sought: Chemical engineering, mechanical engineering, electrical engineering, computer programming, accounting, sales

Contact: Mr Dana Green, Supervisor of Employment Compensation, PO Box 7000, El Dorado, AR, 71731-7000; Phone (501) 862-6411.

MUTUAL LIFE INSURANCE COMPANY OF NEW YORK, INC.
1740 BROADWAY
NEW YORK, NEW YORK 10019-4315

Overview: Provides health and life insurance. Established: 1843.

Key Statistics Assets: $2.0 billion. Number of Employees: 2,800.

Expertise/Education Sought: Accounting, actuarial, marketing, mathematics

Contacts: For college students and recent graduates: Ms Lynn Page, Manager of Human Resources, Glen Point Center West, 500 Frank W Burr Boulevard, Teaneck, NJ, 07666; Phone (201) 907-6986. For individuals with previous experience: Ms Nina Walters, Manager of Human Relations; Phone (212) 708-2000.

MUTUAL OF OMAHA INSURANCE COMPANY
MUTUAL OF OMAHA PLAZA
OMAHA, NEBRASKA 68175

Overview: Provides insurance. Established: 1909.

Key Statistics Number of Employees: 8,000.

Hiring History Number of professional employees hired in 1994: 750.

Expertise/Education Sought: Management, actuarial, general insurance, accounting, finance, information systems

Contact: For individuals with previous experience: Mr Kurt Kline, Employment Manager; Phone (402) 342-7600.

MWR SUPPORT ACTIVITY
3044 CATLIN AVENUE, BUILDING 30
QUANTICO, VIRGINIA 22134

Overview: Manages Marine exchanges, clubs, and recreational facilities. Established: 1903.

Key Statistics Annual Sales: $601.2 million. Number of Employees: 11,391.

Expertise/Education Sought: Retail, hospitality/hotel and restaurant management, accounting, finance

Contact: For individuals with previous experience: Ms Peg Snellings, Manager of Recruitment; Phone (703) 640-3800.

MAXXAM PROPERTIES, INC.
PO BOX 572887
HOUSTON, TEXAS 77257

Overview: Real estate holding company. Established: 1983. Parent Company: Maxxam Group, Inc.

Expertise/Education Sought: Accounting, finance, real estate

Contact: Ms Sharon Romere, Director Human Resources; Phone (713) 925-7600.

NACCO INDUSTRIES, INC.
5875 LANDERBROOK DRIVE
CLEVELAND, OHIO 44124-4069

Overview: Diversified company with mining, industrial equipment, and electric appliance operations. Established: 1913.

Key Statistics Annual Sales: $2.0 billion. Number of Employees: 10,879.

Expertise/Education Sought: Accounting, finance, business, administration

Contact: For individuals with previous experience: Human Resources Department; Phone (216) 449-9600.

NACCO MATERIALS HANDLING GROUP
2701 NORTHWEST VAUGHN, SUITE 900
PORTLAND, OREGON 97210

Overview: Manufactures forklifts.

Expertise/Education Sought: Mechanical engineering, finance

Contact: Ms Clarae Reynolds, Human Resources Administrator; Phone (503) 721-6000.

NALCO CHEMICAL COMPANY
1 NALCO CENTER
NAPERVILLE, ILLINOIS 60563-1198

Overview: Manufactures specialty chemicals. Established: 1920.

Key Statistics Number of Employees: 6,802.

Expertise/Education Sought: Accounting, finance, sales, customer service and support, law, chemistry

Contact: For individuals with previous experience: Ms Karen Nordquist, Manager of Technical Employment; Phone (708) 305-1000.

NASH FINCH COMPANY
7600 FRANCE AVENUESOUTH
MINNEAPOLIS, MINNESOTA 55435-5920

Overview: Wholesale grocery distributor. Established: 1885.

Key Statistics Number of Employees: 11,900.

Expertise/Education Sought: Retail, management information systems

Contact: Mr Richard Prince, Manager of Employment, 7600 France Avenue South, PO Box 355, Minneapolis, MN, 55440-0355; Phone (612) 844-1032.

NATIONAL AMUSEMENTS, INC.
200 ELM STREET
DEDHAM, MASSACHUSETTS 02026-4536

Overview: Owns and operates movie theaters. Established: 1959.

Key Statistics Annual Sales: $1.0 billion. Number of Employees: 18,000.

Hiring History Number of professional employees hired in 1994: 5. 1993: 5.

Expertise/Education Sought: Accounting, advertising, finance, computer programming, program analysis

Contact: Ms Maureen Dixon, Manager of Personnel; Phone (617) 461-1600, ext. 215.

NATIONAL BROADCASTING COMPANY, INC.
30 ROCKEFELLER PLAZA
NEW YORK, NEW YORK 10112-0002

Overview: Operates radio and television stations and networks. Established: 1926. Parent Company: General Electric Company.

Key Statistics Number of Employees: 4,700.

Expertise/Education Sought: Television broadcasting, telecommunications, public relations, sales, computer science

Contact: For individuals with previous experience: NBC Employment Office; Phone (212) 664-5059, ext. 2623.

NATIONAL CITY CORPORATION
1900 EAST NINTH STREET
CLEVELAND, OHIO 44114-3401

Overview: Provides investment banking, mortgages, credit cards, and related financial services. Established: 1845.

Key Statistics Annual Sales: $3.0 billion. Number of Employees: 19,960.

EXPERTISE/EDUCATION SOUGHT: Accounting, finance, auditing, marketing, underwriting

CONTACT: For individuals with previous experience: Ms Darla Terepka, Recruiter; Phone (216) 575-2000.

NATIONAL CITY PROCESSING COMPANY
1231 DURRETT LANE
LOUISVILLE, KENTUCKY 40213-0001

OVERVIEW: Provides data processing services. Established: 1981. Parent Company: National City Corporation.

KEY STATISTICS Annual Sales: $271.0 million. Number of Employees: 4,707.

EXPERTISE/EDUCATION SOUGHT: Data processing, finance, accounting, computer programming

CONTACT: For individuals with previous experience: Mr Ron Tomes, Director of Technical Recruiting; Phone (502) 364-2978.

NATIONAL FUEL GAS COMPANY
10 LAFAYETTE SQUARE
BUFFALO, NEW YORK 14203-0244

OVERVIEW: Distributes petroleum and natural gas products. Established: 1902.

KEY STATISTICS Number of Employees: 3,329.

EXPERTISE/EDUCATION SOUGHT: Accounting, finance

CONTACT: For individuals with previous experience: Human Resources Department; Phone (716) 686-6123.

NATIONAL LINEN SERVICE
1420 PEACHTREE STREET NORTHEAST
ATLANTA, GEORGIA 30309-3002

OVERVIEW: Provides linen rental, lighting, and industrial chemicals services. Established: 1928.

KEY STATISTICS Number of Employees: 22,200.

EXPERTISE/EDUCATION SOUGHT: Sales, customer service and support, human resources, operations, plant management, production management

CONTACT: Ms Michele Benoit, Career Assessment Administrator; Phone (404) 853-1000, ext. 6365.

NATIONAL MEDICAL CARE, INC.
1601 TRAPELO ROAD
WALTHAM, MASSACHUSETTS 02154-7389

OVERVIEW: Provides home health and nursing care services and distributes medical equipment. Established: 1968. Parent Company: W. R. Grace and Company, Inc.

KEY STATISTICS Annual Sales: $2.0 billion. Number of Employees: 18,000.

EXPERTISE/EDUCATION SOUGHT: Accounting, marketing, finance, computer programming, mechanical engineering, data processing, project engineering

CONTACTS: For college students and recent graduates: Mr Tim Kerrigan, Employee Relations Representative-Technical Posiitons; Phone (617) 466-9850. For individuals with previous experience: Ms Sharon Howard, Employee Relations Manager.

NATIONAL SEMICONDUCTOR CORPORATION
2900 SEMICONDUCTOR WAY
SANTA CLARA, CALIFORNIA 95051-0606

OVERVIEW: Manufactures semiconductors and integrated circuits. Established: 1959.

KEY STATISTICS Annual Sales: $2.0 billion. Number of Employees: 22,300.

HIRING HISTORY Number of professional employees hired in 1993: 70.

EXPERTISE/EDUCATION SOUGHT: Electrical engineering, computer engineering, computer science, finance

CONTACTS: For college students and recent graduates: Ms Alexa Fletcher, University Relations and College Recruiting Manager;

Phone (408) 721-5000, ext. 7810. For individuals with previous experience: Mr Robert McLean, Vice President Worldwide Human Resources; Phone (408) 721-4017.

NATIONAL STARCH AND CHEMICAL COMPANY
10 FINDERNE AVENUE
BRIDGEWATER, NEW JERSEY 08807

OVERVIEW: Manufactures starch, adhesives, and resins. Established: 1895. Parent Company: Unilever United States, Inc.

EXPERTISE/EDUCATION SOUGHT: Chemistry, food science, sales

CONTACT: For individuals with previous experience: Ms Donna Lesnowski, Recruiting Specialist; Phone (908) 685-5000, ext. 5178.

NATIONAL STEEL CORPORATION
4100 EDISON LAKES PARKWAY
MISHAWAKA, INDIANA 46454-3440

OVERVIEW: Produces steel. Established: 1929. Parent Company: NKK USA Corporation.

KEY STATISTICS Annual Sales: $3.0 billion. Number of Employees: 9,300.

EXPERTISE/EDUCATION SOUGHT: Finance, sales, marketing

CONTACT: For individuals with previous experience: Ms Michelle Miller, Coordinator of Employment and Manpower Planning; Phone (219) 273-7627; Fax (219)273-7579.

NATIONAL WESTMINSTER BANCORP
175 WATER STREET
NEW YORK, NEW YORK 10038

OVERVIEW: Full service bank. Established: 1949.

EXPERTISE/EDUCATION SOUGHT: Accounting, law, credit/credit analysis, computer programming, human resources, finance, marketing, sales

CONTACT: For individuals with previous experience: Mr John Esposito, Recruiter; Phone (212) 602-1000, ext. 7854.

NATIONS BANK
400 NORTH ASHLEY DRIVE
TAMPA, FLORIDA 33602

OVERVIEW: Commercial bank.

EXPERTISE/EDUCATION SOUGHT: Computer science, computer programming, operations, accounting, finance

CONTACTS: For college students and recent graduates: Ms Maria Taylor-Holland, Manager Management Recruiting; Phone (813) 224-5814. For individuals with previous experience: Ms Mariane Crochet, Vice President of Personnel Management; Phone (813) 224-5483.

NATIONSBANK CORPORATION
100 NORTH TRYON STREET
CHARLOTTE, NORTH CAROLINA 28255-4000

OVERVIEW: Provides commercial, retail, corporate, and investment banking services. Established: 1968.

KEY STATISTICS Assets: $10.0 billion. Number of Employees: 57,463.

EXPERTISE/EDUCATION SOUGHT: Project management, auditing, banking, financial analysis

CONTACT: For individuals with previous experience: Ms Susan Schneider, Senior Vice President of Human Resources; Phone (704) 386-5000.

NATIONSBANK
100 SOUTH CHARLES STREET
BALTIMORE, MARYLAND 21201-2725

OVERVIEW: Commercial bank.

KEY STATISTICS Assets: $230.0 million. Number of Employees: 9,100.

HIRING HISTORY Number of professional employees hired in 1993: 300.

EXPERTISE/EDUCATION SOUGHT: Finance, investment, marketing, information systems, trust

Nationsbank (continued)

CONTACT: For individuals with previous experience: Ms Dianne Coladonato, Vice President for Management Recruitment; Phone (301) 493-7238.

NATIONWIDE INSURANCE ENTERPRISE
1 NATIONWIDE PLAZA
COLUMBUS, OHIO 43215-2220

OVERVIEW: Provides life insurance. Established: 1925.

KEY STATISTICS Number of Employees: 27,800.

EXPERTISE/EDUCATION SOUGHT: Accounting, finance, customer service and support, computer science, actuarial, sales, underwriting, management information systems, claims adjustment/examination

CONTACT: For individuals with previous experience: Mr Randy Surecker, Corporate Recruiter; Phone (614) 249-7321.

NATURAL GAS CLEARINGHOUSE
13430 NORTHWEST FREEWAY
HOUSTON, TEXAS 77040-6095

OVERVIEW: Distributes natural gas products.

KEY STATISTICS Annual Sales: $3.0 billion. Number of Employees: 420.

EXPERTISE/EDUCATION SOUGHT: Accounting, finance, marketing

CONTACT: For individuals with previous experience: Mr Bill Donat, Director of Human Resources; Phone (713) 744-1777.

NAVISTAR INTERNATIONAL TRANSPORTATION
455 NORTH CITYFRONT PLAZA DRIVE
CHICAGO, ILLINOIS 60611-5503

OVERVIEW: Manufactures trucks, engines, and automotive parts. Parent Company: Navistar International Corporation.

KEY STATISTICS Number of Employees: 13,612.

EXPERTISE/EDUCATION SOUGHT: Accounting, management, marketing, human resources, finance, computer programming, management information systems, business management

CONTACT: Ms Kay Carroll, Manager of Human Resources; Phone (312) 836-3597.

NBD BANCORP, INC.
611 WOODWARD AVENUE
DETROIT, MICHIGAN 48226-3408

OVERVIEW: Commercial banking, leasing, and financial services. Established: 1933.

KEY STATISTICS Assets: $3.0 billion. Number of Employees: 18,700.

EXPERTISE/EDUCATION SOUGHT: Business, management, accounting, finance, management information systems

CONTACT: For individuals with previous experience: Dr Therman Smith, Manager of Professional Employment; Phone (313) 225-1000.

NBD BANK
1 INDIANA SQUARE
INDIANAPOLIS, INDIANA 46266

OVERVIEW: National commercial bank.

KEY STATISTICS Number of Employees: 4,799.

EXPERTISE/EDUCATION SOUGHT: Accounting, finance, economics, credit/credit analysis, banking

CONTACT: For individuals with previous experience: Mr Bob O'Neal, Director of Human Resources-Indiana.

NEC AMERICA, INC.
8 OLD SOD FARM ROAD
MELVILLE, NEW YORK 11747

OVERVIEW: Manufactures and markets electronics, communications equipment, computer systems and peripherals. Established: 1963.

EXPERTISE/EDUCATION SOUGHT: Accounting, computer programming, marketing, finance, sales, data processing

CONTACT: For individuals with previous experience: Ms Jane O'Donnel, Manager of Human Resources; Phone (516) 753-7000.

NEC ELECTRONICS, INC.
475 ELLIS STREET
MOUNTAIN VIEW, CALIFORNIA 94039

OVERVIEW: Manufactures semiconductors. Established: 1979. Parent Company: NEC USA, Inc.

KEY STATISTICS Annual Sales: $900.0 million. Number of Employees: 2,000.

EXPERTISE/EDUCATION SOUGHT: Electrical engineering, mechanical engineering, computer science

CONTACT: Ms Jeanne O'Steen, Recruiter, 401 Ellis Street, PO Box 7241, Mountain View, CA, 94043; Phone (415) 960-6000.

NEIMAN MARCUS GROUP, INC.
27 BOYLSTON STREET
CHESTNUT HILL, MASSACHUSETTS 02167-1719

OVERVIEW: Operates chain of department stores. Parent Company: Harcourt General, Inc.

KEY STATISTICS Annual Sales: $2.0 billion. Number of Employees: 16,700.

EXPERTISE/EDUCATION SOUGHT: Law, accounting, finance

CONTACT: For individuals with previous experience: Mr Jerry Hughes, Vice President Human Resources; Phone (617) 232-0760.

NEODATA SERVICES, INC.
833 WEST SOUTH BOULDER ROAD
LOUISVILLE, COLORADO 80027-2452

OVERVIEW: Provides subscription fulfillment, telemarketing, and database information retrieval services.

KEY STATISTICS Annual Sales: $187.0 million. Number of Employees: 4,477.

EXPERTISE/EDUCATION SOUGHT: Customer service and support, finance, accounting, marketing

CONTACT: For individuals with previous experience: Ms Gina Anderson, Staffing Specialist; Phone (303) 666-2880.

NESTLE FROZEN FOOD COMPANY
30003 BAINBRIDGE ROAD
SOLON, OHIO 44139-2205

OVERVIEW: Manufactures frozen foods. Established: 1924.

KEY STATISTICS Annual Sales: $900.0 million. Number of Employees: 13,000.

EXPERTISE/EDUCATION SOUGHT: Administration, accounting, marketing, sales, management information systems, mechanical engineering, industrial engineering, finance

CONTACT: For individuals with previous experience: Ms Lisa Clement, Manager of Recruiting; Phone (216) 349-5757.

NEVADA POWER COMPANY
6226 WEST SAHARA AVENUE
LAS VEGAS, NEVADA 89102-0002

OVERVIEW: Electric utility. Established: 1920.

KEY STATISTICS Annual Sales: $652.0 million. Number of Employees: 1,741.

HIRING HISTORY Number of professional employees hired in 1994: 100.

EXPERTISE/EDUCATION SOUGHT: Accounting, law, computer programming, data processing, electrical engineering

CONTACTS: For college students and recent graduates: Ms Pam Hills, Human Resources Specialist; Phone (702) 367-5000, ext. 5205. For individuals with previous experience: Mr Richard Coyle, Team Leader/Staffing.

THE NEW ENGLAND
501 BOYLSTON STREET
BOSTON, MASSACHUSETTS 02116-3706

OVERVIEW: Provides insurance and investment services. Established: 1835.

KEY STATISTICS Number of Employees: 2,657.

HIRING HISTORY Number of professional employees hired in 1993: 300.

EXPERTISE/EDUCATION SOUGHT: Accounting, marketing, sales, finance, data processing, customer service and support

CONTACTS: For college students and recent graduates: Ms Barbara Burke, Vice President of Human Resources; Phone (617) 578-2000, ext. 2833. For individuals with previous experience: Mr Kevin Cross, Assistant Vice President of Human Resources.

NEW ENGLAND ELECTRIC
25 RESEARCH DRIVE
WESTBOROUGH, MASSACHUSETTS 01582

OVERVIEW: Electric utility. Established: 1898.

EXPERTISE/EDUCATION SOUGHT: Electrical engineering, computer science

CONTACT: Ms Sabrina Boulay, Associate Human Resources Representative; Phone (508) 366-9011.

NEW HOLLAND NORTH AMERICA, INC.
500 DILLER AVENUE
NEW HOLLAND, PENNSYLVANIA 17557-9301

OVERVIEW: Manufactures farm equipment. Established: 1961. Parent Company: FiatAllis North America, Inc.

KEY STATISTICS Annual Sales: $360.0 million. Number of Employees: 4,000.

EXPERTISE/EDUCATION SOUGHT: Finance, accounting, information systems

CONTACT: Mr Ted Lyon, Manager of Recruiting Placement; Phone (717) 355-3983.

NEW UNITED MOTOR MANUFACTURING
45500 FREMONT BOULEVARD
FREMONT, CALIFORNIA 94538-6326

OVERVIEW: Manufactures motors.

KEY STATISTICS Annual Sales: $581.0 million. Number of Employees: 4,157.

EXPERTISE/EDUCATION SOUGHT: Engineering, linguistics, computer programming, finance, marketing

CONTACT: For individuals with previous experience: Ms Tracy Wakefield, Personnel Assistant; Phone (510) 498-5500.

NEW YORK CITY HEALTH AND HOSPITALS CORPORATION
125 WORTH STREET
NEW YORK, NEW YORK 10013-4006

OVERVIEW: Owns and operates hospitals. Established: 1970.

KEY STATISTICS Annual Sales: $3.0 billion. Number of Employees: 49,000.

EXPERTISE/EDUCATION SOUGHT: Data processing, management information systems, accounting, finance, electrical engineering, marketing, mechanical engineering

CONTACT: Ms Gloria Velez, Director of Human Resources; Phone (212) 788-3552.

NEW YORK CITY HOUSING AUTHORITY
250 BROADWAY
NEW YORK, NEW YORK 10007

OVERVIEW: Manages New York City housing projects. Established: 1934.

EXPERTISE/EDUCATION SOUGHT: Law

CONTACT: For individuals with previous experience: Ms Linda Young, Director of Recruitment; Phone (212) 306-8040.

NEW YORK CITY SCHOOL CONSTRUCTION AUTHORITY
3030 THOMSON AVENUE
LONG ISLAND CITY, NEW YORK 11101-3045

OVERVIEW: Provides construction services to area public schools.

KEY STATISTICS Annual Sales: $143.0 million. Number of Employees: 650.

EXPERTISE/EDUCATION SOUGHT: Accounting, finance, data processing, construction engineering, mechanical engineering

CONTACT: For individuals with previous experience: Ms Susan Moran, Manager of Recruitment and Employment; Phone (718) 472-8000.

The Company You Keep.®

NEW YORK LIFE INSURANCE COMPANY
51 MADISON AVENUE
NEW YORK, NEW YORK 10010

OVERVIEW: Provides life insurance and financial services. Established: 1845.

KEY STATISTICS Assets: $8.0 billion. Number of Employees: 7,800.

HIRING HISTORY Number of professional employees hired in 1994: 97.

EXPERTISE/EDUCATION SOUGHT: Accounting, management, finance, information systems, marketing, management information systems, customer service and support

CONTACTS: For college students and recent graduates: Ms Susan Chegwidden, Senior Employment Associate; Phone (212) 576-7178; Fax (212) 447-4292. For individuals with previous experience: Ms Carolyn J Stevens, Assistant Vice President; Phone (212) 576-7093; Fax (212) 447-4292.

CORPORATE PROFILE

New York Life is one of the largest life insurers in the United States and a leader in the financial services industry. The company and its subsidiaries and affiliates are committed to excellence in sales, quality customer service, and product development. This commitment has created a need for talented, results-oriented employees who are willing to grow as the company grows.

Employees are involved in the development, marketing, and administrative support of a broad range of products and services, including individual life insurance; individual annuities; group life and health insurance; pensions; mutual funds; structured finance investment products; and mortgage financing.

Founded in 1845, New York Life has grown by keeping in touch with the needs of its customers while continuing to provide the service and reliability on which the company has built its reputation. To meet these challenges, the company has long maintained a tradition of hiring talented individuals whose career growth is both encouraged and supported.

A career at New York Life offers a variety of opportunities in a competitive, rewarding industry. The dynamics of the marketplace call for a financially sound company with demonstrated flexibility and adaptability. New York Life is that kind of company—proud of its past 150 years and confident of its future.

New York Life is an equal-opportunity employer, M/F/D/V.

NEW YORK OFFICE OF MENTAL HEALTH
44 HOLLAND AVENUE
ALBANY, NEW YORK 12229-5035

OVERVIEW: Statewide department overseeing mental health issues and policies. Established: 1978. Parent Company: Executive Office for the State of New York.

KEY STATISTICS Number of Employees: 29,000.

EXPERTISE/EDUCATION SOUGHT: Psychiatry, psychology, psychotherapy, social work, psychiatric social work, social service, registered nursing, clinical psychology, data processing

CONTACT: Personnel Department/Facilities Personnel Program; Phone (518) 474-2413.

NEW YORK POWER AUTHORITY

1633 BROADWAY
NEW YORK, NEW YORK 10019-6708

OVERVIEW: Utility company. Established: 1931.

KEY STATISTICS Annual Sales: $1.0 billion. Number of Employees: 3,500.

HIRING HISTORY Number of professional employees hired in 1993: 12.

EXPERTISE/EDUCATION SOUGHT: Electrical engineering, law, civil engineering, computer programming, industrial engineering, mechanical engineering, nuclear engineering, accounting

CONTACT: Ms Ann Tivenan, Senior Employment Administrator; Phone (914) 681-6200.

NEW YORK STATE ELECTRIC AND GAS CORPORATION

ITHACA DRYDEN ROAD
ITHACA, NEW YORK 14850

OVERVIEW: Electric and gas utility. Established: 1852.

KEY STATISTICS Annual Sales: $2.0 billion. Number of Employees: 4,000.

EXPERTISE/EDUCATION SOUGHT: Accounting, marketing, finance, management information systems

CONTACT: For individuals with previous experience: Ms Pam Bowman, Human Resources Administrator, PO Box 3287, Ithaca, NY, 14852; Phone (607) 347-4131; Fax (607)347-2016.

NEW YORK TIMES COMPANY, INC.

229 WEST 43RD STREET
NEW YORK, NEW YORK 10036

OVERVIEW: Provides news publications and information services. Established: 1896.

EXPERTISE/EDUCATION SOUGHT: Business administration, journalism, marketing, finance, accounting, human resources

CONTACTS: For college students and recent graduates: Mr Gordon Rust, Manager of Employment; Phone (212) 556-1381. For individuals with previous experience: Ms Brenda Watson, Director of Recruiting and Employment; Phone (212) 556-1888.

NEWPORT NEWS SHIPBUILDING AND DRYDOCK

4101 WASHINGTON AVENUE
NEWPORT NEWS, VIRGINIA 23617

OVERVIEW: Builds ships and nuclear submarines. Established: 1886. Parent Company: Tenneco Interamerica, Inc.

EXPERTISE/EDUCATION SOUGHT: Electrical engineering, mechanical engineering, civil engineering, marine engineering, naval architecture

CONTACT: For individuals with previous experience: Mr Jay O Dunn, Employment Department; Phone (804) 380-2000, ext. 3552.

NIAGARA MOHAWK POWER CORPORATION

300 ERIE BOULEVARD WEST
SYRACUSE, NEW YORK 13202-4250

OVERVIEW: Electric and gas utility. Established: 1937.

KEY STATISTICS Annual Sales: $4.0 billion. Number of Employees: 10,000.

HIRING HISTORY Number of professional employees hired in 1993: 10.

EXPERTISE/EDUCATION SOUGHT: Environmental engineering, computer programming

CONTACT: For individuals with previous experience: Ms Dianne Thompson, Manager of Organizational Staffing; Phone (315) 428-7351.

NIBCO, INC.

500 SIMPSON AVENUE
ELKHART, INDIANA 46516-4750

OVERVIEW: Manufactures plumbing fixtures, piping, and valve fittings. Established: 1976.

KEY STATISTICS Number of Employees: 3,146.

EXPERTISE/EDUCATION SOUGHT: Production management, logistics, systems analysis, data processing

CONTACTS: For college students and recent graduates: Mr Mark Gunther, College Recruiter, PO Box 1167, Elkhart, IN, 46515-4750; Phone (219) 295-3000. For individuals with previous experience: Mr Brian Hulecki, Staffing Coordinator, PO Box 1167, Elkhart, IN, 46515-4750; Phone (219) 295-3000.

NIKE, INC.

1 BOWERMAN DRIVE
BEAVERTON, OREGON 97005-6453

OVERVIEW: Manufactures and markets athletic apparel and footwear. Established: 1964.

KEY STATISTICS Annual Sales: $4.0 billion. Number of Employees: 9,600.

EXPERTISE/EDUCATION SOUGHT: Research and development, administration, production, communications, finance, marketing, sales, management information systems, retail, human resources

CONTACT: Ms My Thi Pham, Human Resources Assistant; Phone (503) 671-6453, ext. 2389.

NIPPONDENSO MANUFACTURING USA

1 DENSO ROAD
BATTLE CREEK, MICHIGAN 49015-1056

OVERVIEW: Manufactures automotive parts and supplies. Established: 1984. Parent Company: Nippondenso America, Inc.

KEY STATISTICS Annual Sales: $493.0 million. Number of Employees: 1,240.

EXPERTISE/EDUCATION SOUGHT: Sales, marketing, accounting, finance, data processing, computer programming

CONTACT: Mr Brad Vanvyl, Supervisor of Human Resources; Phone (616) 965-3322, ext. 2541.

NISSAN MOTOR MANUFACTURING CORPORATION USA

983 NISSAN DRIVE
SMYRNA, TENNESSEE 37167-4405

OVERVIEW: Manufactures cars and trucks. Established: 1980.

KEY STATISTICS Annual Sales: $2.0 billion. Number of Employees: 5,800.

EXPERTISE/EDUCATION SOUGHT: Purchasing, finance, management information systems, accounting

CONTACTS: For college students and recent graduates: Manager of Employment; Phone (615) 459-1400. For individuals with previous experience: Ms Kathy Allen, Professional Recruiter; Phone (615) 459-1400.

NKK USA CORPORATION

450 PARK AVENUE, 25TH FLOOR
NEW YORK, NEW YORK 10022-2642

OVERVIEW: Manufactures steel pipes and sheeting.

KEY STATISTICS Annual Sales: $2.0 billion. Number of Employees: 11,000.

EXPERTISE/EDUCATION SOUGHT: Sales, customer service and support, industrial engineering

CONTACT: For individuals with previous experience: Mr Masal Goda, Vice President of Human Resources.

NORAM ENERGY CORPORATION
525 MILAM STREET
SHREVEPORT, LOUISIANA 71101-3539

Overview: Gas utility. Established: 1928.
Key Statistics Annual Sales: $3.0 billion. Number of Employees: 7,400.
Expertise/Education Sought: Marketing, engineering, accounting
Contact: Ms Bonnie Beard, Manager of Human Resources, PO Box 21734, Shreveport, LA, 71151-0002; Phone (318) 429-2700.

NORDICTRACK, INC.
104 PEAVEY ROAD
CHASKA, MINNESOTA 55318-2324

Overview: Manufactures and distributes exercise equipment. Established: 1986. Parent Company: CML Group, Inc.
Key Statistics Annual Sales: $378.0 million. Number of Employees: 2,300.
Expertise/Education Sought: Accounting, finance, data processing, marketing, sales, product design and development
Contact: For individuals with previous experience: Staffing Department; Phone (612) 368-2500.

NORDSON CORPORATION
28601 CLEMENS ROAD
CLEVELAND, OHIO 44145-1119

Overview: Manufactures industrial equipment for applying paints, adhesives, and coatings. Established: 1909.
Key Statistics Number of Employees: 2,840.
Hiring History Number of professional employees hired in 1993: 20.
Expertise/Education Sought: Finance, accounting, administration, business management
Contact: For individuals with previous experience: Ms Mary Carol, Corporate Human Resources Assistant; Phone (216) 892-1580.

NORFOLK SOUTHERN CORPORATION
3 COMMERCIAL PLACE
NORFOLK, VIRGINIA 23510-2191

Overview: Provides railway freight transportation services. Established: 1894.
Key Statistics Number of Employees: 25,650.
Expertise/Education Sought: Accounting, marketing, data processing, computer science, electrical engineering, civil engineering, mechanical engineering, transportation, logistics
Contact: Mr Eric Garrison, Senior Employment Officer, East City Hall, Avenue Suite 208, Norfolk, VA, 23510-4316; Phone (804) 533-4320.

NORTH AMERICAN VAN LINES, INC.
5001 U.S. HIGHWAY 30 WEST
FORT WAYNE, INDIANA 46818-9799

Overview: Provides transportation and moving services. Established: 1933. Parent Company: Norfolk Southern Corporation.
Key Statistics Annual Sales: $663.0 million. Number of Employees: 2,700.
Expertise/Education Sought: Accounting, data processing, distribution, transportation
Contact: For individuals with previous experience: Ms Karen Bragg-Matthews, Manager of Corporate Employee Relations, PO Box 988, Fort Wayne, IN, 46801-0988; Phone (219) 429-2873.

NORTHEAST UTILITIES
107 SELDON STREET
BERLIN, CONNECTICUT 06067-1616

Overview: Electric utility. Established: 1966. Parent Company: Northeast Utilities Volunteer Association.
Key Statistics Annual Sales: $2.0 billion. Number of Employees: 2,676.
Hiring History Number of professional employees hired in 1993: 100.

Expertise/Education Sought: Engineering, finance
Contact: Ms Ann Johnson-Bly, Manager of Employment, PO Box 270, Hartford, CT, 06141; Phone (203) 665-2278.

NORTHERN AUTOMOTIVE CORPORATION
645 EAST MISSOURI AVENUE
PHOENIX, ARIZONA 85012

Overview: Operates chain of automotive parts stores. Established: 1969. Parent Company: Northern Retail Corporation.
Key Statistics Annual Sales: $591.0 million. Number of Employees: 6,500.
Expertise/Education Sought: Accounting, marketing, finance, law, industrial engineering
Contact: Mr Evan Zang, Director of Corporate Recruiting; Phone (602) 631-7472, ext. 7117.

NORTHERN ILLINOIS GAS COMPANY
1844 FERRY ROAD
NAPERVILLE, ILLINOIS 60563-9662

Overview: Gas utility. Parent Company: NICOR, Inc.
Key Statistics Number of Employees: 2,300.
Expertise/Education Sought: Accounting
Contact: For individuals with previous experience: Mr Jack Flowers, Vice President of Human Resources, PO Box 190, Aurora, IL, 60507; Phone (708) 983-8888.

NORTHERN INDIANA PUBLIC SERVICE COMPANY (NIPSCO), INC.
5265 HOHMAN AVENUE
HAMMOND, INDIANA 46320-1722

Overview: Electric and gas utility. Established: 1912. Parent Company: NIPSCO Industries, Inc.
Key Statistics Annual Sales: $2.0 billion. Number of Employees: 4,300.
Hiring History Number of professional employees hired in 1993: 25.
Expertise/Education Sought: Accounting, business management, economics, marketing, electrical engineering, mechanical engineering, industrial engineering
Contacts: For college students and recent graduates: Ms Violet Sistovaris, Management Development Consultant/College Relations Administrator, 801 East 86th Avenue, Merrillville, IN, 46410. For individuals with previous experience: Management Development.

CORPORATE STATEMENT

NIPSCO is a primary subsidiary of NIPSCO Industries, serving 2.1 million customers across northern Indiana. It is the largest gas distributor and second-largest electric distributor in the state. The company offers career-minded employees various training programs, tuition reimbursement, and low-interest educational loans for employee dependents.

NORTHERN STATES POWER COMPANY OF MINNESOTA
414 NICOLLET MALL
MINNEAPOLIS, MINNESOTA 55401-1993

Overview: Utility company. Established: 1909.
Key Statistics Number of Employees: 7,632.

EXPERTISE/EDUCATION SOUGHT: Electrical engineering, accounting, marketing

CONTACT: For individuals with previous experience: Ms Grady Butts, Manager of Employment.

NORTHERN TELECOM
200 ATHENS WAY
NASHVILLE, TENNESSEE 37228-1397

OVERVIEW: Manufactures telecommunications equipment and systems. Established: 1971.

KEY STATISTICS Annual Sales: $4.0 billion. Number of Employees: 20,000.

EXPERTISE/EDUCATION SOUGHT: Software engineering/development, electrical engineering, computer engineering, computer science, telecommunications, radio frequency engineering, business, marketing

CONTACT: Ms Sally DeSousa, Human Resources Representative/ University Relations Department, US Resourcing Center, Department 1175 NTP, Morrisville, NC, 27560; Phone (919) 992-4610.

NORTHERN TRUST COMPANY
50 SOUTH LA SALLE STREET
CHICAGO, ILLINOIS 60675-1003

OVERVIEW: Provides financial services. Established: 1889.

KEY STATISTICS Annual Sales: $706.0 million. Number of Employees: 6,449.

EXPERTISE/EDUCATION SOUGHT: Accounting, marketing, finance, computer programming, economics

CONTACT: For individuals with previous experience: Ms Roxane Hori, Senior Vice President of People Planning; Phone (312) 630-6000.

NORTHROP GRUMMAN CORPORATION, ELECTRONICS SYSTEMS DIVISION
600 HICKS ROAD
ROLLING MEADOWS, ILLINOIS 60008

OVERVIEW: Researches, designs, develops, and manufactures radar jamming countermeasure systems. Established: 1939.

KEY STATISTICS Annual Sales: $6.0 billion. Number of Employees: 2,648.

CONTACT: For individuals with previous experience: Manager of Staffing, T41.

NORTHWEST AIRLINES, INC.
ST. PAUL INTERNATIONAL AIRPORT
SAINT PAUL, MINNESOTA 55111-3034

OVERVIEW: Provides passenger airline services. Established: 1926. Parent Company: NWA, Inc.

KEY STATISTICS Number of Employees: 42,500.

EXPERTISE/EDUCATION SOUGHT: Aeronautical engineering, aviation, electronics/electronics engineering, flight attendant

CONTACT: For individuals with previous experience: Mr Perliss Johnson, Director of Corporate Human Resources; Phone (612) 726-7273.

NORTHWEST NATIONAL LIFE
20 WASHINGTON AVENUE SOUTH
MINNEAPOLIS, MINNESOTA 55401

OVERVIEW: Provides life insurance. Established: 1885.

KEY STATISTICS Annual Sales: $1.0 billion. Number of Employees: 2,500.

EXPERTISE/EDUCATION SOUGHT: Sales, marketing, computer programming, accounting, credit/credit analysis

CONTACT: Ms Marguerite Samuels, Assistant Vice President of Human Resources; Phone (612) 372-1187.

NORTHWEST TEMPORARY SERVICES
522 SOUTHWEST 5TH AVENUE, 4TH FLOOR
PORTLAND, OREGON 97204-2191

OVERVIEW: Provides temporary employment services.

KEY STATISTICS Number of Employees: 6,000.

EXPERTISE/EDUCATION SOUGHT: Accounting, law, technical

CONTACT: For individuals with previous experience: Human Resources Office, 522 SW 5th Avenue 6th Floor, Portland, OR, 97204; Phone (503) 242-0611.

NORWEST CORPORATION
SIXTH AND MARQUETTE
MINNEAPOLIS, MINNESOTA 55479-3903

OVERVIEW: Commercial bank. Established: 1872.

KEY STATISTICS Number of Employees: 35,000.

EXPERTISE/EDUCATION SOUGHT: Auditing, credit/credit analysis, finance, marketing, mortgage, banking

CONTACT: Ms Chris Kennedy, Senior Vice President of Human Resources; Phone (612) 667-6860.

NORWEST FINANCIAL SERVICES
206 8TH STREET
DES MOINES, IW 50309-3805

OVERVIEW: Provides banking and related financial services. Established: 1897.

KEY STATISTICS Number of Employees: 5,800.

EXPERTISE/EDUCATION SOUGHT: Credit management, credit/credit analysis, financial analysis, management, training and development

CONTACT: For individuals with previous experience: Mr Wilburn Hollis, Manager of Personnel Administration and Employee Relations; Phone (515) 243-2131.

NOVACARE, INC.
1016 WEST 9TH AVENUE
KING OF PRUSSIA, PENNSYLVANIA 19406-1241

OVERVIEW: Provides rehabilitation services.

KEY STATISTICS Annual Sales: $539.0 million. Number of Employees: 7,750.

EXPERTISE/EDUCATION SOUGHT: Rehabilitation, nursing, physical therapy, occupational therapy, social work, psychology

CONTACT: For individuals with previous experience: Ms Kathy Kehoe, Vice President of Human Resources; Phone (610) 992-7200.

NOVACOR CHEMICALS, INC.
690 MECHANIC STREET
LEOMINSTER, MASSACHUSETTS 01453-4402

OVERVIEW: Manufactures plastics. Established: 1937.

KEY STATISTICS Annual Sales: $610.0 million. Number of Employees: 500.

EXPERTISE/EDUCATION SOUGHT: Finance, chemical engineering, marketing, accounting, sales

CONTACT: Mr Scott Loomer, Employment Coordinator; Phone (508) 537-1111, ext. 5009.

NPC INTERNATIONAL, INC.
720 WEST 20TH STREET
PITTSBURG, KANSAS 66762-2860

OVERVIEW: Operates chains of pizzerias and seafood restaurants.

KEY STATISTICS Annual Sales: $337.0 million. Number of Employees: 12,500.

EXPERTISE/EDUCATION SOUGHT: Accounting, law, finance

CONTACT: For individuals with previous experience: Mr Jim Villanaria, Human Resources Director; Phone (316) 231-3390.

NU SKIN INTERNATIONAL
75 WEST CENTER STREET
PROVO, UTAH 84601-4479

Overview: Manufactures skin care and nutritional products.
Established: 1984.

Key Statistics Annual Sales: $424.0 million. Number of Employees:
1,400.

Expertise/Education Sought: Marketing, sales, finance, accounting, data
processing, law, nutrition, emergency services, biology, chemistry

Contact: Ms Liz Dalton, Director of Personnel and Human Resources;
Phone (801) 345-2500.

NUCOR CORPORATION
2100 REXFORD ROAD
CHARLOTTE, NORTH CAROLINA 28211-3484

Overview: Manufactures steel. Established: 1904.

Key Statistics Number of Employees: 5,900.

Expertise/Education Sought: Metallurgical engineering

Contact: For individuals with previous experience: Mr James Coblin,
Manager of Personnel; Phone (704) 366-7000.

NVR, INC.
7601 LEWINSVILLE ROAD
MC LEAN, VIRGINIA 22102-2815

Overview: Provides banking services; speculative builder.

Key Statistics Annual Sales: $573.0 million. Number of Employees:
1,805.

Expertise/Education Sought: Sales

Contacts: For college students and recent graduates: Ms Cindy Hanna,
Recruiting Specialist; Phone (703) 761-2000. For individuals with
previous experience: Mr Joe Madigan, Director of Human
Resources; Phone (703) 761-2000.

NYNEX CORPORATION
1095 AVENUE OF THE AMERICAS
NEW YORK, NEW YORK 10036-3510

Overview: Provides telecommunications services. Established: 1984.

Key Statistics Annual Sales: $13.0 billion. Number of Employees:
76,200.

Expertise/Education Sought: Engineering, systems analysis, sales,
account management, purchasing, planning, marketing, market
research, telecommunications, management

Contact: Mr Tom O'Gara, Manager Human Resources; Phone (212)
395-2500.

NATIONAL CITY BANK
155 EAST BROAD STREET
COLUMBUS, OHIO 43215-3645

Overview: National commercial bank. Parent Company: National City
Corporation.

Key Statistics Number of Employees: 3,219.

Hiring History Number of professional employees hired in 1993: 600.

Expertise/Education Sought: Finance, accounting, actuarial, auditing,
computer programming

Contact: Ms Debra Green, Recruiter; Phone (614) 463-6990.

OCCIDENTAL CHEMICAL CORPORATION
5005 LBJ FREEWAY
DALLAS, TEXAS 75244

Overview: Discovers and produces oil and gas, manufactures chemicals,
and mines coal. Established: 1903.

Expertise/Education Sought: Chemical engineering, process
engineering, data processing, marketing, accounting, law, finance,
auditing, mechanical engineering, management information
systems

Contact: Mr Joe Cousins, Staffing Manager; Phone (214) 404-3800, ext.
3365.

OCCIDENTAL OIL AND GAS CORPORATION
PO BOX 300
TULSA, OKLAHOMA 74102

Overview: Domestic oil and gas exploration and production company.

Expertise/Education Sought: Mechanical engineering, accounting,
finance, chemical engineering, electrical engineering, petroleum/
petrochemical engineering, computer science

Contact: Mr William S Gallagher, Manager of Recruiting and
Placement; Phone (918) 561-3956.

OCCIDENTAL PETROLEUM CORPORATION
10889 WILSHIRE BOULEVARD
LOS ANGELES, CALIFORNIA 90024-4201

Overview: Discovers and produces oil and gas, manufactures chemicals,
and mines coal. Established: 1920.

Key Statistics Number of Employees: 19,627.

Expertise/Education Sought: Accounting, finance, data processing, law,
business administration

Contact: Ms Arlene Wolfe, Supervisor of Human Resources and
Employment; Phone (310) 208-8800, ext. 6501.

OCEAN SPRAY CRANBERRIES, INC.
1 OCEAN SPRAY DRIVE
LAKEVILLE, MASSACHUSETTS 02349

Overview: Manufactures and markets cranberry and other fruit based
foods and beverages. Established: 1930.

Expertise/Education Sought: Sales, marketing, finance, management
information systems, business administration

Contact: Human Resources Department.

OCP INTERNATIONAL, INC.
1270 AVENUE OF THE AMERICAS
NEW YORK, NEW YORK 10020

Overview: Provides legal services.

Expertise/Education Sought: Law, accounting, business administration

Contact: For individuals with previous experience: Ms Claire Sturtvant,
Director of Human Resources; Phone (212) 265-5100.

ODYSSEY MANAGEMENT COMPANY
310 SOUTH INDUSTRIAL BOULEVARD
EULESS, TEXAS 76040-4208

Overview: Provides employee leasing services.

Key Statistics Annual Sales: $100.0 million. Number of Employees:
5,000.

Expertise/Education Sought: Management

Contact: For individuals with previous experience: Mr Bill Plikuhn,
Director of Human Resources.

ODYSSEY PARTNERS
31 WEST 52ND STREET
NEW YORK, NEW YORK 10019-6118

Overview: Holding company. Established: 1951.

Expertise/Education Sought: Accounting, finance, data processing,
marketing, business management

Contact: Ms Mary Parker, Manager of Personnel; Phone (212)
708-0600.

OFFICE MAX, INC.
3605 WARRENSVILLE ROAD
CLEVELAND, OHIO 44122-5203

Overview: Sells discount office equipment and supplies.

Key Statistics Annual Sales: $1.0 billion. Number of Employees: 3,560.

EXPERTISE/EDUCATION SOUGHT: Management, management information systems, finance, accounting, retail management, sales, marketing

CONTACT: For individuals with previous experience: Mr William Ehmann, Director of Recruiting; Phone (216) 921-6900, ext. 6438.

OHIO CASUALTY INSURANCE CORPORATION
136 NORTH 3RD STREET
HAMILTON, OHIO 45025

OVERVIEW: Provides life, property and automobile insurance. Established: 1919.

KEY STATISTICS Number of Employees: 4,800.

HIRING HISTORY Number of professional employees hired in 1993: 23.

EXPERTISE/EDUCATION SOUGHT: Accounting, finance, computer programming, marketing, computer engineering, systems analysis

CONTACT: Ms Marge Brown, Employment Supervisor; Phone (513) 867-3000, ext. 3754.

OHIO POWER COMPANY-COLUMBUS SOUTHERN
301 CLEVELAND AVENUE SOUTHWEST
CANTON, OHIO 44702-1623

OVERVIEW: Electric utility. Established: 1907. Parent Company: American Electric Power Company.

KEY STATISTICS Number of Employees: 5,749.

HIRING HISTORY Number of professional employees hired in 1993: 15.

EXPERTISE/EDUCATION SOUGHT: Electrical engineering, mechanical engineering, marketing, customer service and support, accounting, environmental engineering

CONTACT: Personnel Services Administrator.

OLD KENT FINANCIAL CORPORATION
1 VANDERBURG PLACE
GRAND RAPIDS, MICHIGAN 49506

OVERVIEW: Bank holding company. Established: 1971.

EXPERTISE/EDUCATION SOUGHT: Accounting, computer programming, computer science

CONTACT: For individuals with previous experience: Mr Steve Crandall, Senior Vice President Human Resources; Phone (616) 771-5000.

OLD REPUBLIC INTERNATIONAL
307 NORTH MICHIGAN AVENUE
CHICAGO, ILLINOIS 60601

OVERVIEW: Provides life, casualty, and title insurance.

EXPERTISE/EDUCATION SOUGHT: Accounting, law, sales, finance, computer programming

CONTACT: Mr Charles Strizak, Director of Personnel; Phone (312) 346-8100.

THE OLSTEN CORPORATION
175 BROAD HOLLOW ROAD
MELVILLE, NEW YORK 11747

OVERVIEW: Provides home health care services. Established: 1950.

KEY STATISTICS Annual Sales: $2.0 billion. Number of Employees: 443,600.

EXPERTISE/EDUCATION SOUGHT: Accounting, finance, marketing, sales, health care

CONTACT: For individuals with previous experience: Ms Mary Ellen Betterton, Director of Recruiting.

OMNI HOTELS
500 LAFAYETTE ROAD
HAMPTON, NEW HAMPSHIRE 03842-3347

OVERVIEW: Manages and operates hotels and motels. Established: 1958.

KEY STATISTICS Annual Sales: $500.0 million. Number of Employees: 7,000.

HIRING HISTORY Number of professional employees hired in 1994: 400.

EXPERTISE/EDUCATION SOUGHT: Accounting, management, hospitality/hotel and restaurant management, human resources

CONTACT: For individuals with previous experience: Ms Susan Martinen, Corporate Recruiter; Phone (603) 929-5436.

ONE CALL COMMUNICATIONS, INC.
801 CONGRESSIONAL BOULEVARD
CARMEL, INDIANA 46032

OVERVIEW: Provides long distance telephone communications services. Established: 1982.

KEY STATISTICS Annual Sales: $69.6 million. Number of Employees: 410.

EXPERTISE/EDUCATION SOUGHT: Accounting, finance, sales, data processing, computer programming

CONTACT: For individuals with previous experience: Ms Linda Brumett, Human Resource Recruiter; Phone (317) 843-1300.

ONEOK, INC.
100 WEST 5TH STREET
TULSA, OKLAHOMA 74103-4240

OVERVIEW: Distributes natural gas products. Established: 1933.

KEY STATISTICS Number of Employees: 2,208.

EXPERTISE/EDUCATION SOUGHT: Accounting, finance, marketing, plant management, data processing, petroleum/petrochemical engineering

CONTACT: For individuals with previous experience: Mr H C Williams, Manager of Employment; Phone (918) 588-7365.

OPTICAL DEPARTMENT OF SEARS
18903 SOUTH MILES ROAD
CLEVELAND, OHIO 44128-4245

OVERVIEW: Manufactures eyeglasses and eyewear. Established: 1986. Parent Company: Cole National Corporation.

KEY STATISTICS Annual Sales: $226.0 million. Number of Employees: 2,700.

EXPERTISE/EDUCATION SOUGHT: Accounting, sales, marketing

CONTACT: For individuals with previous experience: Mr Jeff Thompson, Human Resources Representative; Phone (216) 475-8925, ext. 3533.

ORACLE CORPORATION
500 ORACLE PARKWAY
REDWOOD SHORES, CALIFORNIA 94065-1675

OVERVIEW: Develops and markets database and communications software products. Established: 1977. Parent Company: Oracle Systems Corporation.

KEY STATISTICS Annual Sales: $2.0 billion. Number of Employees: 9,247.

EXPERTISE/EDUCATION SOUGHT: Software engineering/development, computer science, design engineering, technology, computer programming, program analysis

CONTACTS: For college students and recent graduates: Mr Larry Lynn, Corporate Recruiter; Phone (415) 506-7000. For individuals with previous experience: Ms Lindsay Quintero, Manager Corporate Recruiting.

ORANGE AND ROCKLAND UTILITIES
1 BLUE HILL PLAZA
PEARL RIVER, NEW YORK 10965-3104

OVERVIEW: Natural gas utility. Established: 1899.

KEY STATISTICS Number of Employees: 1,721.

EXPERTISE/EDUCATION SOUGHT: Accounting, computer programming, plant management, electrical engineering, mechanical engineering, civil engineering, information systems

CONTACT: Mr Nicholas Illobre, Manager of Personnel; Phone (914) 577-2752.

ORE-IDA FOODS, INC.
220 WEST PARKCENTER BOULEVARD
BOISE, IDAHO 83706-3968

OVERVIEW: Manufactures frozen potato, vegetable, and dinner products. Established: 1965. Parent Company: H. J. Heinz Company.

KEY STATISTICS Annual Sales: $794.0 million. Number of Employees: 5,189.

EXPERTISE/EDUCATION SOUGHT: Marketing, finance, accounting

CONTACT: Ms Karey Bertrand, Supervisor of Employment; Phone (208) 383-6330.

ORMET CORPORATION
STATE ROUTE 7, 2 MILES NORTH
HANNIBAL, OHIO 43931

OVERVIEW: Manufactures aluminum products. Established: 1956.

EXPERTISE/EDUCATION SOUGHT: Sales, marketing, accounting, finance, data processing, mechanical engineering

CONTACT: For individuals with previous experience: Personnel Department; Phone (614) 483-1381, ext. 83.

ORTHO DIAGNOSTIC SYSTEMS, INC.
1001 US HIGHWAY 202
RARITAN, NEW JERSEY 08869-1424

OVERVIEW: Provides blood diagnostic services. Established: 1973. Parent Company: Johnson & Johnson.

KEY STATISTICS Annual Sales: $500.0 million. Number of Employees: 1,600.

EXPERTISE/EDUCATION SOUGHT: Laboratory technology, biology, microbiology, chemistry

CONTACT: For individuals with previous experience: Ms Carol Peccarelli, Human Resources Director; Phone (908) 218-8525.

ORTHO PHARMACEUTICAL CORPORATION
ROUTE 202 SOUTH, PO BOX 300
RARITAN, NEW JERSEY 08869

OVERVIEW: Manufactures pharmaceuticals and sanitary paper products. Parent Company: Johnson & Johnson.

EXPERTISE/EDUCATION SOUGHT: Marketing, sales, finance, accounting

CONTACT: For individuals with previous experience: Mr Nick Burkholder, Vice President of Human Resources, (Shared Services Employment), 501 George Street, New Brunswick, NJ, 08903; Phone (908) 524-3451.

OSCAR MAYER FOODS CORPORATION
910 MAYER AVENUE
MADISON, WISCONSIN 53704-4287

OVERVIEW: Produces processed meats and prepared foods. Established: 1883. Parent Company: Kraft General Foods, Inc.

KEY STATISTICS Number of Employees: 11,000.

EXPERTISE/EDUCATION SOUGHT: Marketing, data processing, technical engineering, law, civil engineering, finance, human resources

CONTACT: Human Resources Department; Phone (608) 241-3311.

OSHKOSH B'GOSH, INC.
112 OTTER AVENUE
OSHKOSH, WISCONSIN 54901

OVERVIEW: Manufactures and markets children's clothing. Established: 1895.

KEY STATISTICS Annual Sales: $345.0 million. Number of Employees: 7,000.

EXPERTISE/EDUCATION SOUGHT: Textiles, management, operations

CONTACT: For individuals with previous experience: Corporate Human Resources Department, PO Box 300, Oshkosh, WI, 54902; Phone (414) 231-8800.

OSHKOSH TRUCK CORPORATION
2307 OREGON STREET
OSHKOSH, WISCONSIN 54901-7000

OVERVIEW: Manufactures truck and bus bodies. Established: 1917.

KEY STATISTICS Number of Employees: 2,200.

EXPERTISE/EDUCATION SOUGHT: Accounting, data processing, marketing

CONTACT: Ms Cindy Behm, Manager of Salaried Recruitment, PO Box 2566, Oshkosh, WI, 54903-2566; Phone (414) 235-9150, ext. 2804.

OTIS ELEVATOR COMPANY
10 FARM SPRINGS ROAD
FARMINGTON, CONNECTICUT 06032

OVERVIEW: Manufactures elevators and escalators. Established: 1853. Parent Company: United Technologies Corporation.

EXPERTISE/EDUCATION SOUGHT: Design engineering, electrical engineering, mechanical engineering, software engineering/development, management, sales

CONTACT: For individuals with previous experience: Ms Jane Kennedy, Director of Recruiting; Phone (203) 676-6000.

OUTBOARD MARINE CORPORATION
100 SEA HORSE DRIVE
WAUKEGAN, ILLINOIS 60085-2141

OVERVIEW: Manufactures outboard motors and boats. Established: 1936.

EXPERTISE/EDUCATION SOUGHT: Auditing, marketing, data processing, human resources

CONTACT: Ms Denise Charts, Manager of Human Resources; Phone (708) 689-6200.

OVERNITE TRANSPORTATION COMPANY
1000 SEMMES AVENUE
RICHMOND, VIRGINIA 23224-2246

OVERVIEW: Provides trucking and shipping services. Established: 1935.

KEY STATISTICS Number of Employees: 13,690.

EXPERTISE/EDUCATION SOUGHT: Marketing, computer science, finance, data processing, sales, management information systems, accounting, logistics

CONTACT: Ms Deborah Wickham, Senior Staffing Specialist; Phone (804) 231-8000.

OWENS-CORNING FIBERGLASS CORPORATION
FIBERGLASS TOWER
TOLEDO, OHIO 43659-0001

OVERVIEW: Manufactures glass fiber materials and polyester resins. Established: 1938.

EXPERTISE/EDUCATION SOUGHT: Engineering, manufacturing engineering, industrial engineering, construction engineering, industrial safety, materials engineering

CONTACT: Ms Kathy Zucco, Advanced Employment Specialist; Phone (419) 248-6874.

OWENS-ILLINOIS, INC.
1 SEAGATE
TOLEDO, OHIO 43666-0001

OVERVIEW: Manufactures glass and plastic containers. Established: 1907.

KEY STATISTICS Number of Employees: 28,900.

EXPERTISE/EDUCATION SOUGHT: Chemical engineering, sales, electrical engineering, management, mechanical engineering, plastics engineering, metallurgical engineering

CONTACT: For college students and recent graduates: Mr Gene Escolas, Manager of Training and Development; Phone (419) 247-5000.

OXY CHEMICAL CORPORATION
50005 LBJ FREEWAY
DALLAS, TEXAS 75244

OVERVIEW: Manufactures industrial chemicals.

EXPERTISE/EDUCATION SOUGHT: Mechanical engineering, chemical engineering, electrical engineering, accounting, industrial hygiene, sales, safety

CONTACT: For college students and recent graduates: Mr James Reder, Manager of College Relations, PO Box 80950, Dallas, TX, 75380; Phone (214) 404-3921.

P AND C FOOD MARKETS, INC.
PO BOX 4965
SYRACUSE, NEW YORK 13221

OVERVIEW: Operates chain of food stores. Established: 1944.

HIRING HISTORY Number of professional employees hired in 1994: 25.

EXPERTISE/EDUCATION SOUGHT: Accounting, marketing, finance, business management, law, sales, credit/credit analysis, management information systems

CONTACT: For individuals with previous experience: Mr Mark Sibble, Manager of Employment; Phone (315) 453-8500.

PACCAR, INC.
777 106TH AVENUE NORTHEAST
BELLEVUE, WASHINGTON 98004-5017

OVERVIEW: Manufactures trucks. Established: 1905.

KEY STATISTICS Annual Sales: $3.0 billion. Number of Employees: 12,000.

EXPERTISE/EDUCATION SOUGHT: Accounting, business management, finance, engineering, international finance, data processing, retail

CONTACT: Ms Julie Horsman, Manager of Human Resources; Phone (206) 455-7400.

PACE INDUSTRIES, INC.
405 LEXINGTON AVENUE
NEW YORK, NEW YORK 10174-0112

OVERVIEW: Manufactures air conditioning systems. Established: 1984.

KEY STATISTICS Annual Sales: $470.0 million. Number of Employees: 5,300.

EXPERTISE/EDUCATION SOUGHT: Management, accounting

CONTACT: Mr Henry Porter, Manager of Human Resources; Phone (212) 916-8199.

PACIFIC BELL
140 NEW MONTGOMERY STREET
SAN FRANCISCO, CALIFORNIA 94105-3705

OVERVIEW: Provides telecommunications services. Established: 1984. Parent Company: Pacific Telesis Group.

KEY STATISTICS Annual Sales: $9.0 billion. Number of Employees: 54,026.

EXPERTISE/EDUCATION SOUGHT: Accounting, finance, sales, marketing, data processing

CONTACT: Ms Carolyn Rainey-Golinveaux, Executive Manager; Phone (415) 542-9000.

PACIFIC ENTERPRISES
633 WEST 5TH STREET
LOS ANGELES, CALIFORNIA 90071

OVERVIEW: Natural gas utility.

KEY STATISTICS Annual Sales: $3.0 billion. Number of Employees: 9,800.

EXPERTISE/EDUCATION SOUGHT: Engineering, operations, management

CONTACT: For individuals with previous experience: Ms Cathy Chin, Personnel Services Coordinator, PO Box 60043, Los Angeles, CA, 90060.

PACIFIC GAS AND ELECTRIC COMPANY
77 BEALE STREET
SAN FRANCISCO, CALIFORNIA 94105-1814

OVERVIEW: Electric and gas utility. Established: 1905.

KEY STATISTICS Annual Sales: $11.0 billion. Number of Employees: 23,000.

EXPERTISE/EDUCATION SOUGHT: Accounting, business administration, economics, finance, auditing, computer science, management information systems

CONTACT: For individuals with previous experience: Ms Barbara Coull Williams, Vice President of Human Resources, 201 Mission Street, MC B-32, San Francisco, CA, 94177; Phone (415) 973-6710; Fax (415)973-9181.

PACIFIC MUTUAL LIFE INSURANCE COMPANY
700 NEWPORT CENTER DRIVE
NEWPORT BEACH, CALIFORNIA 92660-6397

OVERVIEW: Provides life, health, and accident insurance. Established: 1936.

KEY STATISTICS Annual Sales: $3.0 billion. Number of Employees: 2,200.

EXPERTISE/EDUCATION SOUGHT: Accounting, actuarial, finance

CONTACT: For individuals with previous experience: Ms Peggy Schmidt, Director of Employment and Staffing; Phone (714) 640-3246; Fax (714)640-3483.

PACIFIC TELESIS GROUP
130 KEARNY STREET
SAN FRANCISCO, CALIFORNIA 94108-4818

OVERVIEW: Provides telecommunications and related services. Established: 1906.

KEY STATISTICS Annual Sales: $9.0 billion. Number of Employees: 55,355.

HIRING HISTORY Number of professional employees hired in 1993: 300.

EXPERTISE/EDUCATION SOUGHT: Computer programming, accounting, computer science, electrical engineering, mechanical engineering, marketing, telecommunications, sales, systems analysis

CONTACT: Mr John Alden, Human Resources Manager, 33 New Montgomery, Suite 11, San Francisco, CA, 94105; Phone (415) 545-1568.

PACIFICARE OF CALIFORNIA
5701 KATELLA AVENUE
CYPRESS, CALIFORNIA 90630-5028

OVERVIEW: Provides health insurance. Established: 1975.

KEY STATISTICS Annual Sales: $2.0 billion. Number of Employees: 2,600.

EXPERTISE/EDUCATION SOUGHT: Management, clinical nursing, social work, claims adjustment/examination, accounting, customer service and support, sales, marketing

CONTACT: For individuals with previous experience: Human Resources Department; Phone (800) 577-5627.

PACIFICORP
700 NORTHEAST MULTNOMAH STREET
PORTLAND, OREGON 97232-4194

OVERVIEW: Electric utility. Established: 1910.

KEY STATISTICS Number of Employees: 13,635.

EXPERTISE/EDUCATION SOUGHT: Marketing, sales, finance, accounting, electrical engineering, mechanical engineering

CONTACT: Ms Della Frazier, Employment Manager, 920 Southwest 6th Avenue, Portland, OR, 97204; Phone (503) 464-6861.

PACKAGING CORPORATION OF AMERICA
1603 ORRINGTON ROAD
EVANSTON, ILLINOIS 60201

OVERVIEW: Manufactures shipping containers, pulp, and paper products. Established: 1959.

EXPERTISE/EDUCATION SOUGHT: Accounting, finance, law, business administration, pulp and paper science, mechanical engineering, industrial engineering, information systems

CONTACT: Ms Kate Cieslak, Administration Manager; Phone (708) 492-5713.

PACKARD BELL ELECTRONICS, INC.
31717 LATIENDA DRIVE
WESTLAKE VILLAGE, CALIFORNIA 91362-4010

OVERVIEW: Manufactures personal computers, software, and peripherals.

KEY STATISTICS Annual Sales: $169.0 million. Number of Employees: 1,400.

EXPERTISE/EDUCATION SOUGHT: Purchasing, accounting, finance, computer science, technical, quality control, production

CONTACT: For college students and recent graduates: Ms Debbie Blum, Manager of Personnel; Phone (818) 865-1555, ext. 987. For individuals with previous experience: Ms Pamela Anderson, Employment Manager, 8350 Fruitridge Road, Sacramento, CA, 95826; Phone (916) 388-6274.

PAINE WEBBER, INC.
1285 AVENUE OF THE AMERICAS
NEW YORK, NEW YORK 10019-6093

OVERVIEW: Brokerage, investment, and related financial services. Established: 1879. Parent Company: Paine Webber Group, Inc.

KEY STATISTICS Annual Sales: $1.0 billion. Number of Employees: 14,400.

EXPERTISE/EDUCATION SOUGHT: Finance, sales, brokerage, computer science, accounting

CONTACT: Corporate Staffing Department, 1000 Harbor Boulevard, 10th Floor, Weehawken, NJ, 07087.

PALL CORPORATION
2200 NORTHERN BOULEVARD
EAST HILL, NEW YORK 11548-1289

OVERVIEW: Manufactures filters. Established: 1946.

KEY STATISTICS Number of Employees: 6,300.

HIRING HISTORY Number of professional employees hired in 1994: 100.

EXPERTISE/EDUCATION SOUGHT: Accounting, industrial engineering, mechanical engineering, electrical engineering, finance, marketing, human resources, computer programming, laboratory technology, manufacturing engineering

CONTACT: Ms Geri Schwab, Manager of Corporate Human Resources; Phone (516) 484-5400.

PAMIDA HOLDINGS CORPORATION
8800 F STREET
OMAHA, NEW BRUNSWICK 68127

OVERVIEW: Owns and operates a chain of discount department stores. Established: 1986.

EXPERTISE/EDUCATION SOUGHT: Accounting, finance, marketing, business management, customer service and support, management information systems

CONTACT: For individuals with previous experience: Mr Brett Williams, Manager of Employment and Employee Relations; Phone (402) 339-2400.

PARISIAN, INC.
750 LAKESHORE PARKWAY
BIRMINGHAM, ALABAMA 35211-4400

OVERVIEW: Operates chain of family apparel and shoes stores. Established: 1880.

KEY STATISTICS Number of Employees: 6,200.

EXPERTISE/EDUCATION SOUGHT: Merchandising, retail, information systems, program analysis, systems analysis, accounting, distribution

CONTACT: For individuals with previous experience: Mr Al Posten, Supervisor of Personnel.

PARKE-DAVIS, DIVISION OF WARNER-LAMBERT COMPANY
201 TABOR ROAD
MORRIS PLAINS, NEW JERSEY 07950

OVERVIEW: Manufactures ethical pharmaceuticals. Established: 1866.

KEY STATISTICS Annual Sales: $2.0 billion. Number of Employees: 4,000.

EXPERTISE/EDUCATION SOUGHT: Business, marketing, life sciences

CONTACT: Human Resources Department.

CORPORATE PROFILE

Parke-Davis is a division of Warner-Lambert Company, one of the foremost producers of ethical pharmaceuticals in the world. The Parke-Davis tradition of caring reaches back 125 years to the days when the motto "Medicamenta Vera" was created. Parke-Davis created some of the finest quality standards in the pharmaceutical industry so that "true medicine" would always reach the patient. Over the years, Parke-Davis products and professionals have helped people worldwide lead longer, healthier, and more productive lives.

The company's best efforts, however, are of little use without skilled communicators to explain their products and their uses to the medical community. This is the role of Parke-Davis pharmaceutical sales representatives, located nationwide. These highly trained professionals are the prime link between Parke-Davis and the physicians who prescribe these medications to patients. Pharmacists also depend heavily on the information offered by their pharmaceutical sales representatives.

Each year, Parke-Davis asks a group of carefully selected graduates to consider becoming pharmaceutical sales representatives. Those who accept the invitation receive outstanding training, significant opportunity for professional growth, and excellent rewards for performance. As one of the People Who Care, a Parke-Davis professional can make a mark providing one of the world's most critical resources—better health care.

For more information, see full corporate profile, pg. 212.

PARKER HANNIFIN CORPORATION
17325 EUCLID AVENUE
CLEVELAND, OHIO 44112-1290

OVERVIEW: Manufactures hydraulic and pneumatic components, aircraft and aerospace equipment, and automotive products. Established: 1924.

KEY STATISTICS Number of Employees: 25,650.

HIRING HISTORY Number of professional employees hired in 1994: 100. 1993: 120.

EXPERTISE/EDUCATION SOUGHT: Mechanical engineering, electrical engineering, audio engineering, accounting, aerospace engineering, agricultural engineering

CONTACT: Mr Duane Crockrom, Manager of Human Resources Development; Phone (216) 531-3000.

PARSONS AND WHITTMORE, INC.
4 INTERNATIONAL DRIVE
RYE BROOK, NEW YORK 10573-1064

OVERVIEW: Manufactures pulp and paper. Established: 1980.

KEY STATISTICS Number of Employees: 1,800.

EXPERTISE/EDUCATION SOUGHT: Computer science, data processing, pulp and paper science, forestry, accounting, finance, sales, marketing

CONTACT: For individuals with previous experience: Mr Richard Martin, Director of Human Resources; Phone (914) 937-9009.

THE RALPH M. PARSONS COMPANY
100 WEST WALNUT STREET
PASADENA, CALIFORNIA 91124-0001

OVERVIEW: Provides engineering services. Established: 1978. Parent Company: Parsons Corporation.

The Ralph M. Parsons Company (continued)

KEY STATISTICS Number of Employees: 3,400.

EXPERTISE/EDUCATION SOUGHT: Accounting, finance, data processing, computer programming, sales, computer graphics

CONTACT: For individuals with previous experience: Ms Melody Wilbur, Employment Supervisor of Human Resources; Phone (818) 440-2000.

PATHMARK STORES, INC.
301 BLAIR ROAD
WOODBRIDGE, NEW JERSEY 07095

OVERVIEW: Operates chain of food stores.

KEY STATISTICS Number of Employees: 27,000.

HIRING HISTORY Number of professional employees hired in 1994: 34. 1993: 30.

EXPERTISE/EDUCATION SOUGHT: Accounting, finance, retail management

CONTACT: Ms Susan McMann, Manager of Employment, PO Box 5301, Woodbridge, NJ, 07095; Phone (908) 499-3000, ext. 4019.

PAYCHEX, INC.
911 PANORAMA TRIANGLE SOUTH
ROCHESTER, NEW YORK 14625-2396

OVERVIEW: Provides payroll processing services and software. Established: 1970.

KEY STATISTICS Annual Sales: $224.0 million. Number of Employees: 2,800.

EXPERTISE/EDUCATION SOUGHT: Accounting, data processing, computer programming, quality control

CONTACT: For individuals with previous experience: Ms Michelle Hall, Recruiter; Phone (716) 385-6666.

PAYLESS CASHWAYS, INC.
2300 MAIN STREET
KANSAS CITY, MISSOURI 64108-2445

OVERVIEW: Operates chain of home improvement stores. Established: 1968.

KEY STATISTICS Annual Sales: $3.0 billion. Number of Employees: 18,903.

EXPERTISE/EDUCATION SOUGHT: Management

CONTACT: For individuals with previous experience: Mr Roger Lee, Director of Administration.

PEARLE, INC.
2534 ROYAL LANE
DALLAS, TEXAS 75229

OVERVIEW: Manufactures and distributes eyeglasses.

EXPERTISE/EDUCATION SOUGHT: Sales, marketing, research, accounting, computer programming

CONTACTS: For college students and recent graduates: Ms Janet Manson, Employment Representative; Phone (214) 277-5136. For individuals with previous experience: Mr Graham London-Carter, Vice President of Human Resources; Phone (214) 277-5534.

PEARSON, INC.
1 ROCKEFELLER PLAZA
NEW YORK, NEW YORK 10020-2002

OVERVIEW: Manages entertainment businesses.

KEY STATISTICS Annual Sales: $862.0 million. Number of Employees: 8,500.

EXPERTISE/EDUCATION SOUGHT: Accounting, finance, management information systems, law, human resources

CONTACT: Mr Randall C Keller, Director of Human Resources; Phone (212) 713-1919.

PECO ENERGY COMPANY
2301 MARKET STREET
PHILADELPHIA, PENNSYLVANIA 19101-1338

OVERVIEW: Electric and gas utility. Established: 1881.

KEY STATISTICS Number of Employees: 9,700.

HIRING HISTORY Number of professional employees hired in 1994: 75. 1993: 71.

EXPERTISE/EDUCATION SOUGHT: Mechanical engineering, electrical engineering, information systems, systems integration, marketing, sales

CONTACT: For individuals with previous experience: Mr Bruce Allhouse, Director of Staffing; Phone (215) 841-4335.

PENN CENTRAL CORPORATION
1 EAST 4TH STREET
CINCINNATI, OHIO 45202-3717

OVERVIEW: Provides property and casualty insurance. Established: 1847.

KEY STATISTICS Number of Employees: 5,400.

EXPERTISE/EDUCATION SOUGHT: Accounting, finance, auditing, law, data processing

CONTACT: Ms Bonnie Tsacalis, Manager of Compensation and Employee Relations; Phone (513) 579-6600, ext. 6709.

THE PENN MUTUAL LIFE INSURANCE COMPANY
INDEPENDENCE PLACE, 600 DRESHER ROAD
HORSHAM, PENNSYLVANIA 19044

OVERVIEW: Provides life insurance.

KEY STATISTICS Number of Employees: 4,850.

HIRING HISTORY Number of professional employees hired in 1994: 12.

EXPERTISE/EDUCATION SOUGHT: Accounting

CONTACT: For individuals with previous experience: Ms Donna Rittmayer, Director of Staffing and Employee Relations; Phone (215) 956-8389.

THE PENN TRAFFIC COMPANY
1200 STATE FAIR BOULEVARD
SYRACUSE, NEW YORK 13209

OVERVIEW: Owns and operates a chain of food stores. Established: 1854.

KEY STATISTICS Number of Employees: 24,200.

EXPERTISE/EDUCATION SOUGHT: Accounting, management information systems, human resources, program analysis, computer-aided design, retail management

CONTACT: For individuals with previous experience: Ms Laurie Theroux, Employment Manager, PO Box 4737, Syracuse, NY, 13221; Phone (315) 453-7284; Fax (315) 453-8583.

PENNSYLVANIA BLUE SHIELD
1800 CENTER STREET
CAMP HILL, PENNSYLVANIA 17011-1702

OVERVIEW: Provides health insurance. Established: 1940.

KEY STATISTICS Annual Sales: $3.0 billion. Number of Employees: 6,200.

EXPERTISE/EDUCATION SOUGHT: Nursing, accounting, auditing, customer service and support, claims adjustment/examination

CONTACT: For individuals with previous experience: Ms Cindy Fox, Manager of Employment.

PENSKE CORPORATION
13400 WEST OUTER DRIVE
DETROIT, MICHIGAN 48239-1309

OVERVIEW: Manufactures truck engines, operates automobile dealerships, and provides truck rental services. Established: 1969.

KEY STATISTICS Annual Sales: $3.0 billion. Number of Employees: 11,000.

EXPERTISE/EDUCATION SOUGHT: Electrical engineering, mechanical engineering, industrial engineering, manufacturing engineering

CONTACT: Ms Joanne Fennicks, Corporate Manager of Salaried Personnel; Phone (313) 592-5000, ext. 7639.

PENSKE TRUCK LEASING COMPANY, LP.
ROUTE 10 GREEN HILLS
READING, PENNSYLVANIA 19603

OVERVIEW: Provides truck rental and leasing services. Established: 1988.

EXPERTISE/EDUCATION SOUGHT: Accounting, administration, finance, project management, law, environmental engineering, sales, production management

CONTACTS: For college students and recent graduates: Ms Tammy Russell, Human Resources Representative; Phone (610) 775-6000. For individuals with previous experience: Mr John W Kaisoglas, Vice President of Employment and Compensation; Phone (610) 775-6202.

PENTAIR, INC.
1500 COUNTY ROAD, B2 WEST
SAINT PAUL, MINNESOTA 55113

OVERVIEW: Manufactures industrial machinery. Established: 1966.

EXPERTISE/EDUCATION SOUGHT: Manufacturing engineering, industrial engineering, electrical engineering, information systems, computer science, computer programming, marketing, finance, accounting, business administration

CONTACT: Ms Debborah Knutson, Director of Recruiting; Phone (612) 639-5206.

PEOPLES ENERGY CORPORATION
130 EAST RANDOLPH DRIVE
CHICAGO, ILLINOIS 60601

OVERVIEW: Gas utility. Established: 1968.

EXPERTISE/EDUCATION SOUGHT: Accounting, mechanical engineering, electrical engineering, civil engineering, computer science, marketing, computer programming, finance, auditing, chemical engineering

CONTACTS: For college students and recent graduates: Ms C James, Senior Personnel Representative; Phone (312) 240-4000. For individuals with previous experience: Mr Ronald Schafer, Supervisor of Employment; Phone (312) 240-4000.

PEOPLES GAS SYSTEM, INC.
111 EAST MADISON STREET, PO BOX 2562
TAMPA, FLORIDA 33602-4719

OVERVIEW: Distributes natural gas. Established: 1978. Parent Company: Lykes Energy, Inc.

KEY STATISTICS Number of Employees: 1,100.

HIRING HISTORY Number of professional employees hired in 1994: 15.

CONTACT: Ms Teri Sturgill, Human Resources Administrator; Phone (813) 273-0074.

PEP BOYS
3111 WEST ALLEGHANY AVENUE
PHILADELPHIA, PENNSYLVANIA 19132

OVERVIEW: Operates retail chain selling automotive parts and supplies. Established: 1921.

KEY STATISTICS Annual Sales: $1.0 billion. Number of Employees: 14,500.

HIRING HISTORY Number of professional employees hired in 1994: 100.

EXPERTISE/EDUCATION SOUGHT: Marketing, purchasing, finance, customer service and support, auditing, law, human resources, retail, management information systems, computer programming

CONTACTS: For college students and recent graduates: Ms Ursula Ballard, Human Resources Generalist; Phone (215) 229-9000. For individuals with previous experience: Mr Thomas Ruggieri, Assistant Vice President of Human Resources; Phone (215) 229-9000.

PEPPERIDGE FARM, INC.
595 WESTPORT AVENUE
NORWALK, CONNECTICUT 06851

OVERVIEW: Manufactures and supplies baked goods. Established: 1937. Parent Company: Campbell Investment Company.

HIRING HISTORY Number of professional employees hired in 1994: 4.

EXPERTISE/EDUCATION SOUGHT: Project engineering, accounting, marketing, computer programming

CONTACT: For college students and recent graduates: Ms Debbie Salvas, Coordinator of Human Resources Services; Phone (203) 846-7265.

PEPSI-COLA GENERAL BOTTLERS
3501 ALGONQUIN ROAD
ROLLING MEADOW, ILLINOIS 60008-3103

OVERVIEW: Manufactures and bottles soft drinks. Established: 1939.

KEY STATISTICS Annual Sales: $1.0 billion. Number of Employees: 4,650.

EXPERTISE/EDUCATION SOUGHT: Accounting, chemical engineering, marketing, finance, mechanical engineering, sales, electrical engineering, law

CONTACT: For individuals with previous experience: Mr Greg Hinton, Manager of Personnel; Phone (708) 253-1000.

PEPSI-COLA, INC.
1 PEPSI WAY
SOMERS, NEW YORK 10589

OVERVIEW: Produces soft drinks. Established: 1902.

EXPERTISE/EDUCATION SOUGHT: Marketing, planning, finance, sales

CONTACT: Mr John Delpino, Director of Prefessional Placement; Phone (914) 767-6000.

PEPSICO, INC.
ANDERSON HILL ROAD
PURCHASE, NEW YORK 10577-1444

OVERVIEW: Manufactures soft drinks and snack foods; operates fast food restaurants. Established: 1898.

EXPERTISE/EDUCATION SOUGHT: Finance, strategic planning, auditing, management information systems

CONTACT: For individuals with previous experience: Mr Ron Parker, Vice President of Corporate Human Resources; Phone (914) 253-2000; Fax (914) 253-2661.

PERCEPTICS CORPORATION
725 PELLISSIPPI PARKWAY
KNOXVILLE, TENNESSEE 37932-3300

OVERVIEW: Manufactures and distributes optical storage equipment. Established: 1989. Parent Company: Westinghouse.

KEY STATISTICS Annual Sales: $22.0 million. Number of Employees: 90.

HIRING HISTORY Number of professional employees hired in 1994: 30.

EXPERTISE/EDUCATION SOUGHT: Image processing, software engineering/development, documentation

CONTACT: For individuals with previous experience: Mr Jim Disney, Director of Human Resources; Phone (615) 966-9200.

PERINI CORPORATION
73 MOUNT WAYTE AVENUE
FRAMINGHAM, MASSACHUSETTS 01701-5800

OVERVIEW: Provides construction and real estate development services. Established: 1895.

KEY STATISTICS Number of Employees: 1,900.

HIRING HISTORY Number of professional employees hired in 1994: 70. 1993: 100.

EXPERTISE/EDUCATION SOUGHT: Civil engineering, accounting

CONTACT: Mr Douglas Mure, Vice President of Human Resources; Phone (508) 628-2223.

PERKINS FAMILY RESTAURANT
6075 POPLAR AVENUE, SUITE 800
MEMPHIS, TENNESSEE 38119

Overview: Owns and operates chain of restaurants.

Key Statistics Annual Sales: $800.0 million. Number of Employees: 33,000.

Expertise/Education Sought: Food services, management

Contact: Ms Teresa Hester, Corporate Human Resources Manager; Phone (708) 766-6400.

PERMANENTE MEDICAL GROUP, INC.
1950 FRANKLIN STREET
OAKLAND, CALIFORNIA 94612-5103

Overview: Provides health care services. Established: 1945.

Key Statistics Annual Sales: $2.0 billion. Number of Employees: 17,000.

Expertise/Education Sought: Management information systems, data processing, computer science, human resources, accounting, finance, marketing

Contacts: For college students and recent graduates: Ms Carli Watney, Director of Personnel; Phone (510) 987-2787. For individuals with previous experience: Ms Angie Aquino-Sales, Recruiter Coordinator; Phone (510) 987-2787.

THE PERRIER GROUP AMERICA
777 WEST PUTNAM AVENUE
GREENWICH, CONNECTICUT 06830

Overview: Distributes bottled water.

Expertise/Education Sought: Accounting, marketing, finance, sales, merchandising, manufacturing, operations

Contact: For individuals with previous experience: Ms Christine Walchuk, Manager of Human Resources; Phone (203) 863-0306.

PETRIE STORES CORPORATION
70 ENTERPRISE AVENUE
SECAUCUS, NEW JERSEY 07094-2567

Overview: Owns and operates women's and children's apparel stores. Established: 1932.

Key Statistics Annual Sales: $1.0 billion. Number of Employees: 17,500.

Expertise/Education Sought: Merchandising, purchasing, accounting, marketing

Contact: Ms Patricia Hughes, Vice President of Human Resources; Phone (201) 866-3600, ext. 7303.

PFIZER, INC.
235 EAST 42ND STREET
NEW YORK, NEW YORK 10017

Overview: Manufactures medical, consumer, and food science products, veterinary drugs, and pharmaceuticals. Established: 1849.

Expertise/Education Sought: Sales, chemistry, computer science, marketing, biology, business administration, human resources

Contact: Ms Faye Williams, Associate Manager of University Relations.

PHAR-MOR, INC.
20 FEDERAL PLAZA WEST
YOUNGSTOWN, OHIO 44503-1498

Overview: Operates chain of discount drug stores.

Key Statistics Annual Sales: $2.0 billion. Number of Employees: 18,275.

Expertise/Education Sought: Accounting, marketing, computer programming, retail

Contact: Mr Greg Eckert, Director of Human Resources; Phone (216) 746-6641.

PHH VEHICLE MANAGEMENT SERVICES
11333 MCCORMICK ROAD
HUNT VALLEY, MARYLAND 21031-1001

Overview: Provides vehicle management services. Established: 1946.

Key Statistics Number of Employees: 4,900.

Expertise/Education Sought: Management information systems, accounting, finance, sales, data processing, customer service and support

Contact: Ms Karen Otto, Employment Specialist; Phone (410) 771-2561.

PHIBRO ENERGY USA, INC.
300 DALLAS, SUITE 3200
HOUSTON, TEXAS 77002-8258

Overview: Refines petroleum. Established: 1985. Parent Company: Salomon, Inc.

Key Statistics Annual Sales: $8.0 billion. Number of Employees: 1,650.

Expertise/Education Sought: Operations, accounting, marketing, chemical engineering, planning

Contact: For individuals with previous experience: Human Resources.

PHILIP MORRIS, INC.
120 PARK AVENUE
NEW YORK, NEW YORK 10017-5592

Overview: Manufactures tobacco products, beer, and packaged foods. Parent Company: Philip Morris Companies, Inc.

Expertise/Education Sought: Sales, finance, engineering, research

Contact: Mr John J Tucker, Senior Vice President of Human Resources; Phone (212) 880-5000.

For more information, see full corporate profile, pg. 214.

PHILLIPS ELECTRONICS
100 EAST 42ND STREET
NEW YORK, NEW YORK 10017

Overview: Manufactures consumer and industrial electronics equipment. Established: 1959. Parent Company: FGP Corporation.

Key Statistics Number of Employees: 35,000.

Hiring History Number of professional employees hired in 1994: 10.

Expertise/Education Sought: Accounting, human resources, law, communications, auditing, tax, treasury management

Contact: For individuals with previous experience: Ms Marlene Weiss, Supervisor of Human Resources; Phone (212) 850-5000.

PHILLIPS PETROLEUM COMPANY
4TH AND KEELER
BARTLESVILLE, OKLAHOMA 74004

Overview: Discovers oil and gas, produces, refines and markets petroleum products. Established: 1917.

Expertise/Education Sought: Business administration, finance, marketing, chemical engineering, mechanical engineering, electrical engineering, petroleum/petrochemical engineering, environmental engineering, geoscience

Contact: For individuals with previous experience: Mr J D Blakemore, Jr, Manager of Employment and College Relations; Phone (918) 661-6600, ext. 1044.

PHILLIPS-VAN HEUSEN
1001 FRONTIER ROAD
BRIDEGWATER, NEW JERSEY 08807

OVERVIEW: Manufactures clothing and jewelry. Established: 1970.

EXPERTISE/EDUCATION SOUGHT: Accounting, finance, marketing, computer programming, merchandising

CONTACT: Ms Betty Chaves, Director of Human Resources; Phone (908) 685-0050, ext. 5282.

PHILLIPS-VAN HEUSEN CORPORATION
1290 AVENUE OF THE AMERICAS
NEW YORK, NEW YORK 10104

OVERVIEW: Manufactures shirts and other apparel. Established: 1859.

EXPERTISE/EDUCATION SOUGHT: Management, human resources, accounting, computer programming, management information systems

CONTACT: Ms Barbara Berkepile, Director Human Resources; Phone (212) 541-5200.

PHYSICIANS MUTUAL INSURANCE COMPANY
2600 DODGE STREET
OHAMA, NEBRASKA 68131-2671

OVERVIEW: Provides medical insurance. Established: 1902.

KEY STATISTICS Annual Sales: $494.1 million. Number of Employees: 1,410.

EXPERTISE/EDUCATION SOUGHT: Accounting, computer programming, systems analysis

CONTACT: For individuals with previous experience: Ms Lise Gjelsten, Vice President of Human Resources; Phone (402) 633-1000, ext. 1151.

PICCADILLY CAFETERIAS
PO BOX 2467, DEPARTMENT PG
BATON ROUGE, LOUISIANA 70821

OVERVIEW: Provides food service. Established: 1944.

KEY STATISTICS Annual Sales: $275.0 million. Number of Employees: 9,000.

HIRING HISTORY Number of professional employees hired in 1993: 200.

EXPERTISE/EDUCATION SOUGHT: Food services, business administration, hospitality/hotel and restaurant management

CONTACT: For individuals with previous experience: Mr Joe Polito, Director of Training; Phone (800) 942-7422.

CORPORATE STATEMENT

Piccadilly Cafeterias, Inc. operates 132 cafeterias located in 16 states. Annual sales are approximately $275 million. The company's real estate division is continually seeking new cafeteria sites to fill expansion plans. All units are corporate owned, providing unit managers the opportunity to advance to the top levels of the company.

PICKER INTERNATIONAL, INC.
595 MINER ROAD
HIGLAND'S HEIGHTS, OHIO 44143

OVERVIEW: Manufactures medical diagnostic equipment. Established: 1930. Parent Company: GEC, Inc.

EXPERTISE/EDUCATION SOUGHT: Marketing, finance, sales, accounting

CONTACT: Mr Mike Moran, Director of Staffing and Recruiting; Phone (216) 473-3524.

PICTURETEL CORPORATION
222 ROSEWOOD DRIVE
DANVERS, MASSACHUSETTS 01923-4590

OVERVIEW: Manufactures video conferencing equipment. Established: 1984.

KEY STATISTICS Annual Sales: $176.0 million. Number of Employees: 811.

EXPERTISE/EDUCATION SOUGHT: Sales, marketing, accounting, research and development, hardware engineering, software engineering/development, computer science, electronics/electronics engineering

CONTACT: For individuals with previous experience: Mr Joe McGrath, Staffing Manager; Phone (508) 762-5000.

PIEDMONT NATURAL GAS COMPANY
1915 REXFORD ROAD
CHARLOTTE, NORTH CAROLINA 28211-3446

OVERVIEW: Distributes natural gas products. Established: 1950.

KEY STATISTICS Annual Sales: $584.0 million. Number of Employees: 1,947.

EXPERTISE/EDUCATION SOUGHT: Computer programming, data processing, accounting, marketing, finance

CONTACT: Mr Darryl Rabon, Supervisor/Employment.

PIER 1 IMPORTS, INC.
301 COMMERCE STREET, SUITE 600
FORT WORTH, TEXAS 76102-4140

OVERVIEW: Operates retail store chain selling housewares, clothing and furnishings. Established: 1962.

KEY STATISTICS Annual Sales: $685.0 million. Number of Employees: 8,227.

EXPERTISE/EDUCATION SOUGHT: Merchandising, accounting, finance, computer programming, advertising, operations, retail management

CONTACT: For individuals with previous experience: Ms Tawney McCarty, Staffing Manager, PO Box 961020, Fort Worth, TX, 76161-0020; Phone (817) 878-8446.

PILGRIMS PRIDE CORPORATION
110 SOUTH TEXAS STREET
PITTSBURG, TEXAS 75686-1532

OVERVIEW: Provides poultry processing services. Established: 1945.

KEY STATISTICS Number of Employees: 10,700.

EXPERTISE/EDUCATION SOUGHT: Accounting, finance, marketing, computer programming, management information systems, data processing

CONTACT: Ms Goldie Harwell, Manager of Employee Relations.

THE PILLSBURY COMPANY
PILLSBURY CENTER, 200 SOUTH 6TH STREET
MINNEAPOLIS, MINNESOTA 55402-1464

OVERVIEW: Manufactures flour, grain, and other food products. Established: 1935.

EXPERTISE/EDUCATION SOUGHT: Sales, marketing, accounting, finance, human resources, operations

CONTACT: For individuals with previous experience: Ms Sandy Ohlson, Director of Personnel Development; Phone (612) 330-4966.

PINKERTON'S, INC.
15910 VENTURA BOULEVARD
ENCINO, CALIFORNIA 91436

OVERVIEW: Provides security and investigation services. Established: 1850.

KEY STATISTICS Annual Sales: $772.0 million. Number of Employees: 47,000.

EXPERTISE/EDUCATION SOUGHT: Systems analysis, accounting, finance, marketing, computer programming, law, administration

Pinkerton's, Inc. (continued)

CONTACTS: For college students and recent graduates: Mr Charlie Maulini, Employee Relations Assistant, 6727 Odessa Avenue, Van Nuys, CA, 91406; Phone (818) 782-5400. For individuals with previous experience: Ms JoAnn McGuff, Senior Manager of Personnel; Phone (818) 380-8800.

PIONEER HI-BRED INTERNATIONAL, INC.
700 CAPITAL SQUARE 400
DES MOINES, IOWA 50309

OVERVIEW: Provides worldwide agrigenetic research services. Established: 1926.

KEY STATISTICS Annual Sales: $1.0 billion. Number of Employees: 4,807.

EXPERTISE/EDUCATION SOUGHT: Sales, marketing, finance, research, product design and development, information systems, communications

CONTACTS: For college students and recent graduates: Mr John Day, Employment Manager; Phone (515) 270-4114. For individuals with previous experience: Human Resource Department, 6800 Pioneer Parkway, Johnston, IA, 50131; Phone (515) 270-4200.

PIPER JAFFRAY, INC.
229 SOUTH 9TH STREET
MINNEAPOLIS, MINNESOTA 55402-3389

OVERVIEW: Investment banking firm. Established: 1974.

KEY STATISTICS Number of Employees: 2,365.

HIRING HISTORY Number of professional employees hired in 1994: 475.

EXPERTISE/EDUCATION SOUGHT: Economics, business administration, accounting

CONTACT: For individuals with previous experience: Ms Dyann Hendrickson, Corporate Employment Representative, PO Box 28, Minneapolis, MN, 55440-0028.

PITNEY BOWES, INC.
1 ELMCROFT ROAD
STANFORD, CONNECTICUT 06926

OVERVIEW: Provides business equipment and business and financial services. Established: 1920.

HIRING HISTORY Number of professional employees hired in 1994: 200.

EXPERTISE/EDUCATION SOUGHT: Software engineering/development, mechanical engineering, electrical engineering, computer programming, systems engineering

CONTACT: For individuals with previous experience: Mr Guss Stepp, Director of Employment; Phone (203) 351-6421.

THE PITTSTON COMPANY
100 FIRST STAMFORD PLACE
STAMFORD, CONNECTICUT 06912

OVERVIEW: Mines, processes, and markets coal and minerals. Established: 1930.

KEY STATISTICS Number of Employees: 22,800.

EXPERTISE/EDUCATION SOUGHT: Marketing, accounting, finance, auditing, data processing, geology, mechanical engineering, computer programming, tax accounting

CONTACT: Mr Edward Cox, Director of Employee Relations; Phone (203) 978-5200.

PITTWAY CORPORATION
200 SOUTH WACKER DRIVE, SUITE 700
CHICAGO, ILLINOIS 60606-5802

OVERVIEW: Manufactures burglar and fire alarm systems and publishes magazines. Established: 1925.

KEY STATISTICS Annual Sales: $650.0 million. Number of Employees: 8,500.

HIRING HISTORY Number of professional employees hired in 1994: 300. 1993: 300.

EXPERTISE/EDUCATION SOUGHT: Accounting, finance, auditing, tax

CONTACT: For individuals with previous experience: Ms Peggy Odegaard, Recruiter; Phone (312) 831-1070.

PIZZA HUT AMERICA, INC.
9111 EAST DOUGLAS
WICHITA, KANSAS 67207

OVERVIEW: Operates chain of pizza restaurants. Established: 1958.

EXPERTISE/EDUCATION SOUGHT: Accounting, marketing, auditing, law, finance, consulting, computer programming

CONTACT: For individuals with previous experience: Employment Manager, PO Box 428, Wichita, KS, 67201.

PLANTATION BOTANICALS, INC.
1401 COUNTY ROAD 830
FELDA, FLORIDA 33930

OVERVIEW: Grows and distributes miniature rosebuds for flower industry. Established: 1964.

KEY STATISTICS Annual Sales: $60.0 million. Number of Employees: 470.

EXPERTISE/EDUCATION SOUGHT: Accounting, finance, data processing

CONTACT: For individuals with previous experience: Mr Marlin Hoffman, Chairman of the Board; Phone (813) 675-2984.

PLASTIPAK PACKAGING, INC.
9135 GENERAL COURT
PLYMOUTH, MICHIGAN 48170-4621

OVERVIEW: Manufactures plastic packaging. Established: 1956.

KEY STATISTICS Annual Sales: $235.0 million. Number of Employees: 1,300.

EXPERTISE/EDUCATION SOUGHT: Sales, marketing, accounting, data processing, distribution, manufacturing, quality control

CONTACT: For individuals with previous experience: Human Resources Department; Phone (313) 455-3600.

PLAYTEX APPAREL, INC.
700 FAIRFIELD AVENUE
STAMFORD, CONNECTICUT 06902-7526

OVERVIEW: Manufactures women's undergarments.

KEY STATISTICS Annual Sales: $329.0 million. Number of Employees: 7,400.

EXPERTISE/EDUCATION SOUGHT: Sales, marketing, finance

CONTACT: Human Resources Department; Phone (203) 356-8000.

PMI FOOD EQUIPMENT GROUP
710 RIDGE AVENUE
TROY, OHIO 45374

OVERVIEW: Supplies equipment, systems and services to world's food industry. Established: 1986. Parent Company: Premark International.

KEY STATISTICS Annual Sales: $1.0 billion. Number of Employees: 9,600.

EXPERTISE/EDUCATION SOUGHT: Accounting, engineering, sales, computer science

CONTACT: Ms Nancy R Smith, Human Resources Administrator; Phone (513) 332-2423.

PNC BANK
500 WEST JEFFERSON STREET
LOUISVILLE, KENTUCKY 40202-2851

OVERVIEW: State commercial bank. Established: 1968.

KEY STATISTICS Assets: $281.0 million. Number of Employees: 2,200.

EXPERTISE/EDUCATION SOUGHT: Finance, accounting

CONTACTS: For college students and recent graduates: Mr Jerry Seelbach, Director of Human Resources. For individuals with previous experience: Ms Allison Laferty, Assistant Vice President Personnel; Phone (502) 581-2679.

PNC BANK
FIFTH AVENUE & WOOD STREET
PITTSBURGH, PENNSYLVANIA 15265

OVERVIEW: Commercial banking and financial services company. Established: 1968.

KEY STATISTICS Assets: $4.0 billion. Number of Employees: 21,060.

EXPERTISE/EDUCATION SOUGHT: Accounting, auditing, finance

CONTACT: For individuals with previous experience: Mr Frank Cepits, Vice President of Human Resources; Phone (412) 762-5047.

POLAROID CORPORATION
549 TECHNOLOGY SQUARE
CAMBRIDGE, MASSACHUSETTS 02139

OVERVIEW: Manufactures photographic and imaging equipment. Established: 1937.

EXPERTISE/EDUCATION SOUGHT: Mechanical engineering, optics, electrical engineering, physics, information systems, finance, chemical engineering, chemistry, computer science

CONTACTS: For college students and recent graduates: Mr Florence B Ramos-Jones, Manager Corporate College Recruiting, 565 Technology Square, Cambridge, MA, 02139; Phone (617) 386-3979. For individuals with previous experience: Mr Joseph G Parham, Jr, Vice President of Human Resources; Phone (617) 386-3214.

POLICY MANAGEMENT SYSTEMS CORPORATION
ONE PMS CENTER, WILSON BOULEVARD
BLYTHEWOOD, SOUTH CAROLINA 29016

OVERVIEW: Provides insurance software systems support services. Established: 1974.

KEY STATISTICS Annual Sales: $453.0 million. Number of Employees: 4,786.

EXPERTISE/EDUCATION SOUGHT: Accounting, marketing, sales, finance, data processing

CONTACT: Mr Wes Daniels, Manager of Recruiting, PO Box 10, Columbia, SC, 29202; Phone (803) 735-4000.

R. L. POLK AND COMPANY
1155 BREWERY PARKWAY
DETROIT, MICHIGAN 48207-2697

OVERVIEW: Markets information services for direct marketers. Established: 1870.

KEY STATISTICS Annual Sales: $386.0 million. Number of Employees: 4,000.

EXPERTISE/EDUCATION SOUGHT: Sales, marketing, computer programming

CONTACT: For individuals with previous experience: Mr David Piwowar, Director of Human Resources; Phone (313) 393-0880.

POLYGRAM RECORDS, INC.
825 8TH AVENUE
NEW YORK, NEW YORK 10019-7416

OVERVIEW: Prepares master records and tapes.

KEY STATISTICS Annual Sales: $268.0 million. Number of Employees: 2,200.

EXPERTISE/EDUCATION SOUGHT: Marketing, law, management information systems, accounting, finance

CONTACT: Mr John Henkel, Manager Human Resources.

PONY EXPRESS COURIER CORPORATION
555077 CENTER DRIVE
CHARLOTTE, NORTH CAROLINA 28217

OVERVIEW: Provides courier services. Established: 1975.

KEY STATISTICS Annual Sales: $156.9 million. Number of Employees: 6,000.

EXPERTISE/EDUCATION SOUGHT: Transportation, sales

CONTACT: For individuals with previous experience: Human Resources; Phone (704) 527-7121.

THE PORT AUTHORITY OF NEW YORK AND NEW JERSEY
1 WORLD TRADE CENTER
NEW YORK, NEW YORK 10048

OVERVIEW: Provides transportation services. Established: 1921.

EXPERTISE/EDUCATION SOUGHT: Transportation, accounting, structural engineering, marketing, finance, public policy and planning, civil engineering, environmental engineering, electrical engineering, mechanical engineering

CONTACTS: For college students and recent graduates: Ms Carol Keppler, Coordinator of College Relations; Phone (212) 435-4687. For individuals with previous experience: Mr Michael Massiah, Assistant Manager of Human Resources; Phone (212) 435-4690.

PORTLAND GENERAL CORPORATION
121 SOUTHWEST SALMON STREET
PORTLAND, OREGON 97204-2995

OVERVIEW: Provides real estate development and construction services.

KEY STATISTICS Assets: $947.0 million. Number of Employees: 2,618.

EXPERTISE/EDUCATION SOUGHT: Management, business management, computer programming, program analysis, drafting, computer-aided design

CONTACT: Ms Neena Kersh, Manager of Staffing Services; Phone (503) 464-7255.

POTOMAC ELECTRIC POWER COMPANY
1900 PENNSYLVANIA AVENUE NORTHWEST
WASHINGTON, D.C. 20068-0002

OVERVIEW: Electric utility. Established: 1896.

KEY STATISTICS Number of Employees: 5,100.

HIRING HISTORY Number of professional employees hired in 1994: 5.

EXPERTISE/EDUCATION SOUGHT: Electrical engineering, technical engineering, accounting, human resources

CONTACT: Ms Carolyn Bostick, Manager Employment; Phone (202) 872-2101.

PPG INDUSTRIES, INC.
1 PPG PLACE
PITTSBURGH, PENNSYLVANIA 15272

OVERVIEW: Produces chemicals, glass, coatings, and resins. Established: 1883.

HIRING HISTORY Number of professional employees hired in 1994: 65.

EXPERTISE/EDUCATION SOUGHT: Management information systems, accounting, chemistry, computer science, human resources, marketing, chemical engineering, electrical engineering, mechanical engineering, civil engineering

CONTACT: Mr Don Stine, Manager of Staffing; Phone (412) 434-3441.

PRAIRIE FARMS DAIRY, INC.
1100 NORTH BROADWAY STREET
CARLINVILLE, ILLINOIS 62626-1183

OVERVIEW: Produces dairy products. Established: 1938.

KEY STATISTICS Annual Sales: $92.8 million. Number of Employees: 1,843.

HIRING HISTORY Number of professional employees hired in 1994: 5.

EXPERTISE/EDUCATION SOUGHT: Biological sciences, agricultural science, accounting

CONTACT: For individuals with previous experience: Mr Thomas Beichler, Vice President of Human Resources; Phone (217) 854-2547.

PRAXAIR, INC.
39 OLD RIDGEBURY ROAD
DANBURY, CONNECTICUT 06810-5113

OVERVIEW: Manufactures industrial gases. Established: 1989.

KEY STATISTICS Annual Sales: $2.0 billion. Number of Employees: 16,766.

EXPERTISE/EDUCATION SOUGHT: Accounting, finance, marketing, chemical engineering, mechanical engineering, electrical engineering

CONTACT: Human Resources Department; Phone (203) 794-3000.

PREMARK INTERNATIONAL, INC.
1717 DEERFIELD ROAD
DEERFIELD, ILLINOIS 60015

OVERVIEW: Manufactures and markets consumer and household products. Established: 1986.

KEY STATISTICS Annual Sales: $3.0 billion. Number of Employees: 24,000.

EXPERTISE/EDUCATION SOUGHT: Management

CONTACT: For individuals with previous experience: Human Resources Department; Phone (708) 405-6000.

PREMIER SALONS INTERNATIONAL
12800 WHITEWATER DRIVE
MINNETONKA, MINNESOTA 55343-9471

OVERVIEW: Operates chain of beauty shops.

KEY STATISTICS Annual Sales: $204.0 million. Number of Employees: 10,000.

HIRING HISTORY Number of professional employees hired in 1994: 5.

EXPERTISE/EDUCATION SOUGHT: Marketing, construction, purchasing, administration, management, computer programming, program analysis

CONTACT: For individuals with previous experience: Mr Bob Sander, Vice President Human Resources.

PRENTICE-HALL LEGAL AND FINANCIAL SERVICES
375 HUDSON STREET
NEW YORK, NEW YORK 10014-7706

OVERVIEW: Publishes legal and financial books, newsletters, and reports. Parent Company: Paramount Communications.

KEY STATISTICS Annual Sales: $933.0 million. Number of Employees: 8,000.

EXPERTISE/EDUCATION SOUGHT: Law, accounting, finance, advertising, marketing

CONTACT: For individuals with previous experience: Ms Bobbie Gill, Assistant Manager of Human Resources; Phone (212) 373-7500.

PRESTON CORPORATION
151 EASTON BOULEVARD
PRESTON, MARYLAND 21655

OVERVIEW: Provides truck freight and shipment services. Established: 1932.

KEY STATISTICS Annual Sales: $547.0 million. Number of Employees: 5,000.

EXPERTISE/EDUCATION SOUGHT: Accounting, finance, sales, marketing, data processing

CONTACT: For individuals with previous experience: Ms Alison Ball, Director of Human Resources Compliance; Phone (410) 673-7151.

PRICE COSTCO
10809 120TH AVENUE NORTHEAST
KIRKLAND, WASHINGTON 98033-5024

OVERVIEW: Sells discounted general merchandise to the public. Established: 1976.

KEY STATISTICS Annual Sales: $8.0 billion. Number of Employees: 22,070.

EXPERTISE/EDUCATION SOUGHT: Accounting, graphic arts, marketing, sales, computer programming, law, finance, business management, customer service and support

CONTACT: Human Resources Department; Phone (206) 803-8100.

PRICE WATERHOUSE
1251 6TH AVENUE
NEW YORK, NEW YORK 10020

OVERVIEW: Accounting and auditing firm. Established: 1890.

EXPERTISE/EDUCATION SOUGHT: Accounting, auditing, human resources, marketing, computer programming

CONTACT: Mr Larry Scott, National Director of Recruiting; Phone (212) 819-5000.

PRIMARK CORPORATION
1000 WINTER STREET, SUITE 4300 NORTH
WALTHAM, MASSACHUSETTS 02154-3809

OVERVIEW: Provides information technology services. Established: 1981.

KEY STATISTICS Annual Sales: $444.0 million. Number of Employees: 3,400.

EXPERTISE/EDUCATION SOUGHT: Human resources, law, accounting, finance, administration

CONTACT: For individuals with previous experience: Ms Diane Robson, Manager of Human Resources; Phone (703) 790-7600.

PRINCE CORPORATION
1 PRINCE CENTER
HOLLAND, MICHIGAN 49423-5407

OVERVIEW: Manufactures and distributes automotive trim and accessories.

KEY STATISTICS Number of Employees: 2,500.

EXPERTISE/EDUCATION SOUGHT: Accounting, finance, data processing, sales, automotive engineering

CONTACT: Mr Robert Farnum, Manager of Staffing; Phone (616) 392-5151.

PRINCESS CRUISES, INC.
10100 SANTA MONICA BOULEVARD
LOS ANGELES, CALIFORNIA 90067-4003

OVERVIEW: Owns and operates cruise ships. Established: 1976.

KEY STATISTICS Annual Sales: $484.0 million. Number of Employees: 5,000.

EXPERTISE/EDUCATION SOUGHT: Sales, marketing, computer programming, data processing, hospitality/hotel and restaurant management, navigation, accounting, finance

CONTACT: For individuals with previous experience: Ms Heidi Dunlay, Manager of Human Resources; Phone (310) 553-1770, ext. 6255.

PRINCIPAL MUTUAL LIFE INSURANCE COMPANY
711 HIGH STREET
DES MOINES, IOWA 50392-0001

OVERVIEW: Manages financial service companies. Established: 1879.

KEY STATISTICS Assets: $12.0 billion. Number of Employees: 14,275.

HIRING HISTORY Number of professional employees hired in 1994: 600.

EXPERTISE/EDUCATION SOUGHT: Accounting, marketing, finance, management information systems, health insurance, underwriting, administration

CONTACT: For individuals with previous experience: Mr T Gordon Welton, Corporate Placement Recruiter; Phone (515) 248-2181; Fax (515)247-5874.

THE PROCTER AND GAMBLE COMPANY
1 PROCTER & GAMBLE PLAZA
CINCINNATI, OHIO 45202

OVERVIEW: Manufactures consumer, health and household products. Established: 1837.

HIRING HISTORY Number of professional employees hired in 1994: 700.

EXPERTISE/EDUCATION SOUGHT: Sales, advertising, marketing, finance, accounting, auditing, systems integration, manufacturing engineering, chemical engineering, purchasing

CONTACTS: For college students and recent graduates: Mr Robert T Pike, College Relations Director; Phone (513) 983-1100. For individuals with previous experience: Mr William Reina, Director of US Recruiting; Phone (513) 983-8583.

PROGRESS SOFTWARE CORPORATION
14 OAK PARK DRIVE
BEDFORD, MASSACHUSETTS 01730-1485

OVERVIEW: Develops application development software. Established: 1981.

KEY STATISTICS Annual Sales: $62.0 million. Number of Employees: 792.

EXPERTISE/EDUCATION SOUGHT: Software engineering/development, accounting, finance, marketing

CONTACT: For individuals with previous experience: Mr Robert Clancy, Director of Human Resources; Phone (617) 275-4500.

PROGRESSIVE CORPORATION
6300 WILSON MILLS ROAD
CLEVELAND, OHIO 44143-2109

OVERVIEW: Provides casualty, business, and life insurance. Established: 1937.

KEY STATISTICS Assets: $2.0 billion. Number of Employees: 5,900.

EXPERTISE/EDUCATION SOUGHT: Claims adjustment/examination, customer service and support

CONTACT: Employment Center; Phone (800) 888-4473.

PROGRESSIVE COUNTY MUTUAL INSURANCE COMPANY
1701 DIRECTORS BOULEVARD
AUSTIN, TEXAS 78744-1054

OVERVIEW: Automobile insurance provider. Established: 1975.

KEY STATISTICS Annual Sales: $143.1 million. Number of Employees: 450.

EXPERTISE/EDUCATION SOUGHT: Accounting, systems integration, finance

CONTACT: For individuals with previous experience: Ms Susan Schwartz, Human Resources Administrator; Phone (512) 441-2000.

PROVIDIAN CORPORATION
400 WEST MARKET STREET
LOUISVILLE, KENTUCKY 40202-3346

OVERVIEW: Provides insurance, financial, and banking services.

KEY STATISTICS Annual Sales: $3.0 billion. Number of Employees: 9,360.

EXPERTISE/EDUCATION SOUGHT: Accounting, marketing, strategic planning, telemarketing, finance, business administration

CONTACT: For individuals with previous experience: Ms Monica Cabell, Human Resources Analyst; Phone (502) 560-2199.

PRUDENTIAL INSURANCE OF AMERICA, INC.
751 BROAD STREET
NEWARK, NEW JERSEY 07102-3777

OVERVIEW: Provides financial services. Established: 1875.

KEY STATISTICS Number of Employees: 105,534.

EXPERTISE/EDUCATION SOUGHT: Computer programming, accounting, finance

CONTACTS: For college students and recent graduates: Ms Ignace Conic, College Recruiter; Phone (201) 802-7139. For individuals with previous experience: Ms Joan Ellen, Director Personnel Administration of Employment; Phone (201) 802-3917.

PRUDENTIAL PROPERTY CASUALTY
23 MAIN STREET
SOUTH PLAINFIELD, NEW JERSEY 07080-2305

OVERVIEW: Provides property and casualty insurance. Established: 1975. Parent Company: Pruco, Inc.

KEY STATISTICS Annual Sales: $1.5 billion. Number of Employees: 5,560.

EXPERTISE/EDUCATION SOUGHT: Computer programming, program analysis, accounting

CONTACT: For individuals with previous experience: Ms Linda Wilson, Manager of Human Resources; Phone (908) 946-5000.

PRUDENTIAL SECURITIES GROUP
199 WATER STREET, 33RD FLOOR
NEW YORK, NEW YORK 10292

OVERVIEW: Provides securities services. Established: 1879.

EXPERTISE/EDUCATION SOUGHT: Accounting, finance, actuarial, auditing, real estate, law

CONTACT: Ms Stephanie Stabile, Manager of Corporate Staffing, 1 New York Plaza, 3rd floor, New York, NY, 10292; Phone (212) 214-1000, ext. 2611.

PRUDENTIAL SECURITIES, INC.
1 SEAPORT PLAZA
NEW YORK, NEW YORK 10292-3526

OVERVIEW: Provides brokerage, investment, and related financial services. Established: 1981. Parent Company: Prudential Securities Group.

KEY STATISTICS Number of Employees: 18,595.

HIRING HISTORY Number of professional employees hired in 1994: 500.

EXPERTISE/EDUCATION SOUGHT: Finance, business, management information systems, accounting, computer science, data processing, marketing

CONTACTS: For college students and recent graduates: Ms Stephanie Stabile, Employment Manager. For individuals with previous experience: Mr John Mueller, Director of Human Resources, 100 Gold Street, 3rd Floor, New York, NY, 10292; Phone (212) 776-4483.

PSI ENERGY, INC.
1000 EAST MAIN STREET
PLAINFIELD, INDIANA 46168-1765

OVERVIEW: Electric utility. Established: 1912. Parent Company: PSI Resources, Inc.

KEY STATISTICS Number of Employees: 4,235.

HIRING HISTORY Number of professional employees hired in 1993: 75.

EXPERTISE/EDUCATION SOUGHT: Electrical engineering, mechanical engineering, accounting, law, computer programming, sales, administration, customer service and support, construction

CONTACTS: For college students and recent graduates: Mr Jerry Depask, Employment Services Coordinator; Phone (317) 839-9611. For individuals with previous experience: Mr Robert Nolan, Manager of Recruiting; Phone (317) 839-9611.

PUBLIC SERVICE COMPANY OF COLORADO
1225 17TH STREET
DENVER, COLORADO 80202-1501

OVERVIEW: Electric and gas utility. Established: 1906.

KEY STATISTICS Annual Sales: $2.0 billion. Number of Employees: 6,507.

EXPERTISE/EDUCATION SOUGHT: Finance, marketing, accounting, electrical engineering, mechanical engineering, human resources

CONTACT: For individuals with previous experience: Ms Diane Romero, Team Leader/Staffing, 1730 Blake Street, Denver, CO, 80202.

PUBLIC SERVICE ELECTRIC AND GAS COMPANY

80 PARK PLAZA
NEWARK, NEW JERSEY 07101

OVERVIEW: Public utility providing gas and electric service in the state of New Jersey. Established: 1903. Parent Company: Public Service Enterprise Group, Inc.

KEY STATISTICS Annual Sales: $6.0 billion. Number of Employees: 11,600.

EXPERTISE/EDUCATION SOUGHT: Computer science, electrical engineering, mechanical engineering, information systems, nuclear engineering

CONTACT: For individuals with previous experience: Mr Al Branca, Employment Manager, 234 Pierson Avenue, Edison, NJ, 08837; Phone (908) 417-2771; Fax (908)417-1159.

PUBLIC SERVICE ENTERPRISE GROUP

80 PARK PLAZA
NEWARK, NEW JERSEY 07102

OVERVIEW: Electric and gas utility holding company. Established: 1985.

EXPERTISE/EDUCATION SOUGHT: Electrical engineering, mechanical engineering, accounting, marketing, finance, sales

CONTACT: For individuals with previous experience: Employment Department; Phone (201) 430-7000, ext. 2771.

PUBLIC SERVICE OF NEW HAMPSHIRE

1000 ELM STREET
MANCHESTER, NEW HAMPSHIRE 03101-1730

OVERVIEW: Provides electric services. Established: 1992. Parent Company: Northeast Utilities Volunteer Association.

KEY STATISTICS Annual Sales: $864.0 million. Number of Employees: 1,640.

EXPERTISE/EDUCATION SOUGHT: Electrical engineering, mechanical engineering, civil engineering, accounting, marketing, finance

CONTACT: For individuals with previous experience: Ms Lori Levesque, Personnel Representative; Phone (603) 669-4000.

PUBLIX SUPER MARKETS, INC.

1936 GEORGE JENKINS BOULEVARD
LAKELAND, FLORIDA 33801-3760

OVERVIEW: Operates chain of food stores. Established: 1921.

KEY STATISTICS Number of Employees: 82,000.

EXPERTISE/EDUCATION SOUGHT: Retail, finance, sales, pharmacy, auditing, marketing

CONTACT: Mr Jim Rhodes, Vice President of Human Resources; Phone (813) 688-2216.

PURINA MILLS, INC.

1401 SOUTH HANLEY ROAD
SAINT LOUIS, MISSOURI 63144-2902

OVERVIEW: Manufactures livestock feed products. Established: 1896.

KEY STATISTICS Annual Sales: $369.0 million. Number of Employees: 2,500.

EXPERTISE/EDUCATION SOUGHT: Accounting, computer programming, sales, finance, management, controlling

CONTACT: Director of Human Resources; Phone (314) 731-2300.

PURITAN-BENNETT CORPORATION

9401 INDIAN CREEK PARKWAY
OVERLAND PARK, KANSAS 66210

OVERVIEW: Manufactures medical devices and other respiratory products. Established: 1913.

KEY STATISTICS Number of Employees: 2,571.

HIRING HISTORY Number of professional employees hired in 1994: 50. 1993: 6.

EXPERTISE/EDUCATION SOUGHT: Data processing, accounting, marketing, sales, mechanical engineering, electrical engineering

CONTACT: For individuals with previous experience: Ms Debbie Schuler, Corporate Human Resources Manager.

PURITY SUPERMARKETS, INC.

101 BILLERICA AVENUE
NORTH BILLERIC, MASSACHUSETTS 01862-1256

OVERVIEW: Operates chain of food stores. Established: 1935.

KEY STATISTICS Annual Sales: $881.0 million. Number of Employees: 6,389.

EXPERTISE/EDUCATION SOUGHT: Accounting, finance

CONTACT: For individuals with previous experience: Ms Julia Clark, Director of Equal Employment Opportunity and Employment; Phone (508) 663-0750.

PENTASTAR SERVICES

5330 EAST 31ST STREET
TULSA, OKLAHOMA 74135-5076

OVERVIEW: Provides car rental and leasing services. Established: 1990.

KEY STATISTICS Annual Sales: $639.0 million. Number of Employees: 5,900.

EXPERTISE/EDUCATION SOUGHT: Accounting, sales, marketing

CONTACT: For individuals with previous experience: Ms Michelle Choquette, Manager Recruitment and Employment; Phone (918) 660-7700.

QUAD GRAPHICS, INC.

W224 N3322 DUPLAINVILLE ROAD
PEWAUKEE, WISCONSIN 53072-4137

OVERVIEW: Provides commercial printing services. Established: 1971.

KEY STATISTICS Annual Sales: $700.0 million. Number of Employees: 6,800.

EXPERTISE/EDUCATION SOUGHT: Marketing, sales, accounting, data processing, information systems, electrical engineering, mechanical engineering

CONTACT: For individuals with previous experience: Ms Lenia Cooney, Director of Recruiting; Phone (414) 246-9200.

THE QUAKER OATS COMPANY

321 NORTH CLARK STREET
CHICAGO, ILLINOIS 60610-4714

OVERVIEW: Manufactures cereal products, processed foods, and pet foods. Established: 1901.

EXPERTISE/EDUCATION SOUGHT: Marketing, logistics, accounting, finance, computer programming, purchasing

CONTACT: For individuals with previous experience: Mr Michael Cohen, Vice President Human Resources Development; Phone (312) 222-7111.

QUALEX, INC.

3404 NORTH DUKE STREET
DURHAM, NORTH CAROLINA 27704-2130

OVERVIEW: Owns and operates photo finishing laboratories. Parent Company: Actava Group, Inc.

KEY STATISTICS Annual Sales: $775.0 million. Number of Employees: 8,000.

EXPERTISE/EDUCATION SOUGHT: Accounting, finance, marketing

CONTACT: For individuals with previous experience: Mr Brian Galpin, Human Resource Representative; Phone (919) 383-8535.

QUALITY SYSTEMS, INC.
4000 LEGATO ROAD, SUITE 1100
FAIRFAX, VIRGINIA 22033

OVERVIEW: Designs and develops integrated defense systems.

CONTACT: For individuals with previous experience: Ms Tina Shaffer, Corporate Recruiting Assistant; Phone (703) 218-1771.

QUEBECOR PRINTING CORPORATION
1999 SHEPARD ROAD
SAINT PAUL, MINNESOTA 55116-3210

OVERVIEW: Provides commercial printing services.

KEY STATISTICS Annual Sales: $695.0 million. Number of Employees: 7,000.

HIRING HISTORY Number of professional employees hired in 1994: 18.

EXPERTISE/EDUCATION SOUGHT: Accounting, customer service and support

CONTACT: For individuals with previous experience: Mr Ralph Ginnola, Human Resources Manager; Phone (612) 690-7200.

QUEBECOR PRINTING USA CORPORATION
125 HIGH STREET 23RD FLOOR
BOSTON, MASSACHUSETTS 02110

OVERVIEW: Provides printing services to publishers and direct marketers. Established: 1990.

EXPERTISE/EDUCATION SOUGHT: Graphic arts, electrical engineering, computer science, business, technical, finance, computer programming, mechanical engineering

CONTACT: For individuals with previous experience: Mr Donald Bush, Vice President Human Resources.

QVC NETWORK, INC.
1365 ENTERPRISE DRIVE
WEST CHESTER, PENNSYLVANIA 19380-5967

OVERVIEW: Provides cable television home shopping services. Established: 1986.

KEY STATISTICS Annual Sales: $1.0 billion. Number of Employees: 4,500.

EXPERTISE/EDUCATION SOUGHT: Accounting, finance, communications, production, sales, business management, graphic arts

CONTACT: For individuals with previous experience: Mr Michael Cavanough, Professional Recruiter; Phone (610) 701-1000, ext. 8456.

RADISSON HOTEL CORPORATION
CARLSON PARKWAY
MINNEAPOLIS, MINNESOTA 55459

OVERVIEW: Owns and operates hotels. Established: 1967. Parent Company: Radisson Hotels International, Inc.

KEY STATISTICS Annual Sales: $2.0 billion. Number of Employees: 45,000.

EXPERTISE/EDUCATION SOUGHT: Accounting, finance, business administration, business management, hospitality/hotel and restaurant management, sales, marketing, operations

CONTACT: Ms Maria Ramsey, Director of Corporate Staffing; Phone (612) 540-5526, ext. 3314.

RALCORP
CHECKERBOARD SQUARE
SAINT LOUIS, MISSOURI 63164

OVERVIEW: Manufactures cereals, baby foods, cookies, and crackers.

KEY STATISTICS Annual Sales: $336.0 million. Number of Employees: 3,500.

EXPERTISE/EDUCATION SOUGHT: Accounting, marketing, customer service and support, sales

CONTACT: For individuals with previous experience: Ms Dina Spooler, Human Resources Coordinator/Recruitment.

RALEY'S
500 WEST CAPITOL AVENUE
WEST SACRAMENTO, CALIFORNIA 95691-2624

OVERVIEW: Operates food stores and retail drug stores. Established: 1935.

KEY STATISTICS Number of Employees: 10,000.

EXPERTISE/EDUCATION SOUGHT: Graphic arts, finance

CONTACT: Mr Sam McPherson, Vice President of Human Resources; Phone (916) 373-6319.

RALLY'S, INC.
10002 SHELBYVILLE ROAD
LOUISVILLE, KENTUCKY 40223-2900

OVERVIEW: Operates chain of fast food restaurants. Established: 1985.

KEY STATISTICS Annual Sales: $174.0 million. Number of Employees: 7,100.

EXPERTISE/EDUCATION SOUGHT: Management

CONTACT: For individuals with previous experience: Ms Kathy Brittain, Director Human Resources; Phone (502) 245-8900.

RALPH'S GROCERY COMPANY
1100 WEST ARTESIA BOULEVARD
COMPTON, CALIFORNIA 90220-5186

OVERVIEW: Operates chain of food stores. Established: 1873. Parent Company: Ralph's Supermarkets, Inc.

KEY STATISTICS Annual Sales: $3.0 billion. Number of Employees: 16,476.

EXPERTISE/EDUCATION SOUGHT: Computer programming, marketing, law, auditing

CONTACT: Ms Sherri Meek, Vice President of Personnel, PO Box 54143, Los Angeles, CA, 90054; Phone (310) 884-9000.

RALSTON PURINA COMPANY
800 CHOUTEAU AVENUE
SAINT LOUIS, MISSOURI 63102-1002

OVERVIEW: Manufactures pet foods and baked goods. Established: 1894.

KEY STATISTICS Number of Employees: 59,516.

EXPERTISE/EDUCATION SOUGHT: Computer programming, accounting, finance, computer science, management, business administration, auditing, program analysis, data processing, software engineering/development

CONTACT: For individuals with previous experience: Employment Department; Phone (314) 982-2962.

RAYTHEON COMPANY
141 SPRING STREET
LEXINGTON, MASSACHUSETTS 02173

OVERVIEW: Manufactures electronic and aircraft products and appliances and provides energy and environmental services. Established: 1922.

EXPERTISE/EDUCATION SOUGHT: Electrical engineering, electronics/electronics engineering, accounting, data processing

CONTACTS: For college students and recent graduates: Mr Donald James, Manager of Corporate Employment; Phone (617) 862-6600, ext. 2376. For individuals with previous experience: Human Resources Department; Phone (617) 862-6600.

RAYTHEON CONSTRUCTORS
160 CHUBB AVENUE 2ND FLOOR
LYNDHURST, NEW JERSEY 07071-3502

OVERVIEW: Provides engineering contracting and consulting services. Established: 1841.

EXPERTISE/EDUCATION SOUGHT: Mechanical engineering, civil engineering, structural engineering, construction engineering, design engineering, architecture

CONTACT: Ms Inez Davis, Human Resource Supervisor; Phone (201) 460-1900.

RAYTHEON SERVICE COMPANY
2 WAYSIDE ROAD
BURLINGTON, MASSACHUSETTS 01803-4607

OVERVIEW: Provides engineering services. Established: 1962.

KEY STATISTICS Annual Sales: $219.0 million. Number of Employees: 5,200.

EXPERTISE/EDUCATION SOUGHT: Technical writing, electrical engineering, software engineering/development

CONTACT: Mr James Dempsey, Manager of Human Resources; Phone (617) 238-2263.

READ-RITE CORPORATION
345 LOS COCHES STREET
MILPITAS, CALIFORNIA 95035-5428

OVERVIEW: Manufactures thin film magnetic disk drive heads. Established: 1981.

KEY STATISTICS Annual Sales: $482.0 million. Number of Employees: 10,448.

EXPERTISE/EDUCATION SOUGHT: Engineering, research and development, process engineering, manufacturing engineering

CONTACT: Professional Staffing Recruiter; Phone (408) 262-2172.

READER'S DIGEST ASSOCIATION, INC.
READERS DIGEST ROAD
PLEASANTVILLE, NEW YORK 10570

OVERVIEW: Publishes books, magazines, and direct mail promotions. Established: 1922.

EXPERTISE/EDUCATION SOUGHT: Journalism, marketing, finance, accounting, human resources, computer programming

CONTACTS: For college students and recent graduates: Ms Kathy Marshall, Staffing Manager; Phone (914) 244-7393. For individuals with previous experience: Ms Susan J Hynson, Senior Staffing Specialist; Phone (914) 238-1000.

RECKITT AND COLMAN
225 SUMMIT AVENUE
MONTVALE, NEW JERSEY 07645

OVERVIEW: Manufactures and distributes cleaning products. Established: 1874.

EXPERTISE/EDUCATION SOUGHT: Industrial engineering, computer programming, packaging engineering, accounting, management information systems, sales, marketing

CONTACT: For individuals with previous experience: Ms Marlene Fried, Manager of Recruitment and Human Resources; Phone (201) 573-5700.

RED ROOF INNS, INC.
4355 DAVIDSON ROAD
HILLIARD, OHIO 43026-2438

OVERVIEW: Operates chain of economy motels. Established: 1973.

KEY STATISTICS Annual Sales: $182.0 million. Number of Employees: 5,400.

EXPERTISE/EDUCATION SOUGHT: Management, hospitality/hotel and restaurant management

CONTACT: For individuals with previous experience: Mr Doug Bruce, Director of Personnel Programs; Phone (614) 876-3200.

REDLAND OHIO, INC.
128 EAST MAIN STREET
WOODVILLE, OHIO 43469

OVERVIEW: Manufactures lime and limestone products.

EXPERTISE/EDUCATION SOUGHT: Accounting, finance, data processing

CONTACT: For individuals with previous experience: Mr Mark Zielinski, Assistant Controller, PO Box 128, Woodville, OH, 43469.

REED ELSEVIER
275 WASHINGTON STREET
NEWTON, MASSACHUSETTS 02158

OVERVIEW: Publishes books, journals, and directories and provides electronic information services.

EXPERTISE/EDUCATION SOUGHT: Accounting, marketing, communications, finance, law, journalism

CONTACT: For individuals with previous experience: Human Resources Department; Phone (617) 964-3030.

RELIANCE ELECTRIC COMPANY
6065 PARKLAND BOULEVARD
CLEVELAND, OHIO 44124-6106

OVERVIEW: Manufactures industrial motors and power supplies for telecommunications equipment. Established: 1904.

KEY STATISTICS Number of Employees: 14,000.

EXPERTISE/EDUCATION SOUGHT: Accounting, purchasing, finance, technical engineering, electrical engineering, systems engineering

CONTACT: For individuals with previous experience: Mr David Burke, Manager of Human Resources; Phone (216) 266-5800.

RELIANCE GROUP HOLDINGS, INC.
55 EAST 52ND STREET, 29TH FLOOR
NEW YORK, NEW YORK 10055-0002

OVERVIEW: Provides insurance and investment services. Parent Company: Reliance Group, Inc.

KEY STATISTICS Annual Sales: $3.0 billion. Number of Employees: 8,550.

EXPERTISE/EDUCATION SOUGHT: Accounting, real estate, finance, investment, management information systems, communications, law

CONTACT: Ms Ann Colleran, Manager of Human Resources; Phone (212) 909-1100.

RELIANCE INSURANCE COMPANY
4 PENN CENTER PLAZA
PHILADELPHIA, PENNSYLVANIA 19103-2501

OVERVIEW: Provides property and casualty insurance. Established: 1970. Parent Company: Reliance Financial Services Corporation.

KEY STATISTICS Number of Employees: 4,000.

EXPERTISE/EDUCATION SOUGHT: Accounting, finance, actuarial, auditing

CONTACT: Mr Dominick Rocchi, Recruiter; Phone (215) 864-4678.

RELIASTAR
20 WASHINGTON AVENUE SOUTH
MINNEAPOLIS, MINNESOTA 55401

OVERVIEW: Provides insurance and financial services.

EXPERTISE/EDUCATION SOUGHT: Sales, marketing, computer programming, accounting, customer service and support

CONTACT: For individuals with previous experience: Ms Marguirita Samuels, Assistant Vice President of Human Resources; Phone (612) 372-5432.

REMEDYTEMP, INC.
32122 CAMINO CAPISTRANO
SAN JUAN CAPISTRANO, CALIFORNIA 92675-3717

OVERVIEW: Provides temporary employment services.

KEY STATISTICS Annual Sales: $121.0 million. Number of Employees: 55,000.

EXPERTISE/EDUCATION SOUGHT: Marketing, management

CONTACT: Human Resources Department; Phone (714) 661-1211.

RENT IT CENTER
2780 BERT ADAMS ROAD
ATLANTA, GEORGIA 30339

OVERVIEW: Provides rental services for home and office furnishings. Established: 1981.

KEY STATISTICS Annual Sales: $649.0 million. Number of Employees: 6,500.

EXPERTISE/EDUCATION SOUGHT: Customer service and support, communications, retail management

CONTACT: For individuals with previous experience: Ms Tracey Williams, Manager Human Resources; Phone (404) 436-9520.

REXNORD CORPORATION
4701 WEST GREENFIELD AVENUE
MILWAUKEE, WISCONSIN 53214

OVERVIEW: Manufactures and markets power transmission components.

EXPERTISE/EDUCATION SOUGHT: Finance, accounting

CONTACT: For individuals with previous experience: Ms Jan Kurowski, Manager Headquarters Staffing; Phone (414) 643-3000.

THE REYNOLDS AND REYNOLDS COMPANY
115 SOUTH LUDLOW STREET
DAYTON, OHIO 45402-1812

OVERVIEW: Provides computer systems integration and design services. Established: 1889.

KEY STATISTICS Number of Employees: 5,636.

EXPERTISE/EDUCATION SOUGHT: Accounting, sales, marketing, computer programming

CONTACTS: For college students and recent graduates: Mr Rick Blackstone, Human Resources Specialist; Phone (513) 443-2642. For individuals with previous experience: Mr William Linesch, Vice President Human Resources, 800 Germantown Street, Dayton, OH, 45407; Phone (513) 443-2642.

REYNOLDS METALS COMPANY
6601 WEST BROAD STREET
RICHMOND, VIRGINIA 23230

OVERVIEW: Produces aluminum, aluminum products, and plastics. Established: 1928.

EXPERTISE/EDUCATION SOUGHT: Accounting, finance, chemical engineering, engineering mechanics, information systems

CONTACT: Ms Maryanne Wince, Headquarters Human Resources Manager; Phone (804) 281-2126.

R. J. REYNOLDS TOBACCO COMPANY
401 NORTH MAIN STREET
WINSTON SALEM, NORTH CAROLINA 27101-3818

OVERVIEW: Manufactures and markets cigarettes. Established: 1875. Parent Company: RJR Nabisco, Inc.

KEY STATISTICS Annual Sales: $5.0 billion. Number of Employees: 9,700.

EXPERTISE/EDUCATION SOUGHT: Data processing, computer programming, accounting, sales, business management

CONTACT: Mr John Lovett, Director of Human Resources and Staffing; Phone (919) 741-6859.

RGIS INVENTORY SPECIALISTS
805 OAKWOOD DRIVE
ROCHESTER, MICHIGAN 48307-1359

OVERVIEW: Provides inventory and related business services. Established: 1960.

KEY STATISTICS Annual Sales: $594.0 million. Number of Employees: 19,000.

HIRING HISTORY Number of professional employees hired in 1993: 150.

EXPERTISE/EDUCATION SOUGHT: Management, accounting, finance, law, data processing, computer programming

CONTACT: Mr Rex Halfpenny, Director of Training; Phone (810) 651-2511.

RHEEM MANUFACTURING COMPANY
405 LEXINGTON AVENUE
NEW YORK, NEW YORK 10174-0112

OVERVIEW: Manufactures heating and air conditioning equipment. Established: 1925. Parent Company: Pace Group, Inc.

KEY STATISTICS Annual Sales: $925.0 million. Number of Employees: 5,100.

EXPERTISE/EDUCATION SOUGHT: Administration, accounting

CONTACT: Mr Henry Porter, Manager of Human Resources; Phone (212) 916-8100.

RHONE-POULENC, INC.
125 BLACK HORSE LANE
MONMOUTH JUNCTION, NEW JERSEY 08822

OVERVIEW: Manufactures specialty chemicals and food. Established: 1948.

EXPERTISE/EDUCATION SOUGHT: Accounting, law, finance, auditing, chemical engineering

CONTACT: For individuals with previous experience: Mr Lee Suydam, Manager of Employee Relations; Phone (908) 297-0100.

RHONE-POULENC RORER, INC.
500 VIRGINIA DRIVE
FORT WASHINGTON, PENNSYLVANIA 19034-3909

OVERVIEW: Manufactures pharmaceuticals. Established: 1947.

KEY STATISTICS Annual Sales: $4.0 billion. Number of Employees: 22,300.

EXPERTISE/EDUCATION SOUGHT: Marketing, industrial engineering, pharmacy, research and development, laboratory technology, sales

CONTACTS: For college students and recent graduates: Ms Susan Tierney, Human Resources Coordinator. For individuals with previous experience: Ms Janet Shapiro, Human Resources Representative, PO Box 852, Collegeville, PA, 19426-0852; Phone (610) 454-8000, ext. 3915.

RICH PRODUCTS CORPORATION
1150 NIAGARA STREET
BUFFALO, NEW YORK 14213-1797

OVERVIEW: Manufactures frozen foods. Established: 1944.

KEY STATISTICS Number of Employees: 5,750.

EXPERTISE/EDUCATION SOUGHT: Sales, human resources, marketing, food services, manufacturing engineering, accounting, public relations, international relations

CONTACT: Mr Peter Coppola, Director of Human Resources Operations, PO Box 245, Buffalo, NY, 14240; Phone (716) 878-8000.

RICHFIELD HOSPITALITY SERVICE, INC.
5575 DTC BOULEVARD, SUITE 300
ENGLEWOOD, COLORADO 80111

OVERVIEW: Provides hotel management services. Established: 1968.

EXPERTISE/EDUCATION SOUGHT: Hospitality/hotel and restaurant management, sales, marketing, management, human resources, purchasing, finance

CONTACTS: For college students and recent graduates: Ms Suzanne Broski, Manager of Staffing; Phone (303) 220-2204. For individuals with previous experience: Mr Bill Clifford, Senior Vice President of Human Resources; Phone (303) 220-2000.

RICHMOND TIMES DISPATCH
333 EAST GRACE STREET
RICHMOND, VIRGINIA 23293-1000

OVERVIEW: Provides newspaper publishing, broadcasting, and cable television services. Established: 1850.

KEY STATISTICS Annual Sales: $601.0 million. Number of Employees: 7,300.

HIRING HISTORY Number of professional employees hired in 1993: 20.

EXPERTISE/EDUCATION SOUGHT: Data processing, marketing, finance, graphic arts, accounting, journalism, hardware engineering, software engineering/development

CONTACT: Ms Allie Bullock, Employment Supervisor; Phone (804) 649-6000.

RICOH CORPORATION
5 DEDRICK PLACE
WEST CALDWELL, NEW JERSEY 07006-6398

OVERVIEW: Manufactures copiers, facsimile machines, cameras, and other office equipment. Established: 1962.

KEY STATISTICS Annual Sales: $912.0 million. Number of Employees: 2,800.

HIRING HISTORY Number of professional employees hired in 1993: 200.

EXPERTISE/EDUCATION SOUGHT: Software engineering/development, computer programming, data processing, finance, digital technology, accounting

CONTACTS: For college students and recent graduates: Mr Tim Tress, Senior Human Resources Administrator; Phone (201) 882-2000. For individuals with previous experience: Ms Joanne Ehman, Manager of Corporate Human Resources; Phone (201) 882-2000, ext. 2233.

RITZ-CARLTON HOTELS, INC.
3414 PEACHTREE ROAD NORTHEAST
ATLANTA, GEORGIA 30326-1164

OVERVIEW: Owns and operates hotels. Established: 1976.

KEY STATISTICS Annual Sales: $710.0 million. Number of Employees: 14,000.

EXPERTISE/EDUCATION SOUGHT: Finance, business, hospitality/hotel and restaurant management, sales, customer service and support, marketing, credit/credit analysis

CONTACT: For individuals with previous experience: Ms Theo Gilbert, Corporate Director of Human Resources; Phone (404) 237-5500.

RJR NABISCO, INC.
1301 AVENUE OF THE AMERICAS
NEW YORK, NEW YORK 10019-6054

OVERVIEW: Manufactures and distributes baked goods, snack foods, and cereals.

KEY STATISTICS Annual Sales: $15.0 billion.

EXPERTISE/EDUCATION SOUGHT: Accounting, human resources, finance, actuarial, business management, computer science

CONTACT: For individuals with previous experience: Ms Rosemary Tice, Personnel Manager.

ROADNET TECHNOLOGIES, INC.
2311 YORK ROAD
LUTHERVILLE TIMONIUM, MARYLAND 21093-2270

OVERVIEW: Provides software services. Established: 1986. Parent Company: United Parcel Service America, Inc.

KEY STATISTICS Annual Sales: $25.5 million. Number of Employees: 312.

EXPERTISE/EDUCATION SOUGHT: Accounting, finance, data processing, computer programming, software engineering/development

CONTACT: For individuals with previous experience: Mr Randy Maenkin, Human Resource Department; Phone (410) 560-0030.

ROADWAY SERVICES, INC.
1077 GORGE BOULEVARD
AKRON, OHIO 44310-2408

OVERVIEW: Provides trucking and shipping services. Established: 1930.

KEY STATISTICS Annual Sales: $4.0 billion. Number of Employees: 46,600.

EXPERTISE/EDUCATION SOUGHT: Risk management, auditing, accounting, purchasing, computer science, information systems, civil engineering

CONTACT: Ms Stefanie Chapman, Human Resources Representative; Phone (216) 384-8184.

ROCHE BIOMEDICAL LABORATORIES
1447 YORK COURT
BURLINGTON, NORTH CAROLINA 27215-3361

OVERVIEW: Provides clinical testing services. Established: 1982. Parent Company: Hoffmann-La Roche, Inc.

KEY STATISTICS Annual Sales: $689.0 million. Number of Employees: 8,400.

EXPERTISE/EDUCATION SOUGHT: Biology, chemical engineering, microbiology, medical technology

CONTACT: Ms Patricia Noell, Personell Administrator; Phone (919) 584-5171, ext. 4635.

ROHM AND HAAS COMPANY
100 INDEPENDENCE MALL WEST
PHILADELPHIA, PENNSYLVANIA 19106-2399

OVERVIEW: Manufactures industrial chemicals, polymers, resins, and Plexiglas. Established: 1909.

KEY STATISTICS Number of Employees: 12,985.

EXPERTISE/EDUCATION SOUGHT: Industrial engineering, chemical engineering, electrical engineering, mechanical engineering, data processing, accounting, finance, marketing

CONTACT: Ms Morissa Guerin, Vice President of Human Resources; Phone (215) 592-2719.

ROLLINS TRUCK LEASING CORPORATION
1 ROLLINS PLAZA
WILMINGTON, DELAWARE 19803

OVERVIEW: Provides truck leasing services. Established: 1954.

KEY STATISTICS Annual Sales: $409.0 million. Number of Employees: 2,676.

EXPERTISE/EDUCATION SOUGHT: Accounting, data processing

CONTACT: For individuals with previous experience: Ms Jean Lawrie, Recruiter; Phone (302) 426-2700.

ROSE'S STORES, INC.
218 SOUTH GARNETT STREET
HENDERSON, NORTH CAROLINA 27536-4600

OVERVIEW: Operates chain of retail stores. Established: 1915.

KEY STATISTICS Annual Sales: $1.0 billion. Number of Employees: 10,000.

EXPERTISE/EDUCATION SOUGHT: Sales, marketing, law, computer programming, accounting, credit/credit analysis, collection, economics, finance

CONTACT: For individuals with previous experience: Ms Frances Burger, Human Resources Specialist; Phone (919) 430-2600.

ROSENBLUTH INTERNATIONAL, INC.
2401 WALNUT STREET
PHILADELPHIA, PENNSYLVANIA 19103-4390

OVERVIEW: Provides travel management services.

KEY STATISTICS Number of Employees: 3,000.

CONTACT: For individuals with previous experience: Human Resources Department; Phone (215) 977-4800.

ROSS-LOOS HEALTHPLAN OF CALIFORNIA
505 NORTH BRAND BOULEVARD
GLENDALE, CALIFORNIA 91203

Overview: Provides health care services.

Expertise/Education Sought: Registered nursing, licensed practical nursing, data processing, physicians

Contact: Ms Barbara Vosen, Director of Recruiting.

ROYAL CARIBBEAN CRUISES, LTD.
1050 CARIBBEAN WAY
MIAMI, FLORIDA 33132-2096

Overview: Operates cruise ships. Established: 1972.

Key Statistics Annual Sales: $1.0 billion. Number of Employees: 6,900.

Expertise/Education Sought: Accounting, finance, sales, marketing, data processing

Contact: Ms Marlynn Schneider, Manager of Employment; Phone (305) 539-6000.

ROYAL CROWN COLA COMPANY, INC.
1000 CORPORATE DRIVE
FORT LAUDERDALE, FLORIDA 33334-3655

Overview: Produces carbonated beverages. Established: 1964. Parent Company: Triarc Companies.

Key Statistics Annual Sales: $374.0 million. Number of Employees: 8,240.

Expertise/Education Sought: Finance, marketing, business development, human resources, business management, law, management information systems

Contact: Ms Susan DeLorenzo, Human Resources Specialist, PO Box 407010, Ft. Lauderdale, FL, 33340; Phone (305) 351-5363.

ROYAL INSURANCE COMPANY
9300 ARROWPOINT BOULEVARD
CHARLOTTE, NORTH CAROLINA 28273

Overview: Provides insurance.

Expertise/Education Sought: Underwriting, marketing, finance, actuarial

Contact: For individuals with previous experience: Mr John Cross, Assistant Vice President of Human Resources; Phone (704) 522-3179.

RUBBERMAID, INC.
1147 AKRON ROAD
WOOSTER, OHIO 44691-2501

Overview: Manufactures housewares, household products, and bath products. Established: 1920.

Key Statistics Number of Employees: 11,978.

Expertise/Education Sought: Technical engineering, manufacturing engineering, marketing, finance, accounting, sales

Contact: For individuals with previous experience: Mr Ted Moore, Recruiter; Phone (216) 264-6464, ext. 5671.

RUSSELL CORPORATION
755 LEE STREET
ALEXANDER CITY, ALABAMA 35010

Overview: Manufactures textiles, knitwear, and clothing. Established: 1902.

Key Statistics Number of Employees: 16,640.

Expertise/Education Sought: Sales, marketing, manufacturing engineering, chemical engineering, mechanical engineering, electrical engineering, accounting, textiles

Contact: For individuals with previous experience: Mr Melvin Ervin, Corporate Staff Representative; Phone (205) 329-5587.

RYAN'S FAMILY STEAK HOUSES
405 LANCASTER AVENUE
GREER, SOUTH CAROLINA 29650-1235

Overview: Operates chain of family restaurants.

Key Statistics Annual Sales: $394.0 million. Number of Employees: 14,000.

Expertise/Education Sought: Retail management

Contact: For individuals with previous experience: Mr Randy Hart, Vice President Human Resources.

RYDER SYSTEM, INC.
3600 NORTHWEST 82ND AVENUE
MIAMI, FLORIDA 33166-6623

Overview: Provides highway transportation services. Established: 1934.

Key Statistics Annual Sales: $4.0 billion. Number of Employees: 37,949.

Expertise/Education Sought: Marketing, finance, accounting, management information systems, auditing, business management, project management, logistics

Contact: Ms Gerri Rocker, Manager of College Relations; Phone (305) 593-4049.

RYKOFF-SEXTON, INC.
761 TERMINAL STREET
LOS ANGELES, CALIFORNIA 90021-1112

Overview: Distributes wholesale foods. Established: 1911.

Key Statistics Number of Employees: 5,430.

Expertise/Education Sought: Sales, marketing, finance, accounting, business administration

Contacts: For college students and recent graduates: Mr Dennis Slipakoff, Manager of Human Resources; Phone (213) 622-4131. For individuals with previous experience: Mr Robert Harter, Senior Vice President of Human Resources and General Councel; Phone (213) 622-4131.

SABRE GROUP, INC.
4200 AMERICAN BOULEVARD
FORT WORTH, TEXAS 76155-2603

Overview: Operates automated airline reservations systems.

Key Statistics Annual Sales: $200.0 million. Number of Employees: 4,000.

Expertise/Education Sought: Computer science, operations research, finance

Contact: For individuals with previous experience: Mr Ed Morgan, Vice President of Human Resources.

SAFETY-KLEEN CORPORATION
1000 NORTH RANDALL ROAD
ELGIN, ILLINOIS 60123-7857

Overview: Recycles hazardous waste. Established: 1961.

Key Statistics Annual Sales: $796.0 million. Number of Employees: 6,400.

Hiring History Number of professional employees hired in 1994: 70. 1993: 70.

Expertise/Education Sought: Accounting, finance, data processing, environmental engineering, computer programming

Contact: Ms Barbara Schuls, Manager of Corporate Employment; Phone (708) 697-8460, ext. 2102.

SAINT JOSEPH HEALTH SYSTEM
440 SOUTH BATAVIA STREET
ORANGE, CALIFORNIA 92668-3907

Overview: Provides health care services. Established: 1923. Parent Company: Sisters of Saint Joseph of Orange.

KEY STATISTICS Annual Sales: $690.0 million. Number of Employees: 7,650.

EXPERTISE/EDUCATION SOUGHT: Accounting, marketing, finance, management information systems, business management

CONTACT: Mr James Counts, Director of Personnel, 505 South Main, Suite 400, Orange, CA, 92668-3907; Phone (714) 647-4997.

SAINT PAUL FIRE AND MARINE INSURANCE COMPANY
385 WASHINGTON STREET
SAINT PAUL, MINNESOTA 55102-1309

OVERVIEW: Provides insurance. Established: 1925. Parent Company: St. Paul Companies, Inc.

KEY STATISTICS Number of Employees: 12,000.

EXPERTISE/EDUCATION SOUGHT: Underwriting, administration

CONTACT: For individuals with previous experience: Mr Carl Braun, Employment Manager-Professional Staffing; Phone (612) 221-7911.

SAKS FIFTH AVENUE
611 FIFTH AVENUE
NEW YORK, NEW YORK 10017-1028

OVERVIEW: Operates chain of specialty retail stores. Established: 1924.

KEY STATISTICS Number of Employees: 8,000.

EXPERTISE/EDUCATION SOUGHT: Merchandising

CONTACT: For college students and recent graduates: Ms Lori Atkins, Manager College Relations; Phone (212) 753-5442.

SALOMON BROTHERS, INC.
7 WORLD TRADE CENTER
NEW YORK, NEW YORK 10048

OVERVIEW: Investment bank. Established: 1874.

KEY STATISTICS Number of Employees: 8,640.

EXPERTISE/EDUCATION SOUGHT: Banking, accounting, finance, underwriting, marketing, real estate

CONTACT: For individuals with previous experience: Mr Bob Dibble, Vice President Corporate Recruitment; Phone (212) 783-0847.

SAMARITAN HEALTH SYSTEM
1441 NORTH 12TH STREET
PHOENIX, ARIZONA 85006-2837

OVERVIEW: Operates general and specialty hospitals, outpatient clinics, specialty clinics, and an HMO.

KEY STATISTICS Annual Sales: $891.0 million. Number of Employees: 12,000.

EXPERTISE/EDUCATION SOUGHT: Pharmacy, finance, economics, radiology, marketing, risk management, accounting, law, food services, human resources

CONTACT: For individuals with previous experience: Ms Theresa Graham, Manager of Recruiting; Phone (602) 495-4000.

SAM'S WHOLESALE CLUB
702 SOUTHWEST 8TH STREET
BENTONVILLE, ARKANSAS 72716

OVERVIEW: Sells discounted general merchandise to the public.

EXPERTISE/EDUCATION SOUGHT: Business management, accounting, information systems, real estate, marketing, law

CONTACT: Mr Dwight Newsome, Manager of Corporate Recruiting; Phone (501) 273-4000.

SAMSONITE CORPORATION
11200 EAST 45TH AVENUE
DENVER, COLORADO 80239-3018

OVERVIEW: Manufactures luggage. Established: 1912.

KEY STATISTICS Number of Employees: 6,000.

EXPERTISE/EDUCATION SOUGHT: Sales

CONTACT: For individuals with previous experience: Ms Gypsy Twillman, Human Resource Specialist.

SAN DIEGO GAS AND ELECTRIC COMPANY
101 ASH STREET
SAN DIEGO, CALIFORNIA 92101-3096

OVERVIEW: Electric and gas utility. Established: 1881.

KEY STATISTICS Annual Sales: $2.0 billion. Number of Employees: 5,000.

EXPERTISE/EDUCATION SOUGHT: Engineering, accounting, finance, communications, marketing, economics

CONTACTS: For college students and recent graduates: Ms Monica Strong, Employment Services - Team Leader, PO Box 1831, San Diego, CA, 92122; Phone (619) 696-4340. For individuals with previous experience: Employment Office; Phone (619) 654-1500.

SANDERSON FARMS, INC.
225 NORTH 13TH AVENUE
LAUREL, MISSISSIPPI 39440-4109

OVERVIEW: Processes poultry; manufactures frozen poultry and other prepared foods. Established: 1955.

KEY STATISTICS Annual Sales: $269.0 million. Number of Employees: 4,100.

EXPERTISE/EDUCATION SOUGHT: Management

CONTACT: For individuals with previous experience: Mr Jessie Walters, Human Resources Manager, PO Box 988, Laurel, MS, 39441; Phone (601) 649-4030.

SANDIA NATIONAL LABORATORIES
1515 EUBANK SOUTH EAST, PO BOX 5800, (MS-1023)
ALBUQUERQUE, NEW MEXICO 87123-1023

OVERVIEW: Engaged in research and development of nuclear technology, the environment, energy, manufacturing, space, the nation's economy, and global security. Established: 1949. Parent Company: Lockheed Martin Corporation.

KEY STATISTICS Number of Employees: 8,500.

HIRING HISTORY Number of professional employees hired in 1994: 225. 1993: 225.

EXPERTISE/EDUCATION SOUGHT: Electrical engineering, mechanical engineering, environmental science, computer science, physics

CONTACTS: For college students and recent graduates: Ms Loyola Leinheiser, Recruiting Coordinator; Phone (505) 844-0979; Fax (505) 844-6636. For individuals with previous experience: Mr Robert H Banks, Recruiting Coordinator; Phone (505) 844-4255; Fax (505)844-6636.

SANDOZ PHARMACEUTICALS CORPORATION
59 STATE HIGHWAY 10
EAST HANOVER, NEW JERSEY 07936-1011

OVERVIEW: Manufactures and markets pharmaceuticals. Established: 1919. Parent Company: Sandoz Corporation.

KEY STATISTICS Annual Sales: $2.0 billion. Number of Employees: 12,000.

EXPERTISE/EDUCATION SOUGHT: Accounting, marketing, finance, law, data processing, management information systems

CONTACT: For individuals with previous experience: Ms Bea Sherman, Associate Director of Staffing; Phone (201) 503-7500, ext. 7155; , ext. 8762.

SANTA FE PACIFIC CORPORATION
1700 EAST GULF ROAD
SCHAUMBURG, ILLINOIS 60172

OVERVIEW: Provides railroad and trucking services. Established: 1983.

EXPERTISE/EDUCATION SOUGHT: Logistics, transportation, marketing, business administration

CONTACT: Ms Yvette Sharp, Senior Human Resources Specialist; Phone (708) 995-6000.

SANTEE COOPER
1 RIVERWOOD DRIVE
MONCKS CORNER, SOUTH CAROLINA 29461-2912

OVERVIEW: Utility company. Established: 1934.

KEY STATISTICS Annual Sales: $589.0 million. Number of Employees: 1,776.

HIRING HISTORY Number of professional employees hired in 1994: 5.

EXPERTISE/EDUCATION SOUGHT: Computer science

CONTACT: Mr Julian Minson, Manager of Employee Relations; Phone (803) 761-8000.

SANUS CORPORATE HEALTH SYSTEMS
400 KELBY DRIVE
FORT LEE, NEW JERSEY 07024-2937

OVERVIEW: Provides health insurance. Established: 1983. Parent Company: NYLife, Inc.

KEY STATISTICS Annual Sales: $1.0 billion. Number of Employees: 2,000.

EXPERTISE/EDUCATION SOUGHT: Underwriting, health insurance

CONTACT: For individuals with previous experience: Ms Jacqueline DeCataldo, Recruitment Specialist; Phone (201) 947-6000.

SARA LEE CORPORATION
70 WEST MADISON STREET
CHICAGO, ILLINOIS 60602

OVERVIEW: Manufactures and markets food, consumer, and household products. Established: 1941.

KEY STATISTICS Number of Employees: 138,000.

EXPERTISE/EDUCATION SOUGHT: Accounting, finance, business management, auditing

CONTACT: Ms Lena Koldras, Corporate Human Resources Supervisor; Phone (312) 726-2600, ext. 8468.

SATURN CORPORATION
100 SATURN PARKWAY
TROY, MICHIGAN 48083-1189

OVERVIEW: Manufactures automobiles. Established: 1985. Parent Company: General Motors Corporation.

KEY STATISTICS Annual Sales: $979.0 million. Number of Employees: 7,000.

EXPERTISE/EDUCATION SOUGHT: Production engineering, design engineering, automotive engineering, mechanical engineering, electrical engineering

CONTACT: For individuals with previous experience: Ms Bonnie Buchanan, People Systems Coordinator, Mail Drop F-10, Spring Hill, TN, 37174; Phone (615) 486-5919.

SAVANNAH FOODS AND INDUSTRIES
2 EAST BRYAN STREET
SAVANNAH, GEORGIA 31401-2655

OVERVIEW: Manufactures, packages, stores, and distributes sugar. Established: 1916.

KEY STATISTICS Number of Employees: 2,185.

EXPERTISE/EDUCATION SOUGHT: Accounting, business, marketing, food science, management, industrial engineering, food engineering

CONTACT: For individuals with previous experience: Ms Betty Miller, Director of Personnel, PO Box 339, Savannah, GA, 31402; Phone (912) 234-1261.

SAVE MART SUPERMARKETS
1800 STANDIFORD AVENUE, PO BOX 4278
MODESTO, CALIFORNIA 95352-4278

OVERVIEW: Operates chain of food stores. Established: 1952.

KEY STATISTICS Number of Employees: 7,000.

EXPERTISE/EDUCATION SOUGHT: Retail, marketing, merchandising, computer programming, management

CONTACT: Mr Michael Silveira, Director of Human Resources and Law, PO Box 4278, Modesto, CA, 95352-4278; Phone (209) 577-1600.

SBARRO, INC.
763 LARKFIELD ROAD
COMMACK, NEW YORK 11725-3185

OVERVIEW: Operates chain of Italian fast food restaurants. Established: 1959.

KEY STATISTICS Annual Sales: $266.0 million. Number of Employees: 8,200.

EXPERTISE/EDUCATION SOUGHT: Administration

CONTACT: For individuals with previous experience: Mr Jim O'Shea, Vice President Human Resources.

SBC COMMUNICATIONS, INC.
175 EAST HOUSTON STREET, SUITE 520
SAN ANTONIO, TEXAS 78205-2233

OVERVIEW: Provides telecommunications products and services. Established: 1984.

KEY STATISTICS Annual Sales: $11.0 billion. Number of Employees: 59,040.

EXPERTISE/EDUCATION SOUGHT: Accounting, finance, sales, telecommunications, data processing

CONTACTS: For college students and recent graduates: Ms David Ortiz, Director of Corporate Recruiting; Phone (210) 351-2468. For individuals with previous experience: Mr Randy Chard, Director of Corporate Staffing; Phone (210) 351-2469.

SCANA CORPORATION
1426 MAIN STREET
COLUMBIA, SOUTH CAROLINA 29201-2834

OVERVIEW: Electric and gas utility.

KEY STATISTICS Annual Sales: $1.0 billion. Number of Employees: 4,788.

EXPERTISE/EDUCATION SOUGHT: Electrical engineering, mechanical engineering, civil engineering, computer programming, accounting

CONTACT: Mr Martin Phalen, Vice President of Human Resources; Phone (803) 748-3109.

SCE CORPORATION
2244 WALNUT GROVE AVENUE
ROSEMEAD, CALIFORNIA 91770-3714

OVERVIEW: Electric utility.

KEY STATISTICS Annual Sales: $8.0 billion. Number of Employees: 16,487.

EXPERTISE/EDUCATION SOUGHT: Auditing, accounting, law, product design and development, sales, marketing

CONTACT: Ms Donna Phillips, Corporate Recruiter; Phone (818) 302-2222.

SCH HEALTH CARE SYSTEM
2600 NORTH LOOP WEST
HOUSTON, TEXAS 77092-8916

OVERVIEW: Owns and operates hospitals and medical centers. Established: 1866.

Key Statistics Annual Sales: $1.0 billion. Number of Employees: 20,000.

Hiring History Number of professional employees hired in 1994: 40.

Expertise/Education Sought: Finance, quality control, health care

Contact: For individuals with previous experience: Ms Kay Saathoff, Personnel Manager; Phone (713) 681-8877.

SCHERING-PLOUGH CORPORATION
2000 GALLOPING HILL ROAD
KENILWORTH, NEW JERSEY 07033

Overview: Manufactures pharmaceuticals and consumer health products. Established: 1864.

Key Statistics Annual Sales: $5.0 billion. Number of Employees: 21,200.

Expertise/Education Sought: Accounting, finance, data processing, sales, research and development, human resources

Contact: For individuals with previous experience: Human Resources Department.

SCHERING-PLOUGH HEALTHCARE PRODUCTS
110 ALLEN ROAD
LIBERTY CORNER, NEW JERSEY 07938

Overview: Manufactures consumer health care products.

Key Statistics Annual Sales: $700.0 million. Number of Employees: 2,500.

Expertise/Education Sought: Finance, management information systems, marketing, sales

Contact: For individuals with previous experience: Ms JoAnne Coakley, Manager of Human Resources; Phone (908) 604-1640.

SCHINDLER ELEVATOR CORPORATION
20 WHIPPANY ROAD
MORRISTOWN, NEW JERSEY 07960-4539

Overview: Manufactures escalators and elevators. Parent Company: Schindler Enterprises, Inc.

Key Statistics Annual Sales: $602.0 million. Number of Employees: 5,360.

Expertise/Education Sought: Electrical engineering, mechanical engineering

Contact: Ms Jonna Davis, Manager of Human Resources; Phone (201) 984-9500.

SCHLEGEL CORPORATION
1555 JEFFERSON ROAD
ROCHESTER, NEW YORK 14623

Overview: Manufactures rubber strips and belting and plastic hardware and building products. Established: 1900.

Key Statistics Number of Employees: 7,000.

Expertise/Education Sought: Design engineering, mechanical engineering

Contact: For individuals with previous experience: Mr Jim Falkner, Human Resources Manager; Phone (716) 427-7200, ext. 5289.

SCHLUMBERGER INDUSTRIES, INC.
PO BOX 75
WEST UNION, SOUTH CAROLINA 29696

Overview: Manufactures electric metering panels and transformers. Established: 1990. Parent Company: Schlumberger Technology Corporation.

Expertise/Education Sought: Accounting, marketing, finance, sales, management information systems

Contact: Ms Suzanne Newell, Manager of Personnel, 180 Technology Parkway, Norcross, GA, 30092-2989; Phone (404) 447-7300.

SCHLUMBERGER, LTD.
277 PARK AVENUE
NEW YORK, NEW YORK 10172

Overview: Provides oilfield services and measurement equipment. Established: 1927.

Expertise/Education Sought: Accounting, marketing

Contacts: For college students and recent graduates: Manager of Recruiting Coordination and University Relations; Phone (713) 623-3020. For individuals with previous experience: Ms Lillian Petty, Personnel Manager; Phone (212) 350-9400.

SCHNEIDER NATIONAL, INC.
3101 SOUTH PACKERLAND DRIVE
GREEN BAY, WISCONSIN 54306

Overview: Provides truck freight and shipping services. Established: 1977.

Key Statistics Annual Sales: $800.0 million. Number of Employees: 10,250.

Expertise/Education Sought: Operations, logistics, business

Contact: Mr Thomas Van Der Steen, Manager of Human Resources; Phone (414) 592-2000, ext. 2545.

SCHOLASTIC, INC.
555 BROADWAY
NEW YORK, NEW YORK 10012

Overview: Publishing company. Established: 1920.

Expertise/Education Sought: Graphic arts, advertising, accounting, marketing, sales

Contact: For individuals with previous experience: Ms Debbie Fuller, Associate Director of Human Resources; Phone (212) 343-6902.

SCHOTTENSTEIN STORES CORPORATION
1800 MOLER ROAD
COLUMBUS, OHIO 43207-1680

Overview: Manufactures furniture. Established: 1972.

Key Statistics Annual Sales: $1.0 billion. Number of Employees: 15,000.

Hiring History Number of professional employees hired in 1993: 10.

Expertise/Education Sought: Accounting, business management, marketing, finance, economics, sales

Contact: For individuals with previous experience: Mr John Miller, Assistant Director of Personnel; Phone (614) 221-9200.

SCHULLER INTERNATIONAL, INC.
717 17TH STREET
DENVER, COLORADO 80202

Overview: Manufactures insulation and roofing products. Established: 1920.

Expertise/Education Sought: Accounting, finance, data processing, computer programming

Contact: Ms Shirley Mahoney, Manager of Employment Practices; Phone (303) 978-2000.

A. SCHULMAN, INC.
3550 WEST MARKET STREET
AKRON, OHIO 44333-2658

Overview: Manufactures and markets plastic resins and products. Established: 1928.

Key Statistics Number of Employees: 1,587.

Hiring History Number of professional employees hired in 1993: 20.

Expertise/Education Sought: Sales, marketing, accounting, management

Contacts: For college students and recent graduates: Mr Steve Copeland, National Sales Manager; Phone (216) 666-3751. For individuals with previous experience: Ms Toy Friedberg, Director of Human Resources; Phone (216) 666-3751.

CHARLES SCHWAB AND COMPANY, INC.
101 MONTGOMERY STREET, 16TH FLOOR
SAN FRANCISCO, CALIFORNIA 94104

OVERVIEW: Provides discount brokerage services. Established: 1971.

EXPERTISE/EDUCATION SOUGHT: Finance, information systems, brokerage, project management, law, computer programming, sales

CONTACT: Human Resources; Phone (415) 627-7000.

SCHWEGMANN GIANT SUPERMARKETS
5300 OLD GENTILLY ROAD
NEW ORLEANS, KENTUCKY 70126

OVERVIEW: Operates chain of food stores. Established: 1946.

EXPERTISE/EDUCATION SOUGHT: Management, accounting

CONTACT: Mr Lee Janies, Director of Human Resources; Phone (504) 947-9921.

SCI SYSTEMS, INC.
2101 CLINTON AVENUE WEST
HUNTSVILLE, ALABAMA 35805-3007

OVERVIEW: Manufactures instrumentation and computer equipment. Established: 1961.

KEY STATISTICS Number of Employees: 12,027.

HIRING HISTORY Number of professional employees hired in 1994: 200.

EXPERTISE/EDUCATION SOUGHT: Computer engineering, software engineering/development, electrical engineering, mechanical engineering, radio frequency engineering

CONTACT: For individuals with previous experience: Mr Kirk Scruggs, Personnel Administrator; Phone (205) 882-4800.

SCIENCE APPLICATIONS INTERNATIONAL CORPORATION
10260 CAMPUS POINT DRIVE
SAN DIEGO, CALIFORNIA 92121-1522

OVERVIEW: Provides high tech security and health and environmental products. Established: 1969.

KEY STATISTICS Annual Sales: $2.0 billion. Number of Employees: 14,965.

EXPERTISE/EDUCATION SOUGHT: Electrical engineering, computer programming, computer science, mechanical engineering, environmental science, data processing, treasury management, finance, accounting

CONTACTS: For college students and recent graduates: Ms Mary Lou Dunford, Corporate Staffing Manager; Phone (619) 546-6000. For individuals with previous experience: Human Resources Department; Phone (619) 546-6000.

THE SCOTT FETZER COMPANY
28800 CLEMENS ROAD
WESTLAKE, OHIO 44145

OVERVIEW: Manufactures household and electrical products. Established: 1914. Parent Company: Berkshire Hathaway, Inc.

KEY STATISTICS Number of Employees: 9,540.

EXPERTISE/EDUCATION SOUGHT: Electrical engineering, design engineering, mechanical engineering, accounting, finance, business management, marketing

CONTACT: For individuals with previous experience: Ms Robin Sabbarese, Personnel Director; Phone (216) 892-3000.

SCOTTY'S, INC.
5300 RECKER HIGHWAY
WINTER HAVEN, FLORIDA 33882-0939

OVERVIEW: Operates chain of home improvement centers. Established: 1924. Parent Company: G.I.B Group.

KEY STATISTICS Annual Sales: $650.0 million. Number of Employees: 6,800.

EXPERTISE/EDUCATION SOUGHT: Retail management, sales

CONTACT: Mr Jim McWilliams, Employment Manager; Phone (813) 297-6155.

THE E. W. SCRIPPS-HOWARD COMPANY
312 WALNUT STREET
CINCINNATI, OHIO 45202-4024

OVERVIEW: Publishes and syndicates newspapers and operates broadcasting stations. Established: 1878. Parent Company: Edward W. Scripps Trust.

KEY STATISTICS Annual Sales: $1.0 billion. Number of Employees: 8,200.

HIRING HISTORY Number of professional employees hired in 1993: 5.

EXPERTISE/EDUCATION SOUGHT: Accounting, sales, marketing, information systems, communications, journalism

CONTACT: Mrs Robyn Hildel, Human Resources Manager; Phone (513) 977-3081.

SEA-LAND SERVICE, INC.
150 ALLEN ROAD
LIBERTY CORNER, NEW JERSEY 07938

OVERVIEW: Provides containerized shipping services. Established: 1956. Parent Company: CSX Corporation.

KEY STATISTICS Number of Employees: 9,440.

EXPERTISE/EDUCATION SOUGHT: Accounting, business, finance, marketing

CONTACTS: For college students and recent graduates: Ms Robin Shaw, Manager of Corporate Employment, Training and Development; Phone (908) 604-3646. For individuals with previous experience: Ms Sheryl Traylor, Director of Human Resources.

SEABOARD CORPORATION
9000 WEST 67TH STREET
SHAWNEE-MISSION, KANSAS 66202

OVERVIEW: Diversified international agribusiness and transportation company engaged in poultry and pork processing, commodity merchandising, baking, shipping, produce storage, and distribution. Established: 1946. Parent Company: Seaboard Flour Corporation.

HIRING HISTORY Number of professional employees hired in 1994: 40.

EXPERTISE/EDUCATION SOUGHT: Chemical engineering, finance, business management, data processing, environmental engineering, human resources

CONTACTS: For college students and recent graduates: Mr Peter Mirakian, Manager of Human Resources; Phone (913) 676-8800; Fax (913) 676-8941. For individuals with previous experience: Ms Susan McMahon-Steiner, Human Resource Manager; Phone (913) 676-8800.

SEAFIRST BANK
800 5TH AVENUE, 33RD FLOOR
SEATTLE, WASHINGTON 98154

OVERVIEW: Provides financial services. Established: 1973.

EXPERTISE/EDUCATION SOUGHT: Accounting, finance, sales, customer service and support

CONTACT: For individuals with previous experience: Staffing Services Department, PO Box 3977, Seattle, WA, 98124.

SEAGATE TECHNOLOGY, INC.
920 DISC DRIVE, BUILDING 1
SCOTTS VALLEY, CALIFORNIA 95066-4542

OVERVIEW: Manufactures magnetic disk drives and computer components. Established: 1978.

KEY STATISTICS Annual Sales: $3.0 billion. Number of Employees: 43,000.

EXPERTISE/EDUCATION SOUGHT: Accounting, marketing, mechanical engineering, electrical engineering, design engineering, finance

Seagate Technology, Inc. (continued)

CONTACT: For individuals with previous experience: Mr Robert Morquecho, Manager of Corporate Human Resources Employment, PO Box 66360, Scotts Valley, CA, 95067-0360; Phone (408) 438-6550.

J. E. SEAGRAM CORPORATION
800 3RD AVENUE
NEW YORK, NEW YORK 10122

OVERVIEW: Produces alcoholic and carbonated beverages. Established: 1933.

EXPERTISE/EDUCATION SOUGHT: Marketing, sales, accounting, finance, business management, human resources

CONTACT: Ms Yvonne Shaw, Director of Human Resources; Phone (212) 572-7000.

SEARS ROEBUCK AND COMPANY
23 SOUTH WACKER DRIVE
CHICAGO, ILLINOIS 60689

OVERVIEW: Operates chain of general merchandise stores. Established: 1886.

EXPERTISE/EDUCATION SOUGHT: Human resources, business management, sales, marketing, retail, finance

CONTACTS: For college students and recent graduates: Ms Barbara Waite, Supervisor of College Recruiting/Merchandising Group, Building 707-9, 3333 Beverly Road, Hoffman Estates, IL, 60179; Phone (708) 286-7016. For individuals with previous experience: Mr Hyman Albritton, Manager Executive Recruiting, Building 707-9/EC-234 A, Hoffman Estates, IL, 60179; Phone (708) 286-7818.

SEDGWICK JAMES, INC.
5350 POPLAR AVENUE
MEMPHIS, TENNESSEE 38119

OVERVIEW: Provides insurance brokerage services.

KEY STATISTICS Annual Sales: $420.0 million. Number of Employees: 5,300.

EXPERTISE/EDUCATION SOUGHT: Information systems, information services, marketing, sales, accounting, tax accounting

CONTACT: For individuals with previous experience: Ms Ann Fields, Manager Corporate Human Resources; Phone (901) 684-3766.

SEI CORPORATION
680 EAST SWEDESFORD ROAD
WAYNE, PENNSYLVANIA 19087-1658

OVERVIEW: Provides information processing and mutual funds management services. Established: 1968.

KEY STATISTICS Annual Sales: $247.0 million. Number of Employees: 1,370.

CONTACT: For individuals with previous experience: Mr Jim Ward, Recruiting Process Leader.

SEI information technology

SEI INFORMATION TECHNOLOGY
212 EAST OHIO STREET
CHICAGO, ILLINOIS 60611

OVERVIEW: Provides information systems consulting services. Established: 1969.

KEY STATISTICS Annual Sales: $29.0 million. Number of Employees: 350.

HIRING HISTORY Number of professional employees hired in 1994: 89. 1993: 50.

EXPERTISE/EDUCATION SOUGHT: Management information systems, information systems, project management, software engineering/development, project engineering

CONTACT: Ms Rebecca Standen, Recruitment Director; Phone (312) 440-8300; Fax (312) 440-8373.

CORPORATE STATEMENT

Founded in 1969, SEI Information Technology is a computer systems consulting organization with a hard-earned reputation for meeting clients' needs through leading-edge technical and business solutions. SEI seeks experienced technology-oriented professionals with solid business management skills to help explore new business opportunities, develop client relationships, aid in product marketing and sales, and assist with general operations initiatives.

SENTARA HEALTH SYSTEM
6015 POPLAR HALL DRIVE
NORFOLK, VIRGINIA 23502-3800

OVERVIEW: Owns and operates hospitals and medical centers. Established: 1982.

KEY STATISTICS Annual Sales: $611.0 million. Number of Employees: 10,000.

EXPERTISE/EDUCATION SOUGHT: Marketing, print production, printing, accounting, administration, business management, customer service and support

CONTACT: For individuals with previous experience: Human Resources Department, Sentara Lee Hospital, 830 Kempsville Road, Norfolk, VA, 23502.

SENTRY INSURANCE
1800 NORTHPOINT DRIVE
STEVENS POINT, WISCONSIN 54481

OVERVIEW: Provides property, life, automobile, health, and commercial insurance. Established: 1913.

EXPERTISE/EDUCATION SOUGHT: Accounting, marketing, finance, actuarial, underwriting, sales, claims adjustment/examination

CONTACT: Ms Liz McDonald, Human Resources Manager; Phone (715) 346-6550.

SEQUA CORPORATION
200 PARK AVENUE
NEW YORK, NEW YORK 10166

OVERVIEW: Manufactures aerospace machinery. Established: 1929.

EXPERTISE/EDUCATION SOUGHT: Environmental science, manufacturing engineering, accounting, finance, marketing, human resources, aerospace engineering

CONTACT: For individuals with previous experience: Ms Carolyn Velechko, Personnel Specialist, 3 University Plaza, Hackensack, NJ, 07601; Phone (201) 343-1122.

THE SERCO COMPANY
4030 LA REUNION PARKWAY, SUITE 150
DALLAS, TEXAS 75212-6014

OVERVIEW: Manufactures dock equipment. Established: 1988. Parent Company: United Dominion Industries.

KEY STATISTICS Annual Sales: $47.0 million. Number of Employees: 325.

HIRING HISTORY Number of professional employees hired in 1994: 10.

EXPERTISE/EDUCATION SOUGHT: Manufacturing engineering, accounting, finance, data processing, payroll, sales

CONTACT: For individuals with previous experience: Mr Jim Mullarkey, Manager of Administration; Phone (214) 905-0707.

SERVICE AMERICA CORPORATION
100 FIRST STAMFORD PLACE
STAMFORD, CONNECTICUT 06904

OVERVIEW: Provides food service and vending machines. Established: 1960. Parent Company: Servam Corporation.

KEY STATISTICS Number of Employees: 18,000.

HIRING HISTORY Number of professional employees hired in 1994: 10.

EXPERTISE/EDUCATION SOUGHT: Accounting, management information systems, sales, finance, marketing, business management, economics, data processing, food services

CONTACTS: For college students and recent graduates: Ms Annmarie Hackett, Director of Compensation; Phone (203) 964-5000. For individuals with previous experience: Mr Jeff Flynn, Corporate Vice President of Human Resources; Phone (203) 964-5000.

SERVICE CORPORATION INTERNATIONAL
1929 ALLEN PARKWAY
HOUSTON, TEXAS 77019-2506

OVERVIEW: Provides funeral and cemetery services. Established: 1962.

KEY STATISTICS Annual Sales: $899.0 million. Number of Employees: 12,716.

HIRING HISTORY Number of professional employees hired in 1993: 50.

EXPERTISE/EDUCATION SOUGHT: Accounting, finance, auditing, law, data processing, human resources

CONTACT: Ms Carol Prescott, Human Resources Representative; Phone (713) 522-5141.

SERVICE LINK, INC.
233 PARK AVENUE SOUTH, 11TH FLOOR
NEW YORK, NEW YORK 10003-1606

OVERVIEW: Provides security guard services.

KEY STATISTICS Number of Employees: 2,500.

EXPERTISE/EDUCATION SOUGHT: Security

CONTACT: For individuals with previous experience: Ms Maria Ortega, Human Resources Director, 500 8th Avenue 8th Floor, New York, NY, 10018; Phone (212) 643-0470.

SERVICE MERCHANDISE COMPANY
7100 SERVICE MERCHANDISE DRIVE
BRENTWOOD, TENNESSEE 37027

OVERVIEW: Operates catalog showroom stores. Established: 1960.

KEY STATISTICS Annual Sales: $4.0 billion. Number of Employees: 22,879.

EXPERTISE/EDUCATION SOUGHT: Management information systems, accounting, purchasing, marketing, management, sales

CONTACT: Mr Mike McPeake, Director of Human Resources; Phone (615) 660-4620.

SERVICEMASTER COMPANY
ONE SERVICEMASTER WAY
DOWNERS GROVE, ILLINOIS 60515

OVERVIEW: Provides building maintenance, sanitation, and industrial services.

KEY STATISTICS Number of Employees: 36,400.

EXPERTISE/EDUCATION SOUGHT: Business management, finance, marketing, chemical engineering, logistics, clinical engineering

CONTACT: Ms Terry Welch, Director for People; Phone (708) 271-1300.

SERVISTAR CORPORATION
SERVISTAR WAY
EAST BUTLER, PENNSYLVANIA 16029

OVERVIEW: Distributes hardware and lumber products. Established: 1935.

KEY STATISTICS Number of Employees: 2,058.

HIRING HISTORY Number of professional employees hired in 1993: 14.

EXPERTISE/EDUCATION SOUGHT: Management information systems, computer programming, finance, accounting, industrial engineering

CONTACT: Mr Charles Rogner, Manager of Recruiting and Training; Phone (412) 283-4567.

SEVERDRUP CORPORATION
801 NORTH 11TH STREET
SAINT LOUIS, MISSOURI 63101

OVERVIEW: Provides architectural and construction engineering services.

EXPERTISE/EDUCATION SOUGHT: Electrical engineering, mechanical engineering, civil engineering, design engineering, environmental engineering, systems integration, architecture, process engineering, project management

CONTACT: For individuals with previous experience: Mr John Busker, Manager of Professional Employment; Phone (314) 436-7600; Fax (314) 436-2959.

SHADY GROVE ADVENTIST HOSPITAL
9901 MEDICAL CENTER DRIVE
ROCKVILLE, MARYLAND 20850-3395

OVERVIEW: Owns and operates hospitals and medical centers. Parent Company: Adventist Healthcare.

KEY STATISTICS Annual Sales: $961.0 million. Number of Employees: 20,359.

EXPERTISE/EDUCATION SOUGHT: Accounting, data processing

CONTACTS: For college students and recent graduates: Ms Jane Prigal, Recruitment Specialist; Phone (301) 279-6240; Fax (301) 217-5001. For individuals with previous experience: Mr Daryl Milam, Director of Human Resources; Phone (301) 279-6256.

SHARP ELECTRONICS CORPORATION
PO BOX 650
MAHWAH, NEW JERSEY 07430

OVERVIEW: Manufactures and markets consumer electronics products, consumer appliances, and office equipment. Established: 1962.

EXPERTISE/EDUCATION SOUGHT: Marketing, sales

CONTACT: For individuals with previous experience: Mr Steve Ness, Manager of Employment; Phone (201) 529-8442.

SHARP HEALTH CARE
3131 BERGER AVENUE
SAN DIEGO, CALIFORNIA 92123-4201

OVERVIEW: General hospital. Established: 1946.

KEY STATISTICS Annual Sales: $634.0 million. Number of Employees: 9,800.

EXPERTISE/EDUCATION SOUGHT: Accounting, marketing, sales, law

CONTACT: Ms Jean Graves, Director of Recruiting/Department of Work Force Programs, 3556 Ruffin Road, Building B, San Diego, CA, 92123; Phone (619) 627-5290, ext. 5276.

SHAW INDUSTRIES, INC.
616 EAST WALNUT AVENUE, PO BOX 2128
DALTON, GEORGIA 30721-4409

OVERVIEW: Manufactures carpet. Established: 1967.

KEY STATISTICS Annual Sales: $2.0 billion. Number of Employees: 21,706.

EXPERTISE/EDUCATION SOUGHT: Sales

CONTACT: Mr Scott Humphrey, Manager of Recruiting, 900 South Harris, Dalton, GA, 20720; Phone (706) 278-3812.

SHAW'S SUPERMARKETS, INC.
140 LAUREL STREET
EAST BRIDGEWATER, MASSACHUSETTS 02333-1764

OVERVIEW: Operates chain of food stores. Established: 1831. Parent Company: J. Sainsbury USA, Inc.

KEY STATISTICS Number of Employees: 16,000.

HIRING HISTORY Number of professional employees hired in 1994: 50. 1993: 50.

EXPERTISE/EDUCATION SOUGHT: Management information systems, finance, computer programming, auditing, merchandising, accounting, marketing

CONTACT: Ms Diane Murphy, Corporate Personnel Manager; Phone (508) 378-7211, ext. 3273.

THE SHERWIN-WILLIAMS COMPANY

101 PROSPECT AVENUE NORTHWEST
CLEVELAND, OHIO 44115-1027

OVERVIEW: Manufactures paints, lacquers and spray paints; operates retail stores. Established: 1866.

KEY STATISTICS Number of Employees: 17,241.

EXPERTISE/EDUCATION SOUGHT: Management, chemical engineering, marketing, finance, business management, purchasing

CONTACTS: For college students and recent graduates: Mr Tom Hopkins, Director of Personnel/Paint Store Group; Phone (216) 566-2980. For individuals with previous experience: Ms Jan Young, Director of Personnel-Corporate; Phone (216) 566-2000.

SHERWOOD MEDICAL COMPANY

1915 OLIVE STREET
SAINT LOUIS, MISSOURI 63103-1625

OVERVIEW: Manufactures and distributes disposable medical products. Established: 1961. Parent Company: American Home Products Corporation.

KEY STATISTICS Annual Sales: $677.0 million. Number of Employees: 6,500.

EXPERTISE/EDUCATION SOUGHT: Accounting, marketing, finance, chemical engineering, mechanical engineering, electrical engineering

CONTACT: For individuals with previous experience: Ms Lola Contestabile, Employment Manager.

SHINTECH INC.

24 GREENWAY PLAZA, SUITE 811
HOUSTON, TEXAS 77046-2401

OVERVIEW: Manufactures polyvinyl chloride resins (PVCs). Established: 1974.

KEY STATISTICS Annual Sales: $600.0 million. Number of Employees: 200.

EXPERTISE/EDUCATION SOUGHT: Management, purchasing

CONTACT: For individuals with previous experience: Ms Carol Andrews, Personnel Supervisor, 5618 Highway 332 East, Freeport, TX, 77541; Phone (409) 233-7861.

SHOE CARNIVAL

8233 BAUMGART ROAD
EVANSVILLE, INDIANA 47711-1599

OVERVIEW: Operates chain of shoe and accessory stores. Established: 1978.

KEY STATISTICS Annual Sales: $215.0 million. Number of Employees: 1,560.

EXPERTISE/EDUCATION SOUGHT: Business administration, business management, management, marketing, retail

CONTACT: For individuals with previous experience: Mr John Merold, Jr, Director of Field Recruiting; Phone (812) 867-6471; Fax (812)867-4055.

CORPORATE PROFILE

Shoe Carnival has over 90 stores in the midwest and midsouth. As the "category killer" of family footwear, each store carries over 40,000 pairs of name-brand shoes. The company guarantees its customers the largest selection and lowest prices on footwear.

Shoe Carnival provides its managers with the technology, training, brand name and private label merchandise, and any other resource or tool needed to maximize sales and profits. Upper-level management delegates decision making to store management, and are committed to growth are guaranteeing career advancement to the top achievers.

Shoe Carnival seeks energetic individuals who are willing to take on new challenges. Applicants should have a B.A. or comparable work experience, strong analytical and communication skills, and a high commitment to customer service and satisfaction. The management team at Shoe Carnival is responsible for the highest average sales volume per unit for any shoe store.

Shoe Carnival managers receive a superior competitive base salary with bonuses. Benefits include a 401(k) plan; stock options; a stock ownership program; medical, dental, life, and disability insurance; a relocation program; management development training that includes a classroom-style seminar; and excellent paid time-off.

SHONEY'S

1727 ELM HILL PIKE
NASHVILLE, TENNESSEE 37210-3777

OVERVIEW: Operates chain of family restaurants. Established: 1959.

KEY STATISTICS Annual Sales: $1.1 billion. Number of Employees: 30,000.

EXPERTISE/EDUCATION SOUGHT: Accounting, marketing, information systems, law, management

CONTACT: For individuals with previous experience: Ms Tracey Stutz, Corporate Human Resources Manager.

SHOWELL FARMS, INC.

10048 PITTS ROAD
SHOWELL, MARYLAND 21862

OVERVIEW: Raises and processes poultry. Established: 1953.

KEY STATISTICS Annual Sales: $340.0 million. Number of Employees: 4,000.

EXPERTISE/EDUCATION SOUGHT: Administration, marketing, accounting

CONTACT: Human Resources Department; Phone (410) 352-5411.

SIEMENS CORPORATION

1301 AVENUE OF THE AMERICAS
NEW YORK, NEW YORK 10019-6022

OVERVIEW: Manufactures electronics and related equipment. Established: 1954.

KEY STATISTICS Annual Sales: $5.0 billion. Number of Employees: 33,444.

EXPERTISE/EDUCATION SOUGHT: Communications, law, management information systems, finance

CONTACT: Ms Ingrid Barrera, Manager of Recruiting; Phone (212) 258-4205.

SIEMENS MEDICAL SYSTEMS, INC.

10950 NORTH TANTAU AVENUE
ISELIN, NEW JERSEY 08830-2704

OVERVIEW: Manufactures and markets medical and diagnostic equipment. Established: 1847. Parent Company: Siemens Medical Corporation.

KEY STATISTICS Annual Sales: $2.0 billion. Number of Employees: 2,200.

EXPERTISE/EDUCATION SOUGHT: Marketing, sales, accounting, finance, management information systems, medical technology, electrical engineering, electronics/electronics engineering, mechanical engineering, law

CONTACT: Mr Cort Montross, Manager of Human Resources; Phone (908) 321-4300.

SIEMENS ROLM COMPANY

4400 OLD IRONSIDES DRIVE
SANTA CLARA, CALIFORNIA 95054-1811

OVERVIEW: Manufactures telecommunications equipment and systems.

KEY STATISTICS Annual Sales: $740.0 million. Number of Employees: 6,000.

HIRING HISTORY Number of professional employees hired in 1994: 100.

EXPERTISE/EDUCATION SOUGHT: Telecommunications, mechanical engineering, electrical engineering

CONTACT: Human Resources Department; Phone (408) 492-2000.

SIGMA ALDRICH CORPORATION
3050 SPRUCE STREET
SAINT LOUIS, MISSOURI 63103-2530

OVERVIEW: Manufactures chemicals, fibers, and metal products. Established: 1975.

KEY STATISTICS Annual Sales: $739.0 million. Number of Employees: 5,110.

EXPERTISE/EDUCATION SOUGHT: Biology, accounting, chemistry, biochemistry, microbiology, chemical engineering

CONTACT: Mr Paul Su, Manager of Staffing Development; Phone (314) 771-5765.

SIGNET BANKING CORPORATION
11013 WEST BROAD STREET
RICHMOND, VIRGINIA 23219-3301

OVERVIEW: Provides commercial and investment banking, consumer finance, and corporate financial services. Established: 1973.

KEY STATISTICS Assets: $1.0 billion. Number of Employees: 5,753.

EXPERTISE/EDUCATION SOUGHT: Accounting, finance, auditing, actuarial, computer programming

CONTACTS: For college students and recent graduates: Ms Marion Moynihan, Assistant Vice President of Human Resources, PO Box 25970, Richmond, VA, 23260-5970; Phone (804) 747-2000. For individuals with previous experience: Mr Greg Paul, Vice President, PO Box 25970, Richmond, VA, 23260-5970.

SILICON SYSTEMS, INC.
14351 MYFORD ROAD
TUSTIN, CALIFORNIA 92680-7039

OVERVIEW: Manufactures semiconductors and related components. Established: 1989. Parent Company: TDK USA Corporation.

KEY STATISTICS Annual Sales: $300.0 million. Number of Employees: 2,100.

EXPERTISE/EDUCATION SOUGHT: Accounting, finance, product design and development, data processing, software engineering/development, design engineering, process engineering

CONTACTS: For college students and recent graduates: Mr Agim Zabeli, Recruiter; Phone (714) 731-7110. For individuals with previous experience: Ms Jennifer Bortele, Staffing Manager; Phone (714) 731-7110, ext. 6252.

SIMON AND SCHUSTER, INC.
1230 AVENUE OF THE AMERICAS
NEW YORK, NEW YORK 10020-1513

OVERVIEW: Publishes books.

EXPERTISE/EDUCATION SOUGHT: Publishing, systems analysis, computer programming, editing, accounting

CONTACT: Mr Alan Gaynor, Associate Director of Staffing, 1 Lake Street, Upper Saddle River, NJ, 07458; Phone (201) 592-2272.

SIMPSON PAPER COMPANY
1301 5TH AVENUE, SUITE 1900
SEATTLE, WASHINGTON 98101-2603

OVERVIEW: Manufactures paper. Parent Company: Simpson Investment Company.

KEY STATISTICS Number of Employees: 4,600.

EXPERTISE/EDUCATION SOUGHT: Pulp and paper science, accounting, sales

CONTACT: Ms Linda Mains, Human Resources Administrator; Phone (206) 224-5000; Fax (206) 224-5210.

SINCLAIR OIL CORPORATION
550 EAST SOUTH TEMPLE
SALT LAKE CITY, UTAH 84102-1005

OVERVIEW: Refines and markets petroleum products. Established: 1952.

KEY STATISTICS Annual Sales: $1.0 billion. Number of Employees: 4,800.

EXPERTISE/EDUCATION SOUGHT: Petroleum/petrochemical engineering, mechanical engineering, management information systems, accounting, transportation

CONTACT: Mr Wendell White, Director of Human Resources; Phone (801) 363-5100.

SINGER SEWING COMPANY
RARITAN CENTER
EDISON, NEW JERSEY 08837

OVERVIEW: Manufactures sewing machines and household appliances.

EXPERTISE/EDUCATION SOUGHT: Accounting, sales, customer service and support, finance, data processing, transportation, marketing

CONTACT: For individuals with previous experience: Mr Terance Brogan, Director Human Resources.

SISTERS OF CHARITY OF LEAVENWORTH HEALTH SERVICES CORPORATION
4200 SOUTH 4TH STREET
LEAVENWORTH, KANSAS 66048-5054

OVERVIEW: Owns and operates hospitals and medical centers. Established: 1972. Parent Company: Sisters of Charity of Leavenworth.

KEY STATISTICS Annual Sales: $754.5 million. Number of Employees: 10,150.

EXPERTISE/EDUCATION SOUGHT: Hospital administration

CONTACT: For individuals with previous experience: Mr Mike Groves, Vice President of Human Resources; Phone (913) 682-1338, ext. 222.

SISTERS OF CHARITY OF NAZARETH
PO BOX 171
NAZARETH, KENTUCKY 40048

OVERVIEW: Owns hospitals.

KEY STATISTICS Annual Sales: $541.0 million. Number of Employees: 10,000.

EXPERTISE/EDUCATION SOUGHT: Administration

CONTACT: For individuals with previous experience: Mr Mark Dundon, President.

SISTERS OF MERCY HEALTH SYSTEMS
2039 NORTH GEYER ROAD
SAINT LOUIS, MISSOURI 63131-3332

OVERVIEW: Owns and operates hospitals and medical centers.

KEY STATISTICS Annual Sales: $1.0 billion. Number of Employees: 15,000.

EXPERTISE/EDUCATION SOUGHT: Data processing, accounting, finance, auditing, management information systems, health care

CONTACT: For individuals with previous experience: Human Resource Department; Phone (314) 965-6100.

SISTERS OF PROVIDENCE OF OREGON
520 PIKE STREET
SEATTLE, WASHINGTON 98101

OVERVIEW: Provides health care services.

HIRING HISTORY Number of professional employees hired in 1994: 5.

EXPERTISE/EDUCATION SOUGHT: Administration, accounting, finance, human resources, public relations, management information systems, law, planning

CONTACT: For individuals with previous experience: Mr Ron Newcomb, Manager of Human Resources, PO Box 11038, Seattle, WA, 98111-9038; Phone (206) 464-4235.

SISTERS OF ST. FRANCIS HEALTH SERVICES
1515 WEST DRAGOON TRAIL
MISHAWAKA, INDIANA 46544-4710

OVERVIEW: Owns and operates hospitals and medical centers. Established: 1974.

KEY STATISTICS Annual Sales: $856.0 million. Number of Employees: 6,923.

EXPERTISE/EDUCATION SOUGHT: Accounting, finance, data processing, auditing, nursing

CONTACT: For individuals with previous experience: Sister Jane Marte Klein, President; Phone (219) 256-3935.

SIZZLER INTERNATIONAL, INC.
12655 WEST JEFFERSON BOULEVARD
LOS ANGELES, CALIFORNIA 90066-7008

OVERVIEW: Operates chain of family restaurants. Established: 1968.

KEY STATISTICS Annual Sales: $488.0 million. Number of Employees: 16,600.

HIRING HISTORY Number of professional employees hired in 1994: 7.

EXPERTISE/EDUCATION SOUGHT: Accounting, law, data processing, computer programming, marketing

CONTACT: Ms Lori Linogon, Corporate Recruiter; Phone (310) 827-2300.

SKF USA, INC.
1100 1ST AVENUE
KING OF PRUSSIA, PENNSYLVANIA 19406-1312

OVERVIEW: Manufactures ball bearings. Established: 1933.

KEY STATISTICS Number of Employees: 5,960.

HIRING HISTORY Number of professional employees hired in 1994: 20. 1993: 20.

EXPERTISE/EDUCATION SOUGHT: Mechanical engineering

CONTACT: Ms Mary Ellen Canavan, Manager of Staffing and Placement; Phone (610) 962-4552.

SKY CHEFS, INC.
524 EAST LAMAR BOULEVARD
ARLINGTON, TEXAS 76011-3999

OVERVIEW: Provides in flight catering services. Established: 1942.

KEY STATISTICS Number of Employees: 6,200.

EXPERTISE/EDUCATION SOUGHT: Food services, administration

CONTACT: For individuals with previous experience: Mr Chris Price, Human Resources Specialist; Phone (817) 792-2123.

SLS, INC.
3333 BEVERLY ROAD
HOFFMAN ESTATES, ILLINOIS 6017-3322

OVERVIEW: Provides freight transportation services. Established: 1939. Parent Company: Sears Roebuck and Company.

KEY STATISTICS Annual Sales: $1.0 billion. Number of Employees: 5,484.

EXPERTISE/EDUCATION SOUGHT: Logistics, transportation, accounting

CONTACT: Ms Roseann Hogenboom, Employment Manager of Equal Employment Opportunity and Benefits, 225 Windsor Drive, Itasca, IL, 60143; Phone (708) 645-5100.

SMART AND FINAL, INC.
4700 SOUTH BOYLE AVENUE
VERNON, CALIFORNIA 90058-3000

OVERVIEW: Distributes wholesale groceries and restaurant equipment and supplies. Established: 1871.

KEY STATISTICS Number of Employees: 3,500.

EXPERTISE/EDUCATION SOUGHT: Computer programming, accounting, purchasing, training and development, production, construction

CONTACT: For individuals with previous experience: Ms Sasha Le, Recruiting Specialist.

A. O. SMITH CORPORATION
11270 WEST PARK PLACE
MILWAUKEE, WISCONSIN 53224-3690

OVERVIEW: Manufactures water heaters, car frames, motors, and fiberglass. Established: 1923.

KEY STATISTICS Number of Employees: 10,800.

HIRING HISTORY Number of professional employees hired in 1994: 5.

EXPERTISE/EDUCATION SOUGHT: Human resources, electrical engineering, marketing, chemical engineering, finance

CONTACT: Ms Donna Cook, Corporate Manager of Human Resources; Phone (414) 359-4000, ext. 4128.

SMITH BARNEY, INC.
1345 AVENUE OF THE AMERICAS
NEW YORK, NEW YORK 10105-0302

OVERVIEW: Provides brokerage and investment services. Established: 1873.

KEY STATISTICS Number of Employees: 25,000.

HIRING HISTORY Number of professional employees hired in 1994: 1,000.

EXPERTISE/EDUCATION SOUGHT: Finance, accounting, underwriting, systems analysis, computer programming

CONTACTS: For college students and recent graduates: Ms Mary Campofranco, Director of Corporate Staffing, 388 Greenwich Street, New York, NY, 10013; Phone (212) 816-8181. For individuals with previous experience: Mr David McNulty, First Vice President of Recruiting; Phone (212) 698-8072.

SMITH AND NEPHEW RICHARDS, INC.
1450 EAST BROOKS ROAD
MEMPHIS, TENNESSEE 38116-1804

OVERVIEW: Designs, markets and manufactures orthopedic implants, trauma, spine, and medical specialty products. Established: 1934.

KEY STATISTICS Annual Sales: $326.0 million.

EXPERTISE/EDUCATION SOUGHT: Marketing, finance, accounting, data processing, mechanical engineering, biomedical engineering

CONTACT: For individuals with previous experience: Mr Steve Ammons, Group Manager of Human Resources; Phone (901) 396-2121.

SMITH'S FOOD AND DRUG CENTERS, INC.
1550 SOUTH REDWOOD ROAD
SALT LAKE CITY, UTAH 84104-5105

OVERVIEW: Operates chain of food and drug stores. Established: 1948.

KEY STATISTICS Annual Sales: $3.0 billion. Number of Employees: 18,800.

EXPERTISE/EDUCATION SOUGHT: Accounting, sales, finance

CONTACT: Mr Kevin Beutler, Human Resources Manager; Phone (801) 974-1245.

SMITHKLINE BEECHAM CLINICAL LABORATORIES
1201 SOUTH COLLEGEVILLE ROAD
COLLEGEVILLE, PENNSYLVANIA 19426-1050

OVERVIEW: Operates clinical and medical laboratory. Established: 1969. Parent Company: Smithkline Beecham Corporation.

KEY STATISTICS Annual Sales: $1.0 billion. Number of Employees: 10,500.

EXPERTISE/EDUCATION SOUGHT: Marketing, finance, accounting, management information systems, data processing, sales

CONTACT: Ms Nancy Shapiro, Director of Human Resources; Phone (610) 454-6000.

SMITHKLINE BEECHAM CORPORATION

1 FRANKLIN PLAZA
PHILADELPHIA, PENNSYLVANIA 19108

OVERVIEW: Manufactures pharmaceuticals and consumer health products. Established: 1830.

EXPERTISE/EDUCATION SOUGHT: Human resources, finance, marketing, management information systems, government affairs/relations, safety engineering, health care

CONTACTS: For college students and recent graduates: Mr Joseph Ambrosino, United States College Recruiter; Phone (215) 751-3238. For individuals with previous experience: Ms Diane Doyle, Manager of Employment and Workforce Planning; Phone (215) 751-4000.

SMITHSONIAN INSTITUTION

1000 THOMAS JEFFERSON STREET
WASHINGTON, D.C. 20560

OVERVIEW: Research and educational center that includes museums, galleries, laboratories, and scholarly organizations. Established: 1846.

KEY STATISTICS Number of Employees: 6,000.

HIRING HISTORY Number of professional employees hired in 1994: 100. 1993: 300.

EXPERTISE/EDUCATION SOUGHT: Computer science, archeology, accounting, natural sciences, history, anthropology

CONTACT: Ms Marilyn Marton, Acting Director of Human Resources; Phone (202) 287-3646.

SNAP-ON TOOLS, INC.

2801 80TH STREET
KENOSHA, WISCONSIN 53141-1410

OVERVIEW: Manufactures hand tools, power tools, tool storage cabinets, and electronic diagnostic and service equipment. Established: 1920.

KEY STATISTICS Number of Employees: 9,000.

HIRING HISTORY Number of professional employees hired in 1994: 75. 1993: 90.

EXPERTISE/EDUCATION SOUGHT: Accounting, marketing, electrical engineering, finance, mechanical engineering, design engineering, data processing, computer programming, computer analysis

CONTACT: Mr Dave Rosenbalm, Senior Human Resources Administrator; Phone (414) 656-4964.

SOCIETY CORPORATION

127 PUBLIC SQUARE, 12TH FLOOR
CLEVELAND, OHIO 44114-1306

OVERVIEW: Commercial banking, insurance, and related financial services. Established: 1845.

KEY STATISTICS Number of Employees: 30,000.

EXPERTISE/EDUCATION SOUGHT: Business management, management, computer science, accounting

CONTACT: Ms Kim Robinson, Manager of College Relations, 127 Public Square 12th Floor, Cleveland, OH, 44114; Phone (216) 689-3433.

SOLA GROUP

2420 SAND HILL ROAD, SUITE 200
MENLO PARK, CALIFORNIA 94025

OVERVIEW: Manufactures eye glass lenses.

KEY STATISTICS Annual Sales: $306.0 million. Number of Employees: 5,370.

EXPERTISE/EDUCATION SOUGHT: Accounting, finance, sales, marketing, manufacturing engineering

CONTACT: For individuals with previous experience: Ms Sharon Spinali, Director of Human Services; Phone (415) 324-6868.

SOLVAY AMERICA, INC.

3333 RICHMOND AVENUE
HOUSTON, TEXAS 77098-3007

OVERVIEW: Manufactures resins, polymers, pharmaceuticals, minerals, veterinary products, automotive products, and chemicals. Established: 1863.

KEY STATISTICS Annual Sales: $1.0 billion. Number of Employees: 4,600.

EXPERTISE/EDUCATION SOUGHT: Environmental engineering, chemical engineering, accounting, management information systems

CONTACT: For individuals with previous experience: Ms Lisa Seeker, Employee Relations Manager.

SONAT, INC.

1900 5TH AVENUE NORTH
BIRMINGHAM, ALABAMA 35203-2610

OVERVIEW: Natural gas drilling and transporting company. Established: 1973.

KEY STATISTICS Annual Sales: $2.0 billion. Number of Employees: 2,300.

EXPERTISE/EDUCATION SOUGHT: Accounting, law, environmental engineering, chemical engineering, mechanical engineering, electrical engineering, marketing, data processing

CONTACT: Ms Denise Sutton, Director of Human Resources, PO Box 2563, Birmingham, AL, 35202-2563; Phone (205) 325-3800.

SONOCO PRODUCTS COMPANY

NORTH 2ND STREET
HARTSVILLE, SOUTH CAROLINA 29550

OVERVIEW: Manufactures packaging tubes, cans, and grocery bags. Established: 1899.

KEY STATISTICS Number of Employees: 16,472.

EXPERTISE/EDUCATION SOUGHT: Chemical engineering, mechanical engineering, electrical engineering, accounting, liberal arts

CONTACT: For individuals with previous experience: Mr H Grady Weaver, Human Resources Manager; Phone (803) 383-7000, ext. 764.

SONY CORPORATION OF AMERICA

9 WEST 57TH STREET, 43RD FLOOR
NEW YORK, NEW YORK 10019-2600

OVERVIEW: Manufactures and markets electronic equipment, office equipment, and home appliances.

KEY STATISTICS Annual Sales: $13.0 billion. Number of Employees: 32,000.

EXPERTISE/EDUCATION SOUGHT: Computer science, manufacturing engineering, accounting, electronics/electronics engineering, marketing, finance, electrical engineering, data processing, sales

CONTACTS: For college students and recent graduates: Mr Rick Lustig, Staffing Specialist, 1 Sony Drive, Park Ridge, NJ, 07656; Phone (201) 930-6660. For individuals with previous experience: Ms Anne Marie Seifert, Manager of Human Resources, 1 Sony Drive, Park Ridge, NJ, 07656; Phone (201) 930-1000.

SONY MUSIC ENTERTAINMENT, INC.

550 MADISON AVENUE
NEW YORK, NEW YORK 10022-3211

OVERVIEW: Produces and markets music and entertainment products. Parent Company: Sony Software Corporation.

KEY STATISTICS Annual Sales: $4.0 billion. Number of Employees: 11,000.

EXPERTISE/EDUCATION SOUGHT: Marketing, sales, information systems

CONTACT: For individuals with previous experience: Recruiting Department; Phone (212) 833-8000.

SONY PICTURES ENTERTAINMENT
10202 WASHINGTON BOULEVARD
CULVER CITY, CALIFORNIA 90232

OVERVIEW: Produces and distributes motion pictures and television programming.

EXPERTISE/EDUCATION SOUGHT: Accounting, finance, marketing

CONTACT: For individuals with previous experience: Human Resources Department; Phone (310) 280-3636.

SOURCE ONE MORTGAGE SERVICES CORPORATION
27555 FARMINGTON ROAD
FARMINGTON HILLS, MICHIGAN 48334-3314

OVERVIEW: Mortgage bank.

KEY STATISTICS Number of Employees: 3,060.

EXPERTISE/EDUCATION SOUGHT: Finance, business management

CONTACT: Ms Debbie MacDonald, Employment Manager.

SOUTH JERSEY INDUSTRIES, INC.
NUMBER ONE SOUTH JERSEY PLAZA
HAMMONTON, NEW JERSEY 08037

OVERVIEW: Distributes and transmits natural gas; mines industrial sand and gravel. Established: 1969.

KEY STATISTICS Annual Sales: $334.0 million. Number of Employees: 1,000.

EXPERTISE/EDUCATION SOUGHT: Accounting, finance, auditing, marketing, computer programming

CONTACT: Mr Cedrick Jeffries, Human Resources Administrator; Phone (609) 561-9000.

SOUTHEASTERN PENNSYLVANIA TRANSPORTATION AUTHORITY
841 CHESTNUT STREET
PHILADELPHIA, PENNSYLVANIA 19106-2326

OVERVIEW: Provides local transit services. Established: 1964.

KEY STATISTICS Annual Sales: $667.0 million. Number of Employees: 9,600.

EXPERTISE/EDUCATION SOUGHT: Accounting, finance, law, data processing, auditing

CONTACT: For individuals with previous experience: Ms Peggy D Fitts, Director of Personnel.

SOUTHERN CALIFORNIA EDISON COMPANY
2244 WALNUT GROVE AVENUE
ROSEMEAD, CALIFORNIA 91770-3714

OVERVIEW: Electric utility. Established: 1887. Parent Company: SCE Corporation.

KEY STATISTICS Annual Sales: $7.0 billion. Number of Employees: 16,487.

EXPERTISE/EDUCATION SOUGHT: Program analysis, computer science, research, education, economics, electrical engineering, civil engineering, mechanical engineering, planning

CONTACT: For individuals with previous experience: Mr Steve Nakajima, Human Resources Department Manager; Phone (810) 302-5144.

SOUTHERN CALIFORNIA GAS COMPANY
810 SOUTH FLOWER STREET
LOS ANGELES, CALIFORNIA 90013-1011

OVERVIEW: Gas utility. Established: 1929. Parent Company: Pacific Enterprises.

KEY STATISTICS Annual Sales: $3.0 billion. Number of Employees: 8,200.

HIRING HISTORY Number of professional employees hired in 1994: 175.

EXPERTISE/EDUCATION SOUGHT: Accounting, finance, marketing, law, economics, electrical engineering, mechanical engineering, civil engineering, environmental engineering, industrial engineering

CONTACT: For individuals with previous experience: Ms Karen Hiller, Personnel Services Coordinator; Phone (213) 244-1200, ext. 3210; Fax (213) 244-1242.

SOUTHERN CALIFORNIA PERMANENTE MEDICAL GROUP
393 WALNUT STREET
PASADENA, CALIFORNIA 91188-1530

OVERVIEW: Provides health care services. Established: 1952.

KEY STATISTICS Annual Sales: $4.0 billion. Number of Employees: 9,500.

EXPERTISE/EDUCATION SOUGHT: Accounting, auditing, data processing, computer programming

CONTACT: For individuals with previous experience: Mr Hugo Aguas, Regional Director of Personnel, 393 Walnut Drive, Pasadena, CA, 91188-4922; Phone (818) 405-5757.

THE SOUTHERN COMPANY
64 PERIMETER CENTER EAST
ATLANTA, GEORGIA 30346

OVERVIEW: Electric utility. Established: 1949.

KEY STATISTICS Annual Sales: $8.0 billion. Number of Employees: 28,000.

EXPERTISE/EDUCATION SOUGHT: Engineering, computer science, accounting, finance, mechanical engineering, electrical engineering

CONTACT: For individuals with previous experience: Ms Mary Gordon Pawlawski, Staffing Specialist; Phone (404) 393-3639.

SOUTHERN MULTI MEDIA COMMUNICATIONS, INC.
115 PERIMETER CENTER PLACE, SUITE 1150
ATLANTA, GEORGIA 30346

OVERVIEW: Provides cable television broadcasting services. Established: 1986.

KEY STATISTICS Annual Sales: $67.0 million. Number of Employees: 500.

EXPERTISE/EDUCATION SOUGHT: Accounting, finance, management

CONTACT: For individuals with previous experience: Mr Rick Seamon, Director of Human Resources; Phone (404) 395-0304.

SOUTHERN NEW ENGLAND TELEPHONE COMPANY
227 CHURCH STREET
NEW HAVEN, CONNECTICUT 06510

OVERVIEW: Provides telecommunications services. Established: 1878. Parent Company: Southern New England Telecommunications Corporation.

KEY STATISTICS Number of Employees: 9,300.

EXPERTISE/EDUCATION SOUGHT: Telecommunications, electronics/ electronics engineering, accounting

CONTACTS: For college students and recent graduates: Ms Carolyn Geter, Carrer Development Staff Manager; Phone (203) 771-7335. For individuals with previous experience: Ms Paula Schiller, Director of Employment and Careers, 367 Orange Street, New Haven, CT, 06510; Phone (203) 771-4355; Fax (203) 771-7050.

SOUTHERN OPTICAL COMPANY
1909 NORTH CHURCH STREET
GREENSBORO, NORTH CAROLINA 27405-5631

OVERVIEW: Manufactures optical products. Established: 1989.

KEY STATISTICS Number of Employees: 470.

EXPERTISE/EDUCATION SOUGHT: Optics

CONTACT: For individuals with previous experience: Mr Jim Price, Director of Human Resources; Phone (910) 272-8146.

SOUTHERN PACIFIC TRANSPORTATION COMPANY
1 MARKET PLAZA
SAN FRANCISCO, CALIFORNIA 94105-1019

Overview: Provides railroad and truck freight services. Established: 1930.

Key Statistics Annual Sales: $3.0 billion. Number of Employees: 16,894.

Expertise/Education Sought: Accounting, marketing, finance, data processing, computer programming

Contacts: For college students and recent graduates: Job Hotline; Phone (800) 873-3744. For individuals with previous experience: Mr Lynn Chapman, Director/Staffing; Phone (415) 541-2623.

SOUTHERN PERU COPPER CORPORATION
180 MAIDEN LANE
NEW YORK, NEW YORK 10038

Overview: Operates copper mines.

Expertise/Education Sought: Geology, mechanical engineering

Contact: Mr Derek Sampson, Human Resources Administrator; Phone (212) 510-2000.

SOUTHLAND CORPORATION
2711 NORTH HASKELL AVENUE
DALLAS, TEXAS 75204-2910

Overview: Operates convenience stores. Established: 1927.

Key Statistics Number of Employees: 32,406.

Hiring History Number of professional employees hired in 1994: 200.

Expertise/Education Sought: Retail

Contact: For individuals with previous experience: Ms Beth Marquardt, Corporate Recruiter.

SOUTHTRUST CORPORATION
420 20TH STREET NORTH
BIRMINGHAM, ALABAMA 35203

Overview: Commercial bank. Established: 1968.

Expertise/Education Sought: Accounting, computer programming, finance, credit/credit analysis

Contact: Ms Anna McLaughlin, Vice President of Personnel; Phone (205) 254-6760.

SOUTHWEST AIRLINES COMPANY
2702 LOVE FIELD DRIVE
DALLAS, TEXAS 75235-1908

Overview: Provides passenger and freight airline services. Established: 1971.

Key Statistics Annual Sales: $2.0 billion. Number of Employees: 15,175.

Expertise/Education Sought: Marketing, sales, finance, accounting, data processing

Contact: Ms DeLisa Catalane, Coordinator of Employment; Phone (214) 904-4000.

SOUTHWEST GAS CORPORATION
5241 SPRING MOUNTAIN ROAD
LAS VEGAS, NEVADA 89120-0001

Overview: Distributes natural gas. Established: 1931.

Key Statistics Number of Employees: 2,318.

Hiring History Number of professional employees hired in 1993: 10.

Expertise/Education Sought: Accounting, finance, marketing, distribution, data processing

Contact: For individuals with previous experience: Ms Linda Mundy, Administrator of Equal Employment Oppurtunity and Affirmative Action; Phone (702) 876-7210, ext. 7196; Fax (702)364-3180.

SOUTHWESTERN BELL MOBILE SYSTEMS
17330 PRESTON ROAD, 100A
DALLAS, TEXAS 75252

Overview: Provides cellular mobile telephone services. Established: 1983. Parent Company: Southwestern Bell Corporation.

Key Statistics Annual Sales: $1.1 billion. Number of Employees: 2,658.

Expertise/Education Sought: Sales, electrical engineering, electronics/electronics engineering

Contact: For individuals with previous experience: Ms Mary Williams, Human Resources Representative; Phone (214) 733-2000.

SOUTHWESTERN BELL TELEPHONE COMPANY
1010 PINE STREET
SAINT LOUIS, MISSOURI 63101-3099

Overview: Provides telecommunications services. Established: 1984. Parent Company: Southwestern Bell Corporation.

Key Statistics Number of Employees: 49,190.

Expertise/Education Sought: Telecommunications, electrical engineering, accounting

Contact: For individuals with previous experience: Mr John Jennings, Managing Director Workforce Development; Phone (210) 351-2527.

SOUTHWESTERN BELL YELLOW PAGES
12800 PUBLICATIONS DRIVE
SAINT LOUIS, MISSOURI 63131-1833

Overview: Publishes telephone directories. Established: 1984.

Key Statistics Annual Sales: $100.0 million. Number of Employees: 2,300.

Expertise/Education Sought: Sales, customer service and support, graphic arts

Contact: For individuals with previous experience: Human Resources Department; Phone (314) 957-2212.

SOUTHWESTERN PUBLIC SERVICE COMPANY
PO BOX 1261
AMARILLO, TEXAS 79170

Overview: Electric utility.

Key Statistics Number of Employees: 2,200.

Hiring History Number of professional employees hired in 1994: 5.

Contact: For individuals with previous experience: Mr Gary McDade, Manager of Employment and Development; Phone (806) 378-2910.

SPALDING AND EVENFLO COMPANIES
1801 COMMERCE DRIVE
PIQUA, OHIO 45356-2674

Overview: Manufactures sporting goods, food containers, juvenile furniture, and rubber nipples. Established: 1981.

Key Statistics Annual Sales: $491.0 million. Number of Employees: 2,970.

Expertise/Education Sought: Business management

Contact: For individuals with previous experience: Mr Dennis Pregent, Director of Human Resources.

SPI PHARMACEUTICALS, INC.
3300 HYLAND AVENUE
COSTA MESA, CALIFORNIA 92626

Overview: Manufactures pharmaceuticals and ophthalmic products.

Expertise/Education Sought: Pharmacy, marketing, finance, accounting, sales

Contact: For individuals with previous experience: Ms Mary Martinolli, Director of Human Resources; Phone (714) 545-0100.

SPIEGEL, INC.
3500 LACEY ROAD
DOWNERS GROVE, ILLINOIS 60515-5432

OVERVIEW: Operates retail outlets and provides catalog mail order services. Established: 1865.

KEY STATISTICS Number of Employees: 11,104.

HIRING HISTORY Number of professional employees hired in 1994: 150.

EXPERTISE/EDUCATION SOUGHT: Marketing, finance, human resources, information systems, law, advertising, merchandising, manufacturing, real estate, retail

CONTACT: Ms Kelly Powell, Manager of Human Resources; Phone (708) 769-3117.

SPORTS AND RECREATION, INC.
4701 WEST HILLSBOROUGH
TAMPA, FLORIDA 33614-5419

OVERVIEW: Sells sporting goods and bicycles. Established: 1988.

KEY STATISTICS Annual Sales: $239.0 million. Number of Employees: 3,000.

EXPERTISE/EDUCATION SOUGHT: Management

CONTACT: For individuals with previous experience: Ms Joan Fernigno, Manager Recruiting.

SPRINGS INDUSTRIES
200 NORTH WHITE STREET
FORT MILL, SOUTH CAROLINA 29715-1654

OVERVIEW: Manufactures rugs and other home furnishings.

KEY STATISTICS Number of Employees: 25,357.

HIRING HISTORY Number of professional employees hired in 1994: 15.

EXPERTISE/EDUCATION SOUGHT: Management information systems, management, finance

CONTACT: Mr R N Scharfenberger, Director of Management Staffing and Development, PO Box 70, Fort Mill, SC, 29716; Phone (803) 547-1500; Fax (803)547-3706.

SPRINT CORPORATION
2330 SHAWNEE MISSION PARKWAY
WESTWOOD, KANSAS 66205-2005

OVERVIEW: Provides telecommunications and related services. Established: 1938.

KEY STATISTICS Number of Employees: 52,200.

EXPERTISE/EDUCATION SOUGHT: Accounting, engineering, sales

CONTACT: For individuals with previous experience: Ms Lonna Lewendoski, Human Resources Recruiting Representative; Phone (913) 624-2946.

SPRINT MID-ATLANTIC TELEPHONE
1411 CAPITOL BOULEVARD
WAKE FOREST, NORTH CAROLINA 27587-7055

OVERVIEW: Provides telephone communication services. Established: 1969. Parent Company: Sprint Corporation.

KEY STATISTICS Number of Employees: 4,308.

HIRING HISTORY Number of professional employees hired in 1994: 60.

EXPERTISE/EDUCATION SOUGHT: Marketing, information services

CONTACT: Ms Janet Holliday, Director Recruitment; Phone (919) 554-5184.

SPRINT/UNITED TELEPHONE NORTHWEST
902 WASCO STREET
HOOD RIVER, OREGON 97031-3103

OVERVIEW: Provider of telecommunications services. Established: 1957. Parent Company: Sprint Corporation.

KEY STATISTICS Annual Sales: $102.0 million. Number of Employees: 630.

EXPERTISE/EDUCATION SOUGHT: Customer service and support, sales, management, technical

CONTACT: Ms Dianne Glaze, Director of Corporate Human Resources; Phone (503) 386-2211.

SPX CORPORATION
700 TERRACE POINT ROAD
MUSKEGON, MICHIGAN 49440-1100

OVERVIEW: Manufactures automotive parts. Established: 1911.

KEY STATISTICS Number of Employees: 8,600.

HIRING HISTORY Number of professional employees hired in 1993: 150.

EXPERTISE/EDUCATION SOUGHT: Accounting, operations, sales, finance, marketing, data processing, electrical engineering, mechanical engineering, materials engineering, industrial engineering

CONTACT: For individuals with previous experience: Mr Steve Lason, Vice President of Human Resources, PO Box 3301, Muskegon, MI, 49443-3301; Phone (616) 724-5000, ext. 5107.

SQUARE D COMPANY
1415 SOUTH ROSELLE ROAD
PALATINE, ILLINOIS 60067

OVERVIEW: Manufactures electrical distribution and industrial control equipment. Established: 1902.

HIRING HISTORY Number of professional employees hired in 1994: 150.

EXPERTISE/EDUCATION SOUGHT: Accounting, finance, human resources, computer programming, industrial engineering, law, business development, information systems

CONTACT: Ms Rita Danker, Manager of Human Resources; Phone (708) 397-2600.

ST. JOE INDUSTRIES, INC.
1650 PRUDENTIAL DRIVE, SUITE 400
JACKSONVILLE, FLORIDA 32207

OVERVIEW: Manufactures corrugated products.

EXPERTISE/EDUCATION SOUGHT: Accounting, marketing, finance, management information systems

CONTACT: For individuals with previous experience: Human Resources Department; Phone (904) 396-6600.

STAFFING NETWORK, INC.
1111 CHARLES WAY
MANCHESTER, NEW HAMPSHIRE 03101-6052

OVERVIEW: Provides employee leasing services.

KEY STATISTICS Annual Sales: $84.0 million. Number of Employees: 4,000.

EXPERTISE/EDUCATION SOUGHT: Accounting, business administration, customer service and support

CONTACT: For individuals with previous experience: Mr Michael Gatsas, President.

STAFFPRO SECURITY, INC.
3662 KATELLA AVENUE, SUITE 110
LOS ALAMITOS, CALIFORNIA 90720-3108

OVERVIEW: Provides security guard services.

KEY STATISTICS Annual Sales: $46.0 million. Number of Employees: 4,040.

EXPERTISE/EDUCATION SOUGHT: Security

CONTACT: For individuals with previous experience: Human Resourcs Office; Phone (310) 596-5949.

A. E. STALEY MANUFACTURING COMPANY
2200 EAST ELDORADO STREET
DECATUR, ILLINOIS 62521-1578

OVERVIEW: Agricultural products processing company. Established: 1898.

KEY STATISTICS Annual Sales: $1.0 billion. Number of Employees: 2,160.

HIRING HISTORY Number of professional employees hired in 1994: 15.

EXPERTISE/EDUCATION SOUGHT: Chemical engineering, merchandising, food science, accounting, chemistry, information systems, research and development

CONTACT: Mr Bruce Raak, Manager Human Resources, PO Box 151, Decatur, IL, 62525-1801; Phone (217) 423-4411.

STANDARD COMMERCIAL CORPORATION

2201 MILLER ROAD
WILSON, NORTH CAROLINA 27893-6860

OVERVIEW: Tobacco leaf merchants. Established: 1916.

KEY STATISTICS Number of Employees: 2,280.

EXPERTISE/EDUCATION SOUGHT: Accounting, finance, marketing, management information systems

CONTACT: For individuals with previous experience: Ms Nancy Haynes, Human Resources Manager; Phone (919) 291-5507, ext. 256.

THE STANDARD PRODUCTS COMPANY

2401 GULLEY ROAD
DEARBORN, MICHIGAN 40124

OVERVIEW: Manufactures automotive products. Established: 1927.

KEY STATISTICS Number of Employees: 9,480.

EXPERTISE/EDUCATION SOUGHT: Technical engineering, mechanical engineering, electrical engineering, manufacturing engineering, administration, management

CONTACT: For individuals with previous experience: Corporate Manager of Employment; Phone (313) 561-1100, ext. 304.

THE STANDARD REGISTER COMPANY

600 ALBANY STREET
DAYTON, OHIO 45408-1405

OVERVIEW: Manufactures business forms and data storage equipment. Established: 1912.

KEY STATISTICS Annual Sales: $722.0 million. Number of Employees: 5,769.

HIRING HISTORY Number of professional employees hired in 1993: 35.

EXPERTISE/EDUCATION SOUGHT: Business management, purchasing, marketing, finance, technical engineering, information services, sales

CONTACT: Ms Sue Hudson, Manager of Human Resources, PO Box 1167, Dayton, OH, 45408-1167; Phone (513) 443-1000, ext. 1543.

STANHOME, INC.

333 WESTERN AVENUE
WESTFIELD, MASSACHUSETTS 01085

OVERVIEW: Manufactures household cleaning products. Established: 1931.

EXPERTISE/EDUCATION SOUGHT: Marketing, finance, accounting, computer programming

CONTACT: Mr Ronald R Jalbert, Vice President of Human Resources; Phone (413) 562-3631, ext. 212.

STANLEY SMITH SECURITY, INC.

3355 CHERRY RIDGE STREET, SUITE 200
SAN ANTONIO, TEXAS 78230-4828

OVERVIEW: Provides armored car and detective services. Established: 1928.

KEY STATISTICS Annual Sales: $114.0 million. Number of Employees: 6,300.

EXPERTISE/EDUCATION SOUGHT: Accounting, management

CONTACT: For individuals with previous experience: Ms Virginia Townsend, Executive Secretary.

THE STANLEY WORKS

100 STANLEY DRIVE
NEW BRITAIN, CONNECTICUT 06053

OVERVIEW: Manufactures hardware and hand tools. Established: 1843.

EXPERTISE/EDUCATION SOUGHT: Electrical engineering

CONTACT: Ms Allison Turkowski, Manager of Human Resources; Phone (203) 827-3942.

STAPLES, INC.

100 PENNSYLVANIA AVENUE
FRAMINGHAM, MASSACHUSETTS 01701-9328

OVERVIEW: Operates chain of office supplies and equipment stores. Established: 1986.

KEY STATISTICS Annual Sales: $2.0 billion. Number of Employees: 15,700.

HIRING HISTORY Number of professional employees hired in 1994: 850.

EXPERTISE/EDUCATION SOUGHT: Distribution, finance, information systems, merchandising, store management

CONTACT: Human Resources - PJO.

For more information, see full corporate profile, pg. 216.

STAR ENTERPRISE

12700 NORTHBOROUGH DRIVE
HOUSTON, TEXAS 77067-2508

OVERVIEW: Markets and distributes refined oil.

KEY STATISTICS Annual Sales: $6.0 billion. Number of Employees: 4,200.

EXPERTISE/EDUCATION SOUGHT: Accounting, marketing

CONTACT: For individuals with previous experience: Mr Floyd Chaney, Director of Human Resources; Phone (713) 874-7000.

STAR MARKET COMPANY, INC.

625 MOUNT AUBURN STREET
CAMBRIDGE, MASSACHUSETTS 02138-4593

OVERVIEW: Operates chain of food stores. Parent Company: American Stores Company.

KEY STATISTICS Annual Sales: $814.0 million. Number of Employees: 7,500.

EXPERTISE/EDUCATION SOUGHT: Management

CONTACT: For individuals with previous experience: Ms Kathy Ferguson, Recruitment Manager; Phone (617) 661-2200.

STATE FARM FIRE AND CASUALTY COMPANY

112 EAST WASHINGTON STREET
BLOOMINGTON, ILLINOIS 61710-0001

OVERVIEW: Provides casualty, automobile, and property insurance. Established: 1935. Parent Company: State Farm Mutual Insurance Company.

KEY STATISTICS Assets: $6.9 billion. Number of Employees: 11,757.

EXPERTISE/EDUCATION SOUGHT: Systems analysis, program analysis, information systems, law, computer programming, actuarial

CONTACT: Mr Kevin Cox, Recruiter; Phone (309) 760-0660.

STATE STREET BANK AND TRUST COMPANY

225 FRANKLIN STREET
BOSTON, MASSACHUSETTS 02110

OVERVIEW: Commercial bank. Established: 1792.

KEY STATISTICS Assets: $2.0 billion. Number of Employees: 9,926.

Expertise/Education Sought: Accounting, finance, computer programming, marketing, sales, management information systems, data processing, analysis

Contact: Ms Nancy Murphy, Vice President and Employment Manager, 1776 Heritage Drive, North Quincy, MA, 02171; Phone (617) 985-8024.

STATER BROTHERS MARKETS

21700 BARTON ROAD
COLTON, CALIFORNIA 92324-4401

Overview: Operates chain of food stores. Parent Company: Stater Brothers, Inc.

Key Statistics Annual Sales: $1.5 billion. Number of Employees: 8,200.

Expertise/Education Sought: Accounting, finance, marketing, management information systems

Contact: Ms Kathy Finazzo, Vice President of Human Resources; Phone (714) 783-5142.

STEELCASE, INC.

901 44TH STREET SOUTHEAST
GRAND RAPIDS, MICHIGAN 49508-7594

Overview: Manufactures and markets office furniture. Established: 1912.

Key Statistics Number of Employees: 13,355.

Hiring History Number of professional employees hired in 1994: 50.

Expertise/Education Sought: Sales, finance, marketing, manufacturing engineering

Contact: Mr Thomas Dryer, Employment Manager; Phone (616) 247-2209.

STEIN MART, INC.

1200 RIVER PLACE
JACKSONVILLE, FLORIDA 32207-1818

Overview: Operates chain of department stores. Established: 1908.

Key Statistics Number of Employees: 4,500.

Expertise/Education Sought: Business management, management, retail management

Contact: For individuals with previous experience: Mr David Kimmel, Vice President of Recruiting and Training; Phone (904) 346-1500.

STERLING WINTHROP

90 PARK AVENUE
NEW YORK, NEW YORK 10016

Overview: Manufactures pharmaceuticals and nonprescription drugs. Established: 1901.

Expertise/Education Sought: Manufacturing, research and development, marketing, finance, engineering

Contact: For individuals with previous experience: Ms Alana M Schuster, Manager of Corporate Employee Relations; Phone (212) 907-2000.

STEWART TITLE GUARANTEE CORPORATION

1980 POST OAK BOULEVARD
HOUSTON, TEXAS 77027-3508

Overview: Provides title insurance. Established: 1970.

Key Statistics Annual Sales: $80.0 million. Number of Employees: 3,400.

Expertise/Education Sought: Business, marketing, accounting

Contact: For individuals with previous experience: Ms Nita Hanks, Senior Vice President of Employee Services; Phone (713) 625-8100.

STOLLE CORPORATION

1501 WEST MICHIGAN STREET
SIDNEY, OHIO 45365-3500

Overview: Manufactures refrigerators and appliance parts. Established: 1976. Parent Company: Aluminum Company of America.

Key Statistics Annual Sales: $750.0 million. Number of Employees: 4,500.

Expertise/Education Sought: Communications, marketing, sales, finance, accounting, computer programming, mechanical engineering, electrical engineering

Contacts: For college students and recent graduates: Mr John Rice, Manager Human Resources Production Staff; Phone (513) 492-1111, ext. 6622. For individuals with previous experience: Mr Lewis Mangen, Manager Human Resources Production Staff; Phone (513) 492-1111, ext. 6063.

STOLT PARCEL TANKERS

8 SOUND SHORE DRIVE
GREENWICH, CONNECTICUT 06830-7242

Overview: Operates truck terminals and provides freight services. Established: 1974.

Key Statistics Annual Sales: $1.0 billion. Number of Employees: 6,700.

Expertise/Education Sought: Logistics, transportation, sales

Contact: Ms Marion Pace, Supervisor of Employee Relations; Phone (203) 625-9400.

STONE CONTAINER CORPORATION

150 NORTH MICHIGAN AVENUE
CHICAGO, ILLINOIS 60601-7568

Overview: Manufactures packaging, pulp, and wood products. Established: 1926.

Key Statistics Number of Employees: 29,000.

Expertise/Education Sought: Accounting, transportation, purchasing, computer programming, finance

Contact: For individuals with previous experience: Ms Susan Hornel, Recruiting Specialist; Phone (312) 580-4649.

STORAGE TECHNOLOGY CORPORATION

2270 SOUTH 88TH STREET
LOUISVILLE, COLORADO 80028-0001

Overview: Manufactures magnetic disk drives and tape drives. Established: 1969.

Key Statistics Annual Sales: $1.0 billion. Number of Employees: 10,100.

Expertise/Education Sought: Computer engineering, electronics/electronics engineering

Contact: Mr David Armstad, Senior Placement Representative; Phone (303) 673-4545.

STRAWBRIDGE AND CLOTHIER

801 MARKET STREET
PHILADELPHIA, PENNSYLVANIA 19107-3199

Overview: Operates chain of department stores. Established: 1868.

Key Statistics Number of Employees: 7,500.

Hiring History Number of professional employees hired in 1994: 50.

Expertise/Education Sought: Merchandising, systems analysis

Contact: Ms Anne Haydon, Manager of Executive Recruiting and Placement; Phone (215) 629-6365.

THE STROH BREWERY COMPANY

100 RIVER PLACE DRIVE
DETROIT, MICHIGAN 48207-4295

Overview: Produces and distributes beer.

Key Statistics Number of Employees: 2,750.

Hiring History Number of professional employees hired in 1994: 20.

EXPERTISE/EDUCATION SOUGHT: Sales, marketing, operations
CONTACT: Mr Glen Konzyn, Director of Human Resources; Phone (313) 446-2000.

STRYKER CORPORATION
2725 FAIRFIELD ROAD
KALAMAZOO, MICHIGAN 49002-1752

OVERVIEW: Manufactures medical equipment and instruments. Established: 1938.
KEY STATISTICS Number of Employees: 3,228.
EXPERTISE/EDUCATION SOUGHT: Accounting, sales, mechanical engineering, design engineering, electrical engineering
CONTACT: Ms Vicki Gordon, Benefits Administrator, PO Box 4085, Kalamazoo, MI, 49003-4085; Phone (616) 385-2600.

STUDENT LOAN MARKETING ASSOCIATION
1050 THOMAS JEFFERSON STREET NORTHWEST
WASHINGTON, D.C. 20007

OVERVIEW: Government student loan association. Established: 1972.
KEY STATISTICS Assets: $2.0 billion. Number of Employees: 4,510.
EXPERTISE/EDUCATION SOUGHT: Accounting, law, technical engineering, computer programming, credit/credit analysis
CONTACT: Ms Janet Mahaney, Director of Recruiting; Phone (202) 333-8000.

SULZER BROS, INC.
200 PARK AVENUE, 16TH FLOOR
NEW YORK, NEW YORK 10166

OVERVIEW: Manufacturers heating, air conditioning, process, and other industrial equipment. Established: 1940.
EXPERTISE/EDUCATION SOUGHT: Marketing, accounting, finance, sales, mechanical engineering
CONTACT: Mr John Bird, Corporate Director of Human Resources; Phone (212) 949-0999.

SUN BANKS, INC.
200 SOUTH ORANGE AVENUE
ORLANDO, FLORIDA 32801

OVERVIEW: Commercial bank.
EXPERTISE/EDUCATION SOUGHT: Accounting, finance, marketing, underwriting, real estate
CONTACT: Ms Michelle Linnert, Manager of Human Resources; Phone (407) 237-4141.

SUN CHEMICAL CORPORATION
222 BRIDGE PLAZA SOUTH
FORT LEE, NEW JERSEY 07024-5798

OVERVIEW: Manufactures inks and chemicals. Established: 1929. Parent Company: DIC Americas, Inc.
KEY STATISTICS Annual Sales: $2.0 billion. Number of Employees: 8,950.
EXPERTISE/EDUCATION SOUGHT: Physics, chemistry, data processing, environmental science, chemical engineering
CONTACT: For individuals with previous experience: Human Resources Department; Phone (201) 224-4600.

SUN COMPANY, INC.
1801 MARKET STREET
PHILADELPHIA, PENNSYLVANIA 19103

OVERVIEW: Manages oil refining, marketing, chemicals, lubricants, and pipeline operations. Established: 1886.
EXPERTISE/EDUCATION SOUGHT: Marketing, finance, accounting, chemical engineering, data processing, mechanical engineering
CONTACT: Ms Lula Hardy, Manager of Professional Employment; Phone (215) 977-3000.

SUNBELT PLASTICS
4611 CENTRAL AVENUE
MONROE, LOUISIANA 71203-6032

OVERVIEW: Manufactures plastics. Established: 1979.
KEY STATISTICS Annual Sales: $50.0 million. Number of Employees: 350.
EXPERTISE/EDUCATION SOUGHT: Chemical engineering, electrical engineering, mechanical engineering, plastics, plastics engineering, accounting, finance, data processing
CONTACT: For individuals with previous experience: Mr John Giffon, Manager of Personnel; Phone (318) 388-2200.

SUNDSTRAND CORPORATION
4949 HARRISON AVENUE
ROCKFORD, ILLINOIS 61108-7987

OVERVIEW: Manufactures aerospace and industrial products. Established: 1910.
KEY STATISTICS Number of Employees: 9,300.
EXPERTISE/EDUCATION SOUGHT: Business administration, mechanical engineering, electrical engineering, manufacturing engineering, materials science, industrial engineering
CONTACT: For individuals with previous experience: Mr Thomas Roland, Human Resources Administrator, 4751 Harrisom Avenue, Rockford, IL, 61108; Phone (815) 226-6295.

SUNRISE HEALTHCARE CORPORATION
5600 WYOMING BOULEVARD NORTHEAST
ALBUQUERQUE, NEW MEXICO 87109-3149

OVERVIEW: Owns and operates nursing homes. Established: 1988. Parent Company: Sun Healthcare Group, Inc.
KEY STATISTICS Number of Employees: 3,015.
CONTACT: For individuals with previous experience: Ms Shena Thorpe, Director of Human Resources; Phone (505) 821-3355.

SUNTRUST BANKS, INC.
25 PARK PLACE NORTHEAST
ATLANTA, GEORGIA 30303-2900

OVERVIEW: Commercial, mortgage, and investment banking. Established: 1866.
KEY STATISTICS Assets: $3.0 billion. Number of Employees: 19,532.
EXPERTISE/EDUCATION SOUGHT: Computer programming, finance, management, accounting, marketing
CONTACT: Ms Diane Borje, Manager of Employment; Phone (404) 588-7711.

SUPER FRESH FOOD MARKETS, INC.
707 RAILROAD AVENUE
FLORENCE, NEW JERSEY 08518

OVERVIEW: Operates chain of food stores. Established: 1982. Parent Company: Great Atlantic & Pacific Tea Company, Inc.
KEY STATISTICS Annual Sales: $900.0 million. Number of Employees: 7,000.
EXPERTISE/EDUCATION SOUGHT: Marketing, accounting, retail, sales
CONTACTS: For college students and recent graduates: Mr John Rongiohe, Personnel Manager, PO Box 68, Florence, NJ, 08518. For individuals with previous experience: Mr Jim Varian, Director of Human Resources; Phone (609) 499-3900.

SUPER RITE FOODS, INC.
3900 INDUSTRIAL ROAD
HARRISBURG, PENNSYLVANIA 17110

OVERVIEW: Operates chain of food stores. Established: 1927. Parent Company: Super Rite Corporation.
KEY STATISTICS Number of Employees: 2,958.
EXPERTISE/EDUCATION SOUGHT: Sales

Super Rite Foods, Inc. (continued)

CONTACT: Ms Pamela Barrick, Manager of Human Resources, PO Box 2261, Harrisburg, PA, 17105; Phone (717) 232-6821.

SUPERVALU, INC.
11840 VALLEY VIEW ROAD
EDEN PRAIRIE, MINNESOTA 55344-3643

OVERVIEW: Distributes and retails foods. Established: 1871.

KEY STATISTICS Annual Sales: $17.0 billion. Number of Employees: 42,000.

HIRING HISTORY Number of professional employees hired in 1994: 13.

EXPERTISE/EDUCATION SOUGHT: Marketing, merchandising, technology, sales, customer service and support

CONTACT: Mr Rick Palmer, Management Staffing, C/O Peterson's, PO Box 990, Minneapolis, MN, 55440-0990; Phone (800) 761-0048.

CORPORATE PROFILE

SUPERVALU *is among the nation's largest food distributors and food retailers. Through 25 wholesale divisions, it supplies 5,500 retail food stores in 48 states. SUPERVALU also owns and operates 296 corporate stores of various names and formats, including Cub Foods, Save-A-Lot, Laneco, and Shop 'n Save.*

Where to find SUPERVALU. *SUPERVALU has divisions and stores across the continental United States, with headquarters in Minneapolis, Minnesota. In addition to 25 wholesale distribution facilities, six regional offices are based in the central, midwest, northern, northwest, southeast, and northeast areas of the country.*

Who SUPERVALU is looking for. *SUPERVALU recruits top-notch candidates for a wide variety of positions. SUPERVALU hires recent college graduates in two ways. The first is directly through the divisions for entry-level positions. The second is through the Recent Graduate Trainee Program. This program is initiated out of SUPERVALU'S home office in Minneapolis, Minnesota. The trainee program offers highly motivated recent graduates a vigorous training plan. This plan focuses on developing trainees in the areas needed to place them in their target position as soon as the training period has been completed. In order to qualify for the program, recent graduates need to have above-average academic standing, solid conceptual abilities, and strong leadership and communication skills. Candidates should be willing to relocate. Some areas with career opportunities available are category management/merchandising, distribution and transportation, retail operations, accounting and finance, advertising and promotion, human resources, and information systems.*

What SUPERVALU has to offer. *SUPERVALU's Recent Graduate Trainee Program involves extensive training. Not only do trainees have development plans that are tailored to fit their experience and interests, but they meet with a business adviser or mentor who helps them make the transition from being a student to being in a business environment. SUPERVALU employees enjoy a competitive benefits package, including tuition reimbursement and 401(k) plans.*

How to connect with SUPERVALU. *For more information about career opportunities with SUPERVALU, Inc., please contact:*

SUPERVALU is an equal opportunity employer and encourages talented individuals from diverse backgrounds to apply.

SWIFT-ECKRICH, INC.
2001 BUTTERFIELD ROAD
DOWNER'S GROVE, ILLINOIS 60515

OVERVIEW: Manufactures processed meat products. Established: 1990. Parent Company: Beatrice Company.

KEY STATISTICS Annual Sales: $2.0 billion. Number of Employees: 15,000.

EXPERTISE/EDUCATION SOUGHT: Operations, management information systems, electrical engineering, mechanical engineering, environmental engineering

CONTACTS: For college students and recent graduates: Mr Wayne Luedke, Manager Human Resources. For individuals with previous experience: Mr Rick Ellspermann, Vice President Human Resources; Phone (708) 512-1000.

SYBRON INTERNATIONAL
411 EAST WISCONSIN AVENUE
MILWAUKEE, WISCONSIN 53202-4409

OVERVIEW: Manufactures dental and orthodontic equipment. Established: 1987.

KEY STATISTICS Annual Sales: $395.0 million. Number of Employees: 3,506.

EXPERTISE/EDUCATION SOUGHT: Accounting, finance, law, human resources

CONTACT: Ms Eileen Short, Director of Human Resources.

SYMBOL TECHNOLOGIES, INC.
116 WILBUR PLACE
BOHEMIA, NEW YORK 11716-2427

OVERVIEW: Manufactures bar code equipment. Established: 1973.

KEY STATISTICS Annual Sales: $360.0 million. Number of Employees: 2,092.

EXPERTISE/EDUCATION SOUGHT: Accounting, marketing, sales

CONTACT: Mr Don Fronzhelia, Director of Human Resources; Phone (516) 563-2400.

SYSCO CORPORATION
1390 ENCLAVE PARKWAY
HOUSTON, TEXAS 77077-2025

OVERVIEW: Markets and distributes wholesale foods. Established: 1969.

KEY STATISTICS Annual Sales: $10.0 billion. Number of Employees: 24,200.

EXPERTISE/EDUCATION SOUGHT: Accounting, finance, management information systems, data processing

CONTACTS: For college students and recent graduates: Ms Lora Silverman, Personnel Coordinator. For individuals with previous experience: Mr Phil Thompson, Technical Recruiter; Phone (713) 584-1390.

SYSTEMS RESEARCH LABORATORIES, INC.
2800 INDIAN RIPPLE ROAD
DAYTON, OHIO 45440

OVERVIEW: Researches and develops advanced technology. Established: 1978. Parent Company: Space Industries International.

KEY STATISTICS Annual Sales: $150.0 million. Number of Employees: 2,700.

EXPERTISE/EDUCATION SOUGHT: Computer science, data processing, accounting, finance, sales, marketing, research and development, mathematics, chemistry

CONTACTS: For college students and recent graduates: Ms Beverly Vallone, Manager of Employment and Equal Employment Opportunity; Phone (513) 426-6000. For individuals with previous experience: Ms Patricia Atchison, Human Resources Manager; Phone (513) 426-6000.

TAD TECHNICAL SERVICES CORPORATION
639 MASSACHUSETTS AVENUE
CAMBRIDGE, MASSACHUSETTS 02139

OVERVIEW: Provides engineering services. Established: 1956.

EXPERTISE/EDUCATION SOUGHT: Electrical engineering, mechanical engineering, drafting, design engineering, technical

CONTACT: For individuals with previous experience: Mr Mark Mahoney, Sales Recruiter; Phone (508) 875-8030.

TALBOTS
520 MADISON AVENUE
NEW YORK, NEW YORK 10022-4301

OVERVIEW: Operates women's and children's clothing stores. Established: 1947.

KEY STATISTICS Annual Sales: $642.0 million. Number of Employees: 4,948.

EXPERTISE/EDUCATION SOUGHT: Accounting, marketing, finance, retail

CONTACTS: For college students and recent graduates: Ms Lynn Martin, Recruiter Specialist, 175 Beal Street, Hingham, MA, 02043; Phone (617) 749-7600, ext. 4151. For individuals with previous experience: Ms Susan White, Manager of Recruitment, 175 Beal Street, Hingham, MA, 02043; Phone (617) 749-7600, ext. 4151.

TAMBRANDS, INC.
777 WESTCHESTER AVENUE
WHITE PLAINS, NEW YORK 10604-3517

OVERVIEW: Manufactures tampons.

KEY STATISTICS Number of Employees: 3,300.

EXPERTISE/EDUCATION SOUGHT: Marketing, sales

CONTACT: For individuals with previous experience: Ms Agnes Canale, Director of Human Resources; Phone (914) 696-6000, ext. 6410.

TAMPA ELECTRIC COMPANY
702 NORTH FRANKLIN STREET
TAMPA, FLORIDA 33602-4418

OVERVIEW: Electric utility. Established: 1899. Parent Company: TECO Energy, Inc.

KEY STATISTICS Number of Employees: 3,130.

EXPERTISE/EDUCATION SOUGHT: Chemical engineering, electrical engineering, industrial engineering, civil engineering, engineering, data processing, mechanical engineering, accounting

CONTACT: Ms Deborah Battista, Senior Coordinator of Recruiting and Cooperative Education, PO Box 111, Tampa, FL, 33601; Phone (813) 228-4111.

TANDEM COMPUTERS, INC.
10600 BRIDGEVIEW COURT
CUPERTINO, CALIFORNIA 95014-2548

OVERVIEW: Manufactures fault tolerant computer systems, communications equipment, and software. Established: 1974.

KEY STATISTICS Annual Sales: $2.0 billion. Number of Employees: 10,413.

EXPERTISE/EDUCATION SOUGHT: Software engineering/development, quality control, finance, sales, marketing, hardware engineering

CONTACT: For individuals with previous experience: Mr Gary Bencomo, College Relations Coordinator, 19333 Vallco Parkway, Cupertino, CA, 95014; Phone (408) 285-6000.

TANDEM TELECOM SYSTEMS, INC.
14231 TANDEM BOULEVARD
AUSTIN, TEXAS 78728

OVERVIEW: Provides custom computer programming services.

EXPERTISE/EDUCATION SOUGHT: Accounting, finance, data processing, software engineering/development

CONTACT: For individuals with previous experience: Mr Michael Anderson, Recruiter; Phone (512) 432-8000.

TAUBMAN COMPANY
200 EAST LONG LAKE ROAD
BLOOMFIELD HILLS, MICHIGAN 48304-2360

OVERVIEW: Operates chain of department stores. Established: 1880.

KEY STATISTICS Annual Sales: $980.0 million. Number of Employees: 15,000.

EXPERTISE/EDUCATION SOUGHT: Accounting, marketing, sales, construction

CONTACT: Human Resources Department; Phone (810) 258-6800.

TAYLOR CORPORATION
1725 ROE CREST DRIVE
NORTH MANKATO, MINNESOTA 56003-1807

OVERVIEW: Provides commercial printing services. Established: 1977.

KEY STATISTICS Number of Employees: 6,000.

EXPERTISE/EDUCATION SOUGHT: Printing, editing, graphic arts, computer programming, systems analysis

CONTACT: For individuals with previous experience: Ms Marie Eckert, Personnel Administrator; Phone (507) 625-2828.

TCI CABLE, INC.
5619 DENVER TECHNOLOGY CENTER PARKWAY
ENGLEWOOD, COLORADO 80111-3017

OVERVIEW: Provides cable television services. Established: 1955.

KEY STATISTICS Annual Sales: $3.0 billion. Number of Employees: 24,000.

EXPERTISE/EDUCATION SOUGHT: Electrical engineering, accounting, marketing, administration, technical

CONTACT: For individuals with previous experience: Human Resources Department; Phone (303) 267-5500.

TCI OF SOUTH FLORIDA
18601 NORTHWEST 2ND AVENUE
MIAMI, FLORIDA 33469-2742

OVERVIEW: Provides telecommunications services. Parent Company: Tele-Communications, Inc.

KEY STATISTICS Annual Sales: $625.0 million. Number of Employees: 1,800.

EXPERTISE/EDUCATION SOUGHT: Telecommunications, television broadcasting

CONTACT: Ms Lucy Lopez, Administrative Assistant to General Manager; Phone (305) 653-5541.

TEACHERS INSURANCE AND ANNUITY
730 3RD AVENUE
NEW YORK, NEW YORK 10017

OVERVIEW: Provides insurance and manages pensions for educational and research organizations. Established: 1918.

EXPERTISE/EDUCATION SOUGHT: Marketing, management information systems, finance, computer programming, real estate, communications, pensions, law, accounting

CONTACTS: For college students and recent graduates: Ms Katherine Reinis, Manager of Training and Development; Phone (212) 490-9000. For individuals with previous experience: Mr Bob Moll, Human Resources Officer; Phone (212) 490-9000.

TECHNICAL AID CORPORATION
109 OAK STREET
NEWTON, MASSACHUSETTS 02164-1456

OVERVIEW: Provides temporary technical emplyment services.

KEY STATISTICS Annual Sales: $381.7 million. Number of Employees: 14,000.

EXPERTISE/EDUCATION SOUGHT: Accounting, finance, management information systems, law, purchasing, marketing, human resources

CONTACT: For individuals with previous experience: Ms Barbara Dempsey, Employment Coordinator.

TECO ENERGY, INC.
PO BOX 111
TAMPA, FLORIDA 33601

OVERVIEW: Electric utility. Established: 1981.

EXPERTISE/EDUCATION SOUGHT: Accounting, finance, marketing, law, data processing

CONTACT: Ms Deborah Batista, Senior Coordinator Recruitment and Corporate Education; Phone (813) 228-4350.

TECUMSEH PRODUCTS COMPANY
100 EAST PATTERSON STREET
TECUMSEH, MICHIGAN 49286-2087

OVERVIEW: Manufactures refrigeration compressors and engines for lawn mowers and snow blowers. Established: 1930.

KEY STATISTICS Number of Employees: 12,376.

EXPERTISE/EDUCATION SOUGHT: Finance, human resources, sales, process engineering, technical engineering, mechanical engineering, electrical engineering

CONTACT: For individuals with previous experience: Mr Thomas Ciminillo, Corporate Staff Representative for Industrial Relations; Phone (517) 423-8411, ext. 551.

TEEPAK, INC.
3 WESTBROOK CORPORATE CENTER
WESTCHESTER, ILLINOIS 60154

OVERVIEW: Manufactures plastic food wrap and sausage casings. Established: 1981. Parent Company: Hillside Industries, Inc.

KEY STATISTICS Number of Employees: 2,200.

EXPERTISE/EDUCATION SOUGHT: Marketing, sales, finance

CONTACT: Ms Mary Karpaty, Manager of Human Resources; Phone (708) 409-3000, ext. 3666.

A. TEICHERT AND SON, INC.
3500 AMERICAN RIVER DRIVE
SACRAMENTO, CALIFORNIA 95864-5802

OVERVIEW: Provides highway and street construction services. Established: 1887.

KEY STATISTICS Annual Sales: $238.0 million. Number of Employees: 1,000.

HIRING HISTORY Number of professional employees hired in 1994: 4.

EXPERTISE/EDUCATION SOUGHT: Civil engineering

CONTACT: Mr Robert Bryant, Manager of Human Resources, PO Box 15002, Sacramento, CA, 95851-1002; Phone (916) 484-3011.

TEKNOR APEX COMPANY
505 CENTRAL AVENUE, PO BOX 229B
PAWTUCKET, RHODE ISLAND 02861-1945

OVERVIEW: Manufactures garden hoses and rubber. Established: 1968.

KEY STATISTICS Annual Sales: $350.0 million. Number of Employees: 1,800.

EXPERTISE/EDUCATION SOUGHT: Accounting

CONTACT: Mr Jack Yando, Director of Human Resources; Phone (401) 725-8000.

TELEFLEX, INC.
630 WEST GERMANTOWN PIKE
PLYMOUTH MEETING, PENNSYLVANIA 19462-1075

OVERVIEW: Manufactures instrumentation equipment, control systems, and electronic measurement systems. Established: 1943.

KEY STATISTICS Number of Employees: 7,920.

EXPERTISE/EDUCATION SOUGHT: Manufacturing engineering, aeronautical engineering, electrical engineering, mechanical engineering, automotive engineering

CONTACT: For individuals with previous experience: Mr Ronald Boldt, Vice President of Human Resources, 155 South Limerick Road, Limerick, PA, 19468; Phone (610) 948-5100, ext. 2878.

TELEPHONE AND DATA SYSTEMS
30 NORTH LA SALLE STREET
CHICAGO, ILLINOIS 60602-2502

OVERVIEW: Distributes telephone and telecommunications equipment. Established: 1968.

KEY STATISTICS Annual Sales: $591.0 million. Number of Employees: 4,343.

HIRING HISTORY Number of professional employees hired in 1994: 30.

EXPERTISE/EDUCATION SOUGHT: Accounting, computer science, computer programming, marketing

CONTACT: Ms Wendy Cerollo, Manager of Human Resources, PO Box 518, Madison, WI, 53705-0518; Phone (608) 845-4000, ext. 4980.

TELESERVICE RESOURCES, INC.
4201 CAMBRIDGE ROAD
FORT WORTH, TEXAS 76155-2625

OVERVIEW: Provides tourist transport, lodging and car rental services.

KEY STATISTICS Annual Sales: $1.0 billion. Number of Employees: 3,500.

EXPERTISE/EDUCATION SOUGHT: Telemarketing

CONTACT: For individuals with previous experience: Mr Doug Ayers, Senior Recruitor; Phone (817) 355-8200.

TEMPLE-INLAND FOREST PRODUCTS
303 SOUTH TEMPLE DRIVE
DIBOLL, TEXAS 75941-2419

OVERVIEW: Manufactures lumber and wood products. Established: 1983. Parent Company: Temple-Inland, Inc.

KEY STATISTICS Annual Sales: $917.0 million. Number of Employees: 5,000.

EXPERTISE/EDUCATION SOUGHT: Accounting, marketing, finance, electrical engineering, mechanical engineering, data processing

CONTACT: For individuals with previous experience: Ms Robin Day, Technical Professional Recruiter; Phone (409) 829-5511.

TENET HEALTHCARE
2700 COLORADO AVENUE
SANTA MONICA, CALIFORNIA 90404-3521

OVERVIEW: Owns and operates hospitals and medical centers.

KEY STATISTICS Annual Sales: $335.0 million. Number of Employees: 9,057.

EXPERTISE/EDUCATION SOUGHT: Accounting, finance, nursing, chemical engineering, electrical engineering, data processing, risk management, law

CONTACT: For individuals with previous experience: Human Resources.

TENET HEALTHCARE CORPORATION
14001 DALLAS PARKWAY, SUITE 200
DALLAS, TEXAS 75240-4346

OVERVIEW: Operates hospitals. Established: 1989.

KEY STATISTICS Annual Sales: $2.0 billion. Number of Employees: 28,200.

EXPERTISE/EDUCATION SOUGHT: Auditing, accounting, information systems

CONTACT: Ms Lourdes Cordero, Director of Human Resources Staffing, 8201 Preston Road, Suite 300, Dallas, TX, 75225; Phone (214) 360-6300.

TENNESSEE GAS PIPELINE COMPANY
1010 MILAM STREET
HOUSTON, TEXAS 77002-5312

OVERVIEW: Supplies natural gas. Established: 1987. Parent Company: Tenneco, Inc.

KEY STATISTICS Annual Sales: $10.0 billion. Number of Employees: 60,000.

EXPERTISE/EDUCATION SOUGHT: Accounting, finance, marketing, systems analysis

CONTACT: Ms Sharon Rogers, Senior College Relations/Specialist; Phone (713) 757-2131, ext. 8282.

TERADYNE, INC.
321 HARRISON AVENUE
BOSTON, MASSACHUSETTS 02118

OVERVIEW: Manufactures electronic systems and software. Established: 1960.

EXPERTISE/EDUCATION SOUGHT: Mechanical engineering, electrical engineering, design engineering, accounting, marketing, sales, computer science

CONTACT: Mr Douglas Scott, Manager of Personnel; Phone (617) 482-2700.

TERRA INDUSTRIES, INC.
600 4TH STREET
SIOUX CITY, IOWA 51101

OVERVIEW: Manufactures fertilizer and chemicals. Established: 1978.

EXPERTISE/EDUCATION SOUGHT: Chemical engineering, accounting, environmental engineering, computer programming, systems analysis, law

CONTACT: For individuals with previous experience: Mr John Birchfield, Vice President of Human Resources; Phone (712) 277-1340.

TEXACO, INC.
2000 WESTCHESTER AVENUE
WHITE PLAINS, NEW YORK 10650

OVERVIEW: Markets and refines petroleum products. Established: 1902.

EXPERTISE/EDUCATION SOUGHT: Engineering, geoscience

CONTACT: For individuals with previous experience: Human Resources Department; Phone (914) 253-4000.

TEXACO REFINING AND MARKETING
10 UNIVERSITY CITY PLAZA
UNIVERSAL CITY, CALIFORNIA 91608-1009

OVERVIEW: Markets and refines oil and gas. Established: 1972. Parent Company: .

KEY STATISTICS Annual Sales: $3.0 billion. Number of Employees: 5,600.

EXPERTISE/EDUCATION SOUGHT: Accounting, marketing, finance, sales, management information systems

CONTACT: For individuals with previous experience: Mr William Heagy, Employee Services Manager.

TEXAS COMMERCE BANK
712 MAIN STREET
HOUSTON, TEXAS 77002

OVERVIEW: Commercial bank. Established: 1950.

HIRING HISTORY Number of professional employees hired in 1994: 50.

EXPERTISE/EDUCATION SOUGHT: Finance, human resources, marketing, sales, data processing, computer programming, accounting

CONTACT: Human Resources Department; Phone (713) 216-4865.

TEXAS INSTRUMENTS, INC.
13500 NORTH CENTRAL EXPRESSWAY
DALLAS, TEXAS 75243-1197

OVERVIEW: Manufactures semiconductors, electronics products, computers, and software. Established: 1930.

KEY STATISTICS Annual Sales: $9.0 billion. Number of Employees: 59,048.

EXPERTISE/EDUCATION SOUGHT: Electronics/electronics engineering, electrical engineering, mechanical engineering, software engineering/development

CONTACTS: For college students and recent graduates: Developmental Placement Programs-College; Phone (800) 439-9533. For individuals with previous experience: Human Resources Department; Phone (214) 995-2011.

TEXTRON AUTOMOTIVE INTERIORS
875 GREENLAND ROAD
DOVER, NEW HAMPSHIRE 03820

OVERVIEW: Manufactures automotive parts. Established: 1830.

KEY STATISTICS Annual Sales: $710.0 million. Number of Employees: 6,000.

EXPERTISE/EDUCATION SOUGHT: Automotive engineering, mechanical engineering, accounting, sales, marketing, electrical engineering, laboratory technology

CONTACTS: For college students and recent graduates: Mr Joseph Paul, Vice President of Human Resources; Phone (603) 433-4142. For individuals with previous experience: Mr Randall Lund, Manager of Human Resources; Phone (603) 742-0720.

TEXTRON, INC.
40 WESTMINSTER STREET
PROVIDENCE, RHODE ISLAND 02903

OVERVIEW: Manufactures aircraft systems and components, automotive parts, industrial products; provides financial services. Established: 1928.

EXPERTISE/EDUCATION SOUGHT: Business management, law, communications, finance

CONTACT: For individuals with previous experience: Ms Patricia J Todd, Director of Human Resources; Phone (401) 421-2800.

TGI FRIDAY'S, INC.
7540 LBJ FREEWAY
DALLAS, TEXAS 75251-1008

OVERVIEW: Operates chain of restaurants. Established: 1975. Parent Company: Carlson Hospitality Group.

KEY STATISTICS Annual Sales: $800.0 million. Number of Employees: 17,000.

EXPERTISE/EDUCATION SOUGHT: Information systems, law, planning, accounting, finance, marketing

CONTACT: For individuals with previous experience: Ms Kathy Cunningham, Corporate Recruitor.

THERMADYNE INDUSTRIES, INC.
101 SOUTH HANLEY ROAD, SUITE 300
SAINT LOUIS, MISSOURI 63105-3406

OVERVIEW: Manufactures welding equipment and metalworking machinery. Established: 1913.

KEY STATISTICS Annual Sales: $271.0 million. Number of Employees: 3,000.

EXPERTISE/EDUCATION SOUGHT: Marketing, sales, accounting, finance

CONTACT: For individuals with previous experience: Mr Matt Roberts, Employee Relations Representative; Phone (314) 721-5573.

THERMO ELECTRON CORPORATION
81 WYMAN STREET
WALTHAM, MASSACHUSETTS 02254-9046

OVERVIEW: Manufactures and distributes plastics, engines, and electrical products. Established: 1956.

EXPERTISE/EDUCATION SOUGHT: Accounting, finance, sales, marketing

CONTACT: For individuals with previous experience: Ms Heidi Doersom, Human Resources Administrator, PO Box 9046, Waltham, MA, 02254-9046; Phone (617) 622-1000.

THERMO KING CORPORATION
314 WEST 90TH STREET
MINNEAPOLIS, MINNESOTA 55420-3630

OVERVIEW: Designs, develops, and manufactures transport temperature control equipment. Established: 1961. Parent Company: Westinghouse Electric Corporation.

KEY STATISTICS Number of Employees: 4,000.

Thermo King Corporation (continued)

EXPERTISE/EDUCATION SOUGHT: Accounting, finance, marketing, sales, mechanical engineering

CONTACTS: For college students and recent graduates: Mr Dale Johnson, Vice President of Strategic Management; Phone (612) 887-2305. For individuals with previous experience: Mr Ronald Berg, Director of Human Resources; Phone (612) 887-2200.

THIOKOL CORPORATION
2475 WASHINGTON BOULEVARD
OGDEN, UTAH 84401-2398

OVERVIEW: Manufactures rocket and missile propulsion systems and related products. Established: 1929.

KEY STATISTICS Annual Sales: $1.0 billion. Number of Employees: 9,300.

EXPERTISE/EDUCATION SOUGHT: Accounting, finance, data processing, human resources, marketing, business management

CONTACT: Mr Tom Rogers, Manager of Human Resources Space Operations; Phone (801) 863-8226.

THOMAS AND BETTS CORPORATION
1555 LYNNFIELD ROAD
MEMPHIS, TENNESSEE 38119-7234

OVERVIEW: Manufactures and distributes electrical and electronic connectors, components, and systems. Established: 1898.

KEY STATISTICS Number of Employees: 8,000.

HIRING HISTORY Number of professional employees hired in 1994: 8.

EXPERTISE/EDUCATION SOUGHT: Industrial distribution, logistics, planning, quality engineering, manufacturing engineering

CONTACT: For individuals with previous experience: Human Resources Manager; Phone (901) 682-7766; Fax (901)680-5161.

J. WALTER THOMPSON COMPANY
466 LEXINGTON AVENUE
NEW YORK, NEW YORK 10017-3140

OVERVIEW: Advertising agency. Established: 1864.

KEY STATISTICS Number of Employees: 7,000.

EXPERTISE/EDUCATION SOUGHT: Sales, marketing, advertising, art direction, film/film production, journalism, communications

CONTACT: For individuals with previous experience: Ms Nancy Temkin, Creative Manager; Phone (212) 210-7000.

THORN APPLE VALLEY, INC.
18700 WEST 10 MILE ROAD
SOUTHFIELD, MICHIGAN 48075-2601

OVERVIEW: Produces pork and other meat products. Established: 1952.

KEY STATISTICS Annual Sales: $729.9 million. Number of Employees: 3,300.

EXPERTISE/EDUCATION SOUGHT: Sales, marketing, accounting, human resources, data processing, management

CONTACT: For individuals with previous experience: Ms s Ann Romine, Recruitment Coordinator; Phone (810) 552-0700.

3COM CORPORATION
5400 BAYFRONT PLAZA
SANTA CLARA, CALIFORNIA 95054-3600

OVERVIEW: Manufactures computer and communications equipment. Established: 1979.

KEY STATISTICS Annual Sales: $827.0 million. Number of Employees: 2,306.

HIRING HISTORY Number of professional employees hired in 1993: 300.

EXPERTISE/EDUCATION SOUGHT: Design engineering, systems engineering, software engineering/development, human resources, management information systems, marketing, manufacturing engineering, finance

CONTACT: For individuals with previous experience: Ms Katherine Fairbanks, Staffing Manager; Phone (408) 764-5000.

THRIFTY PAYLESS, INC.
9275 SOUTHWEST PEYTON LANE
WILSONVILLE, OREGON 97070-9200

OVERVIEW: Operates chain of discount drug stores. Established: 1944. Parent Company: KMart Corporation.

KEY STATISTICS Annual Sales: $3.0 billion. Number of Employees: 17,800.

HIRING HISTORY Number of professional employees hired in 1993: 420.

EXPERTISE/EDUCATION SOUGHT: Pharmacy, pharmacology, pharmaceutical chemistry, business management, finance, management information systems

CONTACTS: For college students and recent graduates: Mr Todd Haines, Manager of Employment; Phone (503) 682-4100. For individuals with previous experience: Mr Rick Johnson, Recruitment Coordinator; Phone (800) 685-6119.

TIDEWATER, INC.
1440 CANAL STREET, SUITE 1600
NEW ORLEANS, LOUISIANA 70112-2711

OVERVIEW: Distributes compressors and petroleum products. Established: 1956.

KEY STATISTICS Number of Employees: 6,900.

EXPERTISE/EDUCATION SOUGHT: Business administration, law, marketing, finance, accounting

CONTACT: Mr Ronald D Smith, Director of Employee Relations; Phone (504) 568-1010.

TIMBERLAND COMPANY, INC.
200 DOMAIN DRIVE
STRATHAM, NEW HAMPSHIRE 03885

OVERVIEW: Markets shoes and related apparel. Established: 1978.

KEY STATISTICS Annual Sales: $419.0 million. Number of Employees: 6,700.

EXPERTISE/EDUCATION SOUGHT: Administration

CONTACT: Ms Vidra Harris; Phone (603) 772-9500.

TIME, INC.
1271 AVENUE OF THE AMERICAS
NEW YORK, NEW YORK 10020

OVERVIEW: Publishes magazines and books. Established: 1922. Parent Company: Time Warner, Inc.

KEY STATISTICS Annual Sales: $4.0 billion. Number of Employees: 6,000.

EXPERTISE/EDUCATION SOUGHT: Analog engineering, marketing, finance, customer service and support, editing

CONTACT: For individuals with previous experience: Ms Carol Ducas, Director of Staffing and Development; Phone (212) 522-4326.

TIME INSURANCE
501 WEST MICHIGAN STREET
MILWAUKEE, WISCONSIN 53203-2700

OVERVIEW: Provides health, life, and disability insurance. Established: 1978. Parent Company: Fortis, Inc.

KEY STATISTICS Annual Sales: $892.0 million. Number of Employees: 4,844.

EXPERTISE/EDUCATION SOUGHT: Computer programming, data processing, human resources, actuarial, accounting, finance, health care

CONTACT: For individuals with previous experience: Ms Mary Girard, Employment Specialist; Phone (414) 271-3011.

TIME WARNER CABLE
160 INVERNESS DRIVE
ENGLEWOOD, COLORADO 80112

OVERVIEW: Provides cable television services. Established: 1968.

HIRING HISTORY Number of professional employees hired in 1994: 150.

EXPERTISE/EDUCATION SOUGHT: Electrical engineering, accounting, telecommunications

CONTACT: Ms Tracey Duffy, Director of Human Resources; Phone (303) 799-1200, ext. 4450.

TIME WARNER, INC.
75 ROCKEFELLER PLAZA
NEW YORK, NEW YORK 10019-6908

OVERVIEW: Diversified media and entertainment company producing books, magazines, music, films, and television programming.

EXPERTISE/EDUCATION SOUGHT: Accounting, finance, marketing, computer programming

CONTACT: Mr Michael Watson, Manager of Human Resources; Phone (212) 484-8000.

TIMEX CORPORATION
PARK ROAD EXTENSION, PO BOX 310
MIDDLEBURY, CONNECTICUT 06762-0313

OVERVIEW: Manufactures watches and parts.

EXPERTISE/EDUCATION SOUGHT: Accounting, marketing, sales

CONTACT: For individuals with previous experience: Mr Robert Ricci, Director Employee Relations.

THE TIMKEN COMPANY
1835 DUEBER AVENUE SOUTHWEST
CANTON, OHIO 44706-2728

OVERVIEW: Manufactures roller bearings and steel. Established: 1898.

KEY STATISTICS Number of Employees: 15,985.

HIRING HISTORY Number of professional employees hired in 1993: 30.

EXPERTISE/EDUCATION SOUGHT: Mechanical engineering, metallurgical engineering, physics, chemistry, marketing

CONTACT: For individuals with previous experience: Mr Lloyd Groves, Manager of Associate Services; Phone (216) 438-3000.

THE TJX COMPANIES, INC.
770 COCHITUATE ROAD
FRAMINGHAM, MASSACHUSETTS 01701-4630

OVERVIEW: Operates chains of off price apparel and houswares stores. Established: 1962.

KEY STATISTICS Annual Sales: $4.0 billion. Number of Employees: 36,000.

EXPERTISE/EDUCATION SOUGHT: Accounting, marketing, finance, human resources, management information systems, retail management, real estate, sales, computer programming

CONTACT: For individuals with previous experience: Mr Bruce Margolis, Director of Human Resources; Phone (508) 390-1000.

TODAY'S TEMPORARY, INC.
18111 PRESTON ROAD
DALLAS, TEXAS 75252-5483

OVERVIEW: Provides temporary employment services. Established: 1982.

KEY STATISTICS Annual Sales: $112.0 million. Number of Employees: 22,750.

EXPERTISE/EDUCATION SOUGHT: Operations, sales

CONTACT: For individuals with previous experience: Ms Karen LaCroix, Director of Human Resources.

TOMPKINS INDUSTRIES, INC.
4801 SPRINGFIELD STREET
DAYTON, OHIO 45431-1084

OVERVIEW: Manufactures windows, doors, lawnmowers, and bathtubs. Established: 1957.

EXPERTISE/EDUCATION SOUGHT: Finance, business management, human resources

CONTACT: For individuals with previous experience: Ms Jean Calhoun, Manager of Human Resources; Phone (513) 253-7171.

TOPS MARKETS, INC.
6363 MAIN STREET
WILLIAMSVILLE, NEW YORK 14221-5898

OVERVIEW: Operates food convenience and deep discount drug store chains. Established: 1962. Parent Company: Ahold USA, Inc.

KEY STATISTICS Annual Sales: $2.0 billion. Number of Employees: 15,000.

EXPERTISE/EDUCATION SOUGHT: Accounting, marketing

CONTACT: Mr John Dobinski, Sr, Director of Personnel, 1885 Harlem Road, Buffalo, NY, 14212; Phone (716) 892-2332, ext. 160; Fax (716)896-2070.

TORCHMARK CORPORATION
2001 3RD AVENUE SOUTH
BIRMINGHAM, ALABAMA 35233-2101

OVERVIEW: Provides health and accident insurance services. Established: 1900.

KEY STATISTICS Annual Sales: $2.0 billion. Number of Employees: 6,052.

EXPERTISE/EDUCATION SOUGHT: Sales

CONTACT: Mr George Thompson, Director of Personnel; Phone (205) 325-4200.

THE TORO COMPANY
8111 LYNDALE AVENUE SOUTH
BLOOMINGTON, MINNESOTA 55420-1136

OVERVIEW: Manufactures turf and lawn care machinery. Established: 1914.

KEY STATISTICS Annual Sales: $794.0 million. Number of Employees: 3,117.

EXPERTISE/EDUCATION SOUGHT: Mechanical engineering, electrical engineering, marketing, accounting, finance, law, data processing

CONTACT: For individuals with previous experience: Mr Rich Lutz, Employment Recruiter; Phone (612) 887-8859.

THE TORRINGTON COMPANY
59 FIELD STREET
TORRINGTON, CONNECTICUT 06790

OVERVIEW: Manufactures bearing and textile machine needles. Established: 1866. Parent Company: Ingersoll-Rand Company.

EXPERTISE/EDUCATION SOUGHT: Mechanical engineering, sales, product design and development, manufacturing engineering

CONTACT: Mr Ken Keane, Manager of Professional Recruiting; Phone (203) 626-2287.

TOSHIBA AMERICA, INC.
375 PARK AVENUE, SUITE 1705
NEW YORK, NEW YORK 10152

OVERVIEW: Manufactures electronic, audio and video equipment. Established: 1965.

KEY STATISTICS Annual Sales: $3.0 billion. Number of Employees: 5,300.

EXPERTISE/EDUCATION SOUGHT: Finance, accounting, public relations, law, computer programming, audio engineering, audiovisual technology, electronics/electronics engineering, mechanical engineering, product design and development

CONTACT: For individuals with previous experience: Ms Lynne Kennedy, Human Resources, 1251 Avenue of the Americas, Suite 4100, New York, NY, 10020; Phone (212) 596-0629.

TOTAL PETROLEUM, INC.
900 19TH STREET, SUITE 2201
DENVER, COLORADO 80202-2523

OVERVIEW: Refines petroleum and petroleum products. Established: 1970. Parent Company: Total Petroleum North America, Ltd.

KEY STATISTICS Annual Sales: $2.0 billion. Number of Employees: 6,700.

EXPERTISE/EDUCATION SOUGHT: Accounting, finance, marketing, data processing, petroleum/petrochemical engineering, plant management

CONTACT: For individuals with previous experience: Mr Robert Belote, Training and Development Manager, PO Box 500, Denver, CO, 80201.

TOWERS, PERRIN, FORSTER, AND CROSBY
245 PARK AVENUE
NEW YORK, NEW YORK 10167-0002

OVERVIEW: Provides management consulting services. Established: 1934.

KEY STATISTICS Annual Sales: $700.0 million. Number of Employees: 5,000.

EXPERTISE/EDUCATION SOUGHT: Benefits administration, human resources, management, health insurance

CONTACT: Mr Patrick Knuff, Director of Staffing, 100 Summit Lake Drive, Valhalla, NY, 10595; Phone (914) 745-4000.

TOYOTA MOTOR MANUFACTURING USA
1001 CHERRY BLOSSOM WAY
GEORGETOWN, KENTUCKY 40324-9564

OVERVIEW: Manufactures cars and trucks. Established: 1986. Parent Company: Toyota Motor Sales USA, Inc.

KEY STATISTICS Annual Sales: $3.0 billion. Number of Employees: 4,750.

HIRING HISTORY Number of professional employees hired in 1993: 100.

EXPERTISE/EDUCATION SOUGHT: Mechanical engineering, electrical engineering, civil engineering, design engineering, computer programming, accounting

CONTACT: For individuals with previous experience: Ms Wendy Warner, Recruitment Specialist; Phone (502) 868-2000.

TOYS R US, INC.
461 FROM ROAD
PARAMUS, NEW JERSEY 07652-3526

OVERVIEW: Operates chain of toy stores. Established: 1948.

KEY STATISTICS Number of Employees: 55,000.

EXPERTISE/EDUCATION SOUGHT: Marketing, sales, advertising, graphic arts, computer programming, customer service and support, management, law, accounting, finance

CONTACT: Mr James Gorenc, Director of Employment; Phone (201) 262-7800.

TRAMMELL CROW COMPANY
2001 ROSS AVENUE
DALLAS, TEXAS 75201

OVERVIEW: Provides property and construction management and leasing services.

KEY STATISTICS Annual Sales: $1.0 billion. Number of Employees: 2,300.

EXPERTISE/EDUCATION SOUGHT: Management, operations, construction engineering

CONTACT: For individuals with previous experience: Human Resources Department; Phone (214) 979-5100.

TRANS WORLD AIRLINES, INC.
1 CITY CENTER
SAINT LOUIS, MISSOURI 63101-1883

OVERVIEW: Provides commercial airline services. Established: 1930.

KEY STATISTICS Number of Employees: 24,500.

EXPERTISE/EDUCATION SOUGHT: Accounting, finance, marketing, sales, law

CONTACT: For individuals with previous experience: Mr Chuck Thibandeau, Senior Vice President-Employee Relations, 11500 Ambassador Drive, Kansas City, MO, 64153; Phone (816) 464-6601.

TRANS WORLD ENTERTAINMENT CORPORATION
38 CORPORATE CIRCLE
ALBANY, NEW YORK 12203-5197

OVERVIEW: Retails specialty music and video products. Established: 1972.

KEY STATISTICS Annual Sales: $493.0 million. Number of Employees: 5,100.

HIRING HISTORY Number of professional employees hired in 1993: 50.

EXPERTISE/EDUCATION SOUGHT: Finance, merchandising, management information systems, marketing, business management

CONTACTS: For college students and recent graduates: Ms Denise DeLuca, Human Resources Coordinator, Department PG; Phone (518) 452-1242. For individuals with previous experience: Ms Paula Langan, Employment Coordinator, PO Box 12-490, Albany, NY, 12212; Phone (518) 452-1242, ext. 4291.

TRANSAMERICA COMMERCIAL FINANCE
225 NORTH MICHIGAN AVENUE
CHICAGO, ILLINOIS 60601

OVERVIEW: Provides commercial loans, financing, and leasing. Established: 1953.

EXPERTISE/EDUCATION SOUGHT: Credit/credit analysis, accounting, information systems, law, marketing

CONTACT: Ms Dornett Wright, Manager of Human Resources; Phone (312) 329-6690.

TRANSAMERICA CORPORATION
600 MONTGOMERY STREET
SAN FRANCISCO, CALIFORNIA 94111-2770

OVERVIEW: Provides insurance, leasing, and related financial services. Established: 1928.

KEY STATISTICS Number of Employees: 10,700.

EXPERTISE/EDUCATION SOUGHT: Accounting, underwriting, actuarial, finance

CONTACT: For individuals with previous experience: Ms Rona King Pehrson, Vice President for Human Resources.

TRANSAMERICA OCCIDENTAL LIFE INSURANCE
1150 SOUTH OLIVE STREET
LOS ANGELES, CALIFORNIA 90015-2211

OVERVIEW: Provides life insurance. Established: 1930. Parent Company: Transmerica Insurance Corporation of California.

KEY STATISTICS Number of Employees: 3,700.

EXPERTISE/EDUCATION SOUGHT: Law, actuarial, finance, marketing, human resources, pensions

CONTACTS: For college students and recent graduates: Ms Christina Rivera, Human Resources Representative; Phone (213) 742-3429. For individuals with previous experience: Ms Lisa Moriyama, 2nd Vice President of Human Resources; Phone (213) 742-2111.

TRANSCO COMPANY
2800 POST OAK BOULEVARD
HOUSTON, TEXAS 77056-6106

OVERVIEW: Provides natural gas pipeline transportation. Established: 1973.

KEY STATISTICS Annual Sales: $3.0 billion. Number of Employees: 4,700.

EXPERTISE/EDUCATION SOUGHT: Mechanical engineering, chemical engineering, electrical engineering, industrial engineering, civil engineering, computer programming, marketing

CONTACTS: For college students and recent graduates: Ms Lorraine Finklea, Personnel Assistant; Phone (713) 439-2000. For individuals with previous experience: Ms Glenna Pierpoint, Manager of Human Resources; Phone (713) 439-2000, ext. 3663.

TRIBUNE COMPANY
435 NORTH MICHIGAN AVENUE
CHICAGO, ILLINOIS 60611-4001

OVERVIEW: Publishes newspapers and electronic information. Established: 1901.

KEY STATISTICS Annual Sales: $430.0 million. Number of Employees: 7,300.

EXPERTISE/EDUCATION SOUGHT: Accounting, finance, marketing, publishing

CONTACT: For individuals with previous experience: Ms Cynthia Vivian, Human Resources Director.

TRIMBLE NAVIGATION, LTD.
PO BOX 3642
SUNNYVALE, CALIFORNIA 94086-2931

OVERVIEW: Manufactures search and navigation equipment. Established: 1978. Parent Company: Trimble Navigation, Ltd.

KEY STATISTICS Annual Sales: $200.0 million. Number of Employees: 832.

HIRING HISTORY Number of professional employees hired in 1994: 80.

EXPERTISE/EDUCATION SOUGHT: Hardware engineering, radio frequency engineering, software engineering/development, firmware engineering, surveying

CONTACTS: For college students and recent graduates: Ms Lorna Chun, Human Resources Representative; Phone (408) 481-6829. For individuals with previous experience: Ms Kathleen Haraughty, Technical Recruiter/Consultant; Phone (408) 481-8958; Fax (408) 481-2874.

TRINITY INDUSTRIES, INC.
2525 NORTH STEMMONS FREEWAY
DALLAS, TEXAS 75207-2400

OVERVIEW: Manufactures railroad cars and steel. Established: 1933.

KEY STATISTICS Number of Employees: 12,600.

EXPERTISE/EDUCATION SOUGHT: Accounting, finance, management information systems, chemical engineering, mechanical engineering, drafting, computer-aided design

CONTACT: For individuals with previous experience: Ms Judy Arrington, Director of Human Resources; Phone (214) 631-4420, ext. 814.

TRINOVA CORPORATION
3000 STRAYER ROAD
MAUMEE, OHIO 43537-9700

OVERVIEW: Manufactures power control components, molded plastics, hoses, fittings, and hydraulic motors. Established: 1916.

KEY STATISTICS Annual Sales: $2.0 billion. Number of Employees: 15,000.

HIRING HISTORY Number of professional employees hired in 1993: 50.

EXPERTISE/EDUCATION SOUGHT: Sales, marketing, finance, data processing, accounting

CONTACT: For individuals with previous experience: Ms Mariam Batke, Manager of Recruitment; Phone (419) 867-2200.

TROPICANA PRODUCTS, INC.
1001 13TH AVENUE EAST
BRADENTON, FLORIDA 34208-2656

OVERVIEW: Produces citrus and other fruit juices. Established: 1949. Parent Company: J. E. Seagram Corporation.

KEY STATISTICS Annual Sales: $1.0 billion. Number of Employees: 3,000.

HIRING HISTORY Number of professional employees hired in 1993: 100.

EXPERTISE/EDUCATION SOUGHT: Sales, program analysis, marketing, data processing, accounting, chemical engineering, mechanical engineering, finance, computer programming

CONTACT: Mr Tom Vorpahl, Director of Human Resources/Operations, PO Box 338, Bradenton, FL, 34206; Phone (813) 742-0338.

TRUCK INSURANCE EXCHANGE
4680 WILSHIRE BOULEVARD
LOS ANGELES, CALIFORNIA 90010

OVERVIEW: Provides insurance. Established: 1935.

EXPERTISE/EDUCATION SOUGHT: Actuarial, accounting, computer programming, data processing, claims adjustment/examination, underwriting

CONTACT: Mr James Griffin, Manager of Human Resources; Phone (213) 932-3200, ext. 3341.

TRUST COMPANY OF GEORGIA
25 PARK PLACE NORTH EAST
ATLANTA, GEORGIA 30303

OVERVIEW: Commercial bank. Established: 1891. Parent Company: Suntrust Banks, Inc.

EXPERTISE/EDUCATION SOUGHT: Business management, marketing, auditing, banking, finance, accounting, human resources

CONTACT: Ms Diane Borje, Vice President of Human Resources, 25 Park Place, Atlanta, GA, 30303; Phone (404) 588-7199.

TRUSTMARK INSURANCE
400 FIELD DRIVE
LAKE FORREST, ILLINOIS 60045

OVERVIEW: Provides life insurance.

EXPERTISE/EDUCATION SOUGHT: Claims adjustment/examination, actuarial, mathematics, information systems, computer programming

CONTACT: For individuals with previous experience: Mr Peter Stern, Associate Director of Human Resources.

TRW FINANCIAL SYSTEMS, INC.
300 LAKESIDE DRIVE
OAKLAND, CALIFORNIA 94612-3540

OVERVIEW: Provides investment advisory services. Established: 1986. Parent Company: TRW, Inc.

KEY STATISTICS Annual Sales: $43.0 million. Number of Employees: 425.

EXPERTISE/EDUCATION SOUGHT: Accounting, finance, data processing, computer programming

CONTACT: For individuals with previous experience: Ms Norma Tannenbaum, Director of Human Resources; Phone (510) 645-3000.

TRW, INC.
1900 RICHMOND ROAD
CLEVELAND, OHIO 44124-3760

OVERVIEW: Manufactures automotive, aerospace, and defense products and information systems. Established: 1901.

KEY STATISTICS Annual Sales: $8.0 billion. Number of Employees: 61,200.

EXPERTISE/EDUCATION SOUGHT: Finance, law, human resources, business management, planning

CONTACT: For individuals with previous experience: Ms Carol Dezzutti, Manager of Human Resources; Phone (216) 291-7000.

TURNER BROADCASTING SYSTEM, INC.
1 CNN CENTER PLAZA
ATLANTA, GEORGIA 30303-2101

OVERVIEW: Operates cable television networks. Established: 1965.

KEY STATISTICS Number of Employees: 5,317.

EXPERTISE/EDUCATION SOUGHT: Television broadcasting, journalism, electronics/electronics engineering, film/film production, journalism

CONTACT: For individuals with previous experience: Ms Julie Cameron, Recruiter; Phone (404) 827-1686.

TV GUIDE
100 MATSON FORD ROAD
RADNOR, PENNSYLVANIA 19088

OVERVIEW: Diversified media and publishing company with operations in newspaper and magazine publishing, television broadcasting, and motion picture production.

EXPERTISE/EDUCATION SOUGHT: Marketing, finance, accounting, publishing, analysis, systems analysis, information systems, advertising, graphic arts, customer service and support

CONTACT: Ms Jeanette Moyer, Manager of Human Resources; Phone (610) 293-8500.

20TH CENTURY INDUSTRIES
6301 OWENSMOUTH AVENUE
WOODLAND HILLS, CALIFORNIA 91367-6488

OVERVIEW: Provides auto and casualty insurance. Established: 1956.

KEY STATISTICS Annual Sales: $1.0 billion. Number of Employees: 2,300.

EXPERTISE/EDUCATION SOUGHT: Claims adjustment/examination

CONTACT: Ms Joyce Goodman, Manager of Employment, PO Box 2000, Woodland Hills, CA, 91365-2216; Phone (818) 704-3700.

TYCO INTERNATIONAL, LTD.
1 TYCO PARK
EXETER, NEW HAMPSHIRE 03833

OVERVIEW: Manufactures fire protection equipment, packaging material, pipes, and electronic components. Established: 1962.

EXPERTISE/EDUCATION SOUGHT: Marketing, finance, management information systems

CONTACT: Mr Dan Casteel, Manager of Industrial Relations; Phone (603) 778-9200.

TYSON FOODS, INC.
2210 WEST OAKLAWN ROAD
SPRINGDALE, ARKANSAS 72762-6999

OVERVIEW: Produces and processes poultry products. Established: 1935.

KEY STATISTICS Number of Employees: 50,619.

EXPERTISE/EDUCATION SOUGHT: Sales, finance, business management, marketing, production, human resources, research and development, accounting

CONTACT: Mr Russel Tooley, Manager of Personnel; Phone (501) 290-4000.

U-HAUL INTERNATIONAL, INC.
2727 NORTH CENTRAL AVENUE
PHOENIX, ARIZONA 85004

OVERVIEW: Provides truck and trailer rental services. Established: 1945.

KEY STATISTICS Number of Employees: 9,150.

EXPERTISE/EDUCATION SOUGHT: Marketing, finance, sales, data processing

CONTACT: Ms JoAnn Hoffman, Manager of Employment; Phone (602) 263-6011.

U.S. BRICK, INC.
8851 HIGHWAY 80 EAST
FORT WORTH, TEXAS 76116

OVERVIEW: Manufactures brick.

HIRING HISTORY Number of professional employees hired in 1994: 5.

EXPERTISE/EDUCATION SOUGHT: Accounting, finance, data processing, auditing, sales, marketing, minerals engineering, plant management

CONTACT: For individuals with previous experience: Ms Patty Sanchez, Personnel Administrator; Phone (817) 244-9191.

US WEST MARKETING RESOURCES GROUP
198 INVERNESS DRIVE WEST
ENGLEWOOD, COLORADO 80112-5202

OVERVIEW: Publishes telephone directories. Established: 1986.

KEY STATISTICS Annual Sales: $295.0 million. Number of Employees: 3,900.

EXPERTISE/EDUCATION SOUGHT: Finance, accounting, marketing, sales, information systems

CONTACT: For individuals with previous experience: Human Resources; Phone (303) 784-2900.

U.S. WEST COMMUNICATIONS, INC.
1801 CALIFORNIA STREET
DENVER, COLORADO 80202-2602

OVERVIEW: Provides telecommunications services. Established: 1984. Parent Company: U.S. West, Inc.

KEY STATISTICS Annual Sales: $9.0 billion. Number of Employees: 49,668.

EXPERTISE/EDUCATION SOUGHT: Data processing, computer programming, sales, communications, accounting, systems integration, customer service and support

CONTACTS: For college students and recent graduates: Mr Paul Trujillo, President and Chief Executive Officer; Phone (303) 896-2021. For individuals with previous experience: Ms Rita Dozal, Director of Staffing; Phone (303) 965-4218.

UARCO
700 WEST MAIN STREET
BARRINGTON, ILLINOIS 60010

OVERVIEW: Provides printed and electronic products, systems, and services. Established: 1894.

KEY STATISTICS Annual Sales: $606.0 million. Number of Employees: 5,158.

EXPERTISE/EDUCATION SOUGHT: Sales, information systems, accounting, engineering

CONTACT: Mr Fritz Kaufman, Personnel Manager; Phone (708) 381-7000.

UJB FINANCIAL CORPORATION
301 CARNEGIE CENTER
PRINCETON, NEW JERSEY 08540-6227

OVERVIEW: Provides commercial banking, investments, and related financial services. Established: 1970.

KEY STATISTICS Assets: $1.0 billion. Number of Employees: 6,219.

EXPERTISE/EDUCATION SOUGHT: Accounting, finance, customer service and support

CONTACT: For individuals with previous experience: Human Resources Department; Phone (609) 987-3200.

ULTRAMAR CORPORATION
2 PICKWICK PLAZA, SUITE 3
GREENWICH, CONNECTICUT 06830-5530

OVERVIEW: Produces, refines, and markets petroleum and petroleum products. Established: 1991.

KEY STATISTICS Annual Sales: $2.0 billion. Number of Employees: 3,100.

HIRING HISTORY Number of professional employees hired in 1994: 5.

EXPERTISE/EDUCATION SOUGHT: Marketing, chemical engineering, process engineering, finance

CONTACT: For individuals with previous experience: Ms Paula Ortega, Human Resources Coordinator, PO Box 93102, Long Beach, CA, 90809-3102; Phone (310) 495-5403.

UNI DISTRIBUTING CORPORATION
60 UNIVERSITY CITY PLAZA
UNIVERSITY CITY, CALIFORNIA 91608

OVERVIEW: Distributes records, tapes, compact discs, and video tapes.
EXPERTISE/EDUCATION SOUGHT: Marketing, sales, finance, accounting, management information systems
CONTACT: Ms Jo Ann Kenney, Director of Employment; Phone (818) 777-4000, ext. 2426.

UNIFI, INC.
7201 WEST FRIENDLY AVENUE
GREENSBORO, NORTH CAROLINA 27410-6237

OVERVIEW: Manufactures texture yarn. Established: 1971.
KEY STATISTICS Annual Sales: $352.0 million. Number of Employees: 6,000.
EXPERTISE/EDUCATION SOUGHT: Engineering science, mechanical engineering, chemical engineering, industrial engineering, physics, biology
CONTACT: For individuals with previous experience: Mr Michael Fogelman, Personnel Manager; Phone (910) 294-4410.

UNIHEALTH AMERICA
3400 RIVERSIDE DRIVE
BURBANK, CALIFORNIA 91505-4155

OVERVIEW: Owns and operates hospitals and insurance companies. Established: 1970.
KEY STATISTICS Assets: $4.0 billion. Number of Employees: 14,000.
HIRING HISTORY Number of professional employees hired in 1994: 100.
EXPERTISE/EDUCATION SOUGHT: Business management, accounting, finance, auditing, actuarial, communications, data processing
CONTACT: Ms Magaly Juarez, Human Resources Manager; Fax (818)238-6000.

UNION BANK
370 CALIFORNIA STREET
SAN FRANCISCO, CALIFORNIA 94104-1402

OVERVIEW: Provides commercial and retail banking services. Established: 1883.
KEY STATISTICS Number of Employees: 7,303.
EXPERTISE/EDUCATION SOUGHT: Finance, business, mathematics, economics
CONTACTS: For college students and recent graduates: Mr Robert Bruce, Manager of College Relations; Phone (415) 445-0224. For individuals with previous experience: Mr Tom Ashby, Vice President of Corporate Staffing, 350 California Street, San Francisco, CA, 94104.

UNION CAMP CORPORATION
1600 VALLEY ROAD
WAYNE, NEW JERSEY 07470

OVERVIEW: Manufactures paper products. Established: 1861.
EXPERTISE/EDUCATION SOUGHT: Chemical engineering, human resources, sales, accounting, safety management, business administration
CONTACT: Ms Arlene Hendrix, Director of Staffing and Career Management; Phone (201) 628-2000, ext. 2249.

UNION CARBIDE CORPORATION
39 OLD RIDGEBURY ROAD
DANBURY, CONNECTICUT 06817

OVERVIEW: Manufactures chemicals and plastics.
HIRING HISTORY Number of professional employees hired in 1994: 100.
EXPERTISE/EDUCATION SOUGHT: Chemical engineering, chemistry, chemical research, mechanical engineering, chemical analysis, polymers, technical engineering, physics, industrial engineering

CONTACT: Mr Donald E Gatewood, Manager of Recruiting and University Relations, Building 82-831, PO Box 8004, South Charleston, WV, 25303-8004; Phone (304) 747-5944.

UNION ELECTRIC COMPANY
1901 CHOUTEAU AVENUE
SAINT LOUIS, MISSOURI 63103-9989

OVERVIEW: Electric utility. Established: 1881.
KEY STATISTICS Annual Sales: $2.0 billion. Number of Employees: 6,300.
HIRING HISTORY Number of professional employees hired in 1994: 14. 1993: 11.
CONTACT: Ms Johnetta Carver, Employment Supervisor; Phone (314) 554-2119.

UNION PACIFIC CORPORATION
EIGHTH AND EATON AVENUES
BETHLEHEM, PENNSYLVANIA 18018

OVERVIEW: Provides railroad and truck freight services. Established: 1969.
KEY STATISTICS Annual Sales: $8.0 billion. Number of Employees: 47,126.
EXPERTISE/EDUCATION SOUGHT: Finance, accounting, management information systems, computer programming, data processing
CONTACTS: For college students and recent graduates: Ms Linda Sudduth, Manager of Human Resources; Phone (610) 861-3200. For individuals with previous experience: Mr Thomas W Kess, Manager of Human Resources; Phone (610) 861-3200.

UNION PACIFIC RAILROAD COMPANY
1416 DODGE STREET
OMAHA, NEBRASKA 68179-0002

OVERVIEW: Provides railroad and truck frieght services. Established: 1869. Parent Company: Union Pacific Corporation.
KEY STATISTICS Annual Sales: $5.0 billion. Number of Employees: 28,000.
EXPERTISE/EDUCATION SOUGHT: Accounting, finance, marketing, data processing, computer programming
CONTACT: Mr Roger Dillon, Senior Manager of Sourcing; Phone (402) 271-3280.

UNION PACIFIC RESOURCE
801 CHERRY STREET
FORT WORTH, TEXAS 76102

OVERVIEW: Refines and distributes coal and other energy products.
EXPERTISE/EDUCATION SOUGHT: Petroleum/petrochemical engineering, accounting, sales, marketing, finance
CONTACT: For individuals with previous experience: Ms Rosemary Berry, Recruiting Manager.

UNION UNDERWEAR COMPANY, INC.
1 FRUIT OF THE LOOM DRIVE
BOWLING GREEN, KENTUCKY 42103

OVERVIEW: Manufactures undergarments and socks. Established: 1985. Parent Company: Fruit of the Loom, Inc.
KEY STATISTICS Annual Sales: $2.0 billion. Number of Employees: 37,000.
EXPERTISE/EDUCATION SOUGHT: Accounting, marketing, finance, sales, manufacturing engineering, electrical engineering
CONTACT: For individuals with previous experience: Mr Marcellus Scott, Corporate Personnel Manager, PO Box 90015, Bowling Green, KY, 42102-9015; Phone (502) 781-6400.

UNISOURCE

825 DUPORTAIL ROAD
WAYNE, PENNSYLVANIA 19087-5525

OVERVIEW: Distributes paper and paper products. Established: 1968. Parent Company: Alco Standard Corporation.

KEY STATISTICS Annual Sales: $41.0 million. Number of Employees: 11,200.

EXPERTISE/EDUCATION SOUGHT: Accounting, finance, business management, computer programming, sales, marketing

CONTACT: For individuals with previous experience: Ms Elizabeth Barrett, Director of Management Information Services and Human Resources; Phone (215) 296-4470.

UNISYS CORPORATION

TOWNSHIP LINE AND UNION MEETING ROADS
BLUE BELL, PENNSYLVANIA 19422

OVERVIEW: Manufactures computers and provides computer systems integration services. Established: 1886.

KEY STATISTICS Number of Employees: 49,000.

EXPERTISE/EDUCATION SOUGHT: Management information systems, marketing, accounting, finance

CONTACTS: For college students and recent graduates: Ms Paula Wolff, Senior Recruiter, PO Box 500, Blue Bell, PA, 19424; Phone (215) 542-4311. For individuals with previous experience: Ms Nancy Devlin, Director of Human Resources, PO Box 500, Blue Bell, PA, 19422; Phone (215) 542-4311.

UNISYS GOVERNMENT GROUP

8201 GREENSBORO DRIVE
MC LEAN, VIRGINIA 22102

OVERVIEW: Provides computer system integration services to government and defense industry.

EXPERTISE/EDUCATION SOUGHT: Engineering, electrical engineering, computer science, computer engineering, systems engineering

CONTACTS: For college students and recent graduates: Ms Therese Suddueth, Manager of Human Resources; Phone (703) 847-3200. For individuals with previous experience: Mrs Barbara Lopez-Nash, Director of Staffing and Planning; Phone (703) 847-3200.

UNITED AIR LINES, INC.

1200 EAST ALGONQUIN ROAD
ELK GROVE, ILLINOIS 60005-4786

OVERVIEW: Provides passenger airline services. Established: 1926. Parent Company: UAL Corporation.

KEY STATISTICS Number of Employees: 75,000.

HIRING HISTORY Number of professional employees hired in 1993: 300.

EXPERTISE/EDUCATION SOUGHT: Finance, management information systems, accounting, business management, auditing, customer service and support, marketing

CONTACT: Mr Jim Houser, Manager of Professional Employment; Phone (708) 952-4000.

UNITED ARTISTS ENTERTAINMENT

9110 EAST NICHOLS AVENUE
ENGLEWOOD, COLORADO 80112-3405

OVERVIEW: Owns and operates movie theaters, produces motion pictures, and provides cable television services. Established: 1926. Parent Company: Oscar I Corporation.

KEY STATISTICS Annual Sales: $1.0 billion. Number of Employees: 12,000.

EXPERTISE/EDUCATION SOUGHT: Accounting, finance, law, marketing, human resources, economics, administration, film/film production, communications

CONTACT: Ms Elizabeth Moravak, Director of Human Resources; Phone (303) 792-3600.

UNITED CITIES GAS COMPANY

5300 MARYLAND WAY
BRENTWOOD, TENNESSEE 37027-5038

OVERVIEW: Distributes natural gas. Established: 1929.

KEY STATISTICS Number of Employees: 1,349.

EXPERTISE/EDUCATION SOUGHT: Accounting, marketing, computer programming, research

CONTACT: Ms Ruby Baldwin, Employment Specialist; Phone (615) 373-0104.

UNITED DOMINION INDUSTRIES

2300 ONE FIRST UNION CENTER
CHARLOTTE, NORTH CAROLINA 28202

OVERVIEW: Provides manufacturing, engineering, and construction services. Established: 1968.

KEY STATISTICS Annual Sales: $2.0 billion. Number of Employees: 12,000.

EXPERTISE/EDUCATION SOUGHT: Accounting, planning, finance, communications, treasury management, systems integration, mechanical engineering, electrical engineering, industrial engineering, construction engineering

CONTACT: Mr Margaret Handlesman, Manager of Corporate Administration; Phone (704) 347-6800.

UNITED HEALTH, INC.

105 WEST MICHIGAN STREET
MILWAUKEE, WISCONSIN 53203-2914

OVERVIEW: Operates long term health care facilities.

KEY STATISTICS Annual Sales: $537.0 million. Number of Employees: 18,000.

EXPERTISE/EDUCATION SOUGHT: Occupational therapy, physical therapy, information systems, accounting, nursing, dietetics, general nursing, home health care, respiratory therapy, pharmacy

CONTACTS: For college students and recent graduates: Professional Recruiter - United Professional Companies; Phone (414) 342-9292, ext. 581. For individuals with previous experience: Mr John Goff, National Recruiter - Unicare Health Facilities; Fax (414)347-4456.

UNITED HEALTHCARE CORPORATION

9900 BREN ROAD EAST
HOPKINS, MINNESOTA 55343

OVERVIEW: Health maintenance organization. Established: 1974.

EXPERTISE/EDUCATION SOUGHT: Computer programming, computer science, accounting, credit/credit analysis

CONTACT: For individuals with previous experience: Ms Tracy Heitner, Manager of Recruitment; Phone (612) 936-7392.

UNITED PARCEL SERVICE

55 GLEN LAKE PARKWAY
ATLANTA, GEORGIA 30328

OVERVIEW: Provides package delivery and courier services. Established: 1907. Parent Company: United Parcel Service America, Inc.

KEY STATISTICS Number of Employees: 300,000.

CONTACT: For individuals with previous experience: UPS Office in Each State.

UNITED STATES GYPSUM COMPANY

125 SOUTH FRANKLIN STREET
CHICAGO, ILLINOIS 60606-4605

OVERVIEW: Manufactures building and construction materials. Established: 1901. Parent Company: USG Corporation.

KEY STATISTICS Number of Employees: 6,200.

HIRING HISTORY Number of professional employees hired in 1993: 40.

EXPERTISE/EDUCATION SOUGHT: Engineering, computer programming, economics, accounting, data processing, finance

CONTACT: Ms Joane Twomey, Director of Development and Training; Phone (312) 606-4000.

UNITED STATES NATIONAL BANK OF OREGON
111 SOUTHWEST FIFTH AVENUE, T-3
PORTLAND, OREGON 97204

OVERVIEW: Commercial bank. Established: 1968. Parent Company: US Bancorp.

KEY STATISTICS Number of Employees: 6,445.

EXPERTISE/EDUCATION SOUGHT: Accounting, finance, auditing, underwriting, real estate

CONTACT: Ms Jennifer Alberti, Employment Specialist; Phone (503) 275-6118.

UNITED STATES SERVICE INDUSTRIES
1424 K STREET NORTHWEST
WASHINGTON, D.C. 20005-2410

OVERVIEW: Provides building maintenance services.

KEY STATISTICS Annual Sales: $32.0 million. Number of Employees: 3,000.

EXPERTISE/EDUCATION SOUGHT: Accounting

CONTACT: For individuals with previous experience: Mr Juan Lopez, Personnel Director.

UNITED STATES SHOE CORPORATION
1 EASTWOOD DRIVE
CINCINNATI, OHIO 45227

OVERVIEW: Manufactures footwear and operates women's clothing stores. Established: 1931.

KEY STATISTICS Number of Employees: 40,000.

EXPERTISE/EDUCATION SOUGHT: Business management, merchandising, accounting, manufacturing engineering, finance, marketing

CONTACT: Ms Sharon Gaffney, Manager of Employment; Phone (513) 527-7000.

UNITED STATES SURGICAL CORPORATION
150 GLOVER AVENUE
NORWALK, CONNECTICUT 06856-1308

OVERVIEW: Manufactures surgical equipment. Established: 1964.

KEY STATISTICS Annual Sales: $1.0 billion. Number of Employees: 6,600.

EXPERTISE/EDUCATION SOUGHT: Nutrition, physical therapy

CONTACT: For individuals with previous experience: Mr Mike Brown, Manager of Employment.

UNITED TECH AUTO HOLDINGS
5200 AUTO CLUB DRIVE
DEARBORN, MICHIGAN 48126-4212

OVERVIEW: Manufactures aviation and automotive equipment. Established: 1978. Parent Company: United Technologies Corporation.

KEY STATISTICS Number of Employees: 38,000.

EXPERTISE/EDUCATION SOUGHT: Automotive engineering, mechanical engineering, electrical engineering, design engineering, marketing, accounting, finance, data processing

CONTACT: For individuals with previous experience: Mr Bill Ilg, Manager of Recruitment; Phone (313) 593-9600; Fax (313)593-9587.

UNITED TECHNOLOGIES CORPORATION
1 FINANCIAL PLAZA
HARTFORD, CONNECTICUT 06101

OVERVIEW: Manufactures advanced technology products for the aerospace, building, and automotive industries. Established: 1928.

EXPERTISE/EDUCATION SOUGHT: Accounting, finance, information systems, law, human resources

CONTACT: Corporate Human Resources; Phone (203) 728-7023.

UNITED TELEPHONE COMPANY OF FLORIDA
555 LAKE BORDER DRIVE
APOPKA, FLORIDA 32703-5899

OVERVIEW: Provides telecommunications services. Established: 1967. Parent Company: Sprint Corporation.

KEY STATISTICS Number of Employees: 4,700.

HIRING HISTORY Number of professional employees hired in 1993: 15.

EXPERTISE/EDUCATION SOUGHT: Accounting, electrical engineering, computer science, marketing, management information systems

CONTACT: Mr Ron Brock, Manager of Recruitment, PO Box 165000, Altamont Springs, FL, 32716-500; Phone (407) 889-6368.

UNITED WISCONSIN SERVICES
401 WEST MICHIGAN STREET
MILWAUKEE, WISCONSIN 53203-3913

OVERVIEW: Provides health insurance. Established: 1939.

KEY STATISTICS Annual Sales: $924.1 million. Number of Employees: 1,526.

EXPERTISE/EDUCATION SOUGHT: Accounting, finance, data processing, nursing, licensed practical nursing

CONTACT: For individuals with previous experience: Ms Lisa Ziebell, Supervisor of Employment; Phone (414) 226-6154.

UNITRIN, INC.
1 EAST WACKER DRIVE
CHICAGO, ILLINOIS 60601-1802

OVERVIEW: Provides life, title, and casualty insurance.

KEY STATISTICS Annual Sales: $1.0 billion. Number of Employees: 7,500.

HIRING HISTORY Number of professional employees hired in 1994: 9.

EXPERTISE/EDUCATION SOUGHT: Accounting, auditing

CONTACT: For individuals with previous experience: Ms Amy Cardella, Human Resources Associate; Phone (312) 661-4600.

UNIVERSAL FOODS CORPORATION
433 EAST MICHIGAN STREET
MILWAUKEE, WISCONSIN 53202-5104

OVERVIEW: Manufactures frozen, canned, and processed foods. Established: 1882.

KEY STATISTICS Number of Employees: 5,450.

EXPERTISE/EDUCATION SOUGHT: Marketing, merchandising, finance, accounting, sales, mechanical engineering

CONTACT: Human Resources Department; Phone (414) 271-6755.

UNIVERSAL HEALTH SERVICES
367 SOUTH GULPH ROAD
KING OF PRUSSIA, PENNSYLVANIA 19406-3184

OVERVIEW: Provides hospital management. Established: 1978.

KEY STATISTICS Annual Sales: $762.0 million. Number of Employees: 9,100.

EXPERTISE/EDUCATION SOUGHT: Accounting, finance, marketing, business, data processing

CONTACT: For individuals with previous experience: Human Resources Management; Phone (610) 768-3300.

UNIVERSITY OF PITTSBURGH MEDICAL CENTER SYSTEMS
200 LOTHROP STREET
PITTSBURGH, PENNSYLVANIA 15213-2536

OVERVIEW: General hospital.

KEY STATISTICS Annual Sales: $802.0 million. Number of Employees: 12,000.

EXPERTISE/EDUCATION SOUGHT: Sales, marketing, occupational therapy, physical therapy

CONTACT: For individuals with previous experience: Mr Conrad Carrioto, Employment Manager; Phone (412) 647-3000.

UNUM LIFE INSURANCE COMPANY
2211 CONGRESS STREET
PORTLAND, MAINE 04102-1941

OVERVIEW: Provides life insurance. Established: 1848.

EXPERTISE/EDUCATION SOUGHT: Computer programming, accounting, sales, communications, marketing, actuarial, claims adjustment/examination, underwriting, human resources, management information systems

CONTACT: Mr Barry Daniels, Recruiter; Phone (207) 770-3216.

THE UPJOHN COMPANY
7000 PORTAGE ROAD
KALAMAZOO, MICHIGAN 49001-0102

OVERVIEW: Manufactures pharmaceuticals, animal drugs, and consumer health care products. Established: 1886.

KEY STATISTICS Number of Employees: 18,600.

EXPERTISE/EDUCATION SOUGHT: Chemical engineering, computer science, chemistry, microbiology, biochemistry

CONTACT: Mr Larry L Harris, Director of Employment; Phone (616) 329-5550.

UPTONS, INC.
6251 CROOKED CREEK ROAD
NORCROSS, GEORGIA 30092-3121

OVERVIEW: Operates chain of family clothing stores.

KEY STATISTICS Annual Sales: $248.0 million. Number of Employees: 3,300.

EXPERTISE/EDUCATION SOUGHT: Management, retail management

CONTACT: For individuals with previous experience: Ms Susan Messner, Regional Manager.

U.S. BANCORP
111 SOUTHWEST 5TH AVENUE
PORTLAND, OREGON 97204

OVERVIEW: Commercial bank. Established: 1968.

EXPERTISE/EDUCATION SOUGHT: Customer service and support, accounting, business, economics, finance

CONTACT: For individuals with previous experience: Ms Judy Rice, Executive Vice President of Human Resources; Phone (503) 275-6111.

U.S. FIDELITY GUARANTY COMPANY
100 LIGHT STREET
BALTIMORE, MARYLAND 21202-1036

OVERVIEW: Provides fire and casualty insurance. Established: 1896.

KEY STATISTICS Number of Employees: 7,560.

EXPERTISE/EDUCATION SOUGHT: Actuarial, accounting, finance, underwriting

CONTACTS: For college students and recent graduates: Ms Betty Hall, Director of College Relations; Phone (410) 547-3863. For individuals with previous experience: Ms Amy Marks, Senior Vice President of Human Resources; Phone (410) 547-3000, ext. 2192.

US HEALTH CORPORATION COLUMBUS
3555 OLENTANGY RIVER ROAD
COLUMBUS, OHIO 43214

OVERVIEW: Owns and operates hospitals. Established: 1983.

KEY STATISTICS Annual Sales: $775.0 million. Number of Employees: 10,000.

EXPERTISE/EDUCATION SOUGHT: Accounting, marketing, finance, management information systems

CONTACT: For individuals with previous experience: Dr Terry Boyd, Director Human Resources; Phone (614) 566-5424.

US HEALTHCARE, INC.
1425 UNION MEETING ROAD
BLUE BELL, PENNSYLVANIA 19422

OVERVIEW: Provides HMO and managed care services.

EXPERTISE/EDUCATION SOUGHT: Management information systems, accounting, sales, applied engineering, imaging technology, claims adjustment/examination, actuarial

CONTACT: For individuals with previous experience: Mr Robert Rosend, Vice President of Human Resources; Phone (215) 628-4800, ext. 5724.

US HOMECARE CORPORATION
141 SOUTH CENTRAL AVENUE
HARTSDALE, NEW YORK 10530-2319

OVERVIEW: Provides home health care and medical equipment rental services.

KEY STATISTICS Annual Sales: $90.0 million. Number of Employees: 3,700.

EXPERTISE/EDUCATION SOUGHT: Accounting, finance, sales, marketing

CONTACT: For individuals with previous experience: Ms Elaine Arbizo, Vice President of Human Resources; Phone (914) 287-4434.

US SPRINT COMMUNICATIONS
8140 WARD PARKWAY
KANSAS CITY, MISSOURI 64114-2006

OVERVIEW: Provides telecommunications and related services.

KEY STATISTICS Annual Sales: $3.0 billion. Number of Employees: 22,000.

EXPERTISE/EDUCATION SOUGHT: Computer science, business administration, marketing, sales, finance, accounting

CONTACTS: For college students and recent graduates: Mr Ben Watson, Senior Vice President of Human Resources; Phone (816) 854-0903. For individuals with previous experience: Mr Tim Stockwell, Director of Human Resources, 6600 College Boulevard, Overland Park, KS, 66211; Phone (913) 624-2157.

US STEEL GROUP
600 GRANT STREET
PITTSBURGH, PENNSYLVANIA 15219-2702

OVERVIEW: Provides raw materials and manufactures steel and steel products. Established: 1901.

KEY STATISTICS Number of Employees: 44,611.

EXPERTISE/EDUCATION SOUGHT: Metallurgical engineering, electrical engineering, mechanical engineering, marketing

CONTACT: Mr Richard Schinagl, Manager of Employment, Recruitment and Policy Development; Phone (412) 433-6688.

US WEST, INC.
188 INVERNESS DRIVE WEST
ENGLEWOOD, COLORADO 80112-2526

OVERVIEW: Provides telecommunications and related services. Established: 1984.

KEY STATISTICS Annual Sales: $10.0 billion. Number of Employees: 60,778.

EXPERTISE/EDUCATION SOUGHT: Data processing, systems integration, marketing, computer programming, sales, electrical engineering, computer engineering, communications, accounting, computer science

CONTACT: Ms Lauerne Morris, Director of University Relations; Phone (303) 754-5318.

USAIR GROUP, INC.
2345 CRYSTAL DRIVE
ARLINGTON, VIRGINIA 22227

OVERVIEW: Provides passenger and freight airline services.

EXPERTISE/EDUCATION SOUGHT: Sales, mechanical engineering, marketing, data processing, human resources, finance

CONTACT: For individuals with previous experience: Mr Joe Burgess, Regional Manager Employee Relations; Phone (703) 418-7463.

UTICA NATIONAL INSURANCE GROUP

180 GENESEE STREET
NEW HARTFORD, NEW YORK 13413

OVERVIEW: Operates insurance companies. Established: 1914.

KEY STATISTICS Annual Sales: $500.0 million. Number of Employees: 1,400.

EXPERTISE/EDUCATION SOUGHT: Computer programming, customer service and support, claims adjusting, economics, actuarial

CONTACT: Mr Thomas J Jasinski, CPCU, Employment Supervisor; Phone (315) 734-2292.

CORPORATE STATEMENT

Utica National Insurance Group is a dynamic, yet conservative multi-line property-casualty insurer based in upstate New York. Its branch offices exist in several major cities. Utica National Insurance offers employees high visibility and a progressive environment.

UTILICORP UNITED, INC.

911 MAIN STREET
KANSAS CITY, MISSOURI 64105

OVERVIEW: Electric and gas utility. Established: 1926.

KEY STATISTICS Number of Employees: 4,737.

EXPERTISE/EDUCATION SOUGHT: Electrical engineering, finance, chemical engineering, accounting, mechanical engineering

CONTACT: Mr Robert Browning, Director of Personnel and Organization, 911 Main, Suite 3000, Kansas City, MO, 64105; Phone (816) 421-6600.

America's Favorite Mail.

VAL-PAK DIRECT MARKETING SYSTEMS, INC.

8605 LARGO LAKES DRIVE
LARGO, FLORIDA 34643-4912

OVERVIEW: Provides direct mail and advertising services. Established: 1968. Parent Company: Cox Enterprises, Inc.

KEY STATISTICS Annual Sales: $160.0 million. Number of Employees: 2,400.

HIRING HISTORY Number of professional employees hired in 1993: 200.

EXPERTISE/EDUCATION SOUGHT: Advertising, marketing, communications, sales, business administration

CONTACT: Ms Lisa Chandler, Recruiting Manager; Phone (800) 294-1455; Fax (813)391-2710.

CORPORATE STATEMENT

Val-Pak seeks sales professionals to present advertising programs to local businesses. It serves 100,000+ clients throughout the U.S. and Canada and mails to over 53 million households an average of seven times annually. Val-Pak is recognized by Sales and Marketing Management *magazine as one of the top five sales forces in the country.*

VALMONT INDUSTRIES, INC.

HIGHWAY 275, PO BOX 358
VALLEY, NEBRASKA 68064

OVERVIEW: Manufactures irrigation systems and light poles. Established: 1945.

KEY STATISTICS Annual Sales: $874.0 million. Number of Employees: 5,030.

HIRING HISTORY Number of professional employees hired in 1994: 5.

EXPERTISE/EDUCATION SOUGHT: Sales, manufacturing engineering, civil engineering, structural engineering, agricultural engineering, mechanical engineering, electrical engineering, marketing

CONTACT: Mr Thomas Whalen, Vice President of Human Resources; Phone (402) 359-2201, ext. 0358.

VALSPAR CORPORATION

1101 SOUTH 3RD STREET
MINNEAPOLIS, MINNESOTA 55415-1211

OVERVIEW: Manufactures and distributes paints and coatings. Established: 1806.

KEY STATISTICS Annual Sales: $694.0 million. Number of Employees: 2,500.

EXPERTISE/EDUCATION SOUGHT: Sales, marketing, finance, chemistry, product design and development, chemical engineering, mechanical engineering, accounting

CONTACT: Mr Paul Mason, Manager of Staffing; Phone (612) 332-7371.

VALUE CITY DEPARTMENT STORES

3241 WESTERVILLE ROAD
COLUMBUS, OHIO 43224-3750

OVERVIEW: Operates chain of discount department stores. Parent Company: Schottenstein Stores Corporation.

KEY STATISTICS Annual Sales: $842.0 million. Number of Employees: 9,600.

EXPERTISE/EDUCATION SOUGHT: Accounting, law, sales, computer programming

CONTACT: Mr Herbert Minkin, Vice President of Human Resources; Phone (614) 478-2200.

VALUE HEALTH, INC.

22 WATERVILLE ROAD
AVON, CONNECTICUT 06001-2066

OVERVIEW: Provides healthcare consulting and information services. Established: 1991.

KEY STATISTICS Number of Employees: 3,300.

EXPERTISE/EDUCATION SOUGHT: Pharmacy, software engineering/development, accounting, sales, finance, marketing

CONTACT: For individuals with previous experience: Mr Bob Patricelli, Chairman and Chief Executive Officer; Phone (203) 678-3400.

VAN WATERS ROGERS, INC.

6100 CARRILLON POINT
KIRKLAND, WASHINGTON 98033-7357

OVERVIEW: Distributes industrial chemicals. Established: 1950.

EXPERTISE/EDUCATION SOUGHT: Sales, accounting, marketing, finance, management information systems

CONTACT: For individuals with previous experience: Ms Mary Barile, Human Resources Coordinator; Phone (206) 889-3400.

VANS, INC.

2095 NORTH BATAVIA STREET
ORANGE, CALIFORNIA 92665-3101

OVERVIEW: Manufactures and sells men's, women's, and children's shoes. Established: 1966.

KEY STATISTICS Annual Sales: $86.6 million. Number of Employees: 2,300.

Vans, Inc. (continued)

Expertise/Education Sought: Business management, marketing, public relations, accounting

Contact: For individuals with previous experience: Ms Jacqie Cleary, Director of Human Resources; Phone (714) 974-7414.

VARITY CORPORATION
672 DELAWARE AVENUE
BUFFALO, NEW YORK 14209

Overview: Manufactures automotive parts, agricultural machinery, and engines. Established: 1847.

Expertise/Education Sought: Manufacturing engineering, automotive engineering, mechanical engineering, electrical engineering, production

Contact: Ms Ruth McManus, Manager of Human Resources; Phone (716) 888-8000.

VENTURE STORES, INC.
2001 WEST TERRA LANE
O' FALLON, MISSOURI 63366

Overview: Operates chain of retail stores. Established: 1970.

Key Statistics Annual Sales: $2.0 billion. Number of Employees: 16,000.

Expertise/Education Sought: Merchandising, computer programming, management information systems, accounting, retail, industrial engineering

Contact: Mr Mike Williams, Director of Executive Recruiting; Phone (314) 281-6646; Fax (314) 281-6049.

VERMONT AMERICAN CORPORATION
NATIONAL CITY TOWER, 101 SOUTH 5TH STREET, SUITE 2300
LOUISVILLE, KENTUCKY 40202

Overview: Manufactures power tool accessories.

Key Statistics Number of Employees: 4,000.

Expertise/Education Sought: Mechanical engineering, sales, marketing, ecology, human resources

Contact: For individuals with previous experience: Mr Elvis Vaughn, Director, Employee Relations; Phone (502) 625-2000.

VIACOM INTERNATIONAL, INC.
1515 BROADWAY
NEW YORK, NEW YORK 10036-5701

Overview: Produces and distributes entertainment and communications products; operates television and radio stations and cable television systems. Established: 1970.

Key Statistics Annual Sales: $675.0 million. Number of Employees: 5,000.

Expertise/Education Sought: Radio broadcasting, communications, journalism, production, television broadcasting, film/film production

Contacts: For college students and recent graduates: Ms Francine Vitrano, Senior Personnel Assistant; Phone (212) 258-6036. For individuals with previous experience: Ms Maria Cottone, Senior Personnel Assistant; Phone (212) 258-6028.

VICTORIA'S SECRET STORES, INC.
8455 EAST BROAD STREET
REYNOLDSBURG, OHIO 43068

Overview: Operates chain of women's apparel stores. Parent Company: Limited, Inc.

Key Statistics Annual Sales: $569.0 million. Number of Employees: 10,000.

Expertise/Education Sought: Marketing, sales

Contact: Ms Terri Bardi, Senior Manager of Recruiting, PO Box 16586, Columbus, OH, 43216; Phone (614) 577-7055.

VIGORO CORPORATION
225 NORTH MICHIGAN AVENUE, SUITE 2500
CHICAGO, ILLINOIS 60601-7601

Overview: Manufactures fertilizers and mineral products. Established: 1991.

Key Statistics Annual Sales: $727.0 million. Number of Employees: 1,400.

Expertise/Education Sought: Marketing, sales, chemical engineering

Contact: Mr B J Lowenthal, Director of Human Resources, 225 North Michigan Avenue, #6 Executive Drive, Collinsville, IL, 62234; Phone (618) 346-7431.

VIKING FREIGHT SYSTEM, INC.
411 EAST PLUMERIA DRIVE
SAN JOSE, CALIFORNIA 95134-1924

Overview: Operates trucking lines in eleven western states.

Key Statistics Annual Sales: $298.7 million. Number of Employees: 4,257.

Expertise/Education Sought: Sales, financial analysis, accounting, management information systems

Contact: For individuals with previous experience: Ms Jennifer Battin, Personnel Manager; Phone (408) 922-2123.

VINCAM HUMAN RESOURCES, INC.
2850 DOUGLAS ROAD
MIAMI, FLORIDA 33134-6901

Overview: Provides employee leasing services.

Key Statistics Annual Sales: $74.9 million. Number of Employees: 8,500.

Expertise/Education Sought: Marketing, sales

Contact: For individuals with previous experience: Mr Vinnie Beneventi, Staffing Manager.

VISHAY INTERTECHNOLOGY, INC.
63 LINCOLN HIGHWAY
MALVERN, PENNSYLVANIA 19355-2143

Overview: Manufactures passive electronic components. Established: 1962.

Key Statistics Number of Employees: 14,500.

Hiring History Number of professional employees hired in 1993: 6.

Expertise/Education Sought: Electronics/electronics engineering, marketing, production management

Contacts: For college students and recent graduates: Ms Martha Mitri, Assistant Manager, Industrial Relations; Phone (610) 644-1300, ext. 2282. For individuals with previous experience: Mr William Spires, Vice President of Human Resources; 644-1300, ext. 2282.

VOLVO GM HEAVY TRUCK CORPORATION
7825 NATIONAL SERVICE ROAD
GREENSBORO, NORTH CAROLINA 27409-9667

Overview: Manufactures trucks. Parent Company: Volvo Cars of North America.

Key Statistics Annual Sales: $1.0 billion. Number of Employees: 4,019.

Expertise/Education Sought: Purchasing, marketing, accounting, credit/credit analysis

Contact: Ms Laura Reddin, Human Resources Special Projects Administrator; Phone (910) 393-2000, ext. 2188.

THE VONS COMPANIES, INC.
618 MICHILLINDA AVENUE
ARCADIA, CALIFORNIA 91107-6300

Overview: Operates chain of food stores. Established: 1906.

EXPERTISE/EDUCATION SOUGHT: Marketing, management, business administration, finance, accounting

CONTACT: For individuals with previous experience: Mr Tom Clayton, Manager of Employment; Phone (818) 821-7551.

VULCAN MATERIALS COMPANY
1 METROPLEX DRIVE
BIRMINGHAM, ALABAMA 35209-6893

OVERVIEW: Manufactures construction materials and industrial chemicals. Established: 1916.

KEY STATISTICS Number of Employees: 6,300.

HIRING HISTORY Number of professional employees hired in 1993: 20.

EXPERTISE/EDUCATION SOUGHT: Finance, auditing, accounting, management information systems, computer programming, data processing, law

CONTACT: Mr Jack Riley, Manager of Human Resources, PO Box 530187, Birmingham, AL, 35253-0187; Phone (205) 877-3000.

WABAN, INC.
1 MERCER ROAD
NATICK, MASSACHUSETTS 01760-2400

OVERVIEW: Owns and operates regional wholesale clubs.

KEY STATISTICS Annual Sales: $4.0 billion. Number of Employees: 16,000.

EXPERTISE/EDUCATION SOUGHT: Accounting, finance, data processing, business management, auditing

CONTACT: Ms Paula Stevens, Assistant Vice President of Staffing; Phone (508) 651-6500.

WACHOVIA BANK OF GEORGIA
191 PEACHTREE STREET NORTHEAST
ATLANTA, GEORGIA 30303-1740

OVERVIEW: Full service bank. Established: 1865. Parent Company: Wachovia Corporation.

KEY STATISTICS Number of Employees: 4,757.

HIRING HISTORY Number of professional employees hired in 1993: 150.

EXPERTISE/EDUCATION SOUGHT: Marketing, accounting, finance, real estate, underwriting

CONTACTS: For college students and recent graduates: Mr Bill Woolery, Assistant Vice President of Human Resources; Phone (404) 332-5721. For individuals with previous experience: Mr Jack Frost, Senior Vice President of Management Employment; Phone (404) 332-5721.

WACHOVIA BANK OF NORTH CAROLINA
301 NORTH MAIN STREET
WINSTON SALEM, NORTH CAROLINA 27101-3819

OVERVIEW: Commercial bank. Established: 1956.

KEY STATISTICS Assets: $3.0 billion. Number of Employees: 15,531.

EXPERTISE/EDUCATION SOUGHT: Operations, finance, accounting, management

CONTACT: For individuals with previous experience: Ms Veronica Black, Senior Vice President of Recruiting; Phone (919) 770-5000.

WACKENHUT CORPORATION
1500 SAN REMO AVENUE
MIAMI, FLORIDA 33146

OVERVIEW: Provides security guard services. Established: 1954.

HIRING HISTORY Number of professional employees hired in 1994: 30.

EXPERTISE/EDUCATION SOUGHT: Accounting, computer science, finance, auditing, human resources, management

CONTACTS: For college students and recent graduates: Ms Vivian Quesada, Employment Specialist; Phone (305) 666-5656. For individuals with previous experience: Mr Jan P Vandersluis, Manager of Corporate Recruiting in Human Resources; Phone (305) 666-5656, ext. 7415.

WAKEFERN FOOD CORPORATION
600 YORK STREET
ELIZABETH, NEW JERSEY 07207-2041

OVERVIEW: Distributes wholesale foods. Established: 1946.

KEY STATISTICS Annual Sales: $40.0 billion. Number of Employees: 4,900.

EXPERTISE/EDUCATION SOUGHT: Business management, finance, marketing, law, accounting

CONTACTS: For college students and recent graduates: Mr Phil Solomon, Senior Recruiting Specialist; Phone (908) 906-5205. For individuals with previous experience: Dr Paula Thomas, Manager of Staffing and Organizational Development; Phone (908) 906-5192.

WALDBAUM, INC.
1 HEMLOCK STREET
CENTRAL ISLIP, NEW YORK 11722

OVERVIEW: Operates chain of food stores. Parent Company: Great Atlantic & Pacific Tea Company, Inc.

KEY STATISTICS Number of Employees: 12,000.

EXPERTISE/EDUCATION SOUGHT: Pharmacy, business

CONTACT: For individuals with previous experience: Ms Ruth Collins, Director of Human Resources; Phone (516) 233-8348.

WALDEN BOOK COMPANY, INC.
201 HIGH RIDGE ROAD
STAMFORD, CONNECTICUT 06905-3417

OVERVIEW: Operates chain of book stores. Established: 1933. Parent Company: Kmart Corporation.

KEY STATISTICS Annual Sales: $1.0 billion. Number of Employees: 11,000.

EXPERTISE/EDUCATION SOUGHT: Computer programming, computer analysis, retail, finance, accounting, marketing

CONTACT: Mr Jim Taylor, Director of Human Resources; Phone (203) 352-2000.

WALGREEN COMPANY
300 WILMONT ROAD, DEPARTMENT 65
DEERFIELD, ILLINOIS 60015-4600

OVERVIEW: Operates nationwide chain of retail drug stores. Established: 1901.

KEY STATISTICS Annual Sales: $9.0 billion. Number of Employees: 62,000.

EXPERTISE/EDUCATION SOUGHT: Retail, management, business, retail management

CONTACT: Personnel Recruitment Department; Phone (708) 405-5889; Fax (708) 405-5995.

CORPORATE STATEMENT

Walgreen Co. is the U.S. chain drugstore industry's leader in sales, profits, store growth, and technology use. With more than 2,000 stores in 30 states and Puerto Rico, the chain serves nearly 2 million customers daily. The company's strategy is to be the nation's most convenient health-care provider.

WALKER INTERACTIVE SYSTEMS
303 2ND STREET
SAN FRANCISCO, CALIFORNIA 94107-1366

OVERVIEW: Develops financial and control application software. Established: 1969.

KEY STATISTICS Annual Sales: $65.0 million. Number of Employees: 481.

EXPERTISE/EDUCATION SOUGHT: Software engineering/development, marketing, accounting

CONTACT: For individuals with previous experience: Human Resources; Phone (415) 495-8811.

WALLACE COMPUTER SERVICES, INC.
HILLSIDE, ILLINOIS 60162-2034

OVERVIEW: Provides commercial printing services; manufactures business forms and office products.

KEY STATISTICS Annual Sales: $588.0 million. Number of Employees: 3,700.

HIRING HISTORY Number of professional employees hired in 1994: 240.

EXPERTISE/EDUCATION SOUGHT: Sales, accounting, management information systems

CONTACT: For individuals with previous experience: Mr Eric Sinn, Manager of Employment; Phone (708) 449-8600.

WALMART, INC.
702 SOUTHWEST 8TH STREET
BENTONVILLE, ARKANSAS 72712

OVERVIEW: Operates chain of discount merchandise stores. Established: 1945.

EXPERTISE/EDUCATION SOUGHT: Retail, accounting, human resources, purchasing, information systems, construction engineering, environmental engineering

CONTACT: Ms Laurie Myers, Director of Personnel; Phone (501) 273-8303.

WALT DISNEY COMPANY, INC.
500 SOUTH BUENA VISTA
BURBANK, CALIFORNIA 91521-0001

OVERVIEW: Produces and distributes motion pictures; owns and operates amusement parks, hotels, and resorts. Established: 1923.

KEY STATISTICS Number of Employees: 62,000.

EXPERTISE/EDUCATION SOUGHT: Finance, management information systems, accounting

CONTACT: Mr Mike Buckhoff, Vice President of Human Resources; Phone (818) 560-1000.

WALT DISNEY WORLD COMPANY
1375 NORTH BUENA VISTA AVENUE
ORLANDO, FLORIDA 32818-5901

OVERVIEW: Owns and operates amusement parks, hotels, and resorts. Established: 1964. Parent Company: Walt Disney Company, Inc.

KEY STATISTICS Annual Sales: $3.0 billion. Number of Employees: 34,000.

HIRING HISTORY Number of professional employees hired in 1993: 222.

EXPERTISE/EDUCATION SOUGHT: Accounting, finance, marketing, electrical engineering, mechanical engineering, industrial engineering, sales, information systems, food services, food science

CONTACT: For individuals with previous experience: Mr Joey Wise, Human Resources Director.

WAMPLER-LONGACRE, INC.
800 COOPER DRIVE
TIMBERVILLE, VIRGINIA 22853

OVERVIEW: Produces and markets poultry products. Established: 1940.

KEY STATISTICS Annual Sales: $712.0 million. Number of Employees: 6,350.

EXPERTISE/EDUCATION SOUGHT: Accounting, information systems, management, human resources, management, operations

CONTACT: For individuals with previous experience: Ms Jane Brookshire, Vice President Human Resources, PO Box 7275, Broadway, VA, 22815.

WANG LABORATORIES, INC.
1 INDUSTRIAL AVENUE
LOWELL, MASSACHUSETTS 01851

OVERVIEW: Manufactures software and provides system integration services. Established: 1951.

EXPERTISE/EDUCATION SOUGHT: Computer programming, finance, marketing, software engineering/development

CONTACT: For individuals with previous experience: Ms Judy Lyttle, Director of Human Resources; Phone (508) 459-5000.

WARNACO, INC.
325 LAFAYETTE STREET
BRIDGEPORT, CONNECTICUT 06601

OVERVIEW: Manufactures women's apparel. Established: 1874.

EXPERTISE/EDUCATION SOUGHT: Data processing, credit/credit analysis, accounting

CONTACT: Ms Lisa Law, Assistant Director of Personnel; Phone (203) 579-8303.

WARNER-LAMBERT COMPANY
201 TABOR ROAD
MORRIS PLAINS, NEW JERSEY 07950

OVERVIEW: Manufactures and markets pharmaceuticals, consumer healthcare products, and other consumer products. Established: 1856.

KEY STATISTICS Annual Sales: $6.0 billion. Number of Employees: 34,000.

EXPERTISE/EDUCATION SOUGHT: Sales, management, business, engineering, finance, accounting, management information systems, data processing, marketing

CONTACT: Mr Raymond Fino, Vice President Corporate Human Resources; Phone (201) 540-2000.

WASHINTON METRO AREA TRANSIT AUTHORITY
600 5TH STREET NORTHWEST
WASHINGTON, D.C. 20001-2651

OVERVIEW: Provides local and suburban transportation services. Established: 1967.

KEY STATISTICS Annual Sales: $328.0 million. Number of Employees: 8,343.

HIRING HISTORY Number of professional employees hired in 1993: 400.

EXPERTISE/EDUCATION SOUGHT: Civil engineering, mechanical engineering, electrical engineering, structural engineering

CONTACT: Ms Lena Young, Manager of Employment Services; Phone (202) 962-2314.

THE WASHINGTON POST COMPANY
1150 15TH STREET NORTHWEST
WASHINGTON, D.C. 20071-0001

OVERVIEW: Publishes newspapers. Established: 1887.

KEY STATISTICS Number of Employees: 6,600.

EXPERTISE/EDUCATION SOUGHT: Accounting, journalism, graphic arts, data processing, business management

CONTACT: For individuals with previous experience: Mr Carl Williams, Director of Personnel; Phone (202) 334-6000, ext. 6466.

WATKINS MOTOR LINES, INC.
1144 WEST GRIFFIN ROAD
LAKELAND, FLORIDA 33805

OVERVIEW: Provides truck transportation services.

KEY STATISTICS Annual Sales: $399.0 million. Number of Employees: 5,200.

EXPERTISE/EDUCATION SOUGHT: Transportation, management information systems, computer science

CONTACT: For individuals with previous experience: Ms Gail Stark, Manager Recruiting Programs, PO Box 95002, Lakeland, FL, 33804.

WAWA, INC.
260 BALTIMORE PIKE
WAWA, PENNSYLVANIA 19063-5699

OVERVIEW: Operates chain of convenience stores located in Connecticut, Delaware, Maryland, New Jersey, and Pennsylvania. Established: 1803.

KEY STATISTICS Annual Sales: $786.0 million. Number of Employees: 10,000.

HIRING HISTORY Number of professional employees hired in 1993: 100.

EXPERTISE/EDUCATION SOUGHT: Customer service and support, retail management, business management, food service management

CONTACT: Ms Andrea Kauriga Burns, Educational Relations Specialist; Phone (610) 358-8723.

For more information, see full corporate profile, pg. 222.

DEL WEBB CORPORATION
601 NORTH 24TH STREET
PHOENIX, ARIZONA 85016-3453

OVERVIEW: Develops real estate and constructs new homes. Established: 1881.

KEY STATISTICS Annual Sales: $510.0 million. Number of Employees: 1,400.

HIRING HISTORY Number of professional employees hired in 1994: 134.

EXPERTISE/EDUCATION SOUGHT: Accounting, marketing, computer programming, production control, administration

CONTACT: For individuals with previous experience: Ms Tommye Ware, Human Resources Manager; Phone (602) 808-8000.

WEGMAN'S FOOD MARKETS, INC.
1500 BROOKS AVENUE
ROCHESTER, NEW YORK 14624-3512

OVERVIEW: Operates chain of food stores. Established: 1921.

KEY STATISTICS Annual Sales: $2.0 billion. Number of Employees: 21,300.

EXPERTISE/EDUCATION SOUGHT: Marketing, sales, management

CONTACT: Mr Gerard Pierce, Director of Human Resources, PO Box 844, Rochester, NY, 14692-0844; Phone (716) 328-2550.

WEIGHT WATCHERS INTERNATIONAL, INC.
500 NORTH BROADWAY
JERICHO, NEW YORK 11753-2196

OVERVIEW: Distributes food products and operates weight loss center franchises. Established: 1978. Parent Company: H. J. Heinz Company.

KEY STATISTICS Assets: $280.0 million. Number of Employees: 10,000.

EXPERTISE/EDUCATION SOUGHT: Management, accounting, finance, logistics, training and development, real estate

CONTACT: For individuals with previous experience: Mr Brian Powers, General Manager of Human Resources; Phone (516) 939-0400, ext. 629.

WEIRTON STEEL CORPORATION
400 THREE SPRINGS DRIVE
WEIRTON, WEST VIRGINIA 26062-4997

OVERVIEW: Manufactures steel. Established: 1909.

KEY STATISTICS Annual Sales: $1.0 billion. Number of Employees: 6,026.

EXPERTISE/EDUCATION SOUGHT: Accounting, marketing, finance, electrical engineering, civil engineering, mechanical engineering, computer science, electrical technology

CONTACT: Mr Jeff Robinson, Corporate Recruiting and Staffing Manager; Phone (304) 797-2000.

WELBILT CORPORATION
225 HIGH RIDGE ROAD
STAMFORD, CONNECTICUT 06905

OVERVIEW: Manufactures commercial kitchen equipment. Established: 1988. Parent Company: .

EXPERTISE/EDUCATION SOUGHT: Accounting, marketing

CONTACT: For individuals with previous experience: Ms Susan Jenson, Director of Human Resources and Benefits; Phone (203) 325-8300.

WELLMAN, INC.
1040 BROAD STREET, SUITE 302
SHREWSBURG, NEW JERSEY 07702

OVERVIEW: Recycles plastic and fibers; manufactures polyester. Established: 1927.

EXPERTISE/EDUCATION SOUGHT: Chemical engineering, design engineering, industrial engineering, finance, accounting, data processing, business administration, mechanical engineering, environmental engineering, electrical engineering

CONTACT: For individuals with previous experience: Mr James Carraway, Manager of Employee Relations, PO Box 188, Johnsonville, SC, 29535; Phone (803) 386-2011.

WELLPOINT HEALTH NETWORK
21555 OXNARD STREET
WOODLAND HILLS, CALIFORNIA 91367-4943

OVERVIEW: Provides health insurance. Established: 1987. Parent Company: Blue Cross of California.

KEY STATISTICS Annual Sales: $2.0 billion. Number of Employees: 2,700.

EXPERTISE/EDUCATION SOUGHT: Finance, accounting, case management, customer service and support, human resources

CONTACT: For individuals with previous experience: Ms Joanne Fink, Director of Recruiting.

WELLS FARGO AND COMPANY
420 MONTGOMERY STREET
SAN FRANCISCO, CALIFORNIA 94163-1205

OVERVIEW: Provides commercial banking services. Established: 1852.

KEY STATISTICS Assets: $5.0 billion. Number of Employees: 19,700.

EXPERTISE/EDUCATION SOUGHT: Accounting, finance, marketing, underwriting, real estate, credit management, information services, operations, information systems

CONTACT: For individuals with previous experience: Ms Una Stephens-Hardy, Manager of Recruitment; Phone (415) 396-5663.

WELLS FARGO ARMORED SERVICE CORPORATION
6165 BARFIELD ROAD
ATLANTA, GEORGIA 30328-4312

OVERVIEW: Provides armored car transport services. Established: 1967.

KEY STATISTICS Annual Sales: $141.4 million. Number of Employees: 5,000.

EXPERTISE/EDUCATION SOUGHT: Management information systems, accounting, law

CONTACT: For individuals with previous experience: Ms Sandy Strong, Assistant Vice President and Director of Human Resources.

WELLS FARGO BANK
420 MONTGOMERY STREET
SAN FRANCISCO, CALIFORNIA 94104-1298

OVERVIEW: Commercial bank. Established: 1968. Parent Company: Wells Fargo & Company.

KEY STATISTICS Number of Employees: 19,700.

EXPERTISE/EDUCATION SOUGHT: Accounting, advertising, data processing, marketing, administration

CONTACT: For individuals with previous experience: Ms Una Stephens-Hardy, Vice President of Recruiting and Placement Services, PO Box 63710, MC 0101-114, San Francisco, CA, 94163; Phone (415) 396-3846; Fax (415)396-5262.

WENDY'S INTERNATIONAL, INC.
4288 WEST DUBLIN GRANVILLE ROAD
DUBLIN, OHIO 43017-2093

OVERVIEW: Operates chain of fast food restaurants. Established: 1969.

KEY STATISTICS Annual Sales: $1.0 billion. Number of Employees: 43,000.

EXPERTISE/EDUCATION SOUGHT: Hospitality/hotel and restaurant management, business management, communications, marketing

CONTACT: For individuals with previous experience: Human Resources Department; Phone (614) 764-3100.

WEST PUBLISHING COMPANY
610 OPPERMAN DRIVE
EAGAN, MINNESOTA 55123-1396

OVERVIEW: Provides publications and on line information services for legal professionals. Established: 1876.

KEY STATISTICS Number of Employees: 6,000.

EXPERTISE/EDUCATION SOUGHT: Computer science, communications, editing, law, journalism

CONTACT: For individuals with previous experience: Ms Barbara Christiansen, Director of Personnel, PO Box 64526, St Paul, MN, 55164-0526; Phone (612) 687-7000.

WESTERN DIGITAL CORPORATION
8105 IRVINE CENTER DRIVE
IRVINE, CALIFORNIA 92718-2937

OVERVIEW: Manufactures magnetic disk drives and computer components. Established: 1970.

KEY STATISTICS Annual Sales: $1.0 billion. Number of Employees: 7,322.

EXPERTISE/EDUCATION SOUGHT: Electronics/electronics engineering, computer science, finance, marketing, mechanical engineering

CONTACT: For individuals with previous experience: Mr Jim Wright, Manager of Human Resources; Phone (714) 932-5000, ext. 5776.

THE WESTERN SOUTHERN LIFE INSURANCE COMPANY
400 BROADWAY
CINCINNATI, OHIO 45202-3312

OVERVIEW: Providees life insurance services. Established: 1948.

KEY STATISTICS Number of Employees: 5,649.

EXPERTISE/EDUCATION SOUGHT: Auditing, underwriting, accounting, marketing, finance, sales

CONTACT: For individuals with previous experience: Ms Cheryl Jordan, Manager of Human Resources; Phone (513) 629-1800.

 Westinghouse

WESTINGHOUSE ELECTRIC CORPORATION
11 STANWIX STREET
PITTSBURG, PENNSYLVANIA 15222

OVERVIEW: Provides electronic control systems, power generation systems, environmental services, refrigeration equipment, and broadcasting. Established: 1886.

KEY STATISTICS Annual Sales: $9.0 billion. Number of Employees: 80,000.

HIRING HISTORY Number of professional employees hired in 1994: 150.

EXPERTISE/EDUCATION SOUGHT: Design engineering, computer science, human resources, finance, accounting

CONTACT: Mr Dalls Frey, Manager of Staffing and Development; Phone (412) 642-6025; Fax (412)642-3950.

CORPORATE STATEMENT

Westinghouse seeks to be the best performing multi-industry company in the world. Core businesses include broadcasting, electronic systems, energy systems, government and environmental services, the Knoll Group (office furniture), power generation, and Thermo King (transport refrigeration).

Substantial concentrations of employees exist in Pennsylvania, Maryland, the Carolinas, Florida, Minnesota, and Washington.

WESTINGHOUSE HANFORD COMPANY
1100 JADWIN AVENUE
RICHLAND, WASHINGTON 99352-3423

OVERVIEW: Operates nuclear energy generation facility. Established: 1970. Parent Company: Westinghouse Electric Corporation.

KEY STATISTICS Annual Sales: $1.1 billion. Number of Employees: 11,208.

EXPERTISE/EDUCATION SOUGHT: Chemical engineering, nuclear engineering

CONTACTS: For college students and recent graduates: Ms Sherry Smith, Employment Director; Phone (509) 376-1481. For individuals with previous experience: Ms Jane Ford, Manager of Recruitment; Phone (509) 376-2378; Fax (509)376-3245.

WESTINGHOUSE SAVANNAH RIVER COMPANY
1993 SOUTH CENTENNIAL AVENUE
AIKEN, SOUTH CAROLINA 29803

OVERVIEW: Nuclear production, waste management, and environmental restoration for the U.S. Department of Energy. Parent Company: Westinghouse Electric Corporation.

KEY STATISTICS Annual Sales: $4.0 billion. Number of Employees: 15,000.

EXPERTISE/EDUCATION SOUGHT: Environmental engineering, environmental science, nuclear medicine, geology, hydrogeology, chemical engineering, nuclear engineering, physics, waste management

CONTACT: Mr W K Sokolo, Manager of Employment; Phone (803) 644-6287.

WESTVACO CORPORATION
299 PARK AVENUE
NEW YORK, NEW YORK 10171

OVERVIEW: Manufactures paper. Established: 1889.

EXPERTISE/EDUCATION SOUGHT: Sales, chemical engineering, process engineering, marketing, finance, physics

CONTACT: Ms Kelley McNamara, Manager of College Recruiting; Phone (212) 688-5000.

WEYERHAEUSER COMPANY
33663 WEYERHAEUSER WAY SOUTH
TACOMA, WASHINGTON 98477

OVERVIEW: Manufactures and markets pulp, paper and wood products; manages and develops real estate; provides financial services. Established: 1900.

EXPERTISE/EDUCATION SOUGHT: Accounting, engineering, human resources, pulp and paper science, forestry

CONTACTS: For college students and recent graduates: Manager of College Recruiting; Phone (206) 924-2602. For individuals with previous experience: Mr Don Oars, Director of Recruiting and Staffing; Phone (206) 924-2345.

WHEATON GLASS INDUSTRIES, INC.
220 G STREET
MILLVILLE, NEW JERSEY 08332-2003

OVERVIEW: Manufactures glass bottles. Established: 1888.

KEY STATISTICS Number of Employees: 6,000.

HIRING HISTORY Number of professional employees hired in 1993: 15.

EXPERTISE/EDUCATION SOUGHT: Electronics/electronics engineering, chemistry, drafting

CONTACT: Ms Etta Lambert, Supervisor of Employment; Phone (609) 825-1400.

WHEELABRATOR TECHNOLOGIES, INC.
LIBERTY LANE
HAMPTON, NEW HAMPSHIRE 03842

OVERVIEW: Provides waste management systems and services. Established: 1985. Parent Company: WMX Technologies, Inc.

KEY STATISTICS Annual Sales: $2.0 billion. Number of Employees: 3,600.

EXPERTISE/EDUCATION SOUGHT: Accounting, finance, marketing, environmental engineering, mechanical engineering, chemical engineering, information systems

CONTACT: Mr Ed Drumm, Director of Benefits and Compensation; Phone (603) 929-3000.

WHEELING-PITTSBURGH CORPORATION
1134 MARKET STREET
WHEELING, WEST VIRGINIA 26003

OVERVIEW: Manufactures steel.

EXPERTISE/EDUCATION SOUGHT: Marketing, finance, accounting, mechanical engineering, chemical engineering, electrical engineering, metallurgical engineering

CONTACT: Mr James Bronchik, Director of Human Resources; Phone (304) 234-2523.

WHEREHOUSE ENTERTAINMENT, INC.
19701 HAMILTON AVENUE
TORRANCE, CALIFORNIA 90502-1334

OVERVIEW: Distributes and markets audio tapes, CDs, and video tapes. Established: 1970.

KEY STATISTICS Annual Sales: $472.0 million. Number of Employees: 7,700.

HIRING HISTORY Number of professional employees hired in 1994: 50.

EXPERTISE/EDUCATION SOUGHT: Operations, field service, finance, analysis, training and development, advertising, project management, merchandising, accounting, management information systems

CONTACT: For individuals with previous experience: Mr Chris Gehrke, Recruiter; Phone (310) 538-2314.

WHIRLPOOL CORPORATION
2000 NORTH HIGHWAY M-63
BENTON HARBOR, MICHIGAN 49022

OVERVIEW: Manufactures consumer appliances. Established: 1929.

EXPERTISE/EDUCATION SOUGHT: Engineering, management information systems, systems analysis, marketing, finance

CONTACTS: For college students and recent graduates: Ms Darla Crawford, Recruiter. For individuals with previous experience: Mr Fred Philpott, Vice President of Human Resources; Phone (616) 926-5000.

WHITE CONSOLIDATED INDUSTRIES
11770 BEREA ROAD
CLEVELAND, OHIO 44111-1686

OVERVIEW: Manufactures refrigerators and household appliances. Established: 1954.

KEY STATISTICS Number of Employees: 30,000.

EXPERTISE/EDUCATION SOUGHT: Marketing, plant management, human resources, finance

CONTACT: For individuals with previous experience: Mr Joseph Burke, Vice President of Human Resources; Phone (216) 252-3700.

WHITING ROLL-UP DOOR MANUFACTURING CORPORATION
113 CEDAR STREET
AKRON, NEW YORK 14001-1038

OVERVIEW: Manufactures roll up doors. Established: 1976.

KEY STATISTICS Number of Employees: 350.

EXPERTISE/EDUCATION SOUGHT: Mechanical engineering, manufacturing engineering, computer programming, accounting, finance, sales, marketing

CONTACT: For individuals with previous experience: Mr Peter Gullo, Personnel Manager; Phone (716) 542-5427.

WHITTMAN-HART
311 SOUTH WACKER DRIVE
CHICAGO, ILLINOIS 60606-5615

OVERVIEW: Provides computer consulting services. Established: 1984.

KEY STATISTICS Annual Sales: $31.0 million. Number of Employees: 325.

EXPERTISE/EDUCATION SOUGHT: Computer science, data processing, finance, accounting, software engineering/development, systems engineering

CONTACT: For individuals with previous experience: Ms Karen Kush, Director of Human Resources.

WICKES LUMBER COMPANY
DEERPATH DRIVE
VERNON HILLS, ILLINOIS 60061-1898

OVERVIEW: Manufactures building materials.

KEY STATISTICS Annual Sales: $847.0 million. Number of Employees: 4,092.

EXPERTISE/EDUCATION SOUGHT: Sales, marketing, accounting

CONTACTS: For college students and recent graduates: Ms Stephanie Kraft, Director of Recruiting; Phone (708) 367-3471. For individuals with previous experience: Mr Bob Adams, Director of Human Resources; Phone (708) 367-6540.

WILDLIFE INTERNATIONAL, LTD.
8598 COMMERCE DRIVE
EATON, MARYLAND 21601

OVERVIEW: Provides environmental research services.

EXPERTISE/EDUCATION SOUGHT: Accounting, finance, environmental research, biology, chemistry

CONTACT: Dr Greg Smith, Director of Laboratory Programs; Phone (410) 822-8600.

WILLAMETTE INDUSTRIES, INC.
1300 SOUTHWEST 5TH AVENUE
PORTLAND, OREGON 97201-5671

OVERVIEW: Manufactures paper, packaging, lumber, and wood products. Established: 1906.

Willamette Industries, Inc. (continued)

KEY STATISTICS Annual Sales: $3.0 billion. Number of Employees: 12,040.

EXPERTISE/EDUCATION SOUGHT: Marketing, finance, accounting, electrical engineering, mechanical engineering, computer programming, chemical engineering

CONTACT: Mr Gregg Newstrand, Regional Personnel Manager; Phone (503) 641-4455.

WILLIAMS COMPANIES, INC.

1 WILLIAMS CENTER FORUM
TULSA, OKLAHOMA 74172-0150

OVERVIEW: Operates oil and gas pipelines and provides telecommunications services. Established: 1908.

KEY STATISTICS Number of Employees: 7,189.

EXPERTISE/EDUCATION SOUGHT: Accounting, finance, law, telecommunications, communications, human resources, auditing, customer service and support, marketing

CONTACT: Ms Mary Walrond, Manager of Employee Relations; Phone (918) 588-2091.

WILLIS CORROON CORPORATION

WALL STREET PLAZA
NASHVILLE, TENNESSEE 37214-3644

OVERVIEW: Provides insurance. Established: 1928.

KEY STATISTICS Number of Employees: 5,600.

HIRING HISTORY Number of professional employees hired in 1993: 452.

EXPERTISE/EDUCATION SOUGHT: Computer programming, accounting, credit/credit analysis, customer service and support, sales, management, health insurance

CONTACT: For individuals with previous experience: Ms Deborah Wilkes, Manager of Employment; Phone (615) 872-3000.

WINN DIXIE STORES, INC.

5050 EDGEWOOD COURT
JACKSONVILLE, FLORIDA 32254-3699

OVERVIEW: Operates chain of food stores.

EXPERTISE/EDUCATION SOUGHT: Retail, merchandising, accounting, business management, finance, marketing, sales, law, computer programming

CONTACT: Mr Adrian Barrow, Human Resources Coordinator; Phone (904) 783-5000.

WISCONSIN ENERGY CORPORATION

231 WEST MICHIGAN STREET
MILWAUKEE, WISCONSIN 53203-0001

OVERVIEW: Electric and gas utility. Established: 1985.

KEY STATISTICS Annual Sales: $2.0 billion. Number of Employees: 5,235.

EXPERTISE/EDUCATION SOUGHT: Accounting, computer programming, data processing, mechanical engineering, electrical engineering, industrial engineering, civil engineering

CONTACT: For individuals with previous experience: Ms Joyce Taylor, Resources Coordinator.

WISCONSIN PHYSICIANS SERVICE INSURANCE

1717 WEST BROADWAY
MADISON, WISCONSIN 53713-1834

OVERVIEW: Provides health insurance. Established: 1977.

KEY STATISTICS Annual Sales: $447.2 million. Number of Employees: 3,000.

EXPERTISE/EDUCATION SOUGHT: Accounting, finance, data processing, law, registered nursing, licensed practical nursing, auditing, managed health care, information services

CONTACT: For individuals with previous experience: Ms Kathy Bennett, Manager of Recruiting, PO Box 8190, Madison, WI, 53713; Phone (608) 221-4711, ext. 5074.

WLR FOODS, INC.

800 CO-OP DRIVE
TIMBERVILLE, VIRGINIA 22853

OVERVIEW: Processes and produces poultry products. Established: 1984.

KEY STATISTICS Annual Sales: $727.0 million. Number of Employees: 6,600.

EXPERTISE/EDUCATION SOUGHT: Business, finance, marketing, sales, accounting

CONTACT: Ms Jane Brookshire, Vice President of Human Resources, Hwy 33, Hinton, VA, 22831; Phone (703) 867-4121.

WMX TECHNOLOGIES, INC.

3003 BUTTERFIELD ROAD
OAK BROOK, ILLINOIS 60521-1102

OVERVIEW: Waste collection and disposal services. Established: 1971.

KEY STATISTICS Annual Sales: $9.0 billion. Number of Employees: 67,300.

EXPERTISE/EDUCATION SOUGHT: Computer programming, computer science, data processing, finance, accounting, sales

CONTACT: Mr Ray Turek, Manager of Human Resources; Phone (708) 218-1725.

WOODWARD AND LOTHROP, INC.

1025 F STREET NORTHWEST
WASHINGTON, D.C. 20013-1414

OVERVIEW: Operates chain of department stores. Established: 1880. Parent Company: Taubman Holdings, Inc.

KEY STATISTICS Number of Employees: 15,000.

EXPERTISE/EDUCATION SOUGHT: Accounting, marketing, finance, sales, business management

CONTACTS: For college students and recent graduates: Ms Joanne Ficco, Personnel Recruiter, 2800 Eisenhower Avenue, Alexandria, VA, 22314; Phone (703) 329-5471. For individuals with previous experience: Ms Heidi Heslop, Management Recruiter; Phone (202) 879-8000.

WOOLWORTH CORPORATION

233 BROADWAY, 24TH FLOOR
NEW YORK, NEW YORK 10279

OVERVIEW: Operates chain of retail stores. Established: 1879.

EXPERTISE/EDUCATION SOUGHT: Accounting, information systems, merchandising, administration, graphic arts

CONTACT: Mr Walter Sprague, Assistant Vice President of Human Resources; Phone (212) 553-2000.

WORLD BANK GROUP

1818 H STREET NORTHWEST
WASHINGTON, D.C. 20433

OVERVIEW: Provides financial assistance and international banking services to developing countries.

EXPERTISE/EDUCATION SOUGHT: Accounting, finance, marketing, law, auditing

CONTACT: For individuals with previous experience: Mr Peter Karp, Director of Human Resources; Phone (202) 473-2000.

WORLD SAVINGS AND LOAN ASSOCIATION

1901 HARRISON STREET
OAKLAND, CALIFORNIA 94612-3574

OVERVIEW: Savings and loan institution. Established: 1963. Parent Company: West Golden Financial Corporation.

KEY STATISTICS Assets: $2.0 billion. Number of Employees: 3,083.

EXPERTISE/EDUCATION SOUGHT: Banking, finance, accounting, credit/credit analysis

CONTACTS: For college students and recent graduates: Ms Susan Lennox, Director of Employee Relations; Phone (510) 446-3068; Fax (510) 446-3072. For individuals with previous experience: Ms Carol Singleton, Benefits Administrator; Phone (510) 446-3969.

WORTHINGTON CUSTOM PLASTICS

800 PENNSYLVANIA STREET
SALEM, OHIO 44460

OVERVIEW: Manufactures injection molded plastics for the automotive industry. Established: 1981.

EXPERTISE/EDUCATION SOUGHT: Administration

CONTACT: For individuals with previous experience: Mr Tom Fiala, Controller.

WORTHINGTON INDUSTRIES, INC.

1205 DEARBORN DRIVE
COLUMBUS, OHIO 43085-4769

OVERVIEW: Manufactures steel, metal cylinders, and plastic. Established: 1955.

KEY STATISTICS Number of Employees: 7,000.

EXPERTISE/EDUCATION SOUGHT: Sales, finance, mechanical engineering, electrical engineering, metallurgical engineering, accounting, management information systems

CONTACT: Mr Ike Kelley, Director of Personnel; Phone (614) 438-3210.

WRIGLEY JR. COMPANY

410 NORTH MICHIGAN AVENUE
CHICAGO, ILLINOIS 60611

OVERVIEW: Manufactures chewing gum. Established: 1891.

EXPERTISE/EDUCATION SOUGHT: Accounting, auditing, marketing, finance

CONTACT: Ms Mary Walls, Personnel Manager; Phone (312) 645-3862, ext. 9250.

WYETH-AYERST INTERNATIONAL, LTD.

555 EAST LANCASTER AVENUE
ST. DAVIDS, PENNSYLVANIA 19087-5221

OVERVIEW: Manufactures pharmaceuticals. Established: 1944. Parent Company: American Home Products Corporation.

KEY STATISTICS Number of Employees: 13,269.

EXPERTISE/EDUCATION SOUGHT: Accounting, marketing, sales, management information systems, chemistry, chemical engineering

CONTACT: For individuals with previous experience: Ms Susan Ford, Supervisor of Employment; Phone (610) 995-4697.

XEROX CORPORATION

DEPARTMENT PET, 800 PHILLIPS ROAD, BUILDING 205-99E
WEBSTER, NEW YORK 14580

OVERVIEW: Manufactures office equipment, software, and document management systems. Established: 1906.

KEY STATISTICS Annual Sales: $15.0 billion. Number of Employees: 92,800.

EXPERTISE/EDUCATION SOUGHT: Computer programming, environmental engineering, electronics/electronics engineering, software engineering/development, chemical engineering, information systems, electrical engineering, mechanical engineering, manufac

CONTACT: Ms Ellie Krieger, Employment/College Relations Manager; Phone (716) 422-6517; Fax (716) 422-2400.

XEROX FINANCIAL SERVICES, INC.

800 LONGRIDGE ROAD
STAMFORD, CONNECTICUT 06904

OVERVIEW: Provides financial and investment services.

EXPERTISE/EDUCATION SOUGHT: Software engineering/development, business, computer science, accounting, electrical engineering

CONTACT: For individuals with previous experience: College Relations - Human Resources, 800 Phillips Road Building 205 99E, Webster, NY, 14580; Phone (716) 423-5090.

XOMED

6743 SOUTHPOINT DRIVE NORTH
JACKSONVILLE, FLORIDA 32216-6218

OVERVIEW: Manufactures medical equipment for eyes, ears, nose, and throat. Established: 1979. Parent Company: Bristol-Myers Squibb Company.

KEY STATISTICS Annual Sales: $36.0 million. Number of Employees: 470.

EXPERTISE/EDUCATION SOUGHT: Electrical engineering, mechanical engineering, industrial engineering, accounting, data processing, marketing, sales, research and development, information services

CONTACT: For individuals with previous experience: Ms Marleen O'Connor, Director of Human Resources.

YORK INTERNATIONAL CORPORATION

631 SOUTH RICHLAND AVENUE
YORK, PENNSYLVANIA 17403-3445

OVERVIEW: Manufactures heating, refrigeration, and air conditioning equipment. Established: 1874.

KEY STATISTICS Annual Sales: $2.0 billion. Number of Employees: 13,800.

EXPERTISE/EDUCATION SOUGHT: Mechanical engineering, electronics/electronics engineering, industrial engineering, manufacturing engineering, computer programming

CONTACTS: For college students and recent graduates: Ms Jo Carol Fink, Director of College Recruiting; Phone (717) 771-6572. For individuals with previous experience: Mr John Tynan, Manager Corporate Staffing; Phone (717) 771-6580.

YOUNG AND RUBICAM, INC.

285 MADISON AVENUE
NEW YORK, NEW YORK 10017-6486

OVERVIEW: Provides advertising and public relations services. Established: 1923.

KEY STATISTICS Number of Employees: 10,000.

EXPERTISE/EDUCATION SOUGHT: Graphic arts, production, marketing, sales, finance, accounting, advertising, law

CONTACT: For individuals with previous experience: Ms Amy Blumenfeld, Manager of Corporate Human Resources; Phone (212) 210-3000.

ZELL/CHILMARK FUND, LP.

2 NORTH RIVERSIDE PLAZA, SUITE 1500
CHICAGO, ILLINOIS 60606-2605

OVERVIEW: Merchant bank.

KEY STATISTICS Annual Sales: $1.0 billion. Number of Employees: 24,000.

EXPERTISE/EDUCATION SOUGHT: Accounting, finance

CONTACT: For individuals with previous experience: Ms Kim Wilson, Human Resources Coordinator; Phone (312) 987-9711.

ZENITH ELECTRONICS CORPORATION
1000 MILWAUKEE AVENUE
GLENVIEW, ILLINOIS 60025-2493

OVERVIEW: Manufactures televisions, VCRs, radios, electronic components, and related products. Established: 1918.

KEY STATISTICS Number of Employees: 25,000.

EXPERTISE/EDUCATION SOUGHT: Purchasing, human resources, finance, research and development, information systems, materials management

CONTACT: For individuals with previous experience: Mr Ed Oakey, Director of Personnel; Phone (708) 391-7000.

ZIMMER, INC.
727 NORTH DETROIT STREET
WARSAW, INDIANA 46580-2746

OVERVIEW: Manufactures orthopedic products. Established: 1972. Parent Company: Bristol-Myers Squibb Company.

KEY STATISTICS Annual Sales: $340.0 million. Number of Employees: 4,450.

HIRING HISTORY Number of professional employees hired in 1993: 20.

EXPERTISE/EDUCATION SOUGHT: Design engineering, sales, computer programming, marketing, finance

CONTACT: For individuals with previous experience: Director of Staffing; Phone (219) 267-6131.

GOVERNMENT EMPLOYERS

BUREAU OF OCEANS AND INTERNATIONAL ENVIRONMENTAL AFFAIRS

2201 C STREET NORTHWEST
WASHINGTON, D.C. 20520

Overview: Monitors U.S. and international ocean and environmental issues.

Contact: For individuals with previous experience: Mr John McGruder, Executive Director; Phone (202) 647-3622.

CENTERS FOR DISEASE CONTROL

1600 CLIFTON ROAD NORTHEAST
ATLANTA, GEORGIA 30333

Overview: Monitors and controls physical and psychological disease. Established: 1946.

Key Statistics Number of Employees: 7,000.

Hiring History Number of professional employees hired in 1993: 75.

Expertise/Education Sought: Behavioral sciences, sociology, public health, statistics, biology, mathematics, pharmacology, epidemiology

Contacts: For college students and recent graduates: Mr Al Parnell, College Relations Coordinator; Phone (404) 488-1218. For individuals with previous experience: Ms Sylvia Botwick, Chief of Recruiting; Phone (404) 639-3311.

CENTRAL INTELLIGENCE AGENCY

1500 WEST BRANCH DRIVE
ARLINGTON, VIRGINIA 22202-8727

Overview: Foreign intelligence agency for United States government.

Expertise/Education Sought: Economics, electrical engineering, international relations, languages

Contact: For individuals with previous experience: Office of Personnel, PO Box 12727, Arlington, VA, 22209; Phone (703) 482-7411.

DEFENSE MAPPING AGENCY

4600 SANGAMORE ROAD
BETHESDA, MARYLAND 20816-5003

Overview: Major combat support agency of the Department of Defense. Established: 1972.

Key Statistics Number of Employees: 7,500.

Expertise/Education Sought: Cartography/photogrammetry, computer science, geography, mathematics

Contact: Mr Gerald Pittman, Chief, Defense Mapping Agency Central Recruitment Branch; Phone (800) 526-3379.

DEPARTMENT OF COMMERCE

14TH STREET AND CONSTITUTION AVENUE
WASHINGTON, D.C. 20230

Overview: U.S. government agency that promotes fair trade and economic growth. Established: 1903.

Key Statistics Annual Budget: $3.0 billion. Number of Employees: 35,000.

Expertise/Education Sought: Law, finance, data processing, accounting, economics, statistics

Contact: Ms H James Reese, Director of Staffing and Recruiting; Phone (202) 482-3453.

DEPARTMENT OF CONSUMER AND REGULATORY AFFAIRS

614 H STREET NORTHWEST
WASHINGTON, D.C. 20001

Overview: U.S. government agency that monitors, investigates, and evaluates consumer product issues.

Expertise/Education Sought: Engineering, maintenance, nursing, registered nursing, business

Contact: For individuals with previous experience: Ms Barbara Gibbs, Acting Chief Employee Servies Division; Phone (202) 727-7471.

DEPARTMENT OF ENERGY

1000 INDEPENDENCE AVENUE
WASHINGTON, D.C. 20585

Overview: U.S. agency that establishes and administers policies regarding energy and natural resources.

Expertise/Education Sought: Nuclear engineering, environmental engineering, chemical engineering, civil engineering, electrical engineering, mechanical engineering, metallurgical engineering, materials engineering

Contact: For individuals with previous experience: Ms Thomisina Matthews, Director of Strategic Initatives; Phone (202) 586-4494.

DEPARTMENT OF HEALTH AND HUMAN SERVICES

200 INDEPENDENCE AVENUE SOUTHWEST
WASHINGTON, D.C. 20201

Overview: U.S. government agency that establishes and administers policies regarding health care and social services.

Expertise/Education Sought: Social work, finance, business management, accounting

Contact: For individuals with previous experience: Ms Theresa Smith, Personnel Officer, 330 Independence Avenue Southwest, Room 1040 Cohen Building, Washington, DC, 20201; Phone (202) 619-0146.

DEPARTMENT OF HOUSING AND URBAN DEVELOPMENT

451 7TH STREET SOUTHWEST
WASHINGTON, D.C. 20410

Overview: U.S. agency that administers programs to help families become home owners or obtain housing.

Expertise/Education Sought: Planning, law, accounting, business administration, finance

Contact: For individuals with previous experience: Ms Olivia Jenson, Director of Personnel; Phone (202) 728-3455.

DEPARTMENT OF JUSTICE, U.S. ATTORNEY GENERAL

1200 PENNSYLVANIA AVENUE
WASHINGTON, D.C. 20530

Overview: U.S. government agency that supervises and directs the administration of justice through the courts of law. Established: 1870.

Key Statistics Number of Employees: 96,000.

Expertise/Education Sought: Criminal justice, law, treasury management, accounting, finance, computer science, control engineering

Contact: For individuals with previous experience: Mr Paul Kremsiek, Deputy Director of Personnel; Phone (202) 514-6788.

DEPARTMENT OF LABOR

200 CONSTITUTION AVENUE NORTHWEST
WASHINGTON, D.C. 20210

Overview: U.S. agency that administers and directs labor policies and programs. Established: 1913.

Key Statistics Number of Employees: 16,500.

EXPERTISE/EDUCATION SOUGHT: Computer science, electrical engineering, industrial hygiene, mathematics, statistics

CONTACT: For individuals with previous experience: For information on specific job vacancies:; Phone (800) 366-2753.

ORGANIZATION PROFILE

The U.S. Department of Labor (DOL) consists of over a dozen different agencies with varied activities that affect the lives of virtually everyone in America. Department of Labor agencies include the Bureau of Labor Statistics, Employment and Training Administration, Employment Standards Administration, Occupational Safety and Health Administration, Mine Safety and Health Administration, Office of the American Workplace, Office of the Inspector General, Office of the Solicitor, Pension and Welfare Benefits Administration, Bureau of International Labor Affairs, Veteran's Employment and Training Service, and Women's Bureau.

A career with the Department of Labor offers a chance for an ambitious person to grow professionally and contribute to the nation's growth as well. DOL offers high-quality training and development opportunities and benefits such as a wellness program, flexible work schedules, dependent care, annual vacation and sick leave, paid holidays, and excellent health and life insurance plans.

Career opportunities at the Department of Labor include professional, technical, and clerical positions. Opportunities exist in the Washington, D.C. area and in field and regional offices throughout the country.

DEPARTMENT OF STATE, BUREAU OF MEDICAL SERVICES
2201 C STREET NORTHWEST
WASHINGTON, D.C. 20520

OVERVIEW: Provides medical related services to the department of state.

HIRING HISTORY Number of professional employees hired in 1994: 3.

EXPERTISE/EDUCATION SOUGHT: Laboratory technology, nursing, physicians

CONTACT: For individuals with previous experience: Ms Rita Torchia, Personnel Officer; Phone (202) 647-3617.

DEPARTMENT OF THE AIR FORCE
PENTAGON
WASHINGTON, D.C. 20250

OVERVIEW: U.S. armed forces organization responsible for ensuring peace and security, focusing on air missions and defense from invasion by air. Established: 1947.

KEY STATISTICS Number of Employees: 46,100.

EXPERTISE/EDUCATION SOUGHT: Mechanical engineering, aviation, law, business administration, computer science

CONTACT: For individuals with previous experience: Colonel Robert Brady, Human Resources Development Director; Phone (703) 614-8488.

DEPARTMENT OF THE ARMY
PENTAGON
WASHINGTON, D.C. 20250

OVERVIEW: U.S. armed forces organization providing land based military protection for the United States.

EXPERTISE/EDUCATION SOUGHT: Accounting, auditing, law, operations research, computer science

CONTACT: For individuals with previous experience: Ms Barbara Hagle, Chief of the Personnel Operations Division, Personnel Services-Washington, 6800 Army/Pentagon, Washington, DC, 20310-6800; Phone (703) 695-3881.

DEPARTMENT OF THE INTERIOR
1849 C STREET NORTHWEST
WASHINGTON, D.C. 20240

OVERVIEW: U.S. agency that directs the use and conservation of public lands and natural resources. Established: 1849.

KEY STATISTICS Number of Employees: 50,000.

EXPERTISE/EDUCATION SOUGHT: Accounting, finance, law, data processing, economics, business management, environmental science, facilities management, land management, computer science

CONTACT: For individuals with previous experience: Ms Sharon Eller, Personnel Officer; Phone (202) 208-6702; 6464.

DEPARTMENT OF THE NAVY
PENTAGON
WASHINGTON, D.C. 20350-1000

OVERVIEW: U.S. armed forces organization providing protection from attack by sea. Established: 1775.

KEY STATISTICS Annual Budget: $70.0 billion. Number of Employees: 541,883.

EXPERTISE/EDUCATION SOUGHT: Technology, finance, accounting, law, auditing

CONTACT: For individuals with previous experience: Ms Dorothy Meletzke, Department Assistant Secretary for Civilian Personnel Policy; Phone (703) 695-2248.

DEPARTMENT OF THE NAVY, NAVAL FACILITIES ENGINEERING COMMAND
200 STOVALL STREET, MAIL CODE 1212
ALEXANDRIA, VIRGINIA 22332

OVERVIEW: Unit of the Department of the Navy responsible for design, construction, and maintenance of all naval shore facilities. Established: 1842.

HIRING HISTORY Number of professional employees hired in 1994: 70.

EXPERTISE/EDUCATION SOUGHT: Environmental engineering, civil engineering, chemical engineering, mechanical engineering, electrical engineering, industrial engineering, fire protection

CONTACT: For individuals with previous experience: Ms Joy A Bird, Director of Professional Development Center; Phone (703) 325-8523.

DEPARTMENT OF TRANSPORTATION, FEDERAL HIGHWAY ADMINISTRATION
400 7TH STREET SOUTHWEST, HP-31
WASHINGTON, D.C. 20590

OVERVIEW: Organization responsible for design, construction, and maintenance of highway systems. Established: 1967.

KEY STATISTICS Number of Employees: 3,600.

EXPERTISE/EDUCATION SOUGHT: Civil engineering, transportation, engineering, environmental engineering

CONTACT: For individuals with previous experience: Ms Pat Stroman, Personnel Staffing Specialist; Phone (202) 366-1168.

ENVIRONMENTAL PROTECTION AGENCY
401 M STREET SOUTHWEST
WASHINGTON, D.C. 20460

OVERVIEW: Provides environmental protection and improvement services.

EXPERTISE/EDUCATION SOUGHT: Environmental engineering, computer analysis, accounting, budgeting, data processing

CONTACT: For individuals with previous experience: Ms Dinah Griggsby, Recruiting Manager; Phone (202) 260-4193.

FEDERAL AVIATION ADMINISTRATION
800 INDEPENDENCE AVENUE SOUTHWEST
WASHINGTON, D.C. 20591

OVERVIEW: Ensures safe and efficient national airspace. Established: 1958.

KEY STATISTICS Annual Budget: $9.0 billion. Number of Employees: 52,736.

EXPERTISE/EDUCATION SOUGHT: Aviation, electrical engineering, security, accounting, finance, safety, business management, operations research, computer science

CONTACT: For individuals with previous experience: Ms Alfreda Brooks, Recruitment Leader; Phone (202) 267-3456.

FEDERAL COMMUNICATIONS COMMISSION

1919 M STREET NORTHWEST
WASHINGTON, D.C. 20554

OVERVIEW: Regulates radio, television, and mass media businesses.

EXPERTISE/EDUCATION SOUGHT: Law, electrical engineering, business administration, business management, data processing

CONTACT: For individuals with previous experience: Mr Michael D'Andrea, Personnel Management Specialist; Phone (202) 418-0126.

FEDERAL EMERGENCY MANAGEMENT AGENCY

500 C STREET SOUTHWEST, FEDERAL CENTER PLAZA
WASHINGTON, D.C. 20472

OVERVIEW: U.S. agency that provides emergency and disaster relief services. Established: 1979.

KEY STATISTICS Number of Employees: 10,000.

EXPERTISE/EDUCATION SOUGHT: Accounting, business administration, computer science, criminal justice, civil engineering, electrical engineering, finance, law

CONTACT: For individuals with previous experience: Mr Barry Socks, Chief of Headquarters Personnel - Operations Division, Room 816.

FEDERAL MARITIME COMMISSION

800 NORTH CAPITOL STREET NORTHWEST
WASHINGTON, D.C. 20573

OVERVIEW: U.S. agency that administers policies and activities regarding maritime transportation. Established: 1961.

KEY STATISTICS Number of Employees: 208.

HIRING HISTORY Number of professional employees hired in 1993: 5.

EXPERTISE/EDUCATION SOUGHT: Surveying, law, transportation, international finance, economics, business administration

CONTACT: For individuals with previous experience: Mr William J Herron, Director of Personnel; Phone (202) 523-5773.

FEDERAL TRADE COMMISSION

6TH STREET AND PENNSYLVANIA AVENUE
NORTHWEST
WASHINGTON, D.C. 20580

OVERVIEW: U.S. agency that enforces fair trade practices.

KEY STATISTICS Number of Employees: 950.

HIRING HISTORY Number of professional employees hired in 1994: 20. 1993: 15.

EXPERTISE/EDUCATION SOUGHT: Marketing, advertising, law, business administration, credit/credit analysis

CONTACT: For individuals with previous experience: Mr Elliot Davis, Director of Personnel; Phone (202) 326-2022.

FOOD AND DRUG ADMINISTRATION

5600 FISHERS LANE
ROCKVILLE, MARYLAND 22085

OVERVIEW: Ensures the safety and effectiveness of medical devices and drugs. Established: 1906.

KEY STATISTICS Annual Budget: $827.0 million. Number of Employees: 9,000.

EXPERTISE/EDUCATION SOUGHT: Health care, chemistry, food chemistry, pharmacology, microbiology

CONTACT: For individuals with previous experience: Ms Delores Beebee, Director of Division Recruiting and Staffing; Phone (301) 443-4116.

GENERAL ACCOUNTING OFFICE

441 G STREET NORTHWEST
WASHINGTON, D.C. 20548

OVERVIEW: Provides financial investigation services.

EXPERTISE/EDUCATION SOUGHT: Economics, accounting, law, finance, auditing

CONTACT: For individuals with previous experience: Ms Francis Garcia, Director of Recruiting; Phone (202) 512-4900.

GENERAL SERVICES ADMINISTRATION

18TH AND F STREETS NORTHWEST
WASHINGTON, D.C. 20405

OVERVIEW: Monitors and evaluates government procurement policies and practices. Established: 1949.

KEY STATISTICS Number of Employees: 18,500.

EXPERTISE/EDUCATION SOUGHT: Finance, accounting, construction engineering, telecommunications, computer science, distribution, purchasing

CONTACT: For individuals with previous experience: Ms Lil Stewart, Director Personnel Operations; Phone (202) 501-0040.

GOVERNMENT PRINTING OFFICE

732 NORTH CAPITOL STREET NORTHWEST
WASHINGTON, D.C. 20401

OVERVIEW: Prints and distributes government documents and publications.

HIRING HISTORY Number of professional employees hired in 1994: 5.

EXPERTISE/EDUCATION SOUGHT: Purchasing, computer science, information systems, printing, publishing, accounting, auditing

CONTACT: For individuals with previous experience: Mr James Curran, Chief of Employment Branch; Phone (202) 512-1124.

INTERNAL REVENUE SERVICE, DEPARTMENT OF TREASURY

1111 CONSTITUTION AVENUE, NORTHWEST
WASHINGTON, D.C. 20224

OVERVIEW: Largest agency of the U.S. Treasury Department; responsible for administration of tax laws. Established: 1791.

KEY STATISTICS Number of Employees: 110,000.

HIRING HISTORY Number of professional employees hired in 1993: 900.

EXPERTISE/EDUCATION SOUGHT: Accounting, computer science, public administration, liberal arts, business

CONTACT: For college students and recent graduates: Ms Diane Moxley, Personnel Management Specialist; Phone (202) 874-6258; Fax (202) 874-6452.

For more information, see full organization profile, pg. 210.

INTERSTATE COMMERCE COMMISSION

12TH STREET AND CONSTITUTION AVENUE
NORTHWEST
WASHINGTON, D.C. 20423

OVERVIEW: Monitors and regulates interstate trade and business policies and practices. Established: 1887.

KEY STATISTICS Number of Employees: 600.

EXPERTISE/EDUCATION SOUGHT: Criminal justice, transportation, law

CONTACT: For individuals with previous experience: Ms Mary Sylvester, Chief of Personnel Management; Phone (202) 927-7288.

MARINE CORPS OFFICER PROGRAMS
#2 NAVY ANNEX BUILDING
WASHINGTON, D.C. 20380

Overview: Administers officer commissioning programs. Established: 1775.

Key Statistics Number of Employees: 200,000.

Expertise/Education Sought: Aviation, computer science, business administration, data processing, law

Contact: For individuals with previous experience: Lt Colonel Charles Boyd, Head Officer/Procurement Branch, Commanding General/Headquarters, #2 Navy Annex Building #2, Washington, DC, 20380.

NASA LEWIS RESEARCH CENTER
21000 BROOK PARK ROAD
CLEVELAND, OHIO 44135

Overview: Conducts research and development in propulsion, space power, and satellites.

Expertise/Education Sought: Finance, management, business, accounting

Contact: For individuals with previous experience: External Recruiting Office; Phone (216) 433-8017.

NATIONAL INSTITUTE OF STANDARDS AND TECHNOLOGY
ADMINISTRATION BUILDING
GAITHERSBURG, MARYLAND 20899

Overview: Promotes public health, public safety, and environmental issues.

Hiring History Number of professional employees hired in 1994: 60.

Expertise/Education Sought: Physics, mechanical engineering, civil engineering, mathematics, computer science

Contact: For individuals with previous experience: Ms Deborah Martin, Staffing Specialist, Personnel and Civil Rights Office, Administration Building 101-A123, Gaithersburg, MD, 20899; Phone (301) 975-2000.

NATIONAL INSTITUTES OF HEALTH
9000 ROCKVILLE PIKE
BETHESDA, MARYLAND 20892

Overview: Conducts studies for the purpose of preventing, detecting, diagnosing, and treating diseases and disabilities.

Expertise/Education Sought: Biology, behavioral research, biotechnology, physics, chemistry

Contact: For individuals with previous experience: Mr Herb Casey, Director Division of Career Resources, Room B-3-C15, Building 31; Phone (301) 496-2403.

NATIONAL PARK SERVICE
1849 C STREET NORTHWEST
WASHINGTON, D.C. 20240

Overview: U.S. agency that administers and maintains national parks, historic areas, and national recreation facilities. Established: 1916.

Key Statistics Number of Employees: 18,474.

Expertise/Education Sought: Automation, accounting, finance, editing, public relations, architecture, history

Contact: Mr Joseph Rogers, Chief of Personnel; Phone (202) 208-6843, ext. 4648.

NATIONAL SCIENCE FOUNDATION
4201 WILSON BOULEVARD
ARLINGTON, VIRGINIA 22230

Overview: Promotes science, engineering, and technical programs.

Hiring History Number of professional employees hired in 1994: 75.

Expertise/Education Sought: Computer science, contracts administration/management, geology, behavioral sciences, education, biology, engineering, economics, physical science, mathematics

Contact: For individuals with previous experience: Ms Janet Silva, Chief of Staffing and Classification Branch; Phone (703) 306-1185; Fax (703) 306-1182.

NATIONAL SECURITY AGENCY
9800 SAVAGE ROAD, M3221
FORT GEORGE G. MEADE, MARYLAND 20755-6000

Overview: Provides national security in communications. Established: 1952.

Expertise/Education Sought: Computer engineering, electrical engineering, computer science, mathematics

Contacts: For college students and recent graduates: Ms Lavertta Tilghman, College Relations Manager, Attention: M322. For individuals with previous experience: Ms Tonya Ross, Manager of Cooperative and Minority Recruiting.

NAVAL AIR WARFARE CENTER AIRCRAFT DIVISION
BUILDING 463
PATUXENT RIVER, MARYLAND 20670-5304

Overview: Conducts aviation research and development.

Hiring History Number of professional employees hired in 1994: 150.

Expertise/Education Sought: Electronics/electronics engineering, mechanical engineering, computer science, aerospace engineering, materials engineering, computer engineering, industrial engineering

Contact: For individuals with previous experience: Ms Pamela Spearow, Professional Recruitment Coordinator, Human Resources Office MS 30.

OCCUPATIONAL SAFETY AND HEALTH ADMINISTRATION
200 CONSTITUTION AVENUE NORTHWEST, ROOM NOAH 3308
WASHINGTON, D.C. 20210

Overview: U.S. agency that ensures the provision and maintenance of safe work places.

Key Statistics Number of Employees: 2,300.

Hiring History Number of professional employees hired in 1993: 10.

Expertise/Education Sought: Industrial hygiene, safety engineering, health and safety

Contact: For individuals with previous experience: Ms Floria Jones, Supervisor of Staffing; Phone (202) 219-8013.

OFFICE OF MANAGEMENT AND BUDGET
725 17TH STREET NORTHWEST
WASHINGTON, D.C. 20503

Overview: Branch of the Executive Office in charge of preparing the national budget.

Expertise/Education Sought: Public policy and planning, economics, law, business administration

Contact: For individuals with previous experience: Mr Steve Weigler, Human Resources Manager; Phone (202) 395-7250.

PEACE CORPS

1990 K STREET NORTHWEST
WASHINGTON, D.C. 20526

OVERVIEW: Provides volunteer services to foreign nations in need.
Established: 1961.

KEY STATISTICS Number of Employees: 1,200.

HIRING HISTORY Number of professional employees hired in 1993: 300.

EXPERTISE/EDUCATION SOUGHT: Medical technology, occupational therapy,
health science, education, training and development, computer
programming, business development, administration, agriculture

CONTACT: For individuals with previous experience: Ms Sharon Barbe
Fletcher, Director of Personnel; Phone (202) 606-8038.

SECURITIES AND EXCHANGE COMMISSION

450 5TH STREET NORTHWEST
WASHINGTON, D.C. 20549

OVERVIEW: U.S. agency that supervises the registration of securities and
regulates the securities industries. Established: 1934.

KEY STATISTICS Number of Employees: 2,700.

HIRING HISTORY Number of professional employees hired in 1994: 300.
1993: 250.

EXPERTISE/EDUCATION SOUGHT: Law, accounting, investment, computer
science

CONTACT: For individuals with previous experience: Mr Fernando
Alegria, Associate Director, Office Administration and Personnel
Management; Phone (202) 942-4000.

SMALL BUSINESS ADMINISTRATION

409 THIRD STREET SOUTHWEST
WASHINGTON, D.C. 20416

OVERVIEW: Provides assistance and loans to small businesses.
Established: 1953.

KEY STATISTICS Number of Employees: 3,000.

HIRING HISTORY Number of professional employees hired in 1993: 20.

EXPERTISE/EDUCATION SOUGHT: Business development, criminal justice, law,
accounting, credit/credit analysis, computer analysis, project
management, investment

CONTACT: For individuals with previous experience: Mr Jose Mendez,
Personnel Staffing Specialist/Recruiter; Phone (202) 205-6790.

U.S. ARMY AUDIT AGENCY, DEPARTMENT OF THE ARMY

3101 PARK CENTER DRIVE
ALEXANDRIA, VIRGINIA 22302-1596

OVERVIEW: Internal audit organization and principal management
consultant to the U.S. Army. Established: 1946.

KEY STATISTICS Number of Employees: 735.

EXPERTISE/EDUCATION SOUGHT: Auditing, accounting

CONTACT: Human Resources Department.

For more information, see full organization profile, pg. 218.

**US Army Corps
of Engineers**

U.S. ARMY CORPS OF ENGINEERS

20 MASSACHUSETTS AVENUE NORTHWEST
WASHINGTON, D.C. 20314

OVERVIEW: Largest public engineering organization. Established: 1775.

KEY STATISTICS Number of Employees: 38,000.

EXPERTISE/EDUCATION SOUGHT: Civil engineering, environmental
engineering, research and development, natural resources,
information systems

CONTACT: Human Resources Department.

For more information, see full organization profile, pg. 220.

U.S. DEPARTMENT OF AGRICULTURE

14TH STREET AND INDEPENDENCE AVENUE
SOUTHWEST
WASHINGTON, D.C. 20250

OVERVIEW: U.S. agency responsible for safety standards for agricultural
products. Established: 1862.

KEY STATISTICS Number of Employees: 110,000.

EXPERTISE/EDUCATION SOUGHT: Marketing, agriculture, biology, sales,
chemistry, management, food science, quality control, accounting

CONTACT: For individuals with previous experience: Ms Marge Brining,
Personnel Specialist; Phone (202) 720-6905.

U.S. GEOLOGICAL SURVEY

12201 SUNRISE VALLEY DRIVE
RESTON, VIRGINIA 22092

OVERVIEW: Earth and science agency. Established: 1879.

KEY STATISTICS Annual Budget: $598.0 million. Number of Employees:
10,000.

HIRING HISTORY Number of professional employees hired in 1994: 35.

EXPERTISE/EDUCATION SOUGHT: Hydrogeology, hydrology, chemistry

CONTACT: Mr Richard C Williams, Chief of Recruiting and Placement;
Phone (703) 648-4000.

U.S. POSTAL SERVICE

475 L'ENFANT PLAZA SOUTHWEST
WASHINGTON, D.C. 20260

OVERVIEW: Provides mail delivery service. Established: 1775.

KEY STATISTICS Number of Employees: 725,290.

EXPERTISE/EDUCATION SOUGHT: Accounting, finance, law, electrical
engineering, mechanical engineering, computer science,
economics, psychology, communications

CONTACT: Mr Stephen A Leavey, Manager of Personnel; Phone (202)
268-2000.

USDA FOREST SERVICE

201 14TH STREET SOUTHWEST
WASHINGTON, D.C. 20250

OVERVIEW: Conserves and manages the USDA national forests and
grasslands. Established: 1905.

KEY STATISTICS Number of Employees: 34,000.

EXPERTISE/EDUCATION SOUGHT: Research, administration, engineering,
physical science, biological sciences

CONTACT: For individuals with previous experience: Mr William Riley,
Director of Personnel, PO Box 96090, Washington, DC,
20090-6090; Phone (202) 205-1760; Fax (703) 235-2529.

EMPLOYER DESCRIPTIONS

In-depth information on the business activities and employment opportunities at some profiled companies and government organizations

AT&T

Connect with the Future

Description of Organization: A worldwide telecommunications corporation providing products, systems, and services for movement and management of information

Number of Employees: 301,000

Academic Fields of Recruitment Interest: Accounting, business, economics, finance, marketing, psychology; M.B.A. fields with technical undergraduate degrees; chemical, computer, electrical, industrial, mechanical, nuclear, and systems engineering; computer science, information systems, math, operations research, statistics; earth sciences, materials science, chemistry, physics

Major Entry-Level Opportunities for New Graduates: Sales and marketing, finance and accounting, business applications/systems programming and management information systems, manufacturing/operations engineering, research and development

BACKGROUND AND OPERATIONS

AT&T is dedicated to being the world's best at bringing people togethergiving them easy access to each other and to the information and services they want and needanytime, anywhere.

AT&T has come a long way from the simple telephone and the voice-only communications network of the past. Today intelligent terminals connect with intelligent networks that are wired and wireless, local and global. Together, they enable people and machines to communicate and share information in an increasingly rich variety of forms: voice, handwriting, video, data, print, or image.

AT&T is a global company that provides communications services and products, as well as network equipment and computer systems, to business, consumers, telecommunications providers, and government agencies. Its worldwide intelligent network carries more than 140 million messages every business day. AT&T Bell Laboratories, the world's most renowned industrial research and development institution, engages in both basic research and product/service development. The company also offers a general-purpose credit card and financial and leasing services. AT&T people work in more than 120 countries.

AT&T is organized into four groups: Communications Services, Network Systems, GIS, and Multimedia Products and Services. Each of these groups is further divided into business units that are designed to meet the needs of unique customer segments. Two of AT&T's business units recently received the Malcolm Baldrige National Quality Award, the first time a company ever received two awards in the same year. Working for one of AT&T's business units means challenge, responsibility, reward, and a variety of career options.

FUTURE DIRECTIONS

AT&T possesses a crucial strength: its global networking capabilities. The company's strategy is to continuously enhance both its own global network and those of other service providers in order to make communications more useful to customers. AT&T aims to build on its strength through innovative, easy-to-use products and services and to continue to provide AT&T quality in the face of intense global and local competition, responding quickly to the needs of vastly different mar-

kets. Global telecommunications markets are expected to double by the year 2000, and AT&T intends to be at the forefront.

EMPLOYMENT OPPORTUNITIES

ENTRY LEVEL

To help prospective employees find the areas that best fit their interests, education, and experience, AT&T's job opportunities are organized in five broad categories, detailed below. AT&T's on-campus interviews are posted under these five recruitment categories. The following describes some typical job assignments for each of the categories.

Sales and Marketing. Successful AT&T salespeople and marketing staffs give customers that competitive edge by understanding their customers' needs and finding ways to fit AT&T's unique mix of products and services to those needs.

AT&T's people face the challenges offered by the convergence of the telecommunications and computer industries. Challenging opportunities exist for individuals interested in winning in diverse, competitive markets. Sales and technical sales support are both excellent entry-level opportunities. The many possibilities range from strengthening product lines where the company is a market leader to becoming a stronger player in markets it has just begun to enter.

Accounting and Finance. To make the right business decisions, AT&T depends on highly skilled and well-trained financial professionals to work as a team in every area of the business. From the day-to-day operations of corporate accounting to the intricacies of internal auditing to overseeing the bottom line, AT&T needs financial managers who can easily adapt to today's fast-changing business world.

Information Systems. AT&T has been a leader in developing information technologies. The Business Applications/Systems Programming and Management Information Systems teams provide AT&T with a "major contender" status, which has led to innovations that have had an impact on the growth of data and information processing. Using leading-edge software and computer systems, programmers and systems analysts work with all parts of the business on a variety of tasks.

Manufacturing/Operations Engineering. AT&T produces high-quality, low-cost products that meet customer needs on time.

The company designs, manufactures, markets, distributes, and services everything needed to build and operate the world's most advanced telecommunications systems.

The company offers a broad range of exciting opportunities in the following fields of manufacturing and operations engineering: design, development, factory/warehouse, field/applications, industrial/manufacturing systems, management, process, product, quality manufacturing control, systems equipment, environmental, and testing engineering.

Research and Development. AT&T has been at the forefront of the telecommunications industry for more than 100 years, drawing on research and development talent of international reputation. Today, scientists and engineers are involved in R&D work at AT&T Bell Laboratories and at the AT&T Network Software Center. The R&D mission is to advance fundamental research in the physical, material, communication, information, and manufacturing sciences in order to provide technology for the marketplace.

Members of AT&T's R&D community work in artificial intelligence; computer hardware and software development; data acquisition through telemetry; information systems planning, design, and development; manufacturing systems; material process control; microelectronics; military systems; photonics; robotics; surface technology; switching and transmission; systems and component engineering; and systems testing and evaluation.

TRAINING

AT&T pioneered and still administers one of the most comprehensive continuing education programs anywhere. The com-
pany provides a wide selection of personalized training programs to help employees keep abreast of fast-changing technological business and marketing developments.

To help employees do their best work, the corporation also offers reimbursement of educational expenses or pays the cost of other academic programs undertaken by eligible employees. Expenses covered include full tuition, laboratory fees, and mandatory recurring fees for formal study at accredited universities, colleges, technical institutes, vocational schools, and other approved institutions.

THE ORGANIZATION AS EMPLOYER

Salaries are among the best in the industry, commensurate with the high qualifications of those employed. Starting salaries are based on academic training and experience. Annual increases are given on the basis of performance.

Supervisors at AT&T work with employees to map out possible career paths. Employees are able to take responsibility for investigating various career options that match with work and geographic preferences worldwide.

AT&T employees receive a comprehensive benefits package that includes paid holidays and annual vacations; dental, vision, and medical expense plans; a tax-deferred savings plan for salaried employees; group life insurance; and accident and sickness disability benefits. AT&T offers progressive benefits plans that address the issues of caring for children, the elderly, and dual-career families.

Flexible working hours help AT&T employees to incorporate personal needs and educational pursuits into their careers. AT&T provides state-of-the-art equipment and services to assist employees in their work. The company's library network makes reference easier and faster. Company-supported clubs and activities help employees to enjoy hobbies and pursue interests.

SUMMER, CO-OP, AND INTERNSHIP PROGRAMS

AT&T accepts résumés for summer positions beginning in November for the following summer. Applicants are asked to forward their résumé and a statement of location and/or work preferences.

Students should check with their campus co-op or placement office for the most recent information on the availability of co-ops or internships with AT&T.

APPLICATION AND INFORMATION

Students interested in AT&T should arrange an interview through their placement office or send a résumé to:

College Recruiting Manager
100 Southgate Parkway, Room 3A01
Morristown, New Jersey 07960

EDS

Description of Organization: Global leader in applying information services

Number of Employees: More than 75,000 worldwide

Headquarters Location: Plano, Texas

Academic Fields of Recruitment Interest: Accounting, business, computer science, engineering, finance, liberal arts, mathematics, information systems

Major Entry-Level Opportunities for New Graduates: Accounting, automotive technology, information systems, operations, programming, software design, systems analysis, systems design, telecommunications

BACKGROUND AND OPERATIONS

EDS is the world's leading supplier of information services. EDS helps customers from the smallest credit union to the world's largest corporation use the power of information and technology to become leaders in an ever-changing marketplace. Founded in 1962, EDS has grown to a company of more than 75,000 employees who support over 8,000 customer contracts with offices in North America, South America, Europe, Asia, and Australia. Revenues for EDS exceeded $10 billion in 1994. In 1984, EDS became an independent subsidiary of General Motors (GM).

EDS contributes in many ways to the success of its customers in the manufacturing, insurance, finance, retail, transportation, health care, energy, and communications industries, as well as in governments at all levels. EDS provides a broad range of services such as management consulting, systems development, systems integration, process management, and systems management.

FOCUS ON DEVELOPMENT

EDS is committed to continuous learning by offering various career planning and development activities for all employees. EDS has the following job families for career growth:

- Engineering
- Consulting
- Sales
- Marketing
- Operations

EDS Centre, Corporate Headquarters, Plano, Texas. For more than thirty years, EDS has helped customers improve their business performance through the application of information technology.

The European IMC, located in Stockley Park, England, controls and monitors the data and voice communications across Europe. It also includes an Information Processing Center that provides many of the company's major United Kingdom customers with information processing services.

- Customer Business Services
- Communications
- Corporate Operations

At EDS, employees' career directions are based on many factors, including performing to reach individual, team, and company goals. An individual's career plan is developed by the employee and manager, which includes tools and activities to help accomplish development goals.

EDS offers continuous development opportunities through professional and technical courses ranging from leadership and sales to finance and methodologies. EDS tailors its educational programs to help employees serve their customers as effectively as possible. Individuals come to EDS with many valuable skills, and the company supplements those skills with ongoing development and real-life experiences.

EDS employees' careers may take a variety of paths rather than follow narrow, rigid career tracks. Because differences are seen as strengths and are viewed as opportunities for innovation, each individual has the opportunity to grow and strengthen EDS's overall capabilities. With a variety of opportunities, EDS promotes from within and offers competitive salaries, paying for performance instead of seniority.

EMPLOYEE BENEFITS

In addition to the professional advantages of working at EDS, the company also offers employees a competitive benefits package. EDS provides a medical plan, dental coverage, life insurance, retirement and stock-purchase plans, an adoption assistance program, and a deferred compensation plan. Because of the GM relationship, EDS has a vehicle purchase program that allows employees to buy new GM automobiles at substantial discounts. Also, employees at major EDS locations enjoy convenient banking services through the EDS Employees Federal Credit Union.

APPLICATION AND INFORMATION

EDS recruits nationwide for entry-level and experienced professionals with business aptitude, technical aptitude, leadership potential, strong academic records, extracurricular achievement, and good communication skills. Applicants are encouraged to send a résumé to one of the following EDS Campus Relations offices:

EDS Campus Relations
5400 Legacy Drive
H4-GB-35, Dept. 3280
Plano, Texas 75024

EDS Campus Relations
700 Tower Drive, 5th Floor
P.O. Box 7019, Dept. 3280
Troy, Michigan 48098

The Plano Information Management Center (IMC) control room. The IMC serves as the command center of the company's global telecommunications network, EDS*NET. Network operators manage voice, data, and video communications.

Traditionally, EDS has focused its development efforts on formal classroom training, but today the company also offers computer-based training, interactive distance learning, and other multimedia tools.

EDS Campus Relations
13600 EDS Drive
Dept. 3280
Herndon, Virginia 22071

EDS Campus Relations
200 Galleria Parkway, NW
Suite 910, Dept. 3280
Atlanta, Georgia 30339

EDS Campus Relations
180 Blue Ravine Road
Suite 1A, Dept. 3280
Folsom, California 95630

EDS is a registered mark of Electronic Data Systems Corporation.

EDS is an equal opportunity employer, M/F/V/D.

Internal Revenue Service

Description of Organization: The largest agency of the U.S. Treasury Department, responsible for administering the nation's tax laws in a fair and equitable manner
Number of Employees: 110,000
Headquarters Location: Washington, D.C.
Academic Fields of Recruitment Interest: Accounting, liberal arts, computer science, public administration, business
Major Entry-Level Opportunities for New Graduates: Positions as Revenue Agent, Revenue Officer, Special Agent, Tax Auditor, Computer Specialist

BACKGROUND AND OPERATIONS

The Internal Revenue Service is the largest bureau within the Department of the Treasury. Its mission is to ensure fair and consistent administration of federal tax laws and and to make the unique American system of voluntary tax compliance work. The IRS is responsible for collecting the majority of the revenues that maintain vital federal programs ranging from national defense to social and domestic improvement.

Most professional employees are located in the district offices where they audit all types of federal returns, review tax cases and make determinations as to proper tax liability, provide assistance to taxpayers, collect delinquent taxes, and investigate possible criminal violations of the tax laws.

The IRS is undergoing significant organizational and technological changes. This means that the best people from all segments of society are needed to make change happen and that it is an exciting time to join this organization. People who are looking to work in an organization where they can make a difference are encouraged to apply.

EMPLOYMENT OPPORTUNITIES

ENTRY LEVEL

The Internal Revenue Service hires a substantial number of college graduates each year to work as Revenue Agents, Revenue Officers, Special Agents, Tax Auditors, and Computer Specialists. Employment possibilities exist in virtually all IRS offices across the country.

Revenue Agents. Revenue Agents plan and conduct on-site examinations of individuals, partnerships, and corporations to determine federal tax liability. Some agents also ensure the compliance of tax-exempt organizations with federal tax law. The work involves regular contact with taxpayers and their representatives, certified public accountants, and tax attorneys.

Revenue Agents must be able to meet the demands of a constantly changing and expanding field of knowledge. Throughout their careers, agents are expected to participate in IRS education and training opportunities as well as self-development activities. In most states, Revenue Agent experience counts toward CPA certification. A degree in accounting that includes at least 30 semester hours in accounting will help an applicant to meet the minimum requirements for the Revenue Agent position.

Revenue Officers. These officers protect the interests of the federal government and ensure compliance with the tax laws through the collection of delinquent tax accounts and delinquent tax returns. Spending a significant amount of their time away from the office in direct contact with taxpayers in all types of occupations, Revenue Officers do their work on a

Most of the Revenue Agent's work is performed outside the office, usually at the taxpayer's place of business.

case-by-case basis. This may involve analyzing financial statements or records, testifying in court, preparing tax returns, or contacting third parties for information.

During the course of a day, Revenue Officers may be involved in setting up a payment plan for the settlement of a company's tax liabilities or tracing the whereabouts of a delinquent taxpayer. The nature of the job requires Revenue Officers to work with a high degree of independence and to exercise mature judgment in making decisions that are in the best interests of the government, yet fair to the taxpayer. This position is not limited to any specific educational major.

Special Agents. Special Agents investigate charges of criminal and civil violations of Internal Revenue laws, generally involving tax fraud. Their investigations determine whether there is sufficient evidence to recommend prosecution for willful attempts to violate federal tax laws or to recommend the imposition of civil fraud penalties.

Special Agents deal with people from all walks of life—owners, officers and executives of large and small businesses, and professionals in all callings, as well as people involved in illegal activities. They also conduct surveillances, serve as witnesses in civil and criminal trials, serve on special task forces, and occasionally participate in making arrests. A certain amount of accounting knowledge is required for this job.

Tax Auditors. Tax Auditors make determinations of tax liability based on information provided by individual wage earners, businesspeople, professionals, and other taxpayers. Tax Auditors work closely with the taxpayers and must be able to apply tax law to individual circumstances and explain why changes in tax liability are being made. Most of the work is performed in an IRS office environment. Any degree qualifies an individual for this position.

Computer Specialists. The IRS has some of the most complex computer needs in the world, and the agency hires a large number of specialists each year. Positions for programmers and analysts are available at the National Office and in the 10 processing service centers around the country. Such jobs often involve the development and testing of complex computer programs for the processing of various types of tax returns, computer system analysis, and computer equipment analysis. In addition, the Service is committed to a growing office automation initiative, and key positions are available in the district and regional offices.

TRAINING

The IRS has one of the largest internal training organizations in the federal government. Each occupation has a custom-designed training program developed by subject-matter experts who have proven themselves to be outstanding performers in their technical field.

Much of the training is now individualized and delivered through the computer-based Automated Training System, which trainees find faster and more interesting than traditional classroom instruction alone. Programs are a mix of classroom and on-the-job instruction, allowing trainees to gain practical hands-on experience working with the techniques and information they have studied.

An extensive Continuing Professional Education program provides additional training throughout an employee's career. Employees keep their skills sharp and up-to-date and equip themselves for more significant responsibilities.

When possible, the Service provides financial assistance to employees for job-related courses offered by colleges and universities or by the U.S. Office of Personnel Management.

The IRS has one of the finest executive and managerial development programs in the federal government. Management training begins at the first supervisory levels, and more advanced training is provided in phases as managers progress

An extensive Continuing Professional Education program provides additional training throughout an employee's career.

to positions of greater responsibility. Those selected for the executive cadres generally are highly skilled professionals who have reached the full working level and shown potential for further advancement.

The Service promotes from within. In fact, most of its senior managers began their careers as entry-level employees in one of the occupations described above.

THE ORGANIZATION AS EMPLOYER

The IRS's philosophy has been to attract the best people and train them well, and the results can be seen in a work force that takes pride in its reputation for high integrity.

Salaries and benefits are comparable to those of other federal agencies. Higher pay rates have been established for some occupations and certain locations.

New employees are covered by the Social Security-based Federal Employees' Retirement System, which features the best elements of private-sector retirement plans. One feature is the Thrift Savings Plan, which gives employees the option of saving up to 10 percent of their basic pay, with matching employer contributions of up to 5 percent. Employees can choose how these tax-deferred savings are invested, and the savings and Social Security credits are completely portable.

There are 10 paid holidays a year, and paid vacations are based on length of government service, including any military time. For the first 3 years of government service, employees earn 13 days of vacation each year; for 4 to 15 years of service, they earn 20 days of vacation each year; and after 15 years, employees are entitled to 26 days of vacation each year. Employees also earn 13 days of sick leave each year, which covers absences for illness, injury, and hospitalization and can be accumulated without limitation.

Employees and their families have the option to enroll in one of many health insurance plans with part of the cost being paid by the government. In addition, federal employees are now covered by Medicare.

CO-OP PROGRAM

The IRS has been an active participant in the Cooperative Education Program since 1966. This program enables students to earn practical work experience and income while continuing with their college studies. Students are introduced to careers in the Service through formal training and by working closely with experienced professionals, and they gain valuable knowledge to complement college courses.

A work force of about 1,000 co-ops is maintained, most of them working toward full-time positions in the major occupations described above.

APPLICATION AND INFORMATION

Most recruitment takes place in the district offices, which have established continuing relationships with schools in their jurisdictions. Interested candidates may apply for a position only during the time periods when a vacancy announcement has been issued. For information about vacancies, applicants should contact the closest IRS personnel office or the OPM Career America Connection at 912-757-3000. For the location of the nearest IRS personnel office, applicants may check with a college placement office or the local telephone directory.

Parke-Davis
Division of Warner-Lambert Company

Description of Organization: Discovers, develops, manufactures, and markets pharmaceuticals and vaccines on a worldwide basis

Headquarters Location: Morris Plains, New Jersey

Academic Fields of Recruitment Interest: All majors (preference given to business/marketing or life science)

Major Entry-Level Opportunities for New Graduates: Positions as pharmaceutical territory managers

BACKGROUND AND OPERATIONS

In the last several decades, a revolution has swept biomedical science. New insights have already led to undreamed-of therapies against killers such as cardiovascular disease, viral infection, and cancer. Now a new generation of pharmaceuticals is on the way—drugs that may "rescue" brain cells after a stroke, slow the progression of Alzheimer's disease, protect arteries from the damage of harmful cholesterol, "switch off" neurologically based diseases, even treat crippling anxiety or addictive substance abuse. Parke-Davis, one of the most respected names in medicine, is right at the front line of this biomedical revolution.

Founded in 1866, Parke-Davis is the ethical pharmaceutical division of the Warner-Lambert Company. Warner-Lambert itself is a global enterprise of more than 35,000 people engaged in the development, marketing, and manufacturing of high-quality health-care and consumer products.

The mission of Warner-Lambert, as expressed through its creed, is to achieve leadership in advancing the health and well-being of people worldwide. The activities of Parke-Davis clearly demonstrate Warner-Lambert's commitment to this mission.

As an example, the involvement of Parke-Davis in cognitive disorders has culminated in FDA approval of Cognex for the treatment of Alzheimer's disease.

Parke-Davis is continuing to make a lasting imprint on cardiovascular medicine through the worldwide marketing of products like Accupril, an ACE-inhibitor for the treatment of hypertension and congestive heart failure. Parke-Davis is also increasing its focus on the special health-care needs of women to meet the demands of this growing market.

These new products reflect Parke-Davis's emphasis on improved R&D productivity. The worldwide R&D staff now numbers more than 2,000 professionals, and R&D investment through this decade will be more than $1 billion for new pharmaceuticals alone.

Parke-Davis is also increasing its investment in sales and marketing to ensure that physicians and patients have the fullest possible access to the fruits of medical research. Parke-Davis now has more than 1,000 professionals serving physicians and other members of the medical profession. However, there is a continuing need for outstanding new graduates to meet the company's commitments in providing superior products and service.

EMPLOYMENT OPPORTUNITIES

Territory Managers. Parke-Davis offers opportunities nationwide for professional territory managers who call on health-care professionals to promote the use of Parke-Davis products. Graduates with B.S./B.A. or M.S./M.A. degrees (business, mar-

keting, or life science preferred) and strong academic standing are encouraged to apply. All candidates should have above average oral communication abilities, good planning skills, results orientation and organizing skills, the ability to work independently, and a strong desire to succeed.

TRAINING

Parke-Davis training is among the best in industry. All new professional territory managers complete an extensive sales training program that consists of several weeks of working directly in a territory with key people and three weeks of classroom training at Parke-Davis headquarters in Morris Plains, New Jersey. Additional training on specific topics is also conducted on an ongoing basis.

THE ORGANIZATION AS EMPLOYER

The continued growth of the company's business in the United States has created a climate where advancement opportunities are numerous.

Warner-Lambert itself is recognized as one of the nation's most desirable employers. It has earned recognition for several years as one of the best companies for working mothers and takes pride in its reputation as a "family-sensitive" company. The company offers a superior educational assistance program to help colleagues continue development. Warner-Lambert provides a competitive and comprehensive benefits program. A company car is also provided to all territory managers.

APPLICATION AND INFORMATION

Parke-Davis encourages applications from both students and experienced graduates. College students should check with their placement offices to see if a Parke-Davis representative will be visiting. If not, interested applicants are encouraged to forward a résumé to one of the following addresses:

PARKE-DAVIS

Women's Healthcare/West
Sales Recruiting
18201 Von Karman Avenue, Suite 630
Irvine, California 92715
Phone: 714-852-1827 or
800-532-2101
Fax: 714-852-1559

PARKE-DAVIS

Women's Healthcare/East
Sales Recruiting
35 Waterview Boulevard, First Floor
Parsippany, New Jersey 07054
Phone: 201-316-0882 or
800-368-0733
Fax: 201-316-5007

PARKE-DAVIS

Northeast Business Unit
Sales Recruiting
35 Waterview Boulevard, First Floor
Parsippany, New Jersey 07054
Phone: 201-263-0063 or
800-368-0733
Fax: 201-263-4828

PARKE-DAVIS

Southeast Business Unit
Sales Recruiting
1050 Crown Pointe Parkway, Suite 1230
Atlanta, Georgia 30338
Phone: 404-396-4080 or
800-354-1712
Fax: 404-392-0821

PARKE-DAVIS

North Central Business Unit
Sales Recruiting
1750 East Golf Road, Suite 490
Schaumburg, Illinois 60173
Phone: 708-240-0205 or
800-242-0205
Fax: 708-240-9324

PARKE-DAVIS

South Central Business Unit
Sales Recruiting
Lincoln Centre Two
5420 LBJ Freeway, Suite 640
Dallas, Texas 75240
Phone: 214-484-5566 or
800-643-5964
Fax: 214-247-6586

PARKE-DAVIS

West Business Unit
Sales Recruiting
18201 Von Karman Avenue, Suite 630
Irvine, California 92715
Phone: 714-852-0905 or
800-356-3391
Fax: 714-852-1559

Philip Morris USA

Philip Morris U.S.A.

Description of Organization: Processes tobacco, manufactures cigarettes, and markets them throughout the United States

Number of Employees: 166,000 worldwide (Philip Morris Companies Inc.)

Headquarters Location: New York, New York

Academic Fields of Recruitment Interest: Accounting; finance; business; marketing; mechanical, chemical, industrial, and electrical engineering; operations research; computer science; chemistry; physics

Major Entry-Level Opportunities for New Graduates: Accountant, financial analyst, engineer, computer programmer, manufacturing supervisor, chemist, territory sales manager

BACKGROUND AND OPERATIONS

Philip Morris Companies Inc. is the world's largest producer and marketer of consumer packaged goods, with major tobacco, food, and beer businesses generating more than $65 billion in 1994 revenues. The principal operating companies are the following:

Philip Morris USA is the nation's leading cigarette manufacturer. For the twelfth consecutive year, it had the highest revenues, income, volume, and share among U.S. tobacco companies. Nearly one out of every three cigarettes sold in the U.S. is a Marlboro, making the Philip Morris brand the nation's best-selling cigarette.

Philip Morris International (PMI) is the leading U.S. exporter of cigarettes. In 1994, PMI gained more volume than all of its international competitors combined.

Kraft Foods Incorporated and **Kraft Foods International** together form the biggest international food company based in the U.S. and the second-largest food company in the world.

Miller Brewing Company is the second-largest U.S. brewer and the third largest in the world.

Philip Morris Capital Corporation (PMCC) is the financial services and real estate portion of the company. Engaging in various financial and investment activities, PMCC is involved in land development and sales in southern California and Colorado through the Mission Viejo Company.

EMPLOYMENT OPPORTUNITIES

SALES OPPORTUNITIES: THE CAREER PATH

Territory Sales Manager (TSM). Sales employees begin the career path at Philip Morris USA as territory sales managers. TSMs sell and implement sales programs and promotions, interact with customers and consumers in retail outlets, analyze retail and customer needs, develop strategies, and establish and build a consultative relationship with customers.

Sales Development Associate. Sales Development Associate is next on the career path for those who distinguish themselves as TSMs. In this assignment, sales development associates gain valuable experience managing people, accounts, and special business projects.

Unit Manager. Moving up to this position requires the ability to inspire team spirit and a commitment to achieving results. Unit managers train, develop, evaluate, and motivate TSMs and are personally responsible for several key accounts.

Senior Account Manager. Senior account manager is the next step along the sales career path. Senior account managers develop business relationships with existing and potential high-volume headquarters accounts.

District Manager. District managers are responsible for managing multimillion-dollar markets, developing their people and the business, achieving sales and promotional objectives in retail and headquarters accounts, and handling more responsibility than many small company presidents.

Section Sales Director. This is a key field management post and the highest-level sales position within a geographic area. This executive assignment entails strategically handling all aspects of the business.

OPERATIONS OPPORTUNITIES

The following positions are utilized within the Operations facilities in Richmond, Virginia; Louisville, Kentucky; and Concord, North Carolina:

Manufacturing and Support Groups. A wide variety of opportunities are available in supervision, mechanical/electrical maintenance, production planning, purchasing, and quality assurance. Experience in a high-speed manufacturing environment is desirable.

Finance. Specialists are involved in a wide range of financial operations, auditing, payroll, accounting, research, and budgets. Accounting and finance backgrounds are required and CPAs are desirable for this position.

Information Services. This area is responsible for the development and maintenance of business manufacturing process control systems. Experience with IBM systems, IMS DB2, and SAP R3 technology is desirable.

Engineering. Engineering's primary responsibility is the development and management of equipment and technology to improve the existing process or to provide new capabilities. Relevant education and experience are required in the fields of mechanical, electrical/electronic, civil, and industrial engineering.

BRAND MANAGEMENT
New York, New York

The brand assistant position involves the development and execution of marketing strategies and plans, including advertising, consumer promotions, retail promotions, direct mail, and new concept development.

An M.B.A. with 2+ years of business experience is desired, preferably in the areas of marketing or sales. Strong strategic, analytical, and creative thinking skills as well as strong presentation skills are required.

OTHER OPPORTUNITIES

MBA Development Program. The MBA Development Program is geared toward those who feel they can make a contribution in a number of different disciplines. For new M.B.A.'s, the program offers a chance to experience a broad range of choices. The program consists of several cross-functional experiences:

Headquarters

New York, New York
- Corporate Affairs
- Finance
- Information Services
- Marketing
- Media
- National Accounts
- Promotion

Operations Facility

Richmond, Virginia
- Business Planning
- Capital Evaluation and Financial Analysis
- Controller's Group
- Information Services
- Leaf Operations
- Leaf Planning and Analysis
- Purchasing
- Research and Development

Cross-functional experiences last six months and may be taken in any order, depending upon the needs of the individual and the company. A typical program consists of four or more rotations and lasts approximately twenty-four months. New York associates will spend about six months in Operations, while Richmond associates rotate to New York for a cross-functional experience in a headquarters function. Upon successful completion of the program, the company strives to place M.B.A. associates in positions that meet their long-term career goals.

MBA Summer Internships. The MBA Development Program also offers opportunities for first-year M.B.A. students seeking a summer internship.

THE ORGANIZATION AS EMPLOYER

Philip Morris is building a team of individuals who value open communication, intelligent risk-taking, and empowerment of the individual.

Philip Morris employees receive a competitive base salary and a highly competitive benefits package that rates in the top 10 percent of U.S. corporations. The package includes medical, dental, vision, and life insurance; a retirement plan; an educational refund; paid vacation days; a 401(k) profit sharing plan; and a relocation assistance package.

APPLICATION AND INFORMATION

Those interested in joining a diverse team where exciting things are happening should consider a challenging and rewarding career with Philip Morris USA. The company recognizes and supports talented individuals who help Philip Morris USA focus on strategic advantage and continuous improvement.

Philip Morris actively recruits on university campuses throughout the country. Applicants interested in meeting with a Philip Morris representative should contact their career services office to find out when a representative will visit the campus. If a representative is unable to visit, applicants should send résumés to one of the following Phillip Morris USA offices:

SALES

Region Recruiter
Philip Morris USA
Three Ravinia Drive, Suite 1560
Atlanta, Georgia 30346

Region Recruiter
Philip Morris USA
5001 Spring Valley Road, Suite 380 West LB30W
Dallas, Texas 75244

Region Recruiter
Philip Morris USA
Woodfield Corp. Center III
300 North Martingale Road, Suite 720
Schaumburg, Illinois 60173

Region Recruiter
Philip Morris USA
100 Walnut Avenue, Suite 401
Clark, New Jersey 07066

Region Recruiter
Philip Morris USA
300 North Lake Avenue, Suite 1100
Pasadena, California 91101

OPERATIONS

Richmond
Employment Department
Philip Morris USA
P.O. Box 26603
Richmond, Virginia 23261

Cabarrus
Employee Department
Philip Morris USA
3321 Highway 29 South
Concord, North Carolina 28027

Louisville
Employment Department
Philip Morris USA
P.O. Box 1498
Louisville, Kentucky 40201

BRAND MANAGEMENT

New York Headquarters
Manager, Executive Recruiting
Philip Morris USA
120 Park Avenue
New York, New York 10017

MBA DEVELOPMENT PROGRAM

New York Headquarters
Manager, Executive Recruiting
Philip Morris USA
120 Park Avenue
New York, New York 10017

Operations
MBA Staffing Specialist
Philip Morris USA
P.O. Box 26603
Richmond, Virginia 23261

Philip Morris USA is an equal opportunity/affirmative action employer and encourages diversity in the workplace.

Staples, Inc.

Description of Organization: A discount retailer with a chain of office superstores, contract and commercial stationery distributors, and a direct mail catalog division, all of which focus on offering deep discounted prices on office supplies to customers ranging from the individual to Fortune 1000 corporations

Number of Employees: 15,700 (full and part-time)

Headquarters Location: Framingham, Massachusetts

Academic Fields of Recruitment Interest: Merchandising, finance, accounting, information systems, logistics, marketing, general business administration, international operations

Major Entry-Level Opportunities for New Graduates: Store management training programs, information systems, finance, accounting, customer service

BACKGROUND AND OPERATIONS

Staples pioneered the office superstore industry in 1986 with the opening of its first store in Brighton, Massachusetts, aimed at providing the same deep discounted prices to the small-business person that previously had been available only to large corporations. Since that time, Staples, Inc., has expanded to include three divisions servicing the needs of businesses ranging in size from the smallest one-person operation to the largest corporations in the country, while maintaining its discount of 40-70 percent on thousands of office supplies, business machines, computers and related products, and office furniture.

Staples: The Office Superstores are located in suburban strip malls and strip centers. These stores offer over 5,000 brand name office products at discounts that average 50 percent off manufacturer's list price. Staple Express is a smaller version of Staples Office Superstores offering 2,700 of the top-selling items aimed at the urban clientele.

Staples Contract and Commercial operates Staples direct mail order, as well as five contract stationers servicing customers ranging in size from small companies to some of the country's largest multisite corporations. Four regional operations are owned and operated by Staples Contract and Commercial: Staples Business Advantage, Spectrum Office Supply, D. A. MacIsaac and Philadelphia Stationers. On a national level, the company operates National Office Supply. The catalog division of Staples Contract and Commercial, Staples Direct, was established in 1990 to service the needs of those customers who prefer the convenience of ordering from the Staples catalog for next-day delivery. By calling 800-333-3330, customers can select from over 5,000 items at the same discounted prices found in Staples Office Superstores. Next-day delivery is free on orders over $50.

Staples operates three superstore businesses outside the continental United States: wholly owned Business Depot in Canada and joint ventures MAXI-Papier Markt Gmbh in Germany and Staples UK in the United Kingdom. Staples' international expansion began in 1991 and continues as a key element in Staples' strategy to expand its geographic diversity and growth platform and enhance its Pan-European purchasing power.

For the fiscal year ended January 29, 1994, Staples reported sales of over $2 billion, a 53 percent increase from the year prior. Staples is listed on the NASDAQ National Market System under the symbol SPLS.

FUTURE DIRECTIONS

Staples: The Office Superstore plans to add ninety additional stores in North America in 1995. As of February 10, 1995, Staples operated 353 North American Superstores and Express units. Stores are located in highly visable sites with large numbers of small and mid-sized businesses (firms with 100 or fewer employees) within a 15-minute drive. There are currently four-teen Staples Express stores located in Manhattan, Boston, and Washington, D.C. These smaller stores are in down town locations with a high density of small and mid-sized businesses. The focus is on walk-in, carry-out business. Several more Express stores will open in 1995.

EMPLOYMENT OPPORTUNITIES

ENTRY LEVEL

The main focus of Staples' recruiting program is the placement of store management trainees in its rapidly expanding North American superstore division. The training program grooms managers for all levels of store management. Opportunities exist for general managers, sales/merchandise managers, operations managers, merchandise team leaders, and operations team leaders.

FOR EXPERIENCED PERSONNEL

The company recruits candidates with related retail experience for corporate employment in merchandising, marketing, and distribution. Positions are available for staff accountants and financial accountants who have backgrounds in consulting, public accounting, or who hold M.B.A. degrees or CPA designations. Information systems positions focus on programmers and systems analysts with background in client server and AS400 environments. Opportunities exist for individuals with logistic, replenishment, and traffic experience.

TRAINING

Staples' store management training programs focus on retail management skills, selling techniques, and product knowledge. Corporate training programs can be either formal or informal and include a variety of on-the-job training assignments supplemented by internal and external seminars.

THE ORGANIZATION AS EMPLOYER

Staples' success is dependent upon the talent and performance of every Staples employee. Therefore the company hires the best-qualified people; gives them the authority to serve their customers; encourages teamwork, personal growth, and professional development; and maintains a build-and-share philosophy toward compensation and employee stock ownership.

Staples recognizes the importance of giving its employees opportunities for career development. All positions below director level throughout the company (stores, corporate, and distribution centers) are posted in all locations. Any employee who meets the requirements and qualifications may apply. This allows Staples to utilize the abundant talent in the current work force, thereby supporting the company policy of promotion from within.

A comprehensive benefits package is provided by the company, and career development is enhanced by programs specifically designed to meet Staples' needs. Tuition refund plans are available for courses offered outside the corporation.

As part of the benefits package, Staples offers a 401K savings plan, comprehensive health care including major medical and dental insurance, long- and short-term disability, and life insurance. An employee assistance program (EAP) is available to provide employees with a positive, professional, and supportive work environment. An employee referral program is in place to encourage current employees to recommend talented individuals for employment with the company.

SUMMER CO-OP AND INTERNSHIP PROGRAMS

The distribution centers have a summer co-op program that allows students to learn the steps involved in getting products to the continually expanding chain of superstores. Interested students should contact Human Resources at the address listed below.

CORPORATE SOCIAL RESPONSIBILITY

Staples is committed to being a good corporate citizen in the communities where it conducts business by providing job opportunities, investing in the community through the buildings and equipment required in-store, supporting manufacturing across the country through solid business growth, and by providing educational experiences for the less fortunate through the company's charitable contribution program.

APPLICATION AND INFORMATION

Staples conducts an extensive college recruiting program to identify candidates for entry-level store management positions. Interested candidates should contact their placement offices for recruiting dates.

Experienced personnel should identify their area of interest and submit their résumés to:

Staples, Inc.
Human Resources-Recruiting-PJO
100 Pennsylvania Avenue
Framingham, Massachusetts 01701-9328

U.S. Army Audit Agency
Department of the Army

Description of Organization: The U.S. Army Audit Agency is a worldwide organization responsible for providing internal audit service within the Department of the Army

Headquarters Location: Alexandria, Virginia

Academic Fields of Recruitment Interest: Accounting/auditing

Major Entry-Level Opportunities for New Graduates: Auditor trainees

BACKGROUND AND OPERATIONS

The U.S. Army Audit Agency is a well-established and highly respected leader in government auditing. The Agency serves as a principal management consultant to the Army, one of the largest and most complex organizations in the United States.

The Agency was established in 1946 and is headquartered in Alexandria, Virginia with offices located throughout the United States and abroad.

The role of the Agency and its employees throughout the world, is to assist the Army in accounting for and managing the public resources entrusted to it. This is done by auditing such areas as procurement and maintenance programs, Army units, Army National Guard and Reserve activities, research and development programs, personnel management activities, financial systems and activities, and morale, welfare, and recreation activities. Audits of these functions include an appropriate mix of performance and financial audits. In addition, the Agency is very active in detecting and preventing fraud, waste, and mismanagement. The Agency's independent approach and professional methods of review provide a valuable perspective on operations and complement all other elements that make up the management process.

Army auditors have the opportunity to participate in highly professional and rewarding auditing activities. All functions of the Army are audited, and the independence of the Agency allows for complete freedom in reporting the results of these audits. The Auditor General, who heads the Agency, reports directly to the Secretary of the Army, thus ensuring the independence of the auditors. Senior managers in the Army have long recognized the value of audit and the professional competence of the Agency. These senior managers, including the Secretary of the Army, generate numerous requests for audit each year and ask the Agency to become involved in some of the most important, complex, and sensitive problems facing the Army. In past years, the Agency has been involved in audits of pricing of spare parts, hazardous wastes, women's roles in the Army, and a variety of functions relating to the Army's combat readiness. Over the last several years, Agency recommendations had the potential to return $35 in monetary benefits to the Army for each $1 of cost incurred by the Agency. In one year, reported potential monetary benefits exceeded $4 billion. As the emphasis on reducing the federal deficit intensifies, auditors will be even more important to Army management.

The Agency has responded to Army management's increasing need for information and data and to the automation processes that accompany this need and is automating the audit process. Portable computers are used by auditors throughout the Agency to create workpapers and spreadsheets and to analyze Army data. Large Army data files can be downloaded onto Agency computers and the information analyzed by the computer to identify problem areas. All auditors are trained in basic computer skills, and some are given high-level computer training. Agency auditors are supported by full-time computer specialists/programmers.

The Agency follows the *Standards for Audit of Governmental Organizations, Programs, Activities, and Functions*, published by the Comptroller General of the United States. Increased use of advanced audit techniques allows the Agency to provide the Army with improved audit results while making the audit process more economical and efficient.

EMPLOYMENT OPPORTUNITIES

ENTRY LEVEL

The Agency offers excellent opportunities for careers in professional auditing. Agency auditors make independent and objective audit analyses of activities, functions, procedures, practices, and internal controls; report on any problems found; and make recommendations for corrective action.

Qualification requirements are specified in the *Office of Personnel Management Handbook X-118*. Current federal government salary rates are published by the Office of Personnel Management and should be available in college placement offices. They may also be obtained from Federal Information Centers.

Auditor, GS-5. The requirement for this entry-level grade is a bachelor's degree in accounting from an accredited college or university; or a bachelor's degree in a related field, such as business administration, finance, or public administration that included or was supplemented by at least 24 semester hours or 36 quarter hours in accounting (up to 6 semester hours of business law may be substituted for a like amount of accounting course work); or four years of accounting experience; or a combination of education and experience fully equivalent to four years of college study; or a certificate as certified public accountant or certified internal auditor, obtained through written examination.

Auditor, GS-7. Candidates may qualify for entry at the GS-7 level if, in addition to the GS-5 requirements, they have completed one year of graduate study in accounting or related fields, such as business administration, finance, or comptrollership; or have one year of professional accounting/auditing experience; or qualify for superior academic achievement.

Career progression within the Agency follows an established career ladder. A career with the Agency begins at the GS-5 or GS-7 grade level. Trainees enter a career program designed to train them to successfully perform assigned audit tasks and to progress to the GS-12 journey-grade level. Based upon their grade when hired and successful performance, auditors may progress from the GS-5 or GS-7 level to GS-12 in three to four years. Promotion to GS-12 is noncompetitive; auditors do not compete against each other for promotions but only have to perform well against their own performance standards to be promoted. Promotions above the GS-12 level are competitive in that the best-qualified auditors are promoted. Advancement to executive and policymaking positions is offered to those who display a high degree of potential.

TRAINING

The Agency's auditor career development program is built around the concepts of on-the-job training, continuing education and training, and self-improvement. The program encompasses diversified assignments, challenging work, classroom training, and participation in professional organizations and activities. The Agency has long been recognized for its excellence in training and has provided advice and assistance on training to other audit agencies throughout the world.

On-the-job training is the most extensive part of the auditor career development program. New hires are assigned to various types of audits and are given close supervision to make sure they understand proper audit standards and learn objective audit techniques. In addition, written performance standards are provided to each auditor; the standards spell out the performance requirements for each auditor grade level. On-the-job progress is assessed on a continuous basis, and employees are given feedback on their successes and on how to improve.

Formal training is used to supplement on-the-job training. It starts with a few days of orientation on the Agency and the Army. After about six months of experience, trainees attend the Introduction to Army Auditing School. This initial training is followed by courses on report writing, statistical sampling, computer skills, and other functions. As an auditor's career progresses, he or she attends the Intermediate Auditor, Senior Auditor, Audit Supervisor, and Audit Management schools. The auditor schools are conducted by the Agency, and the instructors are knowledgeable and competent professional auditors. The Agency is recognized as an official provider of continuing professional education by the National Association of State Boards of Accountancy (NASBA).

THE ORGANIZATION AS EMPLOYER

A career with the Army Audit Agency is challenging and rewarding and offers excellent opportunities for both professional and personal growth. Employees of the Agency work in a progressive atmosphere in which they can develop their career and exercise their creativity.

Auditors who contribute to the successful completion of individual audits are recognized for their efforts, and they receive promotions to higher levels of responsibility and pay. Cash and honorary awards are also used by the Agency to recognize top-level performers.

The Agency's mission requires its auditors to travel to audit sites. These assignments are challenging and take the auditor to interesting and exciting locations. The government pays for all official travel.

Agency auditors are encouraged to pursue advanced degrees in related fields such as finance, economics, and business administration. The Agency fully or partially reimburses the costs of some advanced courses that closely match mission requirements. Auditors are encouraged to attain professional certifications, such as certified public accountant and certified internal auditor, and to actively participate in professional accounting and auditing organizations.

After having been with the Agency for approximately one year, employees are eligible for reassignment to an overseas tour in Germany, Korea, or Hawaii; overseas assignments are voluntary.

As federal government employees, Agency auditors enjoy a wide variety of benefits. They earn 2 weeks (13 work days) of annual vacation during the first 3 years, 4 weeks (20 work days) after 3 years, and 5 weeks (26 work days) after 15 years. Sick leave is accumulated at the rate of 2 weeks (13 days) each year.

New auditors are covered by the Federal Employees Retirement System. This system includes disability and survivor benefits and a tax-deferred Thrift Savings Plan. The Agency contributes to the Thrift Savings Plan. Many comprehensive health plans, including medical and surgical benefits, are provided. Low-cost group life insurance and double indemnity accidental death and dismemberment insurance are also available. The Agency pays a portion of the costs of these insurance plans. In addition, other benefits, such as injury compensation, incentive awards, credit for military service, 10 paid holidays annually, and job security, are offered to the Army auditor.

APPLICATION AND INFORMATION

Graduates interested in becoming a part of the U.S. Army Audit Agency's professional audit staff are encouraged to write to one of the four addresses given below.

Direct inquiries to:

Managing Auditor
U.S. Army Audit Agency
1027 Arch Street, 8th Floor
Philadelphia, Pennsylvania 19107-2317

Managing Auditor
U.S. Army Audit Agency
12140 Woodcrest Executive Drive
St. Louis, Missouri 63141-5046

Managing Auditor
U.S. Army Audit Agency
BWI Commerce Park
7526 Connelley Drive, Suite J
Hanover, Maryland 21076-1663

Managing Auditor
U.S. Army Audit Agency
1222 North Main, Suite 900
San Antonio, Texas 78212-5799

U.S. Army Corps of Engineers
Department of the Army

Description of Organization: The largest public engineering organization in the free world

Number of Employees: 38,000

Headquarters Location: Washington, D.C.

Academic Fields of Recruitment Interest: Business administration and natural resource management

Major Entry-Level Opportunities for New Graduates: Accounting, architecture, environmental protection, human resources, information systems

BACKGROUND AND OPERATIONS

The Corps's dual civil and military missions, dating from the era of George Washington and Thomas Jefferson, have served our nation well for over 200 years. In times of peace, the Corps operates a diverse and challenging civil works program. In wartime, the Corps's capabilities can be mobilized rapidly for expanded military construction.

The Corps also performs a great deal of work for other federal agencies. It reviews designs and specifications for the EPA's wastewater treatment program and provides technical assistance for the toxic-waste cleanup program. The Corps built facilities for NASA at Cape Kennedy and Houston. It is involved in programs for the Departments of Energy and Justice and the Federal Emergency Management Agency.

The activities of the Corps of Engineers embrace virtually the entire range of modern technology, including research, engineering development, investigations and planning, design and construction, operations and maintenance, hydroelectric power production, engineering intelligence, and computer operations. The Corps carries out these diverse activities through a decentralized organization with divisions and districts worldwide. As the premier engineering organization of the Army and a unique national asset, the Corps applies its capabilities toward ensuring defense preparedness, carefully developing water resources, and preserving our natural environment.

FUTURE DIRECTIONS

The Corps of Engineers has the capability to provide essential planning, engineering, and construction support to meet the nation's needs, both military and civil, of the next century. While some of the Corps's traditional missions, such as military construction, are shrinking, others, such as support for other agencies, are increasing. The Corps has the ability, if called upon to serve, to render assistance to the world's developing nations and transfer essential engineering skills to enhance democratic institutions. The Corps also has the ability to help the United States with its decaying infrastructure problems and help ensure development that is environmentally sustainable for future generations. The Corps, as it has in the past, looks to the future for its engineering challenges and opportunities.

EMPLOYMENT OPPORTUNITIES

ENTRY LEVEL

The Corps of Engineers seeks new members with the broadest possible range of disciplinary backgrounds in support of its diverse missions and operations worldwide. Entry-level opportunities in engineering, science, and computer science are available in most Corps locations. In addition, increased salary rates are offered for certain occupations and geographic locations. Candidates who have completed a full four-year curriculum at an accredited college or university leading to a bachelor's degree are qualified for appointment at the GS-5 grade level or, under certain circumstances, at the GS-7 level. Candidates with a master's degree or a doctorate may be qualified for an entry-level appointment at the GS-9 level or higher.

FOR EXPERIENCED PERSONNEL

The Corps typically seeks individuals who have a combination of education and work-related experience in fields that encompass water resource planning and management; engineering investigations and planning; engineering and architectural design; electronic data processing; information science and technology; research and development; real estate acquisition, management, and disposal; financial management; environmental protection; and natural resource management.

TRAINING

In addition to intensive on-the-job training under senior professionals, the Corps provides tuition reimbursement for job-related courses, programs for professional development, and other advanced study opportunities.

THE ORGANIZATION AS EMPLOYER

Because of the diverse responsibilities of the Corps, few careers can offer such a range of opportunities and involvement in both the national and international arenas. In addition to the challenge, the Corps, as part of the executive branch of the government, offers excellent personal benefits, including paid vacation time in the amount of 13 to 26 days per year, based on length of service; sick leave, which is accrued at 13 days per year; and 10 paid federal holidays a year. Federal employees are also covered by an excellent retirement plan, which is transferable and includes tax-deferred savings alternatives; a life insurance program offering variable options; and a choice of a variety of health insurance plans.

STUDENT EMPLOYMENT PROGRAMS

The Corps of Engineers offers a wide range of employment opportunities for students under the Federal-wide Student Educational Employment Program. Students can be employed either full- or part-time on a yearly or seasonal basis. Cooperative education and other career experience positions related to a student's academic major are available, which can lead to permanent appointments with the Corps upon graduation. Also offered are extensive summer employment opportunities in a variety of occupations.

APPLICATION AND INFORMATION

Interested individuals may obtain more information about career opportunities with the U.S. Army Corps of Engineers by writing to, calling, or visiting the Corps Human Resource Office in the geographic area where they are seeking employment.

NORTH ATLANTIC DIVISION

NAD Human Resources Service Center, 1343 Ashton Road, Hanover, Maryland 21076-3102 410-859-3666 (job information line) (Consolidated recruitment for all NAD Districts)

Baltimore District, 10 S. Howard Street, Baltimore, Maryland 21201-1715 410-962-2087

Philadelphia District, Wanamaker Building, 100 Penn Square East, Philadelphia, Pennsylvania 19107-3390 215-656-6870

New York District, 26 Federal Plaza, Room 1923, New York, New York 10278-6090 212-264-0200

Norfolk District, 803 Front Street, Norfolk, Virginia 23510-1096 804-441-7636

NORTH CENTRAL DIVISION

111 N. Canal Street, 14th Floor, Chicago, Illinois 60606-7205 312-353-6330

Detroit District, 477 Michigan Avenue, Detroit, Michigan 48231-1027 313-226-6427

St. Paul District, Army Corps of Engineers Center, 190 Fifth Street East, St. Paul, Minnesota 55101-1638 612-290-5480

Buffalo District, 1776 Niagara Street, Buffalo, New York 14207-3199 716-879-4137

Rock Island District, Clock Tower Building, P.O. Box 2004, Rock Island, Illinois 61204-2004 309-794-5313

OHIO RIVER DIVISION

Federal Office Building, 550 Main Street, Room 9114, Cincinnati, Ohio 45202 513-684-3066

Louisville District, 600 Martin Luther King Place, Louisville, Kentucky 40201-2230 502-582-5886

Pittsburgh District, 2105 William S. Morehead Federal Building, 1000 Liberty Avenue, Pittsburgh, Pennsylvania 15222-4186 412-644-6852

Huntington District, 502 Eighth Street, Huntington, West Virginia 25701-2070 304-529-5666

Nashville District, 801 Broadway, Nashville, Tennessee 37202-1070 615-736-5654

MISSOURI RIVER DIVISION

12565 West Center Road, Omaha, Nebraska 68144-3869

Omaha District, 215 North 17th Street, Omaha, Nebraska 68102-9959 402-221-4077

Kansas City District, 601 E. 12th Street, 700 Federal Building, Room 609, Kansas City, Missouri 64106-2896 816-426-3654

SOUTH ATLANTIC DIVISION

77 Forsyth Street, SW, Atlanta, Georgia 30335-6801, 404-331-6683

Jacksonville District, 400 W. Bay Street, Room 888, Jacksonville, Florida 32232-0019 904-232-3741

Mobile District, 109 St. Joseph Street, Mobile, Alabama 36628-0001 205-690-2524

Savannah District, 100 W. Oglethorpe Avenue, Savannah, Georgia 31402-0889 912-652-5413

Wilmington District, P.O. Box 1890, 69 Darlington Avenue, Wilmington, North Carolina 28402-1890 910-251-4871 910-251-4876 (job information line)

Charleston District, (For information concerning career opportunities in this geographic area, contact the Human Resource Office in Savannah)

LOWER MISSISSIPPI VALLEY DIVISION

820 Crawford Street, Room 300, Vicksburg, Mississippi 39181-0080 601-634-5158

New Orleans District, P.O. Box 60267, New Orleans, Louisiana 70160-0026 504-862-2808

Memphis District, 167 North Main Street B202, Memphis, Tennessee 38103-1894 901-544-3105

Vicksburg District, 820 Crawford Street, Room 300, Vicksburg, Mississippi 39181-0080 601-634-5158

St. Louis District, 1222 Spruce Street, St. Louis, Missouri 63103-2833 314-331-8549

SOUTHWESTERN DIVISION

Human Resource Division Office, 819 Taylor Street, Fort Worth, Texas 76102-0300 817-334-2208 800-453-8907

Tulsa District, 1645 South 101st East Avenue, Tulsa, Oklahoma 74128-0061 918-669-7346

Little Rock District, 700 West Capitol Avenue, Little Rock, Arkansas 72203-0867 501-324-5669

Albuquerque District, Fort Worth District, Galveston District (For information concerning career opportunities in these geographic areas, contact the Division Human Resource Office in Fort Worth)

NORTH PACIFIC DIVISION

220 N.W. 8th Avenue, Portland, Oregon 97209 503-326-3786

Portland District, 333 SW First Avenue, Portland, Oregon 97208-2946 503-326-6976

Walla Walla District, 201 North 3rd, Walla Walla, Washington 99362-1876 509-527-7026

Seattle District, 4735 East Marginal Way, South, Seattle, Washington 98124-2255 206-764-3739

Alaska District, P.O. Box 898, Anchorage, Alaska 99506-0898 907-753-2824

SOUTH PACIFIC DIVISION

630 Sansome Street, Room 952, San Francisco, California 94111-2206 415-705-2430

Human Resource Division Office, 1325 J Street, Suite 1550, Sacramento, California 95814-2922 916-557-5287

Sacramento District, 1325 J Street, Room 1499, Sacramento, California 95814-2922 916-557-6621

Los Angeles District, 300 N. Los Angeles Street, Room 6210, Los Angeles, California 90012 213-894-5340

San Francisco District, 211 Main Street, Room 306, San Francisco, California 94105-1905 415-744-3271

U.S. ARMY ENGINEER DIVISION, HUNTSVILLE

P.O. Box 1600, Huntsville, Alabama 35807-4301 205-895-1230

U.S. ARMY ENGINEER DIVISION, NEW ENGLAND

424 Trapelo Road, Waltham, Massachusetts 02254-9149 617-647-8561

U.S. ARMY ENGINEER DIVISION, TRANSATLANTIC

261 Prince Frederick Drive, Winchester, Virginia 22602 703-665-3732 (Recruitment for Europe, Middle East & Africa)

U.S. ARMY ENGINEER DIVISION, PACIFIC OCEAN

Building 230, Ft. Shafter, Hawaii 96858-5440, 808-438-1098 (Recruitment for Hawaii, Korea & Japan)

WASHINGTON D.C. METROPOLITAN AREA

U.S. Army Humphrey Engineer Center Support Activity, 7701 Telegraph Road, Alexandria, Virginia 22310-3860 703-355-2211

HQ Support Office, 20 Massachusetts Avenue N.W., Washington, D.C. 20314-1000 202-272-0365

CORPS LABORATORIES

U.S. Army Cold Regions Research and Engineering Laboratory, 72 Lyme Road, Hanover, New Hampshire 03755-1290 603-646-4132

Waterways Experiment Station, 820 Crawford Street, Vicksburg, Mississippi 39181-0080 601-634-5069

U.S. Army Construction Engineering Research Laboratory, 2902 Newmark Drive, Interstate Research Park, Champaign, Illinois 61821-1076

U.S. Army Topographic Engineering Center, 7701 Telegraph Road, Building #2592, Alexandria, Virginia 22315-3864 703-355-0255

Wawa, Inc.

Description of Organization: A mid-Atlantic retail chain of convenience stores located in Connecticut, Delaware, Maryland, New Jersey, and Pennsylvania.
Number of Employees: 10,000
Headquarters Location: Wawa, Pennsylvania (Delaware County)
Academic Fields of Recruitment Interest: Retail Management, Restaurant/Food Service Management, and Business Management
Major Entry-Level Opportunities for New Graduates: Management Training Program

BACKGROUND AND OPERATIONS

Wawa, Inc., is an industry leader in convenience store retailing and is continually obsessed with not only meeting but also anticipating and exceeding customer expectations.

Management innovation has always been a mainstay of Wawa. Wawa traces its beginnings to an iron foundry begun in 1803 by the half brother of the current CEO's great-great grandfather. The Wood family then moved into textile manufacturing in the 1850's. By the 1890's the family began dairy farming at its summer home in Wawa, Pennsylvania, where the company is still located today. The dairy business began as a hobby but took on greater importance when the textile business faltered.

The dairy was profitable until the early 1960's, when supermarkets began cutting into home delivery of milk and dairy products. Then the dairy, too, began to decline. Grahame Wood was the visionary who saw a way of saving the dairy by opening stores that would sell its products.

On April 16, 1964, Wawa Dairies opened its first Wawa Food Market. Two more stores were opened later that year and four in 1965. By 1970, 228 stores were successfully operating and paving the way for additional stores. The original store is still operating and has been joined by 517 others in Connecticut, Delaware, Maryland, New Jersey, and Pennsylvania. Meanwhile the dairy processes about 90 million quarts of milk per year, close to 90 percent of which is sold through the Wawa outlets.

Wawa Inc.'s willingness to experiment with new concepts, mostly developed by associates, has eased the company's convenience stores successfully through three decades.

FUTURE DIRECTIONS

Wawa, Inc.'s long-range goals of continued refinement and expansion of market leadership in food service, product diversity, using new technologies and concepts, customer-focused quality, ambitious growth in the market areas it currently occupies, and retaining entrepreneurial management teams will secure its competitive advantage. The company continually pursues strategies for growth and Associates' development.

Wawa is committed to strong decentralized leadership. The company vests regional responsibilities in each operating group. Wawa expects each manager to operate directly and efficiently, to be entrepreneurial, and to develop the human resources needed to achieve objectives.

EMPLOYMENT OPPORTUNITIES

ENTRY LEVEL
The primary thrust of Wawa's recruiting program is to seek quality candidates to train for store management. Also available are flexible part-time Sales Associate positions which can provide supplemental income.

FOR EXPERIENCED PERSONNEL
The company recruits professional candidates with related retail management experience for store management positions.

TRAINING

Training programs are provided for all associates from entry level to incumbents. Training programs offered by the company can either be formal or informal. They include a comprehensive management training program, plus a variety of on-the-job training assignments supplemented by internal and external seminars. Wawa training programs vary in length; they may last up to three years.

THE ORGANIZATION AS EMPLOYER

Wawa is a privately-held company whose culture recognizes the importance of giving its associates the opportunity to grow professionally and personally. Every available opportunity is taken to recognize exceptional performance. Challenging work enables new associates to use their skills as well as learn additional skills through mentors. Associates find the variety of work stimulating, intriguing, and hardly mundane.

A comprehensive benefits program is provided by the company. Profit sharing and savings plans are also available for eligible employees. Compensation is competitive and based on performance. Career development is enhanced through internal and external training programs and tuition reimbursement plans.

SUMMER, CO-OP, AND INTERNSHIP PROGRAMS

Wawa is dedicated to building a quality workforce and is partners with several educational institutions. Interested students should contact their placement office or business studies department for more information.

CORPORATE SOCIAL RESPONSIBILITY

Store managers are generally in the forefront of community charitable and social programs. Associates contribute to several initiatives. Through volunteering for community projects, donating products, environmental efforts, canister collections,

Average Manager Salary

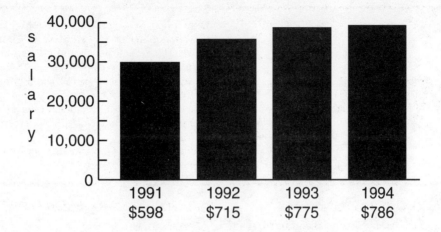

	1991	1992	1993	1994
	$598	$715	$775	$786

and matching corporate funds, each location has high visibility within its community and strives to maintain a reputation as a supportive good neighbor. Wawa believes that neighborhoods are an investment in the future.

APPLICATION AND INFORMATION

Wawa conducts college recruiting to identify candidates for entry-level positions. Interested students should contact their college's placement office for recruiting dates. Written inquiries should be directed to the nearest Wawa regional office:

Wawa Food Markets
Springfield Regional Recruiter
2835-A Route 206 South
Columbus, NJ 08022
800-WAY TO WORK

Wawa Food Markets
Connecticut Regional Recruiter
540 Foxon Road
East Haven, CT 06512
203-467-4838

Wawa Food Markets
Millville Regional Recruiter
821 Columbia Avenue
Millville, NJ 08332
800-607-WAWA

Wawa Food Markets
Claymont Regional Recruiter
99 Wiltshire Road
Claymont, DE 19703
610-569-2101

Wawa Food Markets
Lansdale Regional Recruiter
1857 N. Broad Street
Lansdale, PA 19446-1117
800-822-2111 (in PA)

INDEX BY INDUSTRY

Companies are indexed under the following categories in this section.

Advertising and Public Relations
Agriculture
Automotive
Aviation and Aerospace
Banks
Building Materials
Business Services
Chemicals
Communications
Computer Software
Computer Systems and Peripherals
Construction and Contractors
Consumer and Household Products
Consumer Electronics
Data Processing Services
Defense/Military
Educational Services
Electronics and Electrical Equipment
Engineering Services and Management
Entertainment/Motion Pictures
Environmental Services
Finance and Investments
Food and Beverages
Furniture and Fixtures
Government Organizations
Hardware, Plumbing, Heating and Air
  Conditioning
Hotels, Motels and Restaurants

Industrial Machinery and Equipment
Information Services
Instruments
Insurance
Laboratories
Lumber and Wood
Mail Order and Catalogs
Marketing and Market Research
Medical Equipment and Services
Mining and Metals
Office Equipment
Oil, Gas and Petroleum Products
Optical
Paper and Related Products
Pharmaceuticals
Publishing and Printing
Radio and Television
Real Estate
Retail Trade
Rubber and Plastics
Stone, Clay and Glass Products
Telecommunications
Textiles and Clothing
Transportation and Shipping
Travel
Utilities
Waste Management
Wholesale Trade and Distribution

INDEX BY INDUSTRY

This index classifies companies according to the primary industries in which they operate.

Toshiba America, Inc., 181
Zenith Electronics Corporation, 198

Cost Management Services
U.S. Army Audit Agency,
Department of the Army, 203

Data Processing Services
Alltel Information Services, Inc., 27
Analysas Corporation, 34
Automatic Data Processing, 40
Barnett Technologies, Inc., 44
Ceridian Corporation, 60
Comdisco, Inc., 65
Communications Data Services, 66
Electronic Data Systems
Corporation (EDS), 79
Fleet Services Corporation, 87
M and I Data Services, Inc., 129
National City Processing
Company, 135

Defense/Military
Alliant Techsystems, Inc., 26
Defense Mapping Agency, 199
Department of the Army, 200
General Dynamics Corporation, 92
General Dynamics Land Systems, 92
Harsco Corporation, 100
Hughes Missile Systems
International Company, 106
Lockheed Martin, 121
Lockheed Sanders, Inc., 121
Loral Corporation, 122
Martin Marietta Energy
Systems, 125
Unisys Government Group, 186

Educational Services
Kinder-Care Learning Centers, 117

**Electronics and Electrical
Equipment**
Advanced Micro Devices, Inc., 22
Alcatel Cable Systems, Inc., 25
Alternate Circuit Technology,
Inc., 27
American Power Conversion
Corporation, 31
Amphenol Corporation, 33
AMP, Inc., 33
Amtech Corporation, 34
Anadigics, Inc., 34
Analog Devices, Inc., 34
Anixter Brothers, Inc., 35
Arrow Electronics, Inc., 38
AVX Corporation, 41
Bally Manufacturing
Corporation, 42

A B Chance Company, 21
BICC Cables Corporation, 47
Continental Circuits
Corporation, 68
Cooper Industries, Inc., 68
Cooper Power Systems, Inc., 69
Delco Electronics Corporation, 73
Diebold, Inc., 75
Duracell International, Inc., 77
Electrolux Corporation, 79
Emerson Electric Company, 79
E-Systems, Inc., 77
Eveready Battery Company, Inc., 81
Fujitsu Microelectronics, Inc., 90
GE, 92
Graybar Electric Company, Inc., 96
Hitachi America, Ltd., 103
Hubbell, Inc., 106
Hughes Electronics, 106
Insilco Corporation, 109
Intel Corporation, 109
International Rectifier
Corporation, 111
ITT Defense and Electronics, 112
Litton Industries, Inc., 121
Magnetek, Inc., 124
Mead Data Central, Inc., 127
Micron Technology, Inc., 130
Microsemi Corporation, 130
Minnesota Mining and
Manufacturing Company , 131
Mitsubishi Electric America, 131
Molex, Inc., 132
Motorola, Inc., 133
National Linen Service, 135
National Semiconductor
Corporation, 135
NEC Electronics, Inc., 136
Phillips Electronics, 148
Raytheon Company, 155
Reliance Electric Company, 156
Ricoh Corporation, 158
Siemens Corporation, 166
Silicon Systems, Inc., 167
Square D Company, 172
Teleflex, Inc., 178
Teradyne, Inc., 179
Texas Instruments, Inc., 179
Thermo Electron Corporation, 179
Thomas and Betts Corporation, 180
Trimble Navigation, Ltd., 183
Tyco International, Ltd., 184
Valmont Industries, Inc., 189
Vishay Intertechnology, Inc., 190
Westinghouse Electric
Corporation, 194
Zenith Electronics Corporation, 198

Energy Products and Services
BP America, 53
LaClede Gas Company, 119
Sandia National Laboratories, 160
Sonat, Inc., 169
South Jersey Industries, Inc., 170
Union Pacific Resource, 185

**Engineering Services and
Management**
Albert Kahn Associates, Inc., 114
The Austin Company, 40
Bechtel Group, Inc., 45
Belcan Corporation, 45
Day and Zimmermann, Inc., 72
Dyncorp, 77
Foster Wheeler Corporation, 89
Halliburton Company, 98
Jacobs Engineering Group,
Inc., 112
Lockheed/Martin Services
Group, 121
Morrison Knudsen
Corporation, 133
The Ralph M. Parsons
Company, 145
Raytheon Constructors, 155
Raytheon Service Company, 156
Severdrup Corporation, 165
TAD Technical Services
Corporation, 176

Entertainment/Motion Pictures
American Golf Corporation, 30
Blockbuster Entertainment
Corporation, 48
BMG Music, 51
Cinemark USA, Inc., 62
Gaylord Entertainment
Company, 91
National Amusements, Inc., 134
Pearson, Inc., 146
Sony Music Entertainment,
Inc., 169
Sony Pictures Entertainment, 170
Time Warner, Inc., 181
Walt Disney Company, Inc., 192

**Environmental Agencies (Federal
Level)**
Environmental Protection
Agency, 200
USDA Forest Service, 203

**Environmental Products and
Equipment**
Andover Controls Corporation, 35

Schwegmann Giant
  Supermarkets, 163
Seaboard Corporation, 163
Service America Corporation, 165
Sky Chefs, Inc., 168
The Stroh Brewery Company, 174
Thorn Apple Valley, Inc., 180
Tropicana Products, Inc., 183
Tyson Foods, Inc., 184
Universal Foods Corporation, 187
U.S. Department of
  Agriculture, 203
Weight Watchers International,
  Inc., 193
WLR Foods, Inc., 196
Wrigley Jr. Company, 197

Foundations and Non-Profits
American Red Cross - Biomedical
  Division, 31
Federal Emergency Management
  Agency, 201

Furniture and Fixtures
Andersen Corporation, 35
Bassett Furniture Industries,
  Inc., 44
Haworth, Inc., 101
Herman Miller, Inc., 102
Hon Industries, Inc., 104
Kimball International, Inc., 117
La-Z-Boy Chair Company, 119
Leggett and Platt, Inc., 120
Levitz Furniture Corporation, 120
Mohon International, Inc., 132
Rent It Center, 157
Springs Industries, 172
Steelcase, Inc., 174

Government Organizations
Bureau of Oceans and
  International Environmental
  Affairs , 199
Centers For Disease Control, 199
Central Intelligence Agency, 199
Department of Commerce, 199
Department of Consumer and
  Regulatory Affairs, 199
Department of Energy, 199
Department of Health and Human
  Services, 199
Department of Housing and Urban
  Development, 199
Department of Justice, U.S.
  Attorney General, 199
Department of Labor, 199
Department of State, Bureau of
  Medical Services, 200
Department of the Air Force, 200
Department of the Army, 200

Department of the Interior, 200
Department of the Navy, 200
Department of the Navy, Naval
  Facilities Engineering
  Command, 200
Department of Transportation,
  Federal Highway
  Administration, 200
Environmental Protection
  Agency, 200
Federal Aviation
  Administration, 200
Federal Communications
  Commission, 201
Federal Emergency Management
  Agency, 201
Federal Maritime Commission, 201
Federal Trade Commission, 201
Food and Drug Administration, 201
General Accounting Office, 201
General Services
  Administration, 201
Government Printing Office, 201
Internal Revenue Service,
  Department of Treasury, 201
Interstate Commerce
  Commission, 201
Marine Corps Officer
  Programs, 202
NASA Lewis Research Center, 202
National Institute of Standards and
  Technology, 202
National Institutes of Health, 202
National Park Service, 202
National Science Foundation, 202
National Security Agency, 202
Naval Air Warfare Center Aircraft
  Division, 202
New York City Housing
  Authority, 137
New York Office of Mental
  Health, 137
Occupational Safety and Health
  Administration, 202
Office of Management and
  Budget, 202
Peace Corps, 203
Securities and Exchange
  Commission, 203
Smithsonian Institution, 169
U.S. Army Audit Agency,
  Department of the Army, 203
U.S. Army Corps of Engineers, 203
U.S. Department of
  Agriculture, 203
U.S. Geological Survey, 203
U.S. Postal Service, 203

**Hardware, Plumbing, Heating and
Air Conditioning**
Ace Hardware Corporation, 21
Air-A-Plane Corporation, 24
American Standard, Inc., 32
A. O. Smith Corporation, 168
Carrier Corporation, 58
Duo-Fast Corporation, 77
Heatcraft, Inc., 101
Inter-City Products
  Corporation, 110
Kohler Company, 118
Masco Corporation, 125
Pace Industries, Inc., 144
Rheem Manufacturing
  Company, 157
Schlegel Corporation, 162
Snap-On Tools, Inc., 169
The Stanley Works, 173
Thermo King Corporation, 179
Whiting Roll-Up Door
  Manufacturing Corporation, 195
W.W. Grainger, Inc., 95
York International Corporation, 197

Health Care Services
Advocate Healthcare, 23
Blue Cross and Blue Shield of
  Vermont, 50
Bon Secours Health Systems, 51
Columbia/HCA, 65
Department of Health and Human
  Services, 199
Health Care Retirement
  Corporation of America, 101
Healthcare Services Group,
  Inc., 101
ISS International Service Systems,
  Inc., 111
Kaiser Foundation Health Plan of
  Colorado, Inc., 115
Permanente Medical Group,
  Inc., 148
Ross-Loos Healthplan of
  California, 159
Saint Joseph Health System, 159
United Health, Inc., 186
Value Health, Inc., 189

**Health Maintenance and Preferred
Provider Organizations (HMOs,
PPOs)**
FHP Takecare, 84
Group Health Cooperative of Puget
  Sound, 97
Group Health, Inc., 97
Samaritan Health System, 160
United Healthcare
  Corporation, 186
US Healthcare, Inc., 188

Waste Management

Wholesale Trade and Distribution

GEOGRAPHIC INDEX

An index of profiled companies in alphabetical order by state.

Indiana

Minnesota

Westinghouse Electric Corporation
(Pittsburg), 194
Wyeth-Ayerst International, Ltd.
(St. Davids), 197
York International Corporation
(York), 197

Rhode Island
American Power Conversion
Corporation (West Kingston), 31
Avco Corporation (Providence), 41
Blue Cross and Blue Shield of
Rhode Island (Providence), 50
Cookson America, Inc.
(Providence), 68
Fleet Financial Group
(Providence), 87
Fleet Services Corporation
(Providence), 87
G-Tech Corporation (West
Greenwich), 98
Hasbro, Inc. (Pawtucket), 100
Teknor Apex Company
(Pawtucket), 178
Textron, Inc. (Providence), 179

South Carolina
Blue Cross and Blue Shield of
South Carolina (Columbia), 50
Bowater, Inc. (Greenville), 52
ESAB Welding and Cutting
Products, Inc. (Florence), 81
Fuji Photo Film, Inc.
(Greenwood), 90
Greenwood Mills, Inc.
(Greenwood), 96
Intertech Group, Inc. (North
Charles), 111
Michelin Tire Corporation
(Greenville), 129
Policy Management Systems
Corporation (Blythewood), 151
Ryan's Family Steak Houses
(Greer), 159
Santee Cooper (Moncks
Corner), 161
Scana Corporation (Columbia), 161
Schlumberger Industries, Inc. (West
Union), 162
Sonoco Products Company
(Hartsville), 169
Springs Industries (Fort Mill), 172
Westinghouse Savannah River
Company (Aiken), 194

South Dakota
Citibank South Dakota (Sioux
Falls), 63

Evangelical Lutheran Good
Samaritan Hospital (Sioux
Falls), 81
Gateway 2000 (North Sioux
City), 91
John Morrell and Company, Inc.
(Sioux Falls), 133

Tennessee
Alcoa Fujikura, Ltd.
(Brentwood), 25
A-Plus Communications, Inc.
(Nashville), 36
Arcadian Partners, LP.
(Memphis), 37
Autozone, Inc. (Memphis), 41
Blue Cross and Blue Shield of
Tennessee (Chattanooga), 50
Bridgestone/Firestone, Inc.
(Nashville), 53
Central Parking Corporation
(Nashville), 59
Columbia/HCA (Nashville), 65
Dollar General Corporation
(Nashville), 75
Dover Elevator International
(Memphis), 76
Eastman Chemical Company
(Kingsport), 78
Fedex Corporation (Memphis), 84
First Tennessee National
Corporation (Memphis), 86
Fleetguard, Inc. (Nashville), 87
Gaylord Entertainment Company
(Nashville), 91
GKN North America, Inc.
(Memphis), 94
Guardsmark, Inc. (Memphis), 98
Harrah's Entertainment, Inc.
(Memphis), 99
Inter-City Products Corporation (La
Vergne), 110
International Paper
(Memphis), 111
Kantus Corporation
(Lewisburg), 115
Kraft Food Ingredients Corporation
(Memphis), 118
Magnetek, Inc. (Nashville), 124
Martin Marietta Energy Systems
(Oak Ridge), 125
Mohon International, Inc.
(Paris), 132
Nissan Motor Manufacturing
Corporation USA (Smyrna), 138
Northern Telecom
(Nashville), 140
Perceptics Corporation
(Knoxville), 147

Perkins Family Restaurant
(Memphis), 148
Sedgwick James, Inc.
(Memphis), 164
Service Merchandise Company
(Brentwood), 165
Shoney's (Nashville), 166
Smith and Nephew Richards, Inc.
(Memphis), 168
Thomas and Betts Corporation
(Memphis), 180
United Cities Gas Company
(Brentwood), 186
Willis Corroon Corporation
(Nashville), 196

Texas
ABB Vetco Gray, Inc. (Houston), 21
Affiliated Computer Services, Inc.
(Dallas), 23
Alcon Laboratories (Fort
Worth), 25
American Airlines, Inc. (Fort
Worth), 28
America National Insurance
(Galveston), 28
AMR Corporation (Fort Worth), 33
Amtech Corporation (Dallas), 34
Apple Tree Markets (Houston), 36
Army and Air Force Exchange
Service (Dallas), 38
Associates Corporation of North
America (Irving), 39
Austin Industries Corporation
(Dallas), 40
Baker Hughes, Inc. (Houston), 42
Bank United Texas (Houston), 43
Blue Cross and Blue Shield of
Texas, Inc. (Richardson), 50
Browning-Ferris Industries
(Houston), 54
Builder's Square, Inc. (San
Antonio), 54
Burlington Northern, Inc. (Fort
Worth), 55
Caltex Petroleum Corporation
(Irving), 56
Centex Corporation (Dallas), 59
Central and Southwest Corporation
(Dallas), 59
Champion Healthcare Corporation
(Houston), 60
Cinemark USA, Inc. (Dallas), 62
Coastal Power Production Company
(Houston), 64
Color Tile, Inc. (Forth Worth), 65
Columbia/HCA (Dallas), 65
Compaq Computer Corporation
(Houston), 66
Comp USA (Dallas), 66

INDEX OF HIRING NEEDS

An index of profiled companies by areas of expertise sought.

United Healthcare Corporation, 186
United Health, Inc., 186
United States Gypsum Company, 186
United States National Bank of Oregon, 187
United States Service Industries, 187
United States Shoe Corporation, 187
United Tech Auto Holdings, 187
United Technologies Corporation, 187
United Telephone Company of Florida, 187
United Wisconsin Services, 187
Unitrin, Inc., 187
Universal Foods Corporation, 187
Universal Health Services, 187
Unum Life Insurance Company, 188
U.S. Army Audit Agency, Department of the Army, 203
U.S. Bancorp, 188
U. S. Brick, Inc., 184
U.S. Department of Agriculture, 203
U.S. Fidelity Guaranty Company, 188
US Healthcare, Inc., 188
US Health Corporation Columbus, 188
US Homecare Corporation, 188
U.S. Postal Service, 203
US Sprint Communications, 188
U.S. West Communications, Inc., 184
US West, Inc., 188
US West Marketing Resources Group, 184
Utilicorp United, Inc., 189
Valspar Corporation, 189
Value City Department Stores, 189
Value Health, Inc., 189
Vans, Inc., 189
Van Waters Rogers, Inc., 189
Venture Stores, Inc., 190
Viking Freight System, Inc., 190
Volvo GM Heavy Truck Corporation, 190
The Vons Companies, Inc., 190
Vulcan Materials Company, 191
Waban, Inc., 191
Wachovia Bank of Georgia, 191
Wachovia Bank of North Carolina, 191
Wackenhut Corporation, 191
Wakefern Food Corporation, 191
Walden Book Company, Inc., 191

Walker Interactive Systems, 191
Wallace Computer Services, Inc., 192
Walmart, Inc., 192
Walt Disney Company, Inc., 192
Walt Disney World Company, 192
Wampler-Longacre, Inc., 192
Warnaco, Inc., 192
Warner-Lambert Company, 192
The Washington Post Company, 192
Weight Watchers International, Inc., 193
Weirton Steel Corporation, 193
Welbilt Corporation, 193
Wellman, Inc., 193
Wellpoint Health Network, 193
Wells Fargo and Company, 193
Wells Fargo Armored Service Corporation, 193
Wells Fargo Bank, 194
The Western Southern Life Insurance Company, 194
Westinghouse Electric Corporation, 194
Weyerhaeuser Company, 195
Wheelabrator Technologies, Inc., 195
Wheeling-Pittsburgh Corporation, 195
Wherehouse Entertainment, Inc., 195
Whiting Roll-Up Door Manufacturing Corporation, 195
Whittman-Hart, 195
Wickes Lumber Company, 195
Wildlife International, Ltd., 195
Willamette Industries, Inc., 196
Williams Companies, Inc., 196
Willis Corroon Corporation, 196
Winn Dixie Stores, Inc., 196
Wisconsin Energy Corporation, 196
Wisconsin Physicians Service Insurance, 196
WLR Foods, Inc., 196
WMX Technologies, Inc., 196
Woodward and Lothrop, Inc., 196
Woolworth Corporation, 196
World Bank Group, 196
World Savings and Loan Association, 196
Worthington Industries, Inc., 197
W. R. Grace and Company, Inc., 95
Wrigley Jr. Company, 197
W.W. Grainger, Inc., 95
Wyeth-Ayerst International, Ltd., 197
Xerox Financial Services, Inc., 197
Xomed, 197
Young and Rubicam, Inc., 197
Zell/Chilmark Fund, LP., 197

Account Management
Bank One, Inc., 43
Bozell Jacobs Kenyon Eckhardt, Inc., 53
Cablevision Systems, Inc., 56
McCann-Erickson USA, Inc., 126
Nynex Corporation, 141

Acoustic Engineering
Harman International Industries, Inc., 99

Actuarial
Aegon USA, 23
Aetna Life Insurance Company, 23
Alexander and Alexander of New York, Inc., 25
Allianz Investment Corporation, 26
Allstate Insurance Company, 27
America National Insurance, 28
American Family Assurance Collective, 29
American International Group, 30
American Life Insurance Company, 30
American Motorists Insurance Company, 31
Associates Corporation of North America, 39
Banc One Ohio Corporation, 42
Bankers Trust Company, 43
Bear Stearns Securities Corporation, 45
Blue Cross and Blue Shield of Alabama, 48
Blue Cross and Blue Shield of Connecticut, 48
Blue Cross and Blue Shield of Florida, 49
Blue Cross and Blue Shield of Massachusetts, 49
Blue Cross and Blue Shield of Missouri, 49
Blue Cross and Blue Shield of New Jersey, 49
Blue Cross and Blue Shield of North Carolina, 50
Blue Cross and Blue Shield of Texas, Inc., 50
Blue Cross and Blue Shield of Virginia, 50
Blue Cross Insurance Company, 51
Blue Cross of California, 50
CIGNA Corporation, 62
Commercial Union Corporation, 66
Commonwealth Life Insurance Company, 66
Connecticut Mutual Life Insurance Company, 67
Continental Casualty Company, 68

Administration

Advertising

Chemical, Mechanical, Electrical, And Milling Science Engineers To Fill Production Management Positions

Chemical Research

Chemistry

A. E. Staley Manufacturing
Company, 173
American Cyanamid Company, 29
The American Red Cross, 31
Arcadian Partners, LP., 37
Arco Chemical Company, 37
Armco, Inc., 37
Ashland Chemical, Inc., 39
Ball, Inc., 42
Bayer Corporation, 45
Becton Dickinson and Company, 45
Benjamin Moore and Company, 47
BOC Gases, 51
Burroughs Wellcome Company, 55
Cabot Corporation, 56
Collins and Aikman Product
Company, 65
Cone Mills Corporation, 67
Cosmair, Inc., 69
Courtaulds Coatings, 70
Dow Corning Corporation, 76
Dowelanco, 76
Eastman Chemical Company, 78
Eastman Kodak Company, 78
E. I. DuPont de Nemours and
Company, 77
Elf Atochem North America,
Inc., 79
Engelhard Corporation, 80
Farah USA, Inc., 82
Flexible Products Company, 87
Food and Drug Administration, 201
Fuji Photo Film, Inc., 90
Georgia Gulf Corporation, 93
Glaxo, Inc., 94
Great Lakes Chemical
Corporation, 96
Group Health Cooperative of Puget
Sound, 97
Hardee's Food Systems, Inc., 99
H. B. Fuller, 90
Hercules, Inc., 102
Hoffmann-La Roche, Inc., 103
Hudson Foods, Inc., 106
ICI Americas, Inc., 107
International Flavors and
Fragrances, 110
Intertech Group, Inc., 111
The Kendall Company, 116
Loctite Corporation, 122
Lubrizol Corporation, 123
M. A. Hanna Company, 98
Mallinckrodt Medical, 124
Mayo Foundation, 126
Millipore Corporation, 130
Monfort, Inc., 132
Monsanto Company, 132
Morton International, Inc., 133
Nalco Chemical Company, 134
National Institutes of Health, 202

National Starch and Chemical
Company, 135
Nu Skin International, 141
Ortho Diagnostic Systems, Inc., 143
Pfizer, Inc., 148
Polaroid Corporation, 151
PPG Industries, Inc., 151
Sigma Aldrich Corporation, 167
Sun Chemical Corporation, 175
Systems Research Laboratories,
Inc., 176
The Timken Company, 181
Union Carbide Corporation, 185
The Upjohn Company, 188
U.S. Department of
Agriculture, 203
U.S. Geological Survey, 203
Valspar Corporation, 189
Wheaton Glass Industries, Inc., 195
Wildlife International, Ltd., 195
Wyeth-Ayerst International,
Ltd., 197

Civil Engineering

Advanced Sciences, Inc., 22
Albert Kahn Associates, Inc., 114
Albertson's, Inc., 24
Allied-Signal, Inc., 26
ANR Pipeline Company, 35
A. Teichert and Son, Inc., 178
Austin Industries Corporation, 40
Boston Edison Company, 52
Citgo Petroleum Corporation, 63
Continental Medical Systems, 68
Day and Zimmermann, Inc., 72
Department of Energy, 199
Department of the Navy, Naval
Facilities Engineering
Command, 200
Department of Transportation,
Federal Highway
Administration, 200
DQE, Inc., 76
EG&G Rocky Flats, Inc., 78
Enron Corporation, 80
E-Systems, Inc., 77
Federal Emergency Management
Agency, 201
Georgia Power Company, 93
The Goodyear Tire and Rubber
Company, 95
Halliburton Energy Services
Company, 98
Hawaiian Electric Companies, 100
Indianapolis Power and Light
Company, 108
Jacobs Engineering Group,
Inc., 112
Jones Group, Inc., 114

Kiewit Construction Group,
Inc., 117
Lawrence Livermore National
Laboratory, 119
Lincoln Property Company, 121
Martin Marietta Energy
Systems, 125
McDermott International, Inc., 126
Motorola, Inc., 133
National Institute of Standards and
Technology, 202
Newport News Shipbuilding and
Drydock, 138
New York Power Authority, 138
Norfolk Southern Corporation, 139
Orange and Rockland Utilities, 142
Oscar Mayer Foods
Corporation, 143
Peoples Energy Corporation, 147
Perini Corporation, 147
The Port Authority of New York
and New Jersey, 151
PPG Industries, Inc., 151
Public Service of New
Hampshire, 154
Raytheon Constructors, 155
Roadway Services, Inc., 158
Scana Corporation, 161
Severdrup Corporation, 165
Southern California Edison
Company, 170
Southern California Gas
Company, 170
Tampa Electric Company, 177
Toyota Motor Manufacturing
USA, 182
Transco Company, 182
U.S. Army Corps of Engineers, 203
Valmont Industries, Inc., 189
Washinton Metro Area Transit
Authority, 192
Weirton Steel Corporation, 193
Wisconsin Energy Corporation, 196

Claims Adjusting

Utica National Insurance
Group, 189

Claims Adjustment/Examination

Allianz Investment Corporation, 26
Arthur J Gallagher and
Company, 91
Blue Cross and Blue Shield of
Georgia, 49
Blue Cross and Blue Shield of
Minnesota, 49
Blue Cross and Blue Shield of
Oregon, 50

American Electric Power
    Company, 29
American Family Assurance
    Collective, 29
American Management Systems,
    Inc., 30
Apple Computer, Inc., 36
Battelle Memorial Institute, 44
Bell Atlantic Business Systems
    Services, 46
Bellcore, 46
Cray Research, Inc., 70
Dell Computer Corporation, 73
Diebold, Inc., 75
Harris Corporation, 99
Hitachi America, Ltd., 103
Honda of America Manufacturing,
    Inc., 104
Intergraph Corporation, 110
International Business Machines
    Corporation, 110
LDI Corporation, 119
The Lee Apparel Company,
    Inc., 119
Lin Broadcasting Corporation, 121
Microsoft Corporation, 130
National Security Agency, 202
National Semiconductor
    Corporation, 135
Naval Air Warfare Center Aircraft
    Division, 202
Northern Telecom, 140
Ohio Casualty Insurance
    Corporation, 142
SCI Systems, Inc., 163
Storage Technology
    Corporation, 174
Unisys Government Group, 186
US West, Inc., 188

Computer Graphics
Jacobs Engineering Group,
    Inc., 112
The Ralph M. Parsons
    Company, 146

Computer Operations
Albertson's, Inc., 24
Chicago Title and Trust
    Company, 61

Computer Programming
ADIA Personnel Services, Inc., 22
Adobe Systems, 22
Advanced Logic Research, Inc., 22
Adventist Health Systems/West, 22
Aegon USA, 23
Aflac, Inc., 23
Albertson's, Inc., 24
Alcon Laboratories, 25

Allen-Bradley Company, Inc., 26
Allina Health System, 26
Alltel Information Services, Inc., 27
Altec Industries, Inc., 27
Alumax, Inc., 27
Amcel Corporation, 27
American Airlines, Inc., 28
America National Insurance, 28
American Broadcasting
    Companies, 28
American Electric Power
    Company, 29
American Family Assurance
    Collective, 29
American Management Systems,
    Inc., 30
Ameritech, 32
Ameritech Services, Inc., 33
Ampex, 33
Analysas Corporation, 34
Andersen Corporation, 35
Andrew Corporation, 35
Anstec, Inc., 35
Apple Computer, Inc., 36
Applied Systems, Inc., 36
Arkansas Blue Cross and Blue
    Shield, 37
ASA International, Ltd., 38
Asplundh Tree Expert Company, 39
The Atchison Topeka and Santa Fe
    Railway Company, 40
Atlanta Gas and Light Company, 40
Autodesk, Inc., 40
Automotive Controls
    Corporation, 41
Autozone, Inc., 41
Avco Corporation, 41
Avco Financial Services, Inc., 41
Avis Rent-A-Car System, 41
Baker Hughes, Inc., 42
Banana Republic, Inc., 42
Bankers Life and Casualty
    Company, 43
Bank of Hawaii, 43
The Bank of New York, 43
Bank One, Inc., 43
Battelle Memorial Institute, 44
BDM Technologies, Inc., 45
Bell Atlantic Business Systems
    Services, 46
Beneficial Corporation, 47
Bergen Brunswig Corporation, 47
Big Bear Stores Company, 47
Biosym Technologies, Inc., 48
Blockbuster Entertainment
    Corporation, 48
Blue Cross and Blue Shield Mutual
    of Ohio, 49
Blue Cross and Blue Shield of
    Alabama, 48

Blue Cross and Blue Shield of
    Arizona, 48
Blue Cross and Blue Shield of
    Connecticut, 48
Blue Cross and Blue Shield of
    Delaware, 48
Blue Cross and Blue Shield of
    Maryland, 49
Blue Cross and Blue Shield of
    Michigan, 49
Blue Cross and Blue Shield of
    Minnesota, 49
Blue Cross and Blue Shield of
    National Capitol Area, 49
Blue Cross and Blue Shield of
    North Carolina, 50
Blue Cross and Blue Shield of
    Oregon, 50
Blue Cross and Blue Shield of
    Oregon, 50
Blue Cross and Blue Shield of
    Rhode Island, 50
Blue Cross and Blue Shield of
    South Carolina, 50
Blue Cross and Blue Shield of
    South Carolina, 50
Blue Cross and Blue Shield of
    Texas, Inc., 50
Blue Cross and Blue Shield of
    Utah, 50
BOC Gases, 51
Borg-Warner Automotive
    Corporation, 52
Borland International, Inc., 52
Boston Edison Company, 52
Bradlee's, Inc., 53
Brown-Forman Corporation, 54
Builder's Square, Inc., 54
Burlington Air Express, Inc., 55
Burlington Coat Factory, 55
Burlington Northern, Inc., 55
Burroughs Wellcome Company, 55
Carlson Companies, Inc., 57
Carolina Freight Carriers
    Corporation, 57
Centel Corporation, 59
Central and Southwest
    Corporation, 59
Central Illinois Light Company, 59
Ceridian Corporation, 60
Certified Grocers of California,
    Ltd., 60
Charles Schwab and Company,
    Inc., 163
Charter Medical Corporation, 60
Chicago Title and Trust
    Company, 61
Chubb and Son, Inc., 62
Citicorp Financial Corporation, 63
Claires Boutiques, Inc., 63

Dentistry/Dental Hygiene

Design

Design Engineering

Schottenstein Stores
    Corporation, 162
Service America Corporation, 165
Southern California Edison
    Company, 170
Southern California Gas
    Company, 170
Union Bank, 185
United Artists Entertainment, 186
United States Gypsum
    Company, 186
U.S. Bancorp, 188
U.S. Postal Service, 203
Utica National Insurance
    Group, 189

Editing
Cable News Network, Inc., 55
Gannett Company, Inc., 91
Harper Collins Publishers, Inc., 99
National Park Service, 202
Simon and Schuster, Inc., 167
Taylor Corporation, 177
Time, Inc., 180
West Publishing Company, 194

Education
Arthur Andersen and Company, 38
Bakers and Leeds, 42
Kinder-Care Learning Centers, 117
National Science Foundation, 202
Peace Corps, 203
Southern California Edison
    Company, 170

Electrical Engineering
A B Chance Company, 21
Abbott Laboratories, 21
Adelphia Communications
    Corporation, 22
Advanced Micro Devices, Inc., 22
Advanced Sciences, Inc., 22
Air-A-Plane Corporation, 24
Airborne Express, 24
AK Steel Corporation, 24
AK Steel Corporation, 24
Albany International
    Corporation, 24
Albert Kahn Associates, Inc., 114
Albertson's, Inc., 24
Alcatel Cable Systems, Inc., 25
Alldata Corporation, 25
Allegheny Power Systems, Inc., 25
Allen-Bradley Company, Inc., 26
Alliant Techsystems, Inc., 26
Allied-Signal, Inc., 26
Allied-Signal Technical Services
    Corporation, 26
Alternate Circuit Technology,
    Inc., 27

American Broadcasting
    Companies, 28
American Building Maintenance
    Industries, 28
American National Can
    Company, 31
Ameritech Mobile
    Communications, 32
Ampex, 33
AMP, Inc., 33
Anadigics, Inc., 34
Analog Devices, Inc., 34
The Analytic Sciences
    Corporation, 34
Anchor Glass Container
    Corporation, 34
Andrew Corporation, 35
Anixter Brothers, Inc., 35
A. O. Smith Corporation, 168
Arizona Public Service Company, 37
Arkansas Power and Light
    Company, 37
Armstrong World Industries,
    Inc., 38
Arrow-Communications Labs,
    Inc., 38
Arrow Electronics, Inc., 38
Arvin Industries, Inc., 38
Aspect Telecommunications
    Corporation, 39
Astronautics Corporation of
    America, 39
The Atchison Topeka and Santa Fe
    Railway Company, 40
AT&T Global Information
    Solutions, 39
Baltimore Gas and Electric
    Company, 42
Basin Electric Power
    Corporation, 44
Bassett-Walker, Inc., 44
Bath Iron Works Corporation, 44
BDM Technologies, Inc., 45
Bell Atlantic Corporation, 46
Bellsouth Corporation, 46
Beloit Corporation, 46
B. F. Goodrich, 95
BICC Cables Corporation, 47
Borg-Warner Automotive
    Corporation, 52
Borg-Warner Automotive, Inc., 52
Boston Edison Company, 52
Briggs and Stratton Corporation, 53
Cable Television of Montgomery, 55
Cascade Die Casting Group, Inc., 58
Case Corporation, 58
CBI Industries, Inc., 59
Centerior Energy Corporation, 59
Central and Southwest
    Corporation, 59

Central Illinois Light Company, 59
Central Intelligence Agency, 199
Ceridian Corporation, 60
Chamberlain Manufacturing
    Corporation, 60
Chesapeake Corporation, 61
Cincinnati Bell Telephone
    Company, 62
Cincinnati Milacron, Inc., 62
Clairol, Inc., 63
Clarion Manufacturing
    Corporation, 64
CMS Energy Corporation, 64
Comcast Corporation, 65
Commonwealth Edison
    Company, 66
Compaq Computer Corporation, 66
Computervision Corporation, 66
Consumers Power Company, 68
Cox Enterprises, Inc., 70
Cray Research, Inc., 70
Cummins Engine Company, 71
Curtice Burns Prufac, 71
Day and Zimmermann, Inc., 72
Dell Computer Corporation, 73
Department of Energy, 199
Department of Labor, 199
Department of the Navy, Naval
    Facilities Engineering
    Command, 200
Detroit Diesel Corporation, 74
Devilbiss Health Care, Inc., 74
Diebold, Inc., 75
Dover Elevator International, 76
Dow Corning Corporation, 76
DQE, Inc., 76
Duke Power Company, 76
Duracell International, Inc., 77
Eagle-Picher Industries, Inc., 77
Eastman Chemical Company, 78
Eastman Kodak Company, 78
Eaton Corporation, 78
EG&G Rocky Flats, Inc., 78
E. I. DuPont de Nemours and
    Company, 77
Electrocom Automation, Inc., 79
Electronic Data Systems
    Corporation (EDS), 79
Emerson Electric Company, 79
E. R. Carpenter Company, Inc., 58
ESAB Welding and Cutting
    Products, Inc., 81
E-Systems, Inc., 77
Federal Aviation
    Administration, 200
Federal Communications
    Commission, 201
Federal Emergency Management
    Agency, 201
Federal Paper Board Company, 83

Industrial Distribution
Thomas and Betts Corporation, 180

Industrial Engineering
Allen-Bradley Company, Inc., 26
Allied-Signal, Inc., 26
American General Finance, 29
American Greetings
    Corporation, 30
Arcadian Partners, LP., 37
Arkansas Best Corporation, 37
Arkansas Power and Light
    Company, 37
Austin Industries Corporation, 40
Avco Corporation, 41
Bechtel Group, Inc., 45
BOC Gases, 51
Boston Edison Company, 52
Cawsl Corporation, 58
Cincinnati Milacron, Inc., 62
Collins and Aikman Product
    Company, 65
Dan River, Inc., 72
Day and Zimmermann, Inc., 72
Department of the Navy, Naval
    Facilities Engineering
    Command, 200
Detroit Diesel Corporation, 74
Eastman Chemical Company, 78
Eaton Corporation, 78
EG&G Rocky Flats, Inc., 78
Estee Lauder, Inc., 81
First Brands Corporation, 85
Fuji Photo Film, Inc., 90
Gates Corporation, 91
General Cable Corporation, 92
Georgia Power Company, 93
The Glidden Company, 94
GNB, Inc., 94
Guardian Life Insurance Company
    of America, 98
Halliburton Energy Services
    Company, 98
Hamilton Beach/Proctor-Silex, 98
Haworth, Inc., 101
Herman Miller, Inc., 102
Holnam, Inc., 104
Ingalls Shipbuilding, Inc., 108
Ingersoll-Rand Company, 109
Inter-City Products
    Corporation, 110
Jacobs Engineering Group,
    Inc., 112
Kantus Corporation, 115
The Kelly-Springfield Tire
    Company, 116
Kimball International, Inc., 117
Lafarge Corporation, 119
The Lee Apparel Company,
    Inc., 119

Leggett and Platt, Inc., 120
Libbey Glass, Inc., 120
Lockheed/Martin Services
    Group, 121
Marion Merrell Dow, Inc., 124
Mine Safety Appliances
    Company, 130
M&M/Mars, Inc., 123
Modine Manufacturing
    Company, 131
Naval Air Warfare Center Aircraft
    Division, 202
Nestle Frozen Food Company, 136
New York Power Authority, 138
NKK USA Corporation, 138
Northern Automotive
    Corporation, 139
Northern Indiana Public Service
    Company (NIPSCO), Inc., 139
Owens-Corning Fiberglass
    Corporation, 143
Packaging Corporation of
    America, 144
Pall Corporation, 145
Penske Corporation, 146
Pentair, Inc., 147
Reckitt and Colman, 156
Rhone-Poulenc Rorer, Inc., 157
Rohm and Haas Company, 158
Savannah Foods and Industries, 161
SC Johnson Wax, 114
Servistar Corporation, 165
Southern California Gas
    Company, 170
SPX Corporation, 172
Square D Company, 172
Sundstrand Corporation, 175
Tampa Electric Company, 177
Transco Company, 182
Unifi, Inc., 185
Union Carbide Corporation, 185
United Dominion Industries, 186
Venture Stores, Inc., 190
Walt Disney World Company, 192
Wellman, Inc., 193
Wisconsin Energy Corporation, 196
W.W. Grainger, Inc., 95
Xerox Corporation, 197
Xomed, 197
York International Corporation, 197

Industrial Hygiene
Department of Labor, 199
Healthcare Services Group,
    Inc., 101
Occupational Safety and Health
    Administration, 202
Oxy Chemical Corporation, 144

Industrial Relations
Chevron Corporation, 61

Industrial Safety
Owens-Corning Fiberglass
    Corporation, 143

Information Services
Blue Cross and Blue Shield of
    Virginia, 50
Carson Pirie Scott and Company, 58
Cedars Sinai Medical Center, 59
Commercial Union Corporation, 66
CSC Network/Prentice-Hall Legal
    and Financial Services, 71
Great Lakes Chemical
    Corporation, 96
Mead Corporation, 127
Sedgwick James, Inc., 164
Sprint Mid-Atlantic Telephone, 172
The Standard Register
    Company, 173
Wells Fargo and Company, 193
Wisconsin Physicians Service
    Insurance, 196
Xomed, 197

Information Systems
Ace Hardware Corporation, 21
A. E. Staley Manufacturing
    Company, 173
Alcon Laboratories, 25
Alex Lee, Inc., 25
Allmerica Financial Corporation, 26
Altec Industries, Inc., 27
American Greetings
    Corporation, 30
American Red Cross - Biomedical
    Division, 31
Anixter Brothers, Inc., 35
A. P. Green Industries, Inc., 36
ARAMARK Corporation, 36
ARCO Alaska, Inc., 37
Arkansas Best Corporation, 37
AT&T, 40
Bath Iron Works Corporation, 44
Baxter International, Inc., 44
Belk Enterprises, Inc., 45
Bell Atlantic Corporation, 46
Bellsouth Corporation, 46
Blue Cross and Blue Shield of
    Oregon, 50
Blue Cross and Blue Shield of
    Tennessee, 50
Blue Cross and Blue Shield of
    Vermont, 50
Brink's, Inc., 53
Budget Rent-A-Car Corporation, 54
CACI, Inc., 56
Case Corporation, 58

Leasing

Liberal Arts

Licensed Practical Nursing

Management Information Systems

Mechanical Engineering

Medical Records

Medical Technology

Merchandising

Metallurgical Engineering

Metallurgy

Microbiology

Military/Defense

Minerals Engineering

Mining

Mining Engineering

Molecular Biology
Life Technologies, Inc., 120

Mortgage
Associates Corporation of North
America, 39
Barnett Banks, Inc., 44
First Interstate Bancorp, 86
Marine Midland Banks, Inc., 124
Norwest Corporation, 140

Natural Resources
U.S. Army Corps of Engineers, 203

Natural Sciences
Smithsonian Institution, 169

Naval Architecture
American Commercial Lines, 28
Bath Iron Works Corporation, 44
Newport News Shipbuilding and
Drydock, 138

Navigation
Princess Cruises, Inc., 152

Network Analysis
Alltel Information Services, Inc., 27
Anixter Brothers, Inc., 35
Automotive Controls
Corporation, 41
Bell Atlantic Business Systems
Services, 46
Blue Cross and Blue Shield of
Connecticut, 48
Commerce Bancshares, 66
Dell Computer Corporation, 73
Federal Insurance Company, 83
Federal Reserve Bank of New
York, 83
Fleet Services Corporation, 87
John Alden Life Insurance
Company, 25
John H. Harland Company, 99
Key Bank of New York, 116
Mellon Bank Corporation, 128

Networking
The Beth Israel Hospital
Association, 47
GTE Data Services, Inc., 97

Network Management Systems
GTE Data Services, Inc., 97

Nuclear Engineering
Advanced Sciences, Inc., 22
Baltimore Gas and Electric
Company, 42

Battelle Memorial Institute, 44
Bechtel Group, Inc., 45
Centerior Energy Corporation, 59
Commonwealth Edison
Company, 66
Department of Energy, 199
Duke Power Company, 76
EG&G Rocky Flats, Inc., 78
General Dynamics Corporation, 92
General Public Utilities
Corporation, 93
Martin Marietta Energy
Systems, 125
New York Power Authority, 138
Public Service Electric and Gas
Company, 154
Westinghouse Hanford
Company, 194
Westinghouse Savannah River
Company, 194

Nuclear Medicine
Mayo Foundation, 126
Westinghouse Savannah River
Company, 194

Nuclear Technology
Advocate Healthcare, 23

Nursing
Adventist Health Systems/West, 22
American Home Products, 30
Arkansas Blue Cross and Blue
Shield, 37
Beverly Enterprises, 47
Blue Cross and Blue Shield of
Florida, 49
Blue Cross and Blue Shield of
Kansas, 49
Blue Cross and Blue Shield of
Missouri, 49
Blue Cross and Blue Shield of
Oregon, 50
Blue Cross and Blue Shield of
Texas, Inc., 50
Blue Cross and Blue Shield of
Virginia, 50
Blue Cross of Idaho Health
Service, 51
Columbia/HCA, 65
Continental Medical Systems, 68
Department of Consumer and
Regulatory Affairs, 199
Department of State, Bureau of
Medical Services, 200
Florida Hospital Medical Center, 88
Group Health Cooperative of Puget
Sound, 97
Hawaii Medical Service
Association, 100

Horizon Healthcare
Corporation, 105
In Home Health, Inc., 108
Kaiser Foundation Health of the
Northwest, 114
Kaiser Foundation Health Plan, 115
Kaiser Foundation Health Plan of
Colorado, Inc., 115
Kaiser Foundation Health Plan of
Texas, 115
Methodist Hospital of Lubbock
Texas, 129
Mount Sinai Hospital, Inc., 133
The Multicare Companies, Inc., 133
Novacare, Inc., 140
Pennsylvania Blue Shield, 146
Sisters of St. Francis Health
Services, 168
Tenet Healthcare, 178
United Health, Inc., 186
United Wisconsin Services, 187

**Nursing Management And
Administration**
Horizon Healthcare
Corporation, 105

Nutrition
Bob Evans Farms, Inc., 51
McDonald's Corporation, 127
Nu Skin International, 141
United States Surgical
Corporation, 187

Occupational Therapy
The Beth Israel Hospital
Association, 47
Caremark, Inc., 57
Florida Hospital Medical Center, 88
Harris County Hospital District, 100
Harris Methodist Health
System, 100
Henry Ford Health System, 102
Horizon Healthcare
Corporation, 105
Kaiser Foundation Health of the
Northwest, 114
Lutheran Health Systems, 123
Novacare, Inc., 140
Peace Corps, 203
Thomas Jefferson University
Hospital, 113
United Health, Inc., 186
University of Pittsburgh Medical
Center Systems, 187

Oncology
Montefiore Medical Center, 132
Mount Sinai Hospital, Inc., 133

Systems Analysis

Airborne Express, 24
Airborne Express, 24
Analysis and Technology, Inc., 34
Arkansas Best Corporation, 37
The Bank of New York, 43
Battelle Memorial Institute, 44
Blue Cross and Blue Shield Mutual of Ohio, 49
California Physicians Service, 56
Canadian Pacific Rail System, 56
Capital Blue Cross, Inc., 57
Certified Grocers of California, Ltd., 60
CNA Insurance Companies, 64
Cookson America, Inc., 68
Crowley Maritime Corporation, 71
Federal Insurance Company, 83
First Financial Management Corporation, 86
First of America Bank Corporation, 86
Fleet Services Corporation, 87
Gannett Company, Inc., 91
Glendale Federal Bank, 94
Golden West Financial Corporation, 95
The Goodyear Tire and Rubber Company, 95
GTE Data Services, Inc., 97
GTE Directories Corporation, 97
Harnischfeger Industries, Inc., 99
Hawaii Medical Service Association, 100
Hospital Sisters Health System, 105
Huntington Bank, 107
Manor Care, Inc., 124
McKesson Corporation, 127
Medco Containment Services, Inc., 127
Mellon Bank Corporation, 128
Micro Warehouse, Inc., 129
Nibco, Inc., 138
Nynex Corporation, 141
Ohio Casualty Insurance Corporation, 142
Pacific Telesis Group, 144
Parisian, Inc., 145
Physicians Mutual Insurance Company, 149
Pinkerton's, Inc., 149
Simon and Schuster, Inc., 167
Smith Barney, Inc., 168
State Farm Fire and Casualty Company, 173
Strawbridge and Clothier, 174
Taylor Corporation, 177
Tennessee Gas Pipeline Company, 178
Terra Industries, Inc., 179

TV Guide, 184
Whirlpool Corporation, 195

Systems Engineering

AT&T Global Information Solutions, 39
Eastman Kodak Company, 78
Intermountain Health Care, Inc., 110
Loral Aerospace Corporation, 122
Loral Corporation, 122
Memorex Telex Corporation, 128
Pitney Bowes, Inc., 150
Reliance Electric Company, 156
Unisys Government Group, 186
Whittman-Hart, 195

Systems Integration

Alexander and Alexander of New York, Inc., 25
Alumax, Inc., 27
Bell and Howell Company, 45
Dana Corporation, 72
Deloitte and Touche, 73
Foodmaker, Inc., 88
H. N. Bull Information Systems, 54
Houston Industries, Inc., 106
McDermott International, Inc., 126
PECO Energy Company, 146
The Procter and Gamble Company, 153
Progressive County Mutual Insurance Company, 153
Severdrup Corporation, 165
United Dominion Industries, 186
U.S. West Communications, Inc., 184
US West, Inc., 188
W.W. Grainger, Inc., 95

Tax

Alco Standard Corporation, 25
Avco Financial Services, Inc., 41
Ernst and Young, LLP., 81
Greyhound Lines, Inc., 97
Kaiser Aluminum Corporation, 114
Maritz, Inc., 124
Maxxam Group, Inc., 126
Phillips Electronics, 148
Pittway Corporation, 150

Tax Accounting

Chrysler Credit Corporation, 62
Ernst and Young, LLP., 81
Halliburton Energy Services Company, 98
H & R Block Tax Services, Inc., 48
The Pittston Company, 150
Sedgwick James, Inc., 164

Technical

American Power Conversion Corporation, 31
Ameritech Network Service, Inc., 33
Gateway 2000, 91
H. N. Bull Information Systems, 54
Northwest Temporary Services, 140
Packard Bell Electronics, Inc., 145
Quebecor Printing USA Corporation, 155
Sprint/United Telephone Northwest, 172
TAD Technical Services Corporation, 176
TCI Cable, Inc., 177

Technical Engineering

American Standard, Inc., 32
Avco Corporation, 41
Cooper Power Systems, Inc., 69
Emerson Electric Company, 79
General Instrument Corporation, 93
Harvard Industries, Inc., 100
Kellogg Company, 115
Lyondell Petrochemical Company, 123
Oscar Mayer Foods Corporation, 143
Potomac Electric Power Company, 151
Reliance Electric Company, 156
Rubbermaid, Inc., 159
The Standard Products Company, 173
The Standard Register Company, 173
Student Loan Marketing Association, 175
Tecumseh Products Company, 178
Union Carbide Corporation, 185
W. R. Grace and Company, Inc., 95

Technical Sales

Digital Equipment Corporation, 75

Technical Writing

Combined Insurance Company of America, 65
J. D. Edwards and Company, Inc., 78
Johnson Controls, Inc., 113
Raytheon Service Company, 156

Technology

Department of the Navy, 200
Dun and Bradstreet Corporation, 76
Oracle Corporation, 142
SuperValu, Inc., 176

Technology Research

The Analytic Sciences
   Corporation, 34

Telecommunications

Alltel Corporation, 27
Alltel Information Services, Inc., 27
Alltel Mobile Communications, 27
American Family Assurance
   Collective, 29
Ameritech, 32
Ameritech, 32
Anixter Brothers, Inc., 35
A-Plus Communications, Inc., 36
Aspect Telecommunications
   Corporation, 39
Bellsouth Cellular Corporation, 46
Bellsouth Telecommunications, 46
Cable News Network, Inc., 55
Cablevision Systems, Inc., 56
Centel Corporation, 59
Comcast Corporation, 65
Comdisco, Inc., 65
Cox Enterprises, Inc., 70
First Union National Bank of
   Florida, 87
General Services
   Administration, 201
Greyhound Lines, Inc., 97
GTE Directories Corporation, 97
GTE Service, 97
Home Shopping Network, Inc., 104
MCI Communications
   Corporation, 127
The Mitre Corporation, 131
National Broadcasting Company,
   Inc., 134
Northern Telecom, 140
Nynex Corporation, 141
Pacific Telesis Group, 144
SBC Communications, Inc., 161
Siemens Rolm Company, 167
Southern New England Telephone
   Company, 170
Southwestern Bell Telephone
   Company, 171
TCI of South Florida, 177
Time Warner Cable, 181
Williams Companies, Inc., 196

Telemarketing

ITI Marketing Services, Inc., 111
Providian Corporation, 153
Teleservice Resources, Inc., 178

Television Broadcasting

Adelphia Communications
   Corporation, 22
Cablevision Systems, Inc., 56
Home Shopping Network, Inc., 104

Lifetime TV, 120
National Broadcasting Company,
   Inc., 134
TCI of South Florida, 177
Turner Broadcasting System,
   Inc., 183
Viacom International, Inc., 190

Test Engineering

Lone Star Technologies, Inc., 122

Textiles

Bassett-Walker, Inc., 44
Collins and Aikman Product
   Company, 65
Cone Mills Corporation, 67
Dan River, Inc., 72
Fieldcrest Cannon, Inc., 84
Oshkosh B'Gosh, Inc., 143
Russell Corporation, 159

Therapy

Grancare, Inc., 96

Training And Development

American Red Cross - Biomedical
   Division, 31
Centex Corporation, 59
Edward D. Jones and Company, 114
Field Container Company, LP., 84
Norwest Financial Services, 140
Peace Corps, 203
Smart and Final, Inc., 168
Weight Watchers International,
   Inc., 193
Wherehouse Entertainment,
   Inc., 195

Transfusion Medicine

American Red Cross - Biomedical
   Division, 31

Transportation

ABF Freight System, Inc., 21
Allied Van Lines, 26
Applied Power, Inc., 36
Black and Decker U.S., Inc., 48
Chicago and Northwestern
   Transportation Company, 61
Con-Way Transportation
   Services, 68
CSX Transportation, 71
Dell Computer Corporation, 73
Department of Transportation,
   Federal Highway
   Administration, 200
Emery Worldwide, 80
Federal Maritime Commission, 201
Fort Howard Corporation, 89

Interstate Commerce
   Commission, 201
The Long Island Railroad
   Company, 122
Mayflower Transit, Inc., 126
Norfolk Southern Corporation, 139
North American Van Lines,
   Inc., 139
Pony Express Courier
   Corporation, 151
The Port Authority of New York
   and New Jersey, 151
Santa Fe Pacific Corporation, 161
Sinclair Oil Corporation, 167
Singer Sewing Company, 167
SLS, Inc., 168
Stolt Parcel Tankers, 174
Stone Container Corporation, 174
Watkins Motor Lines, Inc., 192

Travel/Tourism

American-Hawaii Cruises, 30

Treasury Management

Amsted Industries, Inc., 33
Colgate-Palmolive Company, 64
Department of Justice, U.S.
   Attorney General, 199
Exxon Corporation, 82
First Tennessee National
   Corporation, 86
First Union National Bank of North
   Carolina, 87
Follett College Stores
   Corporation, 88
GATX Corporation, 91
Glendale Federal Bank, 94
Houston Industries, Inc., 106
Phillips Electronics, 148
Science Applications International
   Corporation, 163
United Dominion Industries, 186

Trust

Nationsbank, 135

Underwriting

Aegon USA, 23
Alexander and Alexander of New
   York, Inc., 25
Allianz Investment Corporation, 26
American Family Assurance
   Collective, 29
American International Group, 30
American Life Insurance
   Company, 30
Associates Corporation of North
   America, 39
Bank of Boston Corporation, 43

Options, Opportunities & Advice

Peterson's Guide to MBA Programs

Focuses on the practical outcomes of investing in a graduate business education, profiling more than 700 U.S., Canadian, and international MBA programs. Provides the essential details candidates need to help them choose just the "right" program to meet their career goals, their schedules, and their lifestyles.

ISBN 1-56079-366-X, 1,005 pp., 8 1/2 x 11, $19.95

Hidden Job Market 1996

Provides career hunters with vital information on the nation's 2,000 fastest-growing small to mid-size companies—those that are hiring at four times the national rate! The new 1996 edition covers a wide range of high-growth industries such as environmental consulting, home health care, telecommunications, and on-line services, to name just a few.

ISBN 1-56079-517-4, 292 pp., 6 x 9, $17.95

Internships 1996

Includes detailed information on over 40,000 paid and unpaid on-the-job training opportunities for students and adults. For high schoolers, college students, recent graduates, career changers, and those returning to the work force who want to know how to gain experience and entry into their fields of choice through an internship.

ISBN 1-56079-525-5, 557 pp., 8 1/2 x 11, $21.95, 16th edition

I Went to College for *This?*

True Stuff About Life in the Business World—
And How to Get Through It

Garrett Soden

Tells college graduates what to expect during their critical first days and weeks at work, providing them with a wealth of practical advice and some peace of mind.

ISBN 1-56079-339-2, 240 pp., 6 x 9, $11.95

To Order Call: 800-338-3282
Fax: 609-243-9150

NEW ON THE INTERNET

A World of Information and News
Peterson's Education and Career Center
http://www.petersons.com

P Peterson's Princeton, NJ